THE WORLD OF THE FIRST AUSTRALIANS

R01138 21415

THE WORLD OF THE FIRST AUSTRALIANS

An introduction to the traditional life of the Australian Aborigines

by
RONALD M. BERNDT
and CATHERINE H. BERNDT

THE UNIVERSITY OF CHICAGO PRESS

Library of Congress Catalog Card Number: 64-15806
The University of Chicago Press, Chicago
The University of Toronto Press, Toronto 5, Canada

First published in 1964
by Angus and Robertson Ltd,
54/58 Bartholomew Close, London
First Australian edition published 1964
by Ure Smith Pty Ltd, 166 Phillip Street, Sydney

© Copyright 1964 by Ronald M. Berndt
and Catherine H. Berndt

Printed in Australia

65-87227

To Emeritus Professor A. P. Elkin

Foreword

The volume which we called *The First Australians* was published in 1952, reprinted in 1954. It was designed to introduce the Australian Aborigines in a preliminary way, to sketch some of the main points of their life without dwelling on any particular aspect in detail, to stimulate interest in them so that people would want to know more. And in fact it is in response to demands for more—more substance, more detail—that the present volume has been prepared.

Although it concerns the same topic, the similarity between the old and the new ends with the title. It is completely rewritten and expanded. As the sub-title suggests, it gives a comprehensive picture of traditional Aboriginal culture, with special attention to certain areas which the authors know personally. This is how life was lived before the coming of Europeans, or before European influence drastically modified it. The changes which have been wrought as a result of this contact are treated briefly in the final chapter. They will be taken up later in a companion volume which will concentrate entirely on that issue.

Here the major focus is on traditionally-oriented Aborigines, whose way of life is rapidly disappearing. Over most of the Continent it is already a thing of the past.

The material is fully documented, with references. Readers who are interested in the subject as a whole, or in any particular aspect of it, will know exactly where to turn for further information. Although the scope of this volume is fairly wide, and some of the material quite detailed, it is of course impossible in a volume of this size to cover all the literature, or to do more than touch on a number of topics. There are bound to be aspects which readers will want to explore further. To provide for this eventuality, sources are indicated, along with a detailed bibliography.

This is avowedly a text book, or rather an introductory text book, written specifically for people who wish to go beyond the facile exoticism and sentimental half-truths which are becoming part of European-Australian folklore in regard to the Aborigines, with the realities of their way of living ignored or glossed over on the grounds that these are too difficult, too foreign, or too uncongenial, to warrant the trouble of trying to understand them.

We are not suggesting that the Aboriginal heritage is *our* heritage as Western Europeans. Our cultural growth stems from a different direction, and development of an Australian ethos will not depend on the actual content of that Aboriginal past or present, except in a very superficial way. The sentimental movement of the 1940's to recapture a romanticized Aboriginal perspective through stories, poetry, and art, in the search for a peculiarly Australian flavour, was an unsuccessful endeavour to resuscitate something which was never entirely Aboriginal.

Incongruously enough, however, as our State and Commonwealth governments press on toward assimilation for these people—in the sense of eradicating, for all practical purposes, everything of a traditional nature—there is also a contrary movement, not so much among Aborigines and part-Aborigines as among ourselves, as Europeans, to recapture the more exotic aspects of Aboriginal culture. Aboriginal art exhibitions tour the Continent. Tourists crowd about the paintings on Ayers Rock, which a few years ago was a sacred site. In our shops are a few genuine Aboriginal weapons and other things, all but overshadowed by pseudo-Aboriginal art-craft objects of all descriptions, designed to attract local customers and oversea visitors alike. 'Aboriginal' murals appear in commercial offices, Aboriginal names abound for private homes, for ships, and so on. Even songs masquerading as Aboriginal assail our ears. . . . In part these are manifestations of a quest for novelty—the lure of the bizarre, the 'primitive' and 'stone-age'.

But although a lot of this may be Aboriginal in origin or in form, or at least in inspiration, it does not really help to make us any better informed about the Aborigines and their problems. Hanging an Arnhem Land bark painting or an Albert Namatjira on a wall or visiting Aboriginal art exhibitions, or buying a boomerang in a city shop: none of these actions in themselves bring us any nearer to understanding the significance of Aboriginal life, or appreciating the difficulties which face those who today are still caught between two worlds (a cliché which, however, comes uncomfortably close to the truth), even though the very fact of doing these things may point to a sympathy, a *wish* to understand and appreciate. In a more general sense, it may help to achieve a widening of cultural perspective, a greater measure of receptivity to things usually far outside the range of personal experience. Undoubtedly, some aspects of Aboriginal life have influenced us, as Australians, in many respects—not obtrusively, or overwhelmingly, but perhaps more subtly. It is not easy to gauge this yet. Such influences as there are today are mostly haphazard, and will probably become almost unrecognizable as time passes.

Nevertheless, the wealth of Aboriginal traditional culture can contribute to the general development of what is sometimes called, vaguely, the Australian way of life. Firstly, we Australians should know what we are supplanting. This is important in terms of creating not only a national conscience, but also a national consciousness. Secondly, the impact which Aboriginal art, poetry, and oral literature could have on our own has not yet been felt, despite most of the attempts which have been made to translate, or rather transform, them. And thirdly, it should be a permanent reminder to us that European-Australian life is only one variety of Australian life, even though it is so fast becoming the *only* one. There are other ways of doing and seeing and thinking about things. Our way of life is not necessarily superior to all others, although it may seem so to those of us who take its virtues very much for granted and minimize its shortcomings. Yet this kind of ethnocentric outlook is not something peculiar to Western Europeans. It is common the world over, and the Australian Aborigines are no exception. In one respect this is a healthy manifestation, as long as it is confined to a pride in one's traditional background. In another respect it is dangerous, encouraging arrogance, a contempt for foreigners or a hasty rejection of the unfamiliar. But a fuller knowledge of a way of life within our own gates, so to speak, can lead more positively to an understanding of other cultures generally —if not to greater tolerance: the two do not always go hand in hand.

By knowing more about how Australian Aborigines think and behave, we are widening our knowledge of human beings, not just in empirical terms but theoretically as well. We cannot afford to ignore any of the variations on the common theme of man's adjustment to his natural and social environment. In this respect, the present volume has international relevance. And there is an even more immediate if more localized issue: to understand changes which are taking place today in the process of Aboriginal adjustment to the wider Australian society, toward the goal of assimilation, we cannot overlook the continuing influence of their immediate traditional past.

* * * * *

There are few general volumes available on this topic, and for that matter few specific ones. The best known, and the most comprehensive, is by Professor A. P. Elkin, *The Australian Aborigines*

(4th edition, 1964). This has become a classic, and will surely retain its place whatever else is written. Prior to 1938, when that volume was first published, the only reasonably satisfactory overall survey was Basedow's *The Australian Aboriginal*, 1925. (There had been a couple of earlier general ones, but their usefulness was limited.) More recently there have been the first edition of the present book, and F. D. McCarthy's *de luxe* edition, *Australia's Aborigines: Their Life and Culture* (1957*a*). More specific and localized studies are mentioned in the Bibliography at the end of this volume. The arrangement of topics conforms, broadly, to the outline we followed in the earlier *First Australians*. It is a fairly standard sequence; but instead of deliberately reorienting the volume to make it seem 'different' we decided to keep it that way. Because we are concerned with a range of topics and not with a single set of problems or a single theme, the conventional categories should make it easier for people to acquire a general picture.

The present volume is intended to be complementary, and supplementary, to Elkin's *Australian Aborigines* and to McCarthy's study. Inevitably, in focusing on the same range of subject matter, there are some similarities: it would be odd if there were not. But differences in perspective, in treatment, and in content are such that, essentially, it stands by itself. Also, it is not designed to cover all the literature which has been published on the Australian Aborigines. Our approach has been, rather, to rely most heavily on the results of our own work over the last twenty years or so. The main areas covered in this have been: in South Australia, the River Murray, Adelaide city, Ooldea (Great Victoria Desert), and the north of that State from Oodnadatta westward; western New South Wales; in the Northern Territory, the Victoria River district, north-east to Katherine, Army settlements from Larrimah to Koolpinyah, the Daly River, Port Keats, Bathurst Island, western and eastern Arnhem Land; and parts of Western Australia, especially the Western Desert.

Enough comparative material has been included to give a fairly broad coverage, to set local details in wider perspective—to point to diversity, even where this could not be documented without cluttering the text. Also, we have tried to limit the use of Aboriginal terms, but this was not always feasible. Where they occur, they are in a simplified and anglicized form, except that we have kept the *j* symbol for the sound represented in English as 'y'. This applies to proper names too, even when they are not in italics.

Unfortunately, there is no Australia-wide agreement on the spelling of Aboriginal words. To make the matter more difficult, in virtually all Aboriginal languages the sounds some linguists call plosives cannot be clearly divided, as in English, between voiced and voiceless. That is, the Aboriginal sounds fall between those which we write in English as p and b, t and d, k and g. (See, for instance, A. Capell, 'The Classification of Languages in North and North-West Australia', *Oceania,* 1940, Vol. X, No. 3, p. 247.) In recent years there have been moves to standardize the spelling of these sounds, using the ordinary English letters to avoid bringing in new symbols; but while one group of research workers settled on p, t, and k, others had been deciding on b, d, and g. This divergence has persisted. Although a small thing in itself, it is confusing to readers who do not realize that it is simply a question of choice in spelling—not a problem of which most nearly represents the correct sound. We hesitated for some time to commit ourselves to either alternative; but eventually, for the sake of consistency, we agreed to follow Dr. Capell's preference and use the voiced series, b, d, and g. Accordingly, we have adhered to this in most of the Aboriginal words which appear in the present volume. The exceptions are mostly words and names quoted from writers who have used different spelling, 'tribal' names which have become fairly widely accepted in some other form, and several words which have gained some currency in the alternative mode of spelling (Kunapipi, for instance, although Lloyd Warner in his *A Black Civilization,* 1937/1958, refers to this as Gunabibi).

Double quotation marks are used in this volume for direct quotations. Single quotation marks indicate that slight alterations have been made, but that the substance of the quotation is essentially unchanged.

Another point: To avoid too-frequent changes in tense, and also in an attempt to make what we are describing seem less 'museum-like' for all its detail, in the main body of this volume we speak of the traditional picture very largely in terms of the present. The time-scale of events is uneven in Aboriginal Australia. Some of the scenes we ourselves witnessed, not so many years ago, have no counterpart today. Others, long vanished in the south of the Continent, linger in parts of the north. But very few people who read this book are likely to suppose that 'tribal' life is continuing in full swing in such places as Sydney and Melbourne; and if by some chance they do, a glance at these first pages and at the last chapter should be enough to disabuse them.

As far as acknowledgments are concerned it is virtually impossible to select from the long list of persons who have assisted us in so many ways. Most notably of course we are indebted, far more than we can say, to Professor A. P. Elkin, now Emeritus, who over the years has always been warmly ready to offer his advice and encouragement. This is a debt beyond repayment. Our field work and writing were sponsored first, under his aegis, by the Australian

National Research Council, later by the Research Committee of the University of Sydney, and more recently (1956-64) by the Research Grants Committee of the University of Western Australia. Dr. Robert L. Kirk has been kind enough to contribute a section on genetics; Mrs. Thyra Robertson has patiently and carefully typed the final draft of the manuscript. But nothing here could have been written without the active co-operation and friendship of the First Australians themselves. Something of our obligation to them will be met, in a small way, if this book helps toward a better appreciation of these people who in many cases are not yet regarded as full citizens of the Australian Commonwealth, but who are, or were, in fact the real Australians, whose forefathers held this land which now, through what could be called historical accident, we think of as our own.

RONALD M. BERNDT
CATHERINE H. BERNDT

University of Western Australia
June, 1964.

Contents

Illustrations

FIGURES

THE WORLD OF THE FIRST AUSTRALIANS

CHAPTER I

The Aborigines in Time and Space

Although the Australian Aborigines are sometimes called Australoids, they are not a separate human species. It is true that isolation over a long period could eventually have biological repercussions, possibly leading in time to the formation of distinct species. But no human group has been completely isolated from all others over a sufficiently long period for that to take place. This is not to say that there are no physical differences at all between different peoples. Obviously there are: but they are of a relatively minor sort, not enough to mark off *all* the members of a given group from *all* other peoples in the world. Differences in one feature are counterbalanced by similarities in others. As Washburn puts it: "A 'race' is a group of genetically similar populations, and races intergrade because there are always intermediate populations." (Washburn, 1953: 722.) Even the Australian Aborigines, often referred to as the most isolated of all peoples, were not completely cut off from all contact with the outside world. In the north, especially, they had contacts with the Torres Strait and with New Guinea, as well as with some of the Indonesian islands.

ORIGIN

The question of 'who they are' in the broadest sense, how they fit into the general picture of human development from earliest times, is one which cannot be answered simply in a few words. Evidence is still meagre, and interpretations are conflicting. Speaking in general terms, Washburn asserts that: "There are more different theories of man's origin and differentiation now than there were fifty years ago." (Washburn, 1953: 723.) The classification of peoples on the basis of physical appearance and physical measurements has been complicated by the findings of modern genetics, which cut across earlier views, and illuminate previously unsuspected areas of both similarity and divergence between them.

The issue of Aboriginal physical identification is no exception. Blood group research has confirmed alignments which were tentatively mapped out before, but it has negated others. And fossil remains are so few in Australia that the evidence they offer is, so far, suggestive rather than conclusive.

There is a school of thought which holds that the Aborigines represent a distinct line of development: that they are a primitive survival, an anomaly in the modern world. Ruggles Gates held this view for a time. Several writers, such as Sollas, claimed that they alone continued into modern times the ancient Pleistocene stock of Neanderthal Man. But Howells points out that this is making too much of divergences between the Aborigines and other human populations: "it is more reasonable to suppose that if the Australians are of Neanderthal descent, so are other modern races, since the Australians share all those characteristics of Homo sapiens which are generally accepted as separating them from other species". (Howells, 1937: 69.) Abbie also contests that view. (Abbie, 1951: 91-100.)

Apart from a few dissenting voices, then, on one point there is general agreement: that the Aborigines are members of the species Homo sapiens, to which all living races belong. They are representatives of modern man, just as Europeans are. Among the questions asked by those few dissenters are these: Did the stock from which the Aborigines sprang branch off from the main sapiens stem at an early stage of its development? What is its relation to the now extinct types which we know today only through such fossil forms and remains as Pithecanthropus, Cro-Magnon and Solo Man in Europe, Wadjak Man in Java, Peking Man in China, and the range of fossil forms which have been found on the Continent of Africa? How close are the Aborigines to present-day Europeans, or 'Caucasoids'?

One problem which does remain unresolved is, 'Where did they come from', and 'when'? The most persistent claims have been made for southern Asia, with or without specifying any particular areas. Equally, the assumption is widely held that the Aborigines must have been long enough in this Continent to develop the characteristic combination of physical traits which distinguish them to some extent from other human populations. The so-called Australoid strain has been reported from other parts of the world too, in small pockets like some of the tribal people of south India, particularly in the Nilgiri Hills; the Veddahs of Ceylon; perhaps the Ainu of Japan; and parts of Indonesia and New Guinea. But this does not tell us much, if anything, about their relationship to the Australian Australoids. The genetic picture is still incomplete here. (See below.)

What is more, there is no evidence to show how the first of the Aborigines got into Australia, but it was almost certainly by sea. McCarthy (1957*a*: 19) points out that the land bridge between this Continent and Asia "disappeared before it could be used by placental Asian animals"; and it was prior to that time, over a million years ago, "that the marsupial and monotreme fauna reached Australia". McCarthy adds: "The crucial point in regard to man's antiquity in Australia is whether the first migration into the Continent took place during one of the early or in the last of the glacial phases, when more land was exposed and the sea channels to be crossed were not as wide as those of today." Abbie (1960: 404) agrees with Curr that the first arrivals probably came in through "the north-west of the Continent", and that their complete diffusion over the country need not have taken "more than a few hundred years". However, early migratory evidence seems to point more conclusively to the Arnhem Land area and to Cape York.

The origin of the Tasmanians is even more doubtful. One suggestion is that they were the original inhabitants of this Continent, or part of it. Another (see McCarthy, 1957*a*: 24) is that "they drifted from New Caledonia, possibly landing and travelling along the east coast south of Queensland to Tasmania". This last view is

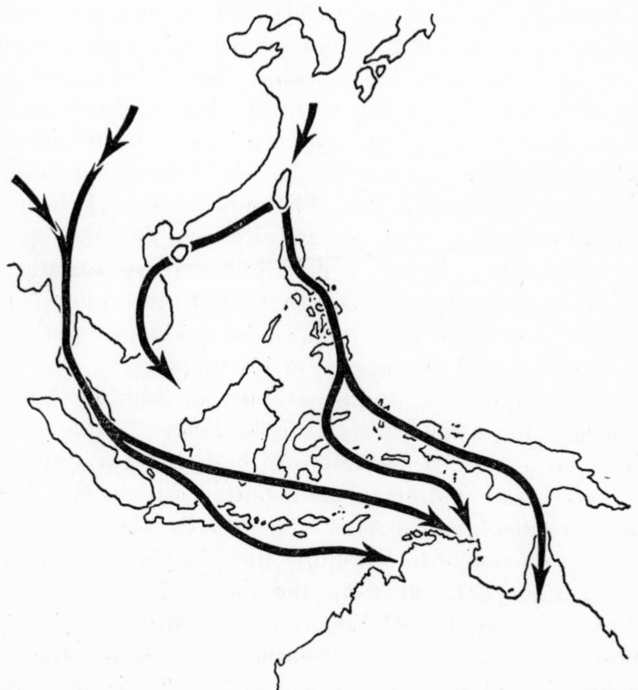

FIG. 1. TENTATIVE MIGRATORY ROUTES INTO AUSTRALIA

supported by Wood-Jones and Abbie as well as by Macintosh (1948: 123-44). To Howells, the Tasmanians are not markedly different from the mainlanders, and could be "an Australian population which has been modified, in part at least, by an incursion of woolly-haired Melanesians from the east". (Howells, 1937: 76.)

In any case, the First Australians possibly brought with them the dog, or dingo, which is not indigenous, and for any long stretches of sea travel had to rely on man. According to Tindale (1959*a*: 44-5), it may have come to Australia with "the first Pleistocene visitors". Dingoes did not reach Tasmania, he says, although this was "part of the mainland in Late Pleistocene times": and while stone remains of what he calls the Kartan phase are "very common" on Kangaroo Island in South Australia, there are no traces of dingo. Nor were any found at Tartanga Island, and at Devon Downs Shelter "the first indisputable remains of the dingo are from Layer IV (Early Murundian)". (See later for Tindale's dating of these 'culture' phases.)

Whether they deliberately set out as explorers to find a new home, or were forced to leave because of population pressures and incoming migrants, we have no way of knowing. But in contrast to the early migrations of sea-faring people like the Polynesians, it seems much more likely that they reached the mainland not so much by design as by accident, such as drifting down as a result of a storm. Both in the past and in the present day, canoes and small boats from nearby Indonesian islands and southern New Guinea have been washed ashore on the Arnhem Land coast. As to when this took place, the question can be settled only by archaeological work, establishing the relative age of fossil human remains. Unfortunately, these are scarce. The most notable of them are the Talgai (Queensland), Cohuna and Keilor (Victoria) specimens. The first stratified sites to be described were at Tartanga-Devon Downs, on the Lower River Murray in South Australia, where work was begun in 1930 (by Hale and Tindale). Fluorine testing of the Keilor skull gave an estimate of 12,500 years.

The whole question of the antiquity of man in Australia is reviewed by Macintosh (1952*a*: 307-39; 1952*b*: 95-105; 1953: 277-96), who has a detailed discussion of the Cohuna cranium, as well as the Talgai teeth and dental arch. But uncertainty still surrounds the dating of these remains. As Elkin (1954: 8) points out, 'although these skulls do not prove antiquity they do suggest an Australian type, somewhat different from the modern Aboriginal. But at present there is no factual evidence of antiquity.' Washburn (1955: 107-8) observes that ancient man must have differed markedly from modern man, and that early Homo sapiens fossils, if alive today, "probably could pass unnoticed in the New York subway". Ancient man spread out, just as early modern man did, but "ancient man (apparently) never reached the New World or Australia". He continues:

> The Wadjak, Cohuna, Talgai series of fossils seems to offer connecting links between early modern man and the Australian. Also of living men the Australian seems to have more in common with generalized early *Homo sapiens*, although the living Australians have evolved along lines of their own. They simply seem to have changed less than the others. Even the Aboriginal Australian is definitely a modern man . . .

ARCHAEOLOGY

Some advance in time-dating early Aboriginal culture phases has been made by McCarthy and Tindale. McCarthy gives a comprehensive summary in his recent volume (1957*a*). Detailed classifications of stone tools have been made, with tentative dating.

TABLE 1*

TIME DEPTH AND CULTURAL CATEGORIES

TIME DEPTH	CATEGORY OR 'CULTURE' NAME			
1,000				
	Murundian (Port Fairy, Victoria: 1777 + or − 175 B.P.)			
2,000				
3,000	Mudukian			
4,000	Pirrian (Devon Down, 4,250 + or − 180 B.P.)			
5,000				
6,000		at Tartangan site: 6,020 + or − 150 B.P.		
	Tartangan	at Menindee: 6,570 + or − 100 B.P.	Kartan isolated on Kangaroo Island	Tasmanian 'culture' isolated on Tasmania
7,000				
8,000		at Cape Martin: 8,700 + or − 120 B.P.		
9,000				
10,000	End of Pleistocene Glaciation			
11,000 and earlier	Kartan	at Fulham; Hallett Cove; Kangaroo Island and Tasmania		

* After Tindale (1959*a*: 37, fig. 1).

Tindale (1941: 144-7; 1957; 1959*a*: 36-51) summarizes culture sequences in south-eastern Australia, with some Carbon 14 dates. This table (above) is a simple adaptation of Tindale's.

McCarthy (1949: 305-19; 1953: 246-8; 1957*a*: 187) reports that twelve prehistoric cultures have been isolated, through "study of their geological locale and the excavation of cave floors in South

Australia, New South Wales and Arnhem Land, but their relationships in point of age and time are not yet determined". He divides these into two series: for coastal south-eastern Australia, Gambieran, Kartan, Bondaian and Eloueran; for the inland series, Tartangan, Pirrian, Mudukian and Murundian.

The sequences cannot be generalized as applying to the whole Continent. For example, the mixed Oenpellian culture is a combination of Pirrian-Mudukian, Eloueran, and some Kimberley elements. (McCarthy, 1957*a*: 188.) The Eloueran, Murundian, Oenpellian, and Milingimbian ("an axe culture", McCarthy calls it) may be "contemporaneous cultures which existed at the time of European occupation", while "the others extend back into the Mesolithic and possibly into the late Palaeolithic periods". But there is a real danger of classifying stone-working techniques with what appear to be similar varieties for prehistoric Europe and elsewhere: there is no uniform time-dating for particular varieties, and a number of stone tools have been dated much earlier, on this basis, than they should be. Mulvaney (1961) has been critical of Tindale's time-sequence categorization as far as Kartan and Tartangan cultures are concerned. Systematically controlled excavations are needed here.

As far as rock paintings and carvings are concerned, and these are to be seen through much of Aboriginal Australia, no key to their age has yet been found. McCarthy (1958: 27-30) mentions that because many rock carvings and incisings (petroglyphs) look old or worn they are often ascribed to a 'prehistoric culture period'. Their antiquity has been the subject of much discussion. Extravagant claims have been made from time to time for the origin of such material.

Take the case of the famous 'Panaramittee Crocodile' carving of the Flinders Range, South Australia, now in the South Australian Museum. Crocodiles lived in Central Australia until Pleistocene times, although the nearest surviving examples are hundreds of miles away. The interpretation which gave this carving its popular name was supported by the fact that the Lake Eyre tribes had myths about the crocodile, *gadimargara*. Also, McCarthy (1958: 29) suggests that early Aborigines in south-eastern Australia could have seen some of the huge creatures which became extinct long before the arrival of Europeans. But according to an old man from the Flinders Range, well acquainted with local traditions, the 'Panaramittee Crocodile' was simply a representation of a magic stick with strings arranged in a network fashion. No one had previously asked the local people what it meant.

Much the same problem faces us in relation to cave paintings.

There are outstanding galleries in various parts of Australia. (See Chapter XII.) Some are obviously very old, and may have been retouched or painted over in more recent times. Or several art styles may be represented on the walls of one cave, raising the question of which came first: whether they existed side by side, or one succeeded another. The beautifully drawn stick figures called *mimi*, near Oenpelli, are an example. A wide variety of them has been illustrated by Mountford (1956), who reports that, as a type, they are "overlaid by the polychromatic X-ray art", and that local people say they are the work of spirits: this, to Mountford, "is an attempt to explain an art style which the aborigines themselves do not use, (and) suggests not only that the *mimi* art is the older, but that it is the work of an extinct cultural group". However, there is no independent evidence on that score. (See Berndt, 1958*a*: 249-61.) Many of these galleries are, or were, sacred sites, still in use in northern and central Australia. In one view, the "facts all point to the diffusion of art ideas from the north to the south over a long period of time"; but just how long is still a matter of speculation. (McCarthy, 1958: 66.)

Large shell mounds such as those on the north coast of Arnhem Land, particularly at Milingimbi, need not have taken thousands of years to build up. (See Elkin, 1954: 7-8.) McCarthy and Setzler (in Mountford, ed., 1960: 215-95) carried out archaeological work in parts of Arnhem Land, finding stone artefacts, bone points and some skeletal material: the stone objects were placed in culture categories and classified, but no dating has been attempted. The material was not plentiful, and "limited almost entirely to the non-perishable chipped stone and bone implements . . ." A point to remember is that the Arnhem Land coast is fairly rich in material culture, as compared with most other parts of Australia; and this includes a very wide range of perishable items—as well as the remarkable galleries of paintings. This is an excellent example of the problems which confront an archaeologist who is trying to explore a people's prehistory but has very few clues to help him. The items that survive may be only a small fraction of those in use at any given period. Nevertheless, provided we do not ask too much of it, archaeological evidence can tell us something about the past. At least, it can offer some thought-provoking suggestions. For instance, excavations have been made at Tandandjal cave, near Beswick Station, Northern Territory. (Macintosh, 1951: 178-204.) Macintosh reports that "the shallowness of the deposit . . . does not suggest great antiquity", but successive layers infer occupation by different groups of people with varying cultural perspectives over the years.

PRIMITIVE?

The Aborigines of today are not survivals with a stone-age culture. They are our contemporaries, modern men and women, motivated by the same basic urges as ourselves, but with a different way of living, a different outlook, different values. And difference does not, necessarily, imply inequality.

The words 'stone-age' and 'primitive' are often used in reference to them, but these words are misleading as well as insidious. For one thing, they have been put forward as an excuse for not trying to understand these people, on the grounds that they are centuries apart from ourselves, or for treating them as something less than human. For another, the same belief has been used obliquely to substantiate the claim that all Aborigines are dirty, superstitious, shiftless, and generally unemployable; that they cannot respond to education, get drunk at the least provocation, and accept prostitution as a normal part of ordinary living. Most of this is entirely untrue; and when it is true this is not because of any innate characteristic, nor because of their 'primitiveness', but because of particular social conditions. Given the circumstances in which many of them have been brought up, it is a wonder that more of them do not conform to this picture.

No modern, contemporary, living man, the Aborigines included, is identical with palaeolithic or neolithic man. To quote Washburn again, the Aboriginal Australian "is definitely a modern man and lacks the peculiarities of the face and limb bone which characterize ancient man". (Washburn, in Hoebel, Jennings and Smith, eds., 1955: 108.) The main responsibility for identifying the two must rest with archaeologists and ethnologists. These specialists emphasized one kind of material, which they came to regard as critical because it provided a clue to intangible aspects of culture which they could not get at in their own field. They became interested in contemporary non-literate peoples. The Australian Aborigines provided the information they wanted because they used stone tools, and because they kept no written records. And so they were equated with early man.

It is true that for certain limited purposes we are justified in drawing general implications. The use of stone tools is undeniably associated with a certain kind of relationship to the natural environment. This point is quite significant. At the same time it should not be taken too far, because over-emphasis on this aspect leads to neglect of many others which are equally important. Although technological complexity is a central theme in our own society, there are other kinds of cultural complexity which do not necessarily coincide with this. Although the Australian Aborigines in their traditional setting used stone tools, had a minimum of

material goods, did not live in houses, hunted and collected their food, this does not make them stone-age or primitive in the accepted archaeological sense of those terms. Apart from anything else, there is the emotional connotation of such words. Inevitably, they are interpreted as meaning crude, rudimentary, underdeveloped, mentally backward, remote in time, and so on. They are not appropriate in respect of any living contemporary group of people, whatever their colour, social organization, or beliefs. The picture is, rather, one of a range of varying physical types and varying societies and cultures, some more complex than others—or complex in different ways.

Part of the trouble has been the assumption that an emphasis on material objects, and on technological achievements, must always go hand-in-hand with highly-developed mental ability or an advanced civilization. The measuring rod here was usually our own Western European-type culture, for a long time depicted as far superior in every way to all others. This view has been profoundly shaken in recent years. One consequence is that we have come to pay much more attention to the relative merits of other societies and cultures. Instead of the term 'primitive' many of us today, if we have to use words of this sort at all, prefer to use the word non-literate (not *il*literate) to distinguish the Aborigines, for instance, from peoples who share a tradition, or norm, of literacy: or non-industrialized, or non-technologically oriented, to contrast them with members of industrialized societies which make use of machine technology. But even these terms are not particularly satisfactory. (For a general discussion of this topic see C. Berndt, 1960: 50-69.)

In this connection there is the question whether the Aborigines are mentally backward or inferior. This is an issue on which it is not easy to be dispassionate, and statements one way or another frequently rest on emotional bias rather than on careful scrutiny of all the available evidence. Accusations framed in these terms are a popular way of disparaging other people, or other societies, which do not subscribe to the same goals or the same means of achieving them. People take their own background of experience and culture very much for granted, and often find it hard to realize that others should have any trouble in acquiring the same familiarity with it. In the same way, adults brought up in another cultural environment have sometimes been likened to children because they are ignorant of things which 'everyone should know': they have to learn the new ways of thinking and behaving, just as children do. But this kind of labelling is always a one-way affair. It rarely occurs to people who take this stand that the adults so described may have had a complex and rich culture of their own, in which they grew to maturity. Even scientists who should have known better were for a long time guilty of this kind of bias: they used their own culture as a universally valid standard, and measured others against it. Too many assessments of intelligence have been made on just this basis—testing in an unfamiliar situation, often artificially constructed, against a range of 'givens' derived from the culture of the persons responsible for designing the test.

Psychologists have been trying for some time to devise satisfactory intelligence tests which are cross-culturally valid: that is, valid in other cultures as well as in our own. So far, in spite of the claims which are sometimes made, none of them are really satisfactory. Porteus (1931, 1933) and others (e.g. Fry and Pulleine, 1931: 153-67) have tried to work out intelligence tests to show along what lines the Australian Aborigines generally, or in specific areas, are higher than some human groups and lower than others—for example, in their capacity to adapt themselves to our way of life. (For a general review of Porteus' work see Elkin, 1932: 101-13.) But this last is a false line of approach. It is useful only in circumstances where adjustment or adaptability is the sole point at issue—in the context of assimilation programmes, for example. But this is not measuring intelligence, except in a very narrow and restricted sense indeed. To be fully acceptable, such testing should take into account a people's own culture, its traditional ways of thinking and acting. One problem here is the matter of incentives. People may not want to co-operate in the tests: they may not see the use of them. If they are not used to test situations, or to the kind of competitive situation to which Europeans (for instance) are accustomed, this may affect their scoring. And difficulties of this sort must always be taken into account.

The most successful cross-cultural tests so far are those which make no claim to measure intelligence, or mental ability, in terms of scaling or evaluating people on this basis. The Rorschach, the Thematic Apperception Test, and so on are, to put it briefly, projective devices for studying personality, categorizing the way in which a person looks at his social and cultural environment, his world. Even these tests have come in for a great deal of criticism, because they are interpreted in a rather arbitrary way, again on the basis of outside standards. But they are broader and less rigid than the others, more useful in helping us to understand people with different values, and different ways of living. Up to the present there has been no systematic testing on this basis in Aboriginal Australia: and we have no satisfactory information in this direction.

It was fashionable at one time to pay a great deal of attention to brain size and weight, which were thought to be closely related to mental and psychological factors. (See Firth, 1956: 31-2.) Quite a few people believed that actual brain capacity and size were fundamental in determining the limits of mental ability. This view is no longer tenable. Perhaps the best statement on it comes, again, from Washburn. He says:

> . . . These are anatomical classifications which are used for anatomical purposes. Since the ends are anatomical in nature, the methods used are anatomical. There is no thought of leaping from anatomy to intelligence, language or religion. A scientist takes the most direct route possible. If one wants to know about intelligence, intelligence should be measured, not cranial capacity. If one wants to know about language, language should be studied, not head form. One gets out of a mill only what goes in, although the form may have changed. When anatomy goes in, only anatomy comes out . . .
> (Washburn, in Hoebel, Jennings and Smith, eds. 1955: 107.)

There is no clear agreement on what is meant by intelligence—except the cryptic assertion that it is whatever the tests are measuring. But it does seem, from the results of many investigations, that the potential ability of all peoples is identical: that all make use of the same mental processes, the same principles of thought, in conceptualizing their environment, although they start off from different premises. There is the old question here of how to assess the effects of heredity as against the effects of environment. Where tests are given to people who share more or less the same social and cultural environment, this factor can be held to some extent constant, and the results are more likely to be comparable. When they are given to people from widely differing environments, we cannot be quite sure what is being measured. We could, perhaps, take one feature which is sometimes classified broadly as intelligence—the ability to extract resources from their particular environment. Study along these lines could lead to the question of adjustment-potential, especially in relation to changing social conditions brought about through alien impact—as among the Australian Aborigines. Any group of normal people (we are not talking here about cases of abnormality, or about the physically or mentally handicapped, such as one finds in any society) can adjust to changing conditions, under favourable circumstances; there is nothing, as far as we know, to hold them back as far as intelligence, or the capacity for intellectual development, is concerned. But any situation of adjustment which involves learning a new way of life is fraught with difficulties which are not always linked with mental ability.

PHYSICAL HOMOGENEITY-HETEROGENEITY

It used to be supposed that the Australian Aborigines were a homogeneous people, substantially of the same stock. More recently it has been recognized that specific conditions such as environment and diet, in addition to mutations and genetic variations, may have led to regional differences among them, with selective breeding preserving or developing local types. One point here is that, to repeat, they did not remain isolated until they were discovered by Europeans. To some extent they were cut off from the rest of the world, from the mainstreams of population movement and cultural change. But there seem to have been spasmodic contacts, perhaps centuries apart, which gradually became more frequent. Tindale comments (1959*a*: 39):

> Not only are the basic types of Australians represented in South Eastern Asia, but most, if not all of the material cultural possessions of Tasmanians and Australians and perhaps all of the basic forms of archaeological stone implements of their ancestors, are of types once in use outside the Australian region. There must be an increasing tendency to see the Australian continental area as only an enclave into which from time to time were projected small samples of the physical types and successive cultural novelties produced by the main bodies of men on the great adjoining Eur-Asiatic continental land mass . . .

A number of writers have echoed these same ideas, but rather less strongly. It is necessary to be cautious here, for there is little factual evidence regarding such contact, outside that which has taken place in historic times—from Indonesia and from New Guinea, for instance. Possibly it is enough to support the contention that these Aborigines have been influenced both physically and culturally by external sources over a long period of time. But we need more archaeological data, and more too on their genetic composition.

The genetic picture

Some details of the genetic picture to date are set out in the Appendix. But in these more general comments, from a human geneticist's point of view, Dr. Robert L. Kirk writes: "Most classifications of human races are based on differences in physical characters such as skin colour, stature, head shape, nose form and hair type. Although the major human races can be adequately described by reference to a series of such physical characters, there are a number of difficulties when similar techniques are applied to the study of relationships between smaller groups. Some characters, stature for instance, are considerably influenced by environmental factors. Further, for none of these physical characters is the method of inheritance completely understood. This defect makes it hard to assess the exact degree of mixing between two different populations.

"For these and other reasons attention has been focused recently on human characters of which the means of inheritance are known, and which are not subject to modification by the environment. The inherited units, or genes, controlling such characters are known as genetic markers. [See Fig. 2.] Amongst these characters are the various blood group systems, inherited differences in certain serum

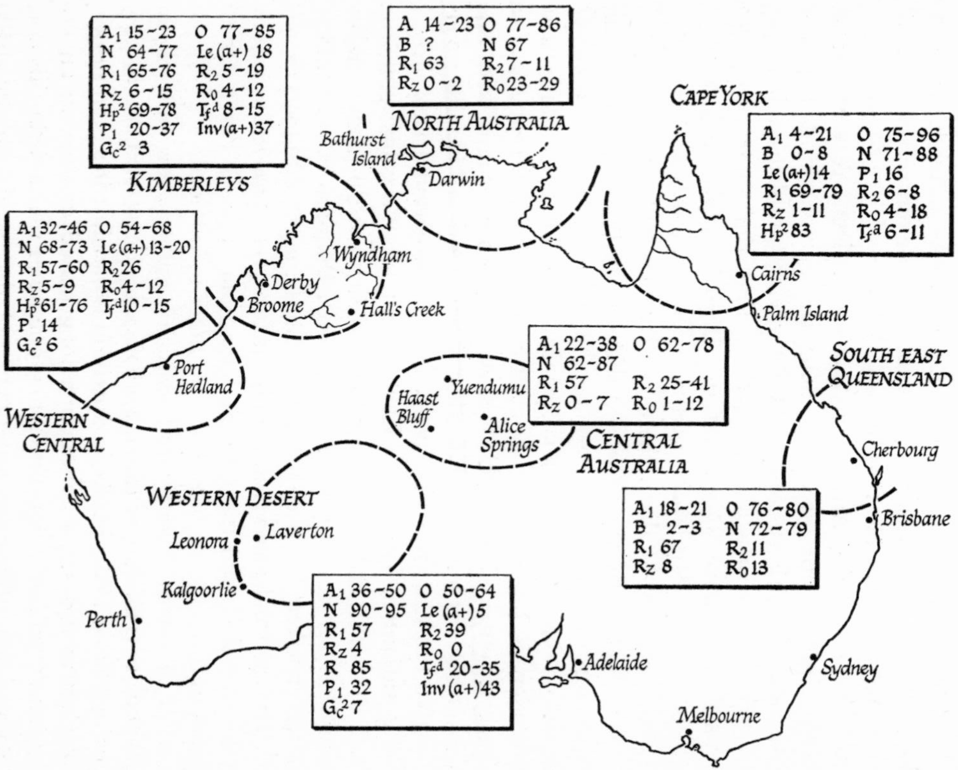

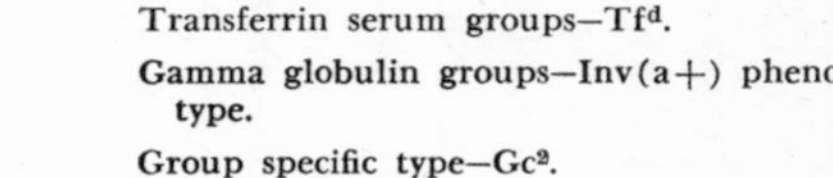

FIG. 2. SUMMARY OF FREQUENCIES FOR VARIOUS MARKER GENES IN AUSTRALIAN ABORIGINAL POPULATIONS

The range of frequencies expressed as percentages is based on available published surveys, together with unpublished observations from studies by Kirk and his colleagues.

Genes shown are:—

- ABO blood groups—A_1, O and B (where group B is present).
- MNS blood groups—N (gene S is absent in all areas).
- RH blood groups—R_1, R_2, R_z, R_0.
- Lewis blood groups—Le(a+ve) phenotype.
- P blood groups—P_1.
- Haptoglobin serum groups—Hp^2.
- Transferrin serum groups—Tf^d.
- Gamma globulin groups—Inv(a+) phenotype.
- Group specific type—Gc^2.

For key see Appendix.

proteins, and different types of haemoglobin. New characters are being discovered each year which fulfil the basic requirements of good genetic markers usable in the study of human populations. In general, however, some years must elapse after the discovery of a new marker before it has been studied in a sufficient number of populations to enable useful comparisons to be made.

"The study of genetic markers so far has failed to indicate the racial stocks with which the Australian Aborigines have close affinities. Perhaps this is not surprising. Isolation of two populations in different environments for as long as 500 generations could readily lead to divergences of considerable magnitude in gene frequencies, even when the selective factors operating are of small magnitude. Future research may indicate the nature of the selective factors involved. If this is accomplished, an attempt can be made to calculate the rate of change of gene frequencies, and to assess the possibilities of divergence from one or another particular ancestral stock. At present it seems possible only to rule out certain affinities as being less probable than others.

"The present day Australian Aborigines, then, are a genetically distinct group, but revealing among themselves considerable and significant variations. And it is in solving problems relating to inter-tribal affinities and migrations that the study of genetic markers may have its greatest use. Two examples may serve to illustrate the potentialities of this approach. Birdsell (1950: 264), commenting on the sharp change in frequency of the blood group gene A eastward from its peak value among the Bidjandjara to a significantly lower value among the Aranda, suggests that the Aranda people have migrated southward relatively recently; and this view is supported by linguistic and other cultural data. In another context, Kirk and Vos, working with groups from the Western Desert and the Kimberleys, have found striking differences between the Western Desert people and groups around Hall's Creek for a variant of the Rh antigen D, and for the gamma-globulin group Gm (b). Both the D variant and the Gm (b) phenotype are completely absent in the Western Desert. Despite the cultural evidence that there has been influence from the north into the Western Desert area, and vice versa, it has not been accompanied by significant gene flow, and the biological isolation of the Western Desert group seems to have been fairly strongly maintained.

"The Western Desert group, which numbers now only about 2,000 persons altogether (Berndt, 1959*a*), is of extraordinary interest to the human biologist. Reproductively isolated, it has been subject to selective forces, possibly over a long period of time, in an undeniably harsh environment. When one notes that it is in this area that one finds the highest frequency of the A_1 gene of the ABO blood group system in Australia, the highest N gene of the MNS system, a very high R_z frequency in the Rh system, the highest transferrin Tf D frequency in the world, is the only population known at present where Gm (b) is completely absent, is the centre of dispersion for the tawny hair gene, and has yielded also the only known example in the world of a person without any detectable Rh antigen, it is tempting to speculate on the respective roles which selection, inbreeding, and genetic drift have played. There is still much to be learnt in this area, as elsewhere in Australia, of value to those interested in the broader problems of human evolution and race formation."

Physical appearance

Looking casually at a cross-section of the Aboriginal population, from the Great Australian Bight to the Arafura Sea, gives an impression of mixed similarities and differences with no sharp dividing line to mark off distinct pockets. However striking the differences may seem in individual cases, in an overall view the transition between these extremes is gradual rather than steep.

One unusual feature of this sort is the extreme hairiness of the people about the Lower River Murray and Lakes district in South Australia, where some men had chest and body hair of nine inches or so in length, some women beards and moustaches. (See Stirling, 1914.) This hairiness diminishes toward the north, where the people appear to be more lightly built, with longer arms and legs. In the Great Victoria Desert, stretching northward from the Transcontinental Railway Line to the central ranges of the Everards, Musgraves, Tomkinsons, Petermanns and Warburtons, they have almost chocolate-coloured skin underneath their surface coating of red or greyish brown dust, sloping foreheads, prominent brow-ridges, characteristically thin shanks. In Central Australia too are people sometimes described as typically Aboriginal, mainly because the Aranda (Arunta) were popularized quite early by Carl Strehlow and by Spencer and Gillen. They have even more distinct brow-ridges, deep-set eyes, broad nostrils. Some of their women and children, like those of the Tanami-Granites 'desert' north-west to Hall's Creek, Billaluna, Balgo, down to the Canning Stock route, and even near Lilla Creek in northern South Australia, have fair or bronze-tinted hair. Toward the borders of the Northern Territory and Western Australia, in this 'desert' country, are a few people with 'Jewish'-like profiles and prominent noses—short men and women, thin and wiry from constant movement in search of food. Further north again, near the coast, they are bigger-boned, taller and heavier. Some are almost European in appearance, except for their brown pigmentation and dark brown eyes, while others again have the 'Centralian' feature of wide nostrils, strong brow-ridge, thick jowls, or receding forehead and chin. On Melville and Bathurst islands are people darker in colour, many of them heavily built, deep-chested and muscular. A few of the old men still wear their clipped tufty beards, fringing the face from ear to ear, unlike any found on the mainland.

In western Arnhem Land too are a number of short people, no more than four and a half to five feet high, from the source of the Liverpool River: some small-boned, delicately shaped, others thick-set and squat. Along the northern Arnhem Land coast the physical range extends from the conventional Centralian type to lighter skinned people reminiscent of Indonesians. There are finely chiselled profiles, straight short noses, broad cheeks, inconspicuous brow-ridges, and lank straight hair: in many cases lips are thinner than those of the more inland groups, and bodies and legs well-developed, against the bony calves of the desert hunters.

Nor is there uniformity in the matter of hair texture, for some have coarse hair, while others have soft, fine strands. Most Aborigines have wavy hair, some curly; and some of the women are proud of the reddish or golden lights which need no red ochre to enhance them.

Thus there is not one Aboriginal type, any more than there is one Australian or European type. There are simply variations within a range. Elkin (1954) and McCarthy (1957*a*) have good descriptions of the physical characteristics of present-day Aborigines and there is no need to duplicate them here. Wagner (1937) and Fenner (1939) comment on physical differences between southern and northern Australian types. But it is one thing to speak of types for the purpose of classification, another to identify them with actual populations. Tindale and Birdsell (1941), and Birdsell alone (1947, 1950), have put forward a tri-hybrid theory, suggesting three distinctive physical types and naming them accordingly: the southern type, 'Murrayians'; the northern, 'Carpentarians'; and 'Barrineans' in north-east Queensland who, they say, may have negrito affinities. All are basically Australoid, but in Birdsell's opinion they are different enough to suggest that they did not converge on Australia from the same starting point. McCarthy (1957*a*: 24), summarizing this material, points out that there are various objections to it, for instance on the grounds that "the distinctions are purely statistical, and that the differences between the three groups can all be readily accounted for by biological processes". (See Abbie, 1961.) Macintosh (1952*c*: 215) notes: "Concepts which speak of region types would seem to be less secure, when suitable representatives of each of these types (i.e., tall, short or medium) occur within the limits of each

Stilted stringybark wet-season or mosquito huts at Buckingham Bay, north-eastern Arnhem Land (1961)

Central Australian wet-weather camp: a bough shelter, the roof serving as a storage platform

(photo: courtesy C. P. Mountford)

Above: Late afternoon camp scene at Balgo, south-eastern Kimberleys, Western Australia (1958)

Right: Women asleep in the shade of a windbreak at Balgo (1958)

Women and children in camp, Warburton Range, Western Australia (1959)

7 or 8 tribes together with intermediate grades and a lack of discontinuity in any one physical trait."

As regards this matter of racial affiliation, one question which troubles some people has to do with throw-backs. Does this apply to persons of Australian Aboriginal stock, they ask, as has been reported in the case of negroes? This question has, of course, a direct bearing on current policies of assimilation. There are two facets to it. One relates to negro throw-backs—the extent to which these occur in fully authenticated cases, as against popular belief or assumptions based on hearsay or partial evidence. (A few such reports, if not all, may have stemmed from efforts to conceal adultery, where a woman had given birth to a child of which her husband was not the father.) The second concerns, specifically, the Australian Aborigines.

Various physical characteristics are involved in any discussion of this sort: hair form and colour, for example; stature; head form; nose shape; the extent to which lips are everted; eye colour; and, of course, blood groups. But popular interest in the main seems to focus on skin colour or pigmentation. A provocative suggestion was made a few years ago by Howells, in keeping with his argument that the Aborigines constitute "a major race which represents an earlier stage in the development of Homo sapiens than does any other existing race". (Howells, 1937: 77.) "Possibly", he says (p. 75), "the early forms of Homo sapiens were as densely pigmented as the Australian and the Negro, the latest types becoming progressively lighter."

Boyd (1950: 308-11), speaking of skin pigmentation in fairly general terms, points to the still unsolved problems relating to its inheritance; but he suggests that in most mixed populations (other than South Africa) "authenticated cases" of so-called throw-backs "are practically non-existent". He underlines the complexity of this issue, in which it seems clear "that more than two genes are involved" (*ibid.*, 41-4, 53). And in regard to the Australians, he asserts the closeness of their relationship to European or "basic white" peoples (*ibid.*, 273-4), expanding on this point in connection with the 'throw-back' question (346): "These stocks are called 'basically white' . . . because on being crossed with white races the offspring suggest that not so many genes (or less dominant genes) for dark pigmentation were present in the dark (or black) ancestors as is the case with the African negroes . . ." Another comment on this score comes from Tindale (1940-41: 66-161), who says:

> [The Aborigines] are fundamentally not negroid in ethnic constitution . . . These dark aborigines have a skin colour whose intensity seems to be controlled by multiple factors so that there is steady dilution of tone with access of white blood. . . .

B

There seems to be no evidence to suggest that their descendants will, through segregation of recessive genes, unwittingly reproduce what have been commonly called 'throw backs' such as has been considered sometimes to occur in the case of the negro-white cross.

Little else can be said on the subject of Aboriginal-European crosses in respect of skin colour, simply because no reliable modern study has been made. The most recent reference is from Gates (1960: 7-50), based on examination of about half a dozen hybrid families at Alice Springs. He concludes: "The observations, taken as a whole, lead to the hypothesis of one main gene for skin pigmentation, together with a minor gene corresponding with the white-brunet. Evidence has also been adduced that the dark skin of the adult aborigines is in considerable measure a matter of tanning."

Disease

A number of earlier writers discuss the matter of disease among the Aborigines—most notably Brough Smyth (1878: 253-69), Curr (1886: 208-34), and Stirling (1911). The best survey, however, is Cleland's (1928). (See also Packer, 1961.) There is not much detailed information as far as Aborigines with little or no alien contact are concerned. Several papers deal with their reactions to various introduced diseases. According to Basedow (1925: xiv), the main dangers lie in syphilis, pulmonary tuberculosis and trachoma, primarily the result of contact. Smallpox, influenza, measles and whooping cough, for instance, are said to have decimated the Aborigines in various parts of the Continent. Cleland (1928: 4) considers that they are no more susceptible to infectious diseases than Europeans, and that the high death rate among them can be explained by such factors as extreme "exposure to weather conditions, unhygienic surroundings, and lack of medical attention". Tuberculosis is possibly a special case, along with syphilis.

Diseases unique to these people are few, and there is no evidence so far that they have built up an inherited immunity or resistance to any infectious disease. Before the coming of Europeans, and of Asians in the north, there were possibly no venereal diseases on the Continent (see R. and C. Berndt, 1954: 208, 213), or common colds. Trachoma may have been present: Dampier (1688) reported that Aborigines on the north-west coast had their eyes half closed to keep out the flies and could not see far unless they held up their heads. Leprosy may have been indigenous, as well as yaws, and Boomerang Legs ("characterized by arthritis, osteitis and periostitis": Cleland, *ibid.*, 6), some skin diseases, and possibly some nutritional diseases, although as far as these last are concerned much more investigation is needed. Several of these appear in mythology and traditional stories of Central Australia and Arnhem Land—

for instance, most notably, Boomerang Legs, trachoma, and possibly leprosy in the north. In the traditional situation, tooth decay was probably uncommon in younger people. On the other hand, although there is little information on this point, it does seem that mental illness and congenital abnormalities of various kinds were not unknown. But 'traditional' and 'indigenous' are ambiguous and relative terms. In regard to disease, as well as to so many other features of Aboriginal life, we cannot speak with any certainty of what happened before outside contact. The traditional past, what people say or believe happened long ago, need not be the same as the historical past, the past as it actually happened; but for much of Australia it represents all the evidence we have.

CULTURAL SIMILARITY AND DIVERSITY

Just as there are physical differences, so there is cultural diversity. This has been foreshadowed in talking about the various prehistoric 'culture' phases, and about the Aborigines' exposure to influences from outside.

Tindale (1959*a*: 38) suggests that early Aboriginal man, gradually spreading across the Continent, may have moved first into the more fertile areas where fresh water was plentiful, leaving the less hospitable parts to be occupied later. McCarthy, in contrast, suggests that

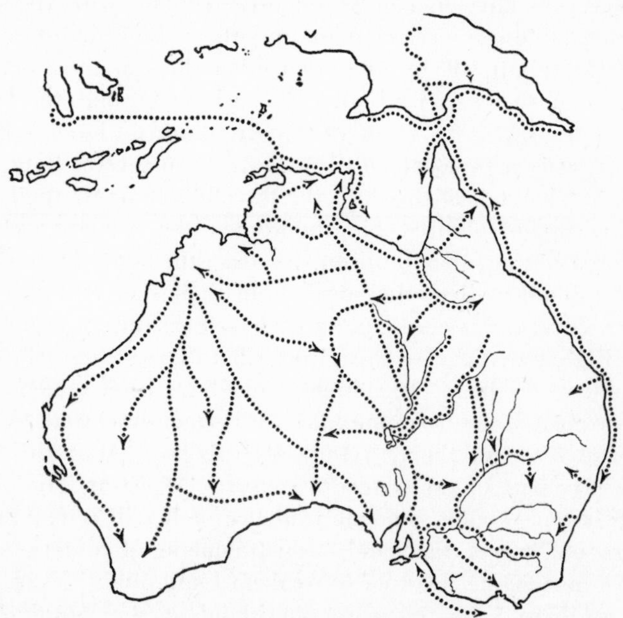

FIG. 3. TRADE ROUTES WITHIN AND BEYOND AUSTRALIA

After McCarthy (1939*a*: 191), with additions. Culture traits as well as ideas spread gradually, from one area to another, often being modified in the process.

when the first immigrants arrived here the whole Continent was well-watered and fertile. (McCarthy, 1957*a*: 19.) This question aside, McCarthy has the best discussion to date on the general topic of diffusion in more recent times. (McCarthy, 1939*a*: 405-38, 80-104, 172-95; 1953: 243-61, including a fairly comprehensive bibliography. And see Koppers, 1955: 171-5.) Diffusion must undoubtedly have been a factor in Aboriginal culture from its very beginnings; but local developments must be considered too. And this dual process —things, ideas, practices, being handed on from one group to another, but being changed, modified or elaborated in the course of acceptance—has permeated all aspects of Aboriginal life.

In what can almost be called historic times people from what is now Indonesia visited the north coast of Arnhem Land, possibly as far back as the fifteenth century, although this dating has been questioned by several writers. (Mountford, 1956: 410.) Current opinion points to three main points of entry for alien influences: Cape York, Arnhem Land and the North-West (Kimberleys). What we are not entirely sure of is when these contacts first took place. McCarthy (1939*a*: 179-83), Haddon (1901-8, 1938), Thomson (1933), and others write of direct and indirect influences from New Guinea on the Cape York Aborigines, through the Torres Strait Islands.

As far as the coastal people of Arnhem Land are concerned, they may very well have had more intensive contact with the outside world, over a longer period, than any other Aboriginal group. (See R. and C. Berndt, 1954.) They remember their first visitors as the Bajini, from the western islands somewhere beyond the Arafura and Timor Seas. The songs of eastern Arnhem Land still commemorate this period, which could have been several hundreds of years ago. They tell of the ships the travellers came in, their golden brown or copper coloured skin, the women they brought with them, the stone dwellings they built on the coast, the cloth they wove and dyed, the small gardens they made, and their special way of spearing fish. Possibly they were early traders from the East Indies, but the Aborigines distinguish them from what they call the 'Macassans', who came after them. Other suggestions have been that they were Bajau or Sea Gipsies, roaming Malay fishermen who were to be met with in all parts of the East India Archipelago. After this, maybe in the early part of the sixteenth century, 'Macassan' (Indonesian) contact began. Today, concrete evidence of it still remains, in the shape of old graves, tamarind trees, fragments of pottery.

In the north-eastern corner of Arnhem Land quantities of pottery fragments have been found on an island at the mouth of Port Bradshaw and along the adjacent mainland. (See R. and C. Berndt, 1951*b*.) Others come from South Goulburn Island. From the shards collected it would seem that these people must have made use of several kinds of pots and bowls, as well as other vessels still unidentified. The 'Macassans' are credited with having introduced them; and according to Aboriginal evidence they even made some on the Australian coast, with the help of local people–who were not, however, interested in doing this by themselves. Excavations by McCarthy and Setzler (in Mountford, ed., 1960: 287-94) revealed none in graves at Bartalumba Bay, or in the shell middens on Milingimbi. A number of specimens obtained in the course of that work have not so far been dated. They could range from 206 B.C. to A.D. 1800. No shards, say McCarthy and Setzler, were in the excavated sites, and no kilns were found: they found nothing to indicate that pottery was made locally. However, up to date, little consistent archaeological work has been done. There were many 'Indonesian' sites, with Malay names, along this Arnhem Land coast; and although we have recorded their approximate positions, most of them have not yet been excavated.

Briefly, then, tradition has it that these visitors came down in large numbers in their praus, with the north-west monsoon. They built settlements of leaf-thatched houses on stilts, in which they lived for part of the year—employing Aborigines, or establishing trading relations with them. All told, their influence on Aboriginal

FIG. 4. THE WORLD OF THE ARNHEM LANDERS AT THE CLOSE OF INDONESIAN CONTACT
After R. and C. Berndt (1954: 39).

life was considerable. It was not simply a matter of the goods they introduced, such as pottery, knives, cloth and sails, and dug-out canoes. More subtly, their impact was reflected in music and song rhythms and in ceremonies, as well as in art forms.

The point here is that Australia was not sealed off from all outside associations. And because of the trading and ceremonial relations which linked neighbouring groups, pressure in one region such as Arnhem Land, Cape York, or the Kimberley coast, must indirectly have had some repercussions in others.

It has been said that Australian Aboriginal languages cannot be linked with any other family of languages, suggesting that they are a purely local development. (Capell, 1956: 2.) If this is so, what does it mean in connection with our discussion of outside contact? Capell reports that these languages differ widely, "both in structure and in vocabulary, among themselves . . . yet there is a basic similarity in certain structural elements and a small but obstinate basic vocabulary". After a detailed survey he concludes by saying, among other things, that "the Australian languages are ultimately one. There is no structural reason for not affiliating Tasmanian with them, but vocabulary contents seem to preclude so doing". "There is insufficient material available for the application of any glottochronological method to compute the directions and rates of

TABLE 2
SUBDIVISIONS OF LANGUAGES IN AUSTRALIA
(After A. Capell, 1956: 99.)

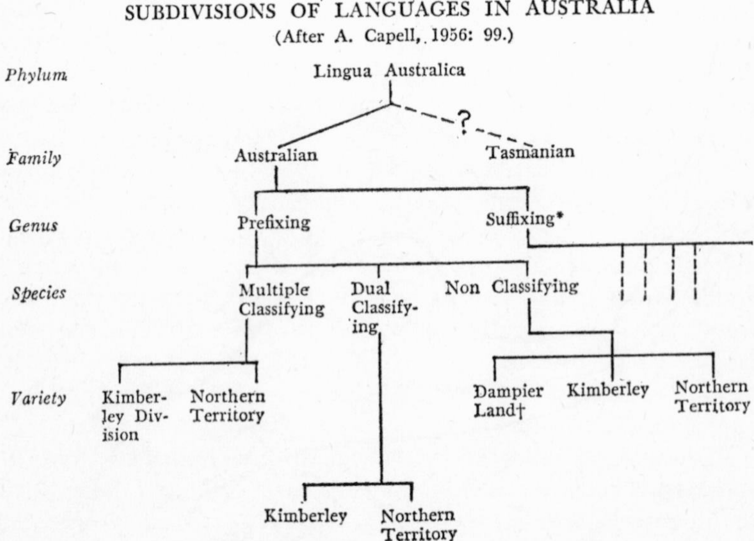

* the sub-divisions of suffixing languages are not yet fully determined.
† and neighbouring southern Kimberleys.

dispersion" (*ibid.*, 95-6). To him (*ibid.*, 95), the two "main divisions" are made up of suffixing and prefixing languages, "and the prefixing has sprung from the suffixing"; within each "there are numerous subdivisions", summarized in the accompanying table, which does not imply a chronological sequence.

The theme then, supported by physical anthropological, archaeological and linguistic data, is variation on a basically common ground—a combination of elements which enables us to speak rather generally about the Australian Aborigines. All over the Continent their way of life could be described as characteristically Aboriginal—but, and this is quite significant, it has been highlighted and enriched by hundreds of local manifestations. Against the common framework there is much diversity. There is, or was, no *lingua franca,* no language by means of which a man can make himself understood from one end of the Continent to the other. Even though Aboriginal languages are basically similar, even if they all belong to one family, this does not mean that they are mutually intelligible. Throughout Aboriginal Australia hundreds of languages were spoken, some made up of a number of dialects. People of one tribe might be unfamiliar with the language spoken only a few miles away. Even when one language covers a wide area, everyone in that area needs to speak or at least understand more than one dialect.

On the whole, the people of each tribe keep much to themselves, meeting those speaking different languages only on ceremonial occasions, or perhaps when permission is granted to strangers to hunt through adjacent territory, or when trading parties come to exchange goods. Although this gives the appearance of tribal isolation, with clear-cut linguistic barriers, such is not always the case, as we shall see later on.

Hand in hand with this diversity of language, distinguishing one tribal group from another, go different patterns of living, each with its peculiar emphasis. Some societies reckon descent primarily through the mother, some through the father, while others attach almost equal importance to both. Rules governing marriage vary from region to region, from tribe to tribe. In one the most favoured mate is a cross-cousin, the daughter of a man's mother's brother or father's sister; in another her daughter is the most desirable wife. And so on.

Environmental differences throughout the Continent have encouraged differences in economic approach, although these can be found even within the same area. There are coastal people, and folk of the inland rivers or fertile jungles; people living among the hills and rocks and thick scrub of the inland, or wandering across comparatively arid wastes, with only occasional waterholes and grassy plains. The way in which they have been forced to obtain their daily sustenance pervades their whole economy—not only the process of food-collecting and hunting, but indeed the whole life of the tribe: for it involves special techniques, special ways of living. Religious experience with its substantiating mythology varies too from one area to another. In some cases a common thread runs from tribe to tribe over a wide stretch of country, its outward manifestations broadly the same—or strikingly different.

What is true for one Aboriginal group, then, does not necessarily hold good for another. There are weapons and utensils, for instance, found only in one tribe: differing techniques for making and decorating spears and spearthrowers, clubs, dilly bags, and digging sticks. Boomerangs may be used in one community as hunting weapons, in another for defloration, in another as clapping sticks to beat rhythmically in time to the singing; and in others they are unknown, or not used at all.

Diversity in language not only fosters different ways of living, behaving, and thinking. Over the years, also, it reinforces and consolidates them. And knowledge of one Aboriginal group (say, in eastern Arnhem Land) does not necessarily mean that we can speak with authority about others—people living in the Great Victoria Desert, or the rain forests near Cairns, or the barren country about the Canning Stock Route.

Aborigines from different regions, different tribes, will not react in exactly the same way to a given situation. Each responds in the light of his own upbringing and background—his traditional heritage, the unique pattern of life developed over countless centuries. And even within one tribe, no two personalities are exactly alike. Everyone has his individual peculiarities, moulded and shaped by his own personal experience.

We must bear these points in mind. They are vital in helping us to understand the Aborigines, with all the rich variety of their life throughout the Continent.

Nevertheless, when contrasted with other peoples of the world, they show a basic similarity which links them together as essentially one. The differences between them recede in importance, as compared with those which mark them off from the invader, the European. Here there is a sharp distinction, not only in physical appearance, but also in outlook and tradition.

The First Australian, faced with the European conqueror, was bewildered. There was no common language, no familiar medium which he could grasp quickly to turn the situation to his advantage. The newcomer in his turn, found little among these people which was congenial. To him they were part of the indigenous environment—people worlds apart from himself, who wandered naked across the land for sustenance, always on the move, building no permanent homes but only flimsy shelters and windbreaks: people with simple weapons, and few material objects.

Because of this background, a product of the Aborigines' close bond with their environment, built up over years of comparative isolation, and because of the gulf which separated them from the Europeans, the newcomers, there was from the very beginning no doubt as to which of the two would dominate the other. Tribes with differing languages and emphases, with no sense of common nationality, could not combine as a war-making unit to drive out the invader. Even had this been possible, they had none of the material goods, the weapons, the political organization, without which they could not hope to succeed.

CHAPTER II

Social Organization and Structure

THE TRIBE AND THE BASIC SOCIAL GROUPS

Aboriginal Australia presents a very different picture today to what it did fifty or a hundred years ago. In the last fifteen or so years, particularly, conditions have been changing very rapidly indeed. This is especially true of such matters as social and tribal organization. For most parts of Australia we should use the past tense in speaking of them, because today they are a thing of the past: but for more remote areas, too, the situation is strikingly different from what it was—and altering even as we write about it. What is more, there are many question marks, particularly in areas with a long history of European settlement. Virtually nothing is known about whole fields of behaviour, and whole regions, and in many cases it is too late to remedy this position.

One general question has to do with the size of the population before European settlement, and its relative density throughout the Continent. Elkin (1954: 10-11) suggests that by 1788 the Aborigines would have numbered 300,000 or so, and from the available information this seems a reasonable estimate. It is not a very high figure, but in view of the kind of life which the Aborigines led we would not expect a large population. The greatest density seems to have been around the coast, where fresh water was likely to be more plentiful and more food was available. When Stokes sailed round Dampier Land (1837-43), about forty years before European settlement, he saw many fires and people (1846: Vol. I, 93, 98). Elkin has assessed the coastal population there at the time of first European settlement as about 1,500—that is, about one person to 4 or 5 square miles; his figure for the Ungarinjin is about one person to 8 or 9 square miles—about 1,000 altogether. According to Brough Smyth (1878: Vol. I, 31, 35), Mitchell (1839: Vol. II, 345) put the whole population of eastern Australia at no more than 6,000 and possibly less. An 1854 estimate of the Aboriginal population of Victoria at its foundation was 7,500. Brough Smyth's own figure was 3,000, or about 18,000 acres per person; another estimate for Victoria was 5,000, or 16 square miles to each person. In the Arnhem Land reserve about ten years ago, an area of 32,000-odd square miles, there were no more than 4,000 or so people, most of them concentrated around the fertile coast and adjoining islands. The Aboriginal population of the region including the fringe points of Jigalong, Wiluna, Leonora, Laverton, the Warburtons and the Rawlinsons, the western edge of the Petermanns and north as far as Lake Macdonald, would be about 1,371 today; or, if we assume that there are still some wandering people in the Carnegie-Canning Stock Route area, as well as in the Rawlinson-Petermann-Blood Ranges and around Lakes Hopkins and Macdonald, the maximum for the whole region, excluding Kalgoorlie, might be 2,000 to 2,200. Before European contact the region would possibly have carried 10,000 persons. The population of the whole Great Victoria and Western Desert, including the central mountainous core, in addition to a further stretch from the Rawlinsons north-west to the Great Northern Highway and the Kimberleys—an L-shaped area, with the upright part of the L in Western Australia and the horizontal part of the L stretching across Western and South Australia—must now be less than 3,200; before European contact it may have carried 18,000 persons. This would cover possibly about 250,000 square miles, and would hold today only about ·00128 persons per square mile, or before white contact ·007 per square mile. Of course, this reveals nothing of the concentration or actual density of population within the area. (See Berndt, 1959*a*: 85-6.)

Even today, the total population figures for full-blood Aborigines represent in most cases only an estimate and not a complete census. When they are in a position to be counted accurately, this in itself means that they are in contact with some kind of settlement—a mission, government centre, pastoral station, town, and so on. And once this takes place, for most Aborigines, they are well on the way to living there for at least part of the time. It is possible that the number of full-blood Aborigines has been over-estimated. Hasluck (1957) suggests that there are now 74,214 Aborigines, or people more Aboriginal than not. Elkin (1959: 30) mentions a minimum figure of 38,321, plus, with 52,857 part-Aborigines—91,178 altogether.

Elkin's table is as follows:

Present-Day Aboriginal Population

	Q'land	N.Terr.	W.A.	S.A.	Vic.	N.S.W.
Aborigines	10,960	15,971	8,655+	2,500	—	235

Part-Aborigines	26,443	1,955	7,196	2,500	1,400	13,363
Totals	37,403	17,926	15,851	5,000	1,400	13,598

It is quite clear that, overall, the full-blood population is declining, in contrast to the growing numbers of part-Aborigines, even though in a few areas it is increasing or at least holding its own: at Bathurst and Melville islands, for example, and in eastern Arnhem Land.

The Tribe

This term 'tribe' is often used loosely for any group of people living and moving about together; and difficulties in definition are increased because in some areas the people themselves have no word which can be translated as an exact equivalent. It has been suggested that by 1788, with an estimated population of about 300,000, there were possibly 500 tribal units. Tindale (1940; 1959*a*: 40) claimed that well over 700 such tribal territories can be recognized. Later he modified this, stating that he personally contacted representatives of 400 tribes, which made up two-thirds of all tribes in Aboriginal Australia. The more conservative figure of 500 seems reasonable, particularly since the units involved may not all have been of the same kind. Some may have been smaller, others larger. It is difficult to assess this when dealing with isolated survivors, in a situation where such things are no more than a memory. The suggestion has been made, in reference to the Western Desert area, that in place of the label 'tribe' it would be more appropriate to speak of dialectal or linguistic units. (R. Berndt, 1959*a*.) This could very well apply to other parts of Australia too, such as western and north-eastern Arnhem Land.

NOTES TO TRIBAL MAP

(An asterisk indicates that either or both of the authors have worked with representatives of the tribe.)

Location number	*Tribal name*	*Tindale's (1940) spelling of tribal name*
1	Aranda*	Aranda
2	Andingari*	Antakirinja
3	Adnjamatana (Adnjamadana)	Wailpi
4	Bidjandjara (Pitjantatjara)*	Pitjandjara
5	Bordaulun	Portaulun
6	'Bringgin' (Brinken) bloc*	Berinken

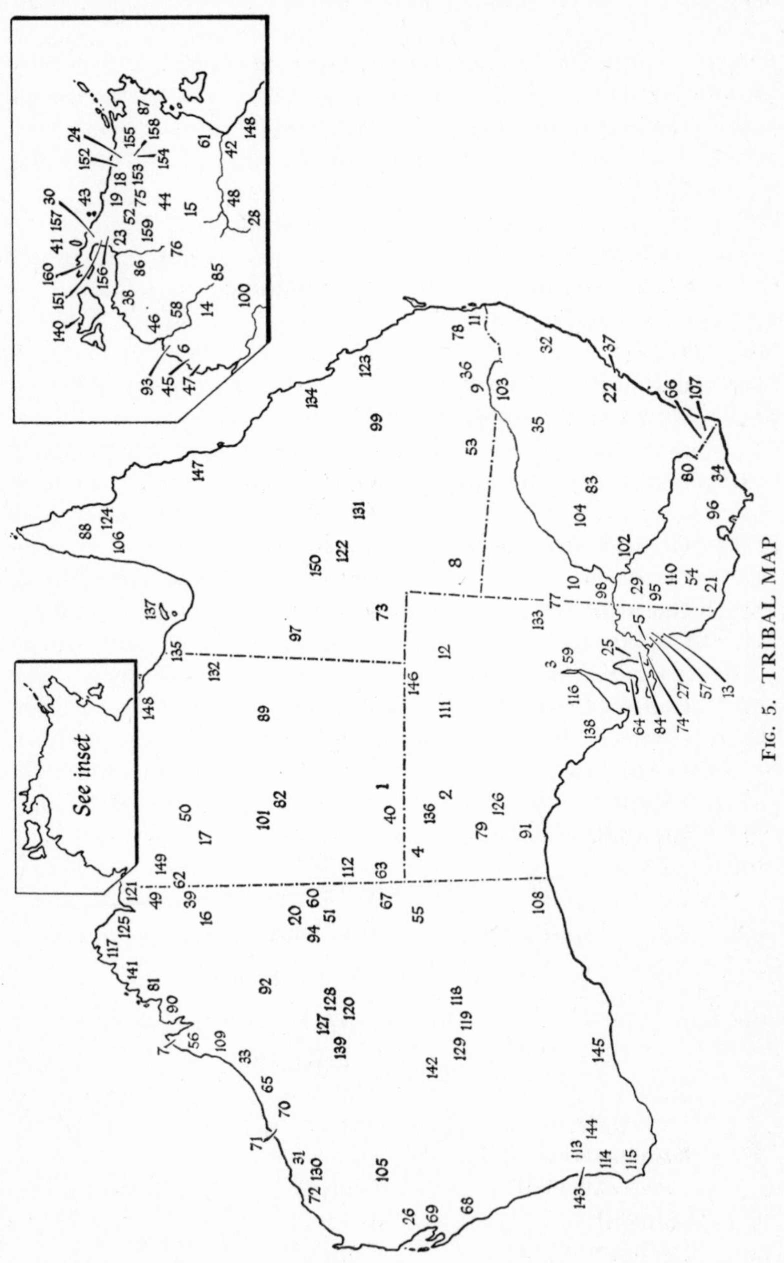

FIG. 5. TRIBAL MAP

Location number	*Tribal name*	*Tindale's (1940) spelling of tribal name*
7	Bard; Bad; Badi	Ba:de
8	Buntamurra (Bundamura)	Puntamara
9	Bigambul	Bigambul
10	Bagindji*	Ba:kendji
11	Chepara	———
12	Dieri*	Dieri
13	Dangani (Tangani)*	Tanganekald
14	Djamadjong (Djamindjung)*	Djamindjung
15	Djawun (Djawin)*	Djauan
16	Djaru*	Djaru
17	Gorindji (Guirindji)*	———
18	Gunbulan; Gunbalang; Walang*	———
19	Gunwinggu; Neinggu*	Gunwinggu
20	Gugudja*	Gogoda
21	Gournditch-mara	Gu:nditjmara
22	Geawegal	Geawegal
23	Gagadju*	Kakadu
24	Gudjalibi (Gadjalibir)*	———
25	Gaurna (lower)	Kaurna
26	Ingada	Ingga:da
27	Jaraldi*	Jarildekald
28	Jangman*	Jangman
29	Jupagalk	———
30	Jiwadja*	Iwaidji
31	Kariera (Gariera)	Kariera
32	Kumbaingeri	Kumbainggiri
33	Karadjeri (Garadjeri)	Karadjeri
34	Kurnai (Gurnai)	Ga:nai (see Tindale, 1940: 197)
35	Kamilaroi (Gamilaroi)*	Kamilaroi
36	Kaiabara	Giabel (?)
37	Katang-Worimi	Worimi
38	Laragia*	Larakia
39	Lungga*	Lungga
(40)	Loridja (Aluridja):* general term for Western Desert bloc	———

Location number	*Tribal name*	*Tindale's (1940) spelling of tribal name*
41	Marlgu*	Ja:ko
42	Mara*	Mara
43	Maung*	Maung
(44)	Maiali (collective name)*	———
45	Mariwuda*	———
46	Mulluk Mulluk (Ngulugwongga)*	Mul:ukmul:uk
47	Murinbada*	Murinbata
48	Mangarei*	Mangarai
49	Malngin*	Malngin
50	Mudbara*	Mudbara
51	Mandjildjara*	———
52	Mangaridji*	———
(53)	Maranoa people (country)	———
54	Mukjarawaint	Ja:dwe; Mukja:dwen
55	Mandjindja (Mandjindji)*	Mandjindja
56	Nyul-nyul (Njulnjul)	Njulnjul
57	'Narrinyeri' Confederacy*	———
58	Nangiomeri*	Nanggumiri (?)
59	Ngadjuri*	Ngadjuri
60	Ngadi (Ngari)*	———
61	Nunggaboju*	Nungubuju
62	Njinin (Njining)*	Njining
63	Ngalia*	Ngalia
64	Narunga*	Nar:angga
65	Njangomada	Nangamada
66	Ngarigo	Ngarigo
67	Nangadadara (Ngadadjara)*	Nga:dadjara
68	Nganda	Nanda
69	Ngugan	———
70	Njamal	Njamal
71	Ngerla	Ngerla
72	Ngaluma	Ngaluma
73	Pitta Pitta	Pitapita
74	Ramindjeri*	Ra:mindjeri
75	Rembranga* (Rembarnga)	Rembarunga

Location number	*Tribal name*	*Tindale's (1940) spelling of tribal name*
76	Togeman (Dogeman or Togiman)*	Tagoman
77	Tongaranka	Dangga:li
78	Turrbal	Jagara
79	Tangara (?)	———
80	Theddora	Jaitmathang
81	Ungarinyin (Ungarinjin)	Ungarinjin
82	Wailbri (Walbiri)*	Walpari
83	Wuradjeri*	Wiradjuri
84	Wagend	Warki
85	Wogeman (Wogiman)*	Wagoman
86	Warei*	———
87	Wulamba bloc ('Murngin'), or Malag*	———
88	Wikmunkan (Wigmungan)	Wikmungkan
89	Waramunga	Waramanga
90	Wuroro (Wororo)	Worora
91	Wiranggu*	Wirangu
92	Wolmeri	Wulumari
93	Wogaidj*	Wo:gait
94	Walmadjeri (Wanmadjeri)*	———
95	Wotjobaluk (Wotjo)	Wotjobalek
96	Wurunjerri	Wurundjeri
97	Workia	Wakaja
98	Wiimbaio	Maraura
99	Wakelbura	Jagalingu
100	Wadaman*	Wardaman
101	Woneiga*	———
102	Wathi-wathi	Wati wati
103	Wollaroi	Weraerai
104	Wongaibon*	Wongaibon
105	Wadjeri	Wadjeri
106	Yir-yoront (Jirjorond)	Jirjoront
107	Yuin	Taua
108	Yerkla-mining	Mirning
109	Yaoro	Jauor (?)
110	Kulin (?)	———

Additional tribal names, not all specifically noted in the main text:

Location number	*Tribal name*	*Tindale's (1940) spelling of tribal name*
111	Arabana	Arabana
112	Bindubi*	Pintubi
113	Balardong	Balardong
114	Bindjareb	Pindjarep
115	Bibelmen	Pi:belmen
116	Banggala	Pangkala
117	Bagu	Ba:gu:
118	Budidjara*	————
119	Badimaia*	————
120	Djargudi*	————
121	Gadjerong	Gadjerong
122	Goa	Koa
123	Gangulu	Kangulu
124	Gandju	Kandju
125	Gwini	Gwini
126	Gogada*	Kokata
127	Guradjara*	————
128	Gadudjara*	————
129	Goara	Go:ara
130	Indjibandi (Indjibandji)	Indjibandi
131	Iningai	Iningai
132	Indjilindji	Indji:lindji
133	Jandruwanda	Jandruwanta
134	Jangga	Jangga
135	Jogula	Jokula
136	Janggundjara*	Jangkundjara
137	Lardil	Lardi:l
138	Nauo	Nauo
139	Njibali	————
140	Tiwi (Diwi)*	Tiwi
141	Wunambal	Wunambal
142	Waula	Waula
143	Wadjug	Whadjuk
144	Wilmen	Wi:lmen
145	Wudjari	Wudjari
146	Wonggangura	Wongkangura
147	Wagamen	Wakamen
148	Waderi*	Wadere
149	Wandjira*	Wandjira

Location number	*Tribal name*	*Tindale's (1940) spelling of tribal name*
150	Wanamara	Wanamara
	Additional	
151	Amurag*	———
152	Burara (Burera)*	Barera
153	Dangbun*	———
154	Djinba	Djinba
155	Djinnang	Jandjinung
156	Eri (Rereri)*	———
157	Gari	———
158	Gunavidji (Gunjibidji)*	Gunavidji
159	Wuningag	———
160	Wurugu	Wurengo

* * * * *

What do we mean by a tribe? Usually it is seen as a combination of a number of features.

1. First, it refers to a group of people who occupy a recognized stretch of country, and claim religious and hunting rights over it by virtue of some supernatural or mythical sanction or charter vested in them; they are related by actual or implied genealogy (see below), and acknowledge common rules which govern their behaviour. Boundaries between them and other units of the same kind are often defined in a general way by natural features. Sometimes, however, it is difficult to know to which tribe a certain territory belongs; or members of one tribe may have hunting rights over country held by another. The picture is not always firmly sketched with no room for ambiguity, particularly in the Western Desert. Contrary to popular belief tribal territories and boundaries are, or were, relatively flexible. Also, people are not invariably afraid to move across the territory of an adjacent tribe. As a rule, they have grounds for fear only if they deliberately or inadvertently interfere with a sacred site.

The area concerned in each case varies a great deal, but much depends on its fertility, the quality and quantity of its natural resources. In north-western South Australia, the middle eastern part of Western Australia, and the central west of the Northern Territory such territories are fairly large, one merging gradually into the other with boundaries left more or less fluid. This is an advantage in places where game and vegetable foods are not concentrated or plentiful. On the Lower River Murray in South Australia, along the Coorong and the Lakes at the river's mouth, such areas were smaller, but richer, and boundaries consequently firmer. The same is the case along the Northern Territory coasts and rivers: in Arnhem Land, on the Daly River and around Port Keats, and on adjacent islands like, Bathurst, Goulburn, Milingimbi and Elcho. Among the tribes which possessed large territories were the well-known Aranda, the Bidjandjara, Dieri, Wailbri and Wuradjeri. Some of the smaller were the Jaraldi, Dangani, Gorindji, Wogeman, Togeman, Marlgu, Gunbalang, Rembranga, Djamindjung, Warei, Mara, Laragia, Maung, Djawun and Jangman.

One way to establish tribal boundaries is to examine the local mythology, for various beings are said to have created most of the physiographic features, which in many cases have become totemic or sacred sites. Tradition dictates who must look after these, and around which of them rites are to be performed and songs are to be sung. When all this is a living reality, the local people can usually draw careful charts of their own and adjacent territories. We ourselves have material of this sort for nearly all the areas in which we have worked during the past twenty years; Tindale too has such 'maps' compiled by Aborigines. Every relevant detail is set out, with special sites clearly marked. Next to travelling all through the tribal territory, noting every rock and billabong, every yam patch and kangaroo hunting ground, every sacred place, and so on, collecting these charts is most rewarding. Ideally, of course, both approaches should be used in conjunction—personal observation, plus native charts: but that is not always possible.

Elkin (1954: 11) has calculated the membership of a tribe as ranging from about 100 to 1,500, and averaging about 500 to 600. Tindale speaks of 500 as the average, but adds that this may be too high.

2. Secondly, the term tribe refers to a group of people who share a common language or dialect, provided they themselves acknowledge this. It is necessary to add this proviso, because in certain cases a linguist might say that there are marked similarities between two or more dialects, or languages, spoken in different areas. The point is that if the people themselves do not recognize these similarities, they are not relevant insofar as classification into tribes is concerned. It is the social recognition of similarities in language, or in other features, which is important here. (We shall return to this question of language a little further on.)

3. Thirdly, following on this last point, we usually associate the term tribe with a group of people who assume that they have more in common with one another than they have with members of other groups, and in consequence of this they may have a collective name for themselves. Or their neighbours may have a special name for them, and they themselves may come to adopt it. For example,

the word Nyul-nyul (Njulnjul) means 'south', but the Nyul-nyul themselves now use this name to identify themselves as a group. Or various directions have been misinterpreted as tribal names: for instance, in reference to the Bidjandjara group of dialectal units in the Western Desert, the terms *jalindjara* or *gajili* (north), *gagarara* (east), *julbarira* (south), *wilurara* (west): *julija* country (roughly to the north-east), *wawulja* (roughly to the north-west), and *jabura* (roughly to the south-west). Tindale (1940: 142-6) discusses this problem.

Not all such names can be translated. In some instances the local people treat them as just names, with no further meaning. Or they may refer to some features which distinguish that group of people from others—not necessarily unique features. For example, Bidjandjara people—the name Bidjandja(ra) is based on the stem *bida*, 'go': that is, those people who use *bida* (or *bidja*) to refer to the action of 'going'. Bidandara, Bidandandara, Bidjadi, Bidjagu, Bidamanggula, Bidala, Widjandja, Widjala, Bidjalgu, are variant forms. There are numerous other examples of this sort. They include the Djaru in the eastern Kimberleys, a term meaning 'speech', or 'talk'; the Didji-dara, in north-western South Australia (*didji*, 'child'); the Lungga (long-faced people); Mariwuda (people of the beach or salt-water); Dieri (man). The language name itself is often used as a label. Take the name Gunwinggu, in western Arnhem Land. The stem, *winggu*, means fresh water; *gun* is a prefix indicating a certain class of nouns, including 'language'. The Gunwinggu refer to all their neighbours in the same way, Maung as Gunmarung, Walang as Gunbalang, and so on; Walang means 'bat' people, living in caves. Their neighbours in turn speak of them by their own labels: the Maung, for instance, call them Neinggu. Or they turn their name into a kind of verb form by adding the third person plural prefix, Biriwinggu, or Gabiriwinggu (*ga-* is a present tense indicator), 'they of the fresh water': or refer to themselves by such labels as Winggu^{c}-winggu, or Ngariwinggu, 'we of the fresh water'.

In other cases there is no overall name, simply local names for many smaller units. Or an overall name may be attached to a number of groups which in fact do not acknowledge that they share a common language. It is doubtful whether that can be taken as a tribal name at all. Strehlow (1947), for instance, suggests that the ethnographic literature on the Aranda makes them appear to be more uniform or more alike in language and culture than they actually are. In such cases it is better to speak of linked tribes, or a cultural bloc, rather than of one large tribal group. Some earlier writers refer to this kind of constellation as a nation; but this is not a good choice, because it suggests a degree of political unity, or at least a consciousness of common interest or identity, not usually present in the case of these rather loosely linked tribes. Nevertheless, in such groupings there is often a more or less common cultural and linguistic background. Their members may go more or less freely through one another's territories, perhaps speak dialects of one language; intermarry; combine, up to a point, to perform rituals; help one another economically; and share the same broad mythology and religious view of life. One of the best known of these is the series of linguistic or dialectal units, sometimes called tribes, whose combined territory extends right across the Western and Great Victoria Deserts. On the Lower River Murray in South Australia there was a similar state of affairs in the 'Narrinyeri' confederacy: *narindjeri* was the local word for man, or human being. This included several smaller units: Jaraldi, Dangani, Ramindjeri, Wagend, Bordaulun, and the lower Gaurna. Also there are the so-called Brinken groups in the Northern Territory, between the Daly and Fitzmaurice rivers.

Tribal names have been changed, in some cases, as a result of alien contact. A notable example is the people now called Mulluk Mulluk; this name comes from 'mullock', meaning rubbish or refuse, from the copper mine which was located in their territory at the end of last century (a commentary, incidentally, on Aboriginal-European relations). Their real tribal name is Ngulugwongga. Very few of them remain today, partly because of a series of punitive expeditions which followed the killing of several Europeans.

Another result of alien impact, and of increasing estrangement from traditional Aboriginal ways, is the attempt to arrive at a general social identification in terms of Aboriginality: labels, not tribal names, like Jamadji ('friend'), Nunga ('people'), Wonggai or Wonggi ('speech'), are used to signify 'people of Aboriginal descent' as contrasted with 'white people'.

4. A fourth point usually associated with the term tribe is that it is large enough for marriage to take place within it. Other small units too regard themselves as being in some way distinct from their neighbours: occupying or holding a certain stretch of country, or having certain customs or performing certain rituals which are not quite the same as those of the groups around them—even a separate dialect perhaps, in a few cases (for example, in north-eastern Arnhem Land). But they are not as a rule classified as tribes unless they fulfil this particular requirement: that a tribe is the largest unit within which there is acknowledgment of social as well as cultural identity, or interdependence, and which is normally self-perpetuating—that is, capable of maintaining its population from its own resources. This need not mean that marriage must always take place within it, although in practice such has probably

been the case more often that not, at least in the past; but it means that the members of that group are independent of outsiders in this respect, whereas many smaller units are not. We may say that such smaller units are exogamous. In other words, their members are expected to marry outside, not among themselves. This is more than a matter of choice: it involves recognition of a rule. Conversely, when we speak of an endogamous unit, the rule relates to marrying within and not outside it: the rule of endogamy may be relevant for a tribe; the rule of exogamy may be relevant to a descent group such as a clan.

A further point in this context, and in summary, is that a tribe is relatively self-contained, with its own social organization and structure. Contact with others may be spasmodic, or confined to trading or ceremonies. Also, its members are often intolerant of the views and behaviour of outsiders. They may say, for instance, that the people of another tribe not far away are cannibals, or indulge in queer practices: that the women have unnatural relations with dogs, or that all their men are powerful sorcerers. Quite often there seems to be a strong underlying concern with being independent of others. But people who rely heavily on their own resources and their traditional background, whose view of the world is turned inward rather than outward, tend to suffer considerably when they come into contact with aliens whose whole way of life is very different—in this case, with Europeans.

5. Nevertheless, in the fifth place, members of a tribe usually regard one another as relatives, as contrasted with outsiders. In other words, their relationships are phrased in terms of kinship. This aspect is important, and we shall come back to it in the next chapter.

Other features could be added to this list, but only as elaborations on these five main points. For instance, the tribe is a territorial and linguistic unit, but it is not particularly important politically or economically; fighting and food-gathering, for example, are matters that concern local groups, clans, or family units. Through the centuries, as far as we can gauge, people seem to have left their original home regions, or changed their tribal boundaries, quite apart from the present situation of what has been called tribal disintegration and the loosening of territorial ties because of culture clash. Notwithstanding this, the true tribal country is that in which the great mythical beings travelled or performed exploits, instituted rituals, created the most important local features, before perhaps disappearing into the ground or the sky or assuming a different shape. Through his links with these beings, an Aboriginal is deeply attached spiritually to his own land. Elkin (1954: 28) puts this very aptly, summing up a relationship which emerges particularly clearly in regard to their religion. He points out that there were, as far as we know, no wars deliberately designed to take over a stretch of country, or to conquer an enemy. In fact, even though the people some distance away may be spoken of disparagingly they are not necessarily enemies. Yet there is spasmodic fighting both within the tribe and outside. There are plenty of examples of tribal fighting, particularly in the northern coastal areas. Also, even though there was no conquest as such there was apparently some movement of population, small groups gradually occupying areas originally possessed by others who had moved away or for some reason no longer occupied all their land.

Even when they leave their own territory, as a result of European contact or the attraction of fringe settlements, the majority of these people do not immediately lose touch with it. They look back to it as their spirit home, and try to return to it now and then for ritual purposes. When they are near death, one of their main wishes is to get back and die in their own country. However, as outside pressures increase, such ties lose their hold. Many Aborigines today, even those who are still traditionally-oriented, do not return to the country of their birth; and quite often this is not because they cannot, but because they do not want to do so. It no longer has any real meaning for them.

Tribal limitations and language variation

It might seem, in looking at the five points relevant to a definition of a tribe, that it is a fairly simple matter to know where one tribe ends and another begins. But if there are differences in language or in behaviour, how do they communicate with one another? The answer to this is a double-barrelled one, because it has to do with their composition, the smaller units of which they are made up.

In the first place, when we speak of communication, we probably think first of language. There are some people even today who talk about 'the Aboriginal language', as if there were only one. How many there are, or were, depends partly on the way in which we distinguish between a language and a dialect. It is not always easy. For instance, in north-eastern Arnhem Land there are a number of small linguistic units, each with its special name. The dialects, or languages, spoken by these groups are different enough so that people who know one of them cannot understand another except by learning it. However, because they are small units, and exogamous as well, most people know at least one or two in addition to their own. Also, the differences are chiefly a matter of vocabulary, and not of structure. But if we take structure as a criterion and say that here we have one broad language-unit with local variations, this plays down the other criterion, of intelligibility—whether or not, or to what extent, one such dialect, or language, can be understood by people who have not specifically learnt it. (We are not considering here individual variation in speech, or minor local differences within a common framework.)

From one point of view it does not matter what term we use here, provided the situation is clearly defined—unless we are trying to indicate how many languages or dialects are spoken in a certain region. It has been said that there were possibly 500 languages in use in Aboriginal Australia at the time of first European settlement. (Capell, 1956: 101, reviews briefly 144 languages.) Five hundred is probably too high a figure, if we consider that many of these languages seem to be fairly closely related, at least on paper, and also have a certain amount of common vocabulary. It is important to remember that 'language' is not necessarily coterminous with 'tribe'.

From the perspective of the people speaking these languages, the extent of this common vocabulary was not normally enough to help them in speaking or even understanding (hearing) languages other than their own, without actually learning them. However, because the Aborigines are, or were, semi-nomadic, moving about in only a limited stretch of territory and not across the whole Continent, this meant that various language-types had an opportunity to become more or less firmly established, particularly in identifying one social group as against another. Also, it would not matter that people in one region could not understand the languages in another hundreds of miles away, because in the ordinary course of events there would be no contact at all between them. In regard to adjacent languages the situation is quite different. It would, perhaps, have been possible to go right across Australia from one language unit to another, using each as a jumping-off point for the next. For one thing, there is often some kind of transition from one language to another, or some common basis against which differences can be understood. For another, there are usually at least some people who can understand or even speak the ordinary language of their neighbours—even if they do so with a foreign accent, or rather ungrammatically. (Strehlow mentions Loridja men in Central Australia who speak Western Aranda—but in a Loridja way.)

We say 'ordinary' language, because within a language itself there may be a special vocabulary, or vocabularies, for use on certain occasions—*apart* from the matter of a sign language, or system of hand signs. In parts of Central Australia, newly initiated boys must use a distinctive set of words while they are in seclusion: and in western Arnhem Land there are separate vocabularies to be used between a man and his actual or classificatory mother-in-law. Other special vocabularies consist of words for sacred matters known only to fully-initiated men, or revealed only at different periods in a man's life as he progresses through ritual stages. Others again are made up of 'singing words', not used in everyday speech. While this is fairly general throughout Aboriginal Australia, it is most highly developed in north-eastern Arnhem Land, among the Miwoidj dialects of the Wulamba bloc.

Reference to neighbours brings us to the second part of the discussion of the limits of one tribe as against another. Differences in the size of tribal territories have had some bearing on their interrelationships. In parts of Central Australia, for instance, where population density is relatively low, people have to travel fairly long distances to come in contact with one another, whereas in regions with a denser population there is more likelihood of contact between a number of different tribes, or different languages, and so more likelihood of their influencing one another. In any case, the largest ceremonial gatherings are normally attended by members of more than one tribe, or more than one language unit, and on such occasions there has to be some means of communication between them. Through such gatherings, myths, rituals, and songs, and various features of social organization, can be passed on gradually from one area to another. They are meeting grounds for exchange of ideas and goods, as well as for social intercourse, even though sacred ritual affords the principal reason for them. But not all members of a tribe, as a rule, speak or understand the language of their neighbours. In any large inter-tribal assembly there are always people who do not understand others, cannot communicate with them directly, and have to depend on interpreters.

This is because, to repeat, a tribe always consists of a number of small units, usually attached to certain localities within its overall territory. The people living at one end of that territory may have quite a lot in common with their nearest neighbours in an adjacent tribe—perhaps as much, for ordinary everyday purposes, as with other members of their own who live some distance away. It is these local groups which are the really effective social units, and in fact usually the effective political and economic units. Especially as regards a larger tribe, the unity within it may be merely nominal, or held up as a kind of ideal: but except on certain ceremonial occasions, the tribe as such does not act as a whole in hunting or food-collecting, or in revenge expeditions, or other forms of fighting and warfare. It is the smaller groups within it which serve as a bridge between one large unit and another, so that really there is no clear-cut demarcation between tribes, or between languages, in ordinary everyday affairs. Distinguishing tribal units is a matter of convenience for us, in helping us to understand Aboriginal social organization, and a matter of convenience for the Aborigines themselves in situations where they feel the need for some broader kind of identification apart from their local ones. It is also the leaders in the various smaller units who have the actual authority in tribal affairs, and at inter-tribal gatherings.

Social groups

Looking at the social arrangements within a tribe, then, as apart from relations between tribes, we find certain divisions which cut across one another, or complement one another. The best accounts are given by Radcliffe-Brown (e.g., 1930-1) and Elkin (e.g., 1954, Chapter IV). The major categories are local descent groups, clans, sections, subsections and moieties. There are others too, which we shall not consider in any detail: for example, the phratry and the patri-line, or patri-lineage. (R. Berndt, 1955.) One would not expect to find all these represented in any one tribe.

1. The *local descent group* has a specific connotation in the literature on the Australian Aborigines. It does not refer simply to a 'group of people living in the same locality', a 'co-resident group'—although this may well be the case too. Rather, it points to a group of people bound to the same locality by ties of a more than transient kind—ties of descent and kinship, as well as of religion. In other words, its members are united by common patrilineal descent, share a given site or constellation of sites, sacred or otherwise, and can trace their relationship genealogically. Its territory is defined not so much by boundaries marking it off from similar units, but by the actual sites which it claims. Ideally, this is inalienable; but members of other local descent groups are not debarred from entry, or from hunting game or collecting food within its precincts, although they may be denied access to a site where sacred objects are stored. This is the land-holding group, linked by special spiritual and ritual ties; and the land itself represents the most obvious, most enduring, and most consistently visible, tangible focus. Executive powers are almost entirely in the hands of initiated men, who control, and have the right to perform, the major totemic rituals and various other religious activities. Women move out of the group at marriage, but are expected to maintain spiritual and emotional ties with their 'country'. They do not relinquish their totemic affiliations merely by leaving it.

We could speak of this as a patrilineal descent group. It is exogamous and, as Elkin says (1954: 80), patri-local as well. However, where the people involved are semi-nomadic it is difficult to speak of 'residence patterns' in the usual sense. Another way of putting this is to say that it is viri-local with a patri-local emphasis. (In 'viri-local' residence a wife goes to live with her husband, but not necessarily in the same place as any of his relatives. When residence is neo-local, this means that the husband and wife need not follow any precedents in choosing where they will live.) Where alien impact has been intensive, the change is toward neo-local 'residence', and the term residence now implies something more permanent.

There has been some controversy as to how widely local patrilineal clans or patrilineal local groups were prevalent in Aboriginal Australia. (See Radcliffe-Brown, 1956; Berndt, 1957: 346-51.) To avoid confusion it is perhaps better to restrict the term 'local descent group' to a unit which not only emphasizes patrilineal descent but makes it a major criterion, while the term clan can be more loosely defined as a unit which stresses either patrilineal or matrilineal descent. An important distinction between the local descent group and the clan is the way relationships within them are defined. In the local descent group, actual genealogical ties are inferred. In the clan, they need not be.

2. The *religious unit* can be variously defined. It may involve several units (clans or local descent groups) which combine to perform rituals associated with a body of mythology they hold in common. In the Western Desert, where the local descent group is associated with one or more spirit beings, this entitles its members to participate in the system of ritual and myth connected with such beings, and shared by a number of local descent groups which 'own' certain sites along their tracks—the focus of collective action on the part of men of a number of local descent groups; each site is the symbol of a relatively wide social and cultural unit. The assumption is that all those sharing a common totem actually constitute a unit: but generally speaking, the local descent groups forming a religious unit are contiguous. This religious unit is what Elkin has called the cult or the lodge.

3. A *clan* is a group of people who claim to be descended in one line from the same putative ancestor or ancestress, not always named and not necessarily in human shape. They may not be able to trace their relationship to one another in genealogical terms, and may not live in the same area; but the clan is virtually always exogamous. Most Aboriginal clans are patrilineal, but there are exceptions. In western Arnhem Land and Bathurst and Melville islands the main emphasis is on matrilineal descent, although the paternal side is not ignored. As Elkin (1954: 87) notes, 'there were matrilineal social totemic clans in south-western Queensland, western New South Wales and Victoria, as well as in eastern South Australia—except along the Lower River Murray and around Adelaide'. The well-defined patrilineal clans such as found in the Jaraldi and Dangani on the Lower River Murray were strikingly

similar to those of north-eastern Arnhem Land, but without the dialect units. (See Warner, 1937/58; Berndt, 1955.)

Elkin demarcates between territorial clans and social clans; these last are probably always matrilineal. The first emphasizes the aspect of country and a person's strong association with it, the place where the nucleus of clan spirits lives and from which his own spirit comes. Actually there are two divisions here, one stressing lineal descent, the other attachment to locality. The second (the social clan) refers primarily to a special relationship between persons because they are all associated with a particular totem or mythological complex—they regard this totem as their 'flesh'.

The members of such a clan, particularly the territorial clan, are most likely to be living in the same neighbourhood or the same stretch of country, because marriage in Aboriginal Australia tends on the whole to be patri-local—that is, a woman on marriage leaves her own home and comes to live with her husband's paternal group: but there are exceptions.

Totemic clan affiliations are more easily understood in the context of religion and mythology, based as they are on the Aborigines' view that all forms of life share certain vital qualities or attributes. This fundamental similarity, they say, was most apparent at the beginning of the world when people and animals and other creatures had not yet assumed separate shapes, or separate physical identities; but the bond between them is still important, and is manifested in various ways, all related back to the creative period as recounted in the most important myths. The point here is that it may influence clan affiliation. People may claim relationship because of their association with certain totems. In many parts of Australia, before a child is born its father may find its spirit in a dream, or through some similar revelation; and that spirit will then be associated with the totem or group of totems, and the corresponding locality, which appeared in the dream. On the other hand, the child's totemic associations, or one of them, may depend on the place at which its mother first realized she was pregnant—for example, at quickening: or on a particular food which caused her to vomit at such a time: this is the case in western South Australia. Among the Aranda, however, it is the locality where a child is born which determines its principal totemic affiliation.

4. The *horde* has been treated in a somewhat confusing way by Radcliffe-Brown (1930: 35-6) and other writers. It is not a landholding group, nor need all its members claim common descent. Rather, it is a mixed group which varies a great deal in size and in composition. Typically, it is made up of male members of a local descent group, *plus* their wives and children, and unmarried female members. They move across the country, hunting and foraging,

traditionally within an undefined radius of the respective cult sites. The maximum figure would be about fifty persons, adults and children; but usually there are far fewer, and certainly that is so today.

The horde is the land-occupying group, and the main hunting and food-collecting unit. It is relatively self-sufficient, and on the move for much of the year, either by itself or in conjunction with one or more others. When various seasonal foods, or fresh water supplies, are concentrated in a particular area, people are likely to congregate there too. When food and water are more evenly distributed, for instance after widespread rains, people also scatter in small parties to take advantage of what the countryside has to offer. At ceremonial seasons a number of hordes come together. Economic factors to some extent determine the size of such meetings —possibly larger in more fertile areas than in the central 'deserts', but ranging from 150 to a maximum of about 400 to 500.

5. The basic unit of everyday social living, and ordinarily the smallest one, is always the *family*—a man, his wife or wives, and their children. In most areas of Aboriginal Australia marriage does not have to be monogamous. A man is allowed, even expected, to have more than one wife at the same time (polygyny). Not all men do. But a few have considerably more than one. This is particularly the case at Bathurst and Melville islands, and in north-eastern Arnhem Land. In rare instances a man might have, simultaneously, from fifteen to twenty wives. This made the family unit a fairly large one, especially with children as well.

6. Another kind of division within the tribe is based on sex. This may seem rather self-evident; but in parts of Victoria, for example, there were what is known as sex totems. Members of each sex have a certain creature or plant as an emblem, identifying them as contrasted with the opposite sex. An attack on the male emblem is equivalent to an attack on all males; this is one of the conventions leading up to marriage or erotic activity. In addition there is the matter of sexual division of labour, the fact that men participate in some activities from which women are excluded, and vice versa. This is particularly noticeable in the religious sphere, in all areas except Melville and Bathurst islands.

7. Another way of grouping persons within a tribe classifies together people of *alternate generations*, or endogamous moieties. It is a social device which, as Elkin puts it, is unnecessary where sections and subsections are present. (See Chapter III.) Examples come from the Broome district, and from the Western Desert. Around Ooldea, for instance, the terms used are *Nganandaraga* or *Nandara* (far western and north-western terms are *Jaldjeli* and *Gumu*) for persons of one's own and grandparents' and grand-

children's generations, and *Dalbuda* (or *Djanamildjan*) for persons of one's father's and children's generations. This division has some bearing on marriage, and also on ceremonial groupings.

8. More widespread than this is the system of classifying everyone within the tribe, and in neighbouring tribes, and in fact all natural phenomena, in two distinct divisions, or *moieties*. Moiety simply means half, but (except as in 7, above) we usually restrict the term to a division which is recognized as exogamous—that is, where a person must marry into the opposite moiety and not into his own. This system of dual organization, as it has been called, provides a clear-cut division for social and ceremonial purposes. The moieties are often named, although the definition does not or should not hinge on this, and often associated with special emblems or totems. Descent in them is either patrilineal or matrilineal: that is, a person is affiliated at birth either with his father's male line, or with his mother's female line.

Radcliffe-Brown (1930-1) suggests that an important function of this division into moieties is that it systematizes kinship arrangements, and that where there are moieties there will also be clans. He also (in Srinivas, 1958: 110 ff.) discusses the moiety system in relation to J. Mathew's (1899) work on the 'Eaglehawk (Kilpara) and Crow (Makwara)'. Associated with these two totemic moiety labels is a copious mythology, with versions differing from one tribe to another. Radcliffe-Brown speaks of the essential oppositeness of moieties and of the social implications of marriage (for example, inter-moiety exchange); but co-operation should be emphasized too.

Named matrilineal moieties have been recorded from only a few regions: in eastern Australia, south of the Gulf of Carpentaria and east of Lakes Eyre and Gairdner, as well as around Perth (Manidjmad, Cockatoo, and Wardangmad, Crow); and in western Arnhem Land. Patrilineal moieties are more common. They are found, for example, in the Northern Kimberleys; around the Daly River; in much of the eastern side of the Northern Territory, including north-eastern Arnhem Land; Cape York Peninsula; in former days (as Elkin states, 1954: 92) in a small isolated region in south-central Victoria; and possibly in a small area around Albany in Western Australia.

CHAPTER III

Social Organization and Structure

(*Continued*)

MORE SOCIAL GROUPS AND KINSHIP

When people talk about Australian Aboriginal social organization, they often emphasize matters of kinship on the one hand, sections and subsections on the other. To outsiders these features may appear exotic or strange, because the first is much less significant in Australian-European society, and the second is entirely absent. But to the Aborigines themselves they are an ordinary part of social living, part of the very fabric of their society.

Sections and subsections

Sections and subsections are often thought to be rather complicated devices which make an already complex social organization much more involved than would seem necessary. It has also been said that they create an effect of compartmentalization, in terms of horizontally conceived classes or statuses, which must make for inflexibility in social action. In actual fact, they seem to have the opposite effect. They ease problems of social relations by establishing further rules which stipulate, although formally of course, what is to be expected from one set of kin against another set. It is always useful to know what to expect from others and, moreover, to know where and how to place them in one's social perspective. This procedure is no more artificial than other systems of social alignment where membership is assigned at birth. It represents a convenient way of classifying people, or placing them in categories, for purposes not only of marriage, or social identification, but also of ordinary everyday behaviour. It is widely distributed. (See Radcliffe-Brown, 1930-1 and Elkin, 1954: 93-104.) J. Mathew (1899: 102-7) lists what he calls 'class-systems' for a large expanse of Aboriginal Australia: exogamous matrilineal and patrilineal moieties, matrilineal and patrilineal 'clans' (which he called phratries), and sections. Thomas (1906: 41-51) gives a comparative list of subsection names for sixteen tribes, while Howitt (1904: 88-293) discusses various social divisions, including sections and subsections.

The section system is, or was, found over much 'of Western Australia, from Derby and the lower Fitzroy down the coast as far as the Gascoyne River, and then south-east to Laverton'. (See Elkin, *ibid.*, 93.) It was spreading across the Great Victoria Desert about Ooldea twenty years ago, although it had not been well integrated there and people did not really understand it. 'The southern Aranda have it; and it covers most of Queensland as well as, traditionally, north-eastern and central New South Wales.' But the subsection system is spreading much more rapidly. It is common in the Kimberleys. From Tanami and the Granites it extends south to the Rawlinson and Warburton Ranges and into the Petermanns, northward into the Victoria River country, to the Fitzmaurice, Katherine and Adelaide rivers, north-east into western Arnhem Land, and on into eastern Arnhem Land. It was new at Milingimbi, Warner reported, in 1926-9. At Yirrkalla, when we were there in 1946, some of the older people refused to recognize it; but now it seems to be completely accepted.

In both cases, descent is indirectly matrilineal. That is, a person's section or subsection depends on his (her) mother's, but is not the same as hers. Where the moiety system is not formalized with named divisions, it may be implicitly recognized in the section and subsection systems. As Radcliffe-Brown (1930-1: 439) points out, "the presence of sections or subsections involves the existence of both patrilineal and matrilineal moieties, though not necessarily named . . ."

In the case of sections, everyone in the tribe belongs from the moment of birth, and even before, to one of four named categories. These influence marriage and kinship relations. Particularly, they group kin 'according to generation levels and cross-cousin relationships'. (Cross-cousins are children of siblings of opposite sex—children of mothers' brothers or fathers' sisters.) 'Each intermarrying pair of sections represents a generation level, and each generation level divides the sections into cross-cousin categories.' (See Elkin, *ibid.*, 96.) The letters used here in outlining these systems are those normally used by Australian anthropologists as a matter of convenience, because the Aboriginal terms for them differ from place to place despite a basic similarity. The sign = connects intermarrying sections, and the arrow sign connects the sections of mother and child. The first example comes from around Broome and La Grange (see Elkin, 1954: 97):

Young woman at Yirrkalla, eastern Arnhem Land, wearing a traditional string breast girdle (1946-7)

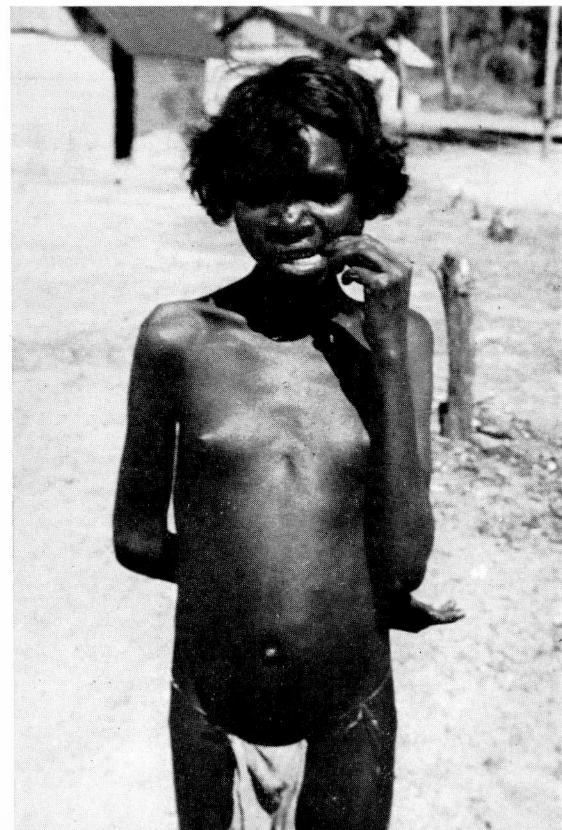

Young married girl, Yirrkalla (1946-7). Traditionally, both men and women wore a minimum of clothing

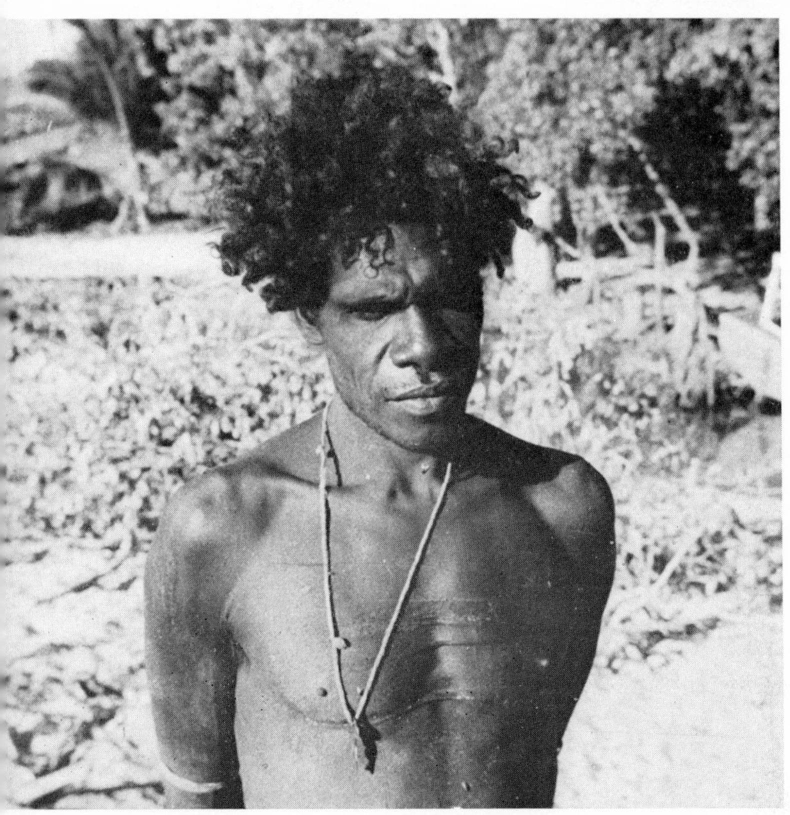

Above: Woman wearing a band to alleviate pains in chest: on beach at Yirrkalla (1946-7)

Left: Yirrkalla man (1946-7). Cicatrizes across the chest were a common feature of varying significance throughout Aboriginal Australia

A	Banaga	=	Burong	B
C	Garimba	=	Baldjeri	D

Explanation: If A, a Banaga man, marries B, a Burong woman, then the children will be Baldjeri; and so on. A's mother is C; B's mother is D; A's father is D; B's father is C. The father's section is not significant in regard to descent. The ideal is that A marries B and so on; but an alternative choice may be C marries B, and then generation levels are out of alignment. The important point is that the division be retained between A and C, and between B and D. This signifies the implicit recognition of moieties, which are exogamous. Marriage would not, normally, take place between the two sections making up one moiety: that is, between B and D, or A and C.

Also significant is the distribution of kin among the four sections. If we take the above pattern, that is, A marries B and the children are D: category A would include not only the person himself but his siblings (brother and sister), father's father, mother's mother, wife's mother's father, son's son and daughter, and others. B would include his wife and her siblings, and his cross-cousins. D would include not only his own children but his father and father's siblings, and his wife's mother. C would include his mother and her siblings, B's father, D's husband or wife as the case might be. Following this pattern, the reader can work out what other kin might be grouped under each section.

There are several variations on this theme. Elkin (1954: 97) mentions one from the De Grey district.

A	Baldjeri	=	Burong	B
C	Garimba	=	Banaga	D

The same principles are involved, but some adjustments are necessary when people from the De Grey intermingle with those from Broome and La Grange. Another example is from Balgo, on the fringe of the Western Desert, near the head of the Canning Stock Route.

A	Jibarga	=	Daruru	B
C	Burungu	=	Burgulu	D

Again, the principles are the same. But at Balgo this section system meets the subsection system and, again, there has to be some rapprochement.

One kind of adjustment between groups with differing section terms takes the form of a six section system. The following example is from Ooldea, in western South Australia.

A	Dararu	=	Banaga	B	First area
C	Garimara	=	Burong	D	
A	Dararu	=	Ibaga	E	Second area
F	Milang	=	Burong	D	

The principles remain the same; by following the arrows and marriage symbols, the division into kin categories and so on can be easily worked out.

The sections, like the subsections, often have totemic associations. In addition some people, in the Great Victoria Desert and in eastern Arnhem Land for instance, have claimed that members of different sections vary in physical appearance, such as skin colour, or hair, or height; but there are no grounds for this.

The subsection system makes use of eight categories instead of four. This example is from Birrundudu and Wave Hill, in the Northern Territory; but these terms are known as far north as Katherine, east toward the Roper River, and down through the Western Desert to Jigalong on the west, the Rawlinson and Warburton Ranges on the south.

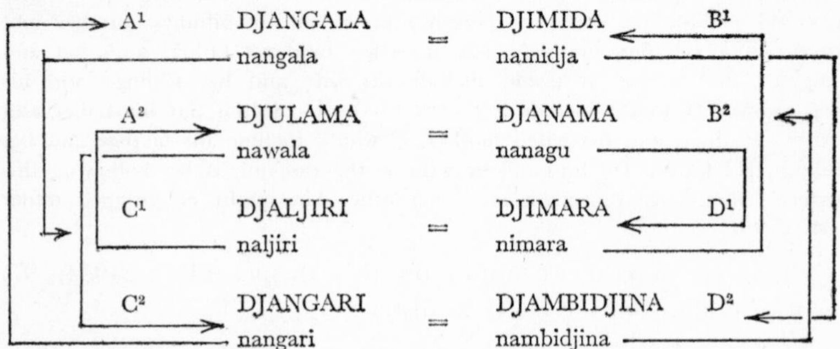

Explanation: This is actually a subdivision of the section system, on the basis of a distinction between cross-cousins and the children of cross-cousins. That is why the capitals have been divided into A1 and A2 and so on. In contrast to the section system, the subsections distinguish between males and females. To show this in the diagram, capitals are used for male terms, lower case for female terms. For example, A1, a DJANGALA man, marries B1, a namidja woman, and their children are DJAMBIDJINA and nambidjina (D2). By taking into account the arrows which link mother with child, as well as the marriage symbols, kin terms can be worked out for each subsection category.

Ideally, in this system an A1 man marries B1, who is his second cousin: his mother's brother's daughter's daughter's daughter or father's sister's daughter's daughter's daughter: or m.f.sr.d.d. or f.f.sr.s.d.; m.m.br.d.d. or f.m.br.s.d. The demarcation between cross-cousins and cross-cousins' children is made in the following way: DJANGALA's mother is nangari, his mother's brother is DJANGARI, his mother's brother's daughter is nanagu (B2) and so is his father's sister's daughter: his mother's brother's daughter's children are DJIMARA and nimara (D1), but they are also his father's sister's daughter's children. If A1, A2, C1, and C2 belong to one matrilineal moiety, those on the opposite side belong to the other. To take DJANGALA again, his cross-cousins and their children both belong to the same unnamed matrilineal moiety, and moieties are exogamous. But there are also implicit, and unnamed, patrilineal moieties: A1, A2, D1 and D2 make up one of these, the remaining terms the other. Different terms are used for various kin within one subsection category. A further point to note here is the exchange of sisters in marriage.

Note: The following abbreviations are used: M. or m., mother; F. or f., father; Sr. or sr., sister; H. or h., husband; Br. or br., brother; D. or d., daughter; S. or s., son.

A simple way of looking at indirect matrilineal descent, in two unnamed matrilineal moieties, is to see it as two separate cycles. One local woman drew a parallel with two circles which could never meet.

nangala	A^1	namidja	B^1
↓		↓	
naljiri	C^1	nambidjina	D^2
↓		↓	
nawala	A^2	nanagu	B^2
↓		↓	
nangari	C^2	nimara	D^1

Explanation: A nangala woman has naljiri daughters, who have nawala daughters, who have nangari daughters, who have nangala daughters: and the same for the other moiety.

Ideally, no matter whom she marries, a nangala woman should have only naljiri daughters (and DJALJIRI sons), and so on. But since not all marriages are 'straight', or between ideally preferred mates, this does in practice affect the subsection affiliation of children born of such unions.

The subsection system in general, showing the demarcation between cross-cousins and children of cross-cousins, can be set out in this way. It rests on the prohibition of cross-cousin marriage.

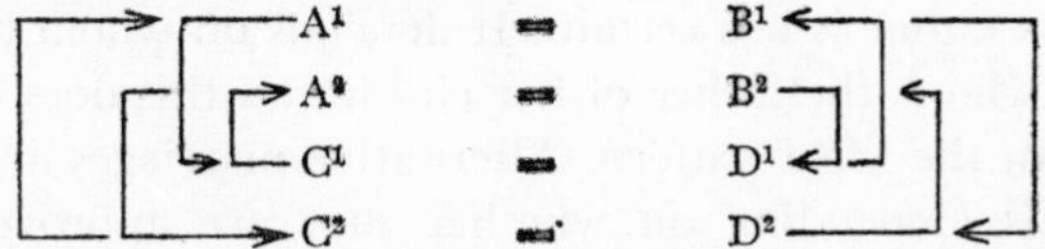

Explanation: The same principles are involved. B^2 is A^1's cross-cousin: the children of A^1's cross-cousin are D^1. D^1, a female, is also A^1's mother's cross-cousin, and her daughter is B^1, the preferred partner for A^1. Further kin correlations may be worked out quite easily on this basis.

How is a child's subsection determined? Supposing a B^1 woman has a child, that child will be given a subsection label from her own matrilineal moiety—in this case, either B^2, D^1 or D^2. B^1 and B^2 are equated for certain purposes. Firstly, patri-moieties may be covertly recognized, just as matrilineal moieties are: thus $B^1 + B^2 + C^1 + C^2$ form one patri-moiety, $A^1 + A^2 + D^1 + D^2$ the other. In other words, the system may be cut diagonally, as we shall see later for north-eastern Arnhem Land, where they are formally recognized. Secondly, B^1 and B^2 stand in actual or classificatory relationship to each other as d.d.-m.m. Thirdly, the subsections are arranged to form pairs of alternating generation levels. Fourthly, for example, B^1 and B^2 are really only section B subdivided, for the purpose of prohibiting cross-cousin marriage: therefore B^1's daughter would not be located in subsection B^2, but in either D^1 or D^2. Fifthly, B^1's mother is of D^1 subsection; and so B^1's child cannot belong to that subsection but must be of the alternate one, D^2. The rule is that, schematically, a child belongs to the *section* of its mother's mother, but of the *alternate division* (subsection).

Distribution of English kin term equivalents, on the basis of demarcating cross-cousins from the children of cross-cousins, and prohibiting cross-cousin marriage, is shown below. It is important to remember that all Aboriginal kin terms recognized in any particular society are divided among the eight subsections. They do not necessarily coincide with the English ones given here.

Ego; Br.; sr.; F.F.; f.f.sr.; S.S.; etc.	A^1	=	B^1	f.f.sr.s.d. (wife); m.m.br.d.d. (wife); preferred form of marriage. f.m.; F.M.Br.; etc.
m.m.; M.M.Br.; etc.	A^2	=	B^2	f.sr.d.; F.Sr.S.; m.br.d.; M.Br.S.; cross-cousins. m.m.br.wife; M.F.; d.d.; etc.
Sr.S.; sr.d.; F.F.Sr.S.; etc.	C^1	=	D^1	w.m.; F.Sr.D.S.; f.sr.d.d.; m.m.br.d.; f.f.sr.s.wife; etc. mother's cross-cousin.
m.; M.Br.; D.H.; s.wife; etc.	C^2	=	D^2	F.; d.; S.; f.sr.; m.br.wife; etc.

Remember that all these diagrams represent ideal systems. The actual situation is more complicated. While a child's subsection (or section) is almost invariably determined by its mother's, the subsection of its father is less certain. It depends on whom the mother marries—or who is the father of her child; and this does not always conform with the ideal pattern. Alternative marriages are, broadly, of two kinds, depending on whether they are approved, or disapproved, in a given society at a given time. (See, for example, Elkin, 1938-40; Kaberry, 1939; C. Berndt, 1950.) Those of the first kind are socially acceptable; they fall within the permitted range of toleration. In certain cases they are called *wadji* (as in the east Kimberleys), a term which can be translated as 'wrong way'; it need not mean wrong in the extreme sense, although it occasionally does. For example, if we take the above diagram: supposing an A^1 man is not available to a woman B^1, A^2 is a legitimate alternative (because A^1 and A^2 are actually two divisions of one section, 'A'). She may even go so far as to marry a C^1 or C^2 man. Although that is not considered desirable, it is not wholeheartedly condemned unless desirable partners are being side-stepped. But if the same woman (B^1) were to marry a man of her own matrilineal moiety, this would be strongly disapproved. Ideally, and traditionally, some severe punishment would be imposed on both partners; but today the sanctions are much weaker. There are fewer opportunities for enforcing them, and less interest in doing so.

It is easy to see why all this calls for a certain amount of ingenuity when groups with slightly different systems meet—for example at inter-tribal gatherings, or these days on cattle or mission stations or in towns, or when one of these systems is introduced into an area where it clashes to some extent with the usual way of classifying relatives, or of arranging marriages. Discussions then can become quite intricate, as people sort out their particular systems and reach a working medium, or a compromise—a process which may take several years.

Semi-moieties

Around the Gulf of Carpentaria are what Radcliffe-Brown (1930-1) called semi-moieties: four named divisions, each consisting of a couple of unnamed patrilineal subdivisions. Elkin (1954: 104-7), discussing these, adds that they extend into Central Australia. Using the same conventional signs (A^1, A^2 etc.), let us look at Radcliffe-Brown's (1930-1: 40-1) Mara example, which was taken directly from Spencer (1914: 60-4) but not adequately explained. Schematically, it can be set out like this:

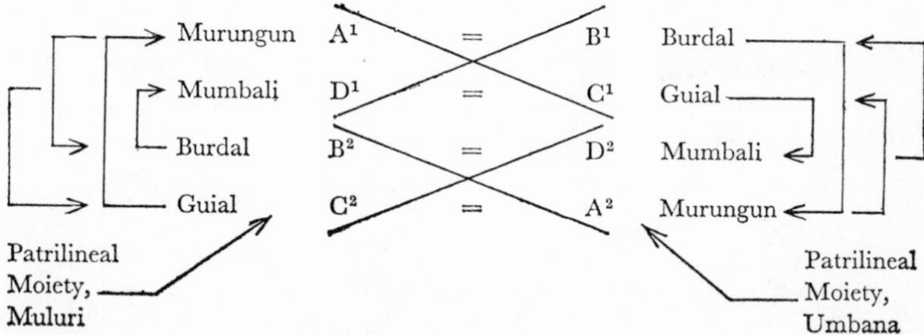

Superficially the organization resembles that of the subsections, and this is quite clear when Spencer's correlation (*ibid.*, 63) with the Mangarei system is taken into account. In the Mangarei tribe the terms (referred to by Spencer) are those used for ordinary subsections, and are similar to those noted by Elkin (1950*a*: 15).

Explanation: Murungun and Mumbali together form a named patrilineal moiety, and so does the other pair (Burdal and Guial). The rule is that a man should not marry a woman of the same semi-moiety as his mother. For example, a Murungun man has a Burdal mother; his wife must be a Guial woman (from the opposite moiety). Alternating generations are clear-cut. Men with, for example, Burdal wives are separated from those with Guial wives, as father from son.

General

A number of general summaries deal with the distribution of various forms of social organization in Aboriginal Australia, especially of moieties, sections, subsections, clans and so on. Those which immediately concern us, and were referred to in compiling the accompanying map, are J. Mathew (1899), Thomas (1906*a*), Howitt (1904: 88-293), Róheim (1925), Radcliffe-Brown (1930-1), Elkin (1938/54), Falkenberg (1948: 22-36; 1962), Lévi-Strauss (1949: 189-287), Service (in Dole and Carneiro, 1960: 416-36).

Howitt's (1904: 88-294) discussion, summarized here, relates principally to south-eastern Australia and the immediate central Australian area.

(*a*) Systems having two classes, with matrilineal descent. These are matrilineal moieties. The Dieri provide an example, with matrilineal and patrilineal totemic units (clans), *madu* and *bindara*; a person has a special relationship with the patrilineal totem of his mother (*maduga*) and the matrilineal totem of his father (also *madu*).

(*b*) Systems having four sub-classes and matrilineal descent: that is, matrilineal moieties, with subdivisions into sections and matrilineal totemic clans. The Kamilaroi provide an example.

The association with matrilineal totemic clans is interesting. Diagrammatically the system is like this:

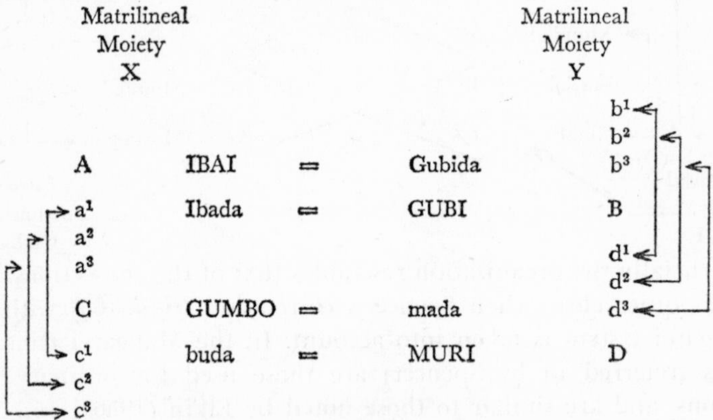

Explanation: Capitals refer to males, lower case to females. 1, 2 and 3 in the case of females refer to totemic clans: b 1, 2, 3 of Moiety Y, kangaroo, possum, goanna, respectively, with the same for d 1, 2, 3; a 1, 2, 3 and c 1, 2, 3 of Moiety X, emu, bandicoot, black snake.

This system is not unlike the Mara semi-moiety organization. A man or woman must belong to the same moiety and totemic clan as his or her mother, but not to the same section. A man of *any* totemic clan belonging to one section may marry a woman from *any* totemic clan of the intermarrying section of the opposite moiety. In matters of descent, however, the mother's clan determines the totemic clan to which the children will belong. There are variations on this theme (see Howitt, 1904: 204 *et passim*) which emphasize the importance of reckoning matrilineal descent. As Radcliffe-Brown notes (1930-1: 231), in this case, 'the sections are not sub-divisions of the whole tribe, but sub-divisions of the totemic clans'.

(*c*) Systems with four sub-classes and patrilineal descent: that is, patrilineal moieties with subdivision into sections and clans.

(*d*) Systems with eight sub-classes and matrilineal descent: that is, subsection systems. (Howitt, *ibid.*, 118, mentions patrilineal descent.)

(*e*) Systems with what Howitt calls anomalous class organization and matrilineal descent, matrilineal moieties, totemic clans and sub-clans.

(*f*) Systems having a two-class system with patrilineal descent: patrilineal moieties, and local groups and/or totemic groups.

(*g*) Systems having what Howitt calls anomalous class organization, with patrilineal descent; sections; totemic clans and/or local groups. Or absence of sections or moieties: possibly with local totemic groups (or clans): restricted inter-clan marriage.

(*h*) Systems without class organization: no moieties, no sections. The Kurnai represent the type-situation. Howitt (1904: 272) speaks of exogamous intermarrying localities.

Howitt gives examples of all these.

Radcliffe-Brown (1930-1: 41-2) makes the following classification, along distributional lines:

'(*a*) tribes having two matrilineal exogamous moieties.

(*b*) tribes having patrilineal moieties.

(*c*) tribes having four sections, which may be divided thus:
i. with named matrilineal moieties.
ii. with named patrilineal moieties.
iii. without named moieties.

(*d*) tribes with eight subsections.

(*e*) tribes with four named patrilineal semi-moieties.

(*f*) tribes with two endogamous alternating divisions (named pairs of sections).

(*g*) tribes without named divisions.'

The following distributional map (Fig. 6) is an assessment of the general situation in Aboriginal Australia up to the present time. It is not a summary of all the material available on this topic, but does articulate most of it. Primarily, it is based on the work of Radcliffe-Brown (1930-1) and Elkin (1938/54; etc.), and in some instances on our own; the Cape York Peninsula area is treated by Sharp (1939).

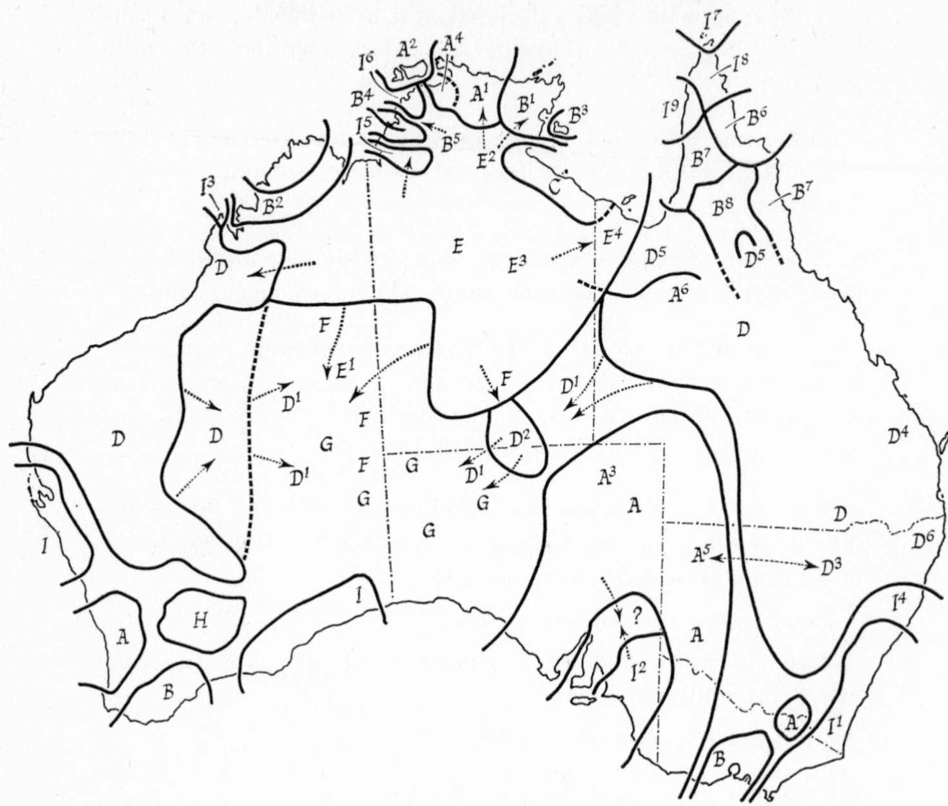

FIG. 6. DISTRIBUTIONAL SPREAD OF AUSTRALIAN ABORIGINAL SOCIAL ORGANIZATION
(See main text for explanation of lettering.)

Note to map. This map shows, in outline, the distribution of some aspects of social organization. It is useful as far as it goes, as a simplified statement which presents only part of the total picture. For one thing, a complete coverage would need to include kinship patterning. We speak of moiety, section, subsection systems, and so on. It would be more accurate to refer to them as sub-systems, with kinship representing another sub-system. Variations in kinship terminology from one tribe to another are linked with variations in other features of social organization, including marriage types. (Radcliffe-Brown, 1930-1: 427.) Also, in making a classification of this sort it is not enough to say, for example, that there are subsections in one area, matrilineal moieties in another. Two or three forms may exist side by side. It is not a matter of one or the other. And alternating generation lines, unnamed, are 'built into' section and subsection systems. (See Elkin, 1940: 213-15.)

Key to map:

A—Matrilineal moieties.

A^1—predominantly matrilineal moieties and phratries (membership non-local); patrilineally-oriented local groups: fairly recent entry of subsections.

A^2—matrilineally based phratries (and/or matrilineal totemic clans); recognition of patri-oriented 'horde'.

A^3—matrilineal moieties; matrilineal totemic clans and patrilineal totemic clans.[1]

A^4—matrilineal phratries, but not named matrilineal moieties: similar to A^2 and close to A^1: see Elkin, 1950*a*.

A^5—matrilineal moieties; matrilineal totemic clans *and* sections (as D), these last possibly introduced. Type: Bagindji.

A^6—matrilineal moiety totemism and sections: also a system of patrilineal totems. (See Sharp, 1939.)

B—Patrilineal moieties.

B^1—patrilineal moieties; patrilineal clans and dialect units: late entry of subsections.

B^2—local patrilineal totemic clans; patrilineal moieties. Type: Ungarinjin.[2]

B^3—local patrilineal totemic clans, with unnamed moieties.

B^4—patrilineal moieties; patrilineal localized totems. Type: Murinbada, Ngulugwongga.

B^5—patrilineal moieties, with associated totems. Type: Warei. Spencer (1914) records four sections.

B^6—patrilineal moieties; absence of sections; patrilineal local totemic clans. (Sharp, 1939.)

B^7—patrilineal moieties; no named sections; patrilineal totemic clans. (Sharp, 1939.)

B^8—patrilineal moieties; four named sections; local patrilineal clans. (Sharp, 1939.)

C—Semi-moieties.

D—Four sections.

D^1—spread of sections.

D^2—section system in southern part of the Aranda, subsection system in northern part. Patrilineal local totemic units, each specifically associated with one moiety. (Radcliffe-Brown, 1930-1: 321-5.)

D^3—sections; matrilineal moieties (named); sections not subdivisions of tribe, as in Western Australia, but of matri-

[1] For detailed notes on area A, extending through eastern and north-eastern South Australia into part of the south-western corner of Queensland and western New South Wales as well as part of western Victoria, see Elkin, 1940: map on p. 421.

[2] For detailed notes on the Kimberley region see Elkin, 1933.

lineal totemic clans. (Radcliffe-Brown, 1930-1: 231.) Type: Wuradjeri, Wongaibon, Gamilaroi.

D^4–named matrilineal moieties; possibly matrilineal totemic clans.

D^5–no named moieties; four named sections; patrilineal clans. (Sharp, 1939.)

D^6–sections; patrilineal local groups. Type: Kumbaingeri.

E–Eight subsections (usually associated with patrilineal local groups).

E^1–continuing spread of subsections.

E^2–named patrilineal moieties. Type: Mangarei.

E^3–patrilineal moieties. Type: Waramunga, etc. (See Spencer, 1914.)

E^4–subsections, organized as unnamed totemic patrilineal moieties and semi-moieties; unnamed 'patri-lineages'. (Sharp, 1939.)

F–Rapprochement between section and subsection systems.

G–Alternating generation levels (endogamous moieties); rapprochement between two differently named section systems, sometimes combined to make a 'six-section' system (see Elkin, 1940); patrilineal local groups.

H–Named pairs of sections (noted by Radcliffe-Brown, 1930-1). However, probably generation levels, as in G.

I–No moieties or sections.

I^1–'exogamous intermarrying localities' (possibly local groups).

I^2–patrilineal totemic local clans.

I^3–patrilineal local groups. Type: Bard.

I^4–patrilineal totemic clans. Type: Katang-Worimi.

I^5–'originally' no moieties or subsections, but possibly patrilineal local totemic groups; recent entry of subsections and subsectional totemism. Type: Nangiomeri.

I^6–patrilineal totemic local clans (units?). Elkin (1950*a*) mentions three named territorial units. Type: Wogaidj, Laragia.

I^7–patrilineal totemic local clans; no moiety or section names. Type: Torres Strait. (Sharp, 1939.)

I^8–absence of named moieties and sections; patrilineal totemic local clans. (McConnel; Sharp, 1939.)

I^9–mainly patrilineal local cult clans. In one tribe, intermarrying territorial divisions. Possibly exogamous matrilineal moieties among some tribes. (Sharp, 1939.)

Broadly, then, and without taking kinship into account, the following seven points emerge from a consideration of this map.

1. A system of dual division is found over a very wide area of the Continent, expressed through the medium of moiety, section, subsection or generation level.

2. In all areas the (or a) basic unit of organization appears to be a local descent group, variously defined, and in nearly every case exogamous.

3. The distribution of various forms of organization offers no key to their origin or mode of diffusion, except in one respect. This concerns the continuing spread of sections and subsections.

4. If we look at the overall picture in terms of patrilineal and matrilineal emphasis, we could say that this last is possibly dominant. Although only a few areas are labelled A, those labelled D and E represent indirect matrilineal descent. Further, in eastern and south-eastern Australia (A, D), with indicated exceptions, matrilineal totemic clans were common.

To balance this, in central and north-central Australia and over the greater part of Western Australia (E, D, F) the emphasis is on patri-local groups. It would be misleading to think of either principle of descent as excluding the other, or completely dominating the general picture, but in any given situation one is likely to be more prominent.

5. Although sections and subsections are based on indirect matrilineal descent, both matrilineal and patrilineal moieties, not always named, are to be found within them. The alternation of generation levels is also written into these systems. (See Radcliffe-Brown, 1930-1; Elkin, 1954.) Section and subsection systems clearly indicate intermarrying divisions. They make clear too the general principle that in nearly all Australian Aboriginal systems, with few exceptions, marriage is formally discouraged between persons of two succeeding generations.

6. The systems discussed here must be considered in relation to kin patterning.

7. Distributional studies on the basis of ecological zones (for example, Service in Dole and Carneiro, 1960) can distort the facts. Take, for example, such a statement as this: "The simplest systems occur in the coastal regions, which are the richest and most densely populated areas. The four- [section] and finally the eight-class [subsection] systems are in progressively poorer and less settled areas . . ." This kind of ordering rests on the assumption that the range from simplest to most complex is equivalent to a progression from absence of moiety or section, to moiety, to section and subsection, and that this extends from coast to inland. The evidence does not support such a view. (*a*) Where there is no moiety or section system there are social totemic units or clans, often part of a complex arrangement of preferential or selective marriage types. (*b*) Where

moieties are indicated, other forms of organization are present too: sections, semi-moieties, phratries, or clans, and so on. (*c*) Section and subsection systems include within them recognition of generation levels and moieties. (*d*) Far from being the most complex arrangement, the subsections simplify social classification and kin recognition; and for this reason, if for no other, they are acceptable in what were previously non-subsection areas.

Western and Eastern Arnhem Land

To make the situation clearer as far as specific units are concerned it is useful to contrast, very briefly, two Arnhem Land systems.

The first is in western Arnhem Land, and the tribes involved are primarily the Gunwinggu and the Maung. (See Elkin, 1950*a*: 1-20; Elkin, R. and C. Berndt, 1951: 253-301.) They have what could be called a moiety-phratry organization, complicated by a subsection system which has come up from further south. The Maung system, particularly, closely resembles the system found at Bathurst and Melville islands, but there the actual moiety name is not used, although the phratries fall into two divisions (see hereunder). Melville and Bathurst islands are atypical as far as Aboriginal Australia is concerned. So are the Maung, for that matter, but they have been strongly influenced, possibly before European times, by mainland people. Insofar as they have totemic affiliations of a sort, they resemble the matrilineal social totemic clans already mentioned.

A phratry, as the term is used here, is not a corporate unit. Its members do not come together collectively, except occasionally at ceremonial times. Its members call one another by kinship terms, but do not claim to share common descent nor to be related to one another except in a classificatory way. (In contrast, members of a clan do maintain that they are united by common descent, even though they may not be able to trace all the steps involved.) In many respects the phratry system resembles the normal section system. All local people belong to one or other of the two moieties, each further divided into two parts. Here is an example:

	Moiety 1		Moiety 2
	NANGARAIDJGU Ngalngaraidjgu		NAMADGU Ngalmadgu
Phratries: A	JARIWURIG njindjariwurig (fire)	C	JARIGARNGULG njindjarigarngulg (stone; water)
		=	
B	JARIJANING njindjarijaning (sun)	D	JARIWURGA njindjariwurga (pandanus)

Explanation: Feminine forms are in lower case, but the Gunwinggu do not use these for the phratry labels. Two categories (phratries) belong to each of the two exogamous moieties, making four altogether: a fifth, 'march fly', sometimes called simply *djoned* in Gunwinggu, has come in from further south-west: from the Amurag, for instance, who recognized the same four but added this fifth, *mandjirimurangaidj*. It is classified in the *namadgu* moiety. Another, *nabiwo*, 'wild bee', in the *nangaraidjgu* moiety, is recognized by the Gunwinggu as belonging to the Djawun tribe; but they do not use it themselves.

A or B marries C or D, and vice versa. Descent is directly matrilineal, so that a child takes the moiety and phatry names of his mother. In preferred marriage A marries C; in an alternative marriage, A marries D.

As in the subsection system, kin terms are distributed between the phratries. Ideally, a Gunwinggu man should marry his m.br.d.s.d., m.br.d.d.d., or m.m.br.d.d. (second choice: m.br.d., f.sr.d.); a Maung man should marry his m.m.br.d.d., or f.f.sr.s.d. The distribution of kinship terms can be easily worked out on this basis.

The subsection system was introduced into this picture, perhaps some time after 1912. It is as follows:

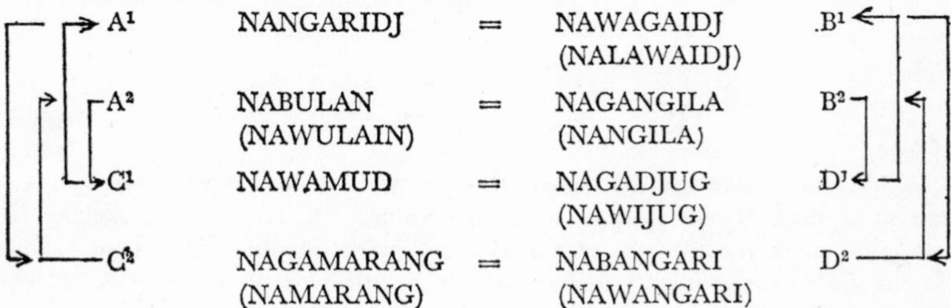

Explanation: The subsections are given in their masculine form: the feminine form takes the prefix *ngal-* instead of the prefix *na-*. The alternative forms in brackets are Maung; but there are other variants too. The same principles are involved as in the other subsection system already outlined. A man and his son's son may not marry women of the same subsection, except in the case of an alternative marriage. Then, however, a man and his grandchildren belong to the same subsection: that is, if A^1 marries B^1 and has a son D^2, who marries C^1 instead of C^2, the children of this union are A^1. This has implications in ritual affairs. In other words, in first choice A^1 marries B^1, in second choice, A^1 marries B^2; both are within the same section subdivisions —marriage outside these would be regarded as irregular.

The subsection system is correlated in this way with the moiety-phratry system.

	NANGARAIDJGU	NAMADGU	
Phratries	A^1	B^1	Phratries
A	A^2	B^2	C
and	C^1	D^1	and
B	C^2	D^2	D

Except in one respect the western Arnhem Land system is heavily weighted in the direction of matrilineal descent. However, these people do have some social intercourse with the north-eastern Arnhem Landers, whose system is predominantly patrilineal in emphasis. Even before the government settlement of Maningreda was set up near the mouth of the Liverpool River, there was contact between them through groups which, from one point of view, combine elements from both sides. People from the Liverpool River-Cape Stewart area moved between the mission stations of Goulburn Island on the west, Milingimbi on the east; and immediately after the last war there was a wave of temporary emigration westward into Darwin, inland through Oenpelli as well as along the coast. The adjustment which has been worked out between the two systems is sketched here without going into details. The eastern Arnhem land moieties (patrilineal descent) are called *dua* and *jiridja*.

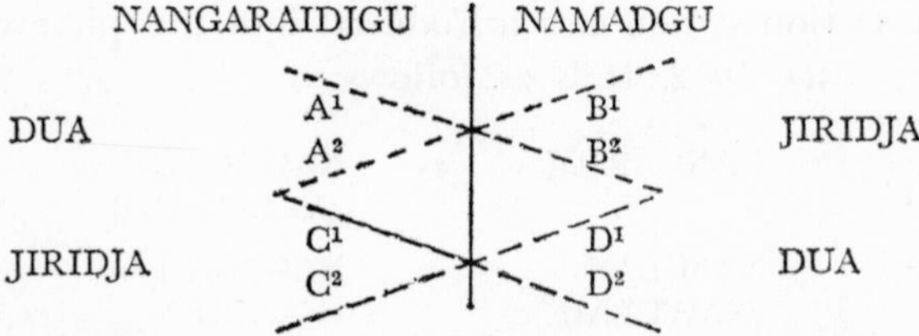

Explanation: The two matrilineal descent cycles of four subsections each, and the patrilineal descent lines of four subsections each, are distinguished by the combination of the two sets of moieties. In these circumstances, a man belongs to his father's ceremonial moiety and is a full heir to his knowledge and rituals, and at the same time is a member of his mother's matrilineal moiety.

Within the primarily matrilineally-oriented society of western Arnhem Land, over and above what happens when the two kinds of system meet, there is also a way of acknowledging patrilineal descent. This is the *namanamaidj* or *jigurumu,* or *ngwoja,* based on locality—a local descent group, in other words. A patchwork of small patrilineal units extends throughout western Arnhem Land, each associated with a named stretch of territory. Should one become extinct its land does not seem to be absorbed into another, although there are cases of overlapping, and of a larger overall *namanamaidj* name including several minor names. *Namanamaidj* affiliation is actually more complicated than this; but essentially it establishes a person's ties with his father's side, and his legitimacy; the traditional rule is that if a child's actual (physical) father is not the mother's husband, at least the two men should belong to the same unit of patrilineal descent. Ideally, with a few exceptions, no man should marry into his own *namanamaidj,* or his mother's; and his mother's *namanamaidj* should be different to that of his wife's mother.

The north-eastern Arnhem Land system, in contrast, is strongly patrilineal. The major units are the *mala*, 'clan', which in a general sense means a group or crowd, and the *mada*, linguistic unit, meaning literally 'tongue'. They overlap in some respects, so that what can be said of the one may apply equally well to the other; and every person in the society belongs by birth to a specific *mada-mala* combination. From one point of view the clans are subdivided into linguistic units, but it would be equally true to put it the other way round, and say that the linguistic units are subdivided to form clans. Every clan and linguistic unit belongs clearly to one or other of the two moieties and acknowledges, in a general way, a common bond with others on its own 'side'. Some *mada* and *mala* stand in a special relationship to others. For instance, they have a bearing on marriage preferences. Also, there are cases of amalgamation, and of the exchange of *mada* and *mala* names. (Western Arnhem Landers like the Gunwinggu sometimes refer to these people collectively as Malag, or Malarg—people who have *mala*, clans. Another such term for them is Miwoidj, or Miwaidj, which they themselves occasionally use for their own constellation of *mada*. Warner called these people Murngin, after the name of a *dua* moiety clan, Murungun. We have called them Wulamba.)

Both kinds of unit are exogamous, and associated with local territories which were created and given to them by the ancestral and spirit beings. Each claims a number of sacred sites and totems, connected in some way with a particular mythical cycle or sequence which may extend through many such units. Each 'owns' parts of various rituals, and various sacred patterns and emblems. The clans and linguistic units have a common structural pattern and a common cultural focus, a common religious and mythological heritage. But territorially the area is relatively large. (See, for example, Warner, 1937/58; Elkin, 1950*a*; R. Berndt, 1951*a*, 1952*a*.) The units which encompass it never gather *en masse* for the performance of ceremonies or for any other purpose.

Within the *mada* territories are special sacred waterholes, totemically associated with the creative beings, and containing a nucleus of spirits which are said to ensure *mala* and *mada* continuity by animating the human material of which its members are composed. Ideally, such spirits are derived from one of the father's ancestral waterholes, to make sure that patrilineal descent is not only a physical but also a spiritual reality. If a child is conceived outside its father's *mada* territory, the animating spirit comes from a waterhole of the country in which conception took place. The child will then be a member of that *mada*, provided this is of the father's moiety. In practice, a child of such 'mixed' birth is never denied admission to his physical father's *mada* and rituals, although these circumstances may prevent him from rising to any sort of leadership there. Because ritual life means so much to these people, a pregnant woman will hastily be brought to her husband's *mada* territory if she is away from it when the birth seems imminent. To be born in the right locality helps to counterbalance the disadvantages of having been conceived elsewhere.

The *mala* belonging to each moiety are territorially independent, within the stretch of country held by the particular *mada* associated with them. They are allied to one another in many other ways, most notably in the religious sphere. Two or three of them may consider themselves to be even more tightly interdependent, especially from an economic point of view: they may also be closely related through kinship. Each *mala* and *mada* has a special name which can be loosely translated. As well, they have what are called 'inside' or esoteric, sometimes sacred, names which should be used only in certain situations—on the ritual ground or in songs, for example. And each has associated with it a series of ritual invocations, called *bugali* (*dua*) or *bugalilji* (*jiridja*). Each *mada* has (or, in effect, is) its own dialect, with a more or less distinctive vocabulary. Because the moieties are exogamous, members of the various clans and linguistic units in one moiety must seek mates from the other and not among themselves. In this sense a person can marry into any one of the *mala* or *mada* of the opposite moiety: but in practice the field is more restricted. The following table sketches the affiliations of two *mada*, one from the *dua* moiety and one from the *jiridja*.

TABLE 3

LINGUISTIC UNITS AND CLANS OF NORTH-EASTERN ARNHEM LAND

DUA MOIETY

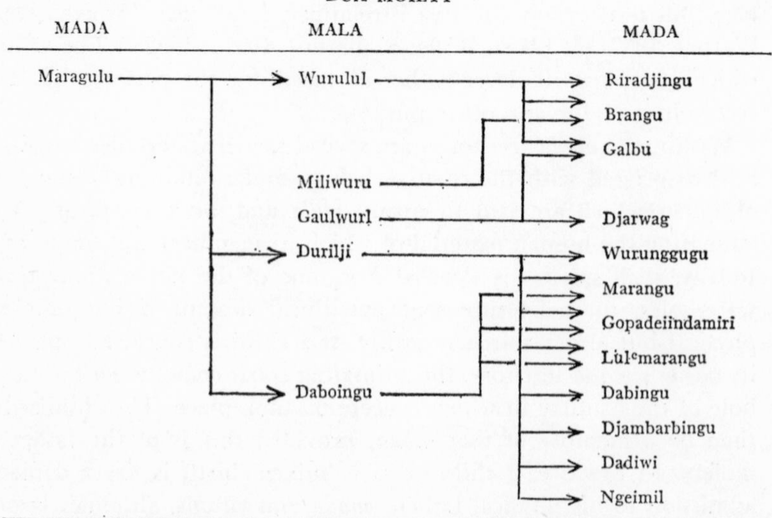

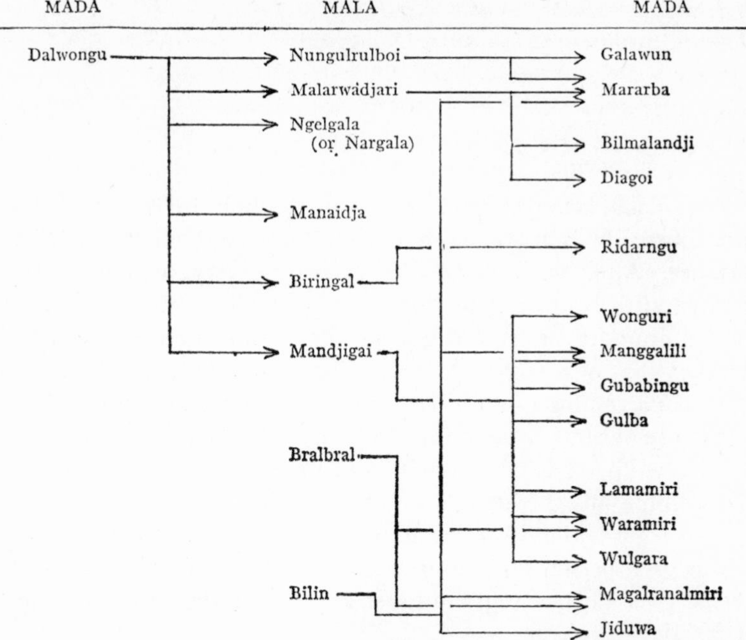

Explanation: One *mada* may be divided among several clans. Maragulu has three: Wurulul, Durilji, and Daboingu. But each of these *mala* is also associated with several other *mada*: Wurulul with Riradjingu, Brangu and Galbu, as well as Maragulu. In turn, those three *mada* are associated with other clans, as indicated. And so on. This cross-cutting of *mala* and *mada* is particularly relevant to ritual life.

The meanings of *mala* and *mada* names come, mostly, from the song cycles; and for that reason they are not always easy to translate in a single word. (Also, as a rule each *mala* has at least one alternative name, either ordinary-everyday or sacred-secret.) Here are a few examples.

Brangu, white cloud

Dalwongu, spring water (with the cry of a swamp bird)

Djarwag, spear wood

Gaulwurl, bushy-topped spearwood tree

Gulba, east wind

Jiduwa, maggots (from decomposing fish)

Malarwadjari, clan of the subincised

Manaidja, honey bee

Mandjigai, sandfly

Manggalili, parrot

Maragulu, gum tree bark

Murungun, red ochre

Nungulrulboi, shoal of young mullet
Riradjingu, long white cloud
Wonguri, parrot calling (on seeing spring water)
Wulgara, swirling of incoming tide
Wurulul, blow fly
Wurunggugu, cry of a pigeon

The *mada* actually receives more attention in everyday social intercourse. It is more often cited as the land-holding unit, for instance. Also, *mada-mala* territories are very accommodating: isolated sites belonging to one moiety may be found in territory of the opposite moiety. Right in the middle of one *mada-mala* territory may be a sacred site belonging to another relatively distant *mada-mala* combination, of either the same or the opposite moiety. There are various reasons for this. For instance, a large *mada* may have split up; or it may have moved to another part of the region and become incorporated in another territory. Each linguistic unit or clan regards the others, as units, from the standpoint of kinship, just as each person takes into account all others within his kinship perspective. This arrangement seems to rest on the acknowledgment of marriage preferences.

Since *mada,* like *mala,* are exogamous, a child's parents must belong to different *mada.* This means that within the nuclear family two dialects are spoken, even apart from the point that the *mada* of the wife's mother and of the husband's mother may not coincide with either of these, or with each other. Generally speaking, as a child grows up he (or she) learns first his mother's dialect, at least in an elementary way, but later puts increasing emphasis on his father's. This pattern of dialect differences has interesting implications as regards bilingualism. On the one hand there is the question of learning, and of personal and social identification. On the other there is the problem of language boundaries. In this situation the dialects have to be similar enough so that people do not lose sight of what they have in common, and can understand something of one another's vocabularies, yet different enough to ensure their distinctiveness, or separateness, as social labels. There is no way of knowing what the linguistic position here may have been to begin with; but certainly today the balancing of sameness and difference, unity and cleavages, as expressed through language, is a process which permeates all social living, from the elementary family to the broader issue of relations between moieties.

The subsection system, which now seems fairly well established, provides additional recognition of indirect matrilineal descent. This is as follows:

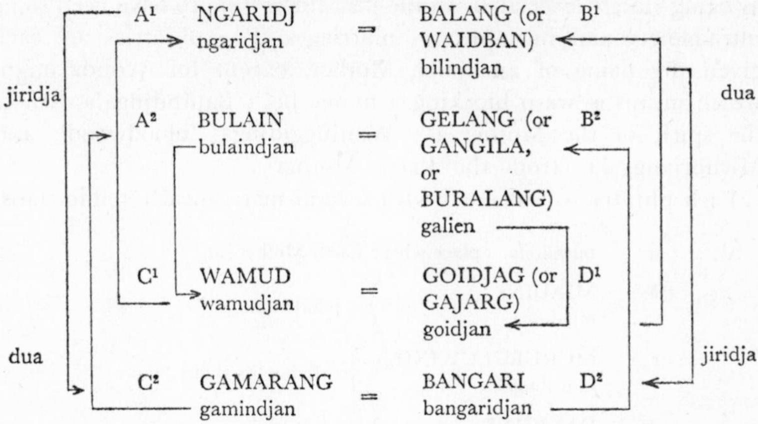

Explanation: The system follows the usual principles. Feminine forms are shown in lower case. However, in this region a man should, ideally, marry a maternal cross-cousin (m.br.d.), and this is provided for. Kinship terms are now classified into eight categories; but the eight subsections operate in four pairs, making it equivalent in this respect to a four section system. There is thus a formal choice between two marriageable partners. And a man's children's subsections depend on the subsection of the woman or women he marries. If he is an A^1 man and marries B^1 and B^2 women, his children's subsections will be D^1 and D^2. The moieties are so arranged that a man's children always belong to the same moiety as himself.

The Bathurst and Melville islands example

The people of Bathurst and Melville islands are sometimes called Tiwi, meaning 'men': *tingi* is a man, or human being, as distinct from a spirit; an ordinary word for a Bathurst and Melville islander is *aragidawamini*, or collectively *aragidawununi* or *djamulubila*. (See Hart, 1930*a*: 167-80; Harney and Elkin, 1943: 228-34; Berndt, 1957: 347-8; Hart and Pilling, 1960. The information given here is from our own field work in that area and differs to a certain extent from Hart's.)

Five phratries (only three were reported by Hart) are now arranged as two intermarrying, unnamed, matrilineal moieties. Thus:

A^1	JARIGA (or MUNUBUGALA)	=	B^1	WONDARUNGUI (or BUDUBUNGALA)
A^2	WUDUNGA (or BUMBIDI, BUNGABIDI)		B^2 (i)	BANINDJUGALA (or WONINGGIDINGA)
			B^2 (ii)	LORILA (or WARUGWAMBILA, MIRUBRIANGGALA)

Today, A^1 and A^2 people may select in marriage a spouse from B^1, B^2 (i) and B^2 (ii), and vice versa: B^2 (i) and B^2 (ii) are classified as being closely associated. In the past there seem to have been some intra-moiety and intra-phratry marriages. The phratries are each given the name of an Earth Mother, except for Wondarungui which means a 'wasp blocking a honey bee'; Banindjugala, 'where the spirit of the Mother is'; Woninggidinga, 'bloodwood'; and Mirubrianggala, 'from the Earth Mother'.

Each phratry is associated with several matrilineal totemic clans:

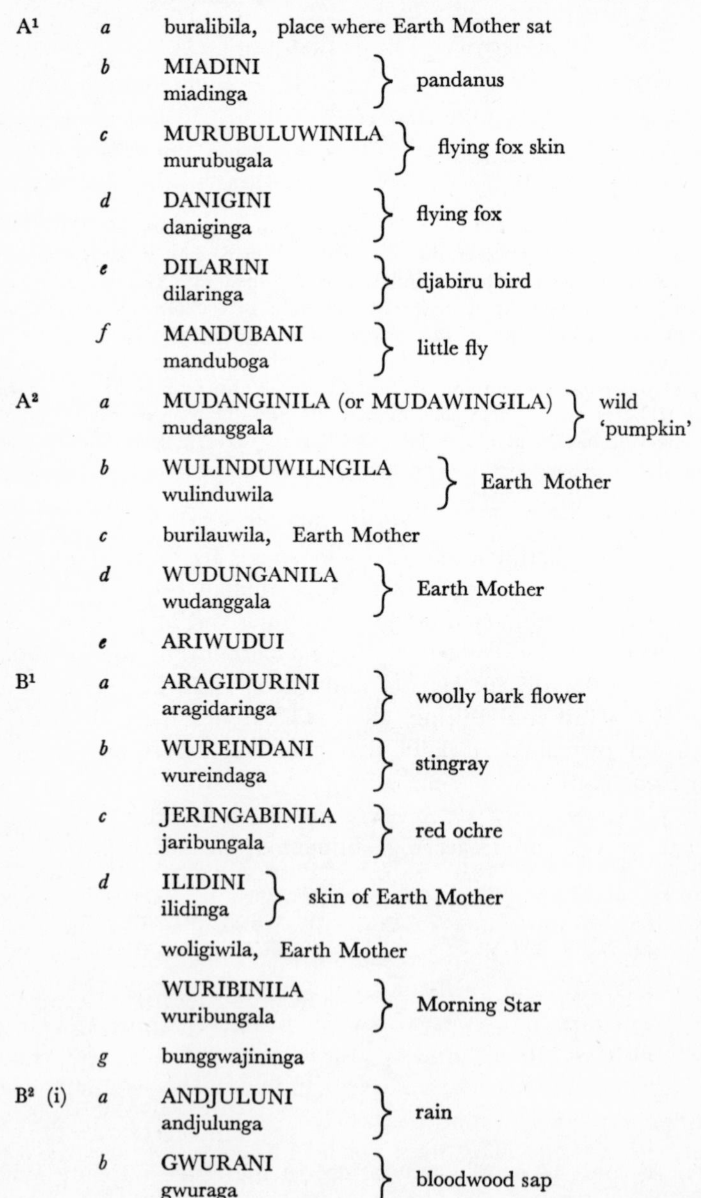

A[1]	*a*	buralibila,	place where Earth Mother sat
	b	MIADINI miadinga	pandanus
	c	MURUBULUWINILA murubugala	flying fox skin
	d	DANIGINI daniginga	flying fox
	e	DILARINI dilaringa	djabiru bird
	f	MANDUBANI manduboga	little fly
A[2]	*a*	MUDANGINILA (or MUDAWINGILA) mudanggala	wild 'pumpkin'
	b	WULINDUWILNGILA wulinduwila	Earth Mother
	c	burilauwila,	Earth Mother
	d	WUDUNGANILA wudanggala	Earth Mother
	e	ARIWUDUI	
B[1]	*a*	ARAGIDURINI aragidaringa	woolly bark flower
	b	WUREINDANI wureindaga	stingray
	c	JERINGABINILA jaribungala	red ochre
	d	ILIDINI ilidinga	skin of Earth Mother
		woligiwila,	Earth Mother
		WURIBINILA wuribungala	Morning Star
	g	bunggwajininga	
B[2] (i)	*a*	ANDJULUNI andjulunga	rain
	b	GWURANI gwuraga	bloodwood sap

B² (ii)	*a*	JARINGGUWUNILA jaringgwungala	Mother leaves her spirit (at a specific place)
	b	BUNGALIWINILA bungaliwila	place name (north)
	c	midjuwila, bird's whistle	
	d	DOGAMBINI dogambunga	small birds
	e	DJABIDJABINI djabidjabunga	march fly

Most of these are given in both masculine and feminine forms. Apparently these clans were not territorially based. But there were local groups (which Hart calls 'hordes', and Hart and Pilling, 1960: 11, 'bands') which were of loose and rather flexible patrilineal descent, rather similar to the *namanamaidj* of western Arnhem Land—a means of maintaining at least nominal association with a person's father's country.

CLASSIFICATION ON THE BASIS OF KINSHIP

Kinship is the basis of social relations, indicating the general range of behaviour expected in any given case. Everyone must be identified in this way. A person coming into a strange group for trading or ceremonial purposes is always allocated a kinship position. The section and subsection systems offer a short-cut to this. If the visitor belongs to a certain subsection, or is allocated one on the basis of what is already known about him, that simplifies matters a great deal.

Throughout Aboriginal Australia kinship is bilateral, which means that there is acknowledgment of both matrilineal and patrilineal descent, although social units such as clan, local descent group, or moiety, emphasize one rather than the other.

Kinship systems

In our own society there is no need for us to trace relationships beyond a certain range, to recognize kinship beyond a certain point. But in classificatory systems, such as we find in Aboriginal Australia, a limited number of kinship terms is used and extended to cover all known persons. In Radcliffe-Brown's definition (1952: 64; see also his discussion in 1930-1), a system of "nomenclature is classificatory when it uses terms which primarily apply to lineal relatives, such as 'father', to refer also to collateral relatives". Two or more 'sisters' are classed as equivalent, and so are a number of 'brothers'; a mother's sister is classed with a mother, a father's brother with a father. This need not lead to confusion, because the terms point to various kinds of relationship rather than to the finer distinctions within them. They say nothing about intensity of feeling, for instance, which would be rather different between actual father and son or mother and daughter on the one hand, distant or nominal father and son or mother and daughter on the other. A person may call a number of women mother, but this does not mean that he does not know which of them is his actual mother who bore him.

In most cases there are two sets of terms: one used by persons directly addressing each other, the other in third person reference. The two sets may be quite distinct; there may be points of similarity; or again, as in the Western Desert, they may be almost identical. A third set of terms may be current too, as in the *gundebi* of western Arnhem Land. This is brought into use mainly in speaking to someone about a third person, using a kinship term which differs from the ordinary terms of address and reference. (A few examples are set out in the outline of the Gunwinggu kinship system.)

Kinship alignments are not fixed and invariant. On the whole, they remain fairly stable. There are exceptions, however. According to circumstances (marriages, or inheritance of kin obligations, to name two possibilities), the terms used between one person and another may alter. But we shall not treat this extra complication here.

The following two diagrams, representing parts of two systems, show how these are arranged. More detailed examples are given by Radcliffe-Brown (1930-1), Elkin (1954), and others. Table 4 illustrates Andingari Kinship (Great Victoria Desert), arranged in simplified form to show the alignment of kin. Basically, it is of Aluridja Type.

Explanation: The system is shown from the standpoint of a man, identified here as 'Ego'. A woman views it a little differently, and uses at least one extra term (for husband's sister/brother's wife). In the table, kin terms are arranged according to generation levels (A and B), and men may exchange sisters in marriage (a custom called *barani* in the Ooldea region). The preferred form of marriage for a man is with a m.m.br.s.d. or f.m.br.d.d.; by tracing the vertical and lateral lines this can easily be seen. A man (Ego) calls his spouse by the term *guri,* which means 'wife'; other *guri* shown in the table are also eligible spouses. Four lines of descent are recognized (see top generation level, A); but only two distinguishing terms are used, as in the grandchildren's generation level. An exception occurs in the case of the daughter's daughter of a m.br.d. or f.sr.d., who is a *guri,* and a man may marry such a woman provided her mother is not married to his own son. Thus in a man's own generation level his male cross-cousin (M.Br.S. or F.Sr.S.) is classified as a 'brother', but his female cross-cousin is *narumba.* (Separate terms for cross-cousins of both sexes are used in the northern part of the Western Desert.) The term *jundal* means 'daughter'. A son's wife is also called this. So are all the wives of men addressed as GADA, including special kinds of GADA such as GADA-WABUDU, or GADA-JUMARI. Suffixes indicate avoidance and restraint. All terms have

TABLE 4

ANDINGARI KINSHIP

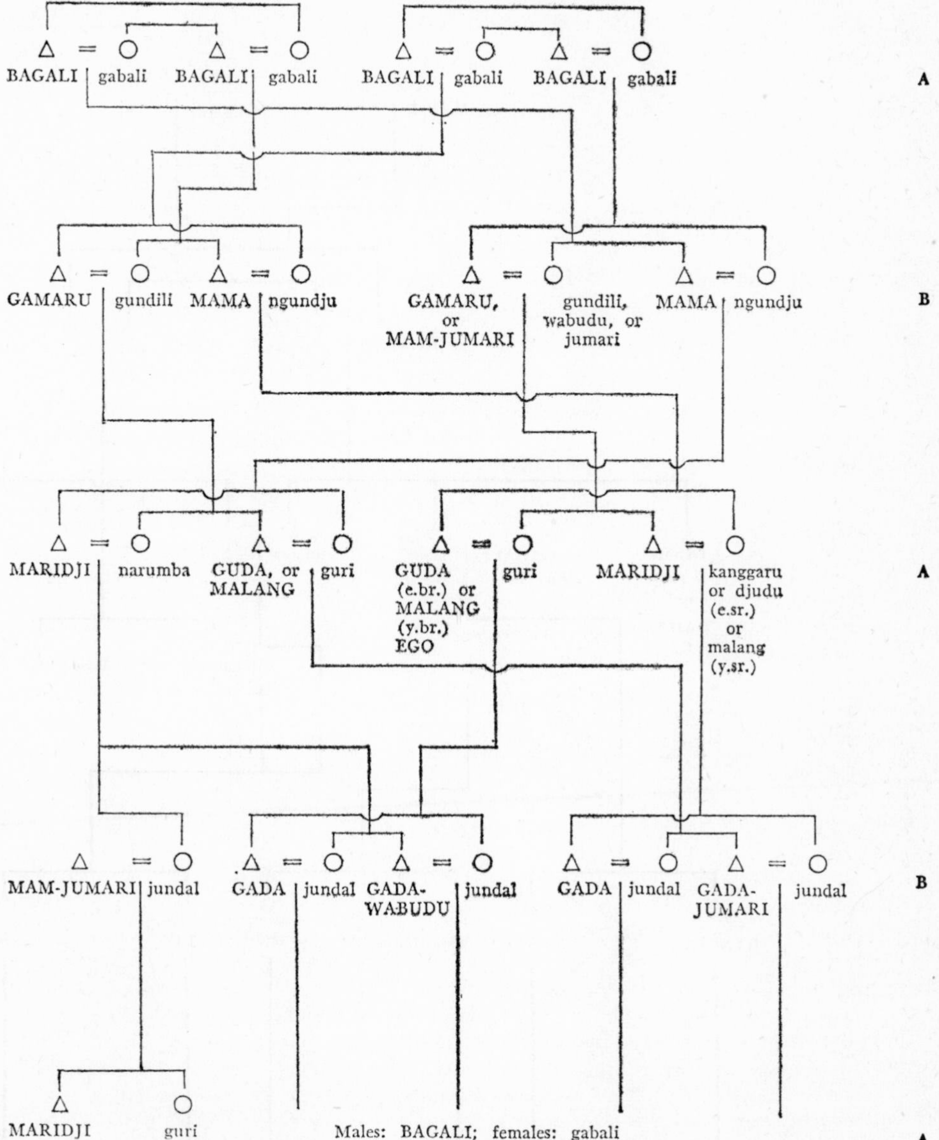

Key: △ = males; ○ = females; kinship terms are shown in capitals for males, in lower case for females; horizontal lines connect siblings; vertical lines connect parents with children. Abbreviation of English kin terms, as above: F. = father; Br. = brother; sr. = sister; S. = son; etc.

TABLE 5

GUNWINGGU KINSHIP

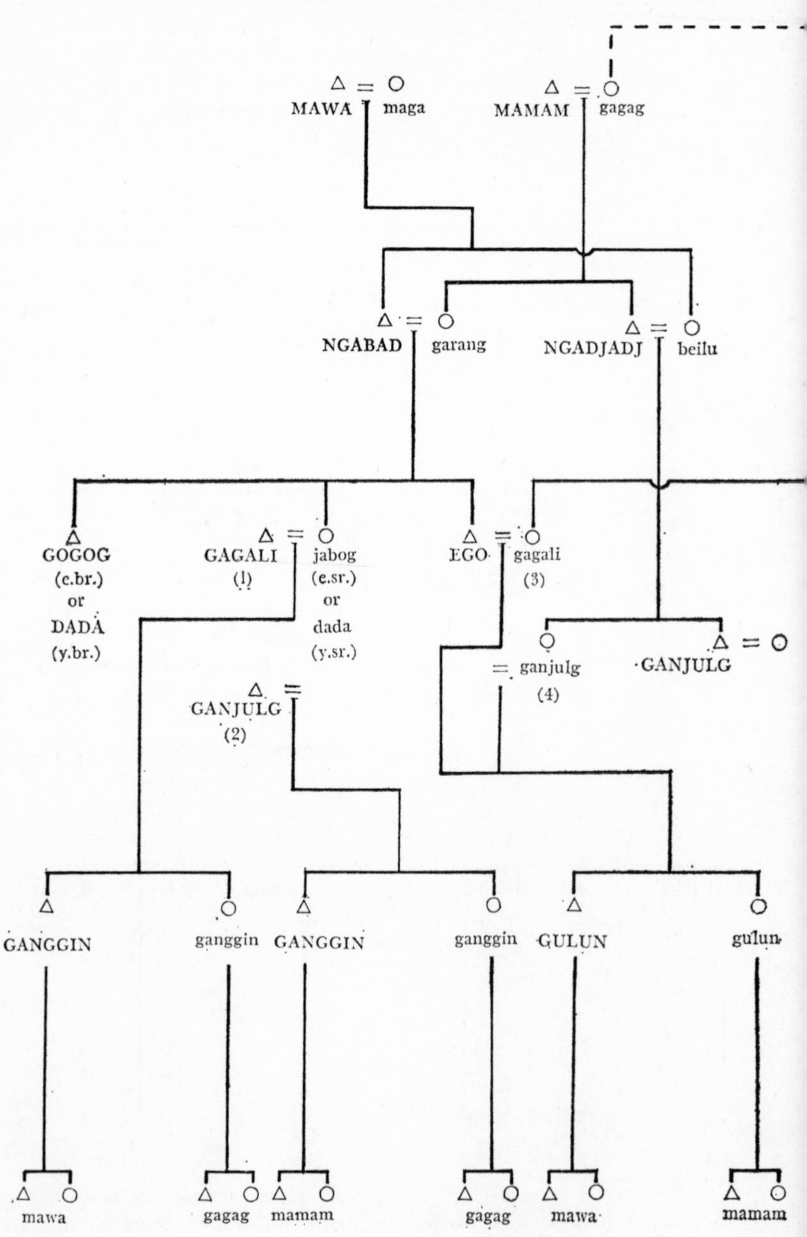

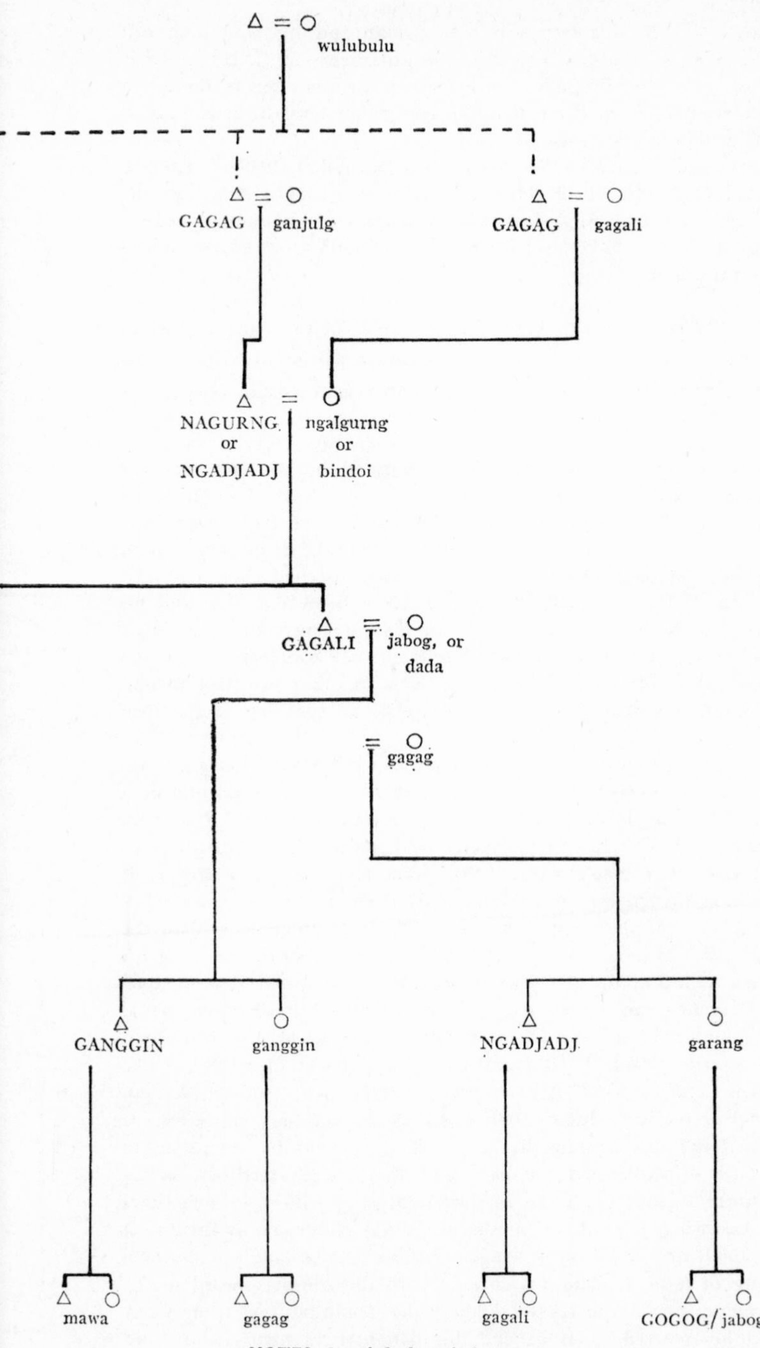

NOTES: 1 and 3, first choice

2 and 4, second choice

reciprocals. For example, a man calls his father's sister *gundili*, and she calls him GADA.

An interesting point in this system is that a man and his wife both call their children by the same terms: like him, she calls her sons GADA and her daughters *jundal*. So do her brothers, and his sisters. In other words, there is a minimum of differentiation in the *descending* generation level B, as contrasted with *ascending* generation level B.

Kin terms vary throughout the Western Desert. (See Elkin, 1938-40: 196-349; 1954: 73; R. and C. Berndt, 1942: 148-52; Douglas, 1958: 111.) Although the terms set out here are known, and several of them commonly used, almost as far north as the east Kimberleys, there are numerous alternatives as well as a few minor variations.

Table 5 shows part of the Gunwinggu (western Arnhem Land) kinship system, arranged in simplified form to illustrate the alignment of kin. Again the point of orientation is a male, shown as Ego.

Explanation of Table 5: This system is complicated by the fact that the Gunwinggu have been influenced by other tribes, not least through intermarriage with them. Two type-marriages are shown in this table. One (first choice) is with a *gagali*, who may be a f.sr.d.d.d., m.br.d.d.d. or m.m.br.d.d.; the connecting links are not detailed here. The second (second choice) is with a maternal or paternal cross-cousin. (See also Table 6 below.) A man and his wife call their children by different terms; but his sister uses the same term for them as he does, *gulun*. Where terms of reference are concerned, the wife's brother uses the same terms for them as she does. In other words, a woman adopts the orientation of her brother (or vice versa) in speaking of her own children.

Here a man, Ego, marries a woman from his own or grandchildren's generation levels. So does his GAGAG (M.M.Br.), who marries either a *ganjulg* or a *gagali*. This underlines an identification between a man and his M.M.Br., which is significant in this society because of its matrilineal emphasis. The perspective is similar in the case of a man's sister. Apart from emphasizing matriliny, it suggests that young women are considered highly desirable as wives; and this, in fact, is what the people themselves often say. It is interesting that the Gunwinggu, like the Maung, have a separate term (reciprocal) for mother's mother's mother, pointing up the importance of the maternal descent line.

Some of these same terms are used in reference, mostly talking about actual relatives: for example, *ngarug ngabad*, my father; *ngarug jabog*, my elder sister. My mother is *ngarug garad*. Then there are general terms of reference like *gongumu*, father; *ngalgongumu*, father's sister; *ngalbaidjan*, mother; *baidjan* or *baidjan-rangem*, mother's brother. (*Baidjan* as an ordinary adjective, or qualifier, means 'big'; but occasionally it is taken, perhaps by extension, to imply this relationship. Women talking about their home territory, as an expanse of country including all the smaller local sites within it, sometimes translated the Gunwinggu words as 'mother-country'.) *Narangem* is used to a girl or woman about her brother, just as *ngaldalug* is a conventionally impersonal way of speaking to a man about his sister, where the ordinary word *dalug*, woman, is given a special quality by adding the feminine prefix, *ngal-*. A man's son may be referred to as *beiwud*, his daughter as *ngalbeiwud*; *wud* is an ordinary word for child, or offspring. A female *gagag* is *ngalginbaleng*; a male *mamam*, *namainmigen*. But another set of third-person reference terms is verb-like, changing for person and number, sometimes incorporating a pronoun-object; insofar as they show tense, they point mainly to a simple past. In this series, for instance, 'your father' is *nguda ngunbonang*; his or her father, *nungga bibonang*, and so on, alluding to the fact that it is the father who 'sees' the spirit child in a dream; when a feminine pronoun-subject is used, *ngaleng bibonang*, the reference is to a father's sister. Your mother is *nguda ngunjaume*; his or her mother, *ngaleng bijaume*; his or her mother's brother, *nungga bijaume; jau* is offspring from the point of view of a mother and mother's brother. For siblings of the same sex, and sometimes collectively for siblings of both sexes, the term could be translated to mean 'standing together', or 'being together'; your brother (where there are two of them), *nguda ngunedangin*; his brother (where there are two of them), *nungga benedangin*. 'Your female *gagag*' is *ngaleng ngundjumdoi*; his or her female *gagag*, *ngaleng bidjumdoi*; his or her male *mamam*, *nungga bigebmainmeng*. 'Your *ganjulg*', addressing two people, is *nguri-modjalgdoren*; *nguri-* is a plural prefix, indicating that the three (or more) of them call one another *ganjulg*.

Gundebi is a little harder to follow, and to use, because when two people are speaking about a third each of them must keep in mind not simply his own kin relationship to that third person, but the other's as well. To start with a simple example: a woman talking to her husband about their own son will refer to him as *nawein* (*ngalwein* for a daughter), and her husband will use the same term. Or a woman talking to her sister about their own mother will speak of her as *ngalngalaingu*, and the sister will do the same—*nangalaingu* for mother's brother. A woman talking to her *maga* about her *gulun*, if her *maga* calls that person own son or daughter (*djedje*, woman speaking), will say *ngorgbeilgu*, and her *maga* will say *ngorgbeil*. Or take a woman talking to a *ganjulg*, a male cross-cousin, about her female *gagag*: if he calls that person *ganjulg*, the speaker will refer to her as *ngalmindjadngo*, and he in reply will refer to her as *ngalmindjadngani*; but if he calls her *maga*, the terms they use will be *ngalwimengwari*, and *jiwimeng*. This is not the place to say more about it, interesting as it is. Illustrating it properly, with a list of terms, would mean overloading the discussion with too many examples. Actually it is much more straightforward than it might seem from this short comment, since in a situation of this sort people are acquainted with one another's relationships as well as with their own—at least in their immediate perspective.

Another set of terms, again, is part of the special vocabulary used between men and women who stand to each other as mother-in-law and son-in-law, *ngalgurng* and NAGURNG. For instance, *nguda ngunmodmeng*, your father; *nguda ngunmulamodmeng*, your mother or mother's brother; *nguda* is the ordinary Gunwinggu pronoun, 'you', and the terms are formed on the same principle as in ordinary reference.

The Gunwinggu system shown in Table 5 is actually much more complex than appears here, if only because of the impact of the subsection system. But this is probably enough to indicate some of its main features. (See Elkin, Berndt and Berndt, 1951.)

Whether or not it is used in conjunction with named moieties, or sections, or subsections, kinship also governs the types of preferred marriage. It does so less strictly today, because the tribes have been scattered and reduced in numbers so that in some regions there are not enough people in the correct intermarrying categories.

TABLE 6

MOIETY DIVISIONS OF THE GUNWINGGU IN RELATION TO KINSHIP

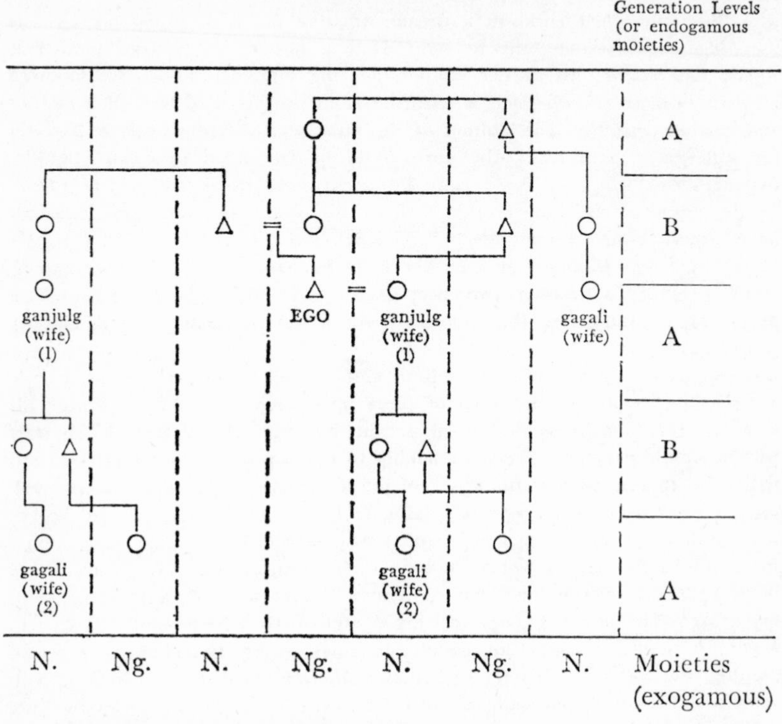

Notes: N. = Namadgu.
Ng. = Nangaraidjgu.
(2) if (1) is not Ego's wife.

The spread of the section and subsection systems has also led to a wider choice of alternatives. But apparently there was always some latitude, and the formally correct type of marriage is not necessarily the most frequent. It represents what people say the preferred marriage-type should be: but there were probably always variations, some permitted and some not. In other words, such a system provides an ideal or construct picture of how kin relationships should be arranged, but from detailed genealogies it is clear that this is not always followed through in practice. In an area where the preferred form of marriage is between a man and his maternal cross-cousin, his mother's brother's daughter, we would not expect to find everyone conforming to it. There may be only a core of preferred marriages, and a scatter of other forms.

Although some work had been done on this topic of kinship before Radcliffe-Brown entered the field, he made an endeavour to put it on a firmer basis, to correct some misconceptions about Australian Aboriginal social organization which were current in the anthropological literature of his day. In 1930-1 he published four papers, later bound as a monograph. This was an attempt to outline the situation, summarizing the available information on it, and clearing the way for further research. It was an exploratory study and should be recognized as such. Although it was a milestone at the time, and is acknowledged as a 'classic' today, this should not blind us to the fact that a number of his generalizations were inadequately supported with ethnographic material. Moreover, he considered only the ideal or the construct picture, and did not explore the matter of variation.

The following paragraphs survey briefly what has been done in Australia since Radcliffe-Brown's day. It is obviously impossible to take into account everything that has been published on this subject.

Radcliffe-Brown discussed fifty separate kinship types, but suggested that throughout the Continent there was actually a single specialized type of system elaborated into a number of sub-types. Elkin (1938-40, 1954) agrees that the Aborigines are essentially homogeneous as far as social organization is concerned. In 1951, Radcliffe-Brown mentioned four key types of marriage system: Kariera, Kumbaingeri, Aranda and Karadjeri. Elkin (1954: 49-79) deals primarily with five: Kariera, Karadjeri, Aranda (or Nyul-Nyul), Aluridja, and Ungarinyin. Their characteristics are as follows:

1. Kariera (Gariera), on the De Grey: cross-cousin marriage allowed.

2. Karadjeri (Garadjeri), around La Grange: marriage allowed only with maternal cross-cousin.

3. Aranda (or Nyul-Nyul, Njulnjul): No cross-cousin marriage, but marriage between certain kinds of second cousins (the children of cross-cousins): ideally, with m.m.br.d.d.

4. Aluridja (also among Bard and north of the Njulnjul): absence of moieties, sections and subsections: cross-cousins called brother and sister, and father's and mother's cross-cousins called by terms for the brothers and sisters of father and mother respectively: cross-cousin marriage prohibited: certain kinds of second cousin eligible, but not the same as in the Njulnjul (ideally, m.m.br.s.d.).

5. Ungarinyin (Ungarinjin), southern boundary of the King Leopold Range: no cross-cousin marriage, but kin terms applied to local groups or clans. That is, the concern is with the relationship between local clans. 'If a man of one clan is a person's mother's brother, then every man in it—irrespective of age—is also his "mother's brother", and every woman in it is his "mother".' It is, as Elkin puts it, a 'vertical system': there are the same terms for succeeding generations, and the type marriage is with a f.m.br.s.d.

Elkin suggests that there are as many types as there are languages in Aboriginal Australia, but that all "are based on similar principles". Differences among them are important too, because they "are associated with variations in marriage rules and in social behaviour". Basic types like these can be used as models, to simplify comparison—provided this is recognized as no more than a first step. Obviously a full comparison must take into account, as well, both the alternative choices which are allowed, and an assessment of the kinds of marriage and other unions which take place in a given population over a period. The structural pattern can be derived from the kind of preferred marriage acknowledged in a particular society, and from the range and distribution of kin terms. However, a number of kinship studies have been concerned more with form or structure than with process. In the conventional chart or table, in such cases, a beginning is always made from a hypothetical Ego, and the patterns that fall into shape around a type-marriage are of a construct kind. We do not always know enough about how persons linked in a particular relationship actually behave in a variety of situations.

Elkin (1938-40, 1938/54) examines specific systems in some detail. He re-analyses, for instance, the Dieri (Lake Eyre) material, drawing attention to some of Radcliffe-Brown's wrong interpretations, and also discusses irregular or alternative marriages, which he accounts for in terms of alien impact. But the keynote of Elkin's work has been his insistence that kinship does not exist in a vacuum. Persons, he says, belong to groups, their membership determined on the basis of sex and age, of community, of language and common culture (tribe), of possession and occupation of a territory (local group, clan and horde), and of kinship position and marital status (family, section, moiety, etc.). It is this structuring of relationships which unites persons within the broader setting of social and economic life 1938/54: 25, 80). He is emphatic, too, that social organization must be seen against a totemic background (1933). Understanding the Dieri kinship system (1938-40: 49), for instance, "requires a knowledge of the tribal totemic beliefs and organization". Pointing out that kinship must be taken into account in considering all marriage arrangements, he underlines its wider social implications. Thus kinship obligations and responsibilities are significant throughout a person's life, stipulating what he (or she) should or should not do in respect of the people he calls relatives of one kind or another—which means everyone in his social perspective—in matters of everyday routine, and in crises, major or minor, such as when they are born, or initiated, or marry, or die. (Elkin, 1938-40: 335, 383.)

Warner's study of north-central Arnhem Land (1937/58), despite some ethnographic weaknesses, has a wealth of material on social organization, kinship and its social and cultural interrelations, and lively and detailed accounts of behaviour between persons. His work has proved particularly stimulating in a narrower sense too, in provoking a controversy which has extended more or less from the date of its publication to the present day. This is the famous 'Murngin' debate. (See, for example, Radcliffe-Brown, 1951, 1956; Lawrence and Murdock, 1949; Lévi-Strauss, 1949; Leach, 1951; Berndt, 1955, 1957.) To Lévi-Strauss the so-called 'Murngin' type of kinship is a focal point in social structural studies, not only because of its intricacy, but because Warner presented a thorough and extensive study of it. (We ourselves have not yet published our data on this region; but see R. Berndt, n.d.)

Ursula McConnel's work on Cape York social organization (1934, 1939-40, 1950) is complementary to Sharp's and Thomson's, but more intensive. One outstanding feature is what she calls a junior marriage system. Among the Wikmunkan (Wigmungan), different terms are used for mother's older and younger brothers. The system rests on recognition of specific age-lines, irrespective of a person's chronological age. Men of an older generation in a younger descent line (for example, an older man belonging to the descent line of his father's younger brother) marry women who are of the younger generation but belong to an older descent line (for example, a woman who stands in relationship to such a man as mother's older brother's daughter), but not vice versa. This makes the system into a downward age spiral, with intermarriage between different generations in the older and younger age-lines (1940: 435). "The system works one way only, i.e. men marry *down* and women marry *up*. Men marry women of their own generation in a younger line, or of a younger generation in an older line, they cannot marry women of an older generation in a younger line" (*ibid.*, 448). "Thus the system works in a unilateral downward-age direction, and only folds back on itself by the marriage of men of the youngest line . . . with women of a younger generation in the oldest line which closes the system in a downward-age spiral" (1950: 108). If by any chance this custom is departed from, the terminology is altered to fit the situation and the kinship pattern is preserved. This junior marriage system, peculiar to the Peninsula tribes, is paralleled in the same area by the junior sororate (when a widower receives a younger sister of his dead wife in her place) and levirate (when a widow passes to her dead husband's younger brother). She underlines, particularly, its unilateral character.

Ursula McConnel (1950: 107-45) is responsible too for a comparison of marriage systems of the Cape York Peninsula, especially in reference to unilateral cross-cousin marriage (that is, marriage with only one kind of cross-cousin, not both), but it has received little attention. Those familiar with Australian kinship material may remember that Radcliffe-Brown (1951) considered the system of the Yir-yoront (Jirjorond), a tribe studied by Sharp (1934*b*), to be an isolated 'Murngin' (Wulamba) type of kinship system: this assumption, as McConnel points out, needs modification in the light of more recent comparative evidence. Further, she presents some actual statements relating to marriage laws, translations from native texts (1940: 438-9). Her aim is to give a description of the system in action (1934: 313-14), deriving from it a general conception of the nature and functioning of the kinship structure. She lists three main assumptions:

1. the primary importance of intimacy in the use of kinship terms: 'it is upon personal intimate ties . . . that the structure of kinship rests';

2. the application of these terms to a wider span of classificatory or indirectly related persons: 'kinship extends far beyond this more intimate situation. . . . the range of kinship (is) an ever widening circle of potentially and indirectly related persons. Such factors are, for example, the sororate and levirate, clan organization and the custom of marrying a woman of definite relationship. These less intimate, potential and indirect relationships' constitute, as it were, outer layers surrounding more personally significant ties;

3. as a continuation of 2, the 'application, in the interests of social order, of the formal kinship pattern to all members of society by means of transferred and derived relationships'; the Aboriginal 'takes the wider links in kinship for granted, and directly applies the formal pattern of kinship to include all members of society without necessarily tracing the links of relationship between them. By this means all members of the society fall into place and are subsumed under the formal pattern of kinship'. In other words, a kinship system is relevant to the total picture of social relationships and takes into account such matters as degrees of intimacy and propinquity, and serves to point to significant ways of behaviour which are signalled by the kinship terms themselves.

Lauriston Sharp's account of Yir-yoront social organization (1934*b*: 404-31) has been used by Radcliffe-Brown in discussion of some general implications. Sharp's treatment is not as detailed as McConnel's nor so extensive in geographic span as Elkin's. It is, however, particularly interesting. "The extent to which kinship patterns regulating emotions and behaviour pervade all aspects of Yir-yoront social life can hardly be exaggerated", says Sharp (*ibid.*, 412). This system is said to be similar to the so-called 'Murngin' system discussed by Warner (1937/58), so that comparatively it is of obvious importance since the latter has been the subject of some controversy (see above). The question of status is significant here, as in all Aboriginal societies to a lesser or greater degree, and this is expressed through specific status relationships. Sharp speaks of " 'weak relationships' balanced by 'strong relationships' ", saying that this "is necessary for a society in which every active individual relationship, at least between males, involves a definite and accepted superiority and inferiority. . . . Even in distant relationships there is always present a recognized element of superordination and

Central Australian man
(photo: courtesy C. P. Mountford)

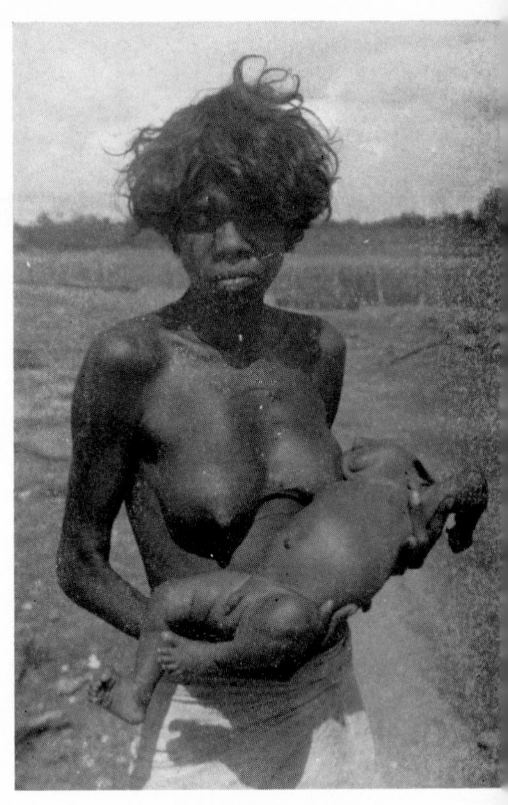

Three different ways in which mothers hold their children. The photograph at right depicts the most convenient position, allowing maximum freedom of movement in food-collecting. Port Keats, south-west of Darwin (1947)

subordination" (*ibid.*, 419). This inequality, inherent in the kinship terminology, is demonstrated in kinship behaviour, and is further exemplified in asymmetrical or unilateral preferential marriage.

Then there is the work of Stanner, who deals with totemism and kinship in the north-western area of the Northern Territory, on the Daly River (1933*a*: 389-405), as well as among the Nangiomeri (1933*b*: 416-17), Djamindjung (1936*a*: 441-51), and Murinbada (1936*b*: 186-216). Radcliffe-Brown considered the Murinbada study to be important because it showed how an indigenous system could incorporate introduced subsections. (This had previously been discussed by Elkin, 1933; 1938-40; 1950*a*: 1-20.) Stanner also emphasizes the gap between ideal and actual kinship systems, which at that time had not been dwelt on to any extent. Phyllis Kaberry (1939: 109 *et passim*) too has paid attention to kinship in the eastern Kimberleys in relation to marriage; the attitudes of individual persons toward it, and the extent to which women consider it as limiting or enhancing their freedom; the situations in which kinship rules are set aside, the frequency of this, in terms of alternative forms of marriage and those classified as 'wrong' (*ibid.*, 115-30), and the adjustments which must be made. These are questions which, she considers, must be discussed before an examination can be made of "the rights, privileges, and duties that are inherent in the marital bond" (*ibid.*, 109).

During and since Radcliffe-Brown's day, the main research on this topic has been done by Elkin, Warner, Lauriston Sharp, Ursula McConnel, Stanner, Phyllis Kaberry, Hart, Piddington, T. Strehlow, Fry, Rose, Thomson, Olive Pink, Tindale, Capell, Lommel and Petri, Falkenberg, Marie Reay, Meggitt and ourselves. Most of this work has been carried out by students originally inspired by Radcliffe-Brown or Elkin, or both, and much of their material and analysis has not yet been published.

Kin behavioural patterns

Kinship terms are only part of any kinship system. Just as important is the behaviour associated with them. Being related to a given person in a particular way means more than simply using the appropriate labels or terms; it means (to repeat) conforming, in greater or lesser degree, to what is regarded as the proper line of conduct in respect of him, or her. This may entail complete avoidance, or restraint and circumspection, a speech tabu, or special duties or rights. It may involve a joking or bantering relationship, or one in which the persons concerned can act with comparative freedom. In addition, there are relationships where mutual cooperation is more than usually significant, either in ordinary affairs or in the sphere of ritual.

In the Western Desert, the term *jumari* connotes 'tabu', or avoidance. (See Table 4.) A man must avoid his *wabudu* or *jumari* (mother-in-law), father-in-law (*wabudu* or *gamaru*), wife's brother or sister's husband (*maridji*), and wife's mother's brother (*mam-jumari*, 'father-tabu'). *Gada-wabudu*, daughter's husband, connotes 'son by initiation'. A man calls his son's wife *jundal*, but her term for him is *mam-jumari*—indicating that a woman should not associate freely with her father-in-law. Among the Bidjandjara-speaking people of the Great Victoria Desert it is a man's prospective father-in-law who cuts the foreskin at his circumcision, and his *maridji* who holds it. Thus the term for wife's father connotes 'initiator': the reciprocal when used for son-in-law is *gada-wabudu*, 'son by initiation', or *gada-jumari*, 'son-tabu'. A special *bulga* relationship is set up between a novice and the *maridji* who holds his foreskin. There may be two or more *wabudu* at an initiation; and this entitles a novice, once he is socially adult, to claim two or more wives. Since these terms extend in a classificatory way throughout the whole group, it is obvious that such relationships must vary a great deal in intensity. Most of them involve special obligations. A man is expected to make gifts, including meat, to his wife's father, mother, and brothers, to compensate them for her loss. He must make payments also to the men who initiate him. When there is an exchange of brothers and sisters in marriage, a tight network of co-operation exists between the respective family circles, and what is given out in the form of payments and gifts to affinal kin actually comes back in one form or another.

Perhaps the most widespread avoidance relationship is the one between a man and his mother-in-law. They are forbidden to utter each other's names. In some cases there is a complete ban on speech between them; or a third person may serve as an intermediary. In others a special vocabulary must be used; in others again, sign language. A woman may turn in her track and face the other way, or hide, if people shout to her that a man she calls daughter's husband is approaching; in pastoral areas in the Northern Territory she may cover her head with paperbark or a handkerchief. The main thing is that two persons who stand in this relationship should avoid face to face contact, or any prolonged or familiar association. The Gunwinggu, for instance, say that if these two stand too close to each other the flies 'go from one to the other, and mingle': therefore they should speak from a little way off—always using the *gungurng* vocabulary, proper between a man and his *ngalgurng*.

This is one solution to the problem of how to maintain social distance between two persons without interfering too much with routine living in a situation where continuous privacy and seclusion are not easy to arrange. In western Arnhem Land, more than in some areas such as the Western Desert, a woman quite often travels and camps in the same party as her daughter and daughter's husband: and this is simplified by the rules which allow her to do so without much inconvenience to the people around them. There are restrictions, too, on the way in which a woman handles the meat she receives from her daughter's husband. But the Gunwinggu example points up very well the opposite side of this picture—the close co-operation of a particular kind which the avoidance rules emphasize. A man may urge his close sister's daughter's daughter, his *gagag*, 'Don't give your daughter to anyone but my son. It's not right to give her to someone who doesn't talk *gungurng* to you, but only talks openly' (that is, in non-restricted language). And a woman can expect help in trouble from her daughter's husband, or betrothed. Conventionally, if anyone abuses her in his hearing he should spring to her defence, and if she is injured or killed in his sight or hearing he must avenge her: 'he can't look at her blood', people say. The bond between two women who are *ngalgurng*, or between two men who stand as *nagurng* to each other, is a rather more diluted mixture of constraint—co-operation. But between those of opposite sex, especially where it has been ratified, so to speak, by the formally correct marriage agreement, it is a positive tie which the apparently negative features serve simply to highlight.

Relationships which call for avoidance and restraint need not be interpreted solely in sexual terms, nor need they express enmity or conflict. It is probably true that they point to areas of social relations in which there is more likelihood of strain than in others because they make mixed demands on the persons concerned. Pressures toward mutual aid, loyalty, common purpose, even strong affection, are countered by pressures toward duties and obligations of a special kind. The possibility of disruption cuts across the ideal of solidarity. Of course this applies to most human relationships, but not equally so. Joking and extreme familiarity provide one framework for coping with it. (Mother-in-law jokes are a feature of many societies.) Tabus, prohibitions, restraints, provide another. But these are not as different as they may seem, and some relationships contain elements of both. The source of strain between two such persons may be their relations to each other in respect of a third (for example the woman who is daughter to one and wife to the other), particularly when their expectations in respect of each other are not evenly matched—when the relationship is an asymmetrical one. Or the emphasis may be more directly on their mutual relationship (for example, as potential husband and wife, or sweethearts). Terms of avoidance do not apply simply to actual consanguineal and affinal relatives, but are extended to include classificatory kin as well.

In some areas, a man's father's sister is a person with whom he can, ideally, be completely frank, in speech if not in action. She may be classified as a female father, as among the Gunwinggu, equivalent for certain purposes to his father's brothers, but for the Gunwinggu this is not a joking relationship. There are other permissive relationships. In the Great Victoria Desert, all women a man calls *guri*, 'wife', are potential wives or sweethearts; but if they are married their husband's permission should be obtained first. The *duwei-galei* cross-cousin relationship in north-eastern Arnhem Land (father's sister's son—mother's brother's daughter) is very similar. So are the *ganjulg* and *gagali* relationships among the Gunwinggu in western Arnhem Land, and the *mamam* among the Maung; between *ganjulg* of both sexes, or between *gagali*, joking of a familiar kind is quite in order.

There is usually a strong emotional bond between a man and his close sister, although it is marked by some constraint as well. In Arnhem Land, for instance, if a man hears his sister scolded or abused, or if her husband beats or quarrels with her in his presence, he will take up his spears and threaten all his sisters, actual and classificatory, including the one directly involved. This is a sanction designed to make sure that women behave circumspectly. The idea is that a man is responsible for the good name of anyone he calls sister, although obviously the closer the relationship the more alert he is likely to be in the matter. Especially in a large camp, a woman can never be sure that none of her 'brothers' are in hearing distance if she is mixed up in an argument. The threat is there, and the assumption is that she should have been more careful than to get involved. She should avoid even the shadow of disagreement, or any action which would shame him. She should not, for instance, allow a brother to see her being intimate with her own husband—although a man is careful to avoid such situations where anyone he calls sister is involved. What is more, in eastern Arnhem Land, a man should only whisper if his actual sister is near. They should never speak directly to each other and he should not utter her name; he may refer to her formally as 'rubbish' (i.e. in eastern Arnhem Land) or 'thing' (as in western Arnhem Land). (Incidentally, name tabus are fairly common in a variety of circumstances.) Nevertheless, men are expected to watch the interests of their sisters, especially close sisters. They look to them to provide husbands for their own daughters, since ideally a man marries his mother's brother's daughter. Another important relationship in this area is the *mari-gudara*, between a man and his sister's daughter's son. In this patrilineally-oriented society it links a man with the patri-line of his mother's mother: it is especially significant in the religious sphere. It represents a strong bond of mutual assistance, in such matters as gift exchange, or help in camp quarelling, as well as in ritual.

There is also the question of incest. General restrictions on sexual relations between close kin exist in all Aboriginal tribes. Particularly, they are proscribed between first-degree or first-order relatives: own parents, own brothers and sisters, own offspring. Circumstances do, or did, vary. For instance, on Bathurst and Melville islands marriage with a sister's daughter or a half-sister from the same father was formerly permitted; it was forbidden, however, by the mission which was established on Bathurst early this century; and the local people's efforts, in going over their genealogies, to 'cover up' marriages now regarded as wrong led to much confusion until these were sorted out. Most Aboriginal societies prohibit or discourage intimacy between a man and, for instance, his father's sister, brother's daughter, sister's daughter, son's wife, son's children, daughter's children, mother-in-law. Again there are exceptions. In some areas a man may have access to his sisters-in-law. In others, a classificatory mother-in-law is a desirable sweetheart, at least surreptitiously; the *djarada* love magic of the central west of the Northern Territory, and the east Kimberleys, makes much of this forbidden but attractive possibility. In north-eastern Arnhem Land a father may marry, temporarily, a woman promised as wife to his son, until his son is socially adult—when, ideally, he hands her over. Alternatively, a man may have one of his father's wives as a sweetheart, with the understanding that he will claim her if his father dies: she may even bear his child. This happened, particularly, in the case of old Wonggu of Caledon Bay. As he grew older, some of his wives had tacitly approved liaisons with his sons; and now that he is dead, a couple of them have passed to a surviving son who had informally asserted his right to them.

A further point, in relation to kin behaviour, is the exchange of wives during certain rituals, or in everyday life. In this last, it serves mainly to cement or establish friendships, or to compensate for some favour received.

Although kinship is the basis of most important relationships between one person and another, there are others as well. Sharing the same personal name, for instance, may be enough to establish a special bond between two people, regardless of whether they belong to the same tribe. The *ngirawad* of the Wagaitj (Wogaidj) is an example; here the persons concerned may not speak to each other until they have ceremonially exchanged goods. (Elkin, 1950*b*: 67-81.) Stanner (1937: 303-7) mentions the same thing for the Daly River-Port Keats region. (See Chapter IV.) In other areas there are no tabus associated with such a relationship. On the Lower River Murray (Jaraldi), sharing a personal name establishes a *mindji* (common name) tie of friendship and mutual aid. *Lundu*, friend, in north-eastern Arnhem Land has a similar connotation. Another kind of bond links 'age-mates', especially those who have undergone the same initiation rites together, or been born or conceived about the same time, or undergone some special experience together.

Stanner (1937: 300) sets out eleven categories, which indicate 'forms of address and reference: personal names; nicknames; kin terms; age-status terms; terms of social status; secret names; terms for membership of social divisions; circumlocutory terms, which fall into several subgroups; metaphorical terms; signs, and expletives'.

Summary

In summary, drawing on the general work of Radcliffe-Brown (1930-1) and Elkin (1940, 1938/54, etc.) and on specific studies as well, ten points are important to remember in considering Australian Aboriginal kinship systems.

1. Kinship is an integral part of the total social organization. People are sorted out, as it were, into categories, and these are indicated by the terminology used in any given tribe. Affines (relatives-in-law) are often classified with consanguineal kin, although qualifying or distinct terms may be used for them, particularly for parents-, brothers-, and sisters-in-law. At least, certain terms indicate potential affines, however close their genealogical relationship. Husbands and wives too are, ideally, related to each other as kin, either actually or in a classificatory sense.

2. Classificatory kinship prevails throughout Aboriginal Australia. An underlying principle here is what Radcliffe-Brown called the 'equivalence of siblings of the same sex'. If one man addresses another by a certain kin term, he will use the same term for his full brothers; a kin term used in relation to a woman will apply to her full sisters too. This equivalence is a formal structural matter. In actual cases differences are recognized, such as special circumstances, or cross-cutting relationships, which ensure that in practice the equivalence is rarely exact, or complete, where adults are concerned. And attitudes vary according to the closeness of the ties. There is no question of confusing a person's 'own' father with a nominal one, or an 'own' brother with a classificatory brother such as a father's brother's son or mother's sister's son. Even though there may appear to be an almost complete identification in some cases, such as between a man and a person he speaks of as his 'own' son, he will probably be ready enough to clarify their relationship by saying, for instance, that the boy's father is his own close

brother, and that he has helped to rear the boy as his own. It is the social aspect which counts.

For other purposes, it is siblings of opposite sex who are 'equivalent'. In a number of systems a man uses much the same terms for his sister's children as she does, and they may reciprocate with terms which identify him socially with her. Correspondingly, he and she use identical terms for his children. The Gunwinggu system, already outlined, is an example. Another comes from north-eastern Arnhem Land, where a man calls his own children *gadu,* they call him *baba* and his sister *mugul* or *mugul-baba*; a woman calls her own children *wagu,* and her brother too uses this term for them.

3. Some relationships are seen as more binding than others. This is particularly the case with siblings of the same sex, where conflict is ideally at a minimum—although brothers may compete for the same women, and this situation is exacerbated in many areas by the levirate. Sibling rivalry is much more apparent in some parts of the Continent than in others; but it is generally modified or kept in check by common religious interests which are of dominant concern. Sisters are often close friends, and this seems to be reinforced rather than otherwise when they are co-wives. Competition for husbands or for sweethearts is not so noticeable in their case, partly perhaps because they can and may share the same husband. A man who wants another wife can, circumstances permitting, add her to his collection. But in every such constellation there can, formally speaking, be only one pivotal husband-figure, or household head; consequently there is more likelihood of competition among men in this sphere.

Children of siblings of the same sex are classified together, but children of siblings of opposite sex may be distinguished terminologically. The structural principle of the equivalence of siblings of the same sex underlies local group organization. For this purpose, a man's father's father, father's father's brothers, father, father's brothers, brothers, father's brothers' sons, sons, and brothers' sons, are classified together. So are his mother, mother's brother, mother's brother's son, and so on. (See Elkin, 1954: 55.)

4. As an extension of the sibling relationship, there are the statuses of mother's brother and father's sister. In nearly all Aboriginal societies these involve special obligations and responsibilities which may be combined with avoidance tabus. Often such persons play an important part in the initiation rituals of their brother's son or daughter, or sister's son or daughter. The relationship between a man and his father's sister is often one of great attachment. However, tabus of one kind or another usually appear in relation to the wives or husbands of these kin. This is usually because of their role in providing wives for their actual or classificatory

nephews, or husbands for their nieces, as the case may be; and this is true whether or not cross-cousin marriage is preferred. In many areas, therefore, these two kin positions—those of M.Br. and f.sr.—are pivotal, and crucial.

5. The relationship between persons belonging to different generation levels is not simply an extension or reflection of the parent-child bond. More generally it signifies difference in status and authority, if not in age, in terms of superordination-subordination. In other words, it suggests horizontal stratification on the basis of status and kinship positioning.

In some cases, persons who stand to each other as grandparent and grandchild are drawn closely together for certain purposes (as those of succeeding generations are for others), and this is often reflected in the terminology used. Generally speaking, this is a symmetrical relationship, in contrast to the possibility of asymmetrical relations for those under (4). It usually signifies mutual aid and respect and, in the case of the grandparent, a teaching-learning relationship. But it may also mean that, as in some cases, it is possible for a person to marry into the generation of a grandchild or grandparent.

Remember that generation levels in this sense are not reckoned in terms of chronological age. They are formal divisions, hinging on relative status. Take a case in which a man marries for the first time at about thirty, has several children and, whether or not he marries in between, takes another wife later at the age of about fifty to sixty. If his first wife came to him at puberty she may still be bearing him children. In other words, there may be a gap of twenty years, if not more, between the surviving children of one mother and father: and it may be wider still between the children of one father but different mothers. This, of course, is not uncommon in other societies; but polygyny complicates it. So does the classificatory system.

Within a person's own generation level are to be found, to some extent at least, 'equals': brothers and sisters, cross-cousins, age-mates and so on. The generation level above him includes those with some authority over him, directly or indirectly: father, mother, father's sister, father's sister's husband, mother's brother, mother's brother's wife, perhaps mother-in-law, father-in-law and so on. Deference, and in some cases avoidance, are relevant here. Even within his own generation level, in some systems, an element of constraint enters into some relationships, for instance in the case of a wife's brother, or a sister's husband. Or constraint and partial avoidance may be the rule between a man and all the women he calls sisters. In the generation below, relations are usually articulated in terms of superordination-subordination: a person's own children, brother's children (who are classified with his own), sister's children, and so on. Here, too, avoidance relatonships are found in some areas, most commonly between a man or woman and the men they call daughter's husband. But a man may be, formally speaking, a generation level above that of his wife's mother—for instance, if he marries his f.sr.d.d.d. In other words, kin positioning and generation level represent only one aspect of the broader picture of status relations.

6. Part of the wider principle of reciprocity is 'reciprocity in marriage'. To Radcliffe-Brown, a marriage was 'a rearrangement of social structure'—perhaps because he saw social structure in terms of a network of relations between persons. If we look at structure in a broader sense (as, in fact, Radcliffe-Brown often did) as encompassing also relations between units, and having some continuity and stability, a marriage which takes place in accordance with the rules, and even one which goes contrary to them in a patterned way, is far from being a rearrangement of this. It is provided for within that structure, part of the patterning. It is, so to speak, a demonstration of the validity of a structure; or the linking together of two families or groups of kin into a rearrangement or reaffirmation of a network of behavioural patterns, obligations and responsibilities. Marriage is not simply a relationship between two persons or two nuclear families, and betrothal arrangements underline this. But among its structural implications is the fact that in all tribes, in one way or another, those who receive a wife must make repayment either then or at some future time, not necessarily in kind. In its simplest form, men exchange sisters or women brothers, as in bilateral (two-sided) cross-cousin marriage. This may mean that a mother's brother's wife is actually a father's sister: and maternal and paternal cross-cousins are often, although by no means always, terminologically equivalent. The principle is similar when the exchange is between different moieties, different clans or local descent groups: it is implicit in the section and subsection systems, at least as a potentiality. On the other hand, this reciprocity may be manifested in delayed exchange. (See Elkin, 1954.)

Marriage reciprocity must be seen in terms not just of exchange of men and women, but of gifts, of rights and privileges, obligations and responsibilities. An elopement, where elopements are not institutionalized, represents a threat to this. It upsets the delicately balanced relationship existing between the persons, or units, involved in that particular cycle of marriage arrangements.

7. The elementary or nuclear family is the basic kinship as well as social unit. It is also, with its core of husband and wife, or wives, the usual medium of achieving sexual satisfaction. Nevertheless, the majority of Aboriginal kin systems are constructed in such a

way as to provide for the potential replacement of spouses and, for that matter, for parent surrogates. Extra-marital relations conventionally fit into this broad framework, with provision in some instances for secondary wives (Dieri) or husbands (western Arnhem Land). In any case there is (was), more or less, in all tribes some opportunity for both men and women to find, outside marriage, sexual partners on a transient-mundane, or transient-ritual, or romantic basis.

8. Kinship is always relevant to person-to-person relationships. Persons are members of social groups or units, but as a rule kinship does not indicate relationship between groups or classes, simply between persons within those groups. An exception here is the relationship between *mada* in north-eastern Arnhem Land. In general, a kinship system is oriented genealogically from the standpoint of any given person, so that virtually everyone in that particular society can be expected to have a slightly different perspective within it.

9. Distinctive kinship patterning is dependent on a number of factors:

(*a*) The number of kin categories distinctly recognized, and terminologically separated out. (In some cases, as for the southern Aluridja, the terms used are few and do little more than indicate sex, generation level, and marriage relationship, whereas in north-eastern Arnhem Land there are twenty-five main terms.)

(*b*) The preferred marriage type, and the series of reciprocal arrangements, or exchanges, associated with it.

(*c*) The question of alternative marriages which are socially acceptable. These may entail reorganization of personal genealogies and kin alignments, with a reshuffling of terms.

(*d*) The question of marriages which are regarded as irregular, and wrong, but not crucially so; and those (including unions regarded as incestuous) which are consistently condemned and, traditionally, subject to severe sanctions.

(*e*) Local descent group, moiety, subsection, section, exogamy, influencing the range of choice in relation to marriage, as well as the kind of terminology used. (See, for example, Elkin, 1940: 371.)

(*f*) The way in which responsibilities, rights, and duties are allocated among various types of kin.

(*g*) The form of totemism operative in the area. (See, for example, Elkin, 1940: 373, in relation to matrilineal social totemism.)

(*h*) The fact that kinship systems are quite often modified to accommodate to the demands of an introduced section or subsection system.

(*i*) Questions of descent.

10. This matter of descent is basic in kinship reckoning. Emphasis

is placed on relationships to and through one parent in terms of unilineal (matrilineal or patrilineal) descent. Kinship, as a whole, is bilateral. Recognition of descent in terms of other social categories may be bilateral, too. But usually one is selected at the expense of the other, or one is 'submerged'.

In Aboriginal Australia kinship is the articulating force for all social interaction. The kinship system of a particular tribe or language unit is in effect a shorthand statement about the network of interpersonal relations within that unit—a blueprint to guide its members. It does not reflect, except in ideal terms, the actuality of that situation; but it does provide a code of action which those members cannot ignore if they are to live in relative harmony with one another. And kinship, in this situation, pervades all aspects of social living. We cannot understand or appreciate traditional life in Aboriginal Australia without knowing something, at least, of its social organization and structure—of which kinship is the major integrating element, or, to put it another way, the fine mesh which holds the society together.

CHAPTER IV

The Basis of Economic Life

The Australian Aborigines are hunters and food-collectors, with no settled dwellings. The impermanent homes they build vary from one area to another; stringy bark or paperbark, sometimes roofed with a smearing of clay; mosquito huts, or stilted wet-season huts for the flooding billabongs of the coastal flats; or caves, as in the rocky hills of western Arnhem Land. This means that they have a special kind of relationship with their natural environment. They are directly dependent on it for survival. We Western Europeans have gone to a great deal of trouble to set up a buffer between ourselves and the physical world around us, trying to ensure that we are to some extent independent of changes in it, to cushion the impact of disasters such as droughts or floods. The Aborigines have their own kind of buffer, in their tools and implements, skills and techniques. This may seem to us quite inadequate, because we are used to a much more elaborate technology. We place so much emphasis on material goods, material wealth, that it is difficult for us to understand people who do not share this interest in accumulating goods almost for their own sake.

It is perhaps for this reason, more than for any other, that Europeans have disparaged the Aborigines and ranked them low in the social scale. They have pointed to the small range of material objects the Aborigines owned, their closeness to nature, and the fact that they did not seriously attempt to change their surroundings. While admitting that the Aborigines were most skilful in taking advantage of their natural resources, they claimed that animals too were able to adapt themselves to their environment without fundamentally altering it. In other words, they were judging the Aborigines on the basis of how far they could control the forces of nature, by practical and not by supernatural means; but in doing this they neglected the richness and complexity of so many other aspects of Aboriginal life.

Because of his way of life, and because, traditionally, he pays far less attention than we do to material objects, the Aboriginal carries with him as few of them as possible. To ensure that he and his family have enough to eat, all a man needs in the bush are his spearthrower and a handful of spears, since he has an intimate knowledge of the ways and habits of the creatures around him. Without this specialized information, his spears and his cleverness in handling them would be useless. He must be able to track with care, to interpret the marks and other evidence left by certain creatures, however faint; to imitate the sounds of animals and birds, to understand the directions of the winds and the importance of the seasons in hunting; and his skill must be constantly maintained by practice. Even where bush foods are fairly plentiful, as along the northern coasts and adjacent islands and the large fresh water rivers, or during good seasons in parts of the inland, the Aboriginal still requires skill and knowledge of the habits of his quarry.

EXPLOITATION OF NATURAL ENVIRONMENT

The Aborigines have been criticized too for not making gardens, and domesticating no animals except the dog. But before European settlers came to Australia there were no other animals which could be domesticated. And although they were not a gardening people, the Aborigines were intimately concerned with the growth cycles of the plants they depended on for food. The Indonesians had gardens, long ago, on the Arnhem Land coast, but the local people were never interested enough to imitate them. An Arnhem Land woman once said in effect, rather patronizingly, as she watched a Fijian missionary working in his mission garden, anxiously concerned because a few of the plants had died: 'You people go to all that trouble, working and planting seeds, but we don't have to do that. All these things are there for us, the Ancestral Beings left them for us. In the end, you depend on the sun and the rain just the same as we do, but the difference is that we just have to go and collect the food when it is ripe. We don't have all this other trouble.'

In some areas such as the Daly River, the Aborigines were careful about exhausting certain yam beds and always left a residue well scattered for the next season's crop. In fact, this practice was much more widespread than is often realized. Their intimate knowledge of the growth of various creatures, as well as of the increase of vegetable and other plants and trees, led many of them to realize that conservation was essential even in times of plenty. They could not afford to be careless. There are cases of what appear to be improvidence, but these are mainly in contact situations. And there are also cases of Aborigines sprinkling seeds around or of preserving certain valuable trees: or saying, for instance, 'The stingray are breeding just now, we won't kill any for food until the new ones have grown.' We speak of the Aborigines as parasites on nature, but are they any more so, fundamentally, than other human beings? Their economy was a subsistence one, but it was not a matter of thoughtless, hand-to-mouth existence, or needless wasting of natural resources.

Holding this view, that nature is their garden, and one which they need not cultivate or 'improve', means of course that the Aborigines were not able to vary the range of foods available. They have had to make use of what is there. But there is actually much more than we might suppose from looking at some of the dry semi-desert areas of the Centre, for instance. And in their own territory, in the kind of country which is familiar to them, if there is anything edible to be found they know exactly where and when and how to find it. At Ooldea in 1941 we listed just a few of the indigenous foods which could easily be obtained in the spinifex area immediately around the Ooldea Soak and mission station. There were 18 varieties of mammals and marsupials; 19 birds; 11 reptiles; 8 insects; 6 water roots; 17 varieties of seed; 3 vegetables; 10 fruits and berries; 4 other plants and fungi, as well as a variety of eggs. And this is a very conservative estimate.

Nevertheless, although there is a fairly large range of foods even in relatively dry regions, it is not simply a matter of picking these up without effort. Many of them are not satisfying except in quantity; tiny grass seeds, or small frogs or lizards. Some areas are harsh. Sweeney (1947: 299) points out that the Wailbri 'have been able to master their desert environment in spite of occasional setbacks: because they have utilized every food resource to the full, and because of their powers of endurance in overcoming "not infrequent" periods of food and water shortage, their community sense, and the evident nutritional value of the desert foods'. Meggitt (1957: 143) notes that vegetable foods normally form 70 to 80 per cent of the usual Wailbri diet. There are not many detailed studies of this aspect, except for descriptive accounts of hunting and food-collecting: for example, Roth (1897: 91-100) for north-central Queensland, and Warner (1937/58: 138-54). However, Cleland (1940, 1957) and others (Irvine, 1957) have made some examination of Aboriginal ecology. The best accounts of Aboriginal food consumption are to be found in Mountford (ed. 1960), and especially important is McCarthy and McArthur's discussion of the amount of time spent in economic activities in Arnhem Land.

It has been suggested that because of their hunting and food-collecting methods the Aborigines must, through the ages, have appreciably altered their natural environment. (Tindale, 1959*a*: 42-3, 50.) Apart from the elimination of 'many of the more vulnerable animals', there was their practice of burning off large stretches of country for hunting, with the possibility of erosion. "Next to the firestick," says Tindale, the digging stick "was probably the most effective instrument in altering the patterns of plant growth, removing a considerable portion of the more edible forms of vegetable life." In contrast, Cleland (1957) considers that 'despite over 10,000 years of occupation, Aboriginal man did not bring about any profound changes in the face of the Continent': this had to wait for the arrival of Europeans.

The question of variety applies also to the substance which is probably most important of all—fresh water. In the coastal areas the quest for water is not usually such a life and death matter as it is in the Centre. This difference is reflected in the various words for 'camp'. Around the coast, in assessing the distance between one place and another people are likely to talk about 'so many camps', or 'so many sleeps', because often the same expression is used for both: *ngura* is a common word for this. But across the dry country of the Great Victoria Desert, distances are measured in 'so many waters': *gabi*, for instance, or *galju*. The named sites are nearly always at waterholes, or rockholes, or soaks. On most of the sacred boards used by the Central people there are designs signifying waterholes, because in this region water means life. It is directly essential, for people who drink it. Indirectly essential too, because both animal and plant life depend on it. But even when there is no surface water, the Aborigines' reputation for being able to find water or moisture, if there is any at all to be found, is well merited. They know just where to look: for instance, in the roots of such trees as the mallee (Howitt, 1904: 51, mentions 'one of the Hakeas'), or in the hollows of other trees, like the bottle or baobab (boab). They can choose the most promising places for digging out soaks, especially in the sandy creek and river beds—for example, the Todd and Alberga, which flow only after heavy rains. Or they may dig for small frogs which have stored water in their bodies during the dry season and are waiting underground for the rains to come again.

When there is no water, as on a dry stretch between camps, there are not many substitutes. There is wild honey, stored by native bees or in the bodies of honey ants, or the 'sugar' which crystallizes on certain leaves, but these are not the same thing. Some people, such as the Gunwinggu in western Arnhem Land, drink wallaby or kangaroo blood, but most consider this too salty—or something special, for secret ritual and not for everyday use. On Bathurst and Melville islands, in a couple of extreme cases when people were short of water while travelling, a man whose wife was breast feeding a child is reported to have drunk some of her milk: but this was very rare indeed. In central Australia wild honeysuckle and other flowers are mixed with water and drunk. (Basedow, 1925: 153.) On the Daly River a drink is made of crushed green ants. And around the Roper, Katherine, and Victoria Rivers a beverage is prepared from pandanus 'fruit', beaten and soaked in water to make a sweetly astringent drink. (Basedow, 1925: 153-4.)

Before the arrival of Europeans, the Australian Aborigines generally did not smoke. Instead, they chewed leaves from one or other of two plants, the *Nicotiana gossei* and *excelsior*, and *Duboisia hopwoodii*, commonly known as *pitcheri* or *pituri*: *balandu* in the Western Desert. (See Johnston and Cleland, 1933-34: 201-23, 268-89.) These leaves were traded over a wide area of the Continent. (McCarthy, 1939*a*: 88-92.) They were chewed and mixed with the ash of special bark to form a quid which was kept behind the ear when not in use. Habitual chewers have a little shelf there. On the north coast, smoking was introduced by the Indonesian traders. The Aborigines of those parts relied on trade tobacco, but also used local leaves, in long wooden pipes or tubes or in crab claws. They say too, although there is no factual evidence to support it, that tobacco was rolled in paper-bark leaves to form a cheroot and smoked long before the arrival of Europeans.

Throughout the Continent, food-collecting and hunting depend on the cycle of the seasons. So, up to a point, does ritual activity. In the Centre, when all the surface waters and all the small water-holes are dry, groups of people gathering about the permanent waters may hold their major rites, scattering again when the rains make fresh water available. The division of the year into seasons depends on the region concerned. In some, eight or nine are named, primarily on the basis of climatic conditions such as heat and cold, the direction of the wind, the amount of rain, and on the kinds of food available. In the northern coastal areas, especially, the divisions are fairly well marked, although they are not fixed. The main difference is between wet season and dry season and between hot and cold, subdivided into such periods as the time when the grass should be burnt off, or the stringy bark trees are in flower, or new grass and new yams are growing.

In the Western Desert there is the same two-fold division: the hot weather, *guli*, and cold weather, *gamaralba* (after Douglas, 1959: 8). Just before *guli* comes *biria-biria*, windy season, and during *guli* the summer storm clouds (*garabuda*) appear. After the hot season come the cold weather clouds *(daligara)*, with the *gagarada*, east wind; then the *djundalba*, fair weather clouds coming from the south after storms. Then rainbows appear, the *djudirangu* symbolizing the monstrous Rainbow Snake, Wonambi. After them come the *juduwari*, winter rain clouds, presaging the return of the windy season. Around Ooldea, too, the cycle follows a desert pattern, but is slightly different: middle of October to April, hot with scattered rains at first, later on becoming dry; May to June, mild weather; June to August, cold and dry; in about September the great winds sweep in from the northern desert, followed in October and November by whirlwinds or willy-willies. In the meantime the countryside has become green, and colourful with wild flowers, so that by September spring, the season of increase, is here. Rites are carried out to maintain and replenish the food supply. It is ceremonial time, when people gather from the surrounding country. Meat is becoming plentiful, the weather is more to their liking, there is excitement over the coming rituals. Men cast off much of their old clothing (Ooldea was in a contact area), women pay more attention to their appearance. Young men and women use flowers to make themselves pretty; it is the time for love-making. There is more singing on the sandridges, more laughing among the women carrying water, and good-humoured bantering between the sexes.

Whatever the area, there is a close and inevitable connection—inevitable in this situation—between the sequence of the seasons and the supply of food. And pervading both of these aspects, linking them in a different dimension, are the myths and rites which in the Aborigines' view sustain and renew them for the benefit of human beings.

PREPARING FOODS

Many Aboriginal languages have a special term for vegetable food as contrasted with meat: *mangari*, for instance, in the East Kimberleys, *mirga* in the Western Desert, and such words as *me* and *mai* over a large stretch of the north. It includes yams and other tubers, grass seeds which are pounded or crushed to make flat cakes, edible leaves, waterlily roots and pods. There are various berries and wild fruits; figs, conkaberries, quondongs, or wild peaches, pandanus nuts, wild 'tomatoes' and so on. On the north coast are such foods as the corms of the tall spike rush, called *ragai* in eastern Arnhem Land. Mussels and small shellfish are found even in some of the inland billabongs and rivers, in the East Kimberleys, for instance. On the coasts are fish, turtles, dugong, stingray, very occasionally stranded whales, and even delicacies like crayfish or lobsters, oysters and clams and other shellfish, limpets, and mangrove worms. Eggs come from mallee hens or jungle fowls, bush turkeys, emus, fresh water tortoises or salt water turtles, seagulls, and crocodiles. Goose egg season on the Daly River is an exciting time as people return to their camps with laden canoes. In parts of Arnhem Land, dozens of flying foxes may be caught in the daytime as they sleep in the mangrove jungles. Right through the Continent, of course, there are kangaroos and wallabies, and many smaller marsupials: creatures like the echidna, and various possums. There are emus, mallee hens, tortoises, lizards and goannas, pythons, and so on. And, of course, the famous witchetty grubs.

When it comes to preparation, the Aborigines know which foods can be eaten raw, and which should be cooked. As a rule they prefer their meat underdone, or rare, and consider that Europeans overcook it. In some regions simple earth ovens were used for certain foods and on certain occasions—in Victoria, for example, and in western New South Wales, ovens with heated stones for cooking emu. More often they preferred to cook on an open fire, on the flames or in the hot coals. Kangaroos, for instance, would ordinarily be singed all over before being divided into pieces and distributed, although they might be cooked in a sand or earth oven, completely covered except for their protruding legs. On the Lower River Murray emu was cooked in this way, with its head left out, so that when steam came from its beak it was judged to be properly done. On the Coorong in South Australia, the black swan, says Ramsay Smith (1924: 191-2), is best when moulting since it does not move about much and is therefore fat and tender. He describes its preparation:

> Ted [an Aboriginal] cleaned out all the intestines, gizzard and heart, from the interior. He then opened the gizzard and scraped away all the inner vegetable-looking lining. He said the intestines were the sweetest part. He cut them through at each end of the loops, thus having two or three sets of about five tubes in each, about eight inches long. He left the mesentery with the fat in it attached to the tubes. Then he 'ran them', i.e. squeezed the contents out, first towards one end, then towards the other. He laid them out on the rocks to dry, with the gizzard, heart and liver. He then, in a couple of minutes or thereby, made a purse out of the skin of each of the feet.

But apart from this matter of routine food preparation, some foods need extra attention before they can be eaten. Among them are various tubers, sometimes called in English 'cheeky yam', which are poisonous if not treated. The process depends on the variety: for instance, one must be soaked, then sliced and spread out to dry in the sun, and then soaked again before cooking.

Another such food is the fruit or nut of the cycad palm, found over much of Northern Australia. This always requires treatment. In Queensland, according to Lumholtz (1889: 164-5), the kernel was pounded, roasted, and then soaked and finally made into a white porridge. In northern Arnhem Land it is soaked for about three to five days, then pounded in a kind of trench in the ground, and moulded into cakes or loaves: these are wrapped in paperbark, and cooked in the hot ashes. After being processed this food keeps for several days, or even several weeks. It is particularly useful at ceremonial times, saving people the trouble of having to go out every day for food—especially when a large crowd has gathered. Cycad palm time coincides with certain ceremonies, and it is especially significant because cycad 'bread' is eaten sacramentally on such occasions.

One fallacy which has been widely circulated is that the Aborigines are improvident with food, that they take no thought for the morrow and never trouble to store or preserve what they have. Up to a point this is so, because most of the foods on which they depend just do not keep. It would not be possible to store them under bush conditions: and most Aborigines prefer to have their food fresh except for such delicacies as well-matured eggs. At the same time, a few foods were treated in this way. All along the north coast, wild plums (*mundudj* in Gunwinggu) were dried in the sun, and then sometimes rubbed with red ochre and dried again. In this condition they would keep for weeks. When they were wanted they would be pounded up, stone and all, moistened at intervals during the process: or else soaked in water. Or they might be mixed with the pounded bones and meat of a kangaroo. On Cape York Peninsula, dried plums were stored in deep holes in the dry sand. In the Great Victoria Desert quondongs, wild peaches, were dried in the sun and kept for some time.

In the Bunya Mountains in Queensland, when bunya nuts were in season they were not all eaten at once. The cone of this tree is large, with an edible 'ovule' in each scale, 'like an almond kernel'. (J. Mathew, 1899: 90.) Net bags would be filled with these and buried in the gravel of a creek bed, to be dug up when required. Grey (1841: Vol. II, 64) also refers to natives of Western Australia as storing zamia nuts by burying them in the ground. Apart from these, several kinds of fish were once smoked and dried beside the Lower River Murray, and around the Stirling River in the Northern Territory: and in the Daly River area there is an excellent way of preserving shark meat for some days, by packing it tightly in leaves and paperbark and squeezing it dry of every drop of moisture.

TECHNIQUES

Apart from the matter of knowing the right seasons, the right times for certain foods, and the right places to find them, there is the question of techniques for getting them or for carrying them. For women, the most important tool is the digging stick, made of some strong wood such as ironwood, pointed at one or both ends, and hardened over a fire. This is used for digging out yams and other roots, or rabbits, or for killing lizards. It is also a fighting stick. In regard to vegetable foods, like roots of lilies or various fruits, a great deal depends on knowing just where to look. Women are familiar with nearly every fruit-bearing tree, every yam patch, and so on, within a certain area, and if they keep an eye on these places they can be reasonably sure of finding food there in season. But where animals or insects and so on are concerned, constant observation is necessary in the bush, keeping one's eyes open all the time. For instance, seeing where a bee has flown into a hollow tree, climbing up, using a rope or vine or just hands and feet, chopping out the honeycomb with an axe; or sometimes the whole tree must be cut down, before extracting the honey.

In hunting animals and birds, a man must be able to interpret all the tracks and other evidence he finds, however faint. He must know how to imitate the sounds these creatures make, and their peculiar habits—as in decoying ducks. He should be adept at gauging the direction of the wind, and moving quietly and quickly through the scrub without disturbing his quarry. In some areas he may rub himself with mud or ochre to disguise himself, or hide the smell of his sweat. His spears and spearthrower are indispensable. So, in many cases, are dogs. In parts of Queensland nets with large mesh were also used in wallaby hunting, and in other areas pits were dug for catching emus (e.g. Roth, 1897: 96-7).

Emus could also be caught by soaking a certain plant in water to which they came to drink: this would stupefy them, so they could be easily caught. The same kind of substance was used for fish. Roth (1897: 95-6) mentions *Tephrosia astragaloides* being used in the Cloncurry and Woonamurra districts of Queensland; in other areas leafy boughs and branches of a gum-tree are used. Basedow (1925: 139) notes that among the northern tribes of Western Australia the emu is caught in this way by means of *Tephrosia purpurea* leaves, while *pitcheri* (tobacco) serves the same purpose in Central Australia (Spencer and Gillen, 1938: 20). Several varieties of leaf are employed in Arnhem Land. One fish poison is from a small plant the Gunwinggu call *djanga,* so potent that people avoid touching it with their hands. They use paperbark in pulling it out from among the rocks, and beat the roots with a stick so that the juice flows into a billabong; 'nobody drinks that water until the new rains come'. In the same way they avoid drinking the water in which they have soaked *mangudu* berries; but this does not prevent their eating the fish.

Over much of Australia, along the coasts and rivers, the Aborigines used to build fish-traps. Barriers of stones, grass, brush, or logs serve as a catchment in which fish are easily caught as the waters recede. Some, particularly in north-eastern Arnhem Land and along the Daly River, are very cleverly arranged, providing large quantities of fish. The Aborigines also make fishing nets of both large and small mesh. Drag-nets, and the large drum variety fastened to buoys, are common in such places as the north coast of the Northern Territory, in Queensland, and among the Lakes people of the Lower River Murray in South Australia. Along the coast and some of the rivers the Aborigines have made fishing spears, lines with bone or wooden hooks, and harpoons, particularly for turtles and dugong: in a few places, such as Cape York, the dugong was virtually a staple food. (See Lumholtz, 1889: 316-22; Basedow, 1925: 135-7; Thomson, 1934: 237-62.) Some harpoons have a wooden buoy attached to mark the kill, in case it should float or swim away after being speared. This kind of activity often entails hours of patient work—standing in the surf waiting to spear stingray, for example.

Whatever is being sought, hunting and food-collecting call for a combination of knowledge and careful observation, in conjunction with the appropriate techniques, and the right kind of material equipment. Plaited baskets, or dilly bags, from pandanus fibre or various grasses, are made in different sizes and shapes according to the use to which they will be put. Some are woven loosely, others so tightly that wild honey and even water can be safely carried in them without spilling. In other cases water is carried in paperbark containers, or baler or nautilus shells, in kangaroo skins, or in the ordinary wooden troughs or 'pitchis' that Aboriginal women over a large part of southern and Central Australia use for carrying food and other belongings: in the case of water, leaves are placed on top to prevent splashing. Or water, sometimes honey, may be carried in bark baskets joined with wax, or in a folded palm leaf.

The Aborigines also make rafts, and stringy bark canoes sewn with fibre. And from their contact with the Indonesians the northern coastal people learnt how to build canoes from hollow logs and tree-trunks—although these had been made at an early period along the River Murray and the Darling, as well as along the Kimberley coast. Some of these log canoes of the north are beautifully shaped, and rather more elaborate than those found in the south, where they were mostly made from large sheets of bark: 'canoe-trees', from which this bark was taken, can still be seen along the Murray. (R. Berndt, 1941: 17-28.) In the north they have cut-in ridges for seats, a variety of paddles, occasionally crude anchors, and 'Macassan-type' sails, originally woven from the leaves of the pandanus palm: one of the largest we have seen was approximately 15 feet by 10 feet. Further inland, the river canoes differ from those used chiefly on the sea: they need sharp prows which can cleave a passage through the grasses, the weeds and the lilies of the billabongs and smaller streams. Some Aborigines make rafts of bark, bamboo or saplings to ferry themselves across the rivers, or along the pools and waterways after heavy rains. The people of Cape York Peninsula had much larger outrigger canoes, some up to 50 feet long, but these were possibly the result of cultural diffusion from New Guinea via the Torres Strait.

The range of directly useful material objects is not large, but even so it would take too much space here to detail all that are used by the different tribes for economic reasons. Basically, for women there is the digging stick. For men there are spears, spear-thrower, and perhaps the boomerang and club. (The boomerang, incidentally, is less widely distributed than is usually believed.) There are stone quarries here and there, as in the Ridarngu country of south-central Arnhem Land, a busy centre for the preparation and trading of spear blades. In some places, such as the east Kimberleys, flaked and serrated spearheads are made from long tapering pieces of quartzite, painstakingly chipped, and mounted mostly on wooden or bamboo shafts with hard wax. Until quite recently, the same care was extended to glass blades, from old bottles. Earlier still, spearheads were often made from white conductors taken from the Overland Telegraph Line. In eastern Arnhem Land, the Aborigines collected nails from drifting timber washed up on the coast, and beat them into shape for their famous shovel-nosed spear blades. Stone axes are not used anywhere in Aboriginal Australia today. Mostly, in the past, they were of dark basalt, with a smooth sharp edge formed by constant grinding, mounted on wooden hafted handles and capable of cutting the hardest wood. Other useful articles are stone adzes, grinding and polishing stones, wedges, chisels, incising tools, drills, shark skin files used as sandpaper for smoothing down wood, and bobbins for winding string of human hair or animal fur.

Some interesting types of stone object can be found in Australia: phallic stones, for example (Mountford, 1939*c*); also, especially in western New South Wales, cylindro-conical stones mostly used in ritual. (McCarthy, 1939*b*.) Another is the *kodja*. (Davidson and McCarthy, 1957: 407-22.) 'This is a flake-axe. It has a stick handle, with a lump of gum at one end into which are inserted either a single sharp flake, or two stones, one sharp and one blunt, on opposite sides of the helve.' Such axes are, or were, found over the south-western part of Western Australia, with occasional appearance of the single-headed *kodja* in parts of northern Western Australia and the Northern Territory. Tindale (1950, 1951), among others, has discussed it. The best general study of Aboriginal technology and material objects has been made by McCarthy (1940: 241-69, 294-320; 1957*a*: 81-97). Much has been written on Australian stone implements, both generally and in relation to particular areas. (See, for instance, Davidson, 1938; McCarthy, Noone and Bramwell, 1946; Mitchell, 1949.)

Another essential item before European contact was the set of fire-making sticks, used as a fire drill or as a fire saw. In a couple of isolated areas, fire was also made by percussion. (See Mountford and Berndt, 1941: 342-4.) Fire is important, for warmth as well as for cooking. A glowing firestick is often carried when travelling, especially throughout Central Australia, and paper-bark torches or flares are used too on the north coast.

COVERING

Over most of Australia the Aborigines wore the very minimum of clothing: in the Centre, for example, nothing at all, except perhaps a human hair or 'wombat' twine waistband in the case of men, or a few feathers intertwined in the pubic hairs, or a pearl-shell. It was chiefly a matter of ornament—'take it or leave it': nudity was preferred. Among the exceptions were the Lower River Murray and other parts of southern and south-eastern Australia, where people had rugs and cloaks of possum and other skins. An illustration of a Kurnai (Gurnai) man wearing a possum rug appears in Howitt (1904: 40, fig. 1, 742). Schürmann (in Woods, 1879: 210) observed that the Port Lincoln people used one or two kangaroo skins, and both he and Taplin (also in Woods, 1879: 43) describe the process of making them. Aborigines around Perth and York and the south-west of Western Australia used kangaroo skin cloaks, sewn with tail sinews. (Curr, 1886: 328, 336, 342.) Around the Daly River area, public coverings were among the gifts given to a newly initiated youth: these were made from bunched threads of twine, attached to a waistband. In western Arnhem Land, women occasionally wore rough skirts of plaited pandanus; both men and women often wore pubic aprons made from soft possum fur twine; and the people about the East Alligator River sometimes slept in large blanket-like mats netted from bush string. On Groote Eylandt, women used sheets of paperbark when they moved about so that they would not be seen publicly by men. Hart and Pilling

(1960: 50) report that, in pre-European days, Bathurst and Melville island women habitually carried pieces of bark, to hold in front of themselves whenever they met a man.

DIVISION OF LABOUR

In talking about obtaining food, preparing and using material objects, we come to the division of labour—who does what, and with whom. In Aboriginal Australia there is a minimum of specialization as far as skills are concerned, and the most striking division is that between the sexes. Observers have sometimes commented on this. Seeing a man going along carrying only his spear and spearthrower, and a wife or two toiling along behind him with a baby or so and a bag or wooden dish full of belongings, they have jumped to the conclusion that woman is a drudge, doing all the work. (See, for instance, Malinowski, 1913: 287-8.) From the local point of view, however, this is a matter of practical necessity. A man must be ready to chase any animal or creature which comes into sight. If he is hampered by a load of belongings and the 'meat' gets away, the whole family suffers—including his wife. Hunting animals, catching larger fish, require alertness as well as endurance, patience, skill: and even so there is no guarantee of success.

Men's hunting activities are more uncertain in outcome than women's food-collecting. For this reason, women contribute, overall, the greater part of the food supply. They can be fairly sure of finding something, except in really desperate drought conditions. Their work is more routine, perhaps, spread over a longer period, but it is more dependable. It suits the way in which a group of women and children can wander rather slowly over a patch of country, gathering a few yams here and a few berries there, perhaps eating a few before putting the others into their carriers—making a day of it, and coming into camp in the late afternoon to build up the fires and start cooking. On the other hand, a man may come into camp empty-handed after working all day. Typically, there is magic associated with hunting, but not as a rule with food-collecting.

This division of labour is not entirely fixed. In the north, a woman may get a kangaroo with her dogs if she has the opportunity; and women hunt for such small meats as goannas and snakes, possums and rabbits. And men may sometimes dig for yams, or collect fruits, if they are hungry or the occasion arises. Tracking down and spearing a kangaroo is probably more exhilarating than digging up a yam: but getting wild honey, or crabs, can be exciting in its own way. Vegetable foods, then, are basic, the main part of the ordinary diet except in some coastal areas: but meat is usually appreciated more. People may eat a meal of yams and still say they are hungry. But a catch of meat or fish is usually spread over a greater number of people than in the case of a basketful of yams. Food-collecting by women is more of an individual affair. Even when a group of women goes out together, each collects food for her own family: herself, her husband and children, and perhaps her parents or some near relative. When several men go hunting together, more than one of them may have rights in the kangaroo or other animal that they kill; but in any case a large animal is usually divided up, even to the extent that the main hunter may keep almost none of it for himself. In other words, a man is more intimately caught up in a network of kin and ritual obligations, which involve giving as well as receiving both food and other goods, and specific services. A woman's responsibilities are not so extensive. The general assumption seems to be that her major duties as a provider should be focused on herself, her husband and children. For one thing, adult men are involved quite heavily in the ritual sphere, as women usually are not—except as general providers at a large ceremony.

Because of the division of labour within every family—with a man providing the main supply of meat, his wife or wives the main supply of vegetables and smaller animals—a husband or wife is, ideally, an economic asset. One cause of quarrelling within a family reflects this expectation: when a woman accuses her husband of not contributing enough meat, or a man complains that his wife never seems to bring in as many yams as other women do. But in the traditional scene there are, or were, few if any drones in an Aboriginal camp. Able-bodied adults must either go out and look for something to eat, or starve. There is no other way of obtaining food. Except, these days, around European settlements, there is no instance of a woman keeping her husband in food while he merely loafs about, nor any case of a woman remaining all her life aloof from general food-collecting enterprises. Food-collecting is part of a woman's domestic routine, just as hunting is part of a man's normal activity.

Children who have not reached puberty are not expected to contribute much to the family supply. They are just learning, people say: and usually their parents provide for them, and attend to various obligations on their behalf. On the other hand, there are old people who can no longer forage for their own food. They are usually looked after by their relatives, especially sons, although in an extreme crisis, such as a prolonged drought, they may in rare cases be regarded as expendable: for example, if there is not enough water for everyone, or if they cannot keep up on a long march. Apart from them, a few people expect to be supplied with food obtained through the labour of others. Principally, there are ceremonial leaders, older men who have authority in the religious sphere. When a boy or young man is initiated, or goes through certain age-grading rituals, he may be shown various sacred designs or totemic emblems, or be taught songs and chants. This puts him under an obligation to the men who reveal these things to him, and he may be obliged to pay them, in the shape of gifts of food, and so on. Men of this standing can demand certain privileges. Then there are native doctors—men who have usually gone through a special initiation, and claim that they can heal the sick or interpret dreams, or make rain, or see spirits which are invisible to anyone else. They are conventionally entitled to demand some return for their services. But normally every adult man is a hunter, able to make his own tools and weapons, even though he does not always do so, and obtain his own meat. And every adult woman is a food-collector, able to make the tools and other objects she uses herself.

An adult Aboriginal, man or woman, should be able to manage alone in the bush if necessary, and barring accidents, for a certain length of time. He is not absolutely dependent on others for the bare necessities of life. The Aborigines, especially in semi-desert conditions, have had to work hard for their living. They do what is humanly possible; but because they live so close to the subsistence level, this is not always enough. There are the seasons to contend with: and so they try to control these too. Many of their rituals are concerned with the increase of the animals and plants on which they depend for food. There is an emphasis on fertility, both human and animal, on trying to ensure that the seasons come and go in a regular way.

Although life is fairly hard, except in the fertile coastal areas, it is not a constant struggle for bare necessities. Nor is it a matter of making crude material objects, of the simplest kind, and leaving it at that. Some of the most ordinary everyday things are quite gracefully and beautifully made, nicely shaped, and even decorated in various ways. (See Chapter XII.) And the obligations on which social life depend are not casual or haphazard affairs. They may sometimes appear to be so, but actually they are quite complex, and quite carefully regulated.

RECIPROCITY

In the past, much has been written about what was called 'primitive communism' in relation to Aboriginal economic life. Even today there are people who speak in these terms. In some pastoral areas, particularly, there are claims that the Aborigines have no sense of ownership: 'Give them something, and you'll see someone else with it next day!' This kind of comment reflects lack of knowledge about social alignments and responsibilities in an Aboriginal community. The Aborigines usually know quite well what individual ownership means. There are objects which are personally owned, and rarely if ever lent or shared: a woman's digging stick, for instance, a man's favourite spears, and various sacred objects. But the Aborigines set much less store than we do by material possessions; and there is in every community an arrangement of obligations which every growing child has to learn. In this network of duties and debts, rights and credits, all adults have commitments of one kind or another. Mostly, not invariably, these are based on kin relationships. All gifts and services are viewed as reciprocal. This is basic to their economy—and not only to theirs, although they are more direct and explicit about it. Everything must be repaid, in kind or in equivalent, within a certain period.

In the Great Victoria Desert, the man who ritually circumcises a boy should later betroth his daughter to him as well, or if the two are already betrothed he should ratify the agreement. Afterward the boy must send more or less regular gifts of food to his prospective parents-in-law. In part, this is compensating them for the future loss of their daughter. In part, it is a deferred payment to the man who initiated him. It is referred to as 'rearing' or 'growing' a wife, because if the betrothed girl is still a baby he may have to wait for some time until she can come to him. For all this period he must supply food to her parents, and consequently to her. If, later on, she elopes with someone else instead, or something goes wrong, he has the genuine complaint that he himself worked to grow her, to nourish her so that she changed from a child to an adult. In parts of the Northern Territory this custom has occasionally been abused, a daughter being betrothed to a man who excels in hunting, or can afford to provide the best gifts: spears, hair belts, parakeet feathers, or European goods. A few girls in north-eastern Arnhem Land have been switched in this way from one betrothal to another. But on the whole the practice has been fairly stable. Hart and Pilling (1960: 15), speaking of Bathurst and Melville islands, emphasize the economic and political value of a daughter: ". . . daughters were an asset to their father, and he invested these assets in his own welfare."

ECONOMIC EXCHANGE AND TRADE

Generally speaking, there are six main kinds of gift exchange.

1. Essentially on the basis of kinship. Ordinarily, a person knows just what is due to certain relatives, close and distant, and what

he can expect from them. There may be a special gift-exchanging relationship, over and above the actual kin connection, between a man and his own or classificatory sister's son, who may be living some distance away, or between a man and his sister's daughter's son (the *mari-gudara* tie mentioned in Chapter III).

One further case here comes from north-eastern Arnhem Land, and is from Warner (1937/58: 63). 'Brothers usually co-operate in making a canoe, a difficult and lengthy business, but a rewarding one because of the high economic value attaching to the finished product. The elder or eldest formally has most control over the canoe, although a determined younger brother may override this. If it were traded to another group, a man's close brothers would consider themselves part-owners of it, even if they had not helped in making it.'

Co-operation among kinsfolk is especially noticeable in crises, or times of stress, most strikingly so after a death and during the subsequent mourning rites. In the Great Victoria Desert, for instance, a dead man's hair is shorn by a wife's brother (*maridji*) and handed over to a tribal sister who makes it into a large quoit-like ring, called *njunjunba*: this is said to contain part of the deceased's spirit. (Berndt and Harvey Johnston, 1942.) A dead woman's hair is cut off by her husband, but again the hair ring is made by the deceased's tribal sister. After the reburial ceremony this *njunjunba* or death-token is given to the widow, or widower as the case may be, and is worn on the arm until the death is avenged. To some extent it resembles the mourning rings of Bathurst and Melville islands. (See Spencer, 1914: plate XXXI.) In the upper part of the Northern Territory, on the Daly River or the Adelaide River for instance, but particularly in north-eastern Arnhem Land, mourning rituals are highly elaborate and prolonged and involve an intricate economic patterning covering different degrees of kin, with large distributions of goods. (See Warner, 1937/58: Chart XVI.) Thomson (1949: 40-1) mentions this too, for north-eastern Arnhem Land. 'The bones of the dead are handled at intervals and on each such occasion the small group of men responsible for this (who are the deceased's father's sister's sons) makes presentations called *gong doid* and *da doid*: the first means "return from hands", referring to those who handle the deceased's bones, and the other "return from mouth".' Such payments are made in each case to male members of the deceased's paternal line and to his mother and wife or wives. Thomson speaks of this as a ritual act to be interpreted as a token payment or "gesture in formal expiation of an infringement of the solidarity of a group, members of which are bound together by the sharing of a special bond".

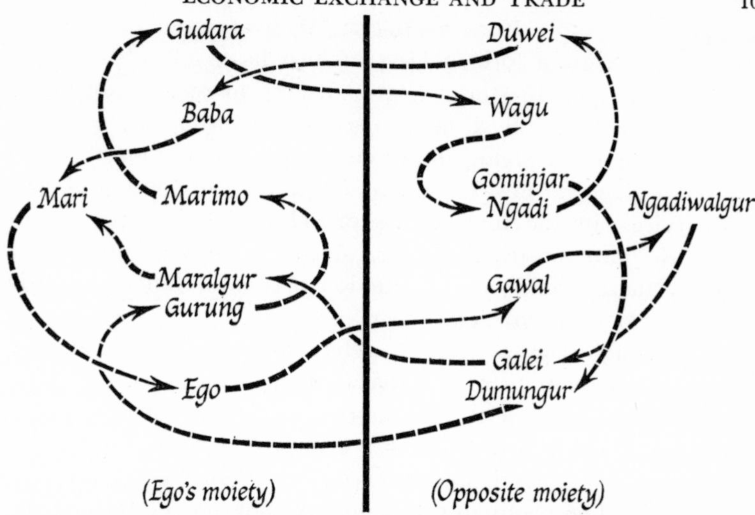

FIG. 7. SERVICES AND GOODS DUE TO PERSONS INVOLVED IN A MARRIAGE ARRANGEMENT

Explanation: general meaning of terms: GUDARA = Sr.D.S.; BABA = F.; MARIMO = F.F.; MARALGUR = M.M.B.S.; GURUNG = F.Sr.D.S.; MARI = M.M.B.; DUWEI = F.Sr.S.; WAGU = Sr.S.; GOMINJAR = D.S.; NGADI = M.F.; GAWAL = M.B.; GALEI = M.B.S.; DUMUNGUR = F.Sr.D.D.S.; NGADIWALGUR = M.M.M.B.S. This diagram demonstrates the chain of duties which links a man with his MARI, his obligations to his wife's father, and the latter's to his daughter's MARI. It shows the MARI as the most important of all Ego's relatives. The key positions are those of GAWAL and MARI —they must be viewed by any given man (as Ego) as positions of superior status. Incoming and outgoing arrows indicate receivers and givers, and from this it will be seen that the MARI receives more than he gives. This is counterbalanced by his sister's marriage with NGADIWALGUR, when the diagram begins to repeat itself in order to ensure a flow of goods from the outside.

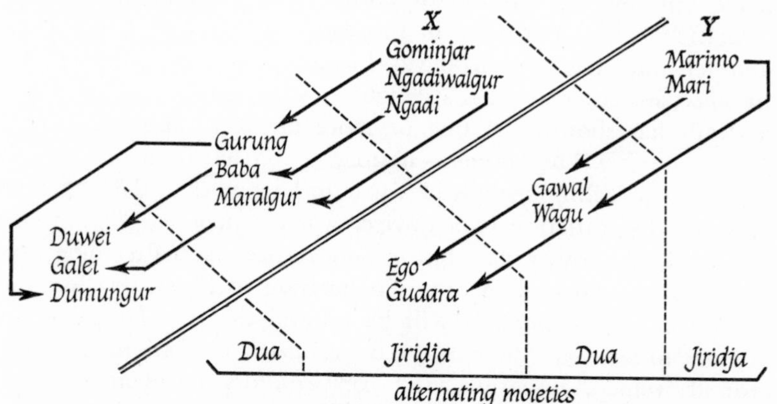

FIG. 8. THE GIVING AND RECEIVING OF WOMEN IN MARRIAGE

Explanation: same kin terms as in Fig. 7. Three groups are found on X side, and two on Y side: Ego receives his wife from his GAWAL, who in turn receives his wife from his own GAWAL, Ego's M.M.B. These signify lines of inheritance. The X and Y lines are recurrent through the generations; thus the MARI, for example, receives his wife from his M.B. in the generation level above him. Seniority in status does not depend on a man's giving his daughter to a male in the generation below; it is ascribed to him through seniority and position in his relevant generation level. A MARI will always have a higher status than a GAWAL, and the latter than an Ego. Such relationships are implicit, not only in the kinship situation, but throughout social life.

Both these examples come from Berndt (1955: 93-5). But see also Warner (1937/58: 108) for a discussion of the daughter-and-gift exchange between father-in-law and son-in-law, in the same area.

Another example from north-east Arnhem Land can be summarized in diagram form, taking up two facets of relations hinging on marriage. The first diagram refers to services and goods due to persons involved in a marriage arrangement, while the second concerns the giving and receiving of women in marriage.

From a glance at Fig. 7 it is easy to see the distribution of goods and services, in the form of reciprocal duties, between persons within the two moieties. This is, of course, only a construct. In actuality there would be a distinction between relatives according to their degree of closeness.

The second diagram (Fig. 8) refers to the same broad topic, specifically in relation to wife-givers and wife-receivers.

2. Gifts made to settle grievances or debts, arising from an offence by a single person or by a group of persons; for instance, to settle a blood feud, and prevent or finalize a revenge. (See Chapter X.) The goods so given may or may not be reciprocated. They may not even be accepted. In some cases of elopement, away from European influence, revenge or punishment by physical violence may be the only approved form of settlement. Occasionally, goods and food are extorted by threat.

An interesting mechanism used in the settlement of debts and grievances was the *kopara,* widely distributed in the north-eastern corner of South Australia. (Elkin, 1931*a*: 191-8.) A *kopara* is brought into action in a variety of circumstances: when gifts have been made but nothing received in return; when a man of one clan (a matrilineal totemic clan, in this case) has received a wife from another, but has not arranged for an equitable exchange—for instance, his sister or sister's daughter; when an inquest following a death has shown that one or more members of another clan are responsible, but no compensatory action has been taken—such as a revenge killing, the gift of a wife to a member of the aggrieved clan, or the initiation of a novice; when a man has circumcised a member of another clan, but has not settled the matter by giving a wife in exchange, unless the circumcision itself was in effect the settlement of a *kopara.* It will be noticed that the *kopara* is an attempt to maintain the network of reciprocal obligations, centring around women, initiation, and compensatory payments after a death. Mutual interdependence in these matters is vital to the people concerned. The *kopara* has a legal quality. Briefly, 'a meeting is arranged by local headmen between those concerned, through intermediaries. Members of the two or more units involved sit round separate fires to discuss the matter: there is a temporary exchange of wives between selected persons of the same moiety. This signifies that the occasion is of great social importance, because only in such circumstances would the normal rule of moiety exogamy be broken. The *kopara* is finally settled when each side gives a wife to a man of the other moiety.'

3. Gifts in return for services, or for goods. A man may make an object, such as a spear or spearthrower, or a woman may make a bag or a length of twine, with or without being specifically asked to do so, and then exchange it for some other article, service, or item of food. A few men here and there may have a reputation for being particularly expert in some task: building a canoe, making feathered string, preparing a dugong or turtle harpoon, and so on. They will expect some 'payment' for their extra help in such matters, even if this is only a share of the meat caught with the harpoon or the fish carried in the canoe. This could almost be called craft-specialization, but of a rather elementary kind. Certainly such specialists would not expect to make a living by that means. We have spoken of native doctors; and others also, conventionally, perform services which require compensation. In north-eastern Arnhem Land there is a fairly well established concept of helpers and helped. A man who goes turtle-hunting may take along some helpers, usually classificatory brothers and age-mates, and they will expect some 'payment'. But this is most highly developed in the ritual sphere.

Again, a group coming into a waterhole outside its own country, in a period of drought, might be received with hospitality by the local people: but this would entail certain obligations. In the same way, access to a red-ochre deposit or a flint deposit would involve an obligation to reciprocate, although in many cases local groups held an economic monopoly over such resources. (See McCarthy, 1939*a*: 87.) Ceremonial handing over of goods in certain circumstances comes into this category. For instance, over the greater part of the Continent, some time after a death there might be a feast and a distribution of goods—hair belts, spears, and so on—to those who had helped with the mortuary ritual.

Probably we could include here gifts associated with the carrying out of ceremonies. Firstly, there are those which are given to the dancers or singers themselves by spectators who enjoyed the performance: in other words, extra presents on a voluntary basis supplementing the more conventional payments. This is not usual, however. In the wet season of 1949-50, when there was a marked drift of population from north-central Arnhem Land into Darwin, small groups from the Liverpool River-Cape Stewart region, travelling overland, halted at Oenpelli on the East Alligator River. In return for hospitality there, they arranged several evening ceremonies. Many of the local people could not understand the words of the songs the visitors sang, but they were enthusiastic about the music and dancing. They showered the dancers with presents, particularly a boy who, they said, was irresistible.

Secondly, there are payments in exchange for rights in dancing and songs, other than those of a secret-sacred kind. The transaction may entitle the purchaser to hand on that particular series to someone else and receive payment for it, or simply to perform the appropriate actions or sing the songs, or both. A number of ceremonies held at Limbunya have been traded down from the Lungga, on the basis of performance rights. Women's ceremonies, centring on such topics as love magic, have come up into the east Kimberleys from the Wailbri and Waramunga and the Mudbara. From there they have spread further north, as well as southwest toward the Canning Stock Route. Through dreams they are elaborated and altered, and the dreamers' names may be added to the songs. Some are handed down from mother to daughter; but most are traded on, in return for payments covering rights to pass them on further still, and to receive gifts for revealing them to others. In such cases the original words of a song are often retained, more or less, even when the people who buy it speak a different language and do not understand the details of what they are singing. The payment covers the general meaning, and the receivers may add their own interpretation, keeping roughly to the words because they fit the tune. The same thing happens with dance steps and themes, which may be elaborated to suit the local situation.

4. Formalized gift exchange, involving trade between various defined partners, in a series which may cover a wide area. More will be said about it later in this chapter. The goods may be retained only temporarily by any one person in the chain. Choice of partners may be voluntary, or outside a person's control. They may stand in a particular relationship to one another, as in 1, above: or as half-brothers, whose mothers call each other sisters, but who belong through their fathers to different local descent groups or clans. Or in the eastern Kimberleys, as among the Guirindji, Lungga, and Djaru, they may be *naragu,* having the same personal name—usually, not always, from totems associated with the subsections. Most people have several names and may therefore have more than one *naragu.* Conversely, the same name may be held by several people; but it is nearly always treated as a person-to-person link. This relationship involves the provision of hospitality when necessary; but some *naragu* may never see each other, although they exchange goods as long as both are alive. The name of one is changed on the death of the other. On the Lower River Murray, in South Australia, the *mindji,* 'one name', relationship involved the same obligations combined with mutual aid. In

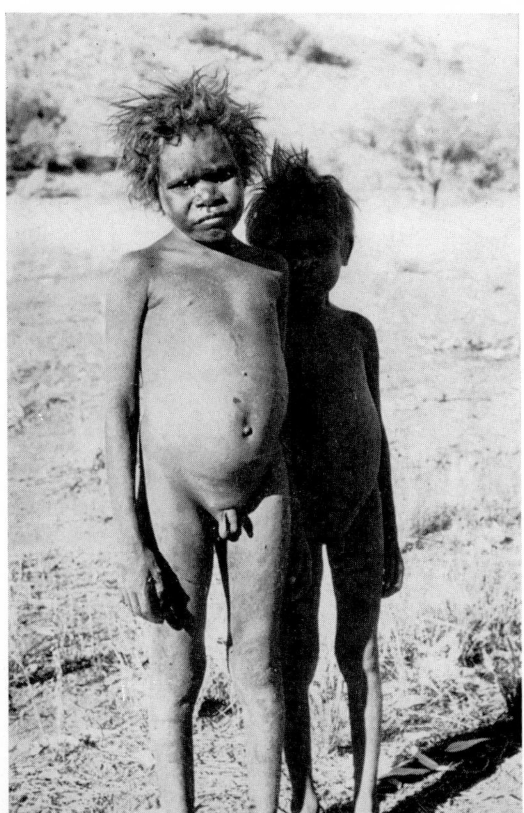

Above: Mother and children asleep, Elcho Island, north-eastern Arnhem Land (1961)

Left: Two brothers at Kathleen Range, east-central Western Australia (1959)

Above: Girls wearing mud 'breasts' to induce the growth of their own, and holding mud 'babies' in paperbark carriers: Milingimbi, north-central Arnhem Land (late 1930s)

(photo: courtesy H. Shepherdson)

Below: Children playing in a tied-up log canoe in the freshwater stream at Yirrkalla (1958)

the Daly River area, the *ngirawad* included, among other things, similar expectations in regard to gifts; for instance, two women of the same name from different mothers were not permitted to speak to each other until they had exchanged goods. (See Chapter III.)

Apart from individual persons, two or more groups may stand in a special trading relationship with one another; but this brings us to the next category.

5. Trade. If we look at any given locality in Aboriginal Australia, in traditional terms, we can see that there is a more or less constant movement of goods, some coming from one direction and some from another. These follow what are called roads or paths (as in category 4). (See Chapter I.) From the perspective of people in any one place, they appear to centre on that place. But if we plan them all out, those on which we have information, we can see that they criss-cross the whole Continent, usually along waterhole routes. As we have seen before, this is significant from the diffusional point of view. For instance, from the Kimberley coast come pearlshells of various kinds, plain and incised, also bamboo necklaces, and certain types of boomerang. They are passed along, on one track, through the eastern Kimberleys: and back from the east come shovel-bladed spears with bamboo shafts, hooked spears, a variety of boomerang, wooden coolamon dishes, dilly bags, and red ochre. The Lungga say they cannot make boomerangs properly: they prefer to import them from the east, west or south-west. The Walmadjeri trade their shields to the east, and Central Australian shields find their way into the Balgo camp near the head of the Canning Stock Route, just as do the typical Western Desert spearthrowers—into an area where the local throwers are quite differently designed. Kimberley pearlshells travelled right across Australia: one road down to Eyre's Peninsula in South Australia, through the Great Victoria Desert and Ooldea: another also to the Great Victoria Desert and Eucla, but via the Gascoyne and the Murchison.

There are hundreds of examples of such trade, all over Australia, and McCarthy (1939*a*) has given a detailed description. Among some tribes, for example the Wuroro (Love, 1936: 191-3), there was usually no separate individual bartering, but a series of group exchanges. The hosts and visitors, after preparing their goods, might sit down about a cleared space. First the visitors would place on a growing heap all the goods they had brought, then the local people would come forward individually and heap up in front of the visitors what they proposed to give them. Then one man after another would take what he wanted.

6. There is also a further category which could be termed

the economics of sacred life. This is relevant to categories 4 and 5 when gift exchange occurs within the context of the large sacred ceremonies: and to category 1, inasmuch as the persons involved stand in particular relationships to one another. It covers a wide range of activities which must be reciprocated or compensated for in some way. Men of one generation level or moiety may help those of the other by singing while they dance, or decorating performers for sacred rituals, expecting the same attentions when their turn comes. Or a ceremonial leader or 'owner' of a particular design or pattern may paint this on the flat blade of a shovel-nosed spear and give it to a man belonging to another clan or local unit—in return he must be given all meat from animals or fish killed by that spear.

In north-eastern Arnhem Land ceremonial leaders are, or were until very recently, able to maintain themselves fairly well by painting sacred designs on the chests of initiates. In fact in most areas, but particularly northern Australia, the various stages of initiation, and later on other sacred rites, through which a man passes must be paid for: viewing the 'high' or most important emblems, seeing certain ritual actions, hearing sacred songs. A man who is not in a position to pay may not see or hear them.

At Balgo, men make small round or oval wooden boards varying in size from about two inches to a couple of feet in diameter, upon which are incised stylized drawings of sections of country with their totemic associations. Each man has several and makes others from time to time, using them to exchange with those belonging to other men. These boards were described to one of us as being 'like photographs'. They are shown and discussed, and finally exchanged. In this way a great deal of information about the country and its mythological affiliations is passed on from one person to another.

CEREMONIAL GIFT EXCHANGE

This topic has already been introduced in categories 4 and 6. Different aspects of it are discussed in the literature: by Stanner (1933-4: 156-75, 458-71) for the Daly River, Thomson (1949) for north-eastern Arnhem Land, and one of us for western Arnhem Land (R. Berndt, 1951*b*: 156-76). Such exchanges are, of course, not confined to the Northern Territory.

The actual contexts in which they take place vary. In the Daly River examples there is an exchange of goods between individual trading partners. In western Arnhem Land there are special trade links between tribal groups. This is inter-tribal trading, not specifically between persons; special ceremonies are connected with it. North-eastern Arnhem Land too has special trading relationships, but exchange of goods is incidental to the main ritual.

On the Daly there are the *merbok* and *kue* exchange. The first is between persons of the same or different tribes, sometimes close relatives. The general *merbok* rule is that an item received by one partner from another is kept for a while, and then passed on to the next. 'A great variety of articles passes along these *merbok* paths', which extend across the country in certain directions. Supply and demand are the basis of this system. For instance, bamboo travels south-west and south of the Daly and does not return except in spear form. 'To receive *merbok* is to place oneself in debt, to be committed to making a return of at least comparable, or preferably greater, value', so that it is a question not merely of trade in the most limited sense, but also of prestige. The time lapse between the receipt of goods and the return gifts, which must not be the same, allows for some speculation, as well as providing an opportunity to gather together one's resources. This last point is particularly important, 'because a man may have several *merbok* partners with claims upon him', just as he has upon others. Further involvement in the network of economic obligations comes with what Stanner has called the *kue*: this is, as he says, 'a ceremonial exchange with a sacramental and legal significance in marriage'. The core is the handing over of gifts between a man and his relatives on one hand, his wife and her relatives on the other. It is held a few years after the marriage, but not until after the birth of children. Conventionally, it serves to ratify and strengthen the union. 'The *kue* is in two parts: firstly, a feast given by the husband for his wife's relatives, and secondly, the gifts they make in return, through her. All who attend the *kue* feast must contribute gifts.' Obtaining these is not easy, especially in view of *merbok* commitments: but a loan *(mima)* may be obtained from a friend, to be repaid later in the shape of similar articles, with no interest such as is necessary in the case of the *merbok*. If a person cannot find anyone willing to lend, he may have to use in the *kue* valuable articles derived from *merbok*, without any hope of an immediate return. For instance, a man may have two *merbok* partners; he receives goods from B, and hopes to pass them on to C. In the meantime he must make return gifts to B, of equal or greater value; he may also have to fulfil his *kue* obligations, without being able to find a *mima*. After a time C begins to press him. If he has more than two *merbok* partners he may be able to juggle things around, but even so he may remain in debt. Fortunately the *merbok* and *kue* paths do not cross frequently; but when they do, a man may have to 'divide his wealth into two parts: one for the reciprocal *kue*, and one for his *merbok* partner on the other side'. It is, as Stanner says, 'a way of cutting one's losses when the two paths cross', but it is not a highly satisfactory way.

In western Arnhem Land members of different tribes may come together for ceremonies which have as their focal point the exchange of special goods. There are six such ceremonies. Each involves a group of people who travel to a place outside their own territory, for the purpose of exchanging items made by themselves or obtained through trade in return for others which they desire. The following diagram presents the picture from the viewpoint of the Oenpelli people, who are predominantly Gunwinggu.

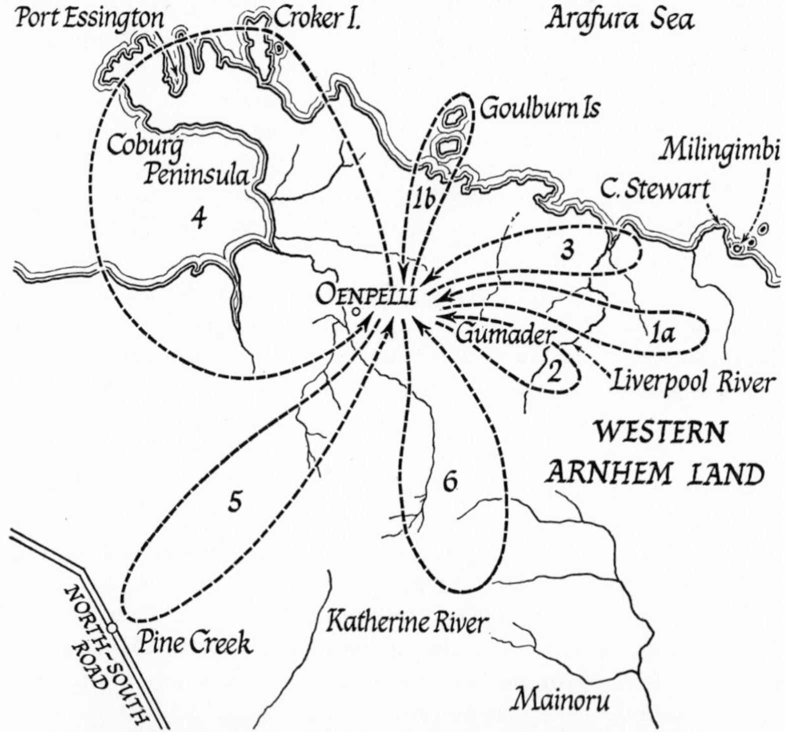

FIG. 9. DISTRIBUTION OF TRADE CEREMONIES IN WESTERN ARNHEM LAND, FOCUSING ON OENPELLI

1a. Eastern *Djamalag*: serrated and shovel-nosed spears; 1b. Northern *Djamalag*: coastal goods, such as nets, lines, baler shells, etc.; 2. *Rom*: baskets, spears, spearthrowers, stone knives, and feathered string; 3. *Midjan*: human hair twine for waistbands; 4. *Wurbu*: breast mats and bags; 5. *Mamurung*: European goods and bamboo spears; 6. *Njalaidj*: stone spear heads and two varieties of red ochre.

In the *djamalag* the dancing is rather less spectacular than in the others, and the emphasis is on sexual freedom. This does not detract from the importance of the economic exchange, since it is viewed as being in itself a form of exchange between members of two trading groups. The culminating feature is the ritual presentation of trade goods. This is an eagerly awaited climax to the dancing and singing, a releasing of emotional tension which has accumulated during the ceremonies. But the exchange itself is not to be viewed simply as a commercial undertaking within the context of the ceremonial: the value of the goods themselves is felt to be enhanced and emphasized, in varying degrees, by the elaboration of the ritual of which they are the centre. The utility of the objects in question is not the only criterion involved in assessing their ultimate value as items of wealth.

In north-eastern Arnhem Land there are no special trading ceremonies such as in western Arnhem Land. Thomson's phrase 'Ceremonial Exchange Cycle' is misleading, in that the economic exchange is nearly always subordinated to the ritual and ceremonial significance. Each man, says Thomson (1949: 70-81), has special trading partners, related to him through classificatory or actual kinship. 'Any given partner acts as a "clearing house" for valuables of certain well-defined types; he holds them for a short period, then passes them to another, in the appropriate direction.' There are five sections of his territory from which a man receives goods. From the first come iron-headed spears and round black pounding stones; from the second, goods of European, and previously Indonesian, origin; from the third, forehead bands, breast mats, hooked spears, 'biting bags' (held between the teeth in fighting), and heavy fighting clubs; from the fourth, spearheads, boomerangs, net bags, possum fur pubic coverings; and from the fifth, hooked spears with bamboo shafts of several varieties, belts of human hair and so on. This exchange, Thomson points out, 'is not to be thought of as a form of barter, although through it goods are circulated over a wide area. It is primarily a matter of prestige. And failure to repay gifts quickly involves a loss of prestige.'

* * * * *

Aboriginal economy, then, relies almost entirely on the natural resources of the countryside. This dependence of man on nature takes the form of a special relationship which comes out quite clearly in religious and totemic beliefs. Aboriginal economy is basically a subsistence economy; people eat what they collect or hunt. But this is not the whole story, as we have seen. Even in the matter of food, the need for a surplus is significant at times—especially in ceremonial terms, when large quantities of food must be available to feed visitors as well as hosts; the use of cycad nut bread is one example. But storage facilities are poor, and only a few foods can be treated in this way. The division of labour between the sexes is significant here, as it is in other aspects of social life. It appears to underline differences, or contrasts, between the activities of men and women, but the pervasive emphasis is on co-operation between them. This is fairly well-balanced, since a man's hunting does not necessarily ensure a steady inflow of food, and his commitments are more extensive, against the relative certainty of a woman's contribution and her few commitments, where food is concerned, outside her immediate family.

If the question of a surplus applies only in a minor degree to the collection of food, it is quite pertinent to more durable goods. We could speak of a trading economy, in a small way, for most of Aboriginal Australia. This point is significant. Although it is true that the Aborigines paid relatively little attention to material possessions, in comparison with most other societies, their concern was far from negligible when we consider it in relation to the range that was open to them; and the quality and quantity of available resources, in conjunction with their total approach to living, one influencing the other, limited the expansion of that range. They did not deliberately reject the material in favour of the spiritual, as a matter of principle. The fact of their interest in material goods is borne out in contact situations, where this aspect is often stressed at the expense of others.

The concept of profit is not highly developed, although it appears in the context of the *merbok*. Mostly, trade rests on conventional assessment of the value of the goods involved: 'These are worth such and such in exchange', rather than, 'Let us see what we can get for them.' At the same time, this concept is not lacking. Nor is haggling or bargaining, especially where a return gift of food or goods is claimed to be inadequate or contributions at a mortuary rite do not come up to expectations. In some circumstances the exchange of gifts, although oriented in terms of obtaining a desired commodity, is not a straightforward commercial transaction. The tangible goods themselves are still important, but in a secondary way. The main thing is the partnership itself, as a social relationship, and the prestige which the partners derive from the exchange. Alternatively, the goods themselves are enhanced in value by virtue of the exchange or the associated ceremony. The intangible or non-utilitarian aspects here count for a great deal.

The network of debtors and creditors which constitutes the *merbok* and *kue* does not actually represent such an unusual situation for Aboriginal Australia. It merely highlights what is implicit in the network of obligations and responsibilities relevant to ties through kinship. The delayed exchange in the *merbok* provides a breathing space for the marshalling of a person's resources, but only on a temporary basis; his obligations must eventually be met. In the same way, a man gives to his kinsfolk in anticipation of a subsequent return, or 'grows up' a girl-child with a view to obtaining, later, her services as a wife. There is always the element of looking ahead, of performing this action or that as part of a framework of assumptions about the ways in which other people will, or should, respond to it. The balancing of advantages and concessions is more obvious in some situations than in others, and above all in the economic sphere.

All labour, male and female, is valued in Aboriginal society, provided it is efficient labour. The canoe builder, the hunter, the wielder of the digging stick, the painter on bark, the maker of a sacred emblem, the singer of songs, the dancer, and so on are praised if they are skilful. But there is no privileged class which is singled out on the basis of birth, or of wealth. Goods are considered to be wealth only if expendable—only if they can be passed on to others. Aside from such matters as food tabus governed by criteria of sex or age or ritual status, all adults of the same local group have equal access to the means of production and, insofar as this phrase is relevant here, to the means of consumption. There are leaders, but they belong to no specially defined class, nor are they maintained by the rest of the community. The same is true for the artist, the songman and the craft worker. They may specialize, but they are not paid on a full-time basis for doing so, they are not in this sense professionals, and they participate in ordinary everyday pursuits almost as much as other men do.

The concept of private property is moderately well-developed, but this does not mean that such property is inalienable. Thus the goods used in gift exchange are personal property only for a certain period, after which the compelling influence of the trading relationship ensures that they are handed on. In the ritual sphere the situation is different. Sacred boards may be personally owned, and so may the valuable feathered string ropes and feather-tasselled spirit dilly bags of eastern Arnhem Land; but most sacred emblems, songs and dances, even though made or performed by particular persons, are owned by the local group or clan as the case may be. There are cases of the selling of clan designs, as in eastern Arnhem Land, in the sense of handing over the sole rights to their reproduction, but this is rare. At Balgo, for instance, the exchange of boards does not constitute exchange of the actual designs engraved on them.

The land upon which these Aborigines depend is not personally owned. There is no private land as such, nor individually owned patches of yams or trees and so on. Land belongs to the local group, the clan, or even the tribe, and is inalienable. In the contact situation, it is the only real wealth these people have which is recognized as such by Europeans. Unfortunately, in nearly all cases it has been taken over entirely by the newcomers, and local rights in it ignored or brushed aside.

CHAPTER V

The Life Cycle: Growing Up

Life in an Aboriginal setting, as elsewhere in the world of human beings, is shaped by the universal sequence of growth and decline. The stages, basically, are the same everywhere, regardless of how many individuals actually complete them all: birth to adolescence, maturity and adulthood; possibly the production of children, who will start up the cycle again on their own account; then old age; and finally, death. Virtually no human society, however, including the Aborigines, is content to see this as a single continuum. The physical or material facts of existence are obvious, and undeniable; but alongside them, or underlying them, these people assume that there are other facts which are not bound in the same way by considerations of time and space: the dimension of spirit, or soul, or life-essence, without which human existence is inconceivable.

COMING INTO BEING

To see this in perspective, we must start off before an Aboriginal child is born and begins his independent existence.

There has been some controversy on the subject of whether or not the Aborigines acknowledge physiological paternity: that is, whether they recognize the role played by the father in procreation. For some areas it has been reported that they do not, or did not before contact with Europeans. Ashley-Montagu (1937*a*: 111; 1940: 111) has stated categorically that they realize sexual intercourse is necessary for conception but do not consider it to be of major importance: that it is not in itself a prerequisite for childbirth, but merely prepares the way for the entry of a spirit child. There is an impressive array of evidence from various anthropologists and others who insist on this view. However, in most of the areas in which we have worked the issue has not been a mystery to these people. Their knowledge may not be exact, and they get some of the details wrong. But in fact, the Aborigines are much more sophisticated about these things because of their frankness in sexual affairs, and because they are intimately concerned with the reproduction of the natural species—human and animal.

In the Great Victoria Desert people say that a number of ejaculations are needed to make a woman pregnant. The semen accumulates, arresting the menstrual flow; it is from this mixture and from the food she eats that the foetus grows, so that a child has a physical affinity with both parents. (See R. and C. Berndt, 1943: 243-9.) Another view is that the father contributes the child's bone substance, the mother its blood and flesh. North-eastern Arnhem Land is a case in point: the bones are likened to sacred emblems or *rangga*: these objects come down to a child in the paternal line, just as his bone substance does. Here children are called *judu* ('semen') or *djamarguli* ('a result of work'—that is, coitus). Warner (1937/58: 23-4) supports this view, pointing out that the 'Murngin' (Wulamba) know about physiological paternity; so does Thomson (1936) for the Wigmungan (Queensland). And see Schmidt (1952: 36-81). Western Arnhem Landers say that it takes five or six ejaculations on successive days to impregnate a woman: the semen is a basis for the foetus, or 'egg', built up through the menstrual flow, through food, and through the breast milk which at this stage flows internally. (R. and C. Berndt, 1951*a*: 80-6.) About this time the father 'brings the spirit child' to his wife through intercourse, which breaks the 'egg', and it is at this point that the foetus begins to take shape: actually, the spirit child is the animator.

However, even when the Aborigines acknowledge a physical bond between father and child, and mother and child, they are likely to regard this as being of secondary importance: something everyone knows about, something they take more or less for granted and do not usually bother to discuss. The really important thing is the child's spirit, the element which gives the flesh animation and life. Often this spirit is not regarded as a single, indivisible entity, but is considered to be capable of appearing in a number of different aspects. Some of these are associated with totemism, and so with the myths and rituals in which a person has a right to share.

We have mentioned conception and birth totemism: when a woman first realizes she is pregnant after eating a certain food in the vicinity of the track of a particular ancestral being, or when there is a mythical and totemic association with the site at which the child is born. (See Chapter VII.) In the Great Victoria Desert, as in other parts of Aboriginal Australia, there are spirit centres, usually waterholes. Spirit children (*didji* or *julan*) may be visible from a distance standing round a fire, but disappear when anyone comes close. Women who want children go to these places and sit waiting with legs apart; or one of them may follow a woman home to her camp. The sites were left, people say, by the mythical beings, and there are suggestions that the children themselves are one manifestation of these. In the Kimberleys (Kaberry, 1939: 41-5) spirit children, *djinganarani*, are not ancestors as they are among the Aranda (Spencer and Gillen, 1938: 125) but 'were placed in the pools by *Galeru*, a Rainbow snake'—which, incidentally, has phallic significance. They are temporarily incarnated as animals, birds, fish, reptiles and so on, and 'conception occurs when one enters a woman through the feet. Or it may be present in food given her by her husband, making her vomit, and later he dreams of it or else of some animal which he associates with it: this becomes the *djering*, or conception totem, of the child which is eventually born.' Kaberry mentions that 'a woman may become ill when handling a dilly-bag, or when a ceremony is being performed, or even when her husband is making a special sacred board; and this becomes the child's totem since it is connected with conception'. In the eastern and southern Kimberleys, as at Balgo, a person's conception totem (e.g. *djarin*) is represented by some physical sign on his or her body: for instance, a man at Birrundudu had double nipples because, he said, his father had given his mother two lily roots, which made her vomit. Or a man may kill a kangaroo by wounding it on the left side of the neck, then give some of the meat to his wife; she vomits; then he dreams of the kangaroo, and the child which is subsequently born has a mark on the left side of its neck. There is a close identification between a person and his conception totem, so that at Balgo, for instance, a man may say, 'I am that kangaroo!'

In north-eastern Arnhem Land there are what can be called Spirit Landings. The spirit children are associated with sacred wells or waterholes, and there is a direct connection between them and the great mythical beings. The spirit of a child takes the form of an animal or fish or some other creature which allows itself to be caught, or escapes in a peculiar way. Soon afterward the man (or his sister) sees it in a dream, in human shape; it addresses him as father, asking for its mother so that it may be born. The father points to her, and it enters her. In western Arnhem Land one site for spirit children is Gumara, on the mainland opposite Goulburn Islands. A man may be diving for trepang when something touches him on the shoulder: he knows at once what it is. Afterward he tells his wife he has found a child: 'It's inside you now; I put it in, that time.' Or a man may go out in his canoe and, seeing a turtle, dive after it with his spear. But a child comes up to him and sits on his shoulder, calling him father, telling him to take it to his mother. Sometimes these children send out large quantities of fish, dugong and so on to attract hunters and prospective fathers. Or they may go inland and ride on the backs of kangaroo, wallaby or buffalo: in this case, the hunter who kills such an animal will see his child-to-be seated upon it.

The spiritual aspect of such beliefs is particularly important, pointing up as it does the social perspective of the child who is eventually born. Some Aborigines say too that they can tell in advance what a child's sex will be. Although we have several dozens of drawings and other accounts relating to this, the sample of actual births is too small to support such a claim. In some areas the key is said to lie in the size and colour of the woman's nipples, or in subtle changes in her face: people on the Lower River Murray and in the middle north of South Australia claimed that it was possible to tell by feeling her belly. No systematic records have been kept, and for the most part it could very well be a matter of being wise after the event.

There seems to be no marked preference for one sex as against the other. A lot depends on the state of affairs in any particular family at a given time. Parents who already have one or two daughters may prefer a son, or vice versa. Generally speaking, reasons can be adduced in favour of either. For a boy, that he will be able to hunt meat and help support his parents as they grow older, or carry on the sacred rituals which come down to him through his father. For a girl, that she will help her parents with vegetable foods, and even if she leaves them at marriage her husband is expected to make gifts of food and other goods to them. Or in a few places, particularly Bathurst and Melville islands, and north-eastern Arnhem Land, girls may be considered particularly valuable as items of wealth or means of creating or cementing alliances.

There is a widespread emphasis on the production of children, or for that matter the young of any creature. This is suggested, among other things, by the distribution of increase rituals and sites. In north-eastern Arnhem Land, especially, many stories and song cycles bring in this topic. Sacred ritual and myth in western as well as eastern Arnhem Land make much of the notion of a Fertility Mother who is concerned with the birth and growth not only of children but of all the natural species, the sequence of the seasons and the continuity of human life. At Yirrkalla one day a wallaby was caught, and brought back to the camp. Men cutting it up for distribution found a foetus inside it. Immediately they began to sing the songs of the clan which had the wallaby as one of its totems, exclaiming at intervals, 'Ah, we are sorry for that wallaby mother with her young, that poor little wallaby baby!' (But this did not stop them from eating it.)

Fertility rites are not necessarily associated with an emphasis on childbearing. In parts of western Arnhem Land which have had a fair amount of outside influence, a number of young women have been reluctant to bear children, considering them a handicap in sweetheart relationships. For reasons other than this, women may not want to have children at all, or no more than two or three. In such cases they may hopefully try herbs which are said to be effective, or physical measures. In western Arnhem Land three were mentioned: drinking hot, almost boiling, water; pounding the belly with stones; and tying rope or cord round the belly and gradually tightening it. Menstruation is also induced, if slow in appearing, by steaming, massage or violent exercise. Women in the Canning Stock Route area of the Western Desert have songs which, they say, can be used to prevent conception. In north-eastern Arnhem Land women occasionally rely on magical means, such as slashing at the afterbirth with a sharp knife while saying, for instance, 'This was the last child. No more!' But some are more cynical. Several women in this region have left their husbands and gone to live with their married daughters or sons, or with others in the same position as themselves; and one of them insisted that the only sure means of avoiding further pregnancies was to keep away from men. Subincision, by the way, is not practised as a method of birth control, nor could it serve that purpose.

Also in this connection, there is the question of infanticide. This has been reported from several areas—by Daisy Bates (1938), for example, for Ooldea, or by Howitt (1904: 748-50) and others. (See Chapter XIII.) But although it does take place occasionally —not usually because a child is not wanted, but because of bad seasons and shortage of food, especially in desert areas—it is, on the whole, rare. It is one thing to carry out contraceptive measures or abortion before a child is born, but not so easy to dispose of a baby once it has a personality of its own and its parents have grown to love it.

The desire to be rid of children, either before or after birth, is more noticeable in areas where Aborigines have had an unhappy history of contact with Europeans. The infant mortality rate was possibly always fairly high. Although the Aborigines' knowledge and skill are adequate in cases of normal childbirth, they do not have the techniques for coping with difficult births: and there are occasions when things go seriously wrong. In addition, the first few months of a child's life are critical, and genealogies from all over the Continent reveal a high death rate among small children. This situation, however, has often been aggravated through European contact, and particularly so in the past, where inadequate medical attention was available. In the Victoria River district of the Northern Territory a few years ago, malnutrition, lack of desire to have children, and a high infant death rate, were a direct result of bad conditions on pastoral stations. (See R. and C. Berndt, 1946; R. Berndt, 1951*c*.)

In some parts of Aboriginal Australia a pregnant woman must observe certain tabus. (There are a number of references to this in the literature. See Spencer and Gillen, 1938: 471; Róheim, 1933: 207-65; Kaberry, 1939: 244; Mountford and Harvey, 1941: 157.) For example, there are some foods which she must not eat, because they may harm the child magically: crayfish or crabs may damage the foetus, or the tendrils of a yam suffocate it. Or any fish caught by a line (since this may strangle the child), or small wallaby or kangaroo from its mother's pouch, is tabu-ed food to a pregnant woman in western Arnhem Land. In other areas there are no food tabus at all (as throughout the Great Victoria Desert). Or (as in north-eastern Arnhem Land) a man must observe a number of such tabus until his wife has borne a child: this naturally heightens his desire to become a father. In some cases magical acts are believed to make childbirth easier, or have some bearing on the child's sex: in western Arnhem Land, a small bag worn round the pregnant woman's neck may contain a miniature spear for a boy, a tiny bag for a girl. While she is pregnant a woman expects more help from her husband and from other women in the same camp, such as her co-wives, but generally speaking her normal activities are not interrupted to any extent.

Practically everywhere the birth must take place outside the main camp in a special shelter or windbreak. The woman may be looked after by her mother, if she is living close enough to come, or her husband's mother, or her co-wives. If she has trouble, a native doctor may be called on to help with songs and spells. In the eastern and southern Kimberleys there are rites and songs to facilitate birth; no man or unmarried girls may be present at the birth, and after it the woman should stay away from her husband for about five days.

Roth (1897: 182-3), Basedow (1925: 61-4), Kaberry (1939: 240-5), and Mountford and Harvey (1941: 157-8) consider points relating to childbirth. In the Great Victoria Desert a woman squats over a hole while older women massage her back. Later the umbilical cord is twisted with the hands and severed with a sharp flint, then formed into a ring to be worn around the child's neck to keep it from crying; the afterbirth is buried in the hole. In western Arnhem Land the husband prepares the birth-camp and brings firewood, water and food. Here she usually remains for two or three weeks. During the actual birth the mother kneels. After it she smokes herself. This is part of the routine cleansing process, which includes the burial of the afterbirth; and the baby is held over a smoking fire face downward to ensure that it will be quiet and good and will not cry too much. (This is done in other areas too: the Western Desert, for instance, where a little sand or earth may be sprinkled into its mouth as well, for the same purpose.) The navel cord is put in a small dilly bag; the mother wears it for a time, then hands it on to a close relative of the child's father, who incorporates it in a sacred dilly bag. Mountford and Harvey (1941: 159) speak of magical properties assigned to the navel cord; so do Spencer and Gillen (1938: 467) and McConnel (1934: 323). In most areas a newly born child is rubbed with ashes to ensure that it will become dark in colouring like its parents.

The period of seclusion varies, from a couple of weeks or so to a day. In desert areas when people are on the move, childbirth and everything associated with it is got over as rapidly as possible. What has become almost a classic case occurred on the north coast at Yirrkalla in 1947. One of us had been taking photographs of various people sitting around in their camps, but exhausted the roll of film in the camera just on reaching a woman who had been pregnant for some months but obviously would not be so for much longer. Telling her I would be back shortly I hurried to change the film in our own camp about 20 or 30 yards away, taking no more than fifteen or so minutes. She was still sitting there, but now she had a newly born baby alongside her. However, this was an exceptional example. What is more, it should not have taken place in the main camp; there was some grumbling about it, though nothing more.

As a rule childbirth is fairly easy, although often women experience difficulty with their first child, and there are cases of a woman being in labour for a long period. Ashley-Montagu (1937*a*: 72-3), on the evidence of several writers (for example, Hooker, 1869; Öberlander, 1863; Palmer, 1884 and Basedow, 1925: 63, as well as Spencer and Gillen), states categorically that childbirth is a comparatively light affair for the woman, "who is usually up and about her regular duties within a few hours after the delivery of the child". It is true that childbirth, especially for the second or subsequent children, may not be such a traumatic experience as for many Western European women: but it is not such an easy business as Ashley-Montagu implies. He goes on to say that "the actual physical experience involved in giving birth to a child is minimized, and the social implications of the birth are . . . magnified", and that the lack of emphasis on childbirth as such minimizes "any notion of the physical ties which might exist between a particular woman and an individual who has been transmitted through her" agency. However, this is not entirely so: birth as a physical experience does receive much attention in many areas: and the second part does not necessarily follow.

A child which is born grossly deformed is rarely permitted to live long. There are no reliable records on an Australian-wide basis for maternal mortality rates in purely indigenous conditions: but certainly numbers of women must have died in childbirth. In such cases the baby will survive only if there is another woman nearby who can feed it. Stillborn children are buried immediately, or in some areas eaten so that the mother will reabsorb the spirit and later give birth again to the same child. Spencer and Gillen (1938: 52) say that twins are not allowed to survive. However, there is not enough evidence on this score. Basedow (1925: 63-4) points out that twins are rarely seen (we have noticed this, too) and that, generally, one twin will be killed at birth. One explanation may lie in the difficulty of feeding and caring for two small children at the same time, especially in a bad season. Interestingly enough, people in the Oenpelli region claim that two cases of Siamese twins occurred there a few generations ago.

Generally speaking, throughout Aboriginal Australia there is a preference for spacing births, at least to avoid having another child while the first is still being nursed. The mother is expected to refrain from sexual intercourse for varying periods, in some areas as long as a year or so, and a woman who becomes pregnant within a few months of bearing a child is likely to be the butt of ridicule and scorn. In a polygynous family the husband need not observe the same restraints; otherwise, he may turn more freely to extra-marital relationships.

CHILDHOOD

Just as we ourselves speak of baby or infant, child, youth or adolescent, and adult, so in most cases there is a special word for a newly born infant, or for one up to a few months old, perhaps another term when he can crawl, another when he is just beginning to walk, and so on. Even at this stage, there is an obvious difference between the social environment of a child in an Aboriginal camp and a child in our own society. An Aboriginal baby is not isolated from the rest of the community. He is not shut away in a house, for instance, allowed out only at intervals, confined for much of the time to the company of two or three adults, and maybe a couple of other children. Because of the way the Aborigines traditionally live, rarely in enclosed huts or houses but in semi-open windbreaks or shelters, a baby is not isolated or secluded. The life of the camp goes on all around him—people talking, playing, eating, quarrelling. Even though at first he is too young to understand or notice, it represents an environment which he probably comes to take very much for granted. From the very beginning, he lives his life to some extent in public. This is not to say that he has no private, or rather personal, life: but personal life goes on in the open, virtually in public.

One question sometimes asked is whether a child finds greater emotional security in a situation of this kind, where his affection is diffused over a number of parents and parent substitutes, so that the loss is not so sharp if his actual parents should disappear from his field of experience. Probably there is no clear-cut answer to this, especially since so many variables are involved; and the whole question is tied up with the kinds of relationship which predominate in that particular society. There may be an advantage in having a pattern of more or less evenly diffused affection over a wide range of persons—rather than concentration on a small number of persons in specific relationships, with very shallow diffusion outside this range. There is not a hard and fast distinction here: but there is a difference in emphasis between what we can isolate as the two extremes.

Toilet training is usually casual. A growing child is expected to learn by example, and eventually by scolding. Adults are usually quite permissive, and show no anxiety about a child who has not learnt to defecate away from the camp by the time he can walk. In areas where personal excrement or leavings are considered good sorcery material, a child's close kin may protect him by attending to the disposal of these themselves. But once he is fully able to walk and run on his own, he is likely to be laughed at and taunted by other children, especially those a little older, as well as by adults, if he 'behaves like a baby': and this normally seems to be effective. In Aboriginal communities defecating is usually a private matter, or at least not carried out in front of members of the opposite sex; but urinating is taken quite casually, and especially so for children and for men; anywhere outside the immediate eating and sleeping area will do. As a semi-nomadic people they have no use for permanent latrines, and in the deserts, particularly, move camp when the surroundings become too dirty for comfort. Or, at least, this is the traditional pattern: but in the contact situation, where camps are almost static, they continue to behave in much the same fashion. The assumption is that even though such material may be used for sorcery it cannot always be traced to specific persons. In any case, before long it merges into the natural environment. An old camp site with no foreign elements like tin or canvas, merely ashes and bones and perhaps heaps of shell, becomes in time virtually indistinguishable from its bush setting.

A baby spends most of his time with his mother, or someone who deputizes for her. She breast-feeds him, carries him with her when she goes looking for food. He may lie in a curved wooden dish held at her side, in some areas lined with a pad of soft paperbark, in others not, especially in desert regions; or he himself may be wrapped in paperbark. In other areas he may be carried in a netbag, slung from her forehead. A little later he may be taught to sit with legs astride her shoulders, hands clutching her hair; even when there is a camp ceremony he may remain there, falling asleep as she dances. Although his mother is especially important at this time, he is not expected to concentrate his affection on her to the exclusion of others. He learns almost as soon as he is born that there are likely to be substitutes who will nurse him and even feed him—for example, women whom his mother calls sister, perhaps her co-wives. Or one of his grandmothers may concentrate her affection on him, caring for him almost to the exclusion of his own mother; she may even breast-feed him when he is thirsty (for instance in the Victoria River country, and parts of western Arnhem Land), with the colourless liquid which continues to flow long after she has ceased to bear children. In the same way, although he has a special relationship with his own father it is not an exclusive relationship. There are other men he calls father, other men who call him son and behave toward him much as his own father does. In some places, because of the bond between alternate generations, his father's father and father's father's brothers are responsible for helping to rear him; or his mother's mother's brother, as in north-eastern Arnhem Land.

A child's world is normally centred on his parents, the people he knows best. He sleeps in their camp by their fire, and they are the persons who most consistently handle and feed him. But there are other people in his world as well, for most of the time. These other people, adults and children, are not far away, and will play and talk with him long before he can distinguish them as separate persons. He may be handed over temporarily to the care of other children, or other adults, who play with him and tease him; but as long as he has not been weaned he remains within reach of his mother, or mother substitute. The environment may change as his family moves about; the scale fluctuates from a handful of people to a crowd of several hundred or so; but the persons closest to him remain largely the same, and wherever they go his parents' camp is home.

Some children are not fully weaned until about five or six, especially if they are youngest in a family; but it is usually around two or three years old, more or less, depending on whether or not the mother is pregnant again. A baby who can sit up by himself is often given odd bones to play with and suck, and by the time he is three or four he depends almost entirely on solid foods. But breast-feeding is something more than this: it signifies a close physical-emotional bond which a child may be reluctant to weaken. In some areas the mother forces the issue by smearing her nipples with a bitter substance to repel him, or pushing him away or driving him off with a shower of pebbles whenever he tries to drink. This is less likely if she has no younger children. In that case the process is more gradual, except that Aboriginal mothers seem on the whole to be more permissive where boys are concerned, just as they often allow baby boys more latitude when it comes to scratching or biting the breast, or rough behaviour generally. But the birth of a new baby, ousting a child from his once privileged position, seems to sharpen his awareness of what he is losing. He can no longer run to his mother, snatch a quick drink and be off again, or cuddle close to her while he sucks, or be pacified with her breast if he falls over or is hurt in play. Now someone else is there, usurping his place. Sometimes there are stormy scenes, with a crying child trying to pull a small brother or sister away from his mother, beating angrily at it. Or later on, perhaps, if his mother is in an indulgent mood and the baby is a little way off, crawling or toddling about or being nursed by someone else, he may climb on to her lap and ostentatiously suck at her breast, jeering at his rival, laughing at its screams of rage, and resisting all attempts to dislodge him. This is a short-lived triumph; the rival always wins, unless removed by an early death —early enough for the *status quo* to be partially restored.

We have seen such examples from the Western Desert across to north-eastern Arnhem Land: a resentful, displaced 'knee baby' gradually acknowledging defeat, and eventually appearing to be reconciled. But it is impossible to say just how frequently this happens. For every obvious case there are many where nothing of the sort is observed—or where observation rests on being in the right spot at the right moment. For example, a child in a rage may turn on a baby brother or sister with whom he had seemed to be on the friendliest terms; or only some odd comment may point up the existence of latent antagonism—current, or recollected long after the child has become an adult. Because this rivalry hinges on competition for the attention of the same mother, or mother substitute, it presupposes the spacing of children in such a way that a new baby is born while its next oldest sibling is still dependent on the breast—physically, or emotionally, or both. The longer the interval between births the less opportunity for such conflict, although the potentiality may be there. There are rare instances, in the Western Desert, of a boy of eight or nine years old clinging to his mother, apparently reluctant to leave her side—and presumably still vulnerable to being emotionally disturbed by the advent of a younger child. Much depends on how the mother herself handles the situation. She may exacerbate it, playing on the jealousy between the two children, or emphasizing and prolonging, over-protectively, the bond between one of them and herself. But if she bears two surviving children within up to three or four years of each other, she cannot give equal attention to both; and this means, inevitably, partial rejection of one while it is still too young to spend enough time away from her—and is therefore constantly confronted by reminders of the changed relationship between them.

It is in this kind of situation that an Aboriginal child learns about his human environment. He spends much of his time during the first couple of years in the company of adults: his mother or father and others living in the same camp. While they are nursing him or playing with him they may teach him short words, trying to get him to imitate them. In some cases there are special 'children's words', simplified or modified versions of adult vocabularies used in talking to children of up to three years old or so (as in the Western Desert, the Victoria River country, and eastern and western Arnhem Land); and sometimes only a child's mother can interpret or translate what he is trying to say. Especially, they will tell him what he should call them, what is his relationship to them, and to the other people who are coming and going around him. Those of us who approach an Aboriginal kinship system or subsection system from the outside may find it hard to understand, or dull. This is because we look at it from the angle of the system itself, or the unfamiliar terms which make up its framework. But an Aboriginal child learns it first in a concrete way, in relation to actual people: and as a rule it is not until he is almost adult that he can really understand the principles involved. In many areas, one of the first terms a child learns is the equivalent of 'mother', even though he may not be able to say it properly. With more or less constant teaching, his circle grows wider and wider. He is told over and over again who certain people are, and what he should call them, and as new people come along he learns to fit them into his picture of the human world. And he learns the hand signs associated with different categories of relatives, as well as husband and wife, so that he can use them as part of the broader vocabulary of hand signs by means of which people are able to communicate from a distance. The following example is taken from our note-books:

Suppose he lives in the eastern Kimberleys and his subsection is *djangala*. Most people will address him or refer to him by this term, and he learns to associate it with himself. He learns also that his mother is *nangari*, and that he is expected to call other *nangari* women mother too. His mother's brother is *djangari*, so most other *djangari* men are also mother's brothers. His sister is *nangala*. He will have to observe some restraint in his behaviour toward her later on—not using her personal name, for instance; but while he is small this is not important. The only real restrictions on his behaviour, in this matter of tabus between persons, are in relation to females he conventionally calls by the term for mother-in-law. Because persons standing in that relationship to him, potential wife's mother, are normally found in the *nimara* subsection, all females in that subsection irrespective of age are tabu to him. This is something he starts learning very early. In the same way, a little girl is taught that she must avoid all males in the subsection which includes those she calls by the classificatory term for son-in-law. If she is of the *nimara* subsection, for instance, she will learn to keep away as as much as possible from all males in the *djangala* subsection, from babies to old men. Of course, when it comes to actual marriage, the matter may be different. The *djangala* boy, when he grows up, may not marry into the correct or preferred subsection but into an alternative one, and this will mean that his actual mother-in-law is not *nimara*. He will avoid her, and use the mother-in-law term in relation to her. But ordinarily he will continue to avoid all *nimara* women as well—because his marriage has not altered the situation in this respect, and in any case it is always possible that he might take a second or third wife from the 'correct' subsection.

However, a child learns not simply the terms associated with various people, but the kind of behaviour he can generally expect from them, and the way in which he must behave toward them. He may be told, 'This is your sister, you call her so-and-so, you should look after her. When you get older you must give her some of the meat you catch, and she will give you vegetable foods . . . You are not to call her name: but when she gets married, her husband will give you gifts: and if her husband treats her badly, you must take her part.' Or he may be shown a little girl going past, and told, 'She is your mother-in-law: you mustn't look at her face to face, or speak to her: but later when she is married you will send her gifts of meat, and if she makes a daughter she may give her to you for a wife.'

This kind of thing is not a matter of formal instruction. Usually a child is not given the complete picture at any one time. The instruction may appear to be casual: but it goes on over a long period, in relation to real persons and actual situations, building up his knowledge of the people around him until he can 'place' them in his scheme of things: and this scheme of things expands as he grows, and his social perspective widens.

In other words, up to a certain age the training of children is quite informal. (See also Kaberry, 1939: 62-76.) A child learns by actually participating in the life of the community, and not so much by learning about participating—as part of life, rather than preparation for life. It is an active, practical process. And he becomes familiar with his natural environment at the same time as his social environment.

Sometimes a mother leaves her small children at home in the camp for old women to look after, especially if she expects to have a long hard day. More often she takes them with her, and of course in moving from one camp to another she has no choice. She may put a baby down on the ground in his wooden dish while she digs for a yam, or give him to an older child to hold: or if the child is just able to walk but cannot manage a long stretch, she may carry him on her shoulders. When she stops, the children may play about, or try to help her. A small girl may be given her own little dilly bag or wooden dish to carry odds and ends of food, helping her to feel important. Children ask questions, watch what their elders are doing, look at the various plants and tracks they see about them. In this way they gradually learn what foods may be eaten, or eaten raw, or need special treatment; what they must not even try to eat; how to make fire; and what the various tracks and signs about them mean, especially in terms of food.

Girls continue to go out with the women, learning how to copy what they do, because this is the pattern they themselves are expected to follow. But boys cannot use the same model: there is no place, traditionally speaking, for men who might try to imitate the food-collecting activities of women and pay no attention to hunting. After a few years, therefore, they spend much more time with adult men. As a rule they are not allowed to participate in wallaby or kangaroo hunts until they have almost reached puberty, because they could not keep up the pace and are likely to get in the way. But a few boys may go out on their own, in small groups, following up various tracks, spearing tiny lizards or spiders or grasshoppers, or birds, making a fire and cooking them: or playing at ceremonies. Sometimes they join with little girls. On the north coast of Arnhem Land, for example, clusters of children play together for hours, in and out of the shallow water, paddling canoes, digging shellfish from the mud at low tide, and so on.

In some areas there are, or were, special children's songs. Many refer to animals, birds, insects, fish, edible plants—things the children are likely to encounter in their everyday life. In western Arnhem Land there are dances to go with them: and people say that younger boys and girls learn them from older children, with no formal teaching at all from adults. There are songs about spirits and ghosts too: and children remember scraps of adult songs, from 'outside' versions of the big religious cycles, or from sweetheart songs, popular in non-sacred ceremonies. (See C. Berndt, n.d.;

R. and C. Berndt, 1942-5: 251-4, 224-6; also 1952-4.) Adults, particularly grandparents, or older children, tell them stories—some based on their own experiences, others traditional, including simplified versions of local myths.

Getting to know these, along with the songs, prepares a boy, in particular, for the more complex series of songs which he must learn before and after his initiation. These early years are in a sense the beginning of his initiation, and a preparation for his future acceptance into the religious-totemic life of the men of his community. This is the case, too, for a girl—although here there are different things to learn.

Sometimes children play at 'husbands and wives'—with separate windbreaks, making little fires and pretending to cook food. Sometimes there are games of adultery, one little boy running off with the wife of another. In these games they are not always careful about the 'correct' categories: they do not always choose those who call them by the general terms for husband or wife. Adults are often rather lenient about this, saying that it does not matter, 'the children are too young to know better'. One thing they are particularly careful about is that those who call each other mother-in-law and son-in-law should not play together. Otherwise they are likely to be quite indulgent about this kind of play.

There are no restrictions on speech between adults in front of children except in the case of sacred matters, and sexual matters are dealt with quite freely. And since there is little privacy in an Aboriginal camp, they may quite often witness the sexual act. In fact, as they get older this may be an absorbing pastime: they have their favourite 'swear' words and imitate sexual activities amongst themselves. When they are still babies, but old enough to respond to the people who handle and talk to them, adults and older children with time to spare may fondle and play with them, tickling their genitals (small children are usually naked), and commenting on their size, joking about sexual relations. A baby boy may be addressed by the term for 'old man', a baby girl as 'old woman': and adults who call them 'husband' or 'wife' may pretend to make erotic advances to them. In some areas children are said to have no sexual desires before they are about five or six years old. This conventional opinion has a parallel in our own society, but in an Aboriginal community there are many more opportunities for small children to experiment in sex. Actually, from about six or seven onward, but particularly when they are sexually mature, they do spend a fair amount of time in erotic play, or in talking about it—even in the pre-pubertal period when the tendency is for the two sexes to keep their play activities more clearly distinct than before.

Aboriginal parents are, on the whole, very indulgent. They pet and spoil their children, and stand a great deal from them in the way of bad behaviour, or even disobedience. When they do punish it is likely to be severe—a sudden slap or a blow, when a mother or father loses patience: but punishment is rarely carried out in cold blood. In western Arnhem Land, drawing on a conventional theme from local mythology, a mother may threaten her child with a thrashing 'in spirit'. This means, simply, hitting his footprints or a tree, making a fine display of rage without touching him at all. It is a warning of what she *could* do, if provoked, but would prefer to avoid. The myths of this area contain many references to the danger of neglecting or ill-treating children (see Chapter XI): and in fact adults do go to some lengths to avoid denying them what they want. In north-eastern Arnhem Land a child who does not get his own way throws himself down on the ground in tantrums, writhing and kicking, crying or whimpering for hours at a time, ignored by everyone nearby, except that every now and then someone may turn and scream exasperation at him. A few girls continue to do this even after puberty. Boys have fewer opportunities for it after their first initiation rite, because from this point onward responsibility for disciplining them begins to pass from the boy's immediate family to the adult men of his particular *mada* and *mala*. But when a child is young, it is his own mother's or father's business to punish him—or not. Should someone else try, even a classificatory mother or father, or one of the father's other wives, or a grandparent, trouble is bound to ensue. If a mother rushes to help her little boy in a fight, and slaps his opponent, this can be the signal for a noisy encounter: other women come running to take sides, and the upshot may be a number of casualties. (Men, however, prefer to keep out of women's fights, unless their own interests are threatened.)

There are minor excitements of a more formal kind in children's lives: in some areas piercing of the nasal septum, in others preliminary initiation rites; but usually life continues in a more routine fashion, with informal teaching and learning. A girl remains very much under the control of her parents until about puberty and marriage, except that her betrothed husband, if she has one, and if he is accessible, has some say in any major issues. In the Western Desert, especially, she may go to his camp to sleep now and then, on the grounds that in this way she gets used to him and his immediate family; but this need not mean that they have full sexual relations or even any physical contact at all.

Aboriginal sleeping arrangements vary. In the Great Victoria Desert, shortly before puberty boys and girls go to their own separate camps, and at this period they play mostly with members of their own sex. Elsewhere, as in north-eastern Arnhem Land, girls stay with their parents while boys, after their first initiation rite, go to the young men's camp under the control of a guardian. In the east and south Kimberleys, boys do not camp apart until after subincision.

MALE INITIATION RITES

The age at which boys begin their initiation is not uniform throughout Australia. In the Great Victoria Desert, when facial and pubic hair appear a boy is termed *djirangga* (meaning, 'a little hair'): as his beard grows longer he is *alguridja* and at sixteen or even older he is 'caught'. (R. and C. Berndt, 1942-5: 254.) Among the Karadjeri (Piddington, 1932*b*: 62) a boy is about twelve years old when he is taken into the bush and decorated from head to foot with human blood; circumcision takes place a year or two later. A western Arnhem Land novice is about the same age; but in north-eastern Arnhem Land a boy is six or eight years old at circumcision. Among the Aranda the first initiation rite takes place at perhaps ten or twelve years of age: Strehlow (1947: 97) mentions fourteen to sixteen.

Generally speaking, however, once he has reached puberty and his facial hair begins to show, a boy is ready for initiation. This does not include the same kinds of sequence everywhere. Nor does it everywhere involve a physical operation; and when there is such, it is not equally painful. But whatever the content of the rites, they always point to a change in status, a transition from one social category to another; and for each person preparing to undergo them for the first time, however much or little mystery is formally associated with them, the experience is very far from being commonplace.

Some boys at this time show a little uneasiness or nervousness; but apart from the fact that they have no choice in the matter, it has been pointed out to them that only in this way can they achieve adult status, be permitted to marry, and assume the responsibilities of family as well as of ritual life. Although most boys have vague ideas about initiation, they know virtually nothing of what happens until they experience it for themselves. The sudden awareness that this so-called ordeal is not far off alters a boy's whole approach to everyday matters. He pays close attention to the actions of his elders, in the hope that some slight unintentional sign or word on their part may give him a clue as to when he can expect it. He may also want to stay nearer his mother. Outwardly, and especially to his friends, he may boast that the old men won't catch him, or that he is impatient for the rites to begin.

In any case, even if he is afraid he is usually resigned and, in a way, anxious for the waiting to be over. If he has not been wild in his childhood, has listened to his elders, shown willingness and ability to remember what he is told, and if his spear is straight and his skill as a hunter is developing, he may not have to wait long for the first rite. But if the older men dislike him, particularly if he has been disrespectful or rude to them, he may be kept waiting for quite a while: or he may be more roughly handled during the actual physical operation, when there is one.

Strehlow (1947: 97) says: "It is only natural that when the time for their initiation arrives, all Aranda boys submit to their ordeal with eager expectation and with a cheerful courage that sustains them more or less successfully in the hour of trial." Even though a boy does not know exactly what will take place, it is quite clear to him that his future in this respect is largely in the hands of the older men, the ritual leaders, who exercise the main authority in his community.

These initiatory rites and ceremonies are not based on caprice, or improvisation. The initiators of today were the novices of yesterday; and although in practice there are slight differences between one performance and the next, the rules which govern them are regarded as fixed and invariant, handed down through generations of men from the great mythical figures themselves. In many cases initiation is patterned on what Elkin (1954: 166) has called "the greatest transition rite of all"—death: a symbolic pre-enactment of death, and of the spiritual revival which it is hoped will follow. As a novice is taken from the main camp where women wail for him, bullroarers are swung in the distance, representing the voice of a being who will swallow him and finally vomit him—a ritual death, with ultimate rebirth to adulthood, and specifically male adulthood. The boy is a boy no longer. Now he is identified with the adult men of his community.

As far as the ritual aspect is concerned, it is mainly a passive transition. The novice achieves new status by having things done to him, not by doing them. Further, it is during this period that relatively formal organized teaching takes place. The initiation rites are a focal point for the disciplining and training of the boy or young man. He is being made into a full member of his society, a custodian of its sacred mythology and ritual. The sentiments on which the unity and cohesion of his group depend are being brought home to him through the shock of participation in what is, to him, a painful or frightening or emotionally overwhelming experience. At the same time, these sentiments are being reinforced in all who are present at the ceremonies. Pain and fear are probably associated with most of the rites involving direct physical operations, but it is doubtful whether, in the ordinary course of events, we could speak of terror or cruelty here. In most of the initiation rites one of us has witnessed, the novices have stood up to the trials quite well, rarely crying or struggling. On the contrary, they appeared to take much pride in their display of fortitude, and in anticipation of their increased status. This is not a matter of their not feeling pain as other people do. Rather, it is a matter of training and tradition. (See Piddington, 1932: 72.) Even a boy whose mother has cuddled and fussed over him whenever he fell over or scratched himself, or carried him astride her shoulders (as in north-eastern Arnhem Land) if he complained of tiredness or sore feet, knows that he cannot expect the same sympathy here. Rewards, or leniency, depend on a show of courage, not weakness. But lack of resistance and protest may be a sign of exhaustion or apathy, not conscious courage. A novice of about six or seven years old who has just gone through a period of intense excitement, perhaps forcibly dragged away from his crying mother (again, as in north-eastern Arnhem Land), may very well be too dazed to realize what is being done to him. In the case of subincision the situation is a little different, and more pain is involved; but those who undergo it are much older, sometimes fully adult.

A youth does not learn all the answers at his first initiation. He continues to learn about sacred ritual and myth, and so on, all through his life, and he may be middle-aged or relatively old before the final revelations are made to him. Initiation merely opens the door to the secret-sacred and esoteric life of the men of his community. The actual process may go on for a long time, in a series of stages. For instance, he may be able to see certain objects but not yet handle them, or witness certain rites but not participate in them. In some areas, such as eastern Arnhem Land, he may go through a series of age-grading rituals, adding to his status as he does so, and at each stage being known by different terms.

Briefly, then, a man is not fully an adult until he has been through the appropriate rituals; and where there are physical operations these provide visible signs of his change in status. A boy who is to be initiated in a traditional situation must accept the necessity of this: he has no alternative. In some cases, in the eastern Kimberleys for instance, he may be taken on a journey before the actual rite: his mother's brother and the group which is to perform the operation may take him around to a number of camps, visiting various sacred sites and holding a number of preliminary ceremonies: and during all this time he is the centre of attention. In other cases a number of boys may be initiated together, as on some occasions in north-eastern Arnhem Land.

Here is a brief list of some of the initiation stages, or types.

Preliminary

In the Great Victoria Desert a novice walks quietly away from the main camp with the initiators, while all the women, and both his parents, lie face downward wailing. In eastern Arnhem Land little boys who are to be circumcised are told that the mythical python, Julunggul, smells their foreskins and has come to swallow them: they take refuge with their mothers and the other women. As the men seize the boys, some of the women grab spears and pretend to defend them, forming a ring around them: others wail

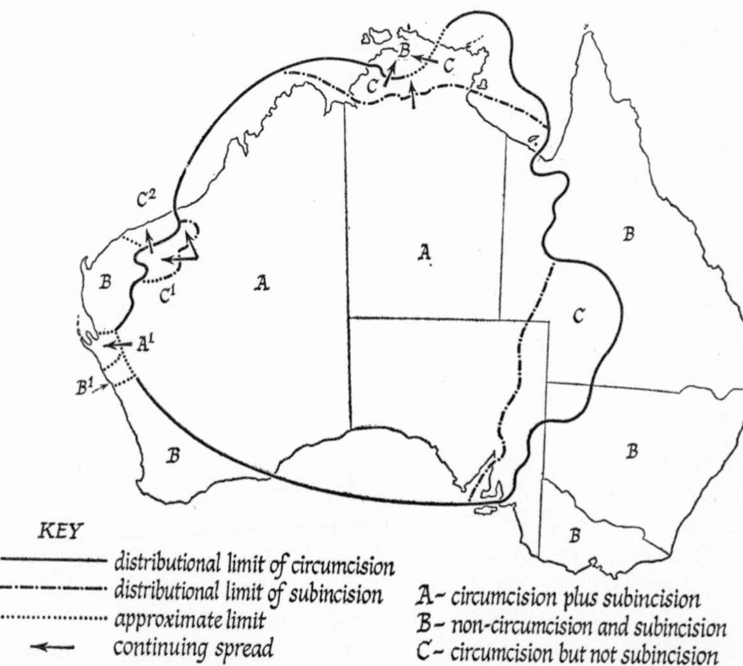

FIG. 10. DISTRIBUTION OF CIRCUMCISION AND SUBINCISION

The map shows the distributional limits of both circumcision and subincision (A). As far as the western limits of this last are concerned they possibly do not coincide with the well-defined circumcision limit. (Tindale, 1940: 150.) In the northern area the ideology of subincision, but not the rite itself, has spread north-east, with the Kunapipi cult: Rose River is the extreme limit of the subincision rite in this area. Again, circumcision myths have spread northward into western Arnhem Land: C indicates circumcision without subincision; B, neither. B¹ refers specifically to the Nganda who were non-circumcising, like the Ingada. However the Wadjeri and Ngugan, and people along the west coast of the Murchison (A¹), practised both. (R. Fink, 'The Changing Status and Cultural Identity of Western Australian Aborigines: a field study of Aborigines in the Murchison District, W.A.', 1955-57, unpublished Ph.D. thesis, Columbia University.) C¹ indicates that the Njamal, and the Njangomada, along with the Indjibandi, Balgu (Bailgu), Bandjima and Njaboli, both circumcised and subincised. Today, however, most (except some members of the southern Njangomada) have dropped subincision. C² indicates that the Kariera, Ngerla, Ngaluma and Madadjinera (or Mardudunera), before European contact, neither circumcised nor subincised, although some individual members of these now practise circumcision. (J. Wilson, personal communication.)

conventionally and some of their close female relatives cry. Eventually, after this mock fight, the boys are removed to the sacred ground.

Depending on the area, messengers may be sent out to summon people, and on their arrival there may be a ritual welcome. And in many areas singing and dancing may continue for weeks before the actual initiation: during this time the novices are segregated away from the main camp.

Tossing rite

This rite, performed over much of Australia, is accompanied by the throwing of fire over the heads of the novices, and also of the women who may be dancing nearby. In the Great Victoria Desert a novice is tossed four times, and the reason given for this is a mythical one: the ancestral being Julana wanted a woman, but succeeded only in frightening her—she flew away. (The tossing symbolizes the flying.) Women representing the mythical Gunggaranggara women dance with shuffling steps making deep grooves in the sand (see Mountford, 1938*a*: Plates XIII and XIV), until men throw firesticks over their heads as they turn and run off through the darkness to their camp, leaving the dancing ground to the men. This is said to express conventional antagonism between the two generation levels. (See Chapter II.) Among the Aranda the tossing constitutes the first initiation rite, and the reason often given is that it is designed to make the novices grow.

Piercing of nasal septum

This practice is widespread, but as an initiation rite it seems to have fallen into disuse. Throughout the Great Victoria Desert it is performed in public without ceremony, as it is in eastern Arnhem Land where it is significant mainly for decorative purposes, and also for the afterlife: the guardians of the Land of the Dead will enquire about this. Among the Aranda it is not part of the initiation rituals, but after the operation a piece of bark is stripped from a nearby tree and thrown in the direction of the sacred conception site of the novice's mother. (See Spencer and Gillen, 1938: 459.) Basedow (1925: 230-1) mentions that the Laragia "pinch a hole through the flesh with their finger-nails" before a child can walk, but that most of the Central Australian tribes use a sharply-pointed bone.

Tooth evulsion

This varies in significance, and in importance. Often it is performed quite simply, in public, particularly throughout northern South Australia. For the Aranda (Spencer and Gillen, 1938: 214) it is 'partly a matter of personal taste and fashion', performed before marriage and after a water ceremony; the explanation given (*ibid.*, 450-8) is that it is designed 'to produce in the face a resemblance to certain dark rain clouds'. The tooth is thrown in the direction of the mother's totemic camp. Roth (1897: 170) also reports that in north-west central Queensland tooth evulsion had no initiatory significance. In other areas, the Northern Kimberley for instance, it appears to be an integral part of ritual. (Basedow, 1925: 232-5.) And in New South Wales it is a central focus of initiation rituals which lead up to the revelation of sacred knowledge. Howitt (1904: 509-642) discusses some of these, such as the *kuringal, burbung and bora.* In the first, novices are shown ground figures which have been moulded out of earth. (See also Falkenberg, 1948: Plates 19 and 23.) These, associated with the mythology, point up the significance of the rites centred around the culture hero named Baiami or Daramulun; and bullroarers are swung—representing the sound of his voice. The tooth is loosened with the finger-nail and knocked or tapped out, and after this the novices witness a series of rites.

Blood Rite

At some point during the initiatory rites throughout most of Aboriginal Australia some form of blood-letting takes place, from either the arm or penis incisure. In some cases red ochre is substituted; but both signify sacredness and symbolize life. Such blood may be likened to menstrual blood. However it is used, for smearing or anointing novices and participants, or for drinking, it is said to give life, strength and courage. Drunk sacramentally, it represents the blood of various mythical beings.

In the Great Victoria Desert during the preliminary initiatory stage blood is drawn from the arm in the first of many rites. The novice is rubbed all over the body with blood and also sips some, before it is passed around and drunk. The drinking signifies the affinity between the participants; it serves as a bond between them, as well as giving strength to the novice. Smearing blood over the body emphasizes the state of ritual death into which the novice has entered. In north-eastern Arnhem Land, novices are completely smeared with red ochre, with sacred clan patterns painted on their chests and white clay masking their faces. In the *djunggawon* initiatory cycle, arm blood symbolizing the blood of the Wawalag sisters is ritually collected in a dish and used as an adhesive for feather down decoration; as it is drawn the great *julunggul* drone pipe is blown. In the myth the Julunggul python smells that blood, and now it is offered to him in the ritual. During other sequences, dancers are painted with blood. In the

Kunapipi (R. Berndt, 1951*a*) novices are taken to the sacred ground where men open their arm veins, sprinkling blood on one another and into a special trench. Again this is the blood of the Wawalag, and symbolizes life. In other rituals in this area, such as the *dua nara* associated with the Djanggawul creative beings (Berndt, 1952*a*), blood and red ochre symbolize the blood of the two Djanggawul sisters, or, alternatively, the 'condensation' of the sun's redness, often represented by the orange-red breast feathers of the *lindaridj* parakeets: when a novice's foreskin is cut, the flow of blood is likened to afterbirth blood.

Depilation

Removal of body or facial hair is found mostly among the non-circumcising tribes: for instance, in parts of eastern Australia (most of Victoria), among the Maung of Goulburn Island, the Bathurst and Melville islanders, as well as among the people of the Lower River Murray in South Australia. In the *jajaurung* rituals all the hair is plucked from a novice's face and pubes. (Howitt, 1904: 613.) For the Encounter Bay and Lower River Murray people these rites are described in detail. (Meyer and Taplin in Woods, 1879.) Hair is left only on the head and chin, or hair from the head is torn out with a spear point and the moustache and most of the beard removed, and then the novices are smeared with grease and red ochre. They may drink water only through a reed and are subject to other prohibitions as well, and remain tabu until the third plucking of the hair. At Bathurst Island, as part of the long and complicated *gulama* yam rituals, men pluck out their beards and moustaches and leave them overnight in water together with sliced yams; the whiskers are associated symbolically with this yam, which is covered with small hairy roots. (Spencer, 1914: 91-115.)

Cicatrization

Scarring, or cicatrization on various parts of the body, is also quite common, but only in some areas is it a part of the actual initiation rituals. For example, in northern Queensland it was usually the only operation carried out. (See Elkin, 1954: 163.) Throughout the Great Victoria Desert it may take place, publicly, at any time after subincision, as a sign that a person is fully initiated. In South Australia, among the Dieri and other Lake Eyre tribes, the *wiljaru* cicatrization rite is of great importance. (Howitt, 1904; Gason and Schürmann in Woods, 1879; Horne and Aiston, 1924.) A young man lies face downward while his initiators cut three to twelve gashes on his back: or in another part of this region arm-vein blood is spurted on the novices' backs and men make marks with their thumbs to indicate where the cicatrices will later be cut. In the *belier* rite of the Laragia two cuts are made on the chest. (Spencer, 1914: 153-7.) Basedow (1907: 10-16) briefly outlines the böllier (*belier*), and a second initiation rite called *mollinya.* In the first, cicatrices are made on the novice's upper arm and thigh: in the second, on either side of the abdomen, each cut extending less than halfway across the front. Generally speaking, the Central Australian tribes do not cicatrize their bodies as much as those further north, and in most cases do not associate it with initiation. At Melville and Bathurst islands, however, extensive scars cover both sides of the back as well as the upper and outer surfaces of the arms and thighs, and horizontal lines across the chest and forehead. Basedow (1925: 238) says that the small V-shaped cicatrices represent the frond of the zamia palm, Spencer (1914: 43) that they represent the barbs on the heavy local spears.

Fire ceremony

As Elkin points out (1954: 174-5), the fire ceremony is widespread. 'Candidates sit around a blazing fire, staring at it until they are almost dazed.' This is partly connected with the throwing of firesticks. But it may take the form of smoking the novices for purificatory purposes, as in the Great Victoria Desert. After subincision, for instance, among the Mangarei, the initiate is smoked. Or pits are made, as among the Dieri. (Berndt, 1953: 191-2.) Fires are lit in these, and over them are put green boughs on which the novices lie. And there are occasions, too, such as in the Great Victoria and Western Deserts, when dancing men move into and over live coals, scattering them in showers.

Circumcision

This rite is perhaps one of the most important. Only a few tribes do not circumcise, and these mainly in small pockets surrounded by circumcising tribes. (Elkin, 1954: 38-9 and Tindale, 1940 indicate the boundaries of this, as well as of subincision. See Fig. 10.) In the Great Victoria Desert men form a 'table' on which the novice is held down: the foreskin, held by one man, is cut off with a stone flake by his *wabudu,* a wife's father, and later eaten by a man especially chosen by the *wabudu.* (R. and C. Berndt, 1945: 265-8.) Nothing is done to stem the flow of blood, which soon dwindles: but the Wiranggu sometimes apply a firestick to the bleeding penis. A Dieri novice urinates into a fire made from special wood, and the steam eases the pain; a Ngadjuri novice lies face downward on a mound heaped with ashes.

Circumcision procedures are described in some detail by a number of writers: Howitt, Roth, Spencer and Gillen, Basedow, Warner, Elkin and others.

Among the Karadjeri there is close mythological substantiation for the major rituals, and two modes of circumcision—the Southern and Northern traditions. (Piddington, 1932*b*: 46-87.) Tindale (1935: 199-224) considers Bidjandjara circumcision rites in the Mann and Tomkinson Ranges. According to Roth (1897: 171), among the Pitta-Pitta (Queensland) a club is fixed in the ground; five or six men gather round, clasping it, and bend forward to make a 'table' on which the novice is placed face upward; the operator, sitting astride his chest, cuts off the foreskin; the flow of blood is arrested by applying hot dry mud. The use of such human tables is common, but they take different forms. (See R. Berndt, 1952*c*: 121-46.) In some areas the prepuce is destroyed or buried, in others eaten, or kept in a specially woven basket as in Arnhem Land. Among the Aranda, circumcision is part of a long series of rites which are held on the *pulla* ground (Strehlow, 1947: 96 *et seq.*); the background to the operation is the twirling sound of bullroarers, the voice of the great spirit, Twanyirika. (Spencer and Gillen, 1938: 244.) The novice is placed on a shield so that blood from the severed foreskin flows on to this.

In north-eastern Arnhem Land (Warner, Berndt), on the last day of the *djunggawon* men paint their spearheads with blood and come with the novices into the main camp where the women are waiting, already decorated. Grass has been arranged on the camp dancing ground. The men encircle it, calling out invocations to the spirits, then cluster tightly around the novices. The women, at one side, wail and sob. Two men lie down on their backs in the centre of the group on the grass, but before the novices are placed on them they are given water to drink and baskets to hold in their teeth to help them in their ordeal; then they are cut, as women dance around the outskirts, knowing what is happening but unable to see it. A day or so later the boys are steamed over a fire covered with damp branches. The foreskin is eventually waxed into a feathered string pendant attached to a sacred dilly bag. Various reasons are given for this rite, usually in mythical terms: one, that it shortens the penis—women as well as men speak disparagingly of the Western Arnhem Landers, and their 'unclean' habit of leaving this long; another, that in the mythical era boys used to sleep with their sisters, and were circumcised as a punishment. Again, it is said to symbolize the severing of the novice's former association with women, putting it on a new and different basis: or the breaking of his umbilical connection with his mother—first, physical birth and physical separation from her; now, ritual rebirth and emotional independ-

Women, with their children, gathering roots on a swamp plain near Milingimbi (late 1930s)
(photo: courtesy H. Shepherdson)

Cycad nuts, in bags, about to be immersed in water (see Chapter IV). At Macassar Well, Milingimbi (late 1930s)
(photo: courtesy H. Shepherdson)

A song man beats his stick rhythmically as he sings to the drone of the didjeridu. Goulburn Island, western Arnhem Land (1961)

ence; but in neither is there any suggestion that this need mean a decline in mutual affection.

Circumcision novices today are identified with those who were born, in the beginning, to the Djanggawul Sisters. A boy who has just had his foreskin cut off is said to have emerged from his Mother, here meaning Djanggawul. At birth a child must be deliberately cut away from his mother; the umbilical connection between them cannot be allowed to lapse gradually. Later, when a boy is circumcised this second cutting signifies that he has been removed from the world which is dominated by females, and by virtue of his rebirth will become more obviously male. For a girl this is not necessary: she is expected to identify with women, not to set herself apart from them. The process of symbolic birth or symbolic weaning from the mother is, in her case, much less dramatic and eventful, if only because its implications are of a minor and largely personal kind.

Subincision

Where subincision is carried out at all, it is particularly important. (See Basedow, 1927: 123-56; Ashley-Montagu, 1937*b*: 193-207; Elkin, 1954: 166; Kaberry, 1939: 99; R. and C. Berndt, 1942-5: 268-70; R. Berndt, 1952*b*: 3-19.) Other terms used for it are 'Sturt's terrible rite' or, more colloquially, 'whistlecock'. Roth, giving examples from the Boulia, Leichhardt-Selwyn and Upper Georgina districts (Queensland), suggests the label 'introcision' because it corresponds with female introcision. (Roth, 1897: 177; J. Mathew, 1899: 121.) According to Kaberry, the Wolmeri and Ngadi at one time practised vaginal introcision, but they continue to perform subincision now without the female rite. In the Great Victoria Desert there is subincision, but no laceration of the vagina. Ashley-Montagu is of the opinion that subincision is practised to resemble the menstrual flow, particularly in view of the intermittent ritual blood-letting which it entails. Certainly the evidence points in this direction. (Compare, for instance, M. Mead, 1950: 102-3.) It is not intended as a contraceptive measure, nor as an excuse for excited emotional display; the rites are sober and quite restrained. In one myth (of Julana and Njirana) an explanation is given in therapeutic terms: the ancestral being's penis itched near the scrotum, and he let out blood to ease it.

Throughout northern South Australia and central Australia the initiand is held down over a human table, his penis held erect while the incision is made underneath it. The significance of the rite lies not so much in the first operation, which is enacted with little ceremony, but in subsequent repetitions of it. In various rites which follow later, men who have pierced their incisures dance so that the blood splashes their thighs. Roth mentions that a novice is placed faced upward on the ground and men, after doing this, dance over him sprinkling him with blood. A fairly full description of Aranda subincision rites is given by Spencer and Gillen (1938: 251-64). Out from Oodnadatta, in the course of certain rituals men congregate around a fire warming themselves, then break off thorns, heat them in the fire and puncture their incisions, splashing the blood over their thighs; they dance toward the novices, showing the wounds. Throughout that area, too, there is the rite of penis-holding. When a man with a subincised penis enters a strange camp, he takes up the hand of each local man in turn, pressing his penis flatly on the palm. This gesture, of offering and acceptance in a close physical contact, signifies the establishment of friendly relations, and is associated with the settling of grievances. (See R. and C. Berndt, 1942-5: 239-66.)

In north-eastern Arnhem Land subincision is not practised, but it is coming into the area through the Kunapipi. (See R. Berndt, 1951*a*.) The name Kunapipi is sometimes said to mean 'subincisure', alternatively the womb of the Fertility Mother: the penis symbolizes the Python or Rainbow or Lightning Snake, the incisure itself the uterus. Symbolically, then, the subincised male member represents both the female and the male organs, which must combine for fertilization to take place. The blood from the cut, either initially or during subsequent piercing, symbolizes both afterbirth blood and menstruation: the parallel is widely acknowledged, across the Northern Territory into the eastern Kimberleys of Western Australia.

Other rites

Various other features are associated with initiation. There are purificatory or cleansing rites; the whole group of people concerned bathes in the same place at the same time, as a climax to the total sequence or at certain points during it. Or the tying of ligatures on the arms, often in preparation for letting blood from them; gifts are presented to the new initiate, a pubic covering, for instance, waistband, pearlshell, or headband. And so on. Strehlow speaks of the painful Aranda practice of tearing off fingernails. (Strehlow, 1947: 112-14.) Aranda novices also have their heads gashed open, and vigorously bitten—to make their hair grow. (Spencer and Gillen, 1938: 251; Strehlow, 1947: 99.) In marked contrast to this is the goose egg rite of the Ngulugwongga on the Daly River, part of a rich complex hinging on fertility and seasonal increase. The small boy who is the centre of attention is given the yolk of a goose egg to eat, then heaped around with eggs until he is almost hidden from sight. He hands these out to his relatives, who have gathered about him. Until adolescence he may eat these eggs freely; then he is sent away for his initiation, centring on circumcision, and only after a couple of years are they available to him again.

EXAMPLES OF INITIATIONS

It is important to remember that the first initiation is simply an introduction to a long series of ceremonies and rituals. After it a man may be classified a social adult, a man as contrasted with a boy, but this in itself is not a simple category; the subdivisions and contrasts within it can be almost equally crucial. Nevertheless, certain religious matters which were unknown to him before, and are formally closed to women, are revealed to him now. Among the things he sees for the first time are various secret-sacred objects. Some appear in the course of the initiatory rituals, others later. All these, like the acts which make up the rituals themselves, have symbolic significance and mythical associations. A novice confronted with some of these, but unaware as yet of their significance, feels that he is on the threshold of a new life—a life which revolves around his religion: a life, moreover, which formally separates him from everyday activity and to some extent from the world of women but also, conversely, draws him closer to the realities of his existence, and closer too to an appreciation of women's part in his society.

In listing the different facets of initiation ritual we have highlighted various foci of interest in the shape of special acts or ritual operations: but around these cluster much ceremony, and all are part of a network of social relations on which we have barely touched.

Among the north-eastern Arnhem Landers, for example, are four major ritual cycles: the *djunggawon, kunapipi, ngurlmag,* and the higher *dua* and *jiridja* moiety *nara.* (See Chapter VIII.) The *djunggawon,* which specifically deals with circumcision, is made up of the following stages: a *julunggul* drone pipe is made and blown, signifying the opening of the rites, and the young novices are taken from the women, painted, and sent on their preliminary journey; women wail over them, dancing about a special Wawalag pole, and again men rush in and take the boys away to the sacred ground; a series of ceremonies is held; the *julunggul* is painted, and blood removed from the participants' arm veins; the dancers are painted with blood, the novices with clan patterns; there are more rituals; presently the actual circumcision takes place in the main camp, followed by dancing, and food tabus are imposed on the boys; they are steamed over a fire, and told about the ritual significance of some of the dances, songs and sacred words; finally the drone pipe is returned to its secret hiding place.

In Western Arnhem Land, there is no physical operation. A youth on reaching puberty is taken to his first *ubar* ritual, which is of general religious significance but is used as an age-grading sequence too. Here he is simply an onlooker attended by guardians, not a participant in the full sense of the word; he must, however, go through certain ritual actions based on the relevant mythology. These initiatory sequences are concerned with instructing the youth in everyday as well as in ritual affairs. The meanings of sacred myths are explained, but not in detail, and the enactment of these by fully-initiated participants helps to impress them on his mind. Usually he goes through three successive rituals, extending over a period of three or four years and sometimes longer: each must be satisfactorily completed before he passes on to the next. The first, beginning with his temporary seclusion, covers a series of totemic performances; during the second, which brings in the sacred *ubar* gong, he himself takes part in an important scene; the last, designed to supplement his knowledge of the associated mythology and the more intricate aspects of its ritual, is often an elaboration of the other two. After he has been through the *ubar* rituals the youth is considered a man, and may marry three or four years later. But as time goes by he gradually becomes more familiar with the *ubar*, and eventually a full participant. Moreover, he can now proceed to the *maraiin* rituals, and after a period of some years participate in them too.

Throughout the Great Victoria and Western deserts the initiation pattern varies in content. It has four main stages. In stage one the novice is taken from the wailing women; fully initiated men draw blood from their veins, paint the novice with it, and drink some themselves. His nasal septum is pierced, the middle tooth in the top row is knocked out, and finally he is painted with red ochre. After this he goes to live in virtual seclusion with other young men, all obliged to observe several prohibitions. A period of nine to twelve months usually elapses before he goes through the second stage, beginning with the tossing rite, and then the presentation of gifts. Initiated men take blood from their arm veins, and fasten feather down over their bodies in sacred designs. They also make a large *wanigi* emblem for later use. When they are ready the women dance, near the circumcision ground, but are dispersed by the throwing of firesticks. The novice is present during a series of totemic rites; for most of the time he is covered up and cannot see them, although he is told the meaning of the songs. Later on the covering is removed and he sees some of the dancing, the first sacred rites he has witnessed; he may also be shown the *wanigi*. Just before dawn he is 'smoked' by dancing men, holding smoking boughs: the men make a path to the human table on which he is to be circumcised. Once the foreskin is cut he is taken back to his seclusion camp, while the main camp moves to another site, as in the case of a death. Two bullroarers are presented to him, and he is allowed to swing them. Then his hair is shaped into a bun, on the foundation of a pad.

Several other rituals are held after his penis is healed: for instance, arm blood is spurted over him, symbolizing his acceptance into the men's sacred life. Later there is his ritual entry into the main camp, where he is welcomed enthusiastically by his parents and close relatives. Conventionally at this time he is taken on a journey to various waterholes situated in his own totemic country. On his return there is an intermediate period, of twelve to twenty-four months, during which he attends post-circumcision rites and is generally instructed in the extensive mythology and so on. When the decision is made to subincise him, he leaves the main camp again to the accompaniment of wailing, and is cut on a human table. There is a period of segregation, followed by rites in which men pierce their incisures and dance with blood-splashed thighs. He can marry now, but usually waits until he has been cicatrized. The intermediate period is taken up with attending more rituals, particularly those concerning blood-letting, and in the course of these his incisure is opened further. There is also ritual feasting, regarded as a form of communion. At this time too he sees the long wooden *djilbilba* boards. The fourth stage, cicatrization, takes place about a year after subincision. After that he is regarded as fully initiated. But although he may actively participate in some rites and ceremonies, there are others of which he is still only a witness, and still others to which he has not yet been admitted.

In other areas, particularly in south-eastern Australia, initiatory rituals are not nearly so complex. Among some Victorian tribes (as reported by Howitt, 1904: 610-12) they include the *jibauk*. Here the novice's mother's brother takes him, covered up and with face hidden, to a large bough windscreen where he and other boys are hung with pubic coverings; his hair is cut, leaving a ridge from back to front; he is smeared with mud and marked with bands of pipeclay, and slung from his neck in a bag is a live possum he has caught and denuded of fur. He stays in seclusion with other young men until his hair has grown about two inches; then his camp is moved gradually, a little distance each day, toward the main camp. During this time he is given a possum skin rug by his sister's husband, and paraded through the main camp, where he is ritually received. He must still attend a further series of rituals.

There is no point in giving further examples. But although there is so much variation in these rituals, the majority contain some common themes: in simplest terms, removal from the main camp and total or partial enforced segregation; performance of some rite to emphasize the fact of transition; revelation of secrets of a religious nature; and finally, return to the main camp as a social adult.

INITIATION OF GIRLS

Girls do not, as a rule, have to go through the same kind of formal training and teaching as boys do. But to say that the central focus is on male initiation does not mean that women have no part in it. On the contrary, they have an important role in much of it, just as they do in other religious rituals. As far as they themselves are concerned, what could be called initiation rituals are often in fact puberty rituals. They too vary a great deal and may even be associated with love magic. In addition there are minor rites and songs connected with the growing of breasts, and other features of physical development.

Speaking very generally, at the first sign of puberty a girl leaves the main camp, and spends several days in a little seclusion hut or shelter some distance away from it. She may have to observe certain food tabus at this time. An older woman or two may be with her, teaching her songs, telling her myths, or instructing her as to how she should behave when she marries. At the end of the seclusion period, depending on the area, she may be led into the main camp nicely decorated and painted. In some places, before this she goes down to the nearest river or billabong at daybreak, and bathes there ritually with a crowd of girls. Other rites too may be connected with puberty. (See below.) In any case, the girl is now a woman, socially as well as physically mature. If she is not already betrothed, or even married, this is the time when arrangements should be made. If she is, or if she has been spending various periods in her husband's camp, this is the time for the marriage to be confirmed. There may not be a spectacular marriage ceremony—sometimes her puberty ritual is taken as covering this: but she may be conventionally handed over to her husband and his kin. In some areas it is not done in that way. A girl may not know when her marriage is to be consummated, although her parents and other relatives may have come to some arrangement about it. She may go out food-collecting as usual, perhaps with an older woman, and be seized by a group of men comprising her future husband and several others whom he calls 'brother'; she therefore calls them husband too, and they have temporary right of access to her before she finally settles down in her husband's camp.

Roth (1897: 174-80) describes various forms which a girl's initiation may take. In the Boulia district (Queensland) a pubescent girl is caught by a number of men; they forcibly enlarge the vaginal orifice by tearing it downward with their fingers, which have possum twine wound round them, then have sexual relations with her, collecting the semen and later drinking it ritually. (Compare, for instance, R. Berndt, 1947: 353.) After this she is permitted to wear a grass necklet and other decorations, and go to her husband. In a different tribe in the same area a stone flake is used, by an old man, to cut part of the perineum; the girl's eyes are covered. She is decorated with bands of charcoal, and red and white feather down fastened on with blood from the wound. The period of sexual relations, again with a group of men, extends until the following morning, and the collected semen is used medicinally. On her return to the camp she may wear special decorations. In the upper Georgina and Leichhardt-Selwyn districts virtually the same rite is carried out. At Birdsville a stick of very hard wood about two feet long, shaped like the apex of a penis, is used to break the hymen and posterior vaginal wall.

The first Boulia initiation is followed by a second ritual which includes dancing; and women are permitted to hit with fighting poles any men against whom they have a grudge, with no fear of retaliation. The ornaments the girl wore at the first stage are now put away. In the third stage different ornaments are used and the girl, together with all the men and women participating, is painted with yellow ochre. Further changes in decorations mark the fourth and final stage. Spencer and Gillen (1938: 92-4) report that when a girl reaches marriageable age she is taken out into the bush, where the rite of *atna-ariltha-kuma* (vulva-cut) is performed. Before the actual cutting a man touches the vulva with a small wooden *tjurunga,* magically to reduce the flow of blood. Afterward the girl is decorated with headband and tail tips of rabbit-bandicoot, necklets, and fur string armlets, and her body is painted all over with a mixture of fat and red ochre. She returns to the main camp, but her husband sends her back to the men who have initiated her and they have coitus with her. (Spencer and Gillen, 269, 457-65, say this is regarded as 'equivalent to male subincision'.) A similar operation followed by sexual relations is carried out by many Central Australian tribes.

Such rites are closely associated with marriage. However, although these are central, there are others as well. The first may have taken place earlier, when the girl's breasts are rubbed with fat and red ochre. There is also the rite of nose-piercing, and of segregation at menstruation: in a sense, too, childbirth can be regarded as one aspect in the series of initiatory rites relevant to females.

Basedow (1907: 13-15; 1925: 252-6) mentions that among the Laragia and Wogaidj a girl goes through a 'smoking ceremony' and ritual bathing, and that north-eastern coastal tribes remove two joints from a finger of a female novice. This is done, although not necessarily as part of initiation, in the Victoria River district as well as on the Daly River, where a ligature of spider web is used: in the second case, the end part of the finger is deprived of circulation and eventually drops off. (And see Howitt, 1904: 746-7.) Basedow describes female initiation rites during which *tjurunga* are used, in one case to touch the girl's body: this is followed by ritual defloration or laceration of the vulva, with either a stone knife or a cylindro-conical stone, such as is used in the Great Victoria Desert. Kaberry (1939: Chapter IX), for the eastern Kimberley tribes and some others, mentions pre-puberty rites, including the piercing of the hymen as a preparation for marriage; other rites of varying complexity which take a girl up to and through her first menstruation—this last involving seclusion, after which she is permitted to take part in women's secret ceremonies; rites relating to pregnancy, birth, and lactation which have their sacred and esoteric aspects. In the Victoria River district too some ritual is associated with crises like birth, the growing of a girl's breasts, and menstruation.

In the Great Victoria Desert the period of seclusion at first menstruation is about a week. During this period certain songs are sung. A little afterward, the girl's future husband asks a 'brother' to take her into the bush. Several women go with her. First she squats over a smoking fire, and then is held down while her hymen is cut. Alternatively, he may deflower her himself. Next day she is painted with red ochre and white clay and decorated with string necklets and a pearlshell. She was 'dead'; but the pearlshell, with its 'life-giving' properties, restores her to life. Cicatrization and piercing of the nasal septum take place not long after this. The essential sequence here is seen as defloration, pregnancy, childbirth. There are rites associated with each, including, in one part of this area, the burning off of pubic hair. In the mythology, circumcision for boys, hymen cutting for girls, take place simultaneously.

Among the Dieri, a boy's foreskin is sometimes handed to the parents of his betrothed wife, who pass it on to the man who cuts the girl's hymen. In the course of the rite or a little later it is put briefly into her vulva, and this is said to establish a sympathetic union between them.

In western Arnhem Land there is no formal rite of defloration, introcision or group bathing for a girl at puberty. When a girl is about seven or eight years of age her nasal septum is pierced; certain tabus are associated with this period, as they are when her breasts are growing, and in fact at various intervals throughout her life from early childhood. Both Maung and Gunwinggu have a choice in the way they refer to a menstruating girl, or woman. They can say bluntly what is involved ('She has blood'), or speak of it indirectly—especially if one of her brothers is within hearing: 'She is sitting down on account of her back', or, 'a stick has pricked her foot'. (C. H. Berndt, 1951; R. and C. Berndt, 1951*a*: 89-91.) At the onset of her first menstruation she is secluded in a special hut made by her husband or husband-to-be. A Maung girl is looked after by her husband's mother or an older sister, who keeps her fire going and makes sure she has plenty of hot, clean sand; again there are certain tabus to be observed, and she uses a plaited oblong mat made by her mother or sister, mother's mother, or father's sister. After about three days she is washed, painted, decorated with armbands, headband, and hair belt and taken to the main camp, where she is introduced as a new woman. One special thing she wears at this time is a band or harness of jungle fibre which is passed round her neck, between and under her breasts. The hut is destroyed by her mother. At subsequent menstrual periods some of the tabus are lifted.

The Gunwinggu use netted bags instead of mats, and the food tabus do not entirely coincide with those of the Maung. There are some parallels: if the girl eats various meats on the mainland (such as wallaby, possum, snake, goanna), the spirits of these animals will suffer and there will be very few of them the following season. But the Gunwinggu emphasize much more sharply the need to avoid water foods, including the lily stems and seeds which the Maung allow the girl to eat at this time (although not the roots). This is because the Rainbow Snake looms large in the perspective of these inland people, especially where blood is concerned. A menstruating girl, like a woman who has just borne a child, must be careful not to attract the Rainbow's attention, by staying close to her fire and not going near a billabong: the fire helps to protect her. At the end of her seclusion her hair and body are completely red-ochred, except for a white forehead band and a white vertical mark on her nose, her armbands, and necklet of jungle beads. A crescent moon is painted in white clay below her breasts, or on her stomach: this, symbolically, regulates the menstrual flow so that it will not continue indefinitely but will reappear with each moon unless she becomes pregnant. Sometimes a Rainbow is painted between her breasts. Now she swings by her hands from a horizontal branch of a nearby tree while women, especially her mother, slap her belly and back ritually with a hard pad of cold river sand wrapped in paperbark; this too is designed to dry up the menstrual flow entirely, to make sure that it does not last too long, or return unexpectedly. The girl's return to the main camp is marked by a ceremony, with men (especially those she calls 'father') beating the sticks, singing, and blowing the didjeridu: it is an occasion she will remember for many years to come. But until the ochre and paint wear off she may not wash in, or drink from, any billabong or stream. If she does so, or if she ever tries to conceal the fact that she is menstruating, she is not the only person who is in danger. The mythology of this region makes much of the power of the Rainbow to swallow or kill people who offend—or attract—it (or her), and babies and young children are especially vulnerable.

The people around and south of the Daly River—Ngulugwongga and Madngala, Wogiman and Nangiomeri, for instance—have some features in common with these rites but, inevitably, there are differences too. Briefly, a girl at first menstruation is secluded in a special hut (afterward burnt by her mother), observes various food tabus, and again must be careful of the Rainbow. When the period is over she is taken before sunrise down to the water, where all the women splash and duck her in noisy excitement. Then she is decorated, painted in red ochre and white clay, with a large painted dilly bag hanging empty in front of her. She is brought triumphantly into the main camp in formal procession, followed by an old woman who jokes and dances, clowning, stamping her feet, throwing her arms about, in contrast to the solemnity of the others: the girl's mother, especially, is crying and wailing, gashing her head with a tomahawk. The girl steps ritually over a row of food (dampers or scones made from white flour are preferred), then sits down while more food is heaped up beside her. Afterward she distributes this. The recipients vary: among the Madngala only the older people were allowed to share it. But in any case, those consistently excluded from it are men who call her 'sister', and particularly her brothers from the same mother.

Men's attitudes to menstrual blood vary throughout the Continent. In the Great Victoria Desert it is dangerous as far as men are concerned; after sexual intercourse with a menstruating woman, people say, a man's hair will turn prematurely white. Generally speaking, however, men do not appear to react to menstruation with disgust or horror; nor are women labelled 'unclean' at this time—although Warner (1937/58) speaks of ritual uncleanness. In the Kimberleys (Kaberry, 1939: 238-9) they are not regarded as unclean, but here too the blood can be dangerous to men. On the other hand, in north-eastern Arnhem Land, even when she is ritually tabu during childbirth or menstruation a woman is sacred for, symbolically, blood is one of the focal interests of religious life. Here, also, at first menstruation a girl is secluded in a hut. She is not expected to move away from it, but if she does she should use two digging sticks in the manner of walking sticks, just as the mythical Djanggawul sisters did when they travelled across the country with their sacred *rangga* poles. (See Warner, 1937/58: 75.) But she is not entirely segregated: if she is already living with her husband, which is most likely the case, she remains in the same camp with him. Her mother red-ochres her, and she is decorated, particularly with a string 'harness', here called *maidga.* Warner mentions (*ibid.*, 310) that at such a time a girl is painted with a flying fox design associated with death: and her ritual death may, perhaps, be implied. In the Rose River area of eastern Arnhem Land, as part of the Kunapipi, young girls are deflowered on the sacred ground with a specially shaped boomerang. The same thing is done symbolically to those who do not need the operation. This is a counterpart of the subincision rite and it is followed by ritual plural intercourse. The Mara of the Roper River have a similar rite. At Groote Eylandt the *labia majora* are cut off, a rite connected with the Wuradilagu cult—which spread, but without this operation, into north-eastern Arnhem Land.

Broadly speaking, then, although girls go through some kind of initiation (or puberty ritual) in most parts of Aboriginal Australia, none of this is so spectacular, formalized, or prolonged as for males. Nor does it involve the whole community in quite the same way. And it lacks the teaching of esoteric details directly relevant to sacred life. Even though there is something of this, the focus is narrower than with the men. Throughout, there is a pervasive theme: a rite, or series of rites, marks the onset of puberty, often highlighted by a physical operation; usually it entails separation from the round of everyday life, a social withdrawal signified by a spatial withdrawal, a movement away from the main camp; the return to that life, as an active participant, but no longer of the same status as before. The change in status is represented by some symbolic action such as ritual bathing, or merely by a public reception, a public acknowledgment. Other rituals take place throughout a woman's life, both before and after this: but it is these which emphasize her state of sexual maturity and ability to bear children, her formal transition from dependent daughter to relatively independent wife and mother.

* * * * *

In Aboriginal societies, most relationships are articulated in kin terms. All activities are carried out in the company of persons who are bound to one another in conventionally defined ways. They not only know what to expect from others, and how they will respond to certain situations, but are reasonably sure that participation and co-operation will be forthcoming if the occasion demands. Over and above the network of obligations and responsibilities linking persons together in, more or less, a mutually satisfying system, there is an atmosphere of familiarity and intimacy possible only in a group which disallows the concept of stranger for anyone within its midst, and even well outside its own social limits.

In initiation, whether for boys or for girls, this emphasis on kin relationship is important. The range of persons involved in male initiation varies quite markedly throughout the Continent, even to the extent that members of a nearby tribal unit may take part; but the basic core of participants is the novice's immediate family of orientation, in conjunction with male members of another family group who have a vested interest in the proceedings. These last are the initiators; if circumcision or some other physical rite is entailed, it is from their ranks that the operator is selected. These persons stand in a certain kind of relationship to one another, and to the novices: all of them are close kin. Around this nucleus is a further circle of kinsfolk who have particular actions to perform —such as enacting totemic rites.

It is not only a boy's male kin who participate, in one way or another. His sisters, his mother, his betrothed wife, and a range of others as well, are conventionally expected to mark the occasion of any ritual crisis in which he is a central figure—just as they are in the event of his death. Their co-operation may take the form of food tabus. In western Arnhem Land, for instance, among such tribes as the Maung, Gunwinggu and Jiwadja, the mother and close sisters of a boy going through the three biggest rituals are subject to the same prohibitions as he is. Or it may take the form of a speech tabu: thus in the same region, the mother of an *ubar* initiate may not raise her voice above a whisper until he has been through the main section of the rites. Or again, and this practice is widespread, they may commemorate a boy's first initiation, his formal transition from childhood to adulthood, and show their sympathy for him at the same time, by scarring their own bodies. For each category of relative a specific part of the body is allocated: and this is not identical for all areas. Among the Maung, for example, a boy's mother cuts three horizontal scars on her belly (this is fairly widespread); his sister, the same on the calf of each leg; his betrothed wife, or any girl who calls him close 'husband', the same on her buttocks, just above the thighs. And so on.

Participation in all these respects, according to local conventions, is traditionally obligatory. The closer the relationship, quite often, the more conscientious or fervent the acceptance of these obligations—thus, a mother may gash her head as well. But the way in which each person should contribute to the smooth running and the success of the occasion is more or less clearly defined. In female initiation the number of persons involved is more restricted; except in the more highly formalized rituals, or the public reception in the main camp, there may be only immediate kin with a sprinkling of affines, or potential affines. Male initiation is a social event; all those present in the camp, or small community, participate in one way or another, and most are actively engaged in dancing, performing certain duties, making emblems, painting body designs, or singing. With the initiation of girls, the focus is usually much narrower.

In social terms, initiation emphazises and underwrites the demarcation between the sexes, and between adults and children. It means increased status for some of those immediately concerned —the novice, the initiators and the parents. Moreover, over and above the social occasion of initiation, of making boys into social adults, and the symbolism inherent in the relevant ritual acts, there is the expectation of some return on the part of many: for the parents, a social adult added to their family; for the novice, a wife from his initiator; for the initiator, a son-in-law, and gifts; for active participants, payment for services rendered. It is not simply a matter of gain, tangible or intangible, for some, gifts and services for others: it means also the assumption of obligations and responsibilities. The socio-economic ramifications of initiation are many.

CHAPTER VI

The Life Cycle: Marriage to Old Age

Conventionally, then, initiation marks a turning point from childhood to adulthood, but not as a simple transition from one undifferentiated state to another. There are grades, or degrees. A boy of six or seven years old is not automatically a man once he has been circumcised, even though this is something which affirms that he is a male in contrast to the state of being a female. Generally speaking it is not until he marries that a man, or a woman, is recognized as fully adult by the rest of the community.

MARRIAGE AND MARITAL RELATIONS

Husband and wife are expected, ordinarily, to become parents, and to rear sons and daughters who will repeat in all essential features their own progress from childhood to adulthood. The whole emphasis in this process, through the initiation rites, for example, is not on being different from previous generations, but on being the same. Of course, there is some variation. The situation never is exactly the same. Even so, these Aboriginal societies are, or were, tradition-oriented. They stress the value of keeping to the forms laid down in the past, rather than building on them with a view to creating something different, or new.

Such societies have been labelled 'repetitive'. Childhood here is a preparation for adulthood, and not merely a prelude to it. A girl can watch the behaviour of her mother and grandmother, confident that when she grows up her life will be very much like theirs. A boy can be reasonably sure that he will follow in the steps of his father and grandfather. There is a security, a certainty, about this which is harder to find in our own society, where specialization has brought with it a much wider range of models for children to imitate, and a son is more likely than not to take up an occupation which differs from his father's. It is not simply that an Aboriginal child learns to be more or less self-supporting economically—able to fend for himself, or herself. It is a matter of taking over the values and ideas and beliefs of earlier generations, modifying them perhaps, but absorbing them in essence, and handing them on in turn to the next generation.

Childhood is, also, a preparation for marriage, to a degree that it is not in our own society. Children grow up in semi-open surroundings, with the whole life of the camp going on about them. Nothing, as a rule, is deliberately concealed from them or closed to them, except certain rites and the objects, songs and myth-material associated with these, or the temporary segregation camps of people going through such crises as menstruation or childbirth. They hear all the details of local quarrels, watch the fights, listen to all the scandal. Children have been called the best informers and the best gossips in an Aboriginal camp. They may practise swear words or obscenities among themselves, delighting in their own daring, or play quite frankly at husbands and wives. To speak of girls being married at puberty, then, does not mean the same thing as it would for a girl in Australian-European society. An Aboriginal girl of that age has been more or less adequately prepared to be a wife, to collect food, to cook for her husband, to care for children, and so on. Less is expected of her than of an older woman, and usually there are others to help in getting food and firewood. When a girl refuses to go to her husband, as sometimes happens, in most cases it is not marriage as such that she is resisting, but the particular husband who has been selected for her.

Sexual Relations

Pre-marital and extra-marital relations shade into each other. Nowhere in Aboriginal Australia, as far as we know, are they totally, and consistently, banned. In many cases they are encouraged—up to a point. Freedom of sexual expression is restricted by rules governing conduct between persons, or categories of persons, and subject to sanctions in varying degrees. But the kinship system itself serves to pin-point the range of the most eligible partners, as well as to disqualify others, while the religious life offers opportunities over and above those available in ordinary everyday activity. The whole subject of sex is treated frankly, as a normal and natural factor in human life.

Marriage as such is not the only circumstance in which people cannot always choose their sexual partners, or the time and place of coming together. A husband can lend his wife to another man without her consent, although usually the matter of consent is incidental where a wife has been brought up to regard this as one of her duties—and may even welcome it for the sake of variety, depending on how attractive she finds the man to whom she is assigned. In other instances where intercourse is prescribed, and formalized, sex has a religious connotation: during the Kunapipi rituals, for instance, in the *gurangara,* or after a girl's initiation, or during the *mindari* of the Dieri. (See Elkin, 1934: 185.) Or the margin of choice may be wider, with participation optional, and more opportunity for personal selection—as in the *djamalag* of western Arnhem Land, and the *lilga* of the Katherine-Daly River area. Or sexual relations may be used as a means of social control, to punish a woman for 'too much running around' by forcing her to be intimate with a number of men, one after another. All these are legitimate forms of licence.

Except where the partners are forbidden to have such close relations in ordinary life (mother-in-law and son-in-law in the Kunapipi, for example), they may perhaps meet on other and less formal occasions as well—in conditions of their own choosing. But although passing liaisons outside marriage are nothing out of the way, and even expected, they should not be carried out blatantly: and assignations are usually made in secrecy, especially when a husband or wife is known to be jealous.

The marriage rules outlined in Chapter III might give the impression that there is no place in Aboriginal Australia for the concept of romantic love. Certainly it is not a dominating theme in everyday life. So much is against it: the formal patterning of marriage preferences, infant and child betrothal, the narrow scope for individual initiative, the restraints written into the kinship system. Nevertheless it has played some part in the lives of a great many traditionally oriented Aborigines. Even in its simplest form, as a matter of fleeting physical attraction, it shows that personal choice is a factor to be reckoned with in spite of conventional measures to keep it within bounds. But just as happens anywhere else, the attraction need not be mutual.

Love magic is believed to be one answer to this. Force is another, but its disadvantages are more obvious. A lot depends on how permanent either or both of the two people concerned want their association to be. They may see it as nothing more than a casual affair. Or one of them, at least, may try to put it on a more formal basis. One possible complication here is that, whether or not the man already has a wife, the girl he wants (or the girl who wants him) is almost certain to have been betrothed to someone else even if she is not actually married. Also, a person may be attracted by someone in a forbidden category. This fact in itself can lend spice to the adventure—if it is only a passing attachment. But it may be fatal if two people in a prohibited relationship try to marry—or could have been fatal, in the past, to either or both.

A short, uncomplicated episode, during a ceremonial gathering for instance, may have no emotional aftermath, or repercussions. Sweetheart relationships, in contrast, are less matter-of-fact and more romantic in tone. The lovers may exchange gifts, or vows; they may be just as jealous as any husband or wife, if not more so. They may 'sing' for each other; or their conversations may be overheard, or reconstructed, by a songman, and later reproduced in the form of a song.

In most areas there are love songs of one kind or another, sung by men, or by women, or by men and women together. Some are of magical intent. (See Chapter IX.) Most of the 'Gossip' songs of western Arnhem Land are about sweethearts, or about affection between men and women, for these subjects have the greater appeal to the composer and his audience. So, in a different and much less direct way, are the 'Rose River' and 'Goulburn Island' love song cycles of north-eastern Arnhem Land. They are more blatant in the *djarada,* which has spread over much of north Australia and has close links with the Kunapipi, or the *ududju* or, futher south, the *jilbindji.* Songs of this kind emphasize erotic aspects: some the excitement of the adventure, or the enjoyment of the act, or the pleasures and vicissitudes of the personal experience itself, others the wider vista of sex-in-relation-to-fertility. Many of them leave little to the imagination—especially those which are designed to stimulate erotic feelings, if not erotic behaviour.

For the most part, the songs dwell on physical characteristics in only a generalized way, which could apply to anyone. Ordinary stories, and myths in prose, are more specific; but even here the allusions are brief, inferences rather than detailed statements. It would be hard to derive from any of these a clear picture of local standards of physical beauty. They must be taken in conjunction with everyday comments on people, everyday actions in relation to them. To see a number of men painstakingly plucking out each little hair from their own chests, expressing distaste at the notion of a hairy body, is to learn something about local attitudes in this respect; or to notice a couple of men, in eastern Arnhem Land, trying consistently to cover up the shining bald patch at the top of their heads, or trimming their little wispy 'Macassan-style' beards.

Standards of beauty vary, from one area to another: but obvious deformities or handicaps—lameness, blindness, deafness, cleft palate, Boomerang Legs, face or limbs eroded by yaws or leprosy—are appraised in much the same way everywhere, as a personal disadvantage. This is not to say that a person need suffer physical hardship in consequence of any or all of them, except in a bad season in poor country when survival of the group is at stake. Other things being equal, such a person is helped and cared for, in the framework of the kinship system within which he, or she, has a place which does not rest on physical appearance, or physical achievements. Nevertheless, over and above these conventional claims, some people are obviously in a much better position than others. To the assets of a healthy body, and clear skin, they add such extras as a good crop of hair or a straight nose (parts of the Arnhem Land coast), or a nose broad and strong across the nostrils (parts of the Western Desert), or moderately long legs and arms (Western Desert). And so on. On the Arnhem Land coast, and in the Western Desert too, to call a woman 'bony' or 'skinny' is to use a term of abuse; but this is a relative matter. Few Aborigines, traditionally, become grossly fat, although there are cases in the contact situation. One woman in the east Kimberleys, for instance, past middle age, grew so heavy that eventually she could not lift herself from the ground; and her daughter, still fairly young but already starting to resemble her, was first neglected and then rejected by her husband—just as men in eastern Arnhem Land have refused to live with wives who are physically displeasing to them.

But whatever the area, and however frankly or otherwise this is expressed, as far as physical attractiveness is concerned the greatest stress is on youth. A girl who has just reached puberty is most desirable as a spouse—one with small, rounded breasts, not yet drooping after years of childbearing; so is a young man, newly initiated. This quality of youth, like physical features which conform with local standards of what is good in a face or a body, is an advantage in love affairs: and it is undoubtedly an asset in marriage, insofar as it puts a person in a better bargaining position in any dispute—although this may be counterbalanced by the jealousy it provokes. In a situation where women are regarded as old at menopause, or even before, the period of youth for them is obviously all too short; and even though they may take various measures to enhance their appearance—rubbing their hair and bodies with fats and red ochre, decorating their hair with gum-nuts, wearing an elegant nose-stick on special occasions—these, of course, like the songs in their love-magic series, have only a limited effectiveness. At the same time, widows past this age do marry men who have deliberately chosen them (as in several Western Desert examples)—and not simply for the contributions they might make to the family economy. Between extreme physical attractiveness and extreme physical ugliness, adolescence and old age, are the majority of ordinary men and women, who seem to have no consistent difficulty in finding sexual partners, and are allocated wives or husbands in accordance with their particular social system, whether or not they want to take any initiative in this respect themselves.

In the Great Victoria Desert the *wongi* allows for intimacy between the sexes from before initiation until marriage, and in some cases afterward as well. In this way young people can have sexual experience during the period before they are allowed to marry: a man, until he is subincised or cicatrized; a girl, until her husband is chosen, or while she is waiting for her betrothed to be initiated. Male and female sweethearts are *wonidjara* and *njidjara*. To attract or retain each other's affection they may use love magic, or the girl may expect small gifts, like pieces of tobacco. Although there appears to be some experimentation with different partners, one feature of the *wongi* is that such an affair may end in marriage. In the case of extra-marital relations, the ideal is that they should be transitory and not interfere with marriage—although they occasionally do so. A married man or woman may take advantage of the *wongi*, in a general way, for the entertainment and novelty of the adventure. More specifically, a man may turn to it at times when he cannot associate with his wife: during menstruation, during pregnancy, and for a period after childbirth, or when he is away visiting another camp where there is someone who stands in the right relationship to him. His wife, on her part, may take advantage of his absence or of his enforced spell of abstinence until the penis incisure heals after cutting. But there is always the risk of elopement should two people become fond of each other, and this can have repercussions outside their immediate circle.

In western Arnhem Land, to take an area where living conditions are very different to those in the desert, the picture of sexual relations outside marriage shows some overall resemblance. A girl may have her first full sexual association at the age of about nine, sometimes earlier, a boy not until twelve to fourteen or so. When a boy and girl have had some preliminary experience together, both may turn to older partners to broaden their range. For the boy this is a matter of prestige, something he can boast about to others of his own age; and his period of pre-marital liaisons may extend until his marriage between about eighteen and twenty-five, sometimes later. But a girl may pass from childhood experiments directly to marriage without any intervening affairs.

There is no way of telling what the indigenous past was like in this region. The impact of 'Macassans', Japanese, and Europeans must have stimulated many changes in the local scene, and especially in this field of relations between the sexes. Oenpelli, for instance, is just across the East Alligator River from the buffalo country, where the original inhabitants are virtually extinct; the local story of Aboriginal contact with the outside world is a depressing and, on the whole, a sordid one. Whatever the reasons, in the Oenpelli-Goulburn Islands area there is a long tradition of relative freedom in sexual affairs. These range from short, matter-of-fact encounters, with no romantic frills, to fairly prolonged liaisons with all the trimmings of romantic love—just as the 'Gossip' songs range from an almost clinical bluntness to sentimental outpourings which say little about the physical aspects of such a relationship, except in drawing attention to the scars and scratches which bear witness to an enjoyable erotic encounter. It is this emotional tie, combining a sexual association with vows of affection and demands for exclusive fidelity, which is signified in the Gunwinggu word *mararaidj*, 'sweetheart'. A man may express violent resentment and jealousy of his sweetheart's husband, while she takes the same stand in regard to his wife. They may declare their faithfulness to each other as 'real' wife and husband, sigh over each other's belongings, confide in go-betweens who are entrusted with carrying small gifts from one to the other. Or they may elope together. Depending on how seriously they feel in the matter, or how ready her husband is to relinquish her, their liaison may be transformed into a publicly recognized marriage—or it may drift to a close, as one or both of them turn to new partners. Whatever the outcome, in an Aboriginal camp such things cannot be kept secret for long, and quarrels flare up from time to time—between the lovers themselves, between one of them and the husband or wife of the other, or between the relatives of any of them who feel that they are directly interested or involved. The 'Gossip' songs afford a safety valve, but they can also exacerbate the situation.

It is a matter for debate whether sexual relations outside marriage, accompanied by gifts, can be classified as prostitution. But prostitution can be defined as the selling of sexual favours without the expectation of marriage, and without the setting up of a specific dyadic relationship, as between sweethearts or lovers: a transient association in which recompense, or payment is crucial. The contract, implied or explicit, is relatively impersonal: one partner can be substituted for another without altering the nature of the arrangement. A specific action, or series of actions, is paid for in a more or less direct way; and the bond between the persons involved is minimized. In contrast, in most instances of pre- and extra-marital relations in Aboriginal Australia the gift, if any, seems to be incidental; however acceptable in itself, it is regarded as a love token rather than a payment. There are possibly exceptions, as some cases seem to suggest; but usually a sexual association between lovers involves mutual obligations—although not to the same extent as in the case of marriage. For instance, in north-east Arnhem Land a man who has been intimate with a woman other than his wife is obliged to give her food on request, or if she visits his camp; but because a wife usually resents this he may try either to evade this obligation or to cope with it surreptitiously. And in western Arnhem Land is what might almost be called an institution of secondary husbands/wives, or 'second class' marriage. In most cases it is not elaborated to this extent, although it is in a few.

Elkin (1938-40: 74-8; 1954: 129-30) speaks of the Dieri *pirauru* system of "secondary marriage". Howitt (1904: 181-7) and Siebert (1910) claim that this is a form of 'group marriage'. Thomas (1906*a*: 110-41) disagrees. So does Malinowski, pointing out that "Every form of licence must be subject to customary rules", and that the *pirauru* relationship is no exception, any more than is wife lending or wife exchange. (Malinowski, 1913: 108-23.) To Elkin (1938-40: 74-7), *pirauru* relationships are "extra-family relationships of a marital type" which are "distinguished from irregular sexual unions", and are governed by specific conventions. The persons immediately concerned must be related to each other in the correct way, and as a rule already have married status before they can enter into an arrangement of this kind. The maximum number of *pirauru* relationships a person may contract is not stipulated, but ritual sanction is necessary in each case.

Perhaps because of the stress on heterosexual relations, there are very few reports of sexual abnormalities in Aboriginal Australia. Possibly there is an element of sexual exhibitionism in some instances of group intercourse; but this is accentuation of a normal interest, or a normal practice, rather than a substitute for more ordinary heterosexual activity. In actual life it is hard to find properly authenticated cases of sodomy or of bestiality, although there are a few stories and myths relating to these—and to male homosexuality. Masturbation and some homosexual experiments are reported among boys or young men who are temporarily segregated from women (Western Desert; Arnhem Land); but although these are not encouraged, the only reaction seems to be the warning that they will weaken themselves if they do this. Men take the part of women in various sacred rites, even engaging in symbolic coitus with male actors: but they do not carry over this identification into everyday life—or at least, not overtly. Homosexual relations among females are rarer still. The close physical contacts which many Aborigines indulge in are deceptive in this respect. They do not necessarily point to sexual intimacy;

and in fact husbands and wives, or sweethearts, avoid caressing each other in public, except in the relative privacy of their own camp or windbreak. Men in certain kin relationships (cross-cousins, for instance) may go about with arms entwined, or hands clasping each other's shoulders. Women sitting together, for example at evening ceremonies in the Western Desert, may be packed tightly together from choice, not necessity, leaning against one another, touching one another's bodies and hair. But this emphasis on proximity to others, or to certain others, is not out of place in a social environment of which people, not material things, are the most important and most obvious component.

Getting married

In Aboriginal Australia, generally speaking, the question of whether or not a person should marry does not arise. It is conventionally expected of everyone as a matter of course, and the main problem is, who will be selected.

A married man is fully, and unquestionably, an adult. Having children confirms his status, even in cases where that is not an acknowledged pre-requisite. And this is so for a woman as well. Marriage and the elementary family of father, mother, and child, are taken very much for granted: but if validation is needed, it can be found in the religious mythology. Even with mother-surrogates and so on, even with the diffusion of responsibility—among relatives when children are very young, among other adults of the local unit or horde as they grow older—the family is the most effective group in which a child's elementary training and socialization take place.

Traditionally speaking, unmarried women are very rare indeed, but there are occasionally unmarried men. It is not, usually, that they do not want to marry, but rather that they have no opportunity of doing so. The reason may be the need to wait for a betrothed wife to mature physically, or disparity in the male-female ratio; or all the eligible women may be already married. A man may have no close relative in the right category whose duty it is to supply him with a wife. Or if he has such a relative, but also has a number of elder brothers, there may not be enough girls to go round. In north-east Arnhem Land a man with several close mother's brothers, or even one mother's brother provided he has plenty of daughters, is in a fortunate position. If he has none, or there are no available daughters, he may be obliged to remain single. These days, increased life expectancy through medical attention and the official curb on violence means that, other things being equal, a man is less likely to predecease his wife or wives so that they pass to someone else. But elopements are less likely to result in bloodshed, and there are pressures against polygyny, so that wives may be more evenly distributed. Also, there are men who express reluctance to marry on the grounds that this would curtail their sweetheart activities. Throughout Aboriginal Australia, conventionally speaking, a man is permitted to have at least two wives concurrently—whereas a woman is formally restricted to one husband at a time. She may have several in succession, however. Over a lifetime, most men and women who survive to middle age can expect to have more than one spouse. A girl betrothed to a man much older than herself is more likely than not to outlive him and go to someone else.

In fact, as far as a woman is concerned there may be virtually no period of her life, except in her old age, when she is not either betrothed or married—or widowed. Hart and Pilling (1960: 14) say that in the traditional past on Melville and Bathurst islands there was no concept of an unmarried female. This holds good fairly generally. The marriage bond may seem, in a few cases, very tenuous indeed. In north-eastern Arnhem Land several women have been rejected by their husbands because they are blind, or crippled: there are others, especially in polygynous families, who spend long periods away from their husbands with their married daughters or other relatives. And some widows refuse to marry again, at forty or so, on the grounds of being too old. But this varies even within one area.

Infant betrothal is common throughout the Continent. In other words, apart from the issue of 'who is to be betrothed to whom', the concept of an ideally correct marriage may include the question of 'when'. If arrangements are made before the girl, in particular, is able to voice an opinion on the matter, this in itself is said to show that the union is more than a whim—that it is a longstanding affair, thoughtfully decided upon, and so has more chance of enduring. The girl now has an extra protector concerned with her welfare; and her parents are assured that, should they die before she becomes an adult, they have done their best to safeguard her future. If their promised son-in-law dies before the marriage is consummated, they can try again; preferably, as a rule, the girl will go to one of his close brothers.

The Gunwinggu of western Arnhem Land speak of a betrothed wife as *gulba-gen, gulba* meaning blood: ideally a girl should be betrothed at birth, before the afterbirth blood has ceased to flow. The framework, or the machinery of selection, is already there. A woman is expected, as a first choice, to give her daughter to one of her mother's mother's brother's sons, not necessarily the eldest. The closer the relationship, the more appropriate the union. After her marriage, therefore, all the interested parties wait for her to give birth to a girl, so that the union can be arranged. If the child is a boy, they will pin their hopes on the next one; but some men have been frustrated by the failure of a potential mother-in-law to bear any daughters at all. The word *gulbagen* is used in a general way for any betrothed wife, regardless of the circumstances of betrothal; but these ideal requirements remain in the background, ready to come to the surface in quarrels. A husband may point out that his wife has no right to be jealous, because she was not betrothed to him in the proper way. Or she may say the same to him, declaring that they are not 'really' married, that theirs is only a sweetheart relationship.

Even where betrothal takes place later than this, ideally it should be settled before a girl reaches puberty. Also, ideally, a husband should be older than his wife. In practice this is not always possible, but when there is a marked discrepancy (for example when a girl has reached puberty while her promised husband is about seven or eight years old) the betrothal is likely to collapse. Child betrothals continue to be arranged in Arnhem Land, and in the Western Desert, but more flexibly than a few years ago. Today people tend to say, 'This is what we would like to happen, but it may not', rather than, 'This is what will happen.'

Whatever the age of the two people immediately concerned, the betrothal agreement is made with deceptive informality. Important as it is, there is usually no ceremony to mark the occasion. And no matter how detailed the discussion, or how careful the arrangements, they can provide no firm assurance that the marriage will in fact be consummated, or that the girl will stay with her husband. If she is at loggerheads with her parents, insisting that she wants to marry someone else, they may try to change her mind, urging that they know what is best for her. But if the girl is determined, even threats of spearing (by her husband and his relatives, or her 'brothers') may not shake her.

There is not enough information on the score of how many young women resent, even if not to the extent of active opposition, marrying men they have not chosen for themselves. Probably they are in a minority, in circumstances where family-arranged unions are accepted as normal, offering a woman comparative economic and social security. The exceptions, commemorated in myth and story as well as in more or less factual accounts, keep the possibility of rebellion alive and at the same time serve as a warning to girls who might try to imitate them. In the mythology of western Arnhem Land, for example, this is a popular theme: the reluctant bride who resists her older husband because she is obsessed with her young sweetheart, and his final revenge. (The sacred Jurawadbad myth, in Chapter VII, makes use of this framework.)

It is to guard against such upsets that in so many Aboriginal societies a girl is taken to her betrothed husband's camp from time to time, in some cases from babyhood on, in the hope that she will get used to him, that when the time comes for marriage he will not be a stranger to her. If in fact she has no special preference for one man rather than another, other considerations can affect the way she looks at her marriage. One is whether her promised husband is active in hunting, whether he can bring in enough meat or fish as his contribution to the family supplies. Another is how he is likely to treat her personally. And another has to do with their sexual relationship. Some women say that a young husband is usually more jealous than an older one, that he keeps too tight a rein on his wife. An old man, they claim, is more tolerant, more ready to turn a blind eye to his wife's sweetheart liaisons provided she does not neglect him, and so allows her to have the advantages of a steady marriage and still have variety in sexual affairs. This savours to some extent of rationalization, an attempt to make the best of a situation, to have it both ways.

But if arranged marriages make for personal discontent or dissatisfaction in individual cases, this affects men as well as women. On the formal level, a man may be just as passive a figure while the negotiations go on around him. Nevertheless, for him the issues are simpler. He does not have to choose between one woman and another when it comes to marriage. If he likes, he can take another wife, although it makes things easier if there is no opposition from the wife or wives he already has. Some women object to sharing a husband, and resist any attempt to make them do so. Others take a contrary stand, often for practical reasons. An older woman may nag at her husband to take a younger wife who can do most of the work. Or a wife may like the idea of a companion who can help in getting food and firewood and looking after the children. A second wife can be useful when the first is ill; and at times when she may not have sexual relations with her husband, she knows that he has a legitimate alternative, one over whom she has some degree of control.

The major ways of arranging or contracting a marriage are: through betrothal arranged entirely by the respective families, whether or not the two principals themselves are consulted about it; through personal selection within a limited range, but with the approval of the families; through elopement; through 'capture'; through the sororate (marrying a deceased wife's sister) or levirate (marrying a deceased husband's brother), or through inheritance of some other sort.

In the first two cases there may be a simple marriage rite, but not necessarily so. Usually for a marriage to be recognized it is enough that a couple should live together publicly and assume certain responsibilities in relation to each other and to their respective families. The cementing of a marriage through the handing over of gifts is significant, as one criterion of the union. But consummation itself may not be enough, and (as on the Daly) a marriage may not be considered a marriage until after the birth of at least one child. (See Chapter IV in reference to the *kue*.) When there are rites, these are unobtrusive. Among the Dieri two firesticks are tapped together. The Adnjamatana place two firesticks beside a betrothed man who is awaiting his wife, and the pair eventually kindle a fire. In both instances one is a grooved 'hearth stick', the other the drill stick for twirling in it—symbolically, female and male, complementary in the process of firemaking. (Mountford and Harvey, 1941: 162.) The Lower River Murray people and the Ngadjuri did much the same, and there are other references in the literature. In western Arnhem Land a girl is sent by her mother to 'take fire' to her new husband's camp. For eastern Arnhem Land, Warner (1937/58: 74-96) speaks of "several degrees of marriage", until finally the girl sets up house with her husband, but the union is not really considered permanent until the first child is born: Warner adds, "it now has become a fully developed family, and except for the wife's being stolen by another man there would be little chance of permanent rupture even if she ran away". In the Great Victoria Desert the rite in which a girl formally takes up residence in her husband's camp is, as usual, a public transaction; but often the man who hands over his sister to her betrothed (his *maridji*, brother-in-law) spears him in the thigh.

Elopement seems to be more common than the ideal picture allows for, and in many instances, in actual practice, accepted as a more or less legitimate way of effecting a marriage, or at least as a possibility not to be condemned out of hand. This potential tolerance may have been reinforced by outside pressures, modifying the indigenous systems; but certainly it is latent in love-magic songs and rites, including the women's *djarada* and *jawalju*. (One popular string-figure in the Victoria River district, among young women idly relaxing in the camp in the late afternoons, was always greeted with laughter: two match-like figures moving rapidly across an open framework—*wadji*, 'wrong side', lovers running away together.)

The runaway couple almost invariably make for another area, preferably one not easily accessible; but in most cases a revenge party will follow them, and perhaps kill or injure either or both. Among the Aranda a woman caught in the act of eloping is severely punished, if not actually killed. Spencer and Gillen (1938: 556-8) say that elopements often lead to conflict between local groups. In any case, the injured husband will expect compensation of some kind; when this takes the form of goods, it suggests that he is being paid to waive his rights in the woman who was previously his wife. In addition, there is always the threat of sorcery; even if, these days, an Arnhem Lander runs away to Darwin with a married woman, people say they are not out of reach of her husband's vengeance. In north-eastern Arnhem Land, although either party can take the initiative in a runaway marriage, from all accounts the woman is more often to blame. The man's relatives may try to send her back to her 'real' husband, to avoid fighting. (See Warner, 1937/58: 86.) She may be led back to him at the end of a length of possum fur string. If he accepts the string, he wants her back; if he cuts it, he does not. String cutting is tantamount, here, to divorce. Or the husband himself may elope with another woman. Among the Kurnai, according to Howitt (1904: 273), this is the only way in which most men can get wives. It must be done secretly; and the woman must be not only willing, but responsible for making the choice. If a man and his friend both have unmarried sisters, they may arrange to elope together. Howitt adds (*ibid.*, 274-6) that Kurnai magic men (*bunjil-yenjin*) arrange elopements by using song-spells, and that during one such ceremony, held to the south of Lake Wellington in about 1855, "ten or a dozen young couples" eloped. He sets out two of the songs, but there does not seem to have been much secrecy about them.

Then there is marriage by capture. Spencer and Gillen (1938: 103-4, 554-5) speak of this as one possible procedure, although among the Aranda a very uncommon one. Occasionally a man seizes a woman from a member of his own group, in which case he may or may not be able to persuade some of his kinsfolk to help him. In north-eastern Arnhem Land this may happen when a man feels that a particular woman he wants has, unfairly, gone to someone else. Or he may simply be attracted to her, and abduct her, killing her husband in the process—without paying any compensation for her unless her father or brothers are strong enough to enforce it; and the same holds good for the relatives of the man he has killed. Skirmishing of this kind takes place as a rule within the same moiety, but mostly between men of different clans and linguistic units. Or, as now and then among the Aranda, a woman may be captured from another area. In this case it may be associated with an avenging party, the men involved being allotted wives of men they have killed. Warner mentions that women may be taken, incidentally, as a result of an ambush in which their husbands are killed—but not as the main object of the attack, although their capture may be regarded as retaliation for an earlier theft of women. Howitt and others too discuss this form of marriage.

Being married

Polygyny is a legitimate form of marriage in Aboriginal Australia: that is, a man can have more than one wife at a time. Nevertheless, the majority of unions are monogamous—one man, one wife. Many writers consider this topic of polygyny: Howitt, for instance, Spencer and Gillen, Malinowski, Elkin, Warner, Kaberry, Berndt, among others. The number of women a man actually has at any given time, in a polygynous marriage, varies a great deal. In most desert regions the maximum is about six, with two or three much more usual; this is so in western Arnhem Land too, except that there is more reshuffling of marriage partners. In north-eastern Arnhem Land the figure is higher: anything up to ten or twelve is not regarded as odd, although actually most men have fewer than this; and the maximum of twenty to twenty-five, in the Cape Arnhem-Caledon Bay area, seems to be represented by only a single case. Hart and Pilling (1960: 17) mention a maximum of twenty-nine for Bathurst and Melville islands.

To some extent this hinges on a man's age, and the stage he has reached in his career. A man who starts off with one wife may gradually acquire others, either through his personal efforts or through inheritance, for instance after the death of an older brother or a father. Or an older brother who feels he has too many wives may hand over one of them, especially one he does not much care for—so putting the younger man in his debt, and at the same time not entirely relinquishing his claims on her, at least informally. Conversely, there are men who prefer not to have more than one wife, or two at the most, even when such opportunities come their way, on the grounds that additional wives bring extra responsibilities and cares which outweigh their advantages.

The reasons for polygynous unions are not wholly sexual. Economic considerations are important. So are prestige, and what can be called political alliances.

In north-eastern Arnhem Land the men with the most wives were originally those with a reputation as fighters, or with access to special trading monopolies. It is usually the forceful person with entrepreneurial learnings who is able to collect wives around him. Because of his reputation, and because he has goods which can be used as gifts in betrothal arrangements, fathers of eligible girls are very ready to negotiate. They may even promise their daughters to several men more or less simultaneously, with an eye to deriving whatever benefits they can, playing one suitor against another, hoping that the situation will eventually resolve itself. And in most cases it does, with the strongest taking the initiative and successfully claiming the girl. One does not find this same juggling with betrothals in desert areas, although there are isolated cases. As Warner points out (1937/58: 77-8, 157-8, 166-7), through the operation of kinship a middle-aged or older man often has a number of young girls as wives—whether or not he claims to be rearing them to marry his sons. (See Chapter III.) Warner (*ibid.*, 77) suggests too that "a man wants as many wives as he can get", if necessary "by stealing them or killing their husbands", or by bullying and bluff—spear-rattling, as this is called: "fighting strength" and "having many wives" are closely correlated. In his view the 'blood feud' kills a sufficient number of young men to allow the system of polygyny to function adequately. From our own work in this region we would not say that it is dependent only on that: the death rate from spearing seems to have been just as high among older men.

In the Kimberleys, Kaberry (1939: 113 *et seq.*) reports "a numerical predominance of men over women": of 174 Lungga unions, 12·6 per cent are polygynous. Her contention is that "the possibility of polygyny" in this region rests (among the Lungga) "not on the decimation of the males in warfare" (Warner's suggestion) but on the "fact that the girls marry at puberty, and the boys at the age of twenty or twentyfive".

These polygynous households, especially the larger ones, are an interesting study in themselves—almost small worlds of their own, in spite of the meshing of ties that link them with other persons and other units outside them. The husband is a central figure, the reason for all these women living together: his relations with each one of them are a matter of direct concern to the others as well. The way he distributes meat, fish, tobacco, anything in fact, is noticed and talked about. Within the family living-space, whether this is defined by a windbreak or a hut, or simply an indeterminate area focusing on one or more small open fires, privacy is not expected nor desired. In any case, privacy in such circumstances is a relative matter, a matter of courtesy—achieved by concentrating on one's own affairs, perhaps hearing or noticing what goes on in the next windbreak but saying nothing about it unless a quarrel or crisis looms up. But among co-wives sleeping in the same camp, there can be no secrecy about which of them their husband chooses to be intimate with, either in the course of the night or in the intervals of hunting and food-collecting during the day. And since he is unlikely to be impartial, this counts in the general assessment of 'who gets most, or least, and of what', an assessment which takes into account preference or neglect where children are concerned as well. The least show of favouritism, however plausibly explained, can lead to arguments; but when co-wives come to blows it is usually against one another, not him. The balance between co-operation and conflict fluctuates according to circumstances. Cliques form, and re-form. In eastern Arnhem Land an older wife or two may go off by themselves for weeks at a time to collect turtle eggs or seagull eggs, or to visit a married daughter; or a couple of wives may care for the younger children so that the others can move about unhampered and bring back enough food for them all.

There is no formal seniority among them, although usually some prestige attaches to being the first wife, or a wife who was promised to that particular husband as a baby and has remained with him since marriage—as contrasted with one who came to him through a sweetheart relationship, or one he took by force from another man. The first wife may try to claim certain privileges, largely of an intangible kind—more say in family discussions, for instance, or greater freedom to 'answer him back'. But this does not make her a favourite wife. In eastern Arnhem Land, particularly, the favourite is most likely to be the youngest, at least until the novelty wears off: and here a man with a large number of wives may arrange his sleeping quarters in a series of concentric circles, the youngest wives in the middle close to himself, older wives on the outside. By this means he can keep an eye on the young ones, those whom other men besides himself find the most attractive, while tactfully ignoring whatever may be going on in the outer circle.

Relations between husband and wife, as persons, do not rest on such formal matters as how the marriage was arranged, and whether or not it is monogamous. Even when there are several wives, this need not exclude affection between the two of them—just as a 'sweetheart marriage' is not inevitably a happy one. This is merely a different way of looking at the institution of marriage, as not simply an exclusive relationship between two people. But it *is* a relationship between two people, even though it brings in others as well. Whether they merely tolerate each other for want of something better, or from sheer inertia, or have a more positive affection for each other, depends to some extent on their personal experience together. If a woman neglects her husband or children, or is always looking for a new erotic experience: if he is so rough and hasty-tempered that she is afraid of him, or so weak that she cannot rely on him in a crisis—that marriage may perhaps last for a long time, but largely as a matter of habit: and it is likely to come to an abrupt end if the opportunity arises. On the other hand, a marriage need not be on the verge of a rupture because husband and wife are constantly quarrelling: in fact, they may prefer it that way.

This is another point on which information on an Australia-wide basis is lacking: the proportion of marriages which endure from their inception until the death of one partner, as against those which are dissolved for other reasons: or the number of unions of various kinds which people in any given area enter into in the course of a lifetime. We ourselves have a great deal of material of this sort, over a period of time, for a few regions: parts of the Western Desert, for instance, and western and eastern Arnhem Land. But for most of the Continent nothing comparable is available; and as far as the traditional past is concerned, it never will be now.

There are marriages which persist into the old age of both partners, with every appearance of devotion between them. This devotion does not take the form of suicide of one of them on the death of the other, except in a few mythical cases (in western Arnhem Land, for instance). But it is marked enough to contrast with the other extreme, in which a husband is responsible for his wife's death—not necessarily deliberately, or in cold blood. There are scattered instances of this: an eastern Arnhem Lander spearing his wife for unfaithfulness; a Gunwinggu man suddenly killing his wife in a state of mental 'blackout' as she slept one night; a Western Desert man playfully hurling spears at his wife and hitting her fatally 'by accident'. But partly because women do not use lethal weapons, except their fighting sticks, and partly because of the conventions governing their relations with men, it is only by indirect means like sorcery that wives are reputed to kill their husbands. In a number of areas men say that it is only by violence that a nagging wife can be silenced, or disciplined: her weapon is her tongue, his a spear or a club—and if an exasperated husband hits his wife too hard, he must bear the consequences.

Marriage means assuming extra responsibilities, setting up a separate household; and for a man, especially, it means the right not simply to express an opinion in local affairs but to have that opinion taken seriously. Although an Aboriginal family unit is not so isolated, so narrowly defined, as its counterpart in Australian-European society, although the boundaries between it and the outside world are more blurred, there is a concentration of obligations and expectations within it which gives it in some degree a special and separate identity.

Each marriage involves the establishment of a new social unit within the overall structure. This is more obvious when both partners are marrying for the first time, less so when a new wife goes to live with a man who has already established such a relationship with one or more others. Then it amounts to adding another elementary family to what is already there: a cluster of elementary families radiating out from its centre, the husband they share in common. The fact that it *is* a cluster of families, of course, increases the number and complexity of relationships within it. There is the relationship between husband and wife, or between husband and each wife, with all that this involves; between each of them, as parents, and each of the children they share, or have 'carried over' from other unions, or adopted; between each of the children themselves; between the wives; and between each family member and each close relative or affine—because these last impinge on them all in different ways.

When a wife comes to live with a new husband, and this usually means living in the same camp as some of his relatives as well, she is not as a rule moving into a new and alien territory at the same time. Whether or not her parents have tried to accustom her to him and his human surroundings early in life, in the great majority of cases all the people to whom she goes, including her husband, are already kin to her. They may not be close: but even if it is only nominal, the tie is there. Certainly a father's sister who is simply that—an aunt, so to speak—is not quite the same as a father's sister who is also a husband's mother. The potentiality may have been latent in their relationship in the first place, but once this is transformed into actuality it gives that relationship a different quality. Inseparable from it, now, are their individual relations with the person who has, from this point of view, come between them. In one sense this reinforces the bond between them. In another it increases the possibility of tension, if not actual conflict. This could be extended, speaking very generally, to all marriages between persons whose families are already linked by close ties of kinship. The assumption is that the positive benefits far outweigh any others: that the cumulative impact of these ties will help to stabilize the union, and that it in turn will reinforce them by carrying them through into the next generation.

Any particular union should be viewed in terms of the eligibility of the two people concerned, against the framework of local rules relating to marriage preferences and acceptable alternatives. These vary from one tribe to another, although there are basic rules common to all. Kinship, exogamy, totemic affiliations, are all aspects which must be considered, among others. Conventionally, marriage is an arrangement between families, not only between persons.

Digging out honey ants, to be placed in the wooden carrying dish in the foreground. Central Australia
(photo: courtesy C. P. Mountford)

A Goulburn Island artist, using a sheet of specially treated bark and a small hair brush, illustrates a local myth (1961)

Children at the sacred rockhole of Wonggarin, near Mount Deering (Kathleen Range, east-central Western Australia). This section of the site, sacred to Njirana and the Gunggaranggara women, is not secret (see Chapter VII). Note child's distended belly (1959)

At the sacred site of Wonggarin, above the rockhole. Here Njirana frightened the Gunggaranggara women with his *wanigi* emblem, which later became this sacred white gum tree (1959)

The metamorphosed stone penis of Njirana (secret-sacred), at Wonggarin (1959). This is anointed with fat and ochre and kept covered

Exhibiting and meditating upon sacred boards removed from their hiding place: Giles, Rawlinson Ranges (1959)

Rain-making ritual. The main performer rubs a pearlshell on the stone before him (on which is crushed grass, moistened with blood), then sucks it, spitting to induce rain. Musgrave Ranges, northern South Australia
(photo: courtesy C. P. Mountford)

Men relaxing after singing sacred songs: before them lie their beating sticks. Warburton Range (1959)

In betrothal, an exchange of gifts between the contracting parties implies their good faith, although in practice it is not as binding as ideal statements suggest. Even where personal considerations are uppermost, as in personally arranged marriages, elopement, and so on, the immediate families are directly implicated. Any form of marriage imposes, on the husband at least, obligations and responsibilities in relation to his wife's immediate kin. If it does not, then it is not, traditionally, a 'real' marriage. This is one criterion distinguishing marriage, as such, from a 'selfish' or individual-centred sweetheart relationship.

The line between marriage and temporary unions is not always easy to establish, either in local terms or in terms of outside definitions; but one criterion is public recognition of the union, as one which is expected to have some continuity, which accords with local views of what a marriage should be, and entails specific rights and obligations. (See R. Berndt, 1962*b*.)

Almost everywhere in Aboriginal Australia a wife is expected to be fertile, to bear children, and to care for them in more than a perfunctory way; but this is not everywhere an essential condition of marriage. There are childless marriages; but women who have borne no children at all seem to be rare. In most cases a mature woman who appears to have none turns out to have had at least one child who died in infancy, or was stillborn, or to have a history of miscarriages, if not of abortions. Presumably there are impotent men, but they seem to be very rare; and sterility among men is even harder to isolate, although there are examples in which women of childbearing age have had no children from one husband but several from the next.

Overall, a man has more rights over his wife than she has over him. He can reject her or leave her if he wishes without giving any grounds for his action except his own inclination. She may leave him temporarily, to visit her parents or for some other purpose: if he has other wives, and does not particularly want her, her absence may drift into permanency. Otherwise she can leave him finally only by elopement, in other words, by entering another union: but if she does this he is quite entitled to proceed against her and her lover. The new union is not regarded as a valid marriage until the first man relinquishes his rights in her, or accepts compensation. Although living together, or camping together, is one of the customary features of marriage, the fact that two people have ceased to do so is not in itself reason enough for assuming that they are no longer married. Further, a man has the right to dispose of his wife's sexual favours as he pleases, with or without her consent: but in doing so he does not relinquish his own claims to her. She cannot, however, do the same where he is concerned. Formally speaking, 'wife lending' has no counterpart in 'husband lending'.

Nevertheless, in one way and another both men and women have some opportunity for extra-marital associations, even if not always to the extent of secondary spouses. And all women are provided for, economically as well as socially. All are part of a family unit, with a definite place in social life. Certainly they depend heavily on men. Even the strongest and most masculine among them are not self-sufficient. And despite the considerable degree of informal authority which women have in their own sphere, including child-rearing, formal control is vested in men. A girl is under the control as well as the protection of her parents and other close relatives. After marriage this responsibility rests largely with her husband, although her father and brothers do not entirely relinquish the first (control), and she expects to be able to turn to them for the second (protection). When she is old, widowed or living apart from her husband, she relies most heavily on her own sons, or the sons of her sisters and brothers, or their sons: or, through her daughters, on her daughters' husbands.

In summary, the status of women, taken as a whole, is not equal to the status of men, taken as a whole; but this tells us only so much. It is more useful, without neglecting such formal considerations, to look at the relations between them in terms of separate and complementary spheres of activity, in marriage as in other aspects of living.

GROWING OLD

In an Aboriginal society, old age brings rewards as well as penalties. It is viewed more leniently, surrounded by less stress and marked by less loneliness, than in our own society. Rather it is assumed to imply added experience, to show that a person, man or woman, is in a position to advise others less well equipped.

On reaching middle-age a man may become a camp boss or headman. And during this phase of life, if he goes through a special initiation and is the right kind of person he may become a native doctor, able to work healing or beneficial magic as well as sorcery. Later, at perhaps fifty-five to sixty years old he may be classed as an elder. But, since as a rule an old man is no longer capable of much in the way of hunting and food-gathering, he comes to rely on his sons and his daughters' husbands. This is considered to be one of the major benefits of having children, who are expected to look after their parents in return for all the care and trouble that have been expended on them. In some cases it may be a sister's daughter's son, grandchild, or sister's son, who shoulders the major part of this responsibility.

If a man has a young wife, this gives him an energetic domestic help to attend to his comforts. At least, this is the way he believes it ought to be. An ideal marriage, from an old man's personal point of view, is one in which a young girl goes first to an elderly husband who can teach her to be a good wife, and perhaps finally hand her on to a younger man. There are differences of opinion about this. But some old women as well as men are not averse to young partners, and in a few areas people declare quite openly that such associations have a rejuvenating effect: that the best way to renew one's youth, or at least to live longer, is to have intercourse with someone who is sexually mature, but otherwise the younger the better. This does not always extend to a wish to marry them. Young wives can prove a nuisance to old husbands. Some elderly men admit frankly that they cannot cope with a lively young woman who not only takes sweethearts but maybe neglects her domestic responsibilities as well. If a man has been especially influential, and has kept up more than a shadow of his earlier reputation, he is in a better position. Old Wonggu of Caledon Bay kept a little entourage of women around him until the very last, including a couple of relatively young ones; but this was partly because as he grew older he grew increasingly permissive about their associations with other men in his own family circle. There are others who appear as pathetic figures. An old man who follows his young wife about, unwilling to let her out of his sight in case she should try to meet a young man, is regarded as a great joke. (There have been a few notorious examples in western Arnhem Land, for instance, and the Great Victoria Desert.) On the other hand, a young-to-middle-aged man who inherits an older wife, or marries her because he cannot get anyone else, may discard her as too old merely because other young men jeer at him for associating with her (as in several cases in north-eastern Arnhem Land).

Sensitive to such slights, or potential slights, considering that the strain of an unevenly balanced marriage is not worth the possible rewards, most old people who no longer have wives or husbands of their own age tend to withdraw from marital responsibilities. In any large camp there are likely to be at least two or three old women living together, and as many old men in their own separate windbreak or hut. The 'old women's camp' may be a centre for visiting women who have left their husbands behind, or even for unmarried girls. It may be no more than a temporary association between people who come together as a matter of convenience; but while it lasts it is a 'household' unit, one of the many which make up the total camp.

It is in the field of sexual relations that the influence of the old is weakest, except where it rests on force—older men may enjoy certain privileges in the sphere of religious ritual. Nevertheless, while diminished sexual attractiveness and the burden of physical disabilities in general are a source of frustration to both men and women, being old has advantages in other respects. An old man who is still active and alert is consulted by his juniors on traditional ways, precedents, performance of ritual, interpretation of myths. Through this he can derive authority and prestige. Not all do, of course, but this is probably one of the ideal expectations of most old men, although circumstances intervene to prevent more than a few of them from reaching this status. The whole system of maintaining authority within a community, and in relations between communities, depends on the older men's being able to control the younger people, not so much through force, as through a common set of beliefs. Contact with the outside world has altered this, in a wide range of ways. For instance, it has led to a cleavage between old people and younger people: and this is the more likely to happen because in our society we do not accord the same respect to the old that, by and large, the Aborigines do—or did. Aboriginal Australia is nominally gerontocratic; that is to say, the authority of the elders is paramount. But we use the term 'nominally' advisedly. It is true that most elders, not all, are viewed as the final repositories of custom and religious belief. But it is also true that middle-aged men are far more powerful in both the religious and secular or mundane spheres. Men become leaders and responsible elders, with a decisive voice in tribal matters, not on the grounds of age alone but because they have something to offer. This is the major criterion.

Aborigines on the whole treat their old people fairly well. But there are cases of neglect; and in desert regions during bad seasons, when a horde is on the move, it may be forced to leave its old people behind to starve or die of thirst. The Aborigines are, generally speaking, kindly folk; but there are many exceptions. Some are surly or quick-tempered, ready to quarrel on the slightest pretext; some are thoughtless and inconsiderate of others, even close kin, or husband or wife, or children; some are greedy or lascivious; some are untrustworthy, sly and irresponsible; some are cruel to the weak, and to animals and so on. Nicknames often point up such traits or commemorate incidents which illustrate them. Traditionally, in fact, throughout the Continent one would be able to find virtually the same range of human characteristics which appear in any society; no society has a monopoly of them.

But, again generally speaking, old men derive their authority and prestige through their knowledge of ritual and mythology. The whole authority system in Aboriginal Australia is based on the gradual acquiring of sacred and ritual knowledge, with the ultimate secrets in the hands of the older men—and, up to a certain point, in the hands of the old women as well. We have said little about old women: but most of what we have said about old men applies to them too. The tabus of avoidance, in kinship, for instance, are modified for the old; and in some areas old women can be present on the men's sacred ground during certain ceremonies, as younger women may not.

The end of the life cycle, insofar as physical existence is concerned, comes at death. Of course this may take place at any time in the course of growing up, or adulthood; but very old people are expected to die, younger people are not. Everywhere, some mortuary rite takes place at death. (See Chapter XIII.) And everywhere there is belief in the survival of the dead person's spirit. Whatever the local views on this, the physical body is always regarded as a temporary manifestation. The life of the spirit, which comes to the fore at certain crises (birth, initiation, and death, for instance), is considered to be just as fundamental, and, in a sense, eternal.

* * * * *

TRANSITION

In the last two chapters we have reviewed briefly various crises in the life of an Aboriginal. From earliest childhood, however haphazard the instruction and training may be, the major focus is on a child's adjustment to the social environment into which he is growing. He must learn how to get on with other persons within his sphere of interaction, in terms of what is expected of him and what he himself can expect from them. Progression into the adult realm means learning a whole range of other things too, most of them directly relevant to the practical issues of living. Pressures toward conformity are exerted on him from infancy, but before initiation the range of tolerated behaviour is much wider than it will ever be again.

Although a child is learning his way around at such a period, the most obvious emphasis is on growing—on becoming physically mature. In some areas children are pushed into the adult world as early as possible: for example, the early initiation of boys in north-eastern Arnhem Land, or small girls helping their mothers in food-collecting expeditions. In others, the process of becoming adults is a much slower one. Children are certainly disciplined throughout this period, but they are not expected to behave as adults. Once they reach puberty, however, the perspective changes: they are on the threshold of adulthood and need to be prepared for it. Adulthood brings increased status, but also increased shouldering of responsibilities. The transition period between childhood with little or no responsibility, and adulthood with much responsibility, is bridged by the initiation rites, which in some cases extend over a couple of years or more. For girls the transition is usually brief. They pass from childhood directly to marriage, whether or not they were previously betrothed. For boys the process is more complex and more arduous, and there is more to be learnt: because at least some of them are expected to become not merely active participants but leaders in the religious life of the community, this does involve more in the way of formal learning and teaching. The difference in role behaviour between the sexes is made clear at the onset of initiation, by the removal of boys from the ordinary camp. This is not merely removal from the influence of women, but a device to accentuate the traumatic nature of initiation, to symbolize the expectation of changes in behaviour over and above the fact of physical change; and the same is done in the case of girls.

Initiation is quite often a long-drawn out affair as far as boys are concerned. A new world is gradually revealed to them, a world the existence of which they only dimly suspected. And although initiation involves training for life, it is training for a special kind of life. They learn more about their place in the local scheme of things, man in relation to man; man in relation to the natural environment; and man in relation to his gods. It is not in initiation that youths learn skills and techniques. The fundamentals of these are assumed to have been learnt before, and only practice will make perfect. But the kind of knowledge which is transmitted through the initiation rituals is the inherited and accumulated store of knowledge handed down from the past—reinterpreted, it is true, to conform with current conditions, but kept as far as possible in the mould of the past.

Initiation is the core of Aboriginal social and cultural life. Among a non-literate people, only through the indoctrination of the young can traditional custom and belief be maintained. Knowledge must be transmitted if such a society is to continue to exist, and this is done most systematically through initiation. The kind of knowledge involved, the content, will be treated in a later chapter. But it should be remembered that not all the answers are obtained at initiation. This is only part of a process which will continue through life, gradually unfolding the store of knowledge which is held by various units making up the tribe or cultural bloc. It is a process which ends only with death. The proportion of time spent on this aspect of social living would be hard to assess,

FIG. 11. *Life Cycle*:
North-east Arnhem Land.

MALES:

1. Infancy and early childhood.
2. First initiation: circumcision: segregation from females.
3. Later initiation.
4. First marriage.
5. Initial parenthood.
6. Further religious revelations.
7. Final religious revelations.
10. Old age.

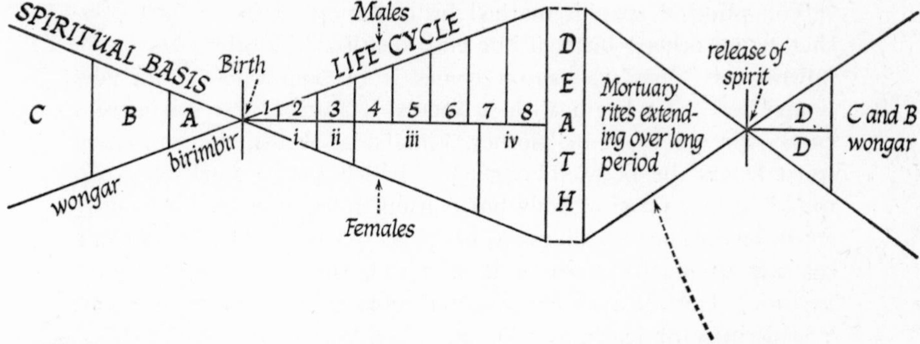

A Unborn spiritual state: resident in clan totemic waterholes.
B Direct relationship of A to Ancestral Beings and spirits, from which they are derived.
C Traditional heritage of the group.
D Land of the Dead: one for each moiety; immortality.

FEMALES:

i Infancy and childhood.
ii Puberty: first marriage.
iii Initial pregnancy: parenthood.
iv Menopause followed by old age.

Spirit still present and can appear to living: divisible into 'good' (human) and trickster (non-human) or *mogwoi* spirits. The latter may remain in the bush to haunt the living and eventually be forgotten.

FIG. 12. *Life Cycle*:
Great Victoria Desert.

MALES:

1. Infancy and childhood.
2. Segregation from females.
3. Initiation: Stage I.
4. ,, ,, II Circumcision.
5. ,, ,, III Subincision.
6. ,, ,, IV Cicatrization.
7. First marriage.
8. Initial parenthood.
9. Increasing participation in religious rituals.
10. Old age.

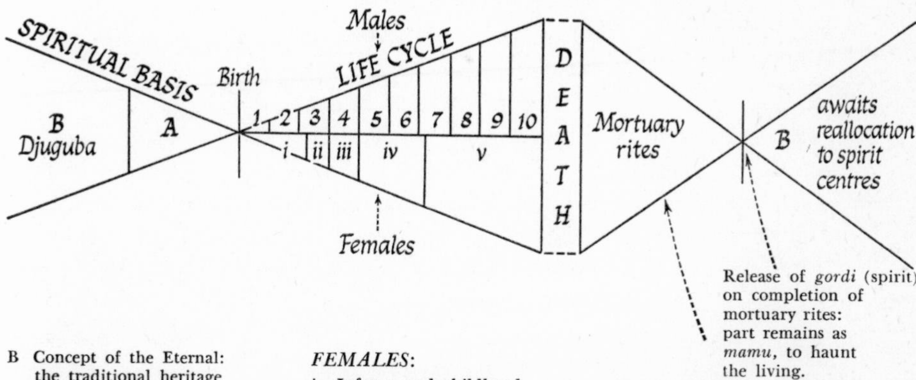

Release of *gordi* (spirit) on completion of mortuary rites: part remains as *mamu*, to haunt the living.

B Concept of the Eternal: the traditional heritage and sacred life, with Mythical Beings.
A *julan* spirit (*gordi*) child centre.

FEMALES:

i Infancy and childhood.
ii Puberty: initiation; cicatrization.
iii First marriage.
iv Initial pregnancy: parenthood.
v Menopause followed by old age.

During which the *gordi* (spirit) undergoes experiences with Wonambi, Rainbow Snake: on friendly terms with *mamu*, trickster spirits; travels around country and visits kinsfolk in dreams.

because so much is devoted to other things: hunting and food-collecting, quarrelling, making love, dancing, singing, making material objects, and so on. It is sufficient to say here that it is a major factor.

The physical span is marked by two major crises, which overshadow all others: birth at one end; death at the other. Each end, however, is 'open': a person comes from 'somewhere', and goes 'somewhere'. To begin with, a foetus is animated, a spirit child enters the womb of its mother. Finally, at death, the animating spirit leaves the body. This general belief, that a spirit takes up residence in a physical body but is itself indestructible, is variously articulated. The two diagrams on page 183 (Figs. 11 and 12), one relating to north-eastern Arnhem Land, the other to the Great Victoria Desert, illustrate one way of looking at this transition, and lead us into the realm of religion.

CHAPTER VII

Religious Belief and Practice: Totemism and Mythology

Religion, in general terms, has to do with such issues as beliefs and practices relating to the supernatural, the meaning of life, and the possibility of survival for the human spirit after the death of the physical body. Usually, also, in conventional definitions of religion, there is some reference to superhuman beings who are said to have special powers, or are not subject to ordinary rules of human behaviour, or are not restricted in time and space in the way that living human beings are. Then there is the question of its relation to magic. One anthropologist has written: "Anyone can make a definition that will separate magic from religion; but no one has yet found a definition that all other students accept: the phenomenal contents of the concepts of religion and magic simply intergrade too much." (Kluckhohn, 1953: 518.) In other words, it is in the intermediate zone where the two merge that definitions become most difficult. Otherwise we can speak of them separately, rather loosely perhaps, but without much fear of being misunderstood.

At the one extreme then, in conventional definitions, there is magic, or those aspects of magic which are almost mechanical, which involve no spirit intervention and no explicit conception of a superhuman power or force, which emphasize individual as against social welfare, and consist of more or less isolated acts, not consciously linked in a wider system of beliefs and rites. At the other extreme, in this kind of conventional definition, there is religion, involving a fairly well systematized body of belief and practice, which may or may not include beliefs about the after-life, and special attitudes toward one or more spirit beings who are thought to control the forces of nature and of the supernatural. Magic and religion then, are not sharply distinct, as Durkheim (1915/54) and others suggested; while magic may not be an integral part of religion, in many cases they are inseparable. There is a growing tendency to regard as religious any system of belief and action which has the qualities of faith and emotional commitment usually associated with religion, whether or not it includes reference to the supernatural.

CONCEPT OF THE SACRED

In most Australian Aboriginal groups there are, or have been, special words referring to a category of belief and action which is recognized as being extremely important. The content and significance of these terms vary from one area to another, and so does the range of aspects they cover. But, at least in regions where the data are fairly reliable, it is clear that they have something in common: they refer to actions which represent relatively well coordinated and defined sequences, of a repetitive kind, directed toward goals which are at least partly explicit. That is, they relate to rituals which are usually described, in translation, by the terms 'religious' or 'sacred': *maraiin* in western Arnhem Land; *mareiin* or *duju* in north-eastern Arnhem Land, *daragu* (*darugu*) or *djudju* in the eastern Kimberleys; *tjurunga* among the Aranda. (Strehlow, 1947: 84-6.) In many Aboriginal societies such terms refer to actions, persons, objects, or verbal material, rather than to belief as such: phenomena which can be seen or heard, rather than phenomena which must be inferred.

In the Aboriginal languages with which we are acquainted, we have not been able to find a separate word for 'believing' as distinct from 'knowing'—although Strehlow notes that the Aranda have such a term (1947: 71): *tnakama*, to believe, to trust. In most cases the basic assumptions which underlie this category of actions and objects, myths and songs, do not seem to have been seriously questioned, to the extent of rejecting them; and outward conformity was the main criterion of acceptance and successful participation. Looking at this kind of situation from the outside, we might say that there was no probing as to the nature of a person's belief, the degree to which this conformed with the beliefs of others. If he behaved in certain defined ways, at certain defined times, this seems to have been sufficient. We do not have enough information as to whether there were any consistent sceptics in the purely indigenous situation. Under alien impact this is another matter.

Beliefs and basic assumptions are handed on almost entirely by word of mouth from one generation to another. There must inevitably be some alteration in the process of transmission, however much emphasis is placed on its fixed, unchanging quality. Even when some individual variation is openly tolerated or acknowledged, it is assumed to be of a minor and incidental kind which does not affect the nature or the main bulk of the material. The overt stress is on stability, on continuity, and on the requirement that what happens in the present should duplicate, in all essential features, what happened in the past—or in the most significant part of that past, when the foundations of human life were established once and for all. This formative or creative period is known by different names but has much the same characteristics, and in each case it is regarded as having critical relevance for the present day. By acting in certain prescribed ways, in accordance with the rules laid down by mythical characters of various kinds who dominated that period, human beings can keep in touch with them or with the power which they continue to exercise. To make such actions more effective, as well as to serve as focal points in remembering and transmitting the relevant material, each group has a range of concrete representations which can be touched, or handled, and observed.

Throughout the Great Victoria Desert the term used for the 'creative period' is *djuguba* or *djugurba (tjukubi)*; in the Rawlinson Range, *duma*; in the Balgo area, *djumanggani*; in the eastern Kimberleys, *ngarunggani*; *bugari* around La Grange and Broome, and *ungud* among the Ungarinjin (Elkin, 1954: 178); *aldjeringa* among the Aranda (Spencer and Gillen, 1938); *mura* for the Dieri; for the Wuradjeri, *maradal* or *galwagi*, but the period before this was *ngerganbu*, 'the beginning of all'; among the Jaraldi, *gulal*; and in north-eastern Arnhem Land, *wongar*. All these have been variously translated as 'creative period', 'ancestral times', 'Dreaming', 'Dreamtime', 'Eternal Dreamtime', and so on.

Briefly, this concept means that the beings said to have been present at the beginning of things still continue to exist. In a spiritual, or non-material fashion, they and all that is associated with them are as much alive today, and will be in the indefinite future, as they were. The term 'eternal' has this connotation. 'Dreaming', in contrast, is a rather unfortunate choice: but it is a direct translation of one of the relevant native words. Where the same term is used for ordinary dreams, as well as this particular time-perspective, this does not mean that people cannot distinguish between the two.* 'Dreaming' does not refer to a dream in the

* The subject of *ordinary dreams* has not been systematically studied in Aboriginal Australia, except in regard to birth, conception and dream totemism, songs obtained during dreams, and dreams associated with native doctors, as well as with spirits of the dead. Ordinary dreams have been noted briefly by R. Berndt (1940*c*: 286-94). Róheim (1945, 1950) discusses in a psychoanalytic framework a number of Central Australian dreams. (See review by R. and C. Berndt, 1946: 67-78, Plates 1-3.) So do Schneider (1941), Schneider and Sharp (1958), for the Yir-yoront. See also Lommel (1951: 187-209.) R. Berndt (1951*a*: 71-84) considers some dreams relating to the Kunapipi rituals (see hereunder). These last were obtained at Yirrkalla, north-eastern Arnhem Land, together with several hundreds of others, most fairly long accounts of food-collecting and hunting exploits, as well as matters of sacred import, sexual adventures, feuds and fighting, spirits, Spirit Landings (see Chapter V), sickness and death, and dreams reflecting mission contact.

narrowest sense; but just as a dream is real to the dreamer, so the doings of the creative beings are real to the believer. Further, although 'eternal' suggests 'timelessness', as it does in a religious context, the Aborigines recognize various time-categories in connection with their everyday activities: days and nights, moons, the sequence or cycle of seasons; immediate and near present, past (historical, pseudo-historical), future (near, far-distant), and so on. Radcliffe-Brown (1945: 38-41) proposed the term World-Dawn or Dawn Beings. This is not satisfactory, because of its static connotation and over-emphasis on the past as such. Radcliffe-Brown was right in pointing out that the beings associated with this epoch are not ancestors in the sense of being bound by genealogical ties to living people. Nevertheless, some of them are said to have produced, from their own bodies or through their own efforts, the progenitors of the present Aborigines. In this general sense it is quite legitimate to speak of them as ancestral or, more accurately, as quasi-ancestral. Not all sacred beings, however, are viewed in that way.

The mythological era, then, is regarded as setting a precedent for all human behaviour from that time on. It was the period when patterns of living were established, and laws laid down for human beings to follow. This was the past, the sacred past; but it was not the past in the sense of something that is over and done with. The creative beings who lived on the earth at that time did perform certain actions then, and will not repeat them: but their influence is still present, and can be drawn on by people who repeat those actions in the appropriate way, or perform others about which they left instructions. This attitude is summarized in the expression 'the Eternal Dreamtime', which underlines the belief that the mythological past is vital and relevant in the present, and in the future. In one sense the past is still here, in the present, and is part of the future as well. In another but relevant context, the spirits of deceased human beings are still alive and indestructible. The mythical characters themselves are not dead. They continue to live, although in different forms, and in different places. Their physical human shape was simply one of a number of manifestations: but they continue to exist as long as men obey their instructions, and act in the ways laid down for them at the beginning. The 'life' of these beings, and the life of the Aborigines as a group or constellation of groups distinct from others, are linked together, the one depending on the other. In other words, there is a close relationship between the religious life and the rest of social life in general.

TOTEMISM

The subject of Aboriginal religion has been discussed most fully by Spencer and Gillen (1938), Radcliffe-Brown (1945, 1952), Warner (1937/58), Elkin (1933, 1954), Berndt (1951*a*, 1952*a*), Strehlow (1947), Stanner (1958, 1959-61). All have suggested, as Durkheim did (1915/54), that a major focus was on totemism. In fact, Aboriginal religion has been labelled as totemic, and a great deal has been written, at second hand, on this subject. Durkheim's classic and brilliant work suffers from just this defect. It was not only written without first-hand knowledge of Aboriginal Australia, but also was severely handicapped by the limitations of his sources. Radcliffe-Brown, among others, relied greatly on Durkheim's theoretical framework. This is not the place to discuss, critically, the work of these writers. But see also Schmidt (1909, 1926-35), Róheim (1925), Haekel (1950).

Totemism is a confusing term, because it has been used in so many different ways. However, it is well-entrenched, and any attempt to substitute another would only add to the confusion. Elkin's (1954: 133) description of totemism is possibly the best. He sees it as: ". . . . a view of nature and life, of the universe and man, which colours and influences the Aborigines' social groupings and mythologies, inspires their rituals and links them to the past. It unites them with nature's activities and species in a bond of mutual life-giving. . . ." He adds that it is 'a relationship between a person or group of persons and (for example) a natural object or species, as part of nature'. Very broadly, it has to do with a view of the world in which man is an integral part of nature, not sharply distinct or differing in quality from other natural species but sharing with them the same life essence. In the formative period, the various species had not finally adopted the shapes in which we see them today. Their physical manifestations were a little more fluid than they are now. Many mythical beings, all through Aboriginal Australia, were either more or less than human according to the way in which we look at it. The life force which they embodied was not limited to a human manifestation, but could find expression also in the shape of some other species. A goanna ancestor may have looked like an ordinary human being, but at the same time he was potentially capable of changing his shape and taking the form of a goanna. This identification in the mythological past has continuing consequences today. Because of it, there is said to be a special relationship between certain human beings and, for instance, that particular kind of goanna.

The general bond between human beings and other aspects of nature is a pervasive one, but for practical purposes it is more limited and more personal in range. Supposing a certain rite is performed with the aim of increasing the supply of goanna: this is not, as a rule, simply a matter of performing a series of actions and expecting them to bring about the desired results more or less automatically, although it sometimes gives this impression. The rite is said to be effective only in the light of the sympathy existing between one or more persons in that community and the goanna ancestor. For that reason, when a conventional distinction is drawn between religion and magic, increase rituals (see Chapter VIII) performed on this basis are sometimes classified in religious rather than in purely magical terms, or at least described as magico-religious.

Personal names may be derived from the totemic complex with which that person is associated, often from the ritual or cult totem acquired or inherited through his, or her, father. And in certain mourning tabus, close kin must avoid eating or using the totems from which the deceased man took his name, or must find new terms for them. Not only animals, birds, reptiles, plants, the sun and moon, and so on, may be treated as totems. According to the way in which the totem was derived it may be a new-born child, or a certain spirit being, or a stretch of country, or a sacred object: or even such concepts as heat or cold, or vomiting, sexual intercourse, or various diseases. Or a person may have one major totem plus a number of subsidiary ones.

The relationship which is labelled broadly as totemic takes a number of different forms. They can be classified in one way under the headings set out by Elkin (1954: 136-55; but particularly his monograph, 1933). We shall adhere to this scheme. We would not expect to find them all in any given Aboriginal community. Nor do the people concerned necessarily distinguish the same categories in a formal way. They are not mutually exclusive. In some areas separate terms are used for them, in others not.

Individual totemism

In this, only one person is involved in a special relationship with some natural species, or some particular member of that species. The relationship is a personal one, not usually shared or inherited, although there are cases of inheritance: a youth may be given a totem at his initiation, as among the Wuradjeri. (Howitt, 1904: 144.) Elkin has distinguished one form as 'assistant totemism', in which a totem animal or creature, for example, may serve as a familiar or 'second self' for a native doctor. Also among the Wuradjeri, a child about the age of ten or twelve years may be taken away from the main camp by a native doctor who 'sings' into him his assistant totem (*bala* or *jarawajewa*, i.e. the 'meat' or totem within him, or the 'spirit animal'). In that case the *bala* is patrilineal in descent. Howitt, and Elkin (1933), say this is widely distributed throughout New South Wales. In Central, North and North-Western Australia, native doctors have spirit snakes, which are associated with the mythical Rainbow. Among the Jaraldi of the Lower River Murray the patrilineally inherited totem serves as an assistant not only in its spiritual but also in its physical form. In western Arnhem Land there are song-makers, or songmen, who specialize in 'Gossip songs' dealing with contemporary people. (See Chapter XI.) A songman of this kind usually attributes each new song to a non-inherited 'familiar', a spirit or creature which reveals it to him during a dream.

Sex totemism

Each sex may have an emblem, such as a bird, animal, and so on, which signifies, conventionally, the solidarity of that sex as distinct from the other. Injuring or killing it is equivalent to challenging or attacking the members of the sex associated with it. The most outstanding example comes from Howitt (1904: 148-51). Among the Kurnai (of Gippsland) the emblems are two birds, one for males and one for females, who regard them as elder brother and elder sister respectively. Among the Kurnai marriage is by elopement, and girls are in a position to refuse their suitors. Conflict between the male-female totems helps to overcome constraint or shyness between young people of marriageable age. Older women may go out and kill a male totem, then display it conspicuously in the camp. This enrages the men, and fighting takes place between young men and women. Later a young man may meet a young woman and call her by the female totem name, asking what that creature eats. Her reply is in such terms as, 'She eats kangaroo', or 'She eats possum.' 'This constitutes a formal offer and acceptance of marriage, and is followed by elopement.' As Elkin observes (1933: 132), although there are cases elsewhere, 'it is usually associated with the south-east of Australia, with matrilineal moieties, and matrilineal social totemic clans'.

Moiety totemism

In Chapter II we discussed moiety divisions, which may be either matrilineal or patrilineal. Each moiety may acknowledge a special bond with some creature, animal, bird and so on, which stands for its members as against the other. This is widely distributed throughout Aboriginal Australia. It is most marked, however, as Elkin points out, in the south-east (Howitt, J. Mathew and others give examples) and south-west of the Continent. In many cases it is expressed through other forms of totemism. In north-eastern

Arnhem Land, for instance, the social and natural environment, and the mythological constellations as well, are distributed between the two moieties. Associated with each are hundreds of items which could be termed totemic, although here again division could be made in terms of major and minor totems. The matrilineal moieties of western Arnhem Land are divided into phratries, each associated with one or more totems.

Section and subsection totemism

It will be remembered from Chapter III that some tribal groups in Aboriginal Australia are divided into four or eight categories, on the lines of indirect matrilineal descent. Each may be conventionally linked or identified with one or more natural phenomena which represent its members in contrast to others. In the eastern Kimberleys there is a "totemic bond of kinship, and a ritual attitude is adopted toward the totem". (Elkin, 1933: 136.) In north-eastern Arnhem Land, each subsection has several totems associated with it: *wamud* has wedge-tailed eagle; *buralang* has rock kangaroo, heron, albatross and wallaby, and so on. But since the subsection system is new to this region, it is not tightly integrated with clan-linguistic unit cult totemism. In the eastern Kimberleys (Kaberry, 1939: 196), although not further south at Balgo, the subsection totems (*naragu*) were 'not treated with any marked respect', nor were there any tabus associated with them: they were treated as namesakes.

Clan totemism

A clan, a group which claims common descent in the male or female line, may also acknowledge a common relationship with one or more natural phenomena. The totem in question serves as a symbol of membership in this unit, both for the persons immediately concerned and for members of other units; it may warn them of approaching danger or trouble; and it may be the central focus of ritual life, with strong territorial and mythological ties.

Elkin (1933: 136-9) draws a distinction between matrilineal social clan totemism, and patrilineal clan totemism. The first is distributed throughout 'eastern Australia, Queensland, New South Wales, western Victoria and eastern South Australia, and a small area in the south-west of Western Australia'. The general term for such a totem is often translated as 'flesh' or 'meat': that is, the person and his totem are 'one flesh'. One distinction between the matrilineal phratries of western Arnhem Land and matrilineal social totemic clans is that the totems belonging to the first are not the centre of cult life, nor do the persons concerned have a special attitude toward them: these two points are significant in social clan totemism. A good example is the *mardu* of the Dieri. This is really an avunculineal cult totem (i.e., of the mother's brother's line); but also in this tribe is patrilineal clan cult totemism, *bindara*. Patrilineal clan totemism is found in 'parts of Western Australia, in the Northern Territory, in Cape York Peninsula, coastal areas of New South Wales and Queensland, central Victoria, north-eastern Australia (for example, the Lake Eyre groups) and along the Lower River Murray and Coorong district'. The best examples are from the latter place, among the Jaraldi, Dangani and so on (see Taplin in Woods, 1879; Radcliffe-Brown, 1918), and north-eastern Arnhem Land (Warner, 1937/58; Berndt, 1951*a*, 1952*a*). In eastern Arnhem Land a combination of aspects, not all directly totemic, is associated with the clan: several totemic cults are relevant to one clan, which may be linked with more than one linguistic unit. (See Chapter III.) Totemic combinations are less marked, but still apparent, in Central Australia.

Local totemism

In this case, people share a common totem by virtue of their association with a particular site, or locality, rather than on the basis of kin relationships or of descent. The totem, or totem-combination, belongs to or is somehow connected with the site. Elkin (1933: 138-43) first made this point in dealing with totemic clans of central and western South Australia. In many cases, especially throughout the Great Victoria Desert, there is totemism determined by the locality at which a child is born: in this sense it is also birth totemism. Because, traditionally, birth nearly always takes place in the local territory of the father, it is patrilineal local (cult) totemism. The real contrast between local totemism and patrilineal cult clan totemism is that descent is not of major importance, although, as Elkin points out, 'there is a tendency for it to become patrilineal'. Perhaps the best example is from the Aranda, but in that case it is the conception and not the birth totem which determines local totemic cult membership. It means that a person, by virtue of his association with a particular site which has mythological affiliations, has a direct link with the totem or sacred figure(s) and so on connected with it. Elkin mentions that such a person's relationship with others who claim a similar connection is, from this point of view, of a secondary kind. However, the fact that different people, irrespective of genealogical ties, have this common association is a force which helps to bind them together.

Conception totemism

Conception totemism may be identified with local totemism.

That is, a child's ritual or cult totem(s) is determined by the totemic and other affiliations of the site at or near which his mother first realized she was pregnant. This is the case among the Aranda. It may be near the track of some ancestral or spirit being, or a place commemorating some important mythical event, and preferably, but not necessarily, associated with the ritual or cult totem of the child's father. Strehlow (1947: 86-96) has a neat summary of this:

> The ownership of the sacred *tjurunga* . . . is determined largely by an accident which none of the tribal elders can control or ward off: it is decided by the 'conception site' of every individual member of a patrilineal totemic clan. It is true that the totemic clans from which the individual owners spring exert certain rights over the local *tjurunga* of which no accident of 'conception' can deprive them. . . . But the conception site occupies by far the most important place in all the complex arguments which centre around the possession of the myths, chants, ceremonies, and sacred objects owned by any large local totemic clan. . . .

On the other hand, in some areas it is said that a man may find a spirit child in a vision or dream, before the mother is pregnant: that is, he may 'know' in advance that a spirit child "is to be incarnated through his wife". (Elkin, 1954: 152.) The child may appear in conjunction with some natural phenomenon, usually one connected with the father himself—with his country, or some social unit to which he belongs: this is the child's conception totem. Or the mother may become sick after eating a certain food and later dream of a spirit child. That particular food will be viewed as the conception totem, because the child is said to have entered her with it, or taken that shape. However, in some cases the spirit may not have totemic affiliations. In north-eastern Arnhem Land, as we have seen in Chapter V, although it takes the form of some natural species the totemic affiliation is oblique, and not directly significant to the child who is later born. In the Great Victoria Desert, the spirit centres at which unborn children live are not totemic, although they were put there by mythological beings and have indirect associations with the Eternal Dreamtime. In the eastern Kimberleys (according to Kaberry, 1939: 42) spirit children were made by a Rainbow Snake, but in anthropomorphic form: at Balgo they are directly totemic and associated with mythological sites.

Birth totemism

This is where a child's ritual or cult totem depends on where it is born, and not on its 'place of conception' (i.e., place where its mother first realized that she had conceived). In the Great Victoria Desert a man tries to make sure that his wife bears her child in his own country, preferably at or near a site on the track of the mythical (totemic) figure most closely associated with himself.

Dream totemism

This overlaps with other varieties: with individual and/or assistant totemism, with conception and birth totemism. A person may be consistently represented, in dreams, by some natural phenomenon with which he is acknowledged to have an especially close link. He may identify himself with a totemic being, in human or other form; in his own dreams, and those of others, the actions it performs are *his* actions, and so on. Alternatively a dream totem, not identified as being his other self, may appear to him in a dream and perform certain services. Examples are the spirit familiars of western Arnhem Land songmen, and the spirit assistants of native doctors. As far as the first is concerned a person may appear in this form, his dream-shape, even after death. In many parts of Australia a person's ritual or cult totem is the one which most frequently appears in this way. This is particularly the case in north-eastern Arnhem Land, but not in the Great Victoria Desert, although there the same word is used for totem and for dream.

Multiple totemism

Multiple totemism is sometimes called classificatory totemism; it may be associated with other kinds of totemism (especially with moiety, clan, section or subsection, phratry or local totemism). All the known universe, or what are considered to be the major aspects of it, is categorized on this basis. A special attitude, usually of a ritual nature, is adopted toward the main totem, entailing a similar approach to all the secondary totems classified with it. This form is fairly common, but has received little notice except from Elkin (1954: 140, 153-4). (Sharp, 1939: 268-75, mentions multiple totemism for the Yir-yoront.) Here are two examples, the first from north-eastern Arnhem Land, the second from the Great Victoria Desert.

The Djanggawul Sisters and Brother walked along the coast until they came to Ngadibalji, where they saw a mangrove bird. Here the Brother left his hair belt: it is now a sandhill. On the sandhill were tracks of wild duck, which were eating wild peanut roots. On the opposite side was a large barren sandhill; and on the surface of this were goanna tracks and the tracks of many birds. A tree with inedible 'apple'-like nuts was growing there too; this is a sacred bullroarer tree. Here the Djanggawul paused and heard the cry of the black cockatoo. Here too is the sacred waterhole which they made, and beside which they camped.

The major totem might be described as the Djanggawul, although they are not really totemic. A man or woman belonging to this site would also have as secondary totems, although they are not specifically graded as such, all the others mentioned here: mangrove bird, hair belt, wild duck, nut tree, black cockatoo. Or he might say that his totem was any one of these, implying association with all the others.

The Wadi Gudjara (Two Men), in the course of their wanderings across the country, reached *gabi* (waterhole) Bindibindina. Here they made camp, ate berries, and picked flowers to put in their hair. They also made *bindi*, sharply pointed sticks with bunched shavings at one end, which they used for decoration. They prepared feather down for putting on their bodies: some of it fell from their hands and became stones. They drew blood from their arms, and some fell to the ground and became red ochre. . . .

The major totem here would be the Wadi Gudjara; and a man or woman belonging to that particular site would have all these other totemic affiliations as well.

TWO MAJOR CATEGORIES

From a different perspective, as Elkin points out (1954: 140-51), all these totemic forms can be classified into two categories: social totemism, and ritual or cult totemism.

In the first there is an emphasis on the social dimension. In other words, totemic affiliation hinges on membership in a particular social unit, of one kind or another, which defines a person's relationship, in totemic terms, to everyone within his social perspective. Social totemism is often concerned with the ordering of marriage and sexual relations, and is 'usually matrilineal in descent'. There are sanctions against marrying a woman or man with the same totemic affiliation, and this rule of totemic exogamy may be substantiated by mythology. Also, a special kind of behaviour may be expected of a person in relation to such a totem. He may not be allowed to kill or eat it, because it is of the same 'flesh' or 'meat' as himself. And it may be considered an elder brother or sister, or even a guardian. Use of the term flesh points up the closeness of the association.

With ritual or cult totemism, the situation differs. The totem is not regarded as 'flesh' or 'meat', and there are usually no prohibitions on killing and eating it. This variety has been found over much of Aboriginal Australia. It is usually patrilineal in descent, although matrilineal cult totemism has been reported for the Cape York Peninsula. (Sharp, 1939: 453-4; 1943: 69.) However, totem exogamy is not important. It may even be considered desirable for husband and wife to have the same totemic affiliation, as in parts of the Western Desert. (R. Berndt, 1959*a*: 100.) In the territory held by each tribe are sacred sites associated with beings who lived in the mythical period. They may be waterholes or rocks or hills (or trees), or caves containing paintings in ochre or blood. Each of them is under the care of a number of adult fully initiated men, who have this right and responsibility because they are associated with it on the basis of birth or conception. These men are custodians of the myth and ritual connected with that site, or cluster of sites, and must lead or perform the rites associated with it.

Before we turn to a brief consideration of mythology, and later of ritual (Chapter VIII), a few significant points relating to totemism generally should be kept in mind. Totems are not necessarily exogamous, but they are more likely to be so where social totemism and not cult totemism is involved. In the past, rather too much emphasis has been placed on this matter. The same is true as regards eating the flesh of one's own totem. A number of examples of this prohibition have been given by Howitt (1904). But in many forms, particularly in cult totemism, even when a man identifies himself with the totem it is eaten quite casually without sacramental intent.

It is also important to remember that not all food tabus, and in almost every Aboriginal society there are some such, relevant to different people during life crises or in a special ritual state, and so on, are necessarily connected with totemism. Moreover, a person's relationship with his totem should not be viewed in isolation: a totem is symbolic or representational of a wider range of associations. A person and his totem possess what we can call a sacred quality in common not simply because of their particular relationship, but because this is part of a broader relationship to the mythological or totemic ancestral beings. The totem, as it were, serves as a link between the human world and the world of myth. It is through this link that man belongs within the stream of the Eternal Dreamtime: is, in a sense, one with those beings. More than this, the mythical figures are sometimes reincarnated through human beings, and the totem symbolizes this concept. Strehlow (1947: 92-3) brings out this point, mentioning, among others, the case of a male honey ant ancestor who once lived at Ljaba and later 'chose to be reincarnated as a woman, named Ljabarinja in his honour'. At Balgo a man discussing his own totem may say, 'That is I, I did so-and-so!' In the Western Desert, in ritual dancing an actor performing the actions relevant to his own totem will not only live the part but actually *be* that totem.

In many cases the natural phenomena which serve as totems are those necessary to the material wellbeing or survival of the people concerned: sun, rain, water, animal and vegetable foods. But this would not account for the wide range of aspects which can be referred to in that way. Sharp (1943: 69) has suggested that "a totem may be any enduring element of the physical or mental environment, either unique conceptual entities, or, more frequently, classes or species of things, activities, states, or qualities which are constantly recurring and are thus considered to be perdurable". Totemism, he says, represents a 'formal relation' between people and the 'persistent elements of the physical environment'. Radcliffe-Brown (1952: 131) has drawn attention to the danger of being content with short formulae: Australian totemism is misrepresented when it is described "as a mechanism by which a system of social solidarities is established between man and nature". This is only one side of the argument. It is, as he has observed, "a representation of the universe as a moral or social order"—which is "an essential part of every system of religion". This is what is meant when we say that totemism is a philosophy: in other terms, it is a set of symbols, a conventional expression of the value system of the society to which it belongs.

MYTHOLOGY

From what has been said so far, we can distinguish four main elements or facets in the organization of Aboriginal religion.

1. Myths, the body of mythology in which the religion finds relatively standardized verbal expression.

2. Rituals (rites), the expression of mythological and other features through organized action of a more or less conventionalized kind.

3. Material objects or representations: these may symbolize or represent certain spirits, or creatures, parts of the human body, and so on.

4. Local sites: the country associated with various beings; the myths and rituals are always to some extent localized.

Ritual and mythology complement each other, even though they never completely coincide. Ritual is an acting out of events or instructions incorporated in myth, and mythology substantiates or justifies or explains a whole range of rituals. Their main concern is with matters in which human beings are most vulnerable: issues of life and death, fertility, and the relations between man and other aspects of nature. We have seen that the Aborigines have a subsistence economy. They are, or were, directly dependent on the earth and what it produces, and on the animals and fish and other creatures which share that earth and its waters with them. There are no human or mechanical intermediaries, except of the most elementary kind, to qualify this dependence or to act as a buffer between them and crises or disasters in their natural environment: not enough water, or too much at one time, or the disappearance of creatures they need for food. In such a situation it is no less than a matter of life and death that the seasons should continue in an orderly, predictable way, that the supply of animal and vegetable food should not diminish.

The word myth is used, popularly, in two contradictory ways. In one it refers to a narrative or story, or series of songs, which is of religious significance; a sacred story, enshrining a special body of beliefs, or setting out instructions from certain sacred or divine beings. In the other it has the meaning of false belief, for example in the saying, 'that's just a myth': an assumption or statement or story based on false premises. This is confusing, because people hearing the term myth in any context are likely to be influenced by the second usage and attach to it the label 'not true'—unless they believe in the religion associated with it. But in this discussion 'myth' is used in the first sense only. It is believed to be true, and of vital significance to human action and human welfare. It may or may not be acted out in ritual, although it frequently is.

In Aboriginal Australia of course, as anywhere else, not all stories could be called sacred. There are ordinary camp stories, or tales, including those which are told to children. Sometimes they are outline versions of the great religious myths, or altered versions of them. What is more, not all the most important myths are known to everyone in the community. The adult men who look after a certain myth or part of a myth may keep it more or less to themselves; they may not let others know the most important details, or they may be the only people allowed to recite it. This is so in many areas, such as north-eastern Arnhem Land, the eastern Kimberleys, Central Australia, north-western South Australia. Thus, among the Aranda, only the men belonging to a certain stretch of country and owning the myths associated with it are entitled to repeat them, and to perform the rituals relating to them. Men from other parts of the territory must ask permission to do so, and have a very good reason for wanting this privilege. Or the 'real' owners may perform the dancing while others assist them in decorating or making sacred objects, or even in singing.

Part of the community may not know the details, or even the outlines, of its major myths. Children, for instance, usually do not, although in areas where boys go through their first initiation rite while fairly young they may be introduced earlier, or in a more serious way, to the myths associated with their own totems and countries. Women may not know all the local myths, even those relating to themselves, although in rare instances there are myths of which only women know the substance. As a rule, most adults have some idea of the main totemic and sacred sites in their particular territories, and the main beings associated with them, if not of all the sacred mythology. Not always, however. According to Strehlow (1947: 93): "The women of the Aranda tribe must remain uninitiated and pass their days in comparative ignorance. No sacred myth ever reaches their ears. Their lips never utter the words of the traditional chants. The ceremonies centring around the lives of their ancestors are carefully hidden from their eyes. . . she may be the owner of the most sacred *tjuruṅga* treasured by her clan, but all knowledge of them is carefully hidden away from her. . . ." We are inclined to consider this a rather formal picture, because in many areas where men say this about women it does not coincide with the actual situation. This does not mean that women would be equally familiar with such myths and rituals. They certainly would not: but frequently they do know something about them.

Even when a myth is known generally, the sacred versions usually contain much more detail, particularly as regards the explanation of symbolism. In virtually all cases there is no single version which is generally accepted as the only correct rendering. Variation, including personal interpretation, is permissible within certain limits. For instance, if men of one local group or linguistic unit are given the opportunity to tell the mythology most intimately associated with them they are likely to provide as many slightly differing versions as there are men. The agreement is likely to be closest on major aspects, and especially so if they are all present at the time and can go over these together. If each person gives his account separately, away from the others, divergence on at least minor points will be more noticeable.

Over much of Australia, sacred myths do not take the form of spoken narratives. They are told through songs, which provide key words, or references, and not full descriptions. A literal translation by itself is not enough, because the meaning lies in the associations of each word. Sometimes these amount almost to a separate vocabulary. In north-eastern Arnhem Land a word used in everyday speech may have several sacred equivalents with slightly different shades of meaning, as well as a further series of ordinary 'singing' words. Songs of this kind are most often sung during sacred rituals, in special sequence. Because nearly all sacred myths and corresponding actions are connected with specific localities, sometimes with sacred objects as well, the songs help people to remember the appropriate details. Nearly every site that is important in some way—waterholes, for instance, particularly in the desert—or has some remarkable feature, such as a special rock formation or an oddly shaped hill, is connected with a myth or section of a myth. As a rule only barren or uninteresting patches of country have no such association.

Myth content

The majority of religious myths have as their framework the wanderings and activities of various beings. Usually such characters are not confined to one area. From the point of view of any one group of people, most of them came from somewhere else, or went off somewhere else, or both. They moved along the waterhole routes or rivers or across country from one place to the next, performing certain actions at each place: putting water there, meeting other spirits, creating people or other living things, making natural features such as rocks or hollows, naming them, instituting rites, singing songs, and so on. These 'Dreaming' tracks stretch in all directions. If the situation we find in such places as the Great Victoria and Western Desert, through the mountainous core of Central Australia and up the Canning Stock Route to the eastern Kimberleys, in the Victoria River area and across the Northern Territory to Arnhem Land is any guide, hundreds of such tracks or roads criss-crossed one another right through the Continent, representing, at least potentially, a network of intercommunication.

Take the Kunapipi series, for example. From the Roper River, it travelled north-west through Rose River to Yirrkalla and Milingimbi, north-west along the Wilton to the Liverpool River and Oenpelli: westward to Katherine, branching north-west again to the Daly River, and southward to Tennant Creek: from Newcastle Waters, west and south-west to Sturt Creek; further tracks lead up to the Victoria and Fitzmaurice rivers, and another to Wyndham. As it moved from one place to another its name changed, and it incorporated something of local mythology. Altogether it has extended through perhaps thirty-five 'tribal' groups.

The Wadi Gudjara wandered across almost the whole Great Victoria and Western Desert, passing through dozens of local group territories and covering possibly twenty-five to thirty dialect or language units.

As a rule no local descent group, clan, or dialect unit owns a complete myth. Even though at first it may appear to do so, what it has is usually only a section, dealing with some of the actions of a certain being. The men over in the next stretch of country may own another section, and can perform the rites associated with that—and so on, all over the country. Members of several local groups come together from time to time to perform their separate, but linked, sections. But the myth is never acted out *in toto* because all its owners could not meet, and in fact would probably not even know one another.

It is obvious, then, that the constellation of ritual, mythology and material representations, with the beliefs expressed through them, is not uniform throughout Australia. Information on this topic is least adequate in the southern part of the Continent, since early observers and recorders were not always reliable. They were inclined to read too much or too little into a given situation, and to pay insufficient attention to native interpretation. With a very few exceptions, they did not observe or record systematically and often omitted or glossed over aspects they considered obscene or shocking. In most of southern Australia today it is no longer possible to check on such material. There have been too many intervening influences. Research into this aspect, in regions where it is no longer a functioning part of everyday life, depends heavily on retrospection and hearsay, with all that this implies. The main point, as far as this chapter is concerned, is that we cannot speak with the same assurance for the areas covered by many of the early writers on this subject as for those in which field work has been more recent.

Some of the tribes of south-eastern Australia, for instance, are reported to have believed in a supreme being, a male god. Howitt (1904: 488-508) went so far as to speak of an 'All Father', and suggested that Nurrundere (Ngurunderi), Nurelli (Nepele), Bunjil, Mungan-ngaua, Daramulun, and Baiame (Baiami) 'all represented the same being under different names'. Not enough is known about the mythology and ritual associated with them. Baiami, among the Kamilaroi, is said to have created everything. Daramulun, in Yuin belief, lived on the earth with his mother, Ngalalbal: 'there were no men or women, only animals, birds, and other creatures. He placed trees on the earth. Then Kaboka, Thrush, caused a flood which destroyed all but a few of the people Daramulun had made. They crawled out of the water on to Mount Dromedary. Daramulun went into the sky, where he now lives, looking down upon the affairs of men'. Such a fragmentary outline could very well have been influenced by alien contact.

At Menindee in 1943 we were unable to obtain the Baiami myth in any detail. He was still well-known, but allusions to him were mainly in the context of initiation and magic, and to his appearance during certain rites. The emu, for instance, was under his direct protection, suggesting a possible totemic affiliation. Guriguda was his wife, mother of Wakend, the Crow. She left the earth in ancestral times and went up into the sky to

Wandanggangura, the place beyond the clouds. It happened in this way. One night she was sitting in the same camp as her son Wakend and his wife, who were eating together. Wakend would give nothing to his mother. Guriguda was angry, but Wakend grew tired of her constant grumbling and speared her in the knee. Instead of pulling out the spear he left it in the wound, and it was on this that she climbed into the sky. Guriguda resembles an ordinary woman, but instead of skin she is covered all over with quartz-crystal, and as she turns rays of light flash in every direction. Her assistant totem (called *jarawajewa,* the 'meat which is within') is the emu, so that she and the emu are identified.

The Ngurunderi myth of the Lower River Murray in South Australia is more complete. This is a version from an old man, Albert Karloan, now dead, the last of his people to be initiated.

The ancestral hero Ngurunderi paddled his bark canoe down the small creek which was later to become the River Murray. He had come from the Darling, following the giant Murray cod. As this fish swam, its tail swept aside the water, widening the river to the size it is today. When Ngurunderi paused to rest the cod swam on into the Lake, and he gave up all hope of catching it. Then he thought of his 'wife's brother', Nepele. Quickly getting into his canoe he rowed to Bumondung, and from there called out to Nepele, who was sitting on a red cliff named Rawugung, Point McLeay. Nepele pushed out his canoe, rowed it to some shoals, and waited with spear in hand. The cod swam down toward Nepele, who speared it opposite Rawugung and placed it on a submerged sandbank there. When Ngurunderi arrived they cut up the cod into many small pieces, throwing each into the water and naming the fish it was to become. Finally they threw the remaining part into the lake saying, 'Keep on being a Murray cod.'

Ngurunderi continued his travels. Eventually he reached Bamundang, where he disembarked and pulled up his canoe: his footprints are still there. Carrying the canoe he walked to Larlangangel, where he left two large mounds of fresh-water mussels. One day, on his way back from Granagung, he saw some people at a place called Ngirlungmurnang. They were frightened of him and hid in the reeds. But Ngurunderi could hear them whispering, and he transformed them into a species of blue bird. At this juncture Ngurunderi's two wives appeared. They were at Gurelbang cooking the *dugeri* (silver bream), tabu to women, and the breeze blowing from that direction carried the smell to him. Having no further use for his canoe, he stood on the two mounds at Larlangangel, and, lifting it up, placed it in the sky where it became the Milky Way. He then set off for Gurelbang. In the meantime the two women, thinking Ngurunderi might smell the fish, had made their escape on a reed-raft, poling their way across Lake Albert to Thralrum, on the western side. There they left the raft, which was metamorphosed into the reeds and yaccas found at that point today, and continued down into the Coorong.

When Ngurunderi reached Gurelbang and found them gone he too made a raft, and followed them into the Coorong. Here he met a malignant spirit named Barambari. Ngurunderi asked whether he had seen the two wives, but Barambari started a quarrel and speared him in the thigh. Ngurunderi laughed, pulled it out and threw it away. Then he threw his club, knocking Barambari unconscious, and thinking he was dead turned to go. But Barambari regained consciousness, and manipulated his magical spearthrower in such a way as to stop Ngurunderi from walking on. Ngurunderi returned, and killed him with his club. He lifted some large gums and other trees, piled them into a heap and set them alight, then lifted Barambari's body and placed it on top of the blazing pyre so it would be completely consumed. Turning around he tried again to walk away, but again could not do so. He picked up all the congealed blood and threw it on the fire, and after that he was able to continue. At Wunjurem he dug a hole in the sand to get fresh water. Kneeling down to drink he put his head against the sand, and this depression was transformed into rock.

Eventually be came to Ngurunduwurgngirl ('Ngurunderi's home'), where he lived for some time, giving up all hope of finding his wives. Later he continued his wanderings down the coast along Encounter Bay, and after a number of adventures was about to cross over from the mainland to Kangaroo Island when he saw his wives starting to do so. It was possible, at that time, to walk across to the island. When they reached the centre Ngurunderi called out in a voice of thunder saying, 'Fall on them, you waters!' Immediately the sea rose, and they were drowned; but they were metamorphosed into Meralang, 'Two Sisters', now called The Pages, north-east of Cape Willoughby on Kangaroo Island. Ngurunderi then went to Kangaroo Island, called Ngurungaui, meaning 'on Ngurunderi's track', referring to the path taken by all spirits on their way to the spirit world. He made a large casuarina tree, under which he rested. Then he walked down to the western side of the island, and threw away his spear into the sea: rocks came up at that place. Finally he dived into the sea to cleanse himself of his old life, and went up into the sky: Waieruwar, the spirit world. But before disappearing, he told the Jaraldi people that the spirits of their dead would always follow the tracks he had made, and eventually join him in the Sky-world.

This is fairly typical of many myths of south-eastern Australia where, as far as the evidence goes, the totemic aspect does not seem to be stressed in this context. In northern South Australia, Central Australia and central Western Australia, through to the southern Kimberleys, shape-changing ancestral beings are common. In some cases, or in some circumstances, the human elements appear to predominate, in others the non-human. Whatever the form one of these characters may adopt, his essential qualities are assumed to remain constant; and his words and his actions carry equal weight. The great Djundagal snake who travelled through the east Kimberleys; Bangal, the creator Bat in the same area, and Moon Man, there of the *djanama* subsection, with his many wives, all *nawala*, who today are the dark patches on the moon's face: these and other mythical figures are more and not less than human. Most often the final change from human to non-human shape comes as a climax, the end of a myth or an episode in a myth, rather than a beginning. Occasionally, it is the other way round.

In the Dieri and Lake Eyre area generally there were the well-known *muramura* beings, who wandered over the country creating and instituting ritual. Howitt (1904: 779 ff.) gives several of these myths. Here, briefly, are two of them.

One tells that in the beginning the earth opened in the middle of Perigundi Lake, and from it emerged one *mardu* (matrilineal clan totem) after another. They lay in the sunshine until they were strong. Then they arose as men, and scattered across the country.

In another the *muramura* Darana, one of the most important of the Dieri totemic beings, lived at Pando, Lake Hope. Once when no rain had fallen for a long time he made rain by singing: the lake and surrounding country were covered with water. When he placed his boomerang-shaped weapon in the ground, the rain stopped. Vegetation came up everywhere and there were many *muluru* (witchetty grubs). Darana gathered them together by singing, dried them, and packed them in bags which he hung on trees. Then he went to meet another *muramura*. In the meantime two youths, the Daraulu, saw the bags and threw boomerangs at them. One hit a bag. The dust from it spread and covered the sun, while the bags shone brightly. All the *muramura* returned in great haste. Seeing what had been done, they killed the two youths, who were revived by Darana but finally killed again by the others; they became two heart-shaped stones. It was decided that the first child born after this incident would be the guardian of the Daraulu. If the stones were scratched, all the people would go hungry. If they were broken, the sky would redden and the dust from the *muluru* would cover the whole earth and kill everyone. (In this connection see T. Vogelsang, 1942: 149-50.)

On another occasion the *muramura* Darana met the *muramura* Wariliwulu, Bat Man, when he was wandering about the country, at a place called Wogadanimuramura at the head of Lake Hope. There is an interesting totemic ceremony associated with the *muramura* Wariliwulu, Galadiri (the Bull Frog), and Bindjidara (young bats). It tells how a great crowd of bats darkens the sky and covers up the sun; this is night. Then they go away into their holes, leaving the sky clear; this is daylight. Among the many other *muramura* is the famous Gadimargara, a mythical animal of crocodile shape which was associated with the *margara*, a yellow-bellied fish.

In the Western Desert, people say, there are still wandering *djugurba* beings like those among the Dieri: partly human, partly animal, reptile, bird, and so on, but in the myths they are thought of as mainly human. Among the most important are the Wadi Gudjara, Two Men, already mentioned. One was Gulgabi or Milbali, the 'white' goanna, the other Jungga, the 'black' goanna. They instituted a number of rites and created many local sites. Then there are Njirana and Julana, names used interchangeably for an ancestral man and his penis; Wadi Malu (Kangaroo Man); Minma Waiuda (Possum Woman); Wadi Gulber ('Blue' Kangaroo Man); Minma Nganamara (Mallee-hen Woman); Wadi Galaia (Emu Man); Minma Mingari (Mountain-devil Woman); Wadi Bera (Moon Man), and many others. The myths associated with all these are very long, and mostly in song versions. Here is an excerpt from one account of the Wadi Gudjara.

The Two Men dig a rectangular pit and place alongside it a *wera*, a wooden dish, which is also the metamorphosed body of Possum Woman. Then they cut their arms, spurt blood into the hole and mix it with sand. They touch each other ritually on the shoulder. One lies down in the pit. They rub blood and sand over each other's heads. Then they go westward, taking the new 'law'. (In another account they sit in the ritual pit and drink blood, just as ordinary men do in this rite, drinking the 'actual blood' of the ancestors as a communion.) The first song in this cycle is:

waiuda lidulidu juldu ngagala ngagala . . .
Possum rattling in hollow tree: blood, blood . . .

(General translation: Possum Woman makes a noise in a hollow tree as it is being burnt down by Djordjor, Night Owl, her betrothed husband. He had sent her away to be made into a woman by the Wadi Gudjara. Later, after she had returned, Djordjor sent her again to the Two Men to get a magical shell, *maban*. However, they were now tabu to her because they had initiated her. She refused to go near them, and instead went westward and turned into a possum. Djordjor was annoyed and followed her: she entered a hollow tree and refused to come out.

In a rage, he burns down the tree. Possum Woman turns into a large wooden *wera* which the Wadi Gudjara later use ritually. The last part of the song refers to the blood they shed, which helps Possum Woman to remain eternally alive.)

Hundreds of such incidents make up the total myth. (See Tindale, 1936: 169-85; Mountford, 1937*a*: 5-28; R. and C. Berndt, 1942-5.) The Wadi Gudjara, Two Men, for instance, chase Minma Nganamara, Mallee-hen Woman, to obtain her eggs, at Mindeljari; Wadi Bera, Moon Man, seduces one of the group of women belonging to Wadi Gudjara, but they later castrate him, and his severed penis is metamorphosed into stone. And so on. The next example is from the Wadi Malu, Kangaroo Man, series, also widespread in this area. It takes place in country between Laverton and the Warburtons.

Wadi Malu is ready to take a young boy named Dugulba out into the bush for circumcision: he looks for him, but cannot find him. He leaves Malubidi waterhole and goes on to Nugali, but still cannot see him. Only Wadi Baba (Dog Man) is there. Malu continues to Widabiwara, and on to Banamaru. From here he sees smoke, but lies down to sleep. This is the smoke made by Dugulba at Bilbin. In the early morning Malu sneaks up: a spark from the fire at Bilbin is carried by the wind and burns his ear. He comes closer and pulls out from himself a small kangaroo to be used as a decoy. Hiding in the bush he watches the boy follow the tracks of the small kangaroo, finally killing it and returning to Bilbin to cook it. While he is doing this Malu enters his camp. The boy offers him food, but he refuses it. Next morning Malu tells him to look for his firesticks (which he has thrown into the bush). As the boy searches Malu seizes him, throws him down on his back and ties him down with a hair belt. He takes him to Janggal, not far from Malubidi, where a number of women are cooking food. Entering with the boy, Malu tells them: 'You women, stay here. I shall take this boy to my countrymen.' He goes on in the direction of Malubidi. In the bush near this waterhole he releases the boy and makes a special ritual camp, paints himself and the boy, whom he hides, and sits down to wait for other members of the initiation party.

People are searching everywhere for Malu's camp and for the boy, but cannot find them. At last one man comes up to it. 'Have you seen that boy?' he asks. 'Um,' replies Malu. When the other presses him he says, 'Yes, but I am waiting.' They wait there together for the other men, who still cannot find them. As they are waiting they sing:

mularumalaru mananari walingu duringbadu . . .
Nose smelling walking along, sinew, circumcised penis . . .

(General translation: referring to circumcision. The sinew refers to a kangaroo leg.)

bila ganina janai bila jalgujalgura . . .
(Holding him there) among the spinifex, among the little bushes, among the dirt. . . .

They remain there. However, some of the Malu men who were looking for them have separated out. One, coming from the north to Bilbin (Minnie Creek, on the Warburton track), is chased all the way from place to place by Wadi Baba, Dog Man, who eventually catches and kills him.

dudingbagadara walgarara wonggaiwonggai . . .
Swinging the mulga club, voices of men . . .

Wadi Malu hears men talking.

ngalweri dagubungu wonggaranggara . . .
(Wadi Malu) goes ahead, quickly, (dog) chasing him . . .

gurangurandu badanu wirilanu . . .
Pulling close to him (Wadi Malu), biting him. . . .

Wadi Malu, tired out, is caught by Wadi Baba at Minnie Creek. Mountford (1939*b*: 78, Fig. 5, Plate II) notes that Wadi Malu's body became a rocky bar across this creek. 'The white quartz intrusions are his fat, and a round hole worn by rotating stones is the socket in the pelvis.'

One Malu man comes from the east, from Galba *gabi*, bringing a novice to Malubidi: they meet another Malu man and the two circumcise the boy. Another goes to Ooldea. Others go to Nini, near Minggulba, where they pierce their subincisures, making blood flow.

guwili wilina guldunu binalanga . . .
Going into the spinifex, piercing, blood flowing . . .

Wadi Nanudi (Turkey Man) is camped near Nini. When all the Malu men have left their camp to go out hunting he takes their fire and hides it in the bush. Returning, they search for their fire. At last they find Nanudi, but he evades their spears and runs off with the fire to Jilildubidi where there is a big waterhole. In the meantime the Wadi Gudjara, having heard he has stolen the fire, follow him. They catch him at a large waterhole further out from Jilildubidi: he tries to escape by entering the water, holding the fire above his head, but they pull him out and throw him to the ground. They take the fire, telling him to continue without it. Nanudi, however, tells the Wadi Gudjara that the Malu really stole the fire from him, and they give him enough to keep warm. . . .

Also typical of this central region is the myth of Njirana and Julana. (Other versions of it are given in Mountford, 1938*a*: 241-54; R. and C. Berndt, 1942-5; and Tindale, 1959*b*: 305-32.)

In the earlier part of their wanderings Julana, the penis, becomes separated from Njirana, the man. It travels under the sand and is always chasing women. At times it assumes human proportions and frightens the Minmara or Gunggaranggara, the Seven Sisters, by swinging a small bullroarer, in an attempt to decoy one woman away from the group. In a section of this very long cycle Minma Mingari, Mountain-devil Woman, is travelling from the west with her pack of dogs which she keeps in a bag. In another direction Njirana has come into Anmangu *gabi* in the Musgrave Range, and making camp settles down to sleep. He is thinking about women. After a while he hears the sound of Minma Mingari urinating at Galan *gabi*. Immediately his penis, Julana, stretches out and travels under the sand to Galan, where it enters her as she finishes urinating. However, she stands up and sings:

> *njirana galunggu babanggu bada aganu baba bai bai njirana . . .*
> Dogs, bite Njirana's penis; dogs, go on, go on . . .

As they bite the penis, Njirana retracts it. The dogs continue biting it, with Minma Mingari following, until they reach Anmangu, where they are all metamorphosed into stone boulders. However, this is not the end of them. They are associated with other places throughout this region. For instance, Wonggarin, on the southern edge of the Kathleen Range, is the most important totemic site for Njirana-Julana and the Gunggaranggara women. It is said that they came from the west with the Wadi Gudjara, the men following the women. As they came along the Wadi Gudjara turned themselves into different things: into wild figs, into goanna, into flowers, and so on. Eventually they reached Rira, the southern edge of the Gibson Desert, near Lake Christopher. They went on to Manguri, on the north-western side of the Rawlinson Range, where the Wadi Gudjara turned into a quoit-shaped object such as women use as a base for carrying wooden dishes on their heads. Then they continued on their travels.

Njirana, however, went after the women. Wherever he went he made fresh water rockholes, at intervals, by urinating. In sandhill country near the Petermanns he found one woman grinding grass seeds, accompanied by a small dog. He lengthened his penis, but the dog thought it was a snake and jumped at it, and the woman hit it with a digging stick. Later he came to Wirindjara (Glen Cumming, near Giles), where the Gunggaranggara sisters were camping in open windbreaks. He extended his penis, but they huddled together in fear. On one side of Glen Cumming he cracked the cliff facing with his penis, trying to get at them. The black coloured stone at this site is menstrual blood from the women: the crack in the rock and other markings were made by Njirana's penis. The Gunggaranggara then went on to Wonggarin, where they made a shelter. Njirana followed them, coming close; the indentation of his buttocks and back can be seen in the rock. He extended his penis again. It travelled along the ground, forming the creek near Wonggarin rockhole. Again the women were frightened and huddled together: his waving penis cracked the rock. Then, to frighten them, he erected a large *wanigi*, a web-shaped emblem he was carrying. This is now a sacred tree, *djugubiribiri*, just above the rockhole. They threw sand, calling out, '*bai, Njirana galu!*': 'Go away, penis of Njirana!' Blinded, it went underground down the creek; but the women continued to throw sand at it;

Above: Newly subincised men rubbing blood on the backs of postulants. Background, group singing: mixed southern Aranda and Bidjandjara. Macumba, northern South Australia (1944)

Left: Ritual act by Malu (Kangaroo) totem men who reenact a part of the Kangaroo and Euro myth sequence. Andingari: at Macumba (1944)

Gujini (Mosquito) totem man with his large *laralara wanigi*, constructed on a spear, of human hair twine and bunches of cockatoo feathers. Southern Aranda: Macumba (1944)

Above: Ritual act by Ganjala (Euro) totem man, decorated in eagle down stuck to his body with blood. This depicts part of the myth in which he arrived at Jay Creek, where he left his body (now a *tjurunga*). Bidjandjara: Macumba (1944)

Below: Ritual act by Baba (Dog) totem men: these are associated with Malu. Andingari: Macumba (1944)

Above: Gujini dancing before his *wanigi*. The stick at his back represents a firestick which, in the myth, he stole from his father's sister. Macumba (1944)

Left: Two Aranda actors representing ancestresses of Akara (in the Simpson Desert), digging out termites. Originally a secret-sacred rite, but revealed to women many years ago as part of the mortuary rites for an Akara woman

(photo: courtesy T. G. H. Strehlow)

on the rock walls are horizontal marks and holes, representing the special *manimani* round sticks they used. It emerged a little distance from the rock-hole, and was metamorphosed as a stone penis—which is now a sacred site, used primarily for increase ritual, as a spirit child centre, and in love magic. It is anointed with fat and ochre and kept covered. In the vicinity of Wonggarin is a sacred store house containing the carved boards of the local group associated with these ancestral beings.

Some of the songs in this long cycle are as follows:

garalu gadi wu bugara . . .
Going down the steep incline . . .

At Garalinga, in the Rawlinsons.

ngadabangara nudjunudju . . .
Sitting under the milkwood tree . . .

At Jalgulga.

wabara bara dilgimana . . .
Twigs crackling (as his penis moves), cracking (the cliff face) . . .

At Wirindjara.

ngarang birugadi guladjirada djulgurulgu . . .
Standing with erect penis, thinking of women . . .

At Wirawira (north of the Rawlinsons).

ngildjibadanga nalagudu . . .
Spearing the stone boulder . . .

Njirana is making a waterhole at Bandajaibanda, in the Rawlinsons.

Over much of Aboriginal Australia there is a fairly consistent belief in the Rainbow Snake, known by various names, but always associated with rain or water. In some areas it is male, in others female. There is considerable variation in the extent to which it is linked with sacred ritual. (See e.g., Radcliffe-Brown, McConnel, Elkin, Piddington, 1930: 342-55.) In parts of the Great Victoria Desert the Rainbow is Wonambi, living in billabongs and rock pools, and playing a major part in the initiation of native doctors. In the Kimberleys he is associated with rock paintings, and with the bringing of rain and spirit children. In eastern Arnhem Land he is always male, and may be identified with the Lightning Snake. In western Arnhem Land the Rainbow is male among the Maung of Goulburn Island: among the mainland Gunwinggu it is sometimes male, more often female. One of her ordinary names is Ngaljod. (Ngal- is a feminine prefix.) She is said to bring floods to drown people who break certain tabus, or children who refuse to stop crying: in myths she could be summoned by people who wanted to destroy a whole camp and indirectly commit suicide at the same time. She is also connected with menstruation and with childbirth. But here, as elsewhere, she may take different forms in different contexts. In one version she is the first Creator, who made all living things.

In the central and desert areas of Australia most ancestral beings have mixed human and non-human identities. On the northern coast they are more often in purely human form, although they are directly and indirectly associated with a large variety of totems.

In western Arnhem Land, among the Gunwinggu, one of the major myths tells of an ancestral woman who is known by a variety of names, most commonly Waramurungundju. She is said to have come over the sea from the north-west, in the direction of Indonesia, at the very beginning of the world. When she landed on the Australian coast she made children, telling them where they were to live and what language they were to speak. She also created much of the countryside and left various natural species or natural features: for example, bees and wild honey in one place, a banyan tree in another. In one version she tried to circumcise the children she had made. At first she was unsuccessful and the children died: in those areas people do not practise circumcision today. But at last she succeeded, and the children survived: in those places, therefore, people continue to circumcise. Because of her creative powers, she is sometimes called 'the Mother'. In some versions she travelled from west to east, finally disappearing in the direction of Yirrkalla. In others she is associated with a man named Wuragag, who came with her from the direction of 'Macassar'. He left her at Melville Island and went on alone to western Arnhem Land, where he eventually met another woman. He had many adventures, and many wives: but finally he turned into a high rocky hill, a landmark which dominates the plains north of Oenpelli. This bears his name, Wuragag, because his spirit remains there; in English it is called Tor Rock.

Much of this inland area, stretching eastward from the East Alligator River, is made up of rocky hills and sandstone ridges, interspersed with river gorges and creeks. These formations are often quite striking. Many of them relate to beings of one kind or another who lived in the mythological era. Ngaljod, the Rainbow, often helped directly in their transformation. After swallowing them she finally vomited their bones, which turned into rocks where their spirits still remain. In translation, 'they came into dreaming'. There is a special term, *djang* in Gunwinggu, for this kind of representation. A *djang* is an object or creature or spirit which contains some power or essence derived directly from the mythological era. Some *djang* sites are hedged with tabus, or said to be dangerous to certain classes of people, such as women, or children, or everyone but the very old. A few are dangerous to everyone, and travellers go out of their way to avoid them. The Gunwinggu word here is *-djamun*, meaning set apart, hedged with prohibitions, not for everyday use; it is applied also to the men's sacred dancing ground, to sacred rites and objects, and to food which has been put aside for ritual consumption. The *djang* are mostly of minor importance, in comparison with beings such as Ngaljod. They are bound to specific localities, and the range of their influence is limited. Some are more widely known than others. Wuragag, for instance, Tor Rock, is a prominent landmark. But even when people know the name of some territory not directly connected with themselves, or their husbands or wives, this need not signify that they are acquainted with the relevant myths, even in outline.

In western Arnhem Land, too, there is the myth of the *ubar*. The *ubar*, a long wooden gong in the shape of a hollow log, is one of the most sacred objects. Among the Gunwinggu it is the uterus of the Mother, sometimes identified with Ngaljod, the Rainbow.

Jurawadbad, a python (sometimes a male Rainbow Snake), is betrothed to a girl named Gulanundoidj, or Minaliwu, but she refuses to sleep with him because she has a young lover, Bulugu, Water Snake. Jurawadbad is angry. He makes an *ubar*, a hollow log, which he leaves lying across a bush track. Then, turning himself into a snake, he enters it. In the meantime Gulanundoidj and her mother are out hunting. They come upon the *ubar*. Thinking there may be a small animal inside, the girl kneels down and peers into the aperture but can see nothing there. She calls to her mother, who also tries, but in this case Jurawadbad opens his eyes and she looks right through them to the other side. Gulanundoidj puts in her hand and Jurawadbad 'bites' her. Then the mother puts in her hand, and is 'bitten' too. As they lie beside the *ubar* dying, Jurawadbad emerges, turns himself into a man again, and departs to another place where ceremonies are in progress (and the myth continues).

Among the Maung at Goulburn Island the mythology is a little different. The *ubar* is still the uterus of the Mother, but there is more emphasis on its phallic aspect: the *ubar* is also the penis of the male Rainbow Snake.

In north-eastern Arnhem Land there are two principal Fertility Mothers, usually in conjunction with a brother. These are the Djanggawul, or Djanggau, Sisters: Bildjiwuraroju, the elder, and Miralaidj the younger.

The myth tells how they and their Brother, named Djanggawul, and in some versions a companion called Bralbral, came across the sea from the north-east. They paused for a while at the island of Bralgu, somewhere in the Gulf of Carpentaria, now the main home of *dua* moiety dead. Then they came on in their bark canoe to the east coast of the mainland, on the path of the rising sun.

The two Sisters, especially, are associated with the sun, which is female in this area although in other regions it is male. In fact in some versions, as at Milingimbi, they are called 'Daughters of the Sun'. They symbolize the sun, with its life-giving properties, essential to the growth of human beings, plants, animals, and so on. This concept is not found to the same degree in other parts of the Continent, such as the central deserts, where the sun's heat can be dangerous to life; but on the north coast the north-west monsoon brings heavy rain during the wet season, and surface water is fairly plentiful.

The Djanggawul Sisters and Brother brought with them a variety of sacred objects, or emblems, which have symbolic associations. The emphasis throughout is on fertility. One such object was a round plaited mat rising like a shallow cone to a peak in the centre, called *ngainmara*, a symbolic uterus. This was perhaps one of the most sacred of all the objects they brought, but it is not used ritually on the men's sacred ground. Such mats are used by women and children, especially, for resting or sleeping under, to keep out rain or mosquitoes or sandflies: or for cover during parts of men's rituals which they are not permitted to witness. It was not unusual a few years ago to see dozens of them scattered here and there in a beach camp, each sheltering a woman or child.

In the myth the conical mat which the Djanggawul brought contained a variety of sacred *rangga* emblems. Some of them are related to creatures or plants or trees which became totemic through their association with the Djanggawul. Another was a sacred dilly bag, also a symbolic uterus. Hanging from it were lengths of feathered string from the *lindaridj* parakeet, representing the rays of the sun—or, in some contexts, an umbilical cord. There were also special patterns, which different clans and linguistic units are entitled to use ritually.

Above all, the Djanggawul are creators. The first human beings, ancestors of the present north-eastern Arnhem Landers, are said to have been born from the Sisters, or taken from the *ngainmara* mat or the sacred dilly bag. They started the practice of giving birth to children as women do today. Later they put finishing touches to them, such as separating out their fingers. They left animals and plants for the people they had made, as well as special sites which serve as reminders of their own physical presence in the area; and they instituted the biggest rituals, the *dua* moiety *nara*. (See Chapter VIII.) Finally, after many adventures, they went westward along the coast into the setting sun. (See Warner, 1937/1958; Berndt, 1952*a*.)

The Djanggawul cycle, which exists in several versions, belongs to members of the *dua* moiety although *jiridja* men participate in it. It is perhaps the most important in north-eastern Arnhem Land. But there are others as well. Laindjung, for instance, came out of the sea on the east coast of the mainland at Blue Mud Bay. The white foam, clinging to him, formed special designs which are used today by some of the *jiridja* clans and linguistic units. Banaidja, or Barramundi fish, is another manifestation. (See R. and C. Berndt, 1948: 317-23.)

Another major constellation is that of the two Wawalag (Wagilag, or Wauwalak) Sisters. They came up into northern Arnhem Land from the neighbourhood of the Roper River. In a few versions they are associated with a man named Wojal or Wudal, or Maiamaia, with boomerang legs, who was travelling in the same direction; but in most versions they came alone, or with the elder Sister's first child and their dog, or dogs. A series of myths relates their adventures. The climax came at a sacred waterhole near the north-central coast, Muruwul, or Miraraminar. The elder Sister gave birth to a child, and the afterbirth blood (or menstrual blood, or both), attracted the attention of a great python which lived in the waterhole.

In one version the Sisters, Waimariwi the elder and Boaliri the younger, with their two female dogs Wulngari and Buruwal, or Muruwul (like the place name), were tired out when they reached the waterhole, and welcomed the shade of the paperbark trees and cabbage palms by the water. They put down their baskets full of stone spearheads, and prepared to get firewood and paperbark for a hut, or shade, and for their sleeping mats, and to cook the food and meat which they and the dogs had caught for their supper. Suddenly, one after another, all these things jumped from the fire and into the well: goannas, roots, wallaby, small land snails. The Sisters realized that something was wrong: 'Oh, elder sister, a snake!' 'Quick, let's go!' But the sky was shut in with clouds: a storm broke, summoned by Julunggul. They washed the baby, to get rid of the smell of blood, but it was too late. Night had fallen. They crouched in the hut by the fire while the rain poured down outside, taking it in turns to dance and to call ritually in an effort to drive away the storm. When the elder Sister danced, crying out '*Gaibaa, Gaibaa, Gaibaa*!' the rain dwindled to almost nothing. When the younger Sister did this, she could check the storm only a little. Then they sang Kunapipi songs, and the storm died down. They were tired: they slept. ('Perhaps they thought the snake had gone: but he was there, waiting.') He sent his son to look: and the report was, 'Father, those two are asleep.' He raised himself up, standing erect, then lowered himself again. His head went into the hut: he wrapped his body around it, around the *molg*, the *banagaga* (two words for the sacred mound, used in ritual; *cf*. also the *ubar banagaga* in Chapter VIII). Then he swallowed them: the two Sisters, the dogs, the children; they slept in his stomach. But an ant bit him: he jumped, and vomited them all. He swallowed the Sisters again, but not the children—because they were *jiridja*, and he and the Sisters were of the *dua* moiety. This version includes also the long conversation between the snakes living at various places, a conventional feature of the myth, in which Julunggul at first denies and then boastfully confesses that he has swallowed the two Wawalag.

A great deal of symbolism appears in the interpretation of this myth. For example, the python, usually called Julunggul in this setting, is a phallic symbol. There is a close parallel with the Rainbow Snake mythology of western Arnhem Land. But the python is, at one level of analysis, the male principle in nature. This is linked with the fluctuation of the seasons, such as the monsoonal rains and floods, and with the increase of human beings and other creatures, and of plants. As in other myths of this area, there is an emphasis on the significance of blood, which has a sacred quality. But the Wawalag are not regarded as creative beings in the same sense as the Djanggawul are. They did not populate the regions through which they passed. In some versions they are described as 'daughters' of the Djanggawul. (See Warner, 1937/1958; Berndt, 1951*a*.)

The concept of a Fertility Mother is quite widely distributed over Aboriginal Australia. (See Elkin, 1954: 215-19; Stanner, 1959-61; and Berndt, 1951*a*; 1952*a*.) Kunapipi (Gunabibi), with which the Wawalag are sometimes associated, is one name for a mythical woman who created human beings and instituted sacred rituals. She too is called the Mother, or Old Woman. The Wawalag are sometimes identified with two of her daughters, called Munga-munga, and the Julunggul python with the python or Rainbow Snake which belongs to the Kunapipi series. Further afield, in the Daly River-Port Keats area and in the central west of the Northern Territory, she is called Galwadi or Gadjeri—among the Guirindji, Malngin, Njining and Djaru, Gugudja and Walmadjeri, from the Victoria River district across into the eastern Kimberleys. (See Meggitt, 1955 and 1962, for the Wailbri.) But the Gadjeri cult and its counterparts seem to have made no headway among the Aranda, with their strongly patrilineal emphasis. Strehlow (1947: 25, 94) reports that the male principle is an important feature of Aranda religious life, to the virtual exclusion, or at least subordination, of the female principle. He refers to the large wooden pole of the northern Aranda, the *tnatantja,* used in sacred ritual, as "the great symbol of masculine fertility", and points out that it is said to have 'shaped the whole landscape': but there is no stress here on the female aspect of human fertility. However, there is the tradition that in the beginning certain women, 'feminine ancestors' as Strehlow calls them, 'used to carry about *tjurunga* (sacred objects), and introduced various sacred rituals.'

The role of women

In the past many writers on Aboriginal life have emphasized the sacredness and secrecy of male ritual activities. They have seen a rigid dichotomy between the sexes, particularly in the religious sphere, and have consequently categorized men as sacred, women as profane. (Cf. Durkheim, 1915/54: e.g. 138; Warner, 1937/1958: 387, 394-8, and others.) We have seen something of the relations between men and women in an Aboriginal society, and the extent to which we can speak of co-operation and complementary expectations.

It is true that men hold the key to religious revelation, and play the executive role in most religious ritual and ceremony: that they are, generally, in possession of the major part of the relevant mythology and songs, and are custodians of the sacred emblems. Nevertheless women are also significant in this sphere. In the first place, they have a part to play in many rituals directed by men, and may have their own as well. In the second place, much of sacred ritual and symbolism relates equally to women as to men. The importance of women in relation to fertility may be a dominant theme, as in Arnhem Land. In the third place there is the persistent claim, which appears in various parts of Aboriginal Australia, to the effect that in the beginning, until they were stolen by men, women owned the most sacred rites and the emblems which are used in them. A fourth and more general point has been made by Kaberry (1939: 277). Writing in reference to the eastern Kimberleys, she says: "The sacred inheritance of the tribe includes the system of totemism, a number of myths of the totemic ancestors . . . the mourning and increase ceremonies, in which both men and women are associated and have their part . . . there can be no question of identifying the sacred inheritance of the tribe only with the men's ceremonies . . ."

The third point is worth mentioning in a little more detail. Among the Aranda, according to Spencer and Gillen (1938: 195-6), many mythical traditions tell how women played an equal part with men, and possessed the sacred emblems. Strehlow writes (1947: 94): ". . . The female ancestors which are celebrated in Aranda myths are usually dignified and sometimes awe-inspiring figures, who enjoyed unlimited freedom of decision and action. Frequently they were much more powerful beings than their male associates . . ." The same is the case over most of the Great Victoria Desert. It is not stated specifically there that women originally possessed all sacred rites and emblems, but this is inferred in the myths telling how women first circumcised such beings as Njirana. Another myth tells how men performed circumcision with a firestick, and as a result many novices died. Galaia (Emu) women came up, however, and pushing aside the firestick showed the men how to use a stone flake. In the Western Desert south of Balgo, women in the mythical era are said to have possessed all sacred ritual, which was later taken from them by men. In western Arnhem Land, the *ubar* ritual belonged at first only to women. In the myth the headwoman, Mingau (a Kangaroo Woman of the fire dreaming), was holding a ceremony with other women when Gandagi (a Kangaroo Man) appeared among them. He stood watching their dancing. At last he drove the women back to the main camp, taking over their sacred emblems. He got together all the men and they began their own ritual: but it was the same as the women's. One version of this myth, from women, insists that Gandagi could not get the steps right until the women taught him how to do them.

The Djanggawul myth in north-eastern Arnhem Land tells how the two Sisters came to Marabai, where they built a shelter and hung inside it their sacred dilly bags, or long baskets, full of emblems. Then they went out to collect mangrove shells. While they were away their Brother and his companions, men whom the Sisters had made (in some versions their brothers, 'fathers', and 'fathers' fathers'), sneaked up and stole the baskets. The Sisters heard the whistle of the *djunmal* mangrove bird, warning them that something was wrong. They hurried back to their shelter to find their belongings gone, and saw on the ground the tracks of the men who had stolen them. They followed these, but had not gone far when the Brother began to beat his singing sticks rhythmically. As soon as they heard the beat of the sticks and the sound of the men singing they stopped, fell to the ground, and began to crawl. They were too frightened to go near that place, fearful not of the men but of the power of the sacred songs. The men had taken from them not only these songs, and the emblems, but also the power to perform sacred ritual, a power which had formerly belonged only to the Sisters. Before that, men had nothing. The myth continues: The elder Sister said, '. . . Men can do it now, they can look after it . . . We know everything. We have really lost nothing, because we remember it all, and we can let them have that small part. Aren't we still sacred, even if we have lost the baskets? . . .'

Such myths reveal something about the relationship between men and women in these societies. In one sense this may be interpreted as a fall from grace on the part of the women, or as a symbolic statement of their subordinate position. But it can also be interpreted as a statement about the dependence of men on women, the insecurity underlying their control of the sacred rites, emblems and myths, and the authority they exercise over women on the basis of that control. In a complementary fashion the converse situation is emphasized in rituals which are still the prerogative of women. (See Kaberry, 1939; Elkin, 1954: 180-4; C. Berndt, 1950*a*.)

CHAPTER VIII

Religious Belief and Practice: Ritual

At first glance, it may seem easy to distinguish between ceremonies that are non-sacred, or 'playabout', and those that are sacred or religious. There are performances intended simply for entertainment and nothing more. Then again, there are ceremonies that may be referred to by a general term, a word which we can translate as 'sacred'. In such cases there can be little doubt as to which is which. But in between are many examples which cannot be described as being just for amusement or pleasure, and yet are not sacred in the way that some of the major rituals are.

So far, we have used the two terms 'ritual' and 'ceremony' without suggesting any distinction between them; but there are advantages in separating them. Firth's definition of ritual is probably the most useful. In his view, ritual is "a kind of patterned activity oriented towards control of human affairs, primarily symbolic in character with a non-empirical referent, and as a rule socially sanctioned". (Firth, 1951: 222.) Monica Wilson (1954: 240) speaks of ritual as meaning primarily religious action. However, it need not be classified as sacred or religious: it can be magical: but it differs from technique in its use of symbolic statement. In other words ritual, whether magical or religious, is stylized and symbolic action carried out with specific ends in view, and having additional meaning and implications for social living either here or in the hereafter. It may take place within or outside the context of ceremony, but in any case is not dependent upon it. A ritual act such as cicatrization, for instance, need not have a ceremonial setting. But ceremony can take place without ritual. As a collective response to situations of seasonal change or life crisis, an occasion of sociability, it might be seen also as a formalized means of emotional release or building up of tensions. It is no less important than ritual, for it may be oriented toward a specific end which is not fully recognized by the people concerned.

THE SACRED SPHERE OF RITUAL

In most areas the Aborigines recognize degrees of sacredness, even if they do not always put it in so many words. They grade some rituals and ceremonies as bigger or more important. This applies also to mythology: certain myths, or certain mythical characters, are regarded as more significant than others. These are the creators, the institutors of rites and customs, the founders of the various Aboriginal ways of life. But this is a continuum, rather than a dichotomy. In terms of sacred and non-sacred, actual situations are often mixed, not entirely the one nor the other. They shade into each other. Even a ceremony which seems to be just an ordinary affair, providing an evening's entertainment in the camp, may be drawing on very much the same themes and the same characters which appear in some of the major rituals. There are numerous examples of this all over Aboriginal Australia. The setting is different, and the attitudes of the people involved are different—they may not be so intense, or so serious: but the division between sacred and secular, or even between sacred and mundane or everyday, is not a hard and fast one.

In the same way, in ritual as in myth (see Chapter VII), magic and religion cannot be rigidly demarcated at the level of empirical reality. The difference is hard enough to establish in our own society, in spite of the ready-made definitions available. We tend to think of religion as an organized body of beliefs and practices involving a supernatural being (for example, a god), an organized body of members (for example, a church), a leader (a minister or priest), and a recognized place of meeting. In contrast, there is a tendency to think of magic as something that is contrary to what we regard as natural laws—pseudo-science (Malinowski)—and as an individual matter, a person performing certain rites because in this way he hopes to achieve something he wants for his own individual ends. Durkheim suggested this as a major contrast between magic and religion.

This fairly conventional or formal framework makes it easier to say what is religion and what is not. But in many other societies, Australian Aboriginal included, the division is even harder to make. There are rituals which seem to belong at neither end of the scale, but are most conveniently labelled magico-religious. Some of the rites we will be treating under the general heading of magic resemble those which are designated as bigger or more sacred. The distinction rests partly on the more impersonal nature of magic, as against the personification of supernatural power in religion, or the emphasis on personal relationships between human and other beings. But this is not wholly satisfactory. Then again, magic is seen as a matter of immediate short-range aims, concerned with specific persons, as against those rituals which concern the welfare of the community in general. At the same time, there is a practical and often immediate slant to many of the big religious rituals as well. For instance, as we saw in relation to mythology, one of the most pervasive themes in Aboriginal religion hinges on the close bond between these people and their natural environment: they try to influence that environment through supernatural means, to make sure that the seasons come and go in the normal way, and that animal and vegetable life persists—because this is necessary for human life. This kind of theme may be overlaid by others; or it may be dominant, as in the case of some of the big fertility cults in northern Arnhem Land. It may appear in love-magic ceremonies performed by women: the *djarada* or the *jawalju,* for instance. The immediate and obvious aim of any such performance may be the obtaining of sweethearts. Each of the women taking part may have her own personal reasons for doing so, but the rituals themselves are placed in a religious or semi-religious context. They may be accorded mythological sanction, special spirit beings may be invoked, or at least mentioned in songs: and there may be special objects. Whether or not we call these sacred depends on our definition, and the extent to which we treat this as an all-or-none affair.

In Aboriginal Australia there has been a tendency on the part of some writers to use the term sacred in a rather restricted way, basing their definitions on the undoubted fact that much of the ritual or sacred life is controlled by adult men. In everyday matters women have a fair measure of responsibility; they take the initiative in attending to their own concerns, such as internal family problems and their own economic and kinship involvements. But they have relatively little formal authority in community affairs, including ritual affairs. Partly for this reason, and partly because men's rituals are on the whole more spectacular and more colourful than women's, some writers have used the term 'sacred' only for rituals from which women are excluded. If a rite or myth or song, or bark or cave painting, is secret to the men of a community, and women and children are conventionally prohibited from seeing it or approaching it, the tendency is to label it 'sacred'. If either women or children are allowed to see it, or to participate in the ritual, the assumption is that it must be profane or secular or non-sacred. This is a one-sided approach, which for the most part does not take into account the context of the rituals, or myths, or paintings, or the ways in which the people themselves use the terms we can translate as 'sacred'.

RITUAL DIVISION OF LABOUR

The dimension of sacred-profane, or sacred-mundane, does not rest on the single issue of the sex of the participants—even though this is an important consideration. The extent of such participation varies according to the area and the circumstances, and also to the general question of how much members of both sexes mix together in everyday life outside the range of immediate family and kin relationships. In the Western Desert, for instance, in any large-scale meetings men and women always sit separately, and despite casual comings and goings the division is quite clear; the ritual pattern can be seen as a reflection, or an extension, of this. At Bathurst and Melville islands there is a marked contrast, not least in the ritual sphere: the sex-based restrictions which permeate religious life in most other parts of the Continent are at a minimum—as they may have been also among the people of the Lower River Murray in South Australia.

Broadly speaking, in any given area ritual performances can be classified under a number of headings, which represent points on a continuum rather than distinct categories.

1. Rituals in which men alone take part, and women do not actively participate at all.

2. Rituals in which men play a major part at some particular place, or site, and women perform a number of subsidiary actions, usually in a different place, and sometimes at a different time.

3. Rituals in which men and women participate together, in the same place at the same time.

4. Rituals in which women alone take part, and men do not actively participate at all.

This does not, except at the extremes, coincide with the 'control' dimension: who is in a position to order or urge others to participate, and if necessary to bring sanctions to bear. It is only in the last (4) that women are fully independent in this respect, answerable to no one except members of their own sex.

Also, the word 'participation' is best interpreted as covering a wide range of possibilities along a 'passive-active' axis, including the facets of seeing, hearing, uttering, or performing various actions. There are rituals or sections of ritual which women may witness, without being expected, or permitted, to do more. Or their contribution may include being painted with appropriate body designs, or observing specific food tabus if a close relative (e.g. son, brother) is going through some stage of his initiation. On other ritual occasions they may join in the singing, or some of it, but not the dancing. Or they may be free to hear certain songs from a distance—or from close quarters, when they may in fact become quite well acquainted with them, but conventionally should not sing them themselves.

Similarly, where men have a separate vocabulary which women are forbidden to use, women may know at least some of the words, and may reveal them in crises.

To take a Western Desert example: one of us (C. H. Berndt), among a group of women at an evening camp ceremony, heard an unfamiliar word during a loud exchange between some men seated nearby, and asked the women what it meant. There was silence for a few moments, then one of them whispered, 'That's a men's word, a *daragu* word, we can't say it.' Next day, however, they translated it into 'ordinary' language; and on several occasions women were heard to use it and similar words in swearing—for instance, after accidentally taking hold of a burning firestick: but only when no men were within earshot.

In many areas there are dancing grounds reserved for men, called variously ring place, centre place, men's shade or shelter, Big Sunday ground, and so on. Ordinarily women are forbidden to enter them. It is here that adult men perform various sacred rituals. This is their part of the division of labour between the sexes. They do, actually, undertake the greater part of the 'work' associated with them. In some areas both men and women refer to what men do on the sacred ground by a word which can be loosely translated as 'work': for instance, *djama*, in north-eastern Arnhem Land. But the rites men perform at such times are designed directly or indirectly to safeguard or promote the welfare of the community as a whole. And in almost every case, women's co-operation is essential. Sometimes they serve merely as an audience, whether or not they are actually present: people in front of whom the men can show off, or from whom they can have secrets. More often, it is their active collaboration which is required, in one form or another. All the men's 'work' may go for nothing if the women do not perform properly their part of the ritual, or (as in Arnhem Land) if they do not supply enough vegetable food to allow the men to concentrate on the performances.

Two other points should be borne in mind in considering religious ritual generally, and more specifically the dominance of men in this field. One is that many of the rites which men carry out themselves away from women imitate, symbolically, physiological functions peculiar to women. The idea is that these are natural to women, but where men are concerned they must be reproduced in ritual form. Apart from the more exotic and elaborate examples of northern Arnhem Land, subincision too is based on this analogy—signifying the menstrual flow; and circumcision in some areas is interpreted as the severing of the umbilical cord, symbolically separating a boy from the influence of his mother. There are numerous other examples. The other point (see Chapter VII) is the mythical claim that at least some of the most important rituals and the sacred objects connected with them were first owned, or destined to be owned, by women: but men took control of them, and that accounts for the situation today.

RITUAL VALIDATION

Aboriginal religious ritual cannot be understood without reference to myth. In the last chapter the emphasis was on mythology; in this, it is on ritual. But the two are interdependent. In Aboriginal Australia all ritual action and, for that matter, most of the symbolism are mythologically based: explanations are given in mythological terms.

Let us put this in another way. If we are looking at a society from the outside, we may notice that its main systems of belief seem to have practical significance beyond what is locally claimed for them. For instance, they may serve to increase social cohesion, or to minimize friction between relatives, or to provide incentives for building up material wealth, and so on. This is not just saying, as extreme functionalists would, that all aspects of culture are interdependent, so that one must influence all the others. It is a matter of pointing to the practical implications of a certain system of beliefs and values, involving consequences which the members of that particular society may consider desirable, or which we may assume to be desirable for them. They may recognize this where short-range affairs are involved, or where the relationship between means and ends seems fairly straightforward: but the principles which underlie the organization are not usually described in pragmatic terms. People do not usually say, 'We do this in order to increase social cohesion' or, 'to minimize friction between relatives', and so on, even though some of them may infer that their actions could have consequences of this kind. Instead, they are likely to refer to some higher authority—for instance, 'the Bible says that we should do this', 'the ancestors said we should do that'. The reference is usually to some supernatural or superhuman power, or force, whether or not this is conceived of in anthropomorphic form. In other words, the norms and values relating to those actions are justified, or validated, by invoking some agency outside the control of ordinary members of that society, and having power to discipline them through negative or positive sanctions. This has been one of the strongest influences in directing and channelling human behaviour, narrowing the range of conformity in what are seen as critical areas of conduct.

The Aborigines are no exception in this respect. The commonest answer to questions about the reason for some ritual act is, 'We do this or that because the Djanggawul, or the Wadi Gudjara, or Ngurunderi, and so on, instructed us to do so: he, or she, established this!' But not all myths are acted out in ritual. Mythology is part of a complex system of belief, which varies from one area to another. Radcliffe-Brown (1952: 155) recommended that "in attempting to understand a religion it is on the rites rather than on the beliefs that we should first concentrate our attention". There is no need to go into this controversy, except to repeat that the two are complementary. But we could say, as far as Aboriginal Australia is concerned, that ritual is one way, although not the only way, in which belief is transformed into action. As Firth (1951: 222) points out: "A distinction is usually drawn between ritual, the mode of action and belief, the mode of conception, in religion". Beliefs—in this context, those expressed through mythology—are the essence of a religion. They remain more or less constantly present among its adherents, at varying levels of awareness, whereas ritual is episodic, carried out only at intervals. Nevertheless the two should be studied in conjunction, as facets of one wider problem area.

Elkin (1954: 148) has suggested that there are two kinds of totemic or religious rituals: those which are commemorative or instructive, or both; and increase rites, where the goal may be a narrowly specific one, focused on a particular species, or may be concerned more broadly with natural and seasonal fertility. But in many cases this is a matter of emphasis. One or other of the two aspects may predominate, or they may be so closely intermeshed that it is difficult to separate them even conceptually. In any event, whether the relevant mythology is spelt out or only cited, it is through spoken statement as well as through material representations that such rituals are substantiated.

MYTH AS EXPLANATION OF RITUAL

Myths, then, may be used to explain or account for certain rites, or to show why various actions are performed: why a certain tribe practises circumcision, or why it does not while its neighbours do. The answer may be that some mythical character gave the order for this, or set the fashion for it. Here are several further examples bearing directly on this point.

Firstly, in the Western Desert there is a myth in which the main characters are Malu (Kangaroo), Ganjala (Euro) and Djurdju (a night bird). Djurdju is a mother's brother of the other two, but he is uninitiated, whereas they are much older and have gone through the full sequence of initiation. At *gabi* Gungara, near the Everards, they passed a number of night owls, *gungara*, and there the two nephews spurted arm blood over Djurdju, who sat shivering. This was the beginning of his ritual death, as Malu and Ganjala proceeded to kill him by 'breaking him up'. Afterward they left him lying dead and went out hunting wallaby, but when they returned they saw that Djurdju was alive and had made a windbreak for himself. Then they showed him the dancing associated with this ritual.

The second example is in two sections, from two closely interrelated series. Their main connecting link is the *dingari*, a word which refers both to the Dreaming, and to a group of mythical beings who are believed to have traversed the whole Western Desert, particularly in the Canning Stock Route region. They are known as far south as Laverton, and as far north as Djamindjung tribal country beyond the Victoria River. Hundreds of songs relate their wanderings and allude to the rituals they introduced, often called by the name *gurangara (kurangara)*. Although in many cases they are referred to collectively, simply as the *dingari*, individual members or individual groups may be singled out in sections of the mythology, or in more detailed discussion. Petri (1960*a*) contrasts the *dingari-gurangara*, which in one sense is associated with darkness, with the *bugari-gara*, the "second period of creation", when the Two Men brought light to the world by pushing the sky away from the earth with their sacred boards.

(*a*) The Ganabuda were a party of women (in some versions, one woman identified with the Gadjeri or Galwadi) in the *dingari* 'mob'. As they travelled from one place to another they danced the *bandimi*. (This is now one of the preliminary rites leading up to circumcision, as in the eastern Kimberleys, where a row of women dances with a shuffling step making parallel grooves in the soft earth.) But Lizard Man, Gadadjilga ('spiny-head'), saw them, and sang *djarada* love magic for them. By this means he was able to catch one of the young Mangamanga girls from among them, and had sexual relations with her. This was *wadji*, wrong. The Ganabuda resented him: and they killed him by breaking off his penis with a *gana* (digging stick). Then they went on, still dancing the *bandimi*, and swinging bullroarers. They owned the sacred objects and the rites connected with them. The older Ganabuda women used to send the girls out to hunt and collect food for them, and in return they showed them the rituals: that is, the girls 'paid' them by supplying them with meat. (This is what men do today: the older ones expect 'pay' from the young men in return for revealing the sacred rituals.) The Ganabuda women had all the *daragu* (sacred things), men had nothing. But one man, Djalaburu, creeping close and watching them secretly one night, discovered that they kept their power (*maia*) under their armbands. He succeeded in stealing this. Next morning the women tried to swing their bullroarers, but they could hardly manage to do so: they had lost their power. After that, Djalaburu led them down to where the men were; the men went up to where the women had been, and took over their responsibility for attending to sacred matters. They changed places.

(*b*) One of the *dingari* men was Lundu, 'kookaburra'. (Petri, 1960*a*, speaks of Lon, the kingfisher.) Coming to Ladjeribang, south of Gordon Downs in Djaru country, he swung a bullroarer. Going further south to Ngandu rockhole, he mixed antbed with blood and used it for painting designs on the bodies of the other *dingari* men. (This kind of painting has a slightly luminous tinge.) He went on to Wonguda, where he swung some *daragu* boards. . . . He continued to Diri swamp, where they painted their bodies again and arranged tall 'pokiti' headdresses. They took part in a ritual here, singing, the actors shaking their chests (like birds shaking their feathers). . . . The *dingari* 'mob' went south again to Galbanu rockhole and spring. Here the old men told the young men to collect meat and 'pay' them. On their return they were first covered with bushes, and when everything was ready they were shown the long *daragu* boards, which were stood upright, decorated with a pattern of emu feathers. The young men came forward and placed the meat they had collected at the foot of the *daragu*. Then the ritual leaders climbed up on the boards and called out invocations.

Thirdly, here is a section of a western Arnhem Land myth relating to the *ubar* ritual.

All the Kangaroo Men lined up and began to jump around and around in a haunched posture, propelling themselves with their arms as kangaroos do; and they saw that their dancing was all right. Then they brought out one man and sat him by himself in the middle of the ground. He began to shiver ritually like an owl. After watching this performance they said, 'Ah, that's very good.' They got two more 'owls'. When they had seen them dancing they said, 'In future, you two must always come and dance.' Many men were there, but these two were especially good. 'We shall call this ritual the *ngurlmag ubar*, it is the most sacred,' they said. *'Ngurlmag! Ngurlmag!* Oh Sacred Uterus of our Mother!' The Goanna got ready for his dance. . . . Then they brought out Blanket Lizard and covered him completely with bushes. The other men got together, chanting loudly, 'Ah! Ah! . . .' and Blanket Lizard stirred in his hiding place. Singing, and the drone of the didjeridu, continued as the Old Kangaroo took up a different pair of beating sticks and walked over to where Blanket Lizard was hidden. The singing and the didjeridu stopped, and the Old Kangaroo began to beat the sticks as he bent over the other and called the sacred names referring to him. . . . Lizard emerged, throwing aside his bushes, and danced all the way down the sacred ground to the sound of the clapping sticks. . . . Then, while the *ubar* gong was beaten, the Old Kangaroo called the power names of the sacred totems:

'I name the blue sky, *bajangudjangul*.'
'I name the sacred *ubar, ubar banagaga*.'
'I name the very old woman, *ngalwariwari*.'
'I name the moon, *wombidjid*.'
'I name the scorpion, *bidjarabul*.'
'I name the long bark fire-torch, *djadagulan*.'
'I name the barramundi fish, *balgungbi*.' And so on.

When he had finished, the men said, 'Everything is all right now!' The *ubar* stopped. The spirit of the Mother had returned to her own camp. The men went back to the main camp, calling out to let the women know they were coming.

This is why we perform the *ubar* now.

The next and final example does not describe the origin of a rite, in this case subincision, but suggests an additional justification for it. The myth says nothing about the esoteric aspects of the practice, but merely asserts that it appeals to women: that men who have not been subincised cannot hope to keep their wives happy and prevent them from having illicit relations with 'wrong way' sweethearts. This is a Djamindjung myth from the Fitzmaurice River area.

Flying Fox, Djinimin, was of the *djanama* subsection, and Rainbow, Djaguld, was *djangala*. Both were men, living at Gimul, not far from the Fitzmaurice River. Flying Fox had two wives, both *nangari,* and both small Rainbows. He was jealous because he suspected both wives found Rainbow more attractive than himself. One day he went out hunting kangaroo, killed one, and cut up the meat to cook on the fire. The two wives came sneaking up to see what he was doing; when they saw that he was safely occupied they hurried off to join Rainbow—although, on the basis of their subsection, they called him 'son'. But Flying Fox came calling out for them, searching, until at last he saw them high on a hill top. 'Why have you climbed up there?' he cried angrily. 'I can't go there, it's too rough!' Those two girls didn't like Flying Fox, because he had not been subincised. Every time he had intercourse with them they used to complain. 'Why don't you subincise your penis? We prefer that. Then it will make an agreeable sound when you have intercourse with us!' Rainbow was subincised; that was why they liked him.

Flying Fox stood below the hill calling to his wives; and they cried back that they would lower a rope so that he could pull himself up on it, carrying the kangaroo on his shoulders to leave both hands free for climbing. He did this, but when he had almost reached the top they cut the rope. He fell back, and was smashed to pieces. Both wives ran away with Rainbow. But Flying Fox began to put himself together. He felt around and found his eyes, his nose, his fingers—all the parts of his body—and remade himself. He was a native doctor: he sang himself well again. Then he took his stone-tipped spears and set off in pursuit. At last he came up to them. He could hear the girls chattering. As he approached, Rainbow tried to placate him, pretending to be glad to see him: 'You're alive! Everything is all right now!' He didn't see the spears. Flying Fox came closer and speared him, so that he fell backward into the water and became a Rainbow Snake. He still lives there today, and he is responsible for making all the fish. But Flying Fox subincised himself, and after that his two wives did not try to leave him again.

Almost every ritual, like almost every important action in everyday life, can be referred back to some myth, which provides a sufficient reason for it so that there is no need to look further.

RE-ENACTMENT OF MYTH

Contemporary ritual is not simply a re-enactment of rites and ceremonies said to have taken place in the prehuman era. It includes events other than these, but also ascribed to mythical beings who lived on earth at that time. Actions of this kind, not separated out as ritual performances in the relevant myths, are translated into ritual form by human actors who repeat them today. The best examples are to be found in Spencer and Gillen (1938), Spencer (1914, 1928), Elkin (1954), Warner (1937/1958), Strehlow (1947) and Berndt. (See Bibliography.)

Strehlow (1947: 108) mentions the *Ingkura* Festival, which extends over several months: "ceremony follows upon ceremony; all the sacred *tjurunga* of the *ingkura* ground must be exhibited both to the members of the resident totemic clan and to visitors from other groups. At Ilbalintja, for instance, the *gurra* (Bandicoot) ceremonies take precedence over all others. They take months to perform. Each one of the numerous local bandicoot ancestors had a separate traditional ceremony connected with his person. The more important *gurra* men usually 'possessed' a large number of *tjurunga*; they figured in several different ceremonies and often carried a number of *tnatantja*-poles. Each one of these poles must be exhibited in a separate performance."

In the Dalwaba (wallaby) cult rituals of the Western Desert, men go out into the bush away from the main camp. Seven actors paint themselves in black and white bands. A *wanigi laralara*, a web-shaped *wanigi* mounted on a pole or several spears, is stuck in the sand at one side of the dancing ground. As the singing begins the Dalwaba men move forward, hopping like wallabies. (Explanation: the Dalwaba are performing a ceremony at a certain waterhole: the actors *are* the ancestral Dalwaba.) A man appears, decorated with red ochre. This is Njirana. He walks toward the *laralara* and, picking it up, sways it from side to side. The Dalwaba are afraid, and bunch together. But they continue with their ceremony and eventually leave the ground. Then Njirana appears again. He carries the *laralara*, holding it from the back and slowly coming forward: then he dances with a shuffling step, his feet making deep grooves in the sand. Upon reaching the chanters he turns abruptly, and dancing to the back of the ground disappears into the bush. (Explanation: Njirana is looking for the leader of the Dalwaba, named Dalbalba.) He returns again, still dancing. As he reaches the centre of the ground Dalbalba appears, and hopping quickly toward Njirana springs on him. The chanting stops, and the two actors retire. (Explanation: Dalbalba surprises Njirana, who later continues in his search for women.)

INCREASE RITUAL

The ultimate reason for present-day behaviour, including ritual behaviour, is that various mythical beings decreed what should be done, perhaps how, and, implicitly or otherwise, why; but there may be also an immediate or practical reason, which their word serves to underwrite.

This is the case with women's love-magic rites. The specific aim of attracting a sweetheart, or renewing a husband's affection, and so on, is one aspect of a broader complex which is sponsored by such mythical characters as Chickenhawk, the fair-haired Munga-munga girls, Possum, or even the Rainbow. Relations between the sexes are seen in general terms, as vital to fertility. Some women, absorbed in their personal problems, disregard this broader framework, just as some husbands do in jealously resenting their wives' participation in the rites. But the viewpoint of others can be summed up in what one woman said about the *djarada* series which had come up to Katherine, in the Northern Territory, through Willeroo from the Victoria River country: 'When we sing about chickenhawk eggs and snake eggs, things like that, we want that chickenhawk, that snake, to have plenty of eggs, plenty of young: and women too, plenty of babies. If some women want to sing for sweethearts, they can sing. But some want to sing for Dreaming; well, they can sing for Dreaming. Some of us don't want to sing for sweethearts all the time, we like to sing for Dreaming.' In the songs which make up this particular *djarada* these various facets are quite apparent: love magic; reference to actions first performed by the mythical sponsors (such as the Munga-munga's encounter with a night-owl); and the fertility-increase aspect.

A much more common and widespread example is that of straightforward increase rites. These are mostly to do with the cult totems already mentioned. Men associated with a particular totem perform rituals intended to renew or maintain the supply of that particular species, sometimes helped by others who play a subordinate part. Increase rituals of a totemic kind are held all over Aboriginal Australia. In some areas they are quite simple, and although they centre on a specific site the performers may not be painted or decorated, or may not use special objects. Here are two examples from the Western Desert.

Minma Didi (a brown bird woman) collected snakes in a skin bag. When it became too full it burst, the snakes came out, and she ran away. A claypan formed where the bag fell, and at *gabi* Daral the snakes were metamorphosed into four large stones with smaller ones alongside. Didi cult totem women are sent out to this site, sometimes accompanied by men. There they lift up the small stones, then drop them again, and make snake tracks leading away from the stones. The movement of the stones frightens out the spirit snakes; they scatter in all directions, enter 'mother' snakes at the breeding season, and are later born.

In another example Minma Nganamara, Mallee-hen Woman, was metamorphosed at Mindeljari: she had been frightened by the Wadi Gudjara. At the top of a granite boulder at this place is her nest, a depression in the stone. A large stone is Nganamara and around her, as smaller stones, are her eggs. Nganamara cult totem men go to the site, climb the boulder to the nest, and paint the stones in white and red ochres. This ensures a plentiful supply of mallee-hens and eggs. Mallee-hen spirits go out in every direction to enter 'mother' mallee-hens and be born. The Wadi Gudjara were the first to perform this rite.

Kaberry (1939: 203) says: "As the totemic ancestors passed through the country they left stones or sometimes a tree, each of which is supposed to contain the *guning* (spirit) of some animal, bird, fish, reptile, tuber, and so on. These sites are called *bud-bud* at Forrest River, and *wulwiny* among the Lunga. By rubbing one of these or striking it with bushes and uttering a spell, the *guning* will go forth and cause the species with which it is associated to multiply."

In parts of the Kimberleys the increase of a given species may be brought about simply by calling the appropriate names, or by touching up the cave paintings relating to it. Or men may go to the relevant site, open their arm-veins, and allow blood to drop on to it. Sometimes they go through actions representing what they hope will take place, such as imitating the behaviour of certain species: or trying to attract them. Elkin (1933: 73; 1954) gives a number of examples. Among the Ungarinjin, for instance, "the increase of the various valuable animal and plant species and the maintenance of the regular operation of various natural phenomena like the sun, moon, stars, wind and rain, is assured" by 'retouching the paintings in the various Wondjina (creative ancestral beings) galleries'. In western Arnhem Land, too, paintings in caves and rock shelters are retouched or new ones added, to ensure increase. Elkin mentions also the artificial arrangement of stones for increase: the designs so formed represent different species. In some areas where this is done, rituals are held and the stones anointed with red ochre or blood, or simply disturbed. Among the Karadjeri the *talu* (increase) for honey, for example, is based on a mythical event. 'The main performers go to a hole known as Nangula and brush it clean, then pierce their arm-veins and subincised penes so that blood flows into it. Each man takes some of the mixture of blood and dust and puts it into a small hole in a stick. They keep the sticks hidden in their hair, and eventually deposit them in trees at various places. The bees will now go out and make honey in those trees.' (Elkin, 1933: 37.)

Probably the best known of the increase rituals are the *intichiuma* of the Aranda and their neighbours. (Spencer and Gillen, 1938: 167-211.) These involve visits to sacred sites, such as the drawings of the witchetty grub totem at Emily Gap, near Alice Springs, and special ritual acts: in that case the uncovering of sacred stones, one representing the chrysalis stage of the grub and the other the egg; songs are sung and the stones are rubbed on the bellies of the performers, indicating repletion. In another a small patch of ground is cleared, and men let blood flow on to it from their arm-veins, then dry to form a hard surface. Upon this the sacred design of the emu totem is outlined in white pipeclay, red and yellow ochre, and powdered charcoal mixed with grease. (In the central west of the Northern Territory such ground drawings are marked out with blood and then decorated with white and red feather down. Strehlow, 1947: Plate 4, illustrates a similar example.) Men wearing decorated *tjurunga* on their heads act the part of *inniakwa*, emu ancestors. Women and children see them from a distance, but flee to the main camp as the men come near. Finally the ground drawing is destroyed. In the Hakea Flower rite, blood is allowed to flow over a stone representing a mass of hakea flowers. Every local totemic group has its own *intichiuma* ceremony, and no two are exactly alike.

In the *mindari* of the Dieri, associated with the *muramura* Warugadi, Emu, two groups take part: *wimabaia*, 'song bird', and *wimabili*, 'song bag'. The *wimabili* men make a large mud-flattened mound, on which are placed white pelican feathers and then black and red ochre dots. Four women are chosen from the two moieties: two are *wimabaia*, and two *wimabili*. In the afternoon ritual they walk across the mound which represents Emu's body. Then all the men begin to sing, telling about Emu, the *muramura* who emerged from Lake Eyre to attend the *mindari*. When the songs are finished the ceremonial leader, an emu cult totem man, breaks up the mound with a club, asking the emu to breed: the broken-up mound 'looks like little emus when they are just born'. Now there will be plenty of emus in season. That night the four chosen women bring water to the men who are gathered on the cleared ceremonial ground. Large boomerangs decorated with red and black ochre dots are placed on the ground before the men. The dancers fill their mouths with the water and spurt it over the boomerangs, which are said to belong to the *muramura* Emu. This rite, called 'watering the boomerangs', is said to make the emus breed and lay eggs. The four women then retire to the bush, where men visit them to have sexual relations. This is part of the increase ritual: the women represent emus being fertilized.

Another rite among the Dieri concentrates on the *badi* grub, of the *badara* box tree. It is connected with the myth of Bat Man, Wariliwulu. The end of a navel cord is wrapped in emu feathers, enclosed in a knitted bag to represent the grub, and hung up in a *badara* tree. Each day for about two weeks a Wariliwulu cult totem man comes, sits down, and 'sings the tree' to make it green, so that later the grubs will come. The singing also makes other grubs breed and become plentiful in the surrounding country. The grub spirits come from the waterhole called Mugaribalgabalgajagubandru, where the *muramura* Wariliwulu lives. (Wariliwulu is also associated with the *muramura* Darana mentioned in the last chapter.)

Increase rites, then, range from single actions such as moving a sacred stone, retouching a painting, invoking a totemic being, to the elaborate ritual of the *intichiuma* and the *mindari*. All increase sites or objects, along with the ritual acts which are carried out, are associated with mythological and totemic characters. The general idea in all these rites is to get in touch with these beings, to draw on their power to achieve the particular goal the performers have in mind. But in order that benefits should accrue, a special attitude toward the supernatural is essential. Moreover, not just anyone can undertake such a ritual successfully. In nearly all cases it must be a person who stands in a defined relationship to that being, for example as a cult totemite; in addition, in this context he is almost always viewed as a descendant of, or a reincarnation of, that being. Beliefs of this kind are not isolated, or haphazard, but part of a coherent system—for nearly all ritual and ceremonial expression in Aboriginal Australia is concerned with defining and establishing or sustaining man's relationship with his environment.

Part of the ritual may involve the use of blood, or its equivalent, red ochre. These two elements symbolize life and animation: the libation of blood, or red ochre, sets free the spirits which are desired. Blood is a significant element in all ritual, increase or otherwise.

In the *mindari* ritual sexual relations are symbolically associated with fertility, and not merely human fertility. Again, this is an aspect which takes different forms in various parts of the Continent. It need not include both men and women, but can be simulated by male actors on the sacred ground. It is much more common than one would suppose from the literature. We shall return to it when we discuss the great fertility cults of Arnhem Land.

Increase ritual need not concern only food. The goal may be rain; or it may be calm weather, as on the north-west coast, where rough conditions interfere with certain kinds of fishing. Or, as in Cape York Peninsula, Queensland, rites may concentrate on the increase of flies, with the idea of annoying or irritating strangers; others again, on the increase of leeches. Some can be performed on any suitable occasion. For others, the usual time is just before the period when the species concerned would normally increase—to make sure that they do. The Aborigines did not try to go contrary to nature, to alter or disturb its course, but simply to keep it going in a normal way.

RITUAL REPRESENTATIONS

In some areas the steps which are taken to bring about increase are much more elaborate. The performers paint and decorate themselves, and their actions take the shape of sacred rituals. Increase rites, then, like the *mindari,* shade into those where the short-range aim of increasing a species is of secondary importance, or not mentioned directly: for example, where the main purpose is to commemorate certain mythical beings, or to instruct younger people about them. Totemic cult rituals and ceremonies are of this type: for instance, the *ingkura* as described by Strehlow (1947), and others by Elkin (1954). Most of these are regarded as bigger or more important than others, and a prominent feature is their use of material symbolic representations: sacred objects which are intimately associated with participants and with the mythological beings are believed to produce particular effects if manipulated in traditionally defined ways.

Those most generally used by men are the bullroarer, varying in size and shape, and the *tjurunga*-type board, ranging in length from about one inch and a half to about twenty feet, either simply or intricately incised, or painted with realistic or conventionalized designs. In any one area there are several types of such boards or bullroarers, each type with its special name. Among the Aranda there are flat stone *tjurunga*; wooden boards; large and small bullroarers; ground paintings; ceremonial poles, *tnatantja*; ceremonial headgear; the *waninga* or *wanigi* emblem; and the sacred earth mound. *Tjurunga* is an Aranda word and, as Strehlow mentions (1947: 84-6), refers not only to sacred objects but also to the relevant ceremonies, myths, songs and so on. Everyone has, or is represented by, a stone or wooden *tjurunga*. These are kept in sacred caves, and in the case of young men there is a special ritual showing when they see their own *tjurunga* for the first time. To quote again from Strehlow (*ibid.*, 116-19), when the elders show a young man his *tjurunga* they tell him that it is his own body: 'This is the ancestor you were when you wandered about in your previous existence.' In the Western Desert there are long wooden *djilbilba* boards; ordinary *wanigi*; *laralara*, web-shaped *wanigi* mounted on a pole or a spear; and *bubing*, bull-roarers: this is a general label and each variety has its own name. Not all boards are secret. The *wanigi* is both sacred and secret in most of the Western Desert, but at Balgo and in the eastern Kimberleys it is used in 'playabout' ceremonies.

Some interesting objects of a rather different kind have been the centre of sacred rites in the Great Victoria Desert. Most of them are of stone. They were first seen by one of us at Ooldea in 1941, and since then we have heard of them at Laverton and the Warburtons. Two dark green stones were the metamorphosed bodies of the Wadi Gudjara. Another was a *djilbilba* board made by the Wadi Gudjara; its spirit shape was taken into the sky by the child Wudulu and is now part of the Milky Way. Others were the eggs of Minma Jungga, Black Goanna Woman, and Minma Milbali, White Goanna Woman. These objects are stored in a sacred storehouse when they are at a particular place. Ordinarily they are passed about from one group to another, travelling around the Great Victoria Desert in an anti-clockwise manner, from west to east and circling back to the west again, along a specified route. Four types of ritual are held in connection with them: meditation, instruction, blood-letting and increase of natural species; and 'driving'. In this last, two totemic headmen, holding the sacred relics, drive ahead of them the women and young men, pausing intermittently to engage in ritual howling. They are re-enacting a mythical incident associated with the Wadi Gudjara at *gabi* Ngigiran, an important religious centre. Other items in this complex include a stone shield made by the Wadi Gudjara; a stone dish, the body of the Waiuda, Possum Woman; another stone dish, symbolizing the body of the Milbali Goanna Woman, into which arm blood is spurted during the relevant ritual, each participant sipping from it and finally rubbing the remainder over their bodies; and the desiccated body of a woman in a flexed position, the 'actual' body of the Milbali Woman.

In some areas the women themselves possess sacred ritual objects: the *miliri* or *giari (kijari)* pole, for instance, among women in the Victoria River district (C. Berndt, 1950*a*), or the *djugubi sanba* or *janbara* at Ooldea. In Arnhem Land, the range of sacred objects is very wide indeed. (See Spencer, 1914; Elkin, Berndt and Berndt, 1950; Warner, 1937/1958; McCarthy, 1948, 1957*a*; and Mountford, 1956.) Among them, in western Arnhem Land, apart from the *ubar* gong there are hundreds of *maraiin* objects: ornately decorated poles with feathered strings attached; beautifully shaped wooden figures of birds, animals and fish, and so on, painted vividly in ochres; objects of bound grass; and painted stones and lumps of hard wild beeswax. In north-eastern Arnhem Land they include *rangga* poles, posts and other objects, profusely decorated and in some cases hung with feathered tassels; the *uwar* gong; long Julunggul Python didjeridus, or drone pipes; and carved human figures. (See Chapter XII.)

The *maraiin* rituals of western Arnhem Land are post-initiatory, and are principally of totemic increase intent. In addition to the range of objects already mentioned, there are others representing parts of the human body, slices of turtle meat, crocodile tongues, emu hearts, wallaby livers, snakes' eggs and so on. When not in use some of them are stored in the bush in rock shelters, or in sacred dilly bags. Other *maraiin* objects are dismantled after use and destroyed. A western Arnhem Land myth tells how these people obtained the *maraiin* ceremonies.

Lumaluma came from the east, swallowing people as he moved from one place to another. In desperation those who remained decided to kill him. As they began to spear him, Lumaluma cried out, 'Don't kill me yet. Leave me for a while, and in return I will show you all the ceremonies I know before I die.' He showed them the *maraiin*, the eastern variant of the *ubar*, the *djunggawon*, *lorgan*, and *gunabibi*, all sacred ceremonies. Then he showed them non-sacred ceremonies: *djadbangari*, *gad* (mortuary sequence), *gunoin*, *barura*, *biridjira*, *bonggwon*, *mindiwala*. Finally came the *buranggang*, the ceremony of his death: the dancing re-enacts the scene when he was fatally speared. Turning away from the dancing place Lumaluma moved down to the beach, into the water, and out to sea. They watched him rising from the water, sending out a spray of water from his wounded body as he cried to them, 'Don't call me Lumaluma any more. I have left the land. I am Nawulnawul, the Whale.' All the people wept.

Spencer (1914: 189) gives a different mythical explanation of the origin of the *maraiin*, which he called *muraian*. However, his descriptions of these rituals tally with those one of us (R. M. Berndt) saw at Oenpelli. Elkin (1961*b*) also discusses a *maraiin* held at Mainoru, in southern Arnhem Land.

Because the range of sacred rituals and ceremonies is so varied, and so rich in detail, it is impossible to cover even in a sketchy way this vital dimension of Aboriginal life. To do that would entail not only a description of the rites, but also analysis of the relevant myths and songs, as well as objects and local sites. Instead we shall single out one type of ritual, outlining the principal actions which take place in it, and the interpretations which people offer for them: and the choice falls on the Arnhem Land fertility cults.

FERTILITY CULTS

We return to the *ubar* of western Arnhem Land, to the ritual counterpart of the myth.

The resonant sound of the *ubar* gong comes clearly across the plains near the East Alligator River: the Mother is calling men to the sacred ground. In the main camp women dance, each holding in her hands an endless piece of string, a cat's-cradle such as young girls use, and calling '*Gaidbaa! Gaidbaa!*' in answer to the beat of the *ubar*. The *ubar* continues, joined by the drone of the didjeridu, and singing begins. First there are individual performances; each man dances separately, with arms outstretched or holding a spear or spearthrower poised in each hand, while others surround him crying out '*Ja, ja, ja!*' to a climax of '*Jei, jei, gogjei, gogjei!*' Women in the camp call back '*Gaidbaa! Gaidbaa!*'

After an interval the second part of the ritual begins. There is silence, and an atmosphere of expectation, until a whistling begins. This accompanies the bringing in of the dancers, one by one. Each is led in by the ceremonial headman, placed in position, and moves his head from side to side while the other bends over him uttering the sacred words of the *ubar*. The whistling is said to be for the wet season, summoning the Rainbow Snake. As the Snake moves his horns are raised, and it is through these that the wind whistles as it starts to blow; the Rainbow arches his body and ascends the sky. He is the harbinger of rain, rejuvenator of the earth: he is the instrument through which the rebirth of nature is achieved, with the help of the Mother.

A long row of actors is formed, all squatting in a haunched posture with heads bent: these are, alternately, male and female wallabies, the animals which appear when the Rainbow sends the wet season. Another actor is placed on the ground and a sacred *maraiin* stone, which is the flesh of the *ubar* Snake, is brought to him to hold: this makes him a living representation of the mythical being. The 'wallabies' then begin to perform as the beat of the clapping sticks changes. They bend toward each other and rub their heads together as they move them from side to side, pause, and shake their bodies. The two end wallabies jump up and dance forward: they are interrupted by the spear of a hunter, which wounds them. All the others jump up one by one, following them. They move around the ground and finally resume their original positions, while the two wounded wallabies throw themselves to the ground. Then they jump up again and all crouch together in a rough circle, bending forward, while the headman calls the sacred invocations. The Rainbow Snake actor moves only a little, on the outskirts. This is followed by more individual dancing and the calling out of '*Ja, ja, ja, gogjei!*' Then all come together again for the calling of the sacred invocations, and after washing off their ochre designs they return to the main camp.

On the following evening the *ubar* sounds again, and again the men leave the camp while women call out ritually. This time the *ubar* is supported on two forked posts at the head of the sacred ground, and beaten by a man standing alongside it. Again the actors are brought in to the accompaniment of whistling: the wallabies are arranged in the attitude of coitus. As the sticks begin to beat, a male wallaby jumps over the back of a female (symbolic coitus) and then over the others. They each do the same, in turn. Finally, all spring up and form a circle: the sacred invocations are called over them. The *ubar* is lifted from the posts. Accompanied by the didjeridu and beating sticks it is carried around, encircling the men, who call out '*Gogjei, gogjei!*' (This re-enacts the incident in which Jurawadbad entered the sacred ground.)

Then the *ubar* is replaced temporarily on its rack. After an interval it is placed lengthways on the ground. Two novices are brought forward, and placed one at each end of it. (This is a re-enactment of part of the Jurawadbad myth: see Chapter VII.) They put their hands inside, then remove them: the *ubar* is lifted up at one end so that an object, a *maraiin* stone, rolls out and touches the hands of each novice in turn (symbolizing the bite of Jurawadbad). While this is happening all the men are gathered around them, and the boys' heads are rubbed or moved from side to side, keeping time with the beat of the didjeridu and clapping sticks. Individual dancing follows. Then two men representing *wiliwili* birds are led forward and placed on the ground back to back. Another, astride a pandanus log, represents a *djurul* bird. When the sticks begin to clap the *djurul* bird shakes itself several times. The two *wiliwili* rub the backs of their heads together, from side to side, and bend forward and around to an upright position. They shuffle down the ground, surrounded by onlookers. Finally they get up and hold hands above their heads to form an arch. In this position they dance down the ground, invocations are called over them, and they reach the *ubar*.

That completes the second day's rites. On following days these are repeated, but after an interval the men go out to the ground again and rearrange it. A stone, the Snake's head, is placed at the apex of the ground and a brush shelter at the other end. Repetition of the wallaby and *wiliwili* dancing is followed by a scene in which a man sits astride a pandanus log near the Snake's head. Holding the log, he bends forward and around, and so back to an upright posture, then shakes his shoulders. (He is Jurawadbad introducing the rite, imitating the actions of the two women in the myth looking into his hollow log, the *ubar*.) Opposite him are the two *wiliwili* birds, who carry out the same actions as before, and then shuffle down the ground toward the shelter. Another two actors, *mulibug* birds, take their place. Then several actors are brought on to the ground. They form a line, each bending forward and holding the back of the man in front. This line represents the Rainbow Snake. It moves forward to the accompaniment of whistling and surrounds the shelter several times, drawing closer to it each time, beating and dragging the bushes (i.e., the Rainbow comes rustling through the bushes). Individual dancing completes the series, and the men return to the camp.

In the final ritual, the men reassemble to the sound of the *ubar*. The wallaby dancing is repeated, but this time they move around the shelter dismantling it and then dance on its remains. Finally, older men pile together the dry boughs and set them alight. The young men dance around the blaze, calling out '*Gogjei, gogjei!*' They must keep away from its smoke, for if it touches them they may weaken. Only the old men pass through the billows of smoke, raking together the remaining branches, keeping the flames alive.

This completes one section of the *ubar*. In the extended series there are many other rites. On the final day all the men come singing into the main camp, in single file. Women meet them, dancing and calling out. Two women climb a pandanus and swing their sacred *lida* object; one or two men also climb a pandanus and call out sacred invocations. Finally all members of the camp bathe ritually in a nearby billabong.

There are too many aspects to mention in detail. For instance, all participants are decorated with special designs. At Oenpelli the actual ceremonial ground is symbolically identified as the Rainbow Snake: the *ubar* is Ngaljod, the Rainbow Snake, who is also the Mother. At Goulburn Island the Rainbow is male, but the ground is the body or uterus of the Mother. Her spirit enters the *ubar*, through which she 'talks', calling all the men to come to her. The men coming on to the ground are re-enacting their original spiritual conception and birth from the Mother. They return to her, becoming sacred through entering her and being in her presence. The *ubar* must be beaten incessantly throughout the ritual, and so men take turns in using the flat-topped pandanus beating sticks. Should the beating stop, this means that her spirit has departed, and the ritual will lose its potency.

Among the actors in these *ubar* rites is one whose role is most unusual for Aboriginal Australia, although it has been reported from other parts of the world. This is the role of clown, or jester. During some of the most serious moments of the Rainbow Snake ritual, an actor moves about the sacred ground poking fun at the dancers, and in fact at the whole proceedings, mimicking their actions and even laughing in their faces. But this licensed joking is confined to himself; and in part it is a test for the novices. Everyone is expected to behave as if he were not there, to avoid showing even a flicker of interest, let alone amusement, at his antics—to be so deeply engrossed in the ritual itself that no distraction of this sort can have any effect.

Another feature of the *ubar* is that women with white hair, 'almost ready to die', are permitted to witness sections of the ritual on the men's sacred ground. Each woman who does so must be accompanied by a close male relative, such as a son, who formally introduces her to the *ubar*: and she herself has no active role in the proceedings. The explanation of this is that by the time she has reached such an advanced age she is reasonably safe: the power of the *ubar*, and of the sacred rites, cannot harm her. Younger women, and children, must be protected; men must mediate between them and the potentially dangerous forces which are basic to human life, but too strong for any but initiated men to cope with directly. Some women say that the *ubar* Mother, like the Kunapipi Mother, prefers to have ritual dealings with men: that she is jealous of women, almost as a co-wife is jealous, but also in the same way that a mother may help and cherish her sons more consistently and for a longer period, if she can, than her daughters —who are expected to be able to fend for themselves at an earlier age. The *ubar* woman is a Mother, concerned for the wellbeing of her adherents: but she is a rival too. Men must be careful in approaching her, making use of the appropriate ritual channels: and this caution is even more imperative for women.

Next, an outline of the north-eastern Arnhem Land *dua* moiety Djanggawul rituals. These have been discussed in some detail by Warner (1937/1958) and Berndt (1952*a*).

A shade or shelter is erected on the sacred ground, and leaders of the *dua* moiety clans and linguistic units prepare the *rangga* emblems. One is the *mawulan* pole, which the Djanggawul Brother used as a 'walking-stick'; when he plunged it into the ground spring water came gushing forth. He did the same with the *djanda* goanna tail, just as the Two Sisters did with their *ganinjari* 'yam' stick or walking-stick. When he used the *djuda*, however, trees sprang up from the ground. These are the basic *rangga* forms, but they have been elaborated into a number of others. Most are decorated in ochres with patterns derived from those first given by the Djanggawul. Also, most have attached to them red parakeet feathered string, symbolizing the rays of the sun, the red sky at sunset, or the blood of the Sisters. The shade of branches symbolizes the *ngainmara* mat, and also a uterus—like the sacred ground itself. The initiates are symbolically *rangga*, or children of the Djanggawul. The preliminary dances represent the rise and fall of the surf, and the sound of the sea, commemorating the original journey from Bralgu to Port Bradshaw. Invocations are called at intervals throughout the dancing and during all the *nara* rituals, and again when the men return to the main camp. The women's role is to provide the men with food: traditionally, cycad palm bread, supplemented by other meats and vegetables.

Soon after these preliminary rituals are held, people from other groups come in: they have been summoned by specially 'signed' message sticks, feathered string, or miniature copies of sacred objects moulded from wild beeswax. Men assemble on the dancing ground to make emblems, and others are removed from the water or mud of sacred sites where they have been stored. These are said to be like *rangga* taken from the Sisters' *ngainmara*, or children from their wombs. They are dried and repainted with designs from water marks which their original counterparts acquired during their journey. In the course of this, the sea dancing is repeated. The songs relate to water from the sacred 'wells' which the Djanggawul made by inserting their *rangga*. This symbolizes coitus between the Brother and Sisters, and the gushing water is the semen which fertilizes both human beings and the earth. It represents too the coming of the heavy rains of the wet season, which is viewed as a period of fertilization.

The first rites in the main sequence relate to totemic species, and do not usually involve *rangga*. Neophytes are instructed. There is a ritual shaving of facial hair. Older men leave short tufts or beards that symbolically represent the fringe of the conical mat, and attach to them red parakeet feathers, like pendant strings from the emblems. In the main camp women, young children, and uninitiated boys gather in a cleared place where they are covered with *ngainmara* mats. Symbolically, they are unborn children of the Djanggawul. Now the men come dancing from the sacred ground and surround them, carrying spears, spearthrowers, and sticks. Invocations are called, mostly the names of places where the Djanggawul Sisters gave birth to the first people. The dancing men poke the mats, and the women and children underneath wriggle in response. Invocations relating to sexual intercourse, childbirth, and so on lead up to the 'birth' itself as they emerge from their mats. They sit watching the men. More invocations are called, and the ritual is over. Again the accent is on fertility. The act of birth, symbolic here, represents in miniature the desired goal: the replenishment of human beings, and the natural species on which they depend.

The next stage is the showing of more totemic dances on the sacred ground. These continue for some weeks. Sections of the myth are re-enacted: for example, there are the animals, birds and other creatures seen at each place through which the Djanggawul passed. The major rituals concern the *djanda* goanna, the *djalga* water goanna, the *lindaridj* parakeet, and spring water. Then the sacred *rangga* are used in dancing and in posturing. The main ones are handled by individual dancers, or by groups of actors who writhe along the ground with the *rangga* clasped to their bodies or held in stylized ways. All the dancers emerge from the sacred shade in which the *rangga* are kept, to the accompaniment of singing or simply to the tapping of the clapping sticks. Some of the most important emerge in silence. In the main camp women gather around a tree or forked stick. Men come down from the sacred ground, calling out ritually. Women answer. The ceremonial leader climbs the tree and women dance around him; clapping the sticks, he calls the invocations. Pairs of dancers then take the part of various creatures, dancing near the tree, in front of the women.

After all this has been going on for some weeks men come, one night, to the main camp bearing flaming torches. This symbolizes the fire which the two Sisters thought had destroyed their sacred bags containing the *rangga*, not realizing at first that they had been stolen. The women dancing around the tree are the Sisters, and the tree is the sacred *djuda* of life-giving properties. The men's totemic dancing by the tree repeats, they say, the actions of the Brother and his companions in their sacred shade: and this in turn goes back to the first performance of all, when the two Sisters danced alone, out of sight of men, while they were still in control of all the sacred emblems and rites.

In the next few weeks the *ngainmara* ritual is repeated in the main camp, and on the sacred ground there are more totemic dances. Neophytes see only the minor emblems. They are painted with sacred patterns, in the manner of corpses, for their ritual death. Then follows ritual bathing. Men representing geese or diving ducks dance down to the billabong or beach and plunge into the water, followed by everyone of all ages. Invocations are called, and when they emerge the men dance various totemic fish. Symbolically this is the wetting of the *rangga* on their journey from Bralgu. At the same time, the people are *rangga* which are put back into a sacred waterhole when the *nara* is completed. There are other symbolic meanings as well. The *nara* proper ends at this point, but it may be followed by other rites. Some are shown to the younger neophytes, by way of instruction. At others the only people present are fully initiated men, familiar with all phases of the *nara*. Then comes sacramental eating of cycad bread on the sacred ground, while invocations are called and the feathered string is removed from the emblems.

The central theme here is, symbolically, both the human sequence which culminates in childbirth, and the cycle of growth and renewal in the natural environment: with the coming of the hot sunshine and rains of the wet season new plants appear, and new foliage, and all the natural species are reborn.

In the same area, the Wawalag mythology underlies three main ritual sequences. The *djunggawon* relates primarily to circumcision. The *gunabibi*, or Kunapipi, has much the same emphasis as the Djanggawul *nara*. The *ngurlmag*, most important of the three, resembles the western Arnhem Land *maraiin* and is mainly revelatory in character. Because the Kunapipi extends so widely, and because so little attention has been accorded such cults in the literature on the Australian Aborigines, our next example outlines the main features of the sequence in this particular area. (See Warner, 1937/1959; R. Berndt, 1951*a*.)

Usually the Kunapipi is held in the dry season when food is plentiful. The assumption is that people are reaping the benefits of performances held in previous years, and at the same time are preparing for the coming wet season and the subsequent growth of food. The rituals may last from two weeks to several months. Messengers are sent out to notify the members of other groups. In the meantime, the hosts go out into the bush. There they prepare the ritual ground, and make a bullroarer, which they

Aranda actors as Emu ancestors, wearing sacred decorated *tjurunga*, in the *tarabulja* non-secret ceremony. Note their pearlshell necklets
(photo: courtesy T. G. H. Strehlow)

Second view of the Aranda actors above. Note the boomerangs held behind their backs
(photo: courtesy T. G. H. Strehlow)

Left: Lightning totem man wearing a 'pokiti' headdress, in the Gadjeri (or Kunapipi) rituals at Birrundudu, central-western Northern Territory (1944-5). (See Chapter VIII)

Below: Men in sacred 'ring place' being decorated for the Djanba (mythical being) series of the Gadjeri rituals. The feather down decorations represent his particular design as well as the special balls he used. Wave Hill, central-western Northern Territory (1944)

anoint with blood to the accompaniment of singing. Some time afterward the first rites take place in the main camp. Men sing the 'outside' or camp version of the Wawalag and Kunapipi songs, while the women dance: non-sacred *garma* or clan songs are also sung. This continues for some weeks.

Then, one evening, the sound of the bullroarer is heard—the voice of Julunggul, the Rock Python, or Rainbow. The Kunapipi leader calls out in answer. So do all the women, just as the Wawalag Sisters cried out when Julunggul came near them. Almost immediately afterward young boys, smeared with red ochre and arm blood, are taken from the main camp to meet Julunggul. He swallows them. By accepting this offering Julunggul is diverted from the main camp and induced to return to the sacred ground. Women wail for the initiates as if they were dead. (Similarly, in the *djunggawon* rituals linked with the same myth, boys who are circumcised are said to be swallowed by the python just as the Wawalag sisters were; and in some versions this is an act of propitiation, to ensure that the whole camp will not be swallowed. Finally the boys are 'vomited', as if they had been reborn after a temporary death.) This goes on until all the boys have been brought to the sacred ground. There intermittent singing and dancing continue through the night, while from a distance women return the calls of the men or answer the sound of the bullroarer. The dances have to do with the creatures which the Wawalag tried to cook, but which escaped from the fire on Julunggul's orders and disappeared into the waters of Muruwul. The sacred ground itself, in the shape of an elongated triangle, is Julunggul's body: and the *nanggaru* hole at its apex represents Muruwul.

The men leave the sacred ground and dance with lighted paperbark torches toward the main camp. On the way they come to where women are crouched under conical mats. Two old women walk up and down, calling out the names of foods which are forbidden to women at this time, and reciting extracts from the Wawalag story. Men of the *jiridja* moiety dance around the mat-covered women. They are Julunggul smelling the blood of the Wawalag; but because there is none they go away, after accepting gifts of food from the women.

Now the visitors are arriving. Women make further gifts of food, and on the sacred ground the *nanggaru* hole is dug. In all the dances which follow, the actors, who are various totemic creatures, enter this hole. Most of them are arranged in pairs of male and female, and they simulate mating. The most important series is the possum dancing, where the men have long bark penes protruding from their hair belts. These rituals continue for some weeks, until a large crescent-shaped trench is dug. This is the *ganala*, the uterus. (In the western Arnhem Land Kunapipi, the walls of this trench are marked with the Snake design.) When it is completed, snake totem actors dance or writhe in the hole: this is followed by the 'mating dance', and others.

In the meantime the two large *jelmalandji* emblems are being prepared, each about twelve to twenty feet long. The basis is a pole, about which are tied pads of grass and paperbark. The outer covering of bark is smeared with arm blood and red ochre, and on this is fastened feather down in a meandering pattern symbolizing Julunggul. A bunch of cockatoo feathers is attached to the top. Both *jelmalandji* have similar designs. One represents the Julunggul, the other the cabbage or wild coconut *gulwiri* palm, which was growing near the Wawalag's shade. The actors too are decorated with feather down. Before the *jelmalandji* are erected the novices are led in, placed in the *ganala*, and covered with bark. Men perform a series of totemic dances while the *jelmalandji* are brought on to the ground and placed beside the *ganala*. The bark sheets covering the novices are removed. The older Kunapipi leaders step forward. Taking sweat from their armpits they rub the palms of their hands across the eyes of the youths, at the same time telling them to look at Julunggul emerging from the waters of Muruwul. Another series of totemic dances is performed before the *jelmalandji*. Then come two actors wearing the tall conically-shaped headdress which represents the pandanus palm the Wawalag saw at Muruwul. This is followed by ritual fire-throwing, the *djamala mareiin*. Firesticks are thrown across the sacred ground and over the *ganala* in which the novices are crouching, symbolizing the lightning sent by Julunggul.

Then actors re-create the scene in which the Wawalag Sisters are swallowed. A pole is brought out and with it two men push over the *jelmalandji*, to the accompaniment of ritual crying: the Julunggul are falling over, after swallowing the Wawalag. The novices are removed from the *ganala* and the *jelmalandji* put in their place. Firesticks are thrown on top, to burn the grass and paperbark surrounding the central poles. Men open their arm-veins and sprinkle blood on one another and into the *ganala*: this is the blood of the Wawalag. Finally they dance around the *ganala*, filling the hole with sand and earth, flattening the ground.

This completes the main section of the Kunapipi, apart from two concluding features: the ceremonial exchange of wives, and the return of the young boys to the main camp.

Ritual licence, widely known as the *gurangara*, is an integral part of the Kunapipi. It is said to establish goodwill, to cement the bonds of friendship, bringing members of different groups closer together. Moreover, it draws women further into the sacred scheme of the Kunapipi, and symbolizes fertility, which is the main aim of the ritual. The partners are not only classificatory wives and husbands, but also persons normally tabu to each other, especially those who call each other mother-in-law and son-in-law. The Kunapipi songs include a series dealing with love magic between such a pair.

There are some brief preliminaries. This time, when the men return to the sacred ground they do nothing but sit down and wait. Presently a group of women comes on to the ground, decorated with feathered string headbands. They dance the bandicoot sequence, then follow their leader in single file back toward the main camp. Symbolically, they are Julunggul approaching the Wawalag. They return in the same way, calling out their sacred term for Julunggul, *'Gidjin!'* The men sit quietly with heads bent. The leader puts up two emblems she and her companions have made secretly: Julunggul, in the shape of miniature *jelmalandji.* They are showing these to the men, treating them as novices. Next they strike the emblems with stringy bark, so that pieces of paperbark from them fly to the ground. In the myth Julunggul sent lightning to attack the Wawalag as they crouched in their hut: it splintered a stringy bark tree so that pieces of wood flew in all directions, and from one of them the first sacred bullroarer was made. After this the women form a dancing line before the men, who begin to sing. They get up and walk over to various women, handing them presents of food, string or ochre, and one couple after another retires to the nearby bush.

The following morning sees the final part of the Kunapipi. Men begin to dance and twirl bullroarers, and set up the *djebalmandji* between the sacred ground and the main camp. Two forked posts are placed upright about six feet apart, supporting a thick ridge pole which is hung with branches so that the space between it and the ground is thickly covered. The novices are placed under the branches, hidden from view, holding on to the ridge pole with their hands. Two Snake men climb on to the forked posts, moving the palms of their hands against their mouths, calling all the men and women to come to the *djebalmandji.* The young novices who have passed through all the main rituals lie passively in the symbolic uterus: soon they will be coming out, will be spiritually reborn.

People assemble on the ritual ground. The women arrive dancing like the Wawalag, driven along by the sound of twirling bullroarers hidden in the surrounding bush. They surround the *djebalmandji,* answering the call of the bullroarers. Then they move off to sit in a bunch some little distance away, and cover themselves and the children with bark and with conical mats while men perform the flying fox dance, calling out like flying foxes. This is said to trick the women into thinking that something else is meant; but it is not really the voice of the flying fox, it is the cry of the Wawalag, frightened of Julunggul. The dancing men surround the covered women and children, and the *djebalmandji*. The two Snake men on the forked sticks cry out. The dancers prod the women with sticks, and throwing aside their coverings they look toward the *djebalmandji* where the young novices are emerging from the branches covered with red ochre, symbolizing blood. The women begin to call out, and return dancing to the main camp. After the *djebalmandji* has been pulled down, the men follow them. There are several other terminating rites. Finally, the men and youths are red-ochred all over. Outline designs of Julunggul are arranged on their backs, and they are brushed with smoking ironwood branches as a form of purification.

The Wawalag mythology is more or less indigenous to the north-eastern Arnhem Land region. The Kunapipi is not, but when it reached here from the south it found an atmosphere congenial to its acceptance—just as it did in western Arnhem Land, where it had much in common with what was already there: the creative Mother Waramurungundju, for instance, Ngaljod the Rainbow and her counterpart the male Rainbow, and many of the assumptions underlying the rites of the *ubar*. With some interchanging of names and shifting of identities it could be fitted easily into the existing patterns, regardless of whether the local social structure emphasized patrilineal descent, as in eastern Arnhem Land, or matrilineal descent, as in western Arnhem Land. The Kunapipi is flexible enough to accommodate a variety of interpretations around its central theme, and even within it. As it passes from one area to another it undergoes certain modifications. New songs may be added, or old ones translated in different ways by people who do not know the language in which these have reached them, although they have been given an account of their meaning.

The Kunapipi which came into the Oenpelli area of western Arnhem Land a few years ago, for instance, included songs of protective magic for people going through the rites for the first time, women as well as men: the spirit of a snake or a small parrot was sung into the back of their heads, so that it could warn them should anyone creep up stealthily to work sorcery on them or spear them in the back. In this particular complex Kunapipi is sometimes identified with Ngaljod, the Rainbow: she is a woman, 'our Mother', but also a snake, and she may take other shapes too. If is difficult to know how literally women in this Arnhem Land region take the conventional accounts of her appearance, and of what happens on the men's sacred ground. Many of them do appear to believe that such accounts are factually as well as symbolically true.

At Oenpelli during a Kunapipi sequence women who were commenting on the songs they were singing, and on the related rites and myth, seemed to be convinced that Kunapipi had in fact emerged from the ground when summoned by the men's cries and the sound of 'her' boomerangs; that she swallowed all the men but kept the young ones longer, letting them out at intervals to eat the food with which the women kept them supplied; that while they remained in her belly, immersed in liquid, they would smooth back their hair to keep the blood out of their eyes; that she would carry them about by night as they slept, because she herself was restless and unsleeping, but was careful about what she hunted for fear it would hurt them—no fish with sharp bones, for instance. Each time she vomited them at daybreak, women said, they were 'born' on to heaps of soft grass which older men had made ready: and as they lay there small and naked, their hands empty of belongings, she would lick them all over until they grew to their full size again. And so on.

But women of this area, like their menfolk, were equally ready to identify Kunapipi with the destructive aspects of Ngaljod when, later, one of the adult men who had been initiated on that occasion died suddenly one day and no other explanation seemed to fit.

Inevitably, ranging over so wide a region—throughout Arnhem Land, across the main north-south road up to the outskirts of Darwin and west to the Daly and Katherine and Victoria rivers, meeting the Galwadi-Gadjeri series from the central western deserts —the Kunapipi constellation is in many respects fluid. But the nucleus, or core, is persistent: there are very much the same paraphernalia, much the same rites, myths and songs. Above all, there is the dominant emphasis on birth, or rebirth: the sacred ground is the 'Mother place' through which men pass to be reborn.

SOCIAL RELEVANCE OF RITUAL

Myth and ritual not only provide the members of an Aboriginal community with a framework through which to perceive their world. They are also an assertion that human life is important, that it has meaning, that it makes sense. Individual persons are born, develop, and die, but that is not the end of it: they belong within a scheme which has continuity as well as comprehensiveness. Myth, as 'spoken or sung ritual', describes and explains what people need to know about this scheme, in a form which can be transmitted with varying degrees of complexity. 'Acted-out ritual' expresses more or less the same content in a different dimension. There is close correspondence between the two, but not necessarily uniformity—if only because of the existence of variants in myth, and the fact that ritual actions too are not immune to changes, or divergences in interpretation.

Much of Aboriginal religion has to do, as we have seen, with the problems of human beings in their spatial and temporal environment. The here-and-now aspects of getting food, having water to drink, surviving hazards of one kind or another, are set in wider perspective. There is reassurance from the past, and hope for the future, an affirmation that man is not entirely helpless, whatever hardships he may suffer at times. There is the conviction that he can intervene to some degree, do something to influence the forces which impinge on him. (The same fundamental confidence, or optimism, underlies sorcery—the belief that people have the ability to manipulate the lives of others, from a distance, even to the extent of disabling them through injury, illness and death: that given more goodwill and less friction between human beings, the incidence of these misfortunes would drop accordingly, because it is human beings rather than impersonal causes such as disease or accident who are primarily responsible for them.) In other words, people are not entirely at the mercy of events: they are less vulnerable than they may seem.

The relationship between human and other beings, or between man and other aspects of nature, is characteristically expressed through such manifestations as totemism, and the widespread assumption that ritual performances on the basis of that relationship can influence the reproduction of human and natural species and maintain the normal course of the seasons. The personal bond between a man and some natural species, or a man and some mythical being, is indispensable if these ritual performances are to succeed in their aims. It is only 'mechanical' rites at the magical end of the continuum which need no such prerequisite.

This sympathy or partial identification between human and other beings helps to soften the rigours of even a harsh environment by making it appear more friendly: bringing its natural features within the realm of the familiar, the personally known and predictable. To survive, the Aborigines have had to be intimately acquainted with their physical environment, its resources, shortcomings, and dangers; but they have gone a step further and established a spiritual relationship with it, as a way of underlining the legitimacy of their own place in it and of the demands they make on it. On one hand this bond expresses their belief in the unity or harmony of living things, in spite of conflicts between them. On the other it upholds the primary importance of human life. The Aborigines, to say it again, are not concerned with dominating their surroundings. Their sacred sites are mostly a matter of natural features such as waterholes, rocks, or stone arrangements which owe little if anything to their endeavours. Their monuments are not buildings or other constructions added to the landscape, but part of that landscape, involving at most a rearrangement or reassembling of some of its elements. They do not live in a man-made environment, but in one where human beings often appear to be dwarfed, physically, by their natural surroundings. Their land is on the whole sparsely populated, even in fertile regions. They have made an impact on it neither through weight of numbers, nor through asserting their control by attempting to change it. Instead, they base their claim to it on the grounds of spiritual and emotional kinship with it.

In general terms, they are not intruders, they have every right to be there. The mythical beings themselves established that right: their title is, consequently, as valid, and goes as far back in time, as that of any of its other inhabitants. Specifically, links with those other inhabitants, and with features of the environment, are divided among sections of the community. In other words they share the privilege, and obligation, of maintaining these particular relationships—as in various forms of totemism, or custodianship of certain sites. But such bonds are not self-sustaining. They must be constantly renewed, just as bonds with all the major beings must be: and the only way in which this can be done is through traditionally prescribed ritual. The mythology points out why, and sometimes how: the ritual translates this into action, at the appropriate times and places. This is the conventional picture. The main stress is on the general issue of man in relation to his natural environment and, by extension, to his supernatural environment, as providing a broader horizon than the narrow span of a human life cycle.

But in the course of coping with all this, no less than in coping with everyday experience, the matter of relations among human beings assumes at least equal significance. There are several facets to this.

One is the question of sharing, or not sharing, responsibility for attending to myths or songs, rituals, or sites—who owns, or controls, or does, or *is*, what, in this connection: who has a special relationship with what mythical being(s).

This has a direct bearing on membership in one unit as con trasted with another, or others—a local descent group, a social or totemic clan, a tribe—on the grounds of common ownership of sacred knowledge, common spiritual if not consanguineal descent, collective responsibility for undertaking a sacred rite, the sharing of a sacred symbol, and so on. Like language, these offer a means of establishing social identity, of justifying or affirming cleavages and common interests, likeness and difference. They constitute, too, another aspect of the division of labour: each unit contributing a certain part, or owning a certain section of a myth or ritual sequence, so that recognition of the broader myth-ritual perspective constitutes also acknowledgment of a broader network of social relations, and of common assumptions about critical issues of human living. Just as within a community men and women are expected to collaborate in ritual as in other affairs, although often in an asymmetrical fashion and certainly on the basis of contrasting or dissimilar contributions, so between social units involved in such a wider constellation, or between different segments of these (e.g. moieties, clans, sections, subsections), co-operation is essential for the overall success of the ritual enterprises in which their members engage. The co-operation may be active or passive, in varying degrees; and it need not involve joint participation in the same place at the same time. Interdependence can very well be manifested in separate or unlike contributions. Responsibility for various ritual sequences may be limited; but the assumption is that these are parts of a whole, however vaguely the boundaries of that whole are defined.

In spite of differential ownership and differential participation within a given community, on the score of sex and age and ritual grading, there is the implicit or explicit assurance that the ultimate benefits of any performance are for everybody in that community, men, women and children. Discrimination enters at the level of means, not of ends. According to the way in which this is interpreted, it could be seen as an attempt by one section of a community (e.g. adult men) to dominate another (e.g. women and children) by drawing on threats of supernatural sanctions, or justifying its own actions by claiming supernatural authority for them. Many instances could be listed in support of such a stand. Women and children have been speared for unknowingly crossing a 'track' along which secret-sacred objects have been carried (as in the Western Desert, or around the Daly River, to cite only two areas); men have been secretly disposed of under the guise of a *maraiin* killing, as punishment for sexual laxity or in the course of a feud, and occasionally their wives and close relatives have been forbidden to make any reference to them under pain of suffering the same penalty (western and eastern Arnhem Land).

Conversely, as between men and women, this discrimination could be viewed as a matter of men's shouldering responsibility for the principal burden of maintaining the religious system (just as they accept liability for the more adventurous and risky task of hunting larger game, or larger sea creatures), undertaking all the most arduous 'work' associated with it, and so leaving women relatively free to attend to the business of bearing and rearing children, and keeping up the supply of vegetables and smaller meats and shellfish. In this view, which is quite widely held, by so doing men are in fact protecting women, both from the difficult and strenuous duties involved, and from the dangers to which human beings are exposed in dealing with powerful forces outside the everyday or mundane range of human experience. Women themselves sometimes adopt this last approach in a parallel situation, when they contend that in excluding certain persons from their *djarada* or *jawalju* ceremonies they are not making the rules but acting in accordance with them: that, for instance, the 'power' involved is too strong for boys once they have been weaned, and can have a harmful effect on babies. The main paraphernalia, such as the long *giari* pole, should be carefully wrapped up and hidden away because of the sickness it could bring to any unauthorized person who handled it or even went near it. And according to some reports anyone, especially a young girl, who talks about the rites to non-participants, specifically to men, is likely to be taken ill and perhaps die: 'Mungamunga will do something to her in a dream.'

Another facet concerns the way in which social relations, including relations between the sexes, are dealt with in ritual and myth: what these media have to say about the arrangement of social units, the rules governing behaviour between persons, the breaking of such rules or the means by which they are enforced, or the types of behaviour which are enjoined or deplored. Frequently, the mythical characters acted in ways which are not normally open to human beings: brother and sister commit incest, brother kills brother, a woman tries to have sexual relations with her son-in-law, people marry 'wrong', and so on. This can be rationalized on the grounds of catharsis through vicarious participation, or the expression of secret wishes, or even the reflection of actual but unacknowledged instances. In any event, such spectacular examples of 'wrong' behaviour are few in comparison with those which are taken to represent 'right' or 'good' behaviour: the division of labour between the sexes in ritual and mundane affairs, the nature of marriage and family relations. The whole panorama of social and cultural life is either spelt out or inferred in myth and ritual, and in the comments and interpretations which supplement them.

Aboriginal religious systems are economically based—not simply in terms of immediate aims (e.g. increase and fertility), but in relation to their organization. All this ritual procedure must be seen against a complicated network of economic obligations, reciprocal duties, payments and receipts, as well as teaching and learning. But these systems also provide a moral basis for action, a set of fundamental principles in accordance with which conduct is directed and channelled. Sacred authority, authority which purports to rest on a religious foundation or to derive from a supernatural source, is a powerful factor in social control, and particularly so in Australian Aboriginal society.

CHAPTER IX

Magic and Sorcery

In magic, there is an assumption that by using special techniques human beings can manipulate or control forces which otherwise are inaccessible. The desired ends are usually short-range, and of a practical kind. In regard to the actual performance, there are four main elements: the material object or substance, that is, the instrument; the verbal action, that is, the spell, which may but need not involve a request or demand to some supernatural being; and the non-verbal action, that is, the rite. Any or all of these may be used in any given case. And fourthly, of course, there is the performer.

Durkheim viewed religion as basically social in origin, as well as in its outward manifestations. The essence of religious feeling, to him, was 'collective consciousness, or conscience', or the sentiments making for social solidarity. He therefore emphasized the individual character of magic. He saw it as an affair of individual performers concerned with furthering their own interests, and this he considered to be anti-social, opposed to the welfare of the larger unit. This distinction is difficult to maintain. Malinowski (1926) suggested that any magical act had a definite, straightforward aim, whereas a religious ritual did not. But this would exclude from the category of religion rites relating to initiation, increase, and fertility, as well as mortuary rites—in which there is always a definite purpose, an expectation of achieving certain ends by such means.

Many anthropologists have written about magic. There is no need to discuss their positions here, except to note that Firth's (1938/56: 156) classification under three main headings is directly relevant to the content of this chapter. The first is productive magic: fertility rites or certain increase rites, rainmaking, love magic, and so on. The second is protective magic, as in healing, or in counteracting the effects of misfortune or accident. Thirdly there is destructive magic, designed to bring sickness, injury or death to human beings, to destroy crops, or damage property. Rainmaking could occasionally come into this category too.

The first two are sometimes called 'white' or beneficial magic, the third 'black' or harmful magic; but when we look at them in a wider context, leaving aside the intentions or claims of the performer, the demarcation is actually not so clear-cut. In some cases the effects of 'black' magic beliefs may be quite beneficial, the effects of 'white' magic beliefs quite harmful. In speaking of destructive magic in Aboriginal Australia we usually call it sorcery, rather than witchcraft. And for the performer or organizer of destructive magic or sorcery the customary term is sorcerer; for the person who more or less regularly carries out beneficial magic, it is native doctor. Native doctors are sometimes sorcerers, and vice versa. A person may claim to be either, or both; or the claim may be made for him—or against him—by others, either in a general way or in respect of some specific incident.

BELIEF IN MAGIC

A question often asked is, 'Do Aborigines really perform sorcery, or magic?' In one sense, it does not matter whether they do or not. If they believe that such performances take place with the results that are claimed for them, this has almost the same social consequences as if they actually did so. It is the belief, influencing their behaviour in relation to one another, which counts—just as it is in regard to their interpretation of signs, or portents. (If people in the Daly River area claim that a queer feeling between the shoulder blades means that a person is going to be speared in the back, or a burning sensation in the stomach means that the woman experiencing it will soon meet her brother—statements like this are interesting in themselves, apart from any other consideration.)

In Aboriginal Australia, as in many other parts of the world, people do carry out certain rites, alone or collectively, in the belief that they are effective. When these are attempts to control or influence the natural environment, as in the case of the large magico-religious festivals of Arnhem Land—to bring rain, or increase the supply of animals and plants—they are based on assumptions which we in our society, generally speaking, do not share. We say that the premises are false, and that this action cannot possibly achieve that result. When it is control over human beings which is desired, the linkage is more obvious to us. A person who claims to have performed magic or sorcery on another is likely to make sure that this information gets around to his intended victim. Granted belief in the power of the relevant rite, or spell, this may indeed be enough. Also, it is easy to account for a failure by saying that 'something has gone wrong'. The ritual or spell was not performed properly, the counteracting magic may have been too strong, or the performer was not in the appropriate state. For example, he may have slept with his wife before a fishing or fighting expedition, or not adhered strictly to the appropriate tabus.

But the strength of magic and sorcery lies in the fact that there are always cases which can be regarded as positive proof. A rainmaker is likely to be most successful if he times his performance to coincide with the onset of a shower. This need not mean that he does this deliberately; but in certain seasons rain can be expected. We might say that it would fall in any case, whether or not any one had performed rain magic, but this is because we exclude magic as a possible cause of rain. In the same way, we do not consider that magic is responsible for the increase of animals, or the growth of crops. We look for other explanations which do not take magic into account, and regard it as irrelevant that rites have been performed just at a time when various species are showing signs of increase.

Where misfortunes to human beings are concerned we adopt the same general approach. On the whole, we prefer to look for empirical or rational explanations. When there are factors which we feel cannot be accounted for in this way we are likely to speak of chance, or fate, or perhaps 'the will of God'. But in many societies, Australian Aboriginal included, this would be regarded as an evasion. Instead, the answer is sought in human terms. In any community there are examples of illness, death, misfortune and injury: and these may be taken as material evidence, showing that sorcery has been effectively performed. The physical cause may seem clear enough: death resulting from an attack by a crocodile or shark, for instance, or injuries received through a fall from a tree. But this may be viewed as a secondary consideration, or consequence, and the real cause may be sought at another level. Why did the crocodile or shark attack that particular person and not another? Why did that man fall from the tree, when most people do not? It is this kind of question to which sorcery is believed to supply an answer. Generally speaking, it rules out the possibility of accident, and actually treats such events on a social level, finding the answer in the friction and antagonisms which are a part of every social situation. Even wounding or death in fighting may be seen in this light. The immediate cause may be a spear thrust; but the real cause may be the hostile action of a third person, who had arranged the situation in advance to ensure that the victim was in the right position at the right time.

Belief in sorcery and other forms of magic, then, rests on the assumption that it is possible for human beings to control, in some measure, natural and supernatural forces. There is an attempt to bring the unpredictable or uncertain into the sphere of the predictable, so that everything which happens to and between human beings can be accounted for in a satisfactory way. But this is also one of the functions of religion. It is important to remember that Aboriginal society, although in a sense it may be magic-ridden, or perhaps it would be better to say 'magico-religious ridden', is not necessarily a sorcery-ridden one. Belief in sorcery is common: and this aspect lives on, in spite of intensive alien contact, when many other aspects of traditional life have disappeared. But people do not go around continually in fear of having sorcery worked upon them: sorcerers do not lurk behind every bush—although one does get that impression from reading some of the literature on these people.

NATIVE DOCTOR-SORCERER

Much has been written about magic and sorcery in Aboriginal Australia. Among the more recent accounts are those by Warner (1937/58), Elkin (1945; 1954: 267-94), Berndt (1942-45). The second is particularly important, as the only general survey on this topic. Elkin has called his volume *Aboriginal Men of High Degree,* and this title is significant. It suggests that such men are possessed of knowledge over and above ordinary members of their society: and further, that this knowledge has to be acquired, that it calls for some effort on their part. The 'men of high degree' are the 'medicine men', the 'clever men' or native doctors.

Elkin's volume has to do primarily with these persons, and not with sorcerers. In everyday life the distinction between native doctor and sorcerer is not sharp, even when there are special terms for each. Kaberry (1939: 250-1), for instance, differentiates between the sorcerer and the *baramambil,* or *baramambin,* who is concerned primarily with healing. To the Gunwinggu in western Arnhem Land a native doctor is *margidjbu,* a sorcerer *mangorang.* (See also Douglas, 1959, for the Western Desert; and for north-eastern Arnhem Land, Warner, 1937/58: 193 ff.) However, this is no real key to separateness of activity. In the Great Victoria Desert and through much of the Western Desert, a native doctor and sorcerer are called *gingin, mabanba,* referring to the *maban* disc, and *nanggaringgu,* referring to sucking out. They combine the function of curing the sick, and helping sorcery victims, with that of carrying out sorcery themselves. Among the Wuradjeri a native doctor was called *wiringan,* 'powerful man', or *buginja,* 'spirit', or 'spirit of the whirlwind', since it was the custom of his spirit-self to travel in a whirlwind; *gigawilan,* or more broadly, *walamira,* 'clever' person. The word *walamira* meant not only clever in the sense of shrewd, but also intellectually clever, and having the ability, through the help of spirit and psychic agencies, to perform wondrous feats, in a way incomprehensible to ordinary people. He was also called *walamira-dalmai,* 'one to whom cleverness has been handed on'. Here, among the Wuradjeri, the native doctor was also the sorcerer.

Native doctors and sorcerers are credited with superhuman or supernatural powers. In the Great Victoria Desert these are dependent on the use of the *maban* disc, while malignant power is called *eradji.* In eastern Arnhem Land the word is *dal,* strength or power.

Not everyone can be a native doctor. It is said to take a specially gifted type of person. Even then, before he can qualify a man must go through a special kind of initiation, over and above the ordinary initiation and age-grading rituals. For sorcery, too, in some areas a separate ritual or mystical experience is said to be necessary. Usually native doctors and sorcerers are men, very occasionally women; but really outstanding or notorious persons in these categories are not common, as contrasted with those who achieve a minor reputation, or perform (or claim to perform) ordinary rites of love magic, sorcery, and so on, but are not regarded as experts in those fields.

Initiation of Native Doctors

This special initiation is broadly similar for the whole Continent, despite a number of differences.

Among the Wuradjeri a person is not eligible to undergo it until he is a social adult. (Berndt, 1947.) From earliest childhood, he must have shown particular leanings toward the 'profession'. Also, he must have been in close association with a reputable practitioner, during a probationary period in which he receives special instruction and is taken in spirit on his teacher's nocturnal wanderings. Later he has his assistant totem (*bala*) sung into him, and is taught the necessary song and ritual concentration which will release it from his body in times of need. Several years afterward, the great Baiami (see Chapter VII) intimates in a dream to the young man's father or father's father that he is willing to receive him. He is then brought to a particular site sacred to Baiami. Other postulants, with their guardians, are present too. After the singing, Baiami appears to them. He is distinguished from other people only by the light radiating from his eyes; but from his mouth he brings forth the sacred water called *gali,* of great power: it is said to be liquefied quartz crystal. This falls on the postulants and enters them, and some little time afterward feathers appear. At that point, Baiami departs. The feathers grow into wings, so that several days later the postulants are ready for Baiami to teach them to fly. He shows them how to use quartz crystal, and sings a piece into their foreheads so that they will have X-ray vision.

Removing fire from his own body, he sings it into their chests. Then he tells them to sing away their wings and return to their guardians. In the final rite he visits them again. This time he removes a thick sinew cord and sings it into each postulant. This is the *maulwa* cord that the doctors use for a variety of purposes. There follows a period in which they try out their powers, and after that they return to the main camp as fully fledged doctors. There are a number of variations on this theme. (Howitt, 1904: 355-425; Elkin, 1945.)

Among the Dieri, power to perform beneficial magic along with sorcery is also said to come to a person through a special experience. (Berndt and Vogelsang, 1941.) A postulant, after subincision, must feel that he wants to be a doctor (*gungi*). After a period of training under a professional *gungi* he receives this power from a spirit, called *gudji*. The *gudji* assumes various shapes, taking possession of a bird or an animal or a whirlwind. Among the Dieri, as among some other tribes, the whirlwind or willy-willy is disliked and sometimes feared. Howitt (1904: 446) tells how a man of the Arabana tribe chased a whirlwind, trying to kill the *gudji* with boomerangs. He reported later that he had had a fight with this spirit, which had growled at him; but soon afterward he died. In the Dieri 'making', it is said, the postulant is taken out into the bush by a *gungi*, especially decorated, to undergo a period of seclusion and meditation. When he leaves the camp he is mourned by his parents; his old life is said to be completely forgotten. He enters a state of trance, during which the spirit visits him and replaces his human mind with a '*gungi* mind'. On the following day the spirit returns and performs certain rites. The next day he completes the making, bestowing on the postulant certain 'powerful' gifts which can be used in performing magic. He has now been reborn. The rites performed by the *gudji* include the insertion of a spirit snake into the postulant's stomach. He is also said to pay a visit to the Sky-world. According to Siebert, in Howitt (1904: 359), *gungi* can fly into the sky world by means of a hair cord: it is there that they drink water which gives them power.

Among the Ngadjuri of the middle north of South Australia a candidate for this position undergoes similar experiences. He meditates, talks with spirits, goes into trance, and sees visions. During the period of his actual seclusion he is considered to be dead, and after completing his initiation he is reborn as a *mindaba* (doctor). Ngadjuri women can be initiated in the same way, with power equal to men's.

In the Great Victoria Desert there are at least two main waterholes associated with the making of native doctors (*gingin*). (Berndt, 1942-45; but see Elkin, 1954: 284-94.) One is *gabi* Djabudi, west of Ooldea, the other Lake Darlot in Western Australia. Like a number of waterholes throughout this region, both are connected with Wonambi, the Rainbow. According to reports of what happens at such a time, the postulant leaves the main camp accompanied only by *gingin*. All his friends and close relatives wail for him as they would for someone newly dead. He is going to receive 'power', *daramara,* meaning 'cut into pieces'. When the party reaches the waterhole he is blindfolded and led to the water's edge. Wonambi, who has been awaiting him, swallows him whole. The *gingin* return to their camp. Some time later they bring food for the Snake. He accepts it, and in return vomits the postulant high into the air, so that he falls at a nearby rockhole. The *gingin* go in search of him, visiting one rockhole after another until they find him in the shape of a small baby: they fly back to their camp carrying him in their arms.

Then follows the fire rite: the baby is placed in the centre of a ring of fires, and the heat makes him grow to adult size. The next stage, prefaced by meditation, is the ritual dislocation or 'cutting' of all his joints with an *eradji* australite. Then into each part which has been cut is inserted a small disc of pearlshell, *maban,* of life-giving qualities, reviving his limbs. They are put into his ears and jaw so that he can understand and speak all languages (although in our experience it did not help any of them with English), so that he can speak to spirits, and to all creatures; into his forehead, so that he will have X-ray vision and be able to divine; and into his stomach, to make him invulnerable. He is then aroused. This completes his formal initiation, but on his return to the main camp he must submit to a test in which all the fully initiated men throw spears at him. The spears, it is said, do not touch him. They glance off, because he is full of the life-protecting *maban.*

In the Birrundudu area of the Northern Territory much the same initiation is reported, except that the postulant and native doctors fly through the air astride the Rainbow. In the eastern Kimberleys, according to Kaberry (1939: 213, 217), the sorcerer obtains knowledge of his craft from the Rainbow Snake and the *djuari,* spirits of the dead; a woman may not be a sorcerer, but she may use a white substance or 'poison' in revenge. Elkin (1945) has discussed the relationship between native doctors and Rainbow or other snakes. Warner (1937/1958: 213-14, 215-16) describes a special spiritual experience through which a north-east Arnhem Lander acquires power to perform magic.

Among the Gunwinggu of western Arnhem Land, a native doctor obtains his power mainly from spirits of the dead. He may have one or even more of these spirits as a familiar, treating it as an oracle to which he can turn for information or advice. In other cases the power is transmitted to him directly, for his own use. The conventional picture is that a man hunting alone one day suddenly encounters the ghost of some close relative: father or father's brother, mother or mother's brother, son or brother's son, or one of his immediate grandparents. At once his spear and thrower fall from his hand and he collapses to the ground. He lies there, weak and unable to move, his eyes fixed on the ghost, which says: 'My son [or father, or sister's son, as the case may be], I have come back to find you. I want to give you power, to make you a *margidjbu*!' It inserts into his head a small thin rod, like a bamboo spear, and breathes power into all his body apertures, telling him to use this for healing. The man cannot speak: his tongue is 'soft, like a baby's', and he can only nod in reply. Then the spirit blows into him again, giving him extra strength: and he rises to his feet, slowly and stiffly as if from sleep. The gift is irrevocable; no subsequent quarrel with that ghost can jeopardize it. But some *margidjbu* have more power than others. A man 'heavy with power' can heal a sick person by following his spirit in a dream, catching it and returning it to his body—on the grounds that the body is useless without its animating spirit. Or he may take the patient in a dream to the land above the clouds and heal him there. In addition, the *margidjbu* should be expert in the physical techniques of diagnosis and healing: massage, bathing, use of appropriate 'medicines'. But the patient must be responsive: he must have confidence in the doctor's ability; and the *margidjbu* must have confidence in his own power. Some men reject a case which they envisage as hopeless because they have been 'called in too late', or because the patient or his relatives are not co-operating. They may tug at a sick man's hair, for instance: if it remains firm, he will live, but if it comes easily away this is a sign that he is beyond treatment. Alternatively, a patient may reject a doctor's attentions, either before or after diagnosis, on the score that they are too costly.

Róheim (1945) also discusses this topic. Spencer and Gillen (1938: 522-33) speak of three distinct 'schools' in the making of medicine men according to whether the rites are performed by *iruntarinia*, spirit doubles of tribal ancestors; by *oruncha*, a special class of spirit, mischievous, but associated with the Dreaming period; or by other native doctors. In the *iruntarinia*, the spirit pierces the postulant's tongue; Spencer and Gillen have a photograph of such a man, showing the hole (Fig. 104). He performs other ritual acts too, and certain tabus are involved. With the *oruncha*, men as well as women are initiated; occasionally women are initiated in the first way. The form of the initiation is the same. In the third procedure, crystals removed from other native doctors are inserted into the postulant, a hole is made under a finger-nail and more crystals pressed in, he is given water containing crystals, and his tongue is cut. Here too he is subject to certain tabus.

The usual theme of magical initiation is ritual death, followed by rebirth as a new person with additional strength and advantages and, particularly important, the power to carry out his professional tasks. In all cases there is the assertion, or inference, that he receives this through some mystical experience. Varying claims are made for such a person, depending on the area concerned. He may be the oracle of his group, foretelling coming events, offering advice, curing patients, making rain, divining the 'murderer' after a death, and counteracting alien magic. In effecting a cure he uses, along with special rites and spells, a variety of objects, such as quartz crystal, pearlshells, australites, bones, and stones; his techniques include sleight-of-hand, ventriloquism, massaging and sucking and, on the Lower River Murray in South Australia, steaming over medicinal herbs. In divining he relies primarily on the small pearlshell disc, and diagnoses illnesses with his X-ray vision. He may be believed to have hypnotic power, supernormal abilities like thought transference, clairvoyance and mind-reading; produce a magical cord, in some cases drawn from the navel, or a spirit familiar as an assistant totem; be able to see and speak with spirits and ghosts; create illusions; fly or travel at an unnaturally fast pace; become invisible, or change into a puff of smoke, a breath of wind, or a reptile. In western Arnhem Land, powerful men are believed to be able to collect the flies that hover about their bodies, so that they can approach someone unobserved, or send a swarm of stinging insects to harass an enemy. In special demonstration ceremonies held among the Wuradjeri, native doctors were said to lie on their backs under a tree, sing out their *maulwa* cords in the same way as a spider does, and then begin climbing until they reached the top of the tree. Elkin, particularly, has given examples of this sort of thing.

BENEFICENT MAGIC

The more general forms of beneficent or non-harmful magic relate to hunting, food-collecting and fishing; rainmaking, and weather control; love magic; magic of jealousy; curing or healing magic; divination after a death; magic to stop quarrels, counteract destructive magic, avert misfortune, evade enemies, keep away snakes, and so on. Rainmaking is important, especially in desert areas. Usually it is carried out with group sanction. It is sometimes possible to identify a native doctor in the Great Victoria Desert by the little bag attached to his beard. In it he keeps such items as quartz crystal, pearlshell, and australites, and as one way of bringing rain he may spread out the contents of his little bag and sing over them. In nearly all areas of Australia the pearlshell is associated with water, with the Rainbow Snake, with clouds and with rain.

There are two other ways of making rain in this desert region. One is by scraping a pearlshell, mixing the powder with fresh grass, and spitting in the direction from which rain is required—all to the accompaniment of singing. The other is through a special rite in which participants wear pearlshells: this is said to attract the rain, and as a few drops fall the *gingin* beckon it to come. There is a shower. That evening there is another ceremony, and the participants wear Wonambi snake headdresses.

Among the Dieri, rain is associated with the *muramura* Darana (see Chapter VII) and some other *muramura.* Blood is allowed to flow, symbolizing rain; and feather down is thrown into the air, to float along, symbolizing clouds. In this rite the *gungi* directly invokes the power of Darana. Rain can also be made in several other ways. A foreskin, carefully preserved from a circumcision and kept in a parcel, is said to be very effective for this purpose. Or goanna fat is rubbed on a youth's body causing steam to rise, form a cloud, and so attract rain. Among the Wuradjeri a native doctor, by means of his special *maulwa* cord, would enter the Sky-world to obtain water from the inexhaustible supply which is stored there (Wantanggangura, the abode of Baiami and the totemic creatures). Among the Aranda, although there are several non-sacred ceremonies relating to rainmaking, the most important is the *intichiuma* of the water totem. (Spencer and Gillen, 1938: 189-93.)

In the Kimberleys (Kaberry and Elkin) rain is associated with Galeru, the Rainbow-Serpent. As Kaberry (1939: 206) says, "The long coils of the snake are charged with the power that is the source of human life, of magic and of the fertility brought to the earth by the rains." Only the old and the initiated in magic can approach him. 'White stones or pearlshell are broken up and wrapped in a grass bundle, and put into a waterhole to make rain.' The Wolmeri, also of the Kimberleys, hold a ceremony in which both men and women participate and a figure of the Rainbow Snake is made. In north-eastern Arnhem Land the Rock Python, Julunggul, is one of the main characters associated with rain. (See Chapter VII.) A native doctor may persuade Julunggul to send rain, or to stop it, but ordinarily there is no special magical procedure apart from those included in the larger cult rituals. In western Arnhem Land the Gunwinggu and others who live in low-lying country subject to flooding have no rain magic; their concern is with averting floods, rather than with causing them. Only the southern Gunwinggu and their neighbours among the hills and rocky escarpments take a different stand.

LOVE MAGIC

Love magic in one form or another, carried out alone or in company, is practised throughout Aboriginal Australia. There is no firm dividing line between stimulatory love songs, designed to excite or arouse the listeners or singers or both without concentrating on specific partners, and those of purely magical intent where a man or woman tries to draw a desired person closer. Throughout much of the Western Desert, and from the eastern Kimberleys across to Newcastle Waters and Katherine, women's secret ceremonies relate directly to love magic. Kaberry (1939: 255-68) discusses the *yirbindji,* which includes the charming of ornaments, body painting, and so on, the rites symbolizing the whole procedure of courtship culminating in coitus. C. Berndt (1950*a*) has also written about such ceremonies (the *djarada, jilbindji* and *jawalju*), which involve healing as well as love magic, and are traditionally linked with mythology. (See Chapter VI.) For both men and women, in most cases separately but occasionally in a combined ceremony, or with simultaneous singing some distance apart, the *djarada* is widely known and practised. It is sometimes called *ududju* in the Northern Territory when associated with a men's love-magic ritual, or *jilbindji* in Central and South Australia. Secular and magico-religious *djarada,* often associated incidentally with the sacred Kunapipi, have entered north-east Arnhem Land from the south. The following are three songs from one of these series, from Yirrkalla; the translation is a general one, since the men who sang them did not know the language in which they were framed and could not always specify the meaning of each word separately.

wogulmanba rarirari bilimanba rarirari . . .
Swelling breasts, protruding nipples . . .

girarang girarang jibarnga luwandinja luwandinja . . .
The fly I send attracts her notice . . .

dibuldibulgula dibuldibulgula gananeindja jabulgali jabulgali . . .
dibuldibulgula gananeindja jalwijalwul gananeindja jalwijalwul . . .
Throat feathers from the emu, blown in the wind . . .
Throat feathers from the emu, tell her to go out into the bush . . .

In the same region there are two other long song cycles relating to love: the 'Rose River' and 'Goulburn Island' cycles. But these are stimulatory rather than magical; the same applies to the 'Gossip' songs of western Arnhem Land (see Chapter VI). As a more direct measure, in north-eastern Arnhem Land, a common practice is to let a length of feathered string fall into the basket of some desired person. If a man belongs to the *dua* moiety and his sweetheart to the *jiridja,* he persuades a woman he can trust to drop into her dilly bag a special white-feathered or possum fur string, associated with her moiety; for a *dua* moiety woman, a red parakeet feathered string would be used. Messages are then exchanged through an intermediary and an assignation arranged. A suspicious husband may make a habit of hunting through his wife's baskets, and if he finds such a feathered string a quarrel is bound to follow. Men have other indirect ways, too, of obtaining women, in the shape of small wooden objects with feathered string attached. *Jiridja* men make models of anchors such as Indonesian visitors to this coast once used. *Dua* men make heads of seagulls or other birds, some holding in their beaks little beeswax models of worms, mice and fish; as the birds catch these foods, so the man hopes to catch the woman he desires. Other love-magic objects are little figures of men and women in various sexual postures.

In one conventional rite the man places the anchor or bird's head near the woman's camp. With the help of two companions he unrolls the ball of string attached to it and stretches it from tree to tree in the main camp, then sits down and sings songs relating to the anchor and to love magic generally. This is a public declaration of his suit. The girl sits in her camp among her relatives wearing a feathered string headdress decorated with drooping feathered pendants. Then he begins to wind back the string, drawing the anchor or bird's head toward him and with it, so these people say, the girl's affection. The rite may be repeated several times before the girl herself is persuaded to come to his camp. It can be performed in a different way. The anchor or bird's head may be hooked or fastened into the girl's hair or around her arm so that she is hooked or caught in full public view and drawn toward him. Or the string, without the attached object, may simply be placed on the ground and stretched out so that one end leads into the girl's camp and the other into his: he then begins to draw it toward him. It is said that the girl has no choice, that she is bound to come to him, because he has caught not only her desire but also her spirit. Much the same rite is carried out surreptitiously in the case of extra-marital liaisons.

In Western Arnhem Land a traditional form of love magic consists of drawing a representation of a desired person on the wall of a rock shelter. If a man wants to attract a woman who is not particularly anxious to have him, he may go to a secluded place and draw her having sexual relations with himself. That same night, so it is said, she will come to his camp: but to retain her affection he must, from time to time, touch up his drawing. This is the conventional account of what happens; but it is doubtful whether anyone actually performs the rite, as contrasted with merely talking about it.

Among the Aranda, according to Spencer and Gillen (1938: 541-3), love magic has to do with obtaining wives: that is to say, a man can legitimately use it only for women who stand in the correct relationship to him. In one variety he incises his own totemic design on a small wooden *tjurunga* of bullroarer type called *namatwinna*. With a couple of companions he takes this into the bush. All night they sing magical songs, inviting a woman to come to him and finally, at daybreak, they swing the *tjurunga*. The humming sound it makes is said to be carried to her, no matter how far away she may be: its power compels her to think of him, and eventually come to him. The same rite may be used to bring about an elopement, as long as the two people concerned stand in the appropriate relationship. Or a man trying to attract a woman will make a charmed headband, *chilara*, decorating it, singing over it, then wearing it in the main camp to catch her eye; she cannot resist it, and by night comes secretly to his camp. Again, he may charm a pearlshell, *lonkalonka*, by singing over it, persuading the lightning to enter it: then he hangs it on a digging stick which he has placed at the non-sacred dancing ground and leaves it there until nightfall. In dancing that evening he wears it as a pubic pendant. Only that one woman sees the lightning flashing on the shell: she is overcome with desire, and takes the first opportunity of coming to his camp or running away with him. Another technique makes use of a 'native horn', as Spencer and Gillen call it, possibly a species of drone pipe or didjeridu: the man holds it in the smoke of a fire during a special rite, charming it, and himself swallows some of the smoke; later on at the evening ceremony, when he blows the horn, the woman he wants is instantly attracted to him.

At Ooldea love magic is associated with the *wongi* (see Chapter VI). It is used by women as well as by men to arouse or renew desire in a husband or lover. There is a fairly wide range of rites, supported by mythology relating to the major mythical beings, the Wadi Gudjara, and Njirana and Julana. There are three main categories, which can be further subdivided.

The first concerns love magic performed by men. In one rite a lock of the girl's hair is sung over. In another a man goes secretly out into the bush, where he makes a sand-drawing of two snakes, a male and a female, and between them a special mark to indicate the girl, then sings over the whole drawing. Another resembles the Aranda headband rite. Or again, the central feature may be a hole the man has dug to symbolize a vulva. If a woman repeatedly looks at a man and teases him, he knows that she wants him: he goes into the bush and sings her. Or he draws male and female snake designs on his chest, with a mark representing the girl, and sings over them. Or he may simply sing in her hearing.

More important, however, are two other rites, the *urumbela* and *madagi*. The *urumbela* are two stone objects, said to have belonged first to the Wadi Gudjara. All that is necessary is to place them on the ground and sing over them. This, people say, is really enough to attract a woman. Usually, however, in the *urumbela* a man makes a small love-magic bullroarer, called *bubibubi* or *madagi*, and incises on it two snakes with the girl's identifying mark, then swings it to the accompaniment of singing. As this is happening she 'feels' and thinks of the man, and later comes to him. The separate *madagi* rite is performed with the help of some elders by a small group of young initiated men, married or otherwise, who want women. The sequence extends over a period of several days. They make a long mound of sand, and inside it an elder places a 'loaded', or previously charmed, *madagi* with string protruding. Several men sit at each end and they begin to sing. Presently one, followed by all the others, jumps to his feet; they open their penis incisures and sprinkle their legs and thighs with blood. Then the singing starts again. As the rite proceeds the power of the *madagi* becomes stronger and the mound itself begins to stir. On the following days they swing the *madagi* at intervals, to intensify the impact on the women.

As an innovation in the Laverton area (Western Australia), a man may make a little wooden 'aeroplane propeller' incised with totemic designs or human figures. (R. Berndt, 1959*c*: 363-4.) He threads string through two holes in the centre and twirls it around, repeating the girl's name; she is said to feel the impact of this immediately in her belly, so that she cannot help desiring him too. (Similarly in Dampier Land a man may swing a *mudamud* love magic bullroarer, introduced from the Fitzroy, to attract a sweetheart. See Elkin, 1933: 56; Klaatsch, 1907.)

In the second category men and women co-operate. In the bush outside the camp a group of women gathers to paint two of their number, accentuating their breasts. (Fairly typical designs are shown in C. Berndt, 1950*a*, and there is an excellent plate in Chewings, 1936, facing p. 120.) They return to the ceremonial ground and dance, until finally they are 'hunted away'. Then the men swing *madagi* attached to the end of spears, so that the spears are jerked in the direction of the women, who are said to feel the jab of the *madagi*-spear in their groins 'so that blood flows'—they think of the men and cannot stay away from them. In another ceremony, several men and women prepare, separately, to go hunting or food-collecting. Some little distance from the camp the women throw aside pretence and go directly to a cleared place in the bush. There they make a long sand mound and then kneel around it, placing on it their headbands as well as pieces of tobacco (or native tobacco) obtained from their husbands or lovers. Near the mound they put the women's sacred object, the *sanba,* associated with a mythical black goanna, to make the rite more effective. The songs that they sing are designed to charm the headbands and tobacco, and to make them, as persons, altogether irresistible. In the meantime the men, out hunting, have not gone too far away to hear the singing: it stirs their desire. That evening a ceremony is held. The men have been given the charmed tobacco. An *indiri* ceremonial pole, a phallic symbol, is erected at one end of the ground, while at the other a large number of women sit in circles singing. At intervals some of them rise, dance toward the pole, then disperse with a cry. After a few hours of this kind of stimulation people pair off for love-making. Another approach is through a *gulagula* expedition of women, excited by the chanting of men. (*Gulagula* is used for any person blatantly in search of sexual adventure.) For example, several women out hunting may hear men performing love magic out in the bush, decide to 'go *gulagula*', and set off to find them. Or a party of men may be helping one of their number to perform love magic for one woman; it happens that she is with a group of others, but the magic is so strong that it draws all of them to the spot where the men are waiting.

In the third category all the performers are women. A young woman and her friends go to a cleared place in the bush, where they make a long sand mound. She sits at one end, and around it the others with legs wide apart. The leader is wearing a white head-band. She puts this on the mound with a piece of tobacco obtained from the man she wants. As they sing, the mound 'rises up', its power charming the tobacco. She takes this and holds it in front of her pubes, simulating the preliminary actions of coitus. While this is happening the man begins to think of her. At first he feels his 'stomach going around'. As the singing continues, the rest of his body is affected. When the women return to camp an intermediary gives him the piece of tobacco, but soon after smoking it he feels giddy. The intermediary, watching, reports this to the young woman. She goes out into the bush, and presently he follows her, impelled by the magic. She ties on her headband, looking at him, and so strong is the magic that blood comes from his penis. They do not speak, or touch each other, but that evening she comes to his camp. Alternatively, a woman may take the same steps by herself, singing over a lock of hair, a piece of tobacco, or some other object belonging to the man she desires. Or her chanting may be sufficient in itself. Other rites are intended to force an unwilling man to change his mind, to recapture the affection of a husband or lover, or even to cool a man's ardour if he is too attentive.

In the majority of love-magic rites no native doctor need be present, at least in his official capacity. There may be leaders—persons who have special claims because they obtained the rite in question through trading or through a dream, or who take the initiative because they are personally interested in the outcome. But most people are in a position to perform simple rites, or have some idea of the techniques purportedly used, in this as in other types of magic. They need not call in a specialist in matters which they feel they can cope with themselves—including sorcery.

SORCERY

An expert in sorcery, whether or not he is a native doctor as well, may be expected to undergo a preliminary experience of some sort before he is acknowledged as such. Some forms of sorcery are said to be open to any adult, or any adult man. Women may help in a rite; but generally speaking, despite exceptions, they are not regarded as responsible for such performances themselves.

The Great Victoria Desert is one region where there is a special sorcery initiation, through which (men say) they come into contact with the mythical characters connected with such practices: in this case Wadi Keniga, Native Cat Man, and Wadi Waiuda, Possum Man. Both Keniga and Waiuda are cult totems and therefore, like all other sacred beings, have religious ritual associated with them. Men of those particular cult totems are responsible, for instance, for initiating men of other totems. The main objects used are the *madagi*, the small incised bullroarer already mentioned, and the *tulu*, a small cylindrical wooden object, incised and tapering at both ends. In the *tulu* initiation postulants lie down at full length in a row in a cleared place among the scrub. There are no fires, but a mystical smoke is said to rise and envelop everyone: they are like dead men. A *tulu* is placed point downward into the navel of each postulant in turn, and sung over; his belly slowly rises up, but is pushed back. After that he is revived. Later he is instructed in the techniques of *tulu* sorcery. In the *madagi* rite men sit round in a circle and sing the object, and are shown how to swing it. The *madagi* are also splashed with arm blood.

In the actual sorcery rite, in contrast to the initiation, a man may use the *tulu* against an unfaithful wife, a 'murderer' accused after an inquest, or a woman who consistently rejects him—or even for killing certain animals and birds. To begin with, a recalcitrant woman may be threatened with *tulu*. If she still refuses, the conventional pattern is this. One day he follows her tracks, watching to see where she urinates. Then, taking out his *tulu*, he pushes it point downward into the damp ground, rubbing it up and down with his fingers and singing. She feels the need to urinate again, but only blood emerges. The haemorrhage continues until she is exhausted, and it is not long before she dies.

A person is vulnerable through anything which has been in close association with him, or her: hair, nail parings, urine, faeces, weapons, food scraps, discarded clothing or other belongings. Among the Kurnai, if a sorcerer is able to obtain anything of this sort from someone he wants to harm, he fastens it to a spearthrower, with hawk's feathers and kangaroo or human fat. Setting this upright in the ground before a fire he sings over it, calling the victim's name: when it falls over, the rite has been successfully concluded. According to Howitt (1904: 363), the Wotjobaluk use a form of sorcery called *guliwil,* meaning a small spindle-shaped piece of wood, which is tied up with human fat, and something connected with the victim—who is represented, together with poisonous snakes, in the incising on the *guliwil.* The bundle is roasted for a long time.

There are many examples of this type of sorcery. Perhaps the best known in the literature is the *ngadungi,* or *ngadhungi,* of the Lower River Murray in South Australia. (Taplin, in Woods, 1879: 23-6.) The main substance used in this is the discarded bones of ducks, swans or other birds as well as the Murray cod. Most people are consequently careful in disposing of such bones, burning them to ensure that they do not fall into the hands of a sorcerer. Should a sorcerer find one, and know who discarded it, he keeps it aside until he wants to use it. Then he makes the bone into a skewer. He mixes fish oil and red ochre into a paste, to make a small lump, and encloses in it the eye of a Murray cod and a piece of flesh from a fresh corpse, attaching the whole thing to the end of the bone and wrapping it up. To improve its potency it is put into the chest of a decomposing corpse and exposed on a mortuary platform. After a time it is removed and placed near a fire, which gradually melts away the paste lump: the victim becomes increasingly ill, and when the lump finally drops away from the bone he dies.

The Pointing Bone

The pointing bone, in one form or another, is widely distributed over the Continent. In Roth's view (1897: 152-8), it is found throughout north-west-central Queensland. There are three parts: the skewer-like bone itself, the connecting string, and the receptacle to keep it in. It can be made from human bone, or from emu, kangaroo, and so on, even from wood. Pointed in the appropriate rite, it causes the victim's blood to move invisibly into the bone and along the connecting string into the receptacle. Conversely the sorcerer's magical object, such as a bone or pebble, moves invisibly from the pointer to the victim, entering him, so that he becomes ill. Similarly, among the Dieri, the victim's soul is drawn into the bone through the blood and a lump of wax or clay attached to the point prevents its escape. Then it is wrapped in emu feathers and *gujamara* leaves and left in the ground for several months. This marks the period of the victim's illness. When it is finally disinterred and ritually burnt, he dies. The actual pointing rite is accompanied by singing. Procedures vary. In the upper Georgina District, as an extra touch, the pointer is given a push in the direction of the victim. Once the victim's blood has been obtained in this way, the sorcerer warms up the receptacle from time to time to make him worse. He holds the victim's life in his hands: burning the receptacle would kill him outright; washing out the contents would cure him.

In the Great Victoria Desert a pointing bone must first be 'loaded'. The sorcerer vomits up some of the *ẹradji,* or magical power, which he keeps in his stomach as a red fluid, and blows it into the bone. Then comes the actual rite. He must be at least forty yards from his victim. Squatting down he winds the unattached end of the human hair twine round his hand and points the stick, *miridalga,* 'death bone', or *gundila,* jerking it toward the victim and singing. The spirit or power in the bone is released. It enters the victim's body. By that same evening he is feeling ill. Next day the sorcerer returns to the bush and heats the bone: the victim becomes correspondingly worse. On the third day the rite is repeated, and that night he dies.

Among the Tongaranka, 'the fibula of a dead man's leg is scraped, polished and ornamented with red ochre, and a cord of his hair attached to it'. (Howitt, 1904: 360.) Among the Aranda and their neighbours, Spencer and Gillen (1938: 534-8) mention pointing sticks and bones known as *injilla, irna, ullinka* (with a hooked end), *ingwania* and *takula.* The *injilla,* used in *kurdaitcha* expeditions, 'is a bone about six inches long with human hair string attached to a small lump of resin at one end; it is placed under the victim's tongue'. The *irna* is a wooden stick. After a preliminary rite the sorcerer stealthily approaches the victim's camp and, unseen, jerks the pointer at him, cursing him: gradually he sickens and dies. The illness is intensified by burning the attached hair string.

Similar in principle to the bone-pointing procedure is the charming of a spear, so that even a superficial wound will lead to the victim's death. Belief in a sorcerer's ability to project a magical substance is relatively common. Among the Wuradjeri it is quartz crystal, *ngalai.* (Berndt, 1947: 71.) They claim that a sorcerer can force out from himself a magical crystal which travels invisibly through the air and enters the victim. It leaves no mark on his body, but he feels a sharp jab of pain. The length of his illness depends on whether the *ngalai* is kept 'cool' or 'warm' by the sorcerer's singing. He can be cured by its removal. Spencer and Gillen (1938: 540) speak of an *ililika,* a hank of magical string, which can be unwound and cracked like a whip in the direction of a victim; its deadly influence is projected through the air. They say also that an object called *tchintu,* sun (*djindu*), is used by the 'Wyingurri' people on the central Western Australia-Northern Territory border. Two incisor teeth of a rat are fixed to a lump of resin, then a length of hair string is added. In the local view it 'contains the heat of the sun, and its power can rapidly burn up a victim if placed on his tracks'. On the Lower River Murray (Taplin, in Woods, 1879: 29-31) there is also the *neljeri,* or *neilyeri,* a sharpened piece of bone or spear placed in the fleshy part of a decomposing corpse, as the *ngadungi* is. Afterward its point is wrapped in hair twine or feathers, soaked in human fat which has been extracted from a corpse for the purpose. A scratch from this poisonous dagger is believed to cause death, but this is not so much magical as direct physical violence.

Kaberry (1939: 249), for the Kimberleys, speaks of small pearlshell discs, *bindjawindja,* 'inserted into a victim's body during a dream: and a stone which may be painted and covered with feathers and sung by a sorcerer'. The Wuradjeri make a death charm by taking hair and fat from a corpse, mixing this into a ball with lace lizard fat, and fastening it to a stick. It is put into action by being unwrapped and spread out on the ground in front of a fire, pointing toward the victim. (Howitt, 1904: 361-5.)

Magic Powder and Other Forms of Sorcery

There is also the 'poison powder' of the Wuradjeri, which a sorcerer makes from the ground-up hip-bone or scapula of a dead woman, taken from the grave by night after the corpse has decomposed. The bone dust is kept in a bag. Or he may dig up her corpse before it reaches that state, after obtaining permission from her spirit, then cut out her uterus, dry it, and grind it to powder. A placenta may be treated in the same way. A pinch of such powder taken in flour or tea or sprinkled on meat is claimed to cause a lingering illness, helped on by small additional doses; a large quantity, to bring death within a fortnight. Yuin and Kamilaroi sorcerers, too, are said to use a kind of powder. (Howitt, 1904: 362.) The Workia people (Queensland) have a 'death powder', *moari,* resembling white ashes, which is placed near where the victim is to sleep or under his blanket. Roth (1897: 159) gives several examples, adding that a specimen of this powder examined at Normanton "was found to be ground glass". The Wurunjerri (Howitt, 1904: 366) believe that illness can be induced by taking *meymet*, pounded flesh from a corpse mixed with cut-up tobacco which the victim unsuspectingly smokes. South of the Daly River there is a belief that a death powder can be mixed in any liquid which a victim unknowingly drinks—with fatal results. In other places people claim that magic powder can be used not in sorcery but as an aphrodisiac: among the Laragia, for instance, dried and powdered bêche-de-mer; at Elcho Island a special powder, traded up from the Roper River, also said to help in hunting and fishing.

The *maulwa* magical cord of the Wuradjeri is another item in the sorcery repertoire. The sorcerer releases it by singing it out, and travelling along the ground it enters the victim's anus so that he doubles up in pain and loses consciousness. According to Roth (1897: 159), 'a triangular pearlshell plate' is used in north-west-central Queensland. The sorcerer comes as close as possible to his victim, pointing the piece of pearlshell toward him, and makes sharp movements in the air, 'to suggest the cutting of his throat and the ripping-up of his belly'.

Image Sorcery

In the Kimberleys, as well as in western and north-eastern Arnhem Land, an effigy may be made from bound grass or paperbark, from ochre or clay, or from wild beeswax. The paperbark figures of eastern Arnhem Land, called *bi*, are painted white, with eyes and mouth in red ochre. The sorcerer stabs a *bi* with a pointed stick to the accompaniment of singing and whips it with a cane or the thin limb of a tree while he calls the name of the victim, who becomes correspondingly ill and finally dies. In a variety of this, the sorcerer draws the figure of a victim on a large stone, with a human head, kangaroo nose and ears, human arms, fingers and legs, a kangaroo foot, and so on. (Warner, 1937/1958: 206-9.) As he does so he speaks to it. The stone is heated in a fire, and 'when it finally breaks the soul of the victim will scream in pain'. Two or three days afterward the victim awakens from sleep feeling weak and ill: 'his body swells, his ears grow large, his nose runs with blood, his elbows and nails split, his skin cracks': he is a leper.

In western Arnhem Land, sorcery figures are drawn on the walls of rock shelters, as well as on sheets of prepared bark. A jealous husband, not necessarily an acknowledged sorcerer, may try to punish an unfaithful wife by drawing her likeness, with an eaglehawk or Rainbow Snake head, several arms, and stingray nails protruding from her body. The conventional sequence is that she becomes ill; as the painting is retouched she becomes worse, and finally dies. Or the figure may represent the woman's lover, or a woman who has rejected a man's attentions. In actual practice, people say, there is no need to do more: the threat of drawing a woman may be enough in itself.

Magical Operations

Revenge expeditions which include sorcery probably do not take place as frequently as they are claimed to do. *Wanmala* is the most common name in the Western Desert, and among the Aranda and some adjacent tribes the *atninga* avenging party is similar. (Spencer and Gillen, 1938: 489-96.) Warner (1937/1958: 163) speaks of warfare for eastern Arnhem Land; but although there are some magical aspects associated with this it is best discussed in relation to the broader topic of law and order (in Chapter X).

However, the *kurdaitcha* (or *gadaidja*) and *illapurinja* are more properly expeditions carried out for the specific purpose of performing sorcery. (Spencer and Gillen, *ibid.*, 476-88.) In the *kurdaitcha* men use special slippers of that name, made from emu feathers stuck together with blood, with an upper rim of netted hair string. To wear them a man must have his small toe dislocated, and in the true *kurdaitcha* shoe there is an opening in the hair network for it. A man setting off to avenge a death in this way is often accompanied by a sorcerer. They are ritually decorated, carrying shields and spears, and at least one *tjurunga* to give courage, strength, and accuracy of aim, as well as to render them invisible to enemies and generally invulnerable. When they come within spearing distance of the person they are after, they hold the *tjurunga* in their teeth and the avenger takes aim. The victim falls: the avenger retreats. Now the sorcerer comes forward. With the aid of *atnongara* crystals and his own power he heals the wound so that no trace of it remains, and revives him with a touch of the *atnongara*. Returning home, the victim knows nothing of what has happened, but in a short time he sickens and dies. In one variation the body is allowed to lie in the sun for a while, then the *kurdaitcha* sucks out blood through an incision in the tongue. Again there is the healing of the wound, the temporary revival, and the return to camp—to die.

An Aranda woman may be an avenger, a *kurdaitcha*, too, although very rarely: the word in that case is *illapurinja*, "the changed one". (Spencer and Gillen, 1938: Fig. 98.) If she is anxious to retaliate, personally, for an injury suffered by one of her relatives, her husband may let her go. She is specially adorned, and carries a long fighting club and a large wooden *tjurunga* he has made for the purpose. While she is away he stands one of her digging sticks in the ground and ties on to it a small tuft of rat tails: if she is killed this falls off, and he at once destroys his camp and moves away. Otherwise, once she finds her victim she creeps up on him from behind and throws her *tjurunga*: it strikes his neck and enters his body, breaking up into little pieces. He collapses. On being revived he suffers intense pain, and unless a native doctor intervenes his death is certain. Spencer and Gillen doubted whether sorcery of this type actually took place. (See also Elkin, 1954: 291-4.)

Djinagabil sorcery, sometimes part of a *wanmala,* resembles the *kurdaitcha.* A man may have eloped with another's wife, transgressed against the religious 'law', or been cited as a 'murderer' after an inquest: women do not seem to be reported as victims of this type of sorcery. The conventional pattern is that a group of men closely related to the person they plan to avenge leave the main camp in the company of a sorcerer. They wear *wibia* shoes, like the Aranda *kurdaitcha,* which have been ritually sung, and of course their small toes have been dislocated. There is a belief that the toe has an eye, which helps the wearer of the *wibia* to find his way. A stick is put horizontally under the foot, extending across under the big toe: this causes him to walk more on the ball of the foot, blurring the track. On the first night out, they ritually mime the death of their intended victim. Otherwise, by night they rest on their backs with feet up on a foot-rest: by day they abstain from drinking water. The journey may take some days because they make a wide detour. They time their arrival near the victim's camp a little before daybreak, and hide behind bushes or undergrowth until he appears. Their aim is to catch him alone, away from others. If he goes out hunting they follow him but do nothing until, perhaps at midday, he pauses to rest. Then they choose one of their number and decorate him as a totemic dog, with ears, and a tail of human-hair twine. The rest of the party begin to chant as the 'dog man', wearing his *wibia* shoes and carrying a firestick, crawls round them and starts off toward his victim. He comes up from behind, springs on him, drags him to the ground, turns him on his back and bites (or chews) his adam's apple.

Versions differ; some say that the victim is first speared all over the body and then bitten by the 'dog'. But in any case, after this first attack the rest of the party creep upon him while the 'dog' runs away. From all reports, they now perform some sort of physical operation. In one, so the story goes, first of all the victim is choked. Then pointed sticks are inserted, one at each side of the collar-bone, and pushed right down. The wounds are healed by rubbing a heated stone over them. This also prevents him from looking around. Arm blood is spurted into his ears, to congeal internally and prevent him from hearing any questions which people may ask when he returns. A short stick is driven in under his tongue, so he will tell no one of his experience. His lower bottom rib on the left-hand side is broken. Small marsupials are hung around his waistband, so there is nothing to suggest to his wife that he has

Actors in the Gadjeri fertility rituals at Birrundudu (1944-5). The body decorations represent falling rain and storm clouds

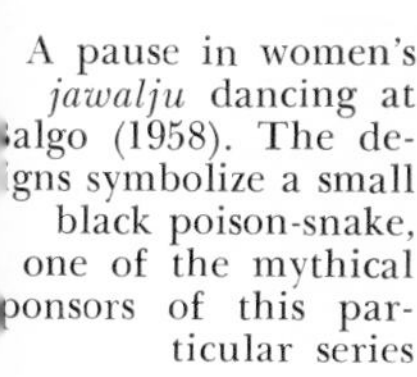

A pause in women's
jawalju dancing at
algo (1958). The de-
gns symbolize a small
black poison-snake,
one of the mythical
ponsors of this par-
ticular series

Women resting in their *jawalju* shade at Balgo (1958). In this area small children were allowed to attend the ceremonies

not been hunting in the usual way. One member of the party then tells the victim's spirit what to say if questioned by others. Finally, a thin stick is pushed down the penis aperture. He revives. They sit behind him. When one of them holds out a spearthrower in the direction of his camp he rises unsteadily and, half-led by his spirit, returns there. The *djinagabil* go back to their own country. The victim shows no outward sign of injury, but that night begins to feel ill. He becomes delirious. The next day he is worse, and on the third he dies.

Belief in this ritual operation is widespread. In south-eastern Australia the emphasis is on the removal of kidney fat. (Howitt, 1904: 367-77.) According to the Wiimbaio, sorcerers from hostile tribes sneak into their camps at night and use a 'strangling net' to drag their victim into the bush. They cut up his belly, remove the kidney or caul fat, and in their place stuff grass and sand. Then they undo the net and let him go home to die. The fat is greatly prized for anointing, on the grounds that the prowess and virtues of the victim will pass to the user. Or a club may be used on the victim, and the fat removed with no sign of an incision.

A Wuradjeri sorcerer uses his *maulwa* cord to catch a victim, who is then turned over on his back quite unconscious. The sorcerer makes a long cut below the last rib on the right side and inserts his hand to cut off a little of the kidney fat. He removes his *maulwa* cord from the victim's intestines, replacing a little piece of it as a substitute for the kidney fat, then returns the rest of it to his own body. He puts a piece of crystal into the victim and sings to close the wound completely. Then, going a little way off, he sings again to revive him, and lets him return home. Presently the small piece of *maulwa* and the crystal begin to grow, increasing day by day until they extend through the victim's body, rotting away the internal organs. While he writhes and groans the sorcerer out in the bush imitates him, intensifying the illness. Finally the crystal returns to the sorcerer. He examines it, and if it is stained with blood he knows that the rite has been successful and the victim is dead. The kidney fat is eaten ritually by fully initiated men to enhance their strength, but must have been obtained legitimately —that is, in the course of revenge. In one variant the sorcerer sends his spirit form in a whirlwind to perform the rite. Much further north too, in the Daly River area, there is the same belief that a sorcerer can remove a victim's kidney fat by making an incision through his ribs with the blade of a shovel spear, afterward magically healing the wound and 'awakening' him: as he roasts the fat, so the victim weakens, and eventually dies.

In the *milin* of the Lower River Murray the sorcerer uses a *plonggi* club with a conically-shaped head. (Taplin, in Woods, 1879:

26-9.) He and a companion creep up on their victim from behind and knock him unconscious with this. Then they hit the joints of his arms and legs, his neck and his chest, ritually breaking the bones. They pull his ears until they crack, making him incapable of telling what has happened. He is now in the power of a malignant spirit which diverts his attention during a fight, or leads him to walk on a poisonous snake, and so on. This rite is sometimes said to be much more elaborate, with caul or kidney fat removed and grass pads substituted, or the *plonggi* used to bruise the chest by repeated blows; but in any case the wound is always magically healed afterward by the sorcerer.

Leaving aside the more obviously magical aspects, it is quite possible that part of the physical operation does take place. Certainly the Aborigines, in areas where this belief prevails, accept the magical side as equally real, and there are unverified rumours which are made more authentic by telling how European doctors have removed spikes from various parts of a sorcery victim's body. We need not accept this as an all-or-nothing matter: elaborations and fantasies can be built up on a slender basis of fact. Whatever actually happens or does not happen, the important point is that people believe it does, and respond accordingly.

In black magic or sorcery the power, or a great deal of the power, is usually thought to lie in the spell, or the curse, or the object that is employed, and not in any force outside it. It really represents another technique for attacking people, on the same level as the spear or fighting stick, but bringing in an additional element, this magical power. The source of the power is significant. In many cases it is associated with the Dreaming, and the great mythical beings. This does not mean that there must be a direct appeal or request to them; but occasionally there is, as in western Arnhem Land in the following section, where the mythical being Nagidgid is specifically invoked by the sorcerer.

Removal of Soul Stuff

Broadly, the Aborigines recognize three general types of magical operation. One is the removal of kidney fat: type area, south-eastern Australia. The second is the insertion of spikes or pointed sticks: type area, Great Victoria Desert. The third is the removal of blood and soul stuff: type area, Arnhem Land. We have already discussed the first two.

In the third, if a western Arnhem Land sorcerer wants to use direct measures instead of working on the victim from a distance, in local belief a number of avenues are open to him. Let us look briefly at one.

First he stabs his victim in the neck, wipes off the blood, and heals the wound with the heated blade of a shovel-nosed spear. He draws blood from the calves of the victim's legs, keeps some, and throws the rest away. Then he may call out to Nagidgid, the spirit patron of sorcerers, asking him to breathe temporary life into the victim after removing his soul, or life. For a period of three days at the longest, Nagidgid can bring the newly dead to life. But during that time they are not alive in the ordinary sense. Their spirits have gone, they walk about like automatons with no recollection of what has been done to them. Before long they feel faint and weak, with aching head and trembling limbs. They refuse food, and lie beside the fire wrapped in paperbark or blankets, feeling the cold creeping upward from their feet; and presently they die. Alternatively, after the wound has been healed the sorcerer may call up either his own snake familiar, or the Rainbow Snake, who emerges from under the ground and eats the discarded blood. He places the victim in the Snake's mouth: but he is only held there, not swallowed. The sorcerer tells the Snake to follow him. He travels above ground, the Snake and victim underneath, until they reach a place where other sorcerers are gathered in a circle, surrounded by a low mound. There the Snake vomits out the victim, as a new-born baby. It begins to lick him so that gradually he becomes a fully grown man again. He returns to his camp, with no recollection of the incident; but after a short period he dies.

In this region the Rainbow Snake is one of the main instruments through which 'professional' sorcerers work, but to do so they must have undergone a special initiation. The victim's experience in the last example resembles in some respects the initiation of sorcerers and native doctors, but many other accounts are less elaborate. The blood the sorcerer keeps may be given later on to a small lizard (with red colouring on the underbelly near the head). He names a certain place, and the lizard goes there and puts it in the roots of a tree. After about two or three years the sorcerer goes to the tree and finds the blood, which has become a congealed stone-like mass, a powerful magical substance. It gives him a clear vision: with its help he can find fish, turtle, and honey easily, and hunt meat successfully. Fragments may be traded.

In eastern Arnhem Land some men wear necklets with a congealed blood pendant, tied in a rag or woven into a tiny basket, to improve their hunting. In the same region people believe that the heart's blood can be magically extracted. (Warner, 1937/1958: 194-5.) In one version the victim is dragged from his camp at night, struggling and choking, by means of a rope slipped around his neck and twisted. One of the sorcerer's companions temporarily takes his place and lies with his wives so that they will not become suspicious. The victim is carried away unconscious to a clearing. There he is placed on the ground—his left side cut open, and his heart pierced with a small sharpened bone or stick. The body is held in such a way that the heart's blood runs into a receptacle: when the heart stops beating, the soul is let out. The sorcerer smooths over the wound with a heated spearthrower and a special substance made from green ants and lizards: the heating and the rubbing continue until no trace of the cut remains. The body is turned over, and green ants bite the protruding intestine so that it retracts into place. The spearthrower, dipped in the blood, is swung above the victim's head, and gradually he revives and sits up. He is hit on the head and told to forget what has been done to him: his tongue is twisted, with the warning that in three days he will die. He is magically cut in two but becomes whole again, and finally returns to lie besides his wives. In the case of a woman the procedure is a little different: the sorcerer opens her vagina and reaches her heart in that way.

In many cases, toward the end of the ritual operation the sorcerer tells the victim just how he or she will die. For example, 'You will be eaten by a crocodile', or a shark, or bitten by a snake, or killed by a spear, or drowned. A woman may be told, 'You will quarrel with your husband, and he will kill you. . . .' After this the victim is revived, and goes back to camp remembering nothing of it. To all appearances he, or she, is alive just like anyone else, but actually this is 'only a body walking about', with no proper spirit or soul. In western Arnhem Land, for instance, people insist that crocodiles, sharks, snakes, and so on, never attack human beings who are really living, those who have souls: they will injure only those who are actually dead already. Anyone who behaves in a reckless or foolhardy way—'asking for trouble', as we might say—is likely to be suspected of this. If nothing happens, people forget about it. If he dies, in one way or another, they may remind one another of their suspicions. Or they may look back, after a death, and be convinced that there were such signs, had they only known. A woman may go to pick wild plums where the grass is thick and snakes may be hiding, taking no notice of others who call her to come back. A man may try to swim across a shark-infested stretch of water, or lose the paddles overboard from a canoe in rough water, or actually capsize the canoe. When an accident happens people will say, in effect, 'Nobody in his right mind would do that kind of thing. Only someone as good as dead would behave in that way'.

In most parts of Aboriginal Australia a few deaths are regarded as entirely natural, especially for the very old. But for the young or middle-aged, the assumption is that death is anything but natural. Someone, therefore, must have been responsible, and according to Aboriginal reckoning it is very unlikely to have been the victim himself.

SIGNIFICANCE OF MAGIC AND SORCERY

In many cases there is the belief that a person who has been 'sorcerized', or bewitched, can be cured by a native doctor. The main exceptions are those types of sorcery involving a ritual operation, especially the magical removal of part of the body or soul. Occasionally it is said that a sorcerer can curtail his activities if he is persuaded or forced to do so.

Because people believe in sorcery, and fear it, it can serve in a general way as a form of social control, a means of upholding or sustaining local rules of behaviour, and also of meting out punishment. Thus it has both positive and negative sides. It is an indirect or extra-physical instrument used as a warning, and threat, against a person regarded as transgressor. An infringement of tribal law, an illicit elopement, a brazen case of adultery, for instance, can trigger off a threat or an accusation of sorcery, which more often than not has further repercussions. A death occurs, an inquest may follow, and a 'murderer' may be named. Killing someone in the appropriate group by spear or sorcery, or claiming to do so, may balance the account; but frequently it does not. A feud is easy to set in motion but not so easy to bring to a halt. Beliefs about sorcery may not be self-sustaining; but proof is never hard to come by, and boasting or acknowledgment of guilt, or irrefutable accusations, help to keep such beliefs alive.

To a member of any given unit—local descent group, clan, linguistic unit, tribe—any supposed act of sorcery against that unit, whatever the provocation, is 'wrong'. Conversely, any supposed act of sorcery performed against outsiders to avenge an injury is 'good'. But over and above the social control aspect of sorcery there is the suggestion that it can be used for personal or selfish ends: that an unscrupulous sorcerer can harm or kill anyone who unwittingly offends him, or that he may do so merely to satisfy a whim without any provocation from the victim. There are sometimes claims that sorcerers may carry out their craft from sheer malice, that they like to see others suffering.

The native doctor's work is, in many respects, at cross-purposes with the sorcerer's. Both have a part to play in their society, but in different ways. A person who claims to be a sorcerer, or has that reputation, may always be regarded as dangerous. He may be seen as abusing his magical knowledge, and too powerful to be wholly trustworthy—or trusted. A native doctor, in contrast, depends very largely on the trust or confidence that is placed in him; of course this does not rest simply on his having a bedside manner; the patient relies on his techniques, his power, and not just on him as a person. When the profession of doctor is combined with that of sorcerer, as in the Great Victoria Desert or among the Wuradjeri, or in parts of Arnhem Land, this is a question of keeping the two social roles separate; but there are bound to be difficulties here.

Doctor and sorcerer alike, to be acknowledged as specialists, must undergo a similar form of initiation to obtain the power they need. It is significant that the same power is seen as underlying both forms of magic. (Elkin, 1954: 290, makes this point too.) In some areas it is not specifically defined, but usually it has its source in the Dreaming, or the traditional past. Magic of both kinds is often supported and substantiated by a body of mythology; it derives its sanction, its validation, from that background. It is linked, either directly or indirectly, with the great creative and ancestral beings, part of the magico-religious, or non-empirical, system of belief and action in that particular society. In such circumstances, magic and religion inevitably overlap. Nor is it always possible to make a demarcation on the basis of social as against personal interests, or benefit.

In terms of the continuum which has been suggested (see Chapter VIII), with magic at one end and religion at the other, much of the activity we have discussed here falls somewhere in between. Love magic is an example. One aspect of the women's secret ceremonies, in certain areas, emphasizes sexual association between men and women. There is a close correspondence between the content of some of these rites, and some of these songs, and actions performed by men in sacred totemic sequences or in the great fertility cults. Both are concerned with fundamental questions, which in local belief are crucial for the welfare of that society and, not least, for its continuance. We might well ask, is one more magical than the other, or more religious? In a religion which focuses attention on life rather than on death, on earthly wellbeing rather than on a hypothetical future state, and on the continuity and persistence of the human spirit, the issues of sexual satisfaction and relations between persons, not to mention the maintenance of the food supply, may be just as relevant as those of relations with a deity, reincarnation, or a state of sinless bliss.

CHAPTER X

Law and Order

Government throughout Aboriginal Australia is, or was, very largely informal and loosely organized. Inevitably, this has had a direct bearing on the maintenance of law and order.

For the majority of Aborigines loyalty is something localized, confined to the land and the people they know. Strangers, Aboriginal or not, are on a different basis, almost tantamount to enemies. Distrust and suspicion permeate relations between tribes living some distance apart, although these are pushed into the background when trading or sacred rituals bring neighbours together on conventionally friendly terms. As a partial counterbalance, when there is consciousness of a shared tradition, of ritual and sacred mythology held in common, this has helped to widen the horizon, drawing more people into the safe, known world of human beings. Quarrels and fights are not lacking, but in such cases they take place within the range of known behaviour, where the rules of killing or making peace are understood and accepted. The pattern or blueprint of behaviour is everywhere in traditional Aboriginal Australia framed in terms of the past. To put it a little differently, the mythical characters instituted a way of life which they introduced to human beings: and because they themselves are viewed as eternal, so are the patterns they set.

The dramatizing of sacred mythology, not on a casual or individual basis but as a collective enterprise, affirms the social identity and solidarity of the units taking part. As well, the combination of positive pressures with absence of serious dissent predisposes members of those units to accept traditional dictates of right and wrong. Through the sanction of religion, a moral rightness is ascribed to the premises on which that society rests.

Not everything that happens in myth, or in the multitude of stories which fall somewhere between the undeniably sacred and the undeniably secular, or mundane, is presented as a model for human beings to imitate in its entirety. The Djanggawul Brother and Sisters commit incest. Jurawadbad kills his own wife and mother-in-law. Bomaboma the trickster rapes a young girl, killing her in the process. Ancestral men steal, from women, the first sacred objects. Njirana spends most of his time following the Seven Sisters, the Gunggaranggara women. The two wives of Balangudjalgngudjalg the White Cockatoo are unfaithful; pretending to go out hunting, they spend all their time playing with other men, until finally he tricks them into entering an inaccessible cave, high in the rocks, then pulls away the tree-ladder and leaves them to die. And so on.

But whether they represent the good or the bad example, the mythical figures are said to have laid down precepts or made suggestions of which people are expected to take notice today. They defined the broad roles to be played by both men and women in such matters as sacred ritual, economic affairs, marriage, child-bearing, death. They warned that if people behaved in such and such a way, certain consequences would surely follow: that various tabus and avoidances had to be observed, that various relatives should not be intimate with one another. They set patterns of behaviour for members of the particular social and cultural group in which their power is acknowledged. The fact that they are regarded as sacred beings gives them a right to dictate in this way, and lends an aura of sanctity to their pronouncements. In some myths statements are framed in terms of what people should do, often as absolute pronouncements. In others they are implicit in the story or songs. A-social behaviour in this setting may point the way to alternative action: if you do that, the result will be this; but these words are not used, the sequence is inferred in the tale itself. Often such behaviour passes without comment, and in fact may not be considered wrong for the particular characters concerned. Although the mythical beings are in a sense 'law-makers', they are also above the law. They are more-than-human, not bound by the rules which restrict ordinary human beings. Being 'outside the law', or above it, is itself an attribute of power and sacred authority. Acts contrary to everyday conventions assume a sacred quality when carried out in particular contexts: a notable example here would be fertility rites involving sexual association between persons who normally avoid each other.

Some of the warnings, or positive suggestions, put forward by the ancestral beings have a practical basis, insofar as they have helped the people concerned to adjust to their particular environment. In many cases, in fact, they appear to embody the accumulated experience of numbers of generations. But this does not of itself ensure their recognition. It is the supernatural sanctions linked with them which underline their significance, and supply cogent reasons for conforming to them.

CONFORMITY

Traditionally speaking, children grow up to accept these dictates more or less unquestioningly. The only conflicting impressions come through outside contact, at ceremonial or trading times, with members of other Aboriginal groups who hold perhaps slightly divergent views. This impact, however, is not on a large enough scale, or continuous enough, or involving sufficiently strong pressures, to have a significant effect on the maintenance of the *status quo*, at least in general or relative terms. This means that within, say, a certain tribe, there are recognized codes of behaviour on which its members are in fundamental agreement. There are, inevitably, some individual differences of opinion among them. In any sphere of belief and action the question of variation must be taken into account, not least as regards the degree to which actuality measures up to the ideal. In most cases there is a range of behaviour which is tolerated without being classified as irregular: this is obvious, for instance, in the choice of marriage partners. (See Chapter III.) Some areas of human activity are more tightly controlled than others. Alternative modes of action need not imply divergent or dissenting views: they may be simply different ways of expressing the same set of ideas or beliefs.

Nevertheless, within any given social unit certain rules and standards are acknowledged, certain patterns of behaviour considered right, as against others which are wrong. Informal as well as formal sanctions are likely to greet any obvious deviation from those patterns—a display of social conscience which is a result of traditional emphasis, and at the same time reinforces and strengthens the power of tradition. Two points should be borne in mind here. Firstly, permitted variation is not the same thing as deviation. Deviation is behaviour which is not tolerated, and against which sanctions of various sorts are exerted. Secondly, stressing this traditional aspect should not be taken to mean that 'Custom is King', that there is no scope for individual variation or individual initiative, as some earlier writers suggested: but it does imply that innovation is at a minimum and that these Aborigines are, in Riesman's sense (1955), 'tradition-directed'.

The members of an Aboriginal society who are supposed to have accumulated most knowledge and experience, and to be most conversant with all features of their own culture, are those fully initiated and no longer young—in many cases, the elders. Wisdom is not assumed to come automatically with increasing age. Personal factors are involved, too. A man, or woman, who by middle life has achieved a reputation for incompetence or foolishness is not normally expected to improve as he grows older. On the whole, however, there is an emphasis on age, especially when it comes to providing a final decision on some debatable point—in much the same way that in our own society precedents are cited as a basis for legal judgments. Other adults do have an informal say, but they are considered to be less familiar with all the issues which may be involved. And because in the great religious sequences men take a more active role than women, some men come to have increased authority as ritual headmen. This lends weight to their opinions. Knowledge of sacred matters is a pre-eminent criterion, and people who qualify on this score are regarded as final authorities, or as human spokesmen for those authorities.

For children, and for minor offences, discipline is maintained largely by the immediate family. (See Chapter V.) Kaberry (1939: 76) mentions that she did not hear "frequent injunctions" to children to do certain things because it was the rule, or the norm, or the traditional way; "in everyday activities, children were told what to do without any preamble, and were slapped if they disobeyed beyond the limits of endurance". This does vary. Restrictions are few for children, and punishment of a severe or prolonged kind is rare. Permissiveness is the theme of childhood. Children are told things and shown things, rather than subjected to a spate of injunctions. For a boy, this relative freedom comes to an abrupt end at the onset of initiation—which also marks a transition, as far as he is concerned, from predominantly parental control. In places where there is little or nothing in the way of physical operations, or ordeals, other means such as food tabus are used to impress on a novice the rules or laws he is expected to remember, and to observe. Quite probably, the experience of deprivation, or physical pain, or threat of pain helps to imprint on a boy's mind the admonitions associated with it. Sometimes, of course, the physical ordeal is not a single event, but a series of events extending over a long period, paralleled by the learning process of which it is simply an external manifestation. When a girl reaches puberty, too, the physical experience may be surrounded with ritual which underlines its social significance, including relatively formal instruction spelling out the proper way for her to behave now she has achieved adult status. She is advised not to stare or smile at other men but stay quietly with her husband, to observe her kinship obligations, to share the food she collects, and so on. This brings together, in essence, what she has been learning in a more diffuse way from early childhood.

Often, then, although there are exceptions, puberty or initiation rituals are an occasion for summing up or emphasizing canons of social behaviour, positive and negative, many of which have already been learnt, and for introducing new admonitions such as in the sphere of ritual. The shift in authority from the immediate family to the wider context of horde, clan, or tribal group does not prevent close kin from taking disciplinary action, but it means that more people are entitled to intervene, and that the actual parents may be overridden, or perhaps not even consulted. Correspondingly, during childhood a boy or girl is not bound by economic and other kinship obligations, even though he is encouraged to become familiar with them and to practise them on a small scale. The responsibility rests with his immediate relatives, especially his parents, just as it does in the matter of teaching and disciplining him. After about puberty, depending on the locality, this picture changes. A young man or woman will continue to receive advice and help, but is now increasingly committed to fulfilling his own obligations, just as he is increasingly held responsible for his own actions.

The sanctions which are drawn upon in the attempt to ensure conformity to accepted moral, ethical, and religious codes may be positive or negative, or a combination of both. The following are some of the most important.

Positive Sanctions

Firstly, there are direct instructions, suggestions, or requests addressed to a growing child almost from the time when he can walk and talk in a reasonably intelligible way, conditioning him to accept certain tenets of behaviour as right and inevitable, and impressing on him the necessity to conform.

Secondly, some outlet is provided for socially harmful or destructive emotions in popular stories which show, according to local standards, a-social activity, such as a mother-in-law abusing a son-in-law. Listening to these allows an opportunity for relaxing the tensions and constraints which permeate various relationships, without being subject to the penalties of actually doing so. Listeners to stories of this kind, especially children and young adults, are able to enjoy the vicarious experience of breaking such tabus, with subsequent re-affirmation of their conformity. It is true that these could set a pattern for imitation, that the bad example could be taken as a model to be followed rather than rejected: but there is not enough reinforcement outside the story-telling situation for this to happen in more than a few cases.

Thirdly, provision for socially sanctioned extra-marital intercourse, especially during certain rituals, or in the convention of wife lending, helps to provide some sexual variety without upsetting the institution of marriage. It does not, however, prevent elopements, or adultery, from taking place outside that context.

Fourthly, rewards are offered for conformity: for example, ritual and secular leadership—the 'big man' or 'big woman', the boss, the elder, the native doctor. Over-conformity to ideal standards is more likely to meet with uneasiness, if not outright criticism. Much depends on personal qualities, on skill and endurance, and, especially, on possession of sacred knowledge together with awareness of its practical implications. Social approval, ranging from lukewarm absence of disapproval to forthright enthusiasm, is accorded such persons as a ritual leader, a good hunter, a man who fulfils his kinship obligations, or a woman who is industrious in food-collecting, solicitous of her children, and faithful to her husband.

Negative Sanctions

On the opposite side, as it were, are the negative sanctions. Because they are not the same throughout the Continent, it is not possible to list them in order of importance.

First, ridicule. This is a powerful weapon, but a two-edged one: it can provoke quarrels or exacerbate them, as well as restrain them. Even less constructively, it is extended to physical deformities or shortcomings for which the person concerned is not responsible: blindness, feeble-mindedness, mental defectiveness. It rarely takes the form of complete ostracism. The only cases we know relate to partial rejection: refusal to take seriously or even to co-operate with people classed as abnormal or 'deaf', foolish, not listening or responding to what they are told, or shown. (See e.g. R. and C. Berndt, 1951*c*: 75-89.) (Just as often, however, people who are blind or crippled or ill are treated with the utmost solicitude, even at great personal inconvenience to their helpers.)

Under this heading too we could include swearing or the use of obscenity. (See Roth, 1897: 184; R. and C. Berndt, 1951*a*: for example 190-1.) Again, this is dangerous to use, and can recoil on the speaker—who may, in extreme instances, be killed instantly. Scandalmongering and gossiping are common pastimes, particularly since much of people's private life is so public: but apart from this, gossip is treated as enjoyable and inevitable, and in fact a necessary part of social relations. Too much of it about a specific person can do him harm, malicious talk can build up trouble; but at the same time it can serve to control or modify the behaviour of people who feel they are vulnerable to it. Husbands suspecting their wives of infidelity, or wives suspecting their husbands, are ready to listen to tales about them. The context is important here: gossiping about whom, with whom, in whose presence, are points which must be considered. There is always the possibility that someone will carry rumours to an interested person, and this in itself is a restraining influence when it comes to behaviour which may be liable to misinterpretation (or correct interpretation, for that matter). Certain actions should not be carried out blatantly if trouble is to be avoided. This applies, above all, to pre- and extra-marital associations—which make up the greater part of most gossip.

Secondly, the brother-sister tabu found in many parts of Aboriginal Australia. In some areas, a man is expected to punish anyone he calls sister if she uses bad language, neglects her economic, family, or ceremonial duties, gets involved in a fight, or is abused in his hearing. This can have a sobering effect on a woman's behaviour when she is near an actual or classificatory brother.

Thirdly, there is fear of the supernatural punishment which may follow, without human agency, the breach of some tabu, or some sacred law—or if singing, dances, or various rites are not properly performed. According to Kaberry (1939: 75): "It is difficult to assess how far *ngarunggani* (the Dreaming) is used not only as a sanction, but also as a threat of supernatural punishment for the infringement of taboos": association with a tabued relative may lead to sore eyes, incest to more or less immediate death, or eating forbidden food to a malignant disease. Most threats of supernatural punishments are framed in diffuse terms: not 'If you do this, which is wrong, the great Djanggawul, Ngurunderi, or some other mythical being, will punish you.' They are usually less explicit: 'If you do this, which is wrong, you'll become ill and die,' implying that it is contrary to the established pattern of life. The creative beings established that pattern, and expect people to follow it: if they do not, the consequences are on their own heads.

Fourthly, there is fear of sorcery, which can be viewed as a powerful legal sanction. Even for minor offences, retaliation may supposedly take the form of sorcery. A corollary to this is fear of being accused of sorcery. If one person has an obvious grudge against another, who suffers some misfortune or illness or perhaps dies, he may be accused of bringing this about by sorcery. If a wife fails to look after her husband or vice versa, or if either of them neglects their children, the same accusation may be made should the spouse, or a child, happen to die. This need not, in every case, involve claims about the actual practice of magical rites.

Around Oenpelli, for instance, if a woman has sweethearts, or even one sweetheart over a long period without her husband's sanction, and he subsequently dies, she is considered to have brought this about either directly, by weakening his heart, or indirectly by being careless about his belongings and leavings so that someone was able to take them for sorcery. A husband, therefore, normally keeps some check on his wife's affairs. While up to a point he may unofficially tolerate them, he retains the right to discover them officially when it suits him, or when he feels it is time to intervene, by 'dreaming' about her activities. This latent threat of 'dreaming', with quarrels that are bound to follow, is possibly a potent factor in restraining married women from having too many lovers.

Fifthly, there is the threat of physical violence, of being injured or killed for some breach of the accepted code of behaviour. But this is sometimes employed to settle a grudge, or satisfy personal desires, under the guise of maintaining conformity to the rules.

In the sixth place, there is the threat of being not simply killed, but also deprived of the usual mortuary rites. A north-eastern Arnhem Lander put to death for some serious offence may be deliberately left lying where he fell, 'for dogs and crows to eat'. There are just enough examples of this to give force to the threat. Of course in feud killings too, especially where the persons concerned belong to different tribes or language-units, a corpse is left untended; but the assumption is that relatives are bound to do something about it, if they find it in time, at least for bone-disposal rites. This is very different to a punishment killing within the same language-unit, where deprivation of rites is part of the punishment, and relatives are prohibited from handling the corpse, under threat of meeting a similar fate.

OFFENCES WITHIN THE TRIBE OR CLAN

Offences within a tribal group can be summarized very loosely under two main headings. In the first place, and of primary importance, are breaches of sacred law—regulations, tabus, codes of behaviour, which are thought to have a clearly supernatural basis. To some extent this conforms to the concept of sin—that is, having a religious connotation. In the second place, there are offences against other persons, or against property. A number of offences seem to fall somewhere between these two, tending toward either extreme according to the seriousness of the implications. For instance, incest offences are also breaches of traditional and supernaturally sanctioned laws, while minor offences do not, in *practice*, have this significance.

Breaches of sacred law

Ritual leaders, meeting secretly, decide on the appropriate punishment—which in extreme cases is death. According to circumstances, two or more of them may take action themselves or delegate it to someone else. They may not tell him at first what they want him to do: the coercion may be more subtle. For instance, he may be given tabued food to eat, and afterward instructed to go and kill a certain person; or a sacred object may be put on his head (Arnhem Land), a form of compulsion against which there is no argument. Supernatural sanctions are occasionally invoked in matters of primarily personal vengeance, which may have wider repercussions. In the Daly River area a stone spearhead may be flung into the sacred ring place, to the accompaniment of ritual invocations, so casting an obligation on all initiated men to co-operate. During the period of early contact there, one man who thought he had a grievance against the European settlers is reported to have done this, and the result was what was described in the Press at the end of last century as the 'Copper Mine Massacre'. In other words, the supernatural authority is cited, or drawn upon, to provoke or substantiate physical action. Kaberry (1939: 76) notes the same point: "When some laws are disobeyed, punishment is inflicted by the old men who are concerned with maintaining the *status quo* and conformity to tradition. They are the instruments of justice. . . ." Occasionally, throughout the Continent, women or children either deliberately or inadvertently see sacred objects or rites which are prohibited to them: the conventional procedure is to spear them immediately, without further deliberation.

For a really serious offence against sacred law, any effective means can be used. A man may be speared in the back on a hunting trip, without warning, by one of his companions. And ideally, whatever is done, there is no redress, no feud: it is framed as punishment, not retaliation.

As an extension of this, group action may be taken against one of its members who does not respond to ordinary sanctions, A young man may be labelled, in effect, uncontrollable, if he refuses to keep away from other men's wives—particularly if those men are ritual leaders. Even if he does not directly break any sacred laws, he is claimed to be a menace to people with whom he comes in contact. If he ignores repeated warnings, the assumption seems to be that nothing more can be done with him, that the usual teaching-and-learning processes and the usual sanctions have failed. In such an extreme case he is, or was, usually killed. A man who elopes with his wife's daughter, or with a close mother-in-law, may be treated in the same way, again with the approval or passive consent of his own group—or, at least, of the adult men of his own group. Women may not even know what is contemplated, and certainly have little say in it.

Offences against property

Offences against property are rare, traditionally, in Aboriginal Australia. (See Sharp, 1934*a*: 38.) Tribal or clan land itself is not transferable, but regarded as being held in trust by living men and women for past, present and future members of that unit. Their ownership, in this special sense of the term, is supernaturally sanctioned. In the same way, deposits of red ochre or stone quarries are traditionally inalienable. Small everyday items like digging sticks, baskets, mats, wooden dishes, fishing spears, and so on, are not normally stolen, although they may be borrowed in accordance with kinship obligations. But offences against dogs, which are regarded almost as members of a family rather than as personal property, may have violent repercussions. (In western Arnhem Land, for instance, in one mythical case, several large camps are said to have been wiped out after a man's special pet dog was unknowingly killed and eaten.)

Ritual stealing is a different matter. Two examples come from north-eastern Arnhem Land, one connected with the making of *dua* moiety feathered string, the other with the *wuramu* ceremony (*jiridja* moiety). Preparing native twine or string is women's work; adding coloured parakeet feathers to it is not. But men do not ask for, or take, the completed lengths of plain twine in a straightforward way. Secrecy is the essence of the transaction—and an expected feature of it. Symbolically, the reference is to the dramatic occasion on which men stole the sacred *rangga* from women in the Djanggawul myth. (See Chapter VII.) In the *jiridja* case a carved *wuramu* figure, a 'Collection Man', is carried through the main camp, and as it passes from hut to hut the men in charge of it take everything portable within reach. Both these forms of stealing are socially approved, in spite of some conventional grumbling about them.

Offences against the person

There are several facets to this.

First: if a woman injures her child in a fit of temper: or allows it to stray, so that it becomes ill or dies, or is never found again: or if she deliberately kills a full-term baby which was healthy and not physically deformed: these are family matters, and she will be punished by her husband, or her co-wives, or both. At least she will be criticized; and the topic will be kept in reserve ready to bring up against her in any dispute or fight. If she bears a child from a man of the same moiety as herself, technically a form of incest, then her husband or co-wives will usually kill it—or would do so, in the past.

Second: running away with another man's wife or, what it amounts to in most cases, another woman's husband. The injured party usually invokes the help of male relatives, if necessary sending out a message stick, or a war stick. This again is primarily a matter for the persons immediately concerned, although the ramifications of the kinship system may involve others as well.

Third: and especially important, there is murder or suspected murder. Generally speaking, there are three means of treating this.

One is by open retaliation in the form of violence. Usually this too is a family matter; the victim's close relatives are expected to avenge him—or, less frequently, her. If one of them is not able to do this himself, perhaps because it would conflict with other kin obligations, he may (as in western Arnhem Land) hand over a special object associated with revenge to some man who is under an obligation to him. This man, whatever his personal feelings in the matter, is bound to carry out the actual killing. In western Arnhem Land the revenge object, the *mai^e^gug*, or *wungbar*, may be bound to the shaft of the spear used for that purpose.

Murders or suspected murders have led, throughout northern Arnhem Land, to so-called blood feuds extending over long periods and breaking out at intervals into open violence. Occasionally, the tribe or the clan as a whole is called in. In north-central and north-eastern Arnhem Land, a high premium is placed on fighting ability. A man who makes it clear that he will not hesitate to throw spears to get what he wants is admired as well as feared. He may even build up his reputation to a point where very few people will care to challenge him openly. To begin with, he may direct someone to kill a certain person. After that there will be another, and then another, plus claims of success in sorcery. If he can continue to get away with such behaviour he may come to a point when actual violence is no longer necessary—when all he need do is look threatening and rattle his spears. So long as he observes the kinship rules, and is careful to conform to sacred laws and ritual obligations, he is rarely punished. Old Wonggu of Caledon Bay, a Djabu-speaking man, had reached this status well before he died a few years ago. Compensation in goods may be offered, or demanded, for a death, but acceptance is no guarantee that revenge will not be attempted. In a situation where fighting qualities are emphasized, even to the extent that prestige can come from spearing a victim in the back, or while he sleeps, there is always danger of a breakdown in group cohesion, and eventually of reaching a state of affairs where physical force is the only recognized criterion. However, it is possibly only the contact situation which has permitted men of this kind to survive in recent years. In the past, men with a reputation for spearing or otherwise killing a number of people, for primarily personal or even family reasons, were as a rule eventually killed themselves. Their fighting careers were eventful but brief, since the cultural factors which allowed them to behave in that way operated also to support their opponents. By their very behaviour, they laid themselves open to retaliation.

Where, for some reason, physical vengeance is not practicable, another course is open. First the 'murderer' is identified to the satisfaction of the victim's relatives. Then one of them performs sorcery, or threatens to do so, or claims to have done so if that particular person becomes ill or dies. (See Chapter IX.)

A third means of treating an actual or supposed murderer, throughout northern Arnhem Land, is the *magarada.* We shall come back to this presently.

In central and southern Australia, grievances are often settled by formally spearing an offender in the thigh—particularly in cases of adultery, elopement and even personal injury: he may even stand quietly, offering no resistance, while the aggrieved party or one of his close kin throws the spear. A careless or angry spearsman may miss the thigh and strike a vital organ, or the wound may become infected, so that in the end the penalty is more drastic than was conventionally anticipated.

In a different context, the desire for revenge can be temporarily diverted into relatively harmless channels, provided it does not get out of hand. In western Arnhem Land a messenger bringing news of a death is caught up in a mock fight with men to whom he announces it. This is regarded as simply a formality, and ideally no blood should be drawn; but there is no reassurance that things will always go smoothly. Close relatives hearing the news for the first time are not expected to react calmly. A dead man's brother, father, mother's brother, a woman's father or brother is carefully watched, and even forcibly restrained in case he uses violence to relieve his feelings, spearing the messenger as a substitute for the murderer. But once this immediate danger is over the messenger joins them in mourning, gashing himself until blood flows as a sign of his sympathy with them.

EMBRYONIC COURT

Although self-help of this sort is the basis of legal procedure in Aboriginal Australia, in most areas more or less formal discussions or meetings are held at irregular intervals to settle grievances. The most convenient time for this is when members of different tribes meet for ceremonies. Except for occasional trading trips, these may be virtually the only occasions on which their members come together. Conventionally there should be no fights at ceremonial times. In practice such gatherings do sometimes break up in fighting, but usually after the conclusion of the main rituals. Ideally, however, this is the time to settle inter-tribal affairs.

In other words, agreement on ways and means of maintaining social order is not confined to members of one tribe, or language-unit. It extends to neighbouring tribes as well, or at least to parts of them, especially if they share the same mythology and ritual. But it is considerably weakened by lack of consistent interaction. While the meetings, within the context of ceremony and ritual, are significant as providing one means of social control, they are not judicially-based bodies.

Formal gatherings in the nature of law courts with judiciary functions do not exist in Aboriginal Australia: there is no formally constituted court of law, comprising special persons vested with authority and power to deal with cases, pass judgment, and impose punishment. The immediate demands of self-help, together with a relatively weak political organization, have militated against such a development. Further, sorcery is not the handmaiden of law, since it usurps one of the court's most cherished functions—that of punishment. As Hoebel (1954) points out, 'the Law has teeth'. But sorcery is only one way of achieving retaliation, and may not even be the most important way. And although constituted courts did not exist in traditional Aboriginal Australia, there were councils which did much the same thing, although far more informally and less systematically.

The nearest approach, as far as we can gather from the material available, is found in the councils of the now virtually extinct Lower River Murray people, such as the Jaraldi and Dangani. Taplin, in Woods (1879: 34-5), speaks of leaders or 'landowners', the *rupulle,* negotiators and spokesmen for the tribe, or patrilineal clan headmen, who may settle disagreements with adjacent tribes, or clans. With the elders, they preside over the *tendi,* a council or court before which offenders are brought for trial. Women play a prominent part. Taplin gives several examples, which tally with cases one of us (R. M. Berndt) recorded at second hand in that area some years ago. In the example Taplin witnessed, two clans met to settle a dispute: their members sat facing each other, and members of other clans were ranged around their *rupulle.* The *tendi* began with a general discussion, with accusers and defendants, and witnesses were called. In Taplin's example no decision was reached, as far as he could tell: whereas in my own cases judgment was passed and punishment meted out.

This rather elaborate system of control seems to have few parallels, although there are suggestions in Howitt of something of the sort in eastern Australia. He speaks (1904: 295-354) of tribal councils, headed by a leader. Among the Wuradjeri a headman can call his people together to consider "the course of action as to murders, abduction of women, adultery, or raids on, or by, other tribes". In the 'Gournditch-mara' tribe the headman settles all quarrels and disputes. Among the Dieri, in contrast to these examples where apparently anyone could be present, special closed meetings are held, attended by heads of local totemic groups, fighting men, native doctors, and elders of some standing. (See also Gason, in Woods, 1879: 265.) Among the matters dealt with are sorcery, murder, breaches of the moral code, offences against sacred ritual, disclosure of secrets of the tribal council or initiation rituals to the uninitiated. A person judged guilty of a major crime is killed by an armed party (*pinya*), sent out by the headman.

Such councils of elders or men of importance, or leaders (tribal, clan, local group, ritual), seem to have been, traditionally, fairly common. But generally they are exceedingly informal and while they meet to settle disputes, among other things, they do not try to handle all types of these, nor do they always act in a judiciary capacity. Roth (1897: 139) differentiates between offences dealt with by the council (that is, offences against the unit as a whole) and those which are settled at a personal level. This distinction is not easy to make. Speaking of the Pitta Pitta (Boulia district, Queensland), he says that the camp council "will take upon itself to mete out punishment in crimes of murder, incest", and indiscriminate use of weapons in the camp itself: in the first two a guilty party is killed, perhaps after being made to dig his own grave, in the last he is crippled with knives. Spencer and Gillen (1938: 15) mention that in meetings called to consider an offence the headmen consult with elders: if the accused is judged guilty, and his crime is a major one, he can expect death: the elders arrange to carry out the sentence by organizing an *ininja* party. Kaberry (1939: 178-9, 272), speaking for the eastern Kimberleys, says that "the horde and not the tribe [and not the local descent group: see Chapter II] is the political unit", which is concerned with government and administration. Men make the decisions, but authority is vested in the headman and the elders. The headman arranges the place and time of meetings: "He and the elders conduct the proceedings centring round the ceremonies" and the settlement of disputes: such meetings provide an opportunity for the thrashing out of grievances. But although political control is vested in the headman and in the elders, this must be qualified: apart from serious charges, many matters are the responsibility of the relevant kinship groups.

A different procedure for settling grievances of a minor sort, in north-eastern Arnhem Land, is what is called the *bugalub*. It resembles the *garma* mortuary rites described by Warner (1937/58: 412 ff.). Persons of either moiety can set it in motion, when they want to clear up some dispute or disagreement or, in a general sense, restore equanimity or balance. (An Elcho Islander who had been taken to Darwin hospital with a severely injured hand called one of these when he returned home.) People gather around a specially prepared ground in the main camp, outlined with mounds of sand: within it a hole has been dug to represent a sacred waterhole associated with the persons responsible for holding the rite. The songs, to the usual accompaniment of clapping sticks and didjeridu, are 'outside' versions of 'inside' (secret-sacred) singing, with the same associations. As one after another in that particular series is sung, women jump up from the place where most of them are sitting together, and dance. Finally the persons concerned (more often men, sometimes women) enter the 'waterhole': and there water is poured over them while invocations are called to the mythical beings connected with that site. This ritual washing is said to heal dissension and make for mutual goodwill between the participants. (At Elcho Island early in 1961, six *bugalub* were held in a matter of two weeks.) The conventional healing of breaches, through contact with the sacred world of myth and ritual, is handled in a way which, apart from the more serious business of the evening, provides popular entertainment and enjoyment for people not directly concerned in it.

The *kopara* of the Dieri and their neighbours is designed for the same purpose, the settlement of grievances, but because of its economic overtones we have discussed it in Chapter IV.

SETTLEMENT BY ORDEAL

While the tribal council is general in one form or another two other procedures, which can be classified as legal in the broad sense of the term, have to do with the settlement of disputes. The first is typified by the north-eastern and western Arnhem Land *magarada* or *manejag*. There is a judicial quality in this, insofar as the major aim is the settlement of a rupture, and all interested parties are represented; but before the holding of this meeting the accused has already been judged guilty, and may even have admitted culpability. Although the *magarada* is spoken of as a peace-making ceremony it is better styled 'trial by ordeal' or 'settlement by combat' or, as in other instances mentioned by Howitt (1904), 'settlement by duel'. Radcliffe-Brown's view (1952: 215-16) would be that this is simply retaliatory action and not law, that a legal system in the narrow sense has not yet been developed. Hoebel (1954: 309), however, sees in the *magarada* a trend toward law: he says that "there is no superior restraining power; it all depends on the self-control of each group" involved. Gluckman's (1955) concept of the 'reasonable man' is significant in this argument.

It does seem fairly clear that this procedure of conventionalized retaliation, socially sanctioned, publicly demonstrated, with the aim of settlement (in terms of indemnity), is a legal one, and closely related to a system of law.

As Warner mentions (1937/58: 174-6), a *magarada* (*makarata*) is not held straightaway after an offence has taken place, but only after people's rage and resentment have had time to cool. Arrangements are always made by the injured party. The two opposing groups, painted in white clay, stand just out of spear-throwing reach, with mangrove jungle or scrub behind for protection if necessary. Members of the aggrieved party advance toward the opposite side in a totemic dance, then walk back. The others do the same. Now they are ready for the 'duel'. Men of the accused's group run irregularly across the ground, and with them run two men who are closely related to both sides. Spears are flung at them—but usually with the stone or iron blades removed. They can dodge, but they must not throw back the spears, or the abuse which accompanies them. This takes the first edge off the injured clan's anger. After a brief lull, the accused man or men runs across the ground. This time the blades are left in the spears, and flung at him one after another. Elders from both sides try to restrain the participants, warning them to keep their tempers in check. Finally, the accused man's party dance across to their opponents. If they spear him in the thigh the matter is at an end, and both groups join in dancing. Ideally the thigh wound is enough, but sometimes the accused is killed. Very occasionally, a fight develops from the conflict of opinion at such a ritual settlement: in which case the feud continues until further attempts are made to curtail it through a *magarada*. If there is no final spearing the case is still open, and further retaliation can be expected.

The *magarada* has its counterparts in other regions—including the conventional thigh-wounding of the Western Desert. Howitt (1904: 333, 335, 338, 342, 348) gives examples of ordeals. Among the Maryborough (Queensland) people, an accused man has only a shield to defend himself. Among the Buntamurra, the close kin of an injured man "fight and thrash the offender". With the Kaiabara, a challenge is sent out by the injured party; if it is accepted they presumably meet in much the same way as for the *magarada*—but without the ritual dancing, which seems to be unique in this context. The Turrbal have "expiatory combats". The Wotjobaluk settle differences immediately by armed combat, fighting until blood is drawn. Howitt gives a further case in which the aggressors are summoned to appear with their kin before members of the injured man's group and face their spears. When the two parties come together, the offender's headman stands between them and tells them not to take unfair advantage of the situation. The offenders, armed only with shields, submit to a shower of spears; as soon as one is wounded the headman tosses "a lighted piece of bark into the air", and this ends the fight. Another example comes from Merri Creek, near Melbourne; in about 1840, two groups met to settle a killing. The accused, armed with his shield, served as a target for spears and boomerangs until hit in the side by a reed spear. At this the headman ran between the two groups calling on them to stop.

As Howitt puts it, "they had had blood, and all were again friends". In the Yuin example, the accused man has two shields. If his offence was murder, he must stand alone; if wounding or sorcery, a companion may support him. His relatives stand at one side of the ground, their opponents opposite. The men chosen to throw spears and boomerangs at him face him in a line, and throw their weapons: when they draw blood, that ends the 'trial by ordeal'.

In another case reported by Howitt the setting was the Tambo River, between Swan Reach and Lake King. Again the two groups were ranged in opposition, and again the accused man was allowed two shields; but he refused to admit guilt. Nevertheless, he had to run the gauntlet of a barrage of boomerangs until one wounded him in the thigh. He flung it back—a breach of convention which could have led to further trouble if women had not "rushed in between the two parties and stopped the fight".

The Tiwi of Bathurst and Melville islands have the custom of a duel during a public trial. (Hart and Pilling, 1960: 80-3.) People sit or stand in a ring about an open clearing. The accuser, painted white and armed with spears, stands opposite the defendant, barely painted and holding few weapons, perhaps none. The accuser then states his case, elaborately, with plenty of abuse, biting his beard (a sign of anger all along the north coast), and finally throws his spears; the other dodges them for some time, then permits one to hit him. He must not react by throwing spears back. Basedow (1925: 165, 167, 172) mentions settlement of grievances in an armed duel which continues until one man falls or both are exhausted. Among the Aranda and Dieri there is a dagger duel, the dagger itself made from a long stone flake with a grip or haft of porcupine resin.

But even though these cases do involve settlement, and special rules are observed during the duel, they are not of the same nature as councils where an authority such as a headman is called in to adjudicate.

In the Kimberleys (Kaberry, 1939: 145-7, 149), matters brought up in inter-tribal discussions have already been thoroughly talked over among the parties concerned. In the example she gives, from Violet Valley, members of the two opposing sides faced each other across the specially prepared 'ring place', while headmen urged restraint. One man called sorcery accusations against another on the opposite side and ran across brandishing his spear, but after a time came back quietly to his own side. His opponent then did the same, asserting his innocence. Other accusations followed between the two groups, from women as well as men, with much abuse and waving of fighting sticks, and some skirmishing. Finally, the headman of the visiting group called an end to the meeting, and they all dispersed to prepare for a ceremony to be held that evening. As Kaberry observes: "Certainly such a settlement lacks the formality of legal proceedings . . . it lacks the embodiment of justice in an official with the power to regulate the marital affairs of individuals of whom he may have no intimate knowledge. . . ." A basic consideration here is that both parties are interested in bringing about a reconciliation. In one sense we can speak here of kin-based legal procedure with the headman acting less as an arbitrator than as a mediator whose business it is to ensure that things do not get out of hand.

INQUEST

Another procedure which has a legal quality is the inquest, often held after a death. It will come up again in the chapter on mortuary proceedings, but something needs to be said about it here. Elkin (1954: 283-4, 302-12, 315-16; 1945) discusses it in some detail. The key figure is usually the native doctor, who through divination or other means claims that he can identify the person or group responsible. Not all deaths are followed by inquests, and not all inquests are followed by retaliation.

The procedures vary too. Among the Lower River Murray people the nearest relative sleeps with his head on the corpse so that he will dream of the 'murderer'. (Taplin, in Woods, 1879: 19-20.) On the following day it is carried on a bier, while he and others surround it and suggest likely names; if the men carrying it feel a movement on its part toward the person who calls one of these names, that is taken as confirmation. Among the Jupagalk, after a man dies the spirit of the 'murderer' is sought in the adjacent bush. (Howitt, 1904: 455, *et seq.*) The Wurunjerri, when no native doctor is available, simply sweep the top of the grave clean, find a small hole, and insert a stick which shows by its slant the direction in which they must search. At Port Stephens the corpse is held on the shoulders of two men, while a third strikes it with a green bough calling the names of various suspects; at the correct name it shakes, making the bearers do the same. Among the Chepara the native doctor sees the culprit in a dream. In other tribes the corpse itself is asked who caused its death (for example, the Bigambul), or the doctor makes a track on the cleared ground under the mortuary platform (for example, the Turrbal) and so interprets the identity of the 'murderer'. With the Wakelbura the earth immediately below the platform is loosened so that the slightest mark will be visible, and examined at intervals. In the eastern and northern Kimberleys, stones are arranged underneath the mortuary platform or tree: when body juices fall on these the doctor can tell from which way the sorcery has come. (Basedow, 1925: 208-9; Kaberry, 1939: 212-

13.) See also Elkin (1954: 305) for the Bad and Ungarinjin. Once guilt has been definitely established, older relatives of the dead person remove the skull or some other bone, paint it with red ochre and blood, bury it in an ant-heap with fire, and sing over it so that the 'murderer' will sicken and die. One way of narrowing the range of responsibility is sometimes used, in the Western Desert, when people come together after an interval in which there have been a number of deaths. Preferably on a dark, still night, small fire-sticks are prepared, one for each dead person, and each stick identified by such points as section or subsection and local affiliation —not by name, since names of the dead are tabu. One after another the sticks are held up in the air: if the sparks fly high and far, someone from another country in that particular direction must be the culprit; but if the sparks fall close by and are soon extinguished, responsibility lies near at hand.

The north-eastern Arnhem Landers say that the 'murderer's' spirit always hovers near the corpse, and a native doctor can easily identify it. (Warner, 1937/58: 196.) Here, too, juices falling from the mortuary platform are used in divination. Or the native doctor watches a stick on which he has put one of the dead person's arm-bands or some of his hair, ready to hit it suddenly with a 'spirit bag' and catch, or at least identify, the 'murderer's' spirit as it jumps from the stick. (Warner, 1937/58: 211.) Spencer and Gillen (1938: 476) say that a dying man may whisper his 'murderer's' name to a native doctor, or this information may be inferred in a general way by examining the grave. In the Western Desert, several months after burial the bones are exhumed and scrutinized for the same purpose. At Laverton, specifically, a corpse may be examined for signs of magical choking, and a native doctor knows from the smell where, roughly, to find the 'murderer'. (Elkin, 1954: 304.) In other cases there is post-mortem examination of internal organs; Elkin discusses some of them.

Inquest proceedings, simple or elaborate, immediate or delayed, are only the first of a series of steps which must be taken if revenge is to be sought. They establish a form of balance by providing an explanation of events, giving the persons most closely associated with a dead man or woman an opportunity to weigh the situation and decide whether they want to carry matters further.

Procedures for settling major differences or identifying sorcerers are of a fairly conventionalized or formalized kind. But side by side with them, or leading up to them, there may be a great deal of informal discussion, with men and women voicing their views openly and noisily in the main camp. If an offence has just been committed and feeling is running high, words may lead to blows, and fighting may break out in earnest. Otherwise talk and argument may go on at intervals for weeks, or even longer. Older men and women usually have a controlling say, in the long run. But angry people are in no humour to look at both sides of an issue, especially to begin with. If a man has a burning grievance against another, he directs public harangue particularly against his antagonist—who may respond in kind, or simply sit with averted face and downcast eyes ignoring him. The rest of the camp will probably go on with its ordinary activities, ostensibly taking no notice, but actually absorbing most of what is said. Even if they do not openly take sides, the incident will supply them with a source of conversation for days and perhaps weeks to come. A good argument, particularly one without too much bloodshed, is the equivalent of a stimulating evening's entertainment.

The north-eastern and north-central Arnhem Landers make full use of the dramatic potentialities here. A man with a grudge may paint himself in ochres and carry a bundle of spears, one fitted ready into the spearthrower to show that, if necessary, he is prepared to back up his claims with force. His supporters, and the defendant and his supporters, may be armed too. Long verbal battles between them, with detailed monologues full of mythical allusions, may go on for night after night, or at intervals over long periods, until the matter is settled in one way or another (through compromise, or bloodshed), or merely drifts off to be resumed later. A man who is violently enraged, and wants to do something more than talk, has a conventional way of asserting himself and frightening or at least startling his opponent at the same time. This is the *maragaridj* or *mari* (meaning anger, or angry). He may engage in some preliminary threats or boasting about what he is going to do, working himself into a state of near-frenzy. When the moment is ripe he snatches up his weapons, rattling a spear in the thrower at arm's length above his head, and runs at full speed toward his opponent, shouting and cursing him: and behind him, making a formal show of restraining him, runs an old woman—a close female relative, such as a father's sister. If he has chosen his setting well, he can approach his victim across a wide clearing with nothing to stop his charge or interfere with the drama of his attack: but he does not always spear to kill. Even though in such cases a man's eyes look glazed and unseeing, and his shouts are hoarse and almost mechanical, he may exercise enough self-control to fling his spear within a couple of inches of his victim—a gesture, not designed even to wound. There may not be enough time for anyone to attempt to check him. Or his antagonist may respond by paying no attention to him at all, simply continuing with what he was doing before—as old Wonggu once did, calmly singing and clapping his sticks at a late afternoon mortuary rite while a Groote Eylandt man with a grudge came running directly at him to fling his shovel-nosed spears.

FEUD AND WARFARE

Law and war are two sides of the same coin. Warfare is armed conflict carried out by members of one social unit (a tribe or clan, for example), or in the name of that unit, against another. Feud, however, is armed conflict which concerns particular families or groups of kin, although it may have repercussions throughout the community and implicate a large number of persons: feud can drift into warfare. Most of Howitt's examples relate to armed combat and duelling, but he also points out (1904: 348, 352-54) that a blood feud can spread and involve the whole tribe. In western and eastern Arnhem Land too some feuds can be traced back over a number of years, with a balance between killings never quite achieved, and all attempts at peacemaking proving ineffective.

Basedow (1925: 183-9) divides warfare in Aboriginal Australia into two categories: inter-tribal fighting and intra-tribal (or inter-clan) feuding. In early days, he says, inter-tribal fighting was fairly common. This is open to dispute, although there are several outstanding instances. (Howitt mentions some, and so do other early writers.) More general, however, are armed expeditions, socially sanctioned, which set out for a definite purpose, such as to avenge the death of a fellow tribesman or clansman or punish an offender. Howitt (1904: 326-30) and Gason (in Woods, 1879: 263-5) describe the Dieri *pinya*, an armed party. It will be recalled that when a person is condemned to death by a special council the headman arranges for a *pinya* to deal with him. Men chosen for this wear a white band round the head, beard tipped with human hair, and diagonal red and white stripes across breast and stomach. They go to the accused man's camp and ask for him. The people there answer at once, because they are afraid; they know the reason for this visit. Members of the *pinya* seize his hand, announce his sentence and lead him aside, where one of them strikes him dead with a large boomerang. (Howitt mentions the case of an accused man pointing to his elder brother to take the blame, because an elder brother stands for and should, ideally, protect a younger.) In other examples the procedure of killing differs, and sorcery may be involved in place of direct violence.

The Aranda avenging party, *atninga*, follows a quarrel between two groups—usually about a woman, or a death ascribed to sorcery. (Spencer and Gillen, 1938: 489-96.) Typically, say Spencer and Gillen, the attackers enter their opponents' camp fully armed, but fight with words, not weapons; after a time things quieten down, and the affair subsides. But occasionally they come to blows. Or the *atninga* wait in hiding to spear their victims. In one case the *atninga* men were hopefully offered women in the ordinary way, but rejected them—a sign of their hostile intentions. But after discussions had gone on for a couple of days or so they reached an agreement: in return for the death of three men (two had married wrongly, a third had boasted of killing members of the *atninga*'s tribe), the local men would not only go unharmed but would even help the killers. Accordingly, two of the men were speared through trickery; the third, suspicious, had escaped the night before. After that, the avengers danced around the bodies while the others watched passively. This example contains a number of details, such as a special term (*immirinja*) for the actual killers, as contrasted with the decoys (*alknalarinika*). And the avengers later made an excited ritual entry into their home camp, greeted by old women dancing and wielding fighting clubs.

Sending women over to the camp of visitors whose intentions are doubtful is fairly common. Ostensibly this is a friendly gesture, to appease an enemy. But now and then it is designed to put the visitors off guard and leave them vulnerable to attack. Members of a revenge expedition may capture wives and daughters and sometimes young sons of the men they kill. Howitt (1904) mentions a number of instances. The Geawegal (on the Hunter River) keep captured women who belong to the correct intermarrying classes. Other examples come from the Maryborough region (Queensland), south-east South Australia, south-western Victoria, on the Yorke Peninsula and in Gippsland, among other areas. The issues have often been confused here, and it is likely that many of the cases cited can be classified as marriage by capture: that is, a party of men going out specifically to obtain a woman, in contrast to a party which is bent on revenge and carries off its victims' widows almost as a side-issue.

In the Western Desert, a *wanmala* expedition may be sent out for much the same reasons as the *atninga*—particularly to avenge a sorcery death, or track down and kill a runaway wife and her lover. Several men, summoned by a native doctor or sorcerer, go into the nearby bush to paint themselves and prepare their special *wibia* shoes. When they are ready there is a short ceremony in the main camp: women sit beating time for them while they brandish and rattle their spears. Then they leave, flinging spears as they go. They hold other ceremonies, too, foreshadowing the fight which will take place when they reach their victim's camp. And they sing songs sponsored by the mythical Wadi Banbanbalala, Bell Bird Man, who 'makes *wanmala*'; in everyday life, people who hear a bell bird calling may say uneasily that a *wanmala* must be nearby. During the *wanmala* journey the elders carry bundles of spears.

In conventional accounts, they reach the victim's camp, enter it stealthily and take him by surprise, encircling him. Then, holding their spears poised ready to kill him at the final word, the older men sing:

> *guna majula ranggaranggalu nangani gudjaludjalu*
> *baramaja majula laurula bundila wedjawedja*
> *dudrururu guna majula . . .*
>
> Faeces! Sing, laugh, he's the one we're going to spear. Sing, sing! Let all our spears go flying, spinning. Faeces! Sing!

Among the Tiwi of Bathurst and Melville islands, if duels fail to resolve a dispute, the result may be a full-scale fight between two armed groups of men. (Hart and Pilling, 1960: 83-7.)

But the most highly organized warfare in Aboriginal Australia is found in north-eastern and north-central Arnhem Land. (See Warner, 1937/1958: 155-90.) The war-making unit here is the clan or the linguistic unit and the immediate source of the trouble, generally, an inter-clan killing or a woman. An interesting point, supported by our own material, is that most fighting takes place between neighbouring clans of the same moiety. As Warner suggests, "Feuds between clans of opposite moieties are more likely to die out for lack of the stimulus provided by competition for women. Such clans are likely to allow a *magarada* to be held. . . ." He adds: "Kinship solidarity extends warfare but also has the opposite tendency: that of limiting its scope when it has reached very large proportions. All the clans are interrelated, and generally many will find their loyalties divided. . . ." The immediate aim of most fighting in this region is that the 'enemy' should be made to suffer the same injury that it has inflicted—that is, compensation in like terms.

At least six types of armed attack are recognized, and named. They are listed by Warner. Not all can be termed warfare. The *magarada*, for instance, is primarily settlement by ordeal even though it may bring, not peace, but further fighting. *'Nirimaoi julngu'*, camp fights, hinging on adultery accusations, involve loud talking rather than serious injury or death. In *narub* or *djawald* a victim is killed or wounded in his sleep. Whatever personal grievance prompted the attack, responsibility for it is ascribed to the clan as a whole—even though the men concerned do not worry about obtaining even informal sanction for it beforehand. *Miringu* (or *maringo*, death adder, as Warner calls it) is much closer to warfare in the usual sense of the word. The reason is usually an inter-clan killing. To begin with, members of a *miringu* party perform magical rites, such as going through the motions of finding and spearing an image of their victim, drawn on the ground or moulded from clay and identified by name. They use a bone, from the dead man they plan to avenge, to tell them which direction they should take, then set off in snake-like formation to the victim's camp, surrounding it in a traditionally prescribed way before killing him, and perhaps others as well. This *miringu* is comparable to the Desert *wanmala*, the Dieri *pinya*, and Aranda *atninga*.

Two other types of fighting in north-eastern Arnhem Land are the *milwerangel* and the *gaingar*. The first is prearranged, and involves a number of clans. The *gaingar*, on a larger scale and on a regional basis, is very rare indeed, the outcome of intense anger and upset built up through long feuding—and conventionally intended (says Warner) to be 'a spear fight to end spear fights' and so bring peace to all the people of that area. This too is preceded by magical rites, with specially decorated spears, symbolizing each moiety, which are later sent out as an invitation and a challenge. Any kind of ruse is permissible in this fighting, and the number of deaths expected from it is higher than in any other variety—although still not much more than a dozen or so at a time.

MAINTENANCE OF ORDER

Measures for the maintenance of law and order, for reinforcing social solidarity and cohesion, are nearly always on a local basis. Sanctions employed by a clan, a tribe, or a linguistic group, may have no force outside it, except where several of these are linked in acknowledgment of a common culture pattern or close trading alliance, or consciously share a common sacred and ceremonial bond. Where no such associations are recognized, and there is no linguistic similarity, a stranger would have no effective ritual status. Even if he were assigned a place in the kinship organization he would be attached to it only by very tenuous ties: his adopted relatives would be less ready to defend his rights than those of people more closely connected with them.

To repeat, then, the maintenance of order in pre-contact times, and in the very few areas that are relatively little affected by contact, has had only local and restricted application. Authority is limited, and qualified by claims of kinship which override more impartial considerations of social welfare. 'Justice' is dependent on these factors. The first response to an injury is the desire to retaliate in kind, to hit back in terms of self-help. But other issues intervene: why was that particular person injured or killed, and in what circumstances? Who was he and who are his kin? Who are the other interested parties? Who is the aggressor (or aggressors), who are his kin, and what were his reasons for doing this? As soon as these questions are asked, it becomes necessary to discuss the matter with others: 'Under such conditions what shall we do, how may we avenge this injury, this slight, this death?' But when such questions are raised, with attention to precedent, to what has been done in other similar cases, we have the basis of law and regulation. In all Aboriginal societies there are certain approved mechanisms—the council, the meeting, the *magarada* or ordeal, armed combat and the duel, and the inquest—whereby infraction may be resolved. None of them, however, is wholly satisfactory, because the authority system is not usually strong enough to impose its own penalties—although there are indications that it was, actually, much stronger than is sometimes thought.

Despite the overriding importance of kinship there is enough evidence available to speak of authority (even if it is weak) and of government (insofar as law and order are maintained within limits). The element of self-help is much more apparent here, the absence of central authority more marked, than in many other societies. Weak or strong as the case may be, this is politics. (See Chapter II; also R. Berndt, 1959*a*: 103-4.) Sharp (1958: 1-8) refers to the Yir-yoront as 'people without politics'. "There are," he observes, "roles, and rules for the roles, and a system of law with specified kin serving as public agents with authority to act in defined circumstances, and provision for changes in the roles and rules through public action or inaction. But all this is simply kinship. . . ." Hiatt (1959: 186-7) says more or less the same thing. Of course, this is indisputable: kinship is significant in Aboriginal Australia, in this sphere as in others. But it is like saying (for example) that there is no religion, no magic, no economics, only kinship. To take this extreme stand is to ignore, on the one hand (although Sharp did not), the fact that people are categorized in units the members of which are interdependent, and that relations both within and between those units may not be framed only, or predominantly, in kinship terms; and on the other hand both the content of actions, and the ways in which kin relationships are used.

Howitt (1904: Chapter VI) was possibly the first writer on the Australian Aborigines to emphasize the importance of law and order and tribal government, although a number of earlier writers had considered the question for specific areas. Hoebel (1954: 301-9, in his chapter on 'The Trend of the Law') admits that 'rudimentary law-ways' are there, but takes the view that 'they are almost inchoate', that the line between private and criminal offences is hazy, and that the Aborigines tend to respond to legal action with physical aggression. To some extent this is true; but much retaliation in Aboriginal Australia is at the level of magic or sorcery and, as we have seen, the sanctions involved are not wholly physical. There seems to be a general tendency to resolve serious ruptures without extending them. Although retaliation is the essence of law, the controls operate in such a way as to restrict regional spread and limit the number of killings. In this context kinship is a mitigating influence but also, even more, a resolving influence. Not all wrongs committed against property, person, or social units are countered, or resolved, by immediate action of a 'legal' sort. There is not only variation in response to the same offence. How active, or how passive, that response is depends on circumstances, on factors which go beyond the persons immediately involved.

In general terms, it is not the range of criminal and other acts which is significant in considering the whole question of law in this context. The range is relatively narrow in Aboriginal Australia. Women, revenge for death or injury, breaches of sacred laws and marriage rules, and a few other points of minor importance, constitute virtually the total subject matter of legal procedure. This is far more limited than in some societies where property and material objects are more obviously significant. Where these are present in great quantities, they are potentially the subject of legal action to guard the rights of their possessors. This may mean an elaboration of legal procedure; but it is not, as we can see in measuring it against the position in Aboriginal Australia, necessarily relevant to the development of law in a chronological sense. The real test of law should rest on consideration of how an infringement or breach, of whatever nature, is resolved on an equitable basis, within the cultural perspective. Do the persons involved consider such and such a fair settlement? Are they satisfied? Do they feel that compensation, in goods or in physical or magical retaliation, is adequate and fulfils their expectations sufficiently to heal the breach? What loopholes are left for further action? These questions are of some importance in considering the rule of law and the maintenance of order in any society. When we ask them against the background of evidence from Aboriginal Australia, it is not hard to see that there is plenty of what we can call legal procedure and even judicial action, but that law itself is weak. There are too many loopholes which provide opportunity for feud to develop.

Traditional custom is a powerful factor, but personal decision within that framework is often an overriding influence which cuts across other personal decisions, other interests. Also, the fact that religion is one of the major emphases in Aboriginal life, and that it supports the quasi-gerontocratic system of authority, does not mean that everything else is entirely subordinated to it. The religious system depends for its continued existence principally on male recruits, but it is supported by the community as a whole. It rests, for the most part, on consensus and not on force. Outside of religious matters, the headman, elders, ritual leaders, native doctors, sorcerers, and so on, must depend on ordinary members of the society to up-

Men smeared with mud and pipeclay standing around a symbolic waterhole while invocations are called: a section of a mortuary sequence held at Yirrkalla (1947). (See Chapter XIII)

Participant (Wonggu) decorated for a mortuary ritual. He wears a special 'Macassan-style' beard interwoven with red parrakeet feathers, and bunches of leaves are tied to his arms: Yirrkalla (1947)

Above: Two mortuary poles, decorated with the linguistic group and clan designs of two dead persons, propped in position awaiting the placement of the bones: Yirrkalla (1947)

Below: Circumcision novices for the *djunggawon* rituals (see Chapter V). Each is painted with his sacred linguistic group and clan designs, which identify him as a member of one unit in contrast to another: Yirrkalla (1947)

hold their judgment and decisions or advice. They cannot always, constitutionally, enforce their opinions, and are indeed themselves handicapped by ties of kinship and clanship, and quite often by conflicting loyalties.

In all the cases we have outlined, while there is so much verbal emphasis on revenge, it is plausible to infer that underlying this is the more general aim of achieving order, or balance. An injury is done, the *status quo* is upset: retaliation provides a means whereby this may be restored. In other words, peace should follow the application of law. But if this fails and dissension continues—if, for instance, a feud cannot be resolved—then we have a state of war, or potential war. Warfare in the broader sense is infrequent in Aboriginal Australia, and most examples which have been classified as such are often no more than feud. Feud, however, is an extension of law—it is one attempt to resolve divergent or conflicting interests. Members of a *wanmala, pinya, atninga,* and so on, may specifically set out to achieve settlement, to punish an offender, real or supposed; but their right to punish may not be acknowledged, and the consequence may be retaliatory action of the same kind. Nevertheless, because a *wanmala* does not always succeed in its aim, and in fact exacerbates the situation, this does not invalidate its significance as a legal mechanism. Feud can turn to warfare; and here again, as in the idealized claims for the north-eastern Arnhem Land *gaingar,* the aim is to achieve peace, through the settlement of differences.

CHAPTER XI

Art and Aesthetic Expression

Art and aesthetic expression are often separated out as special subjects, to be studied apart from others. There is the suggestion that art has to do with aesthetic expression, and not so much with other kinds of expression: that it is non-utilitarian, not concerned with practical ends or aims. Artists are often demarcated quite sharply from craftsmen; and the phrase 'art for art's sake' points to one approach which is strongly entrenched.

There are peoples who do not draw this distinction, or at least not in so many words or to the same extent. Among them are the Australian Aborigines. While they find aesthetic pleasure in certain forms of activity, this is not as a rule an end in itself. It is usually associated with other aims. They are not self-conscious about this aspect which we call art. Concern with techniques, with the matter of how a thing is done, is important to them—although much less so than content, or subject matter. But people who do not share that tradition, and have little interest in that content, usually impose their own, different, criteria: they look at the various items which come their way, and if these seem to fall short of their standards in terms of technique they label them undeveloped, or crude.

Mostly, in speaking of art we think of graphic and plastic art, especially in the fields of painting, carving and sculpture. But it is quite legitimate to include dramatic art, poetic art, the art of story-telling, and so on. Here we treat this broader coverage, exploring four categories: poetry-song; oral literature; dramatic performance; and visual art such as painting and carving. (C. Berndt, 1961*a*, has recently made a brief survey of this field.)

Even though no Australian Aboriginal language has any special term which can be translated directly as 'art', there are words for painting or drawing and for carving (cutting), as well as for song, story or tale, and ceremonial performances (dancing and so on). For that matter, there is no separate word for 'artist', although in some places there is for songman. Generally speaking, although the majority of men can paint, carve and incise, within their local tradition, there are usually some who are regarded as being better than others, or as having the right to make certain emblems, for instance, rather than others. They hold these rights through age, status or ritual prestige, or membership of a particular unit, and not necessarily because they can make them better than other people—although this may in fact be the case, if only in consequence of long practice. In other words, there is no professional category or occupational class of artists, none who earn their living because they paint or draw and sell to others: this is an outcome of the contact situation, and not a traditional development. Artists in Aboriginal Australia do perform various tasks for some tangible or intangible reward—for ritual or magical reasons; or because they have been commissioned to do so, or because the system of interlocking obligations compels them, and there are penalties for evasion, no less severe for being non-formalized. Compensation may be involved: but this is not on an unequivocally commercial basis, although some of the essential ingredients of that are there.

Aboriginal art, and the people who play an active part in shaping it, must be seen in context. Aboriginal artists draw or carve, and so on, for only part of their time: for the rest, they carry out other activities, including hunting. Like a native doctor, however successful or renowned, and whatever his reputation, such a man cannot withdraw from his responsibilities as an ordinary member of his community. There are men who can paint or carve better than others; diagnose illnesses and effect cures; dance; compose and sing songs; make canoes and net bags; or tell stories—just as some women are particularly good at singing, or dancing, or plaiting mats. But this points to personal qualities and ability, rather than to a professional class of persons who practise specific skills in this broad field of the arts. There is some evidence of craft specialization, especially in the north, but this is not general. Militating against such a development is the basic economic structure of Aboriginal societies. There are songmen, and even dancers, who are in more or less constant demand; but they could not make a living from composing, or singing, or dancing.

SINGING AND POETIC EXPRESSION

Apart from Strehlow's study of Aranda songs (1933: 187-200; 1947; unpublished) and Elkin's of Arnhem Land music and song (1954: 261-6; 1953-6), and the references hereunder, there is not a great deal of published material on this topic. Tindale (e.g. 1937: 107-20) has some interesting songs from the south-east of South Australia (Dangani), among other areas. He divides them into eight types: 'dream songs or *begere*, relating the adventures of ancestral beings; magical songs; songs associated with sickness and death; totemic songs; hunting songs; dramatic songs and epics; fighting songs; and those dealing with "public opinion" '. Father Worms (1957: 213-29) also discusses song-poetry of the Yaoro and Bad, north-western Australia: these are primarily exoteric songs, quite simple in construction and content, but very pleasing. (Bibliographical references to esoteric songs published by Worms are contained in that article.) A number of works do mention songs and singing, and occasionally give an anglicized rendering or a few lines of vernacular text. (For example, Taplin, in Woods, 1879: 39; Howitt, 1904: 413-25; Basedow, 1925: 379-85; Roth, 1897: 120-5.) An interpretation of Aboriginal songs has been made by Harney and Elkin (1949).

Many Aboriginal myths are told in song, not as prose narratives. These sacred songs, as they may be called, are usually sung in a special setting: on the men's dancing ground, or in association with ritual sequences. Each is incomplete in itself: it is one of a series, to be understood only in relation to the rest of that series. But there is also a great deal of singing at other times—in fact, on nearly all occasions when people come together, particularly during the evenings, often well into the night. There are songs for almost all occasions, and the range of subject matter is as varied as life itself. A man or woman sometimes sings alone, especially in mourning, but usually in company. Around the northern coasts and rivers there is much more emphasis on individual singing, and individual songmen: one singer, beating his clapping sticks, often accompanied by a didjeridu player, whether or not he has an audience gathered about him. Conversely, throughout the centre and much of the south the convention is different. A person may sing to himself, or herself, as he goes along, just as children may try out songs informally in play. But the tradition is one of group singing—men together, or women together, or both, with no singling out of individual performers. The distinction is not a rigid one: it depends partly on circumstances. There is some group singing in the north, just as there is individual singing further south.

In some ordinary camp singing there may be only a small extended family, or a group of young men, enjoying an evening's entertainment. On other occasions, when more formal ceremonies have been arranged, the groups are larger and include dancers as well. When they hear the sound of sticks clapping, or a didjeridu blowing, for instance (tuning up), people come drifting in twos and threes to the space which has been cleared for dancing. There they sit down on the ground, arranging themselves in socially significant patterns: usually men and women sit a little apart, but choices within these groupings may be made on the basis of close kinship, or membership of the same subsection, moiety, and so on. In many cases the people who are present are simply members of the audience, and do not participate directly except to express appreciation; but just as often, especially in central areas, the audience is a participant one, ready to join in the singing, clap their thighs to the rhythm, or jump up to dance.

The commonest instrument is a pair of clapping sticks, which in one form or another is widely distributed. These may be boomerangs —a pair held by each member of a group of singers and beaten together, or rattled, in time to the music. In north-eastern Arnhem Land the wood used to make such sticks is chosen for its resonant quality. They sometimes bear painted designs, and those of *dua* moiety men may be decorated with feathered strings as well. In western Arnhem Land they are carved in a variety of shapes, indicating the spirit familiars of the songmen—animals, birds, and so on. Spencer and Gillen (1938: 604) mention a special variety of clapping sticks called *trora*. (See also Brough Smyth, 1878: Vol. 1, 356.) As another kind of accompaniment to the singing, boomerangs, clubs or lengths of wood may be used to pound on the ground. In north-eastern Arnhem Land a large pad of bound paperbark is treated in this way: it represents the barramundi, one manifestation of the ancestral being Banaidja, or Laindjung, and the noise of its pounding is the sound made by this fish. Skin pads, like small drums, were used on the Lower River Murray, South Australia. Among the 'Narinjeri' skin rugs were rolled up tightly and beaten with the fist. (Taplin, in Woods, 1879: 37.) In the Leichhardt-Selwyn and Cloncurry districts (Queensland), instead of beating their thighs women use a kind of drum or small pillow made of possum skin, filled with such things as feathers and rags, and beaten with the flat of the hand. (Roth, 1897: 120.) Elkin (1954: 249) notes that "the Papuan type of hand-drum with the ends closed with iguana skin, has been introduced into Cape York Peninsula". (See also Thomson, 1933.)

The trumpet or drone pipe, the didjeridu as it is often called, is widespread, particularly throughout the north, and extending southward. According to Basedow (1907: 47-9), Wilson (1835: 87) speaks of the drone pipe in referring to a native dance at Raffles Bay. Stokes (1846: Vol. 1, 394) notes it for the Port Essington people in 1838, adding that 'they blow through it with their noses': this, of course, is not so. It is mentioned also by Leichhardt (1847: 534), for Raffles Bay in 1845, MacGillivray (1852: Vol. I, 151) and others. Basedow (1925: 375-6) reported it among the coastal people "between the Gulf of Carpentaria and Cambridge Gulf, and as far inland as Wave Hill on the Victoria River". He says, "to serve the requirements of a single night's performance, a green stem of a native hibiscus might be cut off and the thick bark removed *in toto* in the form of a pipe". (See also Worms, 1953: 278-81.) But in 1945, from Wave Hill to Birrundudu and Gordon Downs in the east Kimberleys, only young men played it (and young women included it in their series of string figures, or cat's-cradles); older men regarded it as new-fangled and would have nothing to do with it. At Balgo early in 1958 it was used rarely: but two years later it was very popular indeed. A small trumpet is reported for the Aranda. (Spencer and Gillen, 1938: 606-7.) It is placed to the mouth, and singing through it intensifies the volume. This differs from the drone pipe used in the north, which can produce a range of sounds. (See Elkin, 1954: 248.)

Then there is the hollow wooden log, or gong, the *ubar* or *uwar* of both western and eastern Arnhem Land: it is placed in the cleft of two forked sticks and beaten with a short length of wood. Like the more elaborate versions of the drone pipe, it is used only on the sacred ground, has symbolic significance, and is often intricately decorated with ochres and sometimes with feathered strings.

Bullroarers cannot, strictly speaking, be classed as musical instruments, although they are, literally, sound instruments. There are many types, nearly all swung in a ritual context (sacred or magical). Rattles are used occasionally: in the Kimberleys, for instance, large baobab nuts, dried and incised. (Basedow, 1925: 374.) Another kind of rattle, says Basedow, is found all along the north coast: 'a large convoluted shell with a small pebble inside, or even a number of shells threaded on a string'; the only such examples we have seen were at Oenpelli in western Arnhem Land. Fresh or dried leaves are tied round the ankles, or arms, or below the knee, to rustle as the performers move. And rasps, "washboard-like notched sticks", scraped with a rubbing-stick, are favoured by the Yaoro, Bad, Njulnjul, Garadjeri and Njangomada. (Worms, 1957: 213.)

Most songs are associated, at least potentially, with action sequences of some kind. Sacred songs often have their corresponding rites, or stipulated actions or movements. But others too may represent part of a ceremonial complex where song and dance are, ideally, inseparable. Thus in the women's *djarada* and *jawalju* there are opening and closing songs; songs which should be sung during preliminary body painting, or while the participants are sitting down before the dancing begins, or performing certain steps, or using certain objects; others should be sung only by members of certain subsections. And so on.

Within limits, there is no lack of variety in tunes and rhythms, as between areas, or local traditions, and between different song series. Some are exceedingly complex in structure, and represent mature development restricted, primarily, through paucity of instrumental accompaniment. Research in this direction is only beginning. (See E. H. Davies, 1927, 1932, 1947; T. A. Jones, 1956-7; Strehlow, 1955; A. P. Elkin and T. A. Jones, 1958.) The best collections of Aboriginal music are now in Sydney, Adelaide and Perth.

Selection of songs

Over much of Aboriginal Australia the songs are usually short; and each is repeated many times, the words altered to suit the rhythm. In eastern Arnhem Land they are longer, but still include a fair amount of repetition. Linguistic units (*mada*) of the same moiety share a broadly similar body of mythology, expressed through song, but each has its own tunes and rhythms, and its own arrangement of words to suit them. In any particular song cycle, therefore, several *mada* may be saying very much the same thing, but not in quite the same way.

Generally speaking, the Aborigines have no poetry in the sense of spoken verse. Their counterpart to this is in the form of song, or chants. In sacred songs especially, the style, the way of saying things, is not a prosaic literal affair: there is a heavy use of symbolism; a single word may convey a whole range of images—most notably in short compressed songs where each word has a number of mythical and other implications apart from its literal meanings. This is not always clear in translation. It is difficult to translate poetic images from another culture, keeping the local flavour but at the same time making them both intelligible and significant to outsiders, without including some comments on the context, on the structure of the original language, and on special features of various words. The construction of songs often shows considerable technical skill, in the choice and arrangement of words, the use of metre and stress in the total patterning, the matching of sounds—and the relation of the whole to a particular tune, or to its musical accompaniment. Strehlow (1947) has gone into this with great care for the Aranda, showing how different word forms convey subtle distinctions in meaning; but it applies to sacred songs, and to others as well, all over Aboriginal Australia.

Some of the ordinary rain-magic singing of the deserts is permeated by simple imagery. A Walmadjeri cycle, for example, from Ganingara well, a rain centre on the Canning Stock Route, is largely made up of words of this sort: clouds building up, wind blowing from the right direction, the patter of rain drops, little streams starting to run, brimming waterholes, wet ground, and storms.

A contrasting example from north-eastern Arnhem Land is the Djanggawul mythology. The Djanggawul are associated with the light and warmth of the sun: they came on the rays of the rising sun, and finally disappeared into the sunset. The things they brought with them are central points in a complex of symbols. A length of twine, with orange-coloured birds' feathers worked into it, is sometimes referred to in the songs as a cluster of living birds. The feathers 'are' the birds; but they are also the rays of the sun. This string, prominent in the *dua* moiety *nara* rituals, is one of the most precious items of wealth in the traditional sense. (Members of the *jiridja* moiety use white birds' feathers.) In the same area, there is an emphasis on the sacredness of blood, as life. Many mythical allusions to this are expressed in song. A vivid sky at sunset may be likened to the blood of the Wawalag Sisters, or of a circumcision novice; to the blood of a kangaroo killed by another mythical figure, or eaten raw by inland groups in the Wudal cycle. There are numerous examples of this kind.

These songs are organized in cycles ranging in size from a dozen or so to two or three hundred parts. For each creature or thing there is a series of names, with slightly different meanings. In addition there are 'outside' and 'inside' words, singing words, invocations, 'big' names and 'small' names, and so on. Their principal characters are spirit beings in human shape, and in fact all the most important living things in the local environment—everything which 'has a name', in the sense of being *manigai^{e}mir*, mentioned in song. Some are major figures, creators like the Djanggawul. Others are subsidiary, in varying degrees. The actions which together make up the central thread, or the framework, may be located mainly in the prehuman era—despite their relevance to the present.

Wudal, for instance, or Maiamaia, came north long ago through the rocky gorges of central Arnhem Land from the 'Wawalag' country. The song cycle which focuses on his journey tells first of the dry stretches he traversed, thirsting for water—the expanse of pebbles glinting in the sun, the sharp stones hurting his feet. Other songs commemorate his association with wild honey: bees, flowering gum trees, their leaves eaten by caterpillars; the blanket lizard Wudal saw on the trunk of one of these trees; the birds and other creatures which were disturbed when he cut down their 'home' to get honey to put into his long baskets; the billabong of fresh, still water from which he drank; the spirit people who lived near it, looking at their reflections in the water, dancing and singing around the conventionalized pole-figures of the Wawalag Sisters, eating raw kangaroo meat—leading up to the final song, the Red Cloud. Other actions are 'contemporary', 'always' going on, their characters 'always there'. The spirit beings who people this region live side by side with their human counterparts. Garmali, for example, forever fishing from his canoe; or Rabaraba, collecting oysters at low tide among the rocks, cracking and eating them, humming and crying to herself. In all these songs, the sequences are carefully arranged and even the apparent digressions interwoven with the central theme.

The most satisfying way to show this would be to take a whole cycle, following it through from beginning to end: but most of them are too long and too detailed to condense into a few pages. Instead, let us look at four examples, extracts from longer series, shortened and modified in translation, without dwelling on the specific allusions, local and mythical, which amplify their main points.

The first comes from a song cycle of the Wonguri linguistic unit, Mandjigai (sandfly) clan—here we give the second and the final songs. The content, in outline, is fairly simple. Moon, an ancestral man, lived near the clay-pan of the Moonlight at the Place of the Dugong by Arnhem Bay: when he died he went down into the sea, where his bones became a nautilus shell. Ever since this mythical event took place Moon repeats his death, casting away his bone, and is reborn. (See R. Berndt, 1948*a*: 16-50.) The story is unfolded in a leisurely way, with much attention to local details rather than to plot; and it includes a number of place and other names which also have meanings, not easily translated without extra discussion. (Here as in other examples the division into lines is sometimes rather arbitrary, a matter of convenience in setting out.)

> They are sitting about in the camp, among the branches, along the back of the camp:
> Sitting in rows in the camp, in the shade of paperbark trees:
> Sitting in rows, like new white spreading clouds:
> In the shade of paperbark trees, they are sitting resting like clouds.
> People of the clouds, living there like mist, like mist sitting resting with arms on knees,
> In toward the shade, in the Lily Place, the shade of the paperbarks.
> Sitting there in rows, those Wonguri-Mandjigai people, paperbarks along like a cloud.
> Living on cycad nut bread, sitting there with white-stained fingers,
> Sitting in there resting, those people of the Sandfly clan . . .
> Sitting there like mist, at that Place of the Dugong . . . and of the Dugong's Entrails . . .
> Sitting resting there in the Place of the Dugong . . .
> In that Place of the Moonlight Clay-pan, and at the Place of the Dugong . . .
> There at that Dugong Place they are sitting along in rows.

In the last song, the Evening Star sinks in the west.

> Up and up soars the Evening Star, hanging there in the sky.
> Men watch it, at the Place of the Dugong, the Place of the Clouds, the Place of the Evening Star.

Far off, at the Place of Mist, the Place of Lilies, the Place of the Dugong.
The lotus, Evening Star, hangs there on its long stalk held by the Spirits.
It shines on that Place of the Shade, on the Dugong Place, and on to the Moonlight Clay-pan . . .
The Evening Star shines, back toward Milingimbi, over the Wulamba people . .
Hanging there in the distance, toward the Place of the Dugong,
The Place of the Eggs, of Tree-Limbs-Rubbing-Together, Place of the Moonlight Clay-pan . . .
Shining on its short stalk, the Evening Star: always there at the clay-pan, at the Place of the Dugong . . .
There, far off, the long string hangs at the Place of the Evening Star, the Place of Lilies.
Away there at Milingimbi . . . at the Place of the Full Moon,
Hanging above the head of that Wonguri headman:
The Evening Star goes down across the camp, among the white gum trees . . .
Far away in those places near Milingimbi . . .
Goes down among the Ngurulwulu people, toward the camp and the gum trees,
At the Place of the Crocodiles, Place of the Evening Star, away toward Milingimbi . . .
Evening Star going down, lotus flower on its stalk . . .
Going down among all the western clans . . .
It brushes the heads of the uncircumcised people . . .
Sinking down in the sky, the Evening Star, the lotus . . .
Shining on to the foreheads of all those headmen . . .
On to the heads of all those Sandfly people . . .
It sinks into the place of the white gum trees, at Milingimbi.

Another example, from the same region but from the Ridarngu linguistic unit, has the wet season as its theme:—

1. Fresh water running, splashing, swirling,
Running over slippery stones . . . clear water . . .
Carrying leaves and bushes before it . . .
Swirling around . . .

2. Water running, running from pool to pool . . .
Water running in streams,
Foaming, carrying leaves and bushes before it . . . churning,
Bubbling up among the Miljarwi clansfolk.
Water flowing over the rocks . . . flowing each side of the termite mounds,
Running fast toward Nalibinunggu clansfolk . . . Ridarngu . . . Gaiilindjil . . . Ridarngu,
Toward the Bunangaidjini Wonguri . . .[1]
Fast-running water.

3. *Bilgawilgajun!* (We invoke the Spirits!)
Water dammed up by barriers of stone at Buruwandji . . . at Mumana, at Bungarindji,[2]

[1] Clan names are mentioned, one associated with the Wonguri, the others with the Ridarngu.

[2] In hill country near the headwaters of the Goyder River.

Breaking out, foaming, like sacred feathered armbands . . .
Carrying away the debris . . .
Sound of rushing water . . . running,
Smaller streams joining together, roaring down . . .
Washing out tree roots at Buruwandji . . . running past the Rocks.

The next example, also from north-eastern Arnhem Land, comes from the 'Goulburn Island' love song cycle. The Lightning Snakes play across the sky at the beginning of the monsoonal season.

The tongues of the Lightning Snakes flicker and twist, one to the other . . .
Flashing among the cabbage palm foliage . . .
Lightning flashing through clouds, flickering tongue of the Snake . . .
Always there, at the wide expanse of water, at the place of the sacred tree . . .
Flashing above the people of the western clans,
All over the sky their tongues flicker, above the Place of the Rising Clouds, the Place of the Standing Clouds,
All over the sky, tongues flickering, twisting . . .
Always there, at the camp by the wide expanse of water . . .
All over the sky their tongues flicker: at the place of the Two Sisters, the place of the Wawalag.
Lightning flashing through clouds, flickering tongue of the Lightning Snake . . .
Its blinding flash lights up the cabbage palm foliage . . .
Gleams on the cabbage palms, and their shining leaves . . .

The next concerns the Morning Star, Banumbir, in a version from the Djambarbingu and Galbu linguistic units. It is associated primarily with mortuary rites. The central feature is a long pole, hung with feathered string and balls of white feathers representing Morning Star(s). In this translation, alternative names are omitted.

1. Banumbir, Morning Star . . .
Rising, rising . . . attached to its string . . .
Above Wuguludjeju, Baleibalei.[3]

2. Following the water, following the water all the way,
Feathered ball on its string . . . rising,
Shining brightly at Wuluri,[3]
Coming from Bralgu.

3. Ghosts, lifting their arms as they dance . . .
Dancing along . . . with hooked finger-nails[4]
Dancing there in the darkness . . . in pitch darkness . . . at Bralgu,
At Wuguludjangaru . . . at Baleibalei.

4. Morning Star, rising; it hangs from the tree[5]
Morning Star . . . coming from Dunumanbi, from Bralgu . . . shining on Baleibalei . . .

[3] The Morning Star shines over these Galbu places at Caledon Bay.

[4] The spirits handle the string to which is attached the feathered ball, the Banumbir.

[5] The spirits climb a tree and release the Banumbir on the end of its string.

Following the water . . .[6]
Seagull feathers . . . spoonbill feathers.

5. Making that Star . . .
See the hands of Mainggulumang, Morning Star maker
At Bralgu, at Dunumanbiri,
Ghost hands, like clapping sticks.
Gumbajinaju, Rirweibuma[7]
Making the Star . . . fastening short strings to the main length,[8]
Fastening short strings with feathered balls like flowers . . .

The symbolism is richer here, perhaps, than in some other parts of Australia, but the principles are the same.

In song as in story, people do not merely say what they feel is necessary in a matter-of-fact way. And they make use of the natural world about them to express their ideas. Broadly, there are two kinds of song. One is claimed to be traditional in both form and content, handed down through the generations from the mythical era without being changed in the process. The other, much less widespread, is attributed to individual 'composers', either contemporary or nearly so.

On Melville and Bathurst islands, during mortuary rituals or at the big yam festivals which include initiation rites, various people are expected to come forward and sing short songs, with dancing to match—mourners, for instance, or close kin of a boy being initiated. Song language is not the same as ordinary speech, although some words appear in both; and apart from that, here again the literal translation is not sufficient. Many of the best songs are attributed to people who died as much as fifty years or so ago. Others are quite recent: but these are few in number, and likely to become even fewer as the years go by.

In the following song a woman is grieving for her dead husband: she sang one morning, when the posts had been painted and placed in position around his grave, ready for the ceremonial dancing. She presented it in the shape of a dialogue, as if he first asked a question, she replied to it—and so on. (C. Berndt, 1950*b*.)

'Why do you come here every day to my grave?'
'Because' (she says) 'your posts are painted and ready.
Come on, get up from that grave!
I saw you there dancing just now,
Shaking yourself in the dance!'
'Why not come to me here?' (he asks).

[6] It comes across the water from Bralgu. The Star is a feathered ball made from white seagull and spoonbill feathers.

[7] Alternative names for this spirit.

[8] The main string has short lengths attached to it, with a Morning Star at the end of each. Several such Stars are sent to different parts of the eastern Arnhem Land mainland.

'I'm not old, I'm too young!' (she tells him).
'Well, I'm here, I am waiting for you . . .
I'm glad my wife's coming near me.
You'll be thirsty, I can't give you water,
I'm taking you to a dry and waterless country.'

These are simple songs, built up on traditional lines, but dealing with local affairs in an everyday framework. The singers touch lightly on personal experiences, sometimes including their own names. They achieve their impact largely through direct personal statements, compactly handled, interspersed with comments on the natural environment: the splashing of the waves as a canoe moves through them, a whirlwind catching up the leaves, a falling star. One man underlined the importance of mourning tabus, in singing angrily about how such a tabu was broken. Telling how he was taken unawares in the bush one day, struck on the head while wearing his *bugamani* mourning armbands, he ended with the climax: 'I throw away my *bugamani* armbands, the *bugamani* is over!' (i.e., 'If the mourning signs aren't respected, I won't bother with them!')

The images and symbols which are used in myth and in sacred songs come very easily into this setting—although the allusions here are brief and glancing, not long-sustained.

Rather different are the mourning songs of north-eastern Arnhem Land. There are ordinary clan songs, and those dealing with the *dua* and *jiridja* moiety Lands of the Dead, sung by men to the accompaniment of clapping sticks and didjeridu. Women use the same songs at times of emotional stress, sorrow or happiness. A mother whose child is ill, or dead, or setting off on a long journey, sings extracts from a series belonging to her own *mada,* or the child's father's. She sings in a conventional wailing tone, sobbing, and breaking off every now and then to chant some remarks of her own—such as telling how the child became ill, or blaming someone for it. But she may wail the same song, in the same way, sometimes gashing her head so that blood flows down her face, if the child comes home after a long absence. This next example is part of the Wawalag cycle. The song which provides the framework brings in the *djurwalag,* an unidentified brown bird which, people say, calls out at sunset when it sees the red sky, the blood of the Wawalag Sisters. The word *wongar* indicates that it is not an ordinary bird but belongs to the realm of Dreaming, or myth. This particular version is Djambarbingu. The singer is a Dajurjur *mada* woman, but her own mother was Djambarbingu, and so is her husband, the dead child's father. She is weeping for this child, her only daughter, who was just starting to crawl. (C. Berndt, 1950*b*.)

Ah, the *wongar* bird is speaking, through Djambarbingu country,
There at Bambula and Lalamandja!
Presently he will call out, through all those places . . .
Hear the cry of the bird!
There at Djerambal, and Ngudngud, and Gurgajubdun . . .
Ah, my daughter's face! Her eyes! My daughter, there alone!
My daughter, her limbs and body dead and lost to me!
Ah, there at Ngurmili, Lalamandja, Djerambal . . .
Blood-red sky at sunset!
Whose is that mark, that sign on his face?
The *djurwalag* bird spits at the setting sun and the red sky.
His voice goes out to Djerambal and Gurgajubdun, and to the sacred shade.
Ah my daughter, my daughter!
You lie there alone, no longer close to my breast!

In western Arnhem Land, the most popular and most numerous individual compositions are the 'Gossip' songs. These deal with contemporary events, and above all with romantic or sweetheart relationships. The songman's familiar—an owl, snake, frog, bird, or a dead child—comes to him at night and sings to him in a dream; when he wakes up he tries out his new song, and later sings it publicly. Actually, of course, a good songman is alert to all the gossip and song potential for miles around. No names are mentioned, but the songmen have specific cases in mind, and the listeners enjoy the game of identifying the characters—and sometimes starting fresh gossip sequences in the process.

The three following are examples:

1. I'm thinking and thinking of him, I wish he'd come back.
   I wish I could see his face . . .
   It would make me feel happy inside.

(A woman is talking to herself, 'I am thinking of my sweetheart; I wish he'd come back; if only I could see his face again I would be happy.') In Gunwinggu.

2. 'Go, look for her tracks!' he says.
   'Perhaps she has crossed the creek,' he thinks,
   Brooding about her.

(A man's sweetheart has gone away: he pines for her: he asks a friend to follow her tracks—perhaps she will return. He is thinking of the time she was with him.) In Gunbalang.

3. Look! There's a fire burning at Wandjili,
   It reminds me . . .

(Two girls are talking together: one sees a fire in the distance at Wandjili, near Barclay Point (on the mainland, opposite Goulburn Island). This reminds her of her sweetheart and their pleasure together at that place.) In Gunbalang.

The next is a Laragia lament for country which is no longer theirs. The Laragia originally occupied the Darwin area (Basedow,

1907), but are now virtually extinct. It was sung by an old Laragia man, at Adelaide River.

Waves coming up, high waves coming up against the rocks,
Breaking, shi! shi!
When the moon is high with its light upon the waters,
Spring tide, tide flowing to the grass,
Breaking, shi! shi!
In its rough waters the young girls bathe.
Hear the sound they make with their hands as they play!

Over the greater part of Aboriginal Australia, particularly in the Centre, most songs are ascribed to a traditional origin and not to contemporary composers. Usually they are arranged in cycles, a few words to each song. The following is a section from the sacred Dulngulg cycle of the Mudbara tribe, east of the Victoria River country, Northern Territory. Each line represents one song, which is repeated over and over before the singers move on to the next.

Day breaks: the first rays of the rising Sun, stretching her arms.
Day breaks, as the Sun rises to her feet.
Sun rising, scattering the darkness; lighting the land . . .
With disc shining, bringing daylight, as birds whistle and call . . .
People are moving about, talking, feeling the warmth.
Burning through the Gorge, she rises, walking westward,
Wearing her waistband of human hair.
She shines on the blossoming coolibah tree, with sprawling roots,
Shady branches spreading . . .

The next examples are from the Warburton Range, Western Australia: they are in Ngalia, and part of the Wadi Gudjara cycle. (See Chapter VII.) In this case we have included the actual words of the song, with a straightforward interpretation of each.

1. *maralamarala* *djigalbuga* *bindinibindiri* *marabindi*
hair waving/ grass seed, 'three cornered jack'/ star/
white crystal nose bone/

Explanation: The Wadi Gudjara are running, their hair blown by the wind, across a plain where there are many of these grass seeds. Their white nose bones flash in the sun like twinkling stars.

2. *baba balana baril barildja gildjunarana jalwandura . . . lunda*
dog/ pointing toward/ lying down/ fell over/ broke /
skin/ . . . . leg/

Explanation: The Wadi Gudjara spear a dog.

3. *mungarundu* *bindiri* *barabara*
growing dark/ star/ bright/

Explanation: The Wadi Gudjara reach *gabi* Darama, in the Canning Basin, as stars appear.

4. *djara manggula liwinda dari gagararalu*
shield/ pick up (got)/ posturing (with it)/ heel/ from the east/

Explanation: They take up their shields.

5. *baindjera baibai gara*
painting . . . .

Explanation: Women from the north-west, from *gabi* Dadiwanba, paint themselves.

6. *guduna ngaranga dainmara*
one (woman)/ standing/ dancing/

Explanation: Women associated with the Wadi Gudjara are dancing.

7. *giwan bungu jiliwiri*
ashes/ strike ('tree bark')/ broken part of tree from which branch taken/

Explanation: The Wadi Gudjara make a fire at *gabi* Wadulba, south-west of the Warburtons, and later scatter the ashes when they move on.

DANCING AND DRAMATIC PERFORMANCES

'Corroboree' has passed into English as a word for all Aboriginal ceremonies and rituals and entertainments involving singing and dancing, and social effervescence generally. Howitt (1904: 413) says it is probably derived from "some tribal dialect in the early settled districts of New South Wales, and has been carried by the settlers all over Australia". Haygarth (1850: 103), among others, spells it as 'corrobory', and seems to imply that it is a word used in the Sydney district. However, it is too vague a term, lumping sacred and non-sacred together in an undifferentiated way, without adding anything distinctive to compensate for using it.

Many early descriptions of dancing and dramatic performances (ceremonies and rituals) were marred by misunderstandings, misinterpretations, and prejudices deriving from the writers' cultural background at that particular time. We read statements like these: ". . . at other times the songs will consist of the vilest obscenity. I have seen dances which were the most disgusting displays of obscene gesture possible to be imagined, and although I stood in the dark alone, and nobody knew that I was there, I felt ashamed to look upon such abominations . . . The dances of the women are very immodest and lewd . . ." (Taplin, in Woods, 1879: 37-8.) Or, "Some corroborees are lewd in the extreme, and it is generally understood that at such times sexual restrictions are shamefully, or from the native point of view shamelessly, relaxed." (Mathew, 1899: 140.) Needless to say, this is not the case with the majority of these performances. The exceptions, when normal rules may be relaxed, have already been referred to. (See Chapter VIII.)

A certain amount of what could be covered under this sub-heading has already been considered. In religious ritual, the re-enactment of myths or sections of myths is a dramatic performance in itself. So, in many cases, are initiation sequences, and some love magic. There are great differences between sacred and non-sacred dancing and dramatic performance: partly on the basis of more marked solemnity in the first, but also in regard to the significance and symbolic meaning of the dancing and posturing, and the matter of participation. But the dividing line cannot be sharply drawn. Much ritual and ceremony of sacred significance is performed in the main camp, with group participation.

A great deal has been written about the dance and the so-called corroboree in Aboriginal Australia, but mostly in an impressionistic or sketchy way. Few anthropologists have been in a position to record the complicated and varied dance steps and hand movements. The best account is by Elkin (1954: 256-61), but actually the variety is far greater than he indicates. Focusing on the non-sacred, Thomas (1906*b*: 120-8) gives some examples at second-hand. Basedow, who travelled widely throughout Aboriginal Australia (1925: 377-85), gives others. In one of these, a crocodile ceremony of the Cambridge Gulf people, a row of men stand with legs apart, while a 'crocodile' actor wriggles between them. Reaching the first man he lies flat, legs close together like a tail, arms bent with palms flat on the ground, then raises the front of his body, booming harshly to imitate the cry of a crocodile. Basedow describes briefly, too, a dance at Forrest River in which crow actors hop around an old man representing a carcase; a Laragia and Wogaidj caricature of women's wailing; a popular Fowler's Bay scene in which a man imitates a woman collecting food; and several dances from Melville and Bathurst islands: jungle fowl, kangaroo and a mock fight. Curr (1886: I, 403) reports that women of the 'Yircla Meening' tribe dance with "a wommera in their right hands".

Spencer (1914: 32-4) suggests that in Aboriginal communities the evenings are nearly always occupied with singing and dancing. This is certainly true for most of the areas in which we have worked where the people are traditionally oriented. There are exceptions, of course. People may be dispersed in small groups, scattered over a wide area; or the majority of men may be engaged on sacred matters or rituals away from the main camp, or simply out fishing. And on some mission and pastoral stations and towns there are restrictions, self-imposed and otherwise. Spencer also mentions the lively Melville Island dancing; the buffalo dances especially, with their vigorous stamping and leaping, can be an exciting experience for spectators as well as performers. In a very different style, some of the Wogaidj camp dancing is outstanding for the elegant and graceful hand movements of the women.

North-eastern and western Arnhem Land women may dance

holding cat's-cradles or lengths of string. (Basedow, 1925: 373, observed this on the Daly too.) But this varies according to the content of the songs and the nature of the performance. On the eastern side, each song in the 'outside' versions of the long sequences shared among the linguistic groups has its appropriate actions. Mostly, this is a matter of standing on one spot, and moving the hands or feet or both to the rhythm. *Girdjir* is the usual word for it. In the sandfly sequence, for instance, as the songman claps his sticks and sings and the didjeridu is blown, women stand swaying slightly to the music, making stylized gestures of scratching. In a wasp sequence they grasp each ear, nodding their heads sideways, as the song tells how the buzzing of the wasp irritates people trying to rest in the midday heat. For one of the Wudal songs, they imitate a person putting wild honey into a long basket. And so on.

Women, on the whole, play a more unobtrusive part in a ceremony, dancing in the background or to one side. Men are more energetic and versatile, their performances usually more spectacular. Dancing may be solo or in groups, open or closed to audience participation. Small children sometimes join in, a boy with the men, a girl with the women; in north-eastern Arnhem Land a baby may fall asleep on its mother's shoulders, clutching her hair, as she bobs and sways to the singing. The dancing associated with a long song cycle may take a few days or several weeks—in which case the dancing itself may be repetitive, or vary only slightly.

In the southern Kimberleys, as at Balgo, some camp ceremonies are a preliminary part of initiation sequences; but there are many others, coming from all directions: the Canning Stock Route to the south-west, the desert country to the south and east, the east Kimberleys to the north. In one of these the dancers wear conically-shaped headdresses superimposed with blood and feather down on a basis of brush and human-hair twine, and wear or carry a *wanigi* object. (See Chapter XII.) They prepare themselves behind a screen of bushes, and as they dance huge heaps of dry grass are set ablaze, flaming up so that the singing-audience can see the decorations quite clearly. It is not unusual to find such a public showing of objects or decorations which are secret in other areas, or even in other situations in the same area.

In parts of the Kimberleys, for instance, incised boards are used in this public way—even though in the same area similar boards with different designs are secret. But throughout the Western Desert as far as Port Hedland, a feature of certain ceremonies is that short sequences within them are closed to women and children. At a given signal they must crouch down, covering their heads completely, while a few men keep watch to make sure that nobody peeps. The singing continues; but the decorations, or the objects used, or the dancing, differ from what has gone before. After five minutes or so, sometimes longer, the restrictions are lifted; the huddled groups of women and children sort themselves out again, shaking the dust or sand from their hair, and the ceremony proceeds. Alternatively, a sequence formerly closed may be declared open. This happened in the case of one scene in a ceremony staged at Adelaide River Army settlement, in 1945, by a group of men from the so-called Brinken tribes around Port Keats. Women sat clapping their thighs, watching intently, as a cluster of men danced around the main actor, who held on his shoulders, as a mother does a child, a little puppet of bound grass. This had only recently been changed from a secret to a public performance: but women were warned, before attending, that simply by being present they were liable to become pregnant—and the prospect deterred some of them.

The basis of many ceremonies is a dream. A man, occasionally a woman, claims to have had a set of songs and dance-steps shown to him in a dream; and as 'boss' of that series he can expect to receive compensation for passing on this revelation to others. It may be a rearrangement of an existing song-and-dance combination, or it may introduce new features based on his own observation or experience—new tunes or rhythms, or body decorations, or objects, or new content. Native doctors or 'clever' men, or women with a background of participation in love-magic rites, are especially likely to report dreams of this kind.

Ceremonies so derived include a fairly wide range of types, some linked with mythical figures of major importance, others with minor figures, and still others having no explicit connections with any of these. Those in the last two categories are particularly vulnerable to change, or to being superseded by others; but in the process they may travel a long way from their acknowledged home. Even more than in the case of sacred rites or sacred cults, ordinary camp ceremonies are transmitted from one Aboriginal group to another over immense areas. In the course of this, the song-words may remain more or less intact even though singers and audience have only a general or hazy notion of their meaning—a feat of rote-memory on which a number of writers have commented. (Cf. Roth, 1897: 117-18.) This is a source of frustration to people looking for exact translations; but to those who receive it as part of a ceremonial complex of singing and dancing, the general rendering may be enough to give coherence to the whole without worrying about particular details. As one woman at Balgo pointed out, when pressed for specific interpretation of every word in a series to clarify inconsistencies in translation, 'We don't see the people who started these songs, we can't ask them: we get them from others in between, and they are the ones who tell us.' The nearer the place of origin, the greater the likelihood of finding someone who knows the language in which they are composed; but some songs travel well beyond the reach of such intermediaries, and attempts at word-for-word translation may be no more than guesses. This applies to gestures and dance-steps too. Some are accepted as straightforward representations—especially where the subject matter is indisputably erotic. In others the symbolic significance is more obscure: members of the audience may have to ask, if they are sufficiently curious, but even then there may be nobody competent to explain with any degree of assurance.

The ceremonies include statements about how other people live, or what people do in other places, as well as about local happenings—the 'Afghan' and camel sequences in the Victoria River country, for instance, some of which have been traded up from the desert to the south. A little to the west of this, at Limbunya on the Stirling River, other series have come down from the direction of the north-west coast, mainly through the Lungga people. One of these, in 1944, focused on the killing of a crocodile—about 10-12 feet long, of paperbark bound with twine; the central dancer balanced it on the palms of his hands above his head, swaying in time to the singing, while others made rhythmic gestures of spearing it. Also from the Lungga came songs about boats seen at Wyndham, 'Chinamen' living there, a fisherman trying to sell his catch (fish made of bark, dangling from each side of a pole carried on a man's shoulders). Among the objects used in the dancing were *wanigi*: one a rectangle topped by a small triangle, another made from a red spotted handkerchief attached to the central cross; another, of wool bound in the conventional diamond shape, was passed from hand to hand among a circle of men reclining around a fire, each in turn peering at it, moving it rhythmically from side to side—a 'paper', read by the manager of one of the East Kimberley cattle stations. This was a tacit comment—a simple parody, or imitation. Another, from Wave Hill, was more humorous, and more cynical.

In one scene a policeman, a 'man with chains', was shown trying to bring in 'witnesses' for a court case. The actors here were men, representing attractive young women all roped ('chained') together by the neck in a long line. The policeman led the way, dancing slowly around the clearing; but every now and then when he was looking the other way a small raggedy actor, a 'bagman' or 'swaggie', would come sneaking up from behind and try to take away one of the girls. The policeman, turning and seeing him, would drive him away, kicking at him and lashing out with a stick, with a great deal of noise and commotion: he wanted the girls for himself. The side play, gestures and impromptu remarks of the actors, punctuating the singing, kept the audience in a state of hilarious laughter for over an hour.

Dramatic scenes of this general kind, depicting and interpreting the changed circumstances in which the Aborigines found themselves, have been reported from places all over the Continent. Taplin, in Woods (1879: 38-9) mentions one about the figurehead of a ship, another about a train; Basedow (1925: 382) a ceremony outlining events at Fort Dundas about a century before; and Howitt (1904: 422-4) has other examples; so does Roth (1897: 117). In situations of stress, ceremonies provide an outlet in which the Aborigines can try to look on the humorous side, mimicking the people who for most of the time appear to have such power over them, and showing that they are still, essentially, undefeated in spirit.

In all these cases, when the scene calls for women their part is taken by men, who decorate themselves accordingly: it is only in women's secret ceremonies that a woman may take the place of a man. In all non-sacred camp dancing, even though other implications may be involved, the primary intention is that it should be entertaining: and here the range is relatively wide. The performances may be quietly enjoyed with a minimum of excitement: at the other extreme they may be riotous. Further, in these ordinary ceremonies the attitudes of the dancers perhaps come closest to what we (as western Europeans) are used to. A dancer may try to attract the attention of the spectators, especially those of the opposite sex; or in the northern part of Australia, where there is more emphasis on individual performers, a dancer may be concerned with keeping up his reputation, dancing better than others. At the same time, this does not warrant our speaking of Aboriginal dancing as professional. Gifts are made occasionally to individual performers, but no Aboriginal could, traditionally, earn a living simply by acting or dancing.

It is becoming the habit to speak of such performances as examples of Aboriginal ballet. But non-sacred, or for that matter sacred, ceremony and ritual are not comparable. If they are ballet, this is ballet of a very specialized kind. The audience may or may not participate. There is no organized training involved here: dance steps and movements, songs and organization of acts and so on are learnt through observation and practice during the ceremonies themselves: the situation is very different indeed to the European ballet.

In summary, as far as the content of such ceremonies is concerned, three major divisions may be made.

1. Ceremonies which involve the re-enactment of myths or stories: these are presented in a stylized form and all actions are symbolically significant. The dance, the song and the ceremony as a whole are interdependent.

2. Dance movements, individually or collectively performed, in relation to specific songs, but not having mythical substantiation.

These may be regarded as traditional, but as having no specific meaning other than that; it is the dance and the rhythm which count and not the explanation of it.

3. Imaginative and inventive dancing and songs composed to translate for public enjoyment, if not information, contemporary events of everyday living. Many of the dramatic performances with songs and musical accompaniment are of this sort, and they are not necessarily a result of alien impact. Only a small percentage concern themselves with contact situations; the majority relate directly to the ongoing life of the camp.

ORAL LITERATURE

Although myths may be told in narrative form, especially to novices during initiation rituals, this happens more often in the case of other stories—those which are less obviously sacred. There are ordinary stories which people make up and tell, or those based on actual experiences of living persons—including dreams; but here we will be considering stories which are handed down from one generation to another. They are traditional in the sense that they come from the past and mostly concern totemic anthropomorphic creatures, ancestral beings and spirits, although some are quasi-historical, or concern the adventures of immediate ancestors which may be, as it were, pushed back into the Dreaming era. What is more, they are traditional *because* they are believed to have come down from the past unchanged. But because the Aborigines are non-literate, because traditionally they do not use any form of writing and must rely on transmission through word of mouth, there is much variation.

Myths and stories handed on in this way are even more vulnerable to personal interpretation than in the case of written material. This is true for sacred and secular examples alike, although it is likely that song rhythms and tunes have a conventionalizing effect on the transmission of ideas in song form. The question of variation is a fascinating one. It would lead us into too many digressions to explore it here, but it should be borne in mind in looking at all these examples of myth and story. There are divergences on major or minor points, or both, not only between social units in the same or in different areas, but also between persons within those units. At the same time there is a fair measure of stability, or continuity. Some of the story versions we recorded at Milingimbi for instance, in the late 1940's, do not vary greatly from those which Warner obtained there in the 1920's. We did not ask specifically for these stories, but they were told as part of the local repertoire; and a couple of them are included here partly for that reason, as well as for their intrinsic interest.

The division between sacred mythology and ordinary stories is not easy to make. As we have seen from Chapter VII, sacredness is a matter of degree. Rough and ready criteria, as far as myth is concerned, would be its association with ritual and its presentation in song form. In addition, the subject matter is a significant clue: sacred mythology deals with creative beings, formation of the countryside (usually), specific instructions for the holding of rites and ceremonies and so on. On the other hand, many ordinary stories do offer explanations of why things are as they are: and many non-sacred ceremonies are validated by myths which can be expressed through song. Or, to take another example, one myth may be presented in its song form on the sacred ground, and acted out in a sequence of dances, while its prose form can be told in everyday situations. Some myths have 'outside' and 'inside' versions: those which are used only in sacred ritual when special interpretation is given of certain features and incidents, when symbolic allusions are made, or when sacred words are added; while the ordinary versions are available to everyone. There may even be a children's version. Thus apart from the 'outside' Djanggawul singing, at Milingimbi there is a children's story of the Sun, Moon's wife, who travels across the sky each day laden with parakeet feathered string, walking slowly with her *mawulan* and *ganinjiri* walking sticks, moving the dark clouds aside with her hands, until she reaches the red sky in the west and swims back under the sea, in the shape of a fish, to her little daughter waiting at home. This practice of having different degrees of exclusiveness in myth content is quite common in Aboriginal Australia, and has not been sufficiently appreciated by many investigators. Some published collections give no indication on this point, which is signficant in evaluating this kind of material in social terms.

Very little systematic work has been done on Aboriginal oral literature. There was the earlier work of K. L. Parker (1896, 1898), as well as sections in Woods (1879: 55-61 etc.), Roth (1897: 125-8), Howitt (1904: e.g. 779-806), Spencer and Gillen (1938), Spencer (1914), Worsnop (1897), R. H. Mathews (1899), C. Strehlow and Leonhardi (1907-21), and a number of others.

J. Mathew (1899: 14-22, 146-8) took as his theme the 'Eaglehawk and Crow' myth which is widely distributed throughout the Continent in one form or another—although the identity of the two major characters varies. Mathew's discussion centred mainly on dual organization. He believed this myth was a symbolic expression of a fundamental dichotomy in Aboriginal society. In nearly all versions Eaglehawk and Crow were in conflict. (See Radcliffe-Brown in Srinivas, 1958: 110-27). In other words, to him the myth expressed the moiety cleavage. While Mathew's empirical material was not entirely accurate, and while he jumped to conclusions and made hasty speculations on a slender basis, he was not content to record the myths without considering what they meant in social terms. This was a significant development, which is much less apparent in other work of that period on Australian Aboriginal mythology. True, he was looking for social origins, and his methodology was not well developed: but he was thinking in terms of social facts. During that period most published Aboriginal myth versions were considered out of their social context and, with some exceptions, were drastically watered down for public consumption.

Since that time, most works on the Australian Aborigines have included some reference to mythology and stories, directly or otherwise. Róheim, for instance (1925, 1945: mainly in the context of psychoanalytic theory), Basedow (1925), Warner (1937/58: particularly 519-65), Elkin (1938/54), Kaberry (1939), Tindale (1936, 1938, 1959*b*), Petri (1954), Mountford (1956, 1958), Capell (1939, 1960*a, b*), Lommel (1952) and others. Ursula McConnel (1931, 1935*b*, 1936, but particularly 1957) was the first to publish a systematic series of myths. Her material came from one tribe, the Wik Mungkan of Cape York Peninsula: unfortunately their social context and their content are not adequately analysed (see review by C. Berndt, 1958). Nevertheless this does provide a better insight into the subject than any of the earlier attempts.

Apart from the anthropological approach to mythology and oral literature, other writers have published books and pamphlets on what are called Aboriginal myths, legends and stories. Some are presented in simplified form, as being better suited to children than to adults. Others are romanticized or distorted, considerably anglicized, and viewed out of context: they belong under the title of Australian-European literature, rather than Aboriginal.

In some culture areas of Aboriginal Australia anything up to four or five hundred and more myths and stories are known: not by everyone, but by those few who are particularly interested. In others there may perhaps be no more than a couple of dozen or so. In western Arnhem Land, almost every topographical feature has mythical associations. (See, for example, R. and C. Berndt, 1951*a*.) In north-eastern Arnhem Land there are hundreds of stories, often with slight variations in theme, emphasis, or characters according to locality. (Catherine Berndt, 1952: 216-39, 275-89.) The right to tell certain ordinary stories as well as myths may be restricted, on the basis of clan or local group membership. But to balance this there is ample evidence to suggest that many stories have been widely diffused, and borrowing is nothing out of the way.

The time and place for stories is, most often, around the camp fires at night, or at any period when people can spare an hour or two for relaxation. And they are told, primarily, for pleasure. Occasionally they serve other purposes too. They may be admonitory or instructive, pointing a moral, or imparting information in an agreeably easy way. Some stories are directed principally at children, who may learn them, for instance, from their grandparents. Others are principally for adults—which does not mean that children cannot hear them too. Nor, traditionally, is telling stories an occupation for women, and for men who are too lazy to do anything else—as Roth asserts in his Queensland study (1897: 125). Some people, are, of course, more adept at this than others. They can hold an audience spellbound even when the tales they tell are familiar in every detail. And there are men, and women, who can make the most colourful adventure sound dull and prosaic—just as there are persons here and there who declare that they can't sing: they are ready to make a noise of sorts in company but avoid as far as they can any solo performances. Unlike painting and woodcarving, or for that matter singing on special occasions, the teller of a story does not, in a traditional setting, expect gifts or material rewards in return. He may be a specialist, or an expert, but he is not a professional.

Wherever there is a tradition of oral story-telling, we can legitimately speak of it as a dramatic art—a statement which makes little sense when a story is simply a set of words on a printed page, designed for the eye alone. An Aboriginal story-teller draws on visual effects too, but as a supplement to his spoken words, not a substitute for them. In this live, flesh-and-blood, situation there is no impersonal barrier between him and his listeners: he can communicate with them directly, and personally. And in doing so he has at his command all the local repertoire of gestures, hand and body movements, facial expressions, changes in tone, supplemented perhaps by embellishments of his own. He may jump to his feet at a moment of excitement, subside to the ground again, pause, suddenly raise his voice or lower it to a whisper: and he may not object to questions which give him an opportunity to expand or elaborate some particularly interesting theme. But in any case the actual words he uses are only a skeleton, a framework upon which the narrative itself is built up and comes to life.

In considering oral literature, three main aspects should be taken into account. One is form or structure, which has two facets: the sequence of events and incidents, the way the plot hangs together; and the language in which these are framed. There may be a certain degree of formalization as contrasted with ordinary everyday speech. Generally, this is a question of style. Over and above personal idiosyncrasies, each language has its characteristic structure, its agreed-upon modes of expression; and, specifically, there are conventions, either more or less flexible, as to what is appropriate in story-telling. Secondly, there is the content or subject matter. Some narratives are a shorthand summary of events, leaving a great deal to the imagination of the listeners. The plot may be so well known that only an outline is necessary. Other stories again go into considerable detail, dwelling on seemingly irrelevant aspects: a tortuous plot, numerous characters coming and going. Some are well-rounded and neatly told, others are carelessly conceived, with loose ends, the threads not caught together, ending before explanations are made. Much depends, here, on the skill of the narrator.

There are stories about tricksters and malignant spirits, tales of illicit love and amorous adventure. And there are simple statements telling how the natural species adopted the shapes they have today, or how certain topographical features came about; how human beings became as they are, both physically and culturally: how they became vulnerable to death, were able to bear children and so on, or how they came to adopt certain customs and beliefs. Some are arranged as sagas, of Odyssean quality—tales relating to the Land of the Dead, travels to far-distant and mythical lands, adventures with spirit beings. In addition, there is the question of choice of theme. In western Arnhem Land for, instance, the emphasis is on the Rainbow Snake, swallowing people in a great flood which inundates the surrounding country. Catastrophe is a dominant theme, casting a cloak of gloom over nearly all the tales. In some areas there is a preponderance of stories dwelling on social relationships, an emphasis on persons rather than on cultural details. In others, it is the natural environment rather than people: the characters are of secondary importance.

Thirdly, there is the link between a myth or story and its social context. How far does its content shed light on interpersonal relations, and relations between groups, in that particular society? Here, as in the sacred mythology, the characters may do things considered 'wrong' for the story-tellers and their listeners. Relationships normally tabued are exposed to ridicule, or relatives who should help and support each other do just the opposite. There are stories of incest, intimacy between a man and his mother-in-law, quarrels between parents and children, between brothers, or between sisters. Other stories, or other parts of the same stories, point to 'good' behaviour: what people should do in a variety of situations. In all of them there is co-operation as well as conflict, social solidarity as well as social cleavages. But knowing the content of a story, what it says about these relationships, is only part of the problem. There is the question of how that particular story fits into the broader framework of other stories and comparable material, both generally, and on the same topic. Above all, there is the question of under what circumstances, by whom and to whom, are stories told, and how do people respond to them: what they say and do in relation to them, or as a direct or indirect consequence of them.

But although we raise these questions, they cannot be answered here without going into too many specific details of places and persons, areas of divergence and convergence between different versions—in fact, consideration of the whole range of social living from that particular point of view. Instead, again, we shall set out a number of examples to give some idea of the content of these non-sacred or not-quite-sacred stories.

Selection of stories

The stories which follow were recorded in the vernacular, and in nearly all cases are more detailed than in the short translations given here. The first few concern the natural species, how they came to be as they are now: but this theme overlaps with, and leads into, others—including the topic of spirits, malignant or unpredictable, who inhabit the same world as human beings.

Echidna and Tortoise. Gunbalang, western Arnhem Land. There are several very different versions of this story.

In the beginning, Echidna Woman, Wombilbaia, and Freshwater Tortoise Man, Mangili, were in human shape. But one day, at a place on the Marganala Plain in Jiwadja tribal territory, they quarrelled about a snail. Both wanted to eat it. At last Tortoise, in a rage, picked up a bundle of light bamboo spears and threw them at Echidna: they stuck in her back and became quills. Echidna retaliated by picking up a large flat stone and throwing it at Tortoise: it stuck to his back, like a shell. That is how they became what they are today.

The First Bees. Northern Gunwinggu.

Once they were men, all those bees. Three of them belonged to the *namadgu* moiety: Manjalg, a Jiwadja man from the coast, was *jarigarngurg*; Gubalag and Lorlban, both *jariwurga*, came from Djinba country to the south-east. Two other bee men, Djawun speakers from the south-west, belonged to the *nangaraidgu* moiety: Gadderi, *jariburig* phratry, and Nabiwu, of the Djawun phratry *nawulgain*. They all came together at one place, where Wuragag now sits as Tor Rock, to exchange trade gifts such as hairbelts and spears. But they quarrelled about these gifts; the *namadgu* men started it. They fought with spears and sticks. The Djawun men had sharp pointed bamboo spears, and spearthrowers. Manjalg had a Melville Island throwing stick, and a barbed Jiwadja spear, and a fighting stick. The two from the east had mangrove spears with stone tips, sticks, and stone boomerangs. They kept fighting, until the *namadgu* men's sticks were all broken to pieces. The *nangaraidgu* men still had spears, because they had been thinking there might be a fight; that's why they brought so many. They gave some to the others, so they could keep on fighting . . . They were there alone, there was nobody to restrain them. They kept throwing spears at one another. When dawn came they didn't go out hunting, but stayed in camp all day, fighting. At last they fell to the ground and just lay there, simply bodies.

But sweat still came from them: it was like wild honey. As time passed little wings grew, and hairs emerged. Gubalag spoke first: 'Don't stay lying down like that!' He tried to run, and bit those two, Nabiwu and Gadderi: he had changed ('made himself'). As for their bodies, lying dead after they had speared one another, in the holes they had made in their bellies they saw bees crawling, their own honey bees. Their bodies were dead: but their spirits flew up like bees. Their speech was like the speech of bees, as they spoke to one another: 'Let us not go on fighting. Let us become bees, and go off to find separate trees.' That's what they did. Their bodies, with their spearthrowers and spears, turned into stone; they put themselves *djang*, and still they stand there. But their spirits flew away for ever. They farewelled ('sent away') one another, eating from flowers to make honey. And people, we human beings, taste it and say, 'This is real honey.' Those first people tasted it, long ago. They showed us, we new people: and we continue to eat it, following their lead. All these things—vegetable foods, fish, kangaroo, other meats: they showed us, those first of people; and we, when we have come into being, we eat all those things as they taught us.

Becoming a Crocodile (1). Maung, Goulburn Islands.

At Unganba, between Sandy Creek and Junction Bay on the north-west coast of Arnhem Land, in Maung country, a group of people were travelling along. Eventually they came to Inimeiarwilam, meaning 'He pulled a bark canoe', at the mouth of the King River. The name commemorates their actions at this place, where they pulled a bark canoe down to the water and started to ferry people across. They had to make several trips. One man kept asking to be taken over, but each time he was refused. When most of them had crossed he was still sitting there, brooding. 'I'll turn myself into a crocodile (*gunbiribiri*),' he thought. So he swam over to the other side—but he was not entirely a crocodile yet. 'I'll do something to make myself into a real crocodile.' He went to Aniwunggalainjun, a little further up-stream.

There he heated some ironwood roots over a fire, peeled off the bark and pounded it until it became soft, then went on pounding and moulding until it was like hard wax. He placed this on his nose, making it longer and blunter, like a crocodile's, then plunged into the water and became a real crocodile. By this time the bark canoe was bringing over another load of travellers. The man-crocodile swam toward it, capsized it, killed them and ate them. Then he emerged and spoke to everyone: 'I'll do the same to all the people I catch, I'll kill and eat them.' His spirit went up into the Milky Way, where three small stars represent him, and three larger stars the bark canoe he turned over. Among those he ate were three young girls. They became three hard lumps at the back of his head: and today, it is said, they warn the crocodile of approaching danger.

Stories like this account for the behaviour of creatures harmful to man by tracing it back to some grudge, or grievance, which left an enduring bitterness. The crocodile adopted his present shape because he could not get his own way: he turned against human beings, and nothing they might do now can alter his stand. In the same way, Jurawadbad became a poisonous snake because his young wife rejected him; but nobody else is safe from him either. For comparison, here is another crocodile tale which has the same theme, but expresses it through very different subject matter.

Becoming a Crocodile (2). Ngulugwongga, Daly River. One version of this story appears in R. and C. Berndt (1946: 69-70).

Crocodile Man, Bindagbindag, was married to Whistle Duck Woman, Balmad. Two daughters were born to them, both crocodiles: but when the girls were old enough Bindagbindag neglected Whistle Duck and had sexual relations with them. This was at Banggar, on the western side of the Daly River.

He used to go out fishing in his bark canoe, and when he returned he would call out from the bank for them to come and pick up the fish. The two girls would come down, followed by their mother. As they waded out to get the fish Bindagbindag would have intercourse with them in the water. Their mother saw this, but made no trouble. Every day when he went out fishing the same thing happened: and she just watched.

But at last she decided what she would do. She made a rope of grass, secretly, when the two girls were out looking for bush foods. When they came back, she hid it. She was angry.

One day the old man said, 'I'll leave you now, before daybreak, and I'll be back at sundown': he went out in his canoe. While he was away the mother showed the rope to the two girls. The three of them climbed into a banyan tree, and so up into the sky.

On his return Bindagbindag found the camp empty. He called out to the two girls. At last the elder girl called back from the sky, 'My mother and sister and I are up here.' 'What am I going to do?' he asked. The younger sister cried, 'Look for the rope. My mother is going to lower a rope. She will throw it to you—take hold of it.'

The old man replied that he would go back and get the fish. But what he did was to stick 'nails' (scales?) all over himself, just as a crocodile has knobs on its back. Then he went back to the banyan tree, and called out that he was ready. Whistle Duck lowered the rope: as she threw it, it made a noise like a swinging bullroarer. He jumped up to catch it. Whistle Duck began to pull up the rope; but the elder sister didn't want her father, because he was always having intercourse with her. Only the smaller sister wanted him. When at last they had drawn him up quite close to them, Whistle Duck took from her belt a mussel shell 'knife' and started to cut the rope. The younger sister snatched the knife from her hands, but she had others. She tricked her daughter into looking the other way, and cut the rope quickly.

Crocodile fell back on to the ground, smashing all his bones. He lay there for a long time. Then he began to fix up his body. 'It's better that I should stay in the water,' he said. 'Before, I was like a man. I'm nothing now, all broken up. So I'll remain in the water, and everyone will be afraid of me.' He sang himself into a crocodile. He waited until a wild dog came down to drink, grabbed it, and killed it. 'Well, this is what I'm going to do all the time—that old woman did me an injury, so now I'll frighten everyone.' The rope is still in the sky, as the Milky Way; a black patch is the banyan tree, with the old woman and two girls camped under it. And Crocodile's spirit is up in the sky too.

Emu and Djabiru. North-eastern Arnhem Land. One version of this story is recorded by Warner (1937/58: 543-5).

Two Men, Emu (Wulban) and Djabiru (Gandji), were living at Dalmia by Arnhem Bay, in Gubabingu linguistic group territory. Djabiru was married to Emu's daughter. Emu used to make hooked spears, Djabiru pronged fishing spears. One day Djabiru and his wife went out for stingray, promising to bring back some for Emu. They were able to get a great deal of this, and when they returned to their camp they made a fire and cooked it. But they ate all the delicacies, such as liver and fat, leaving only the flesh. This they wrapped up in paperbark bundles and carried over to Emu's camp. Emu's other children saw them coming, and called out, 'Here they come, father, we'll have plenty of stingray now!' Emu's daughter took the bundles over to him and he opened them. 'But there is no fat, no liver! There is only meat. Have you two eaten it all?' 'No,' she replied. 'That's all we got, father.' 'There is no fat at all,' repeated Emu. 'You two have certainly eaten it!' Angrily he grabbed his club and the two men began to fight. Djabiru picked up a length of pandanus and hit Emu's arms, breaking the bones. That is why the emu now has short arms (wings). Then he found a large smooth stone resembling an emu egg: he threw it at Emu, who swallowed it. That is why emu eggs are so hard today. Emu picked up a bundle of the hooked spears he had been making, but Djabiru flew away into the sky. Seizing his thrower, Emu tried to spear him, but he had flown too high. Then Emu picked up a short spear, a throwing javelin, connected it to his spearthrower and magically propelled it through the sky. It caught Djabiru in the anus, entered it and came out of his mouth. That is why the djabiru bird has a long beak today. 'This is my spear for fishing,' said Djabiru, and went to live in the sea-water swamps. Emu went off in the opposite direction, to live in the bush.

Bell Bird and Emu's Nest. Bidjandjara, Great Victoria Desert.

Wadi Banban, Bell Bird Man (*banbanbalala*), coming to *gabi* Beri, saw an emu's nest with two eggs in it. He gathered bushes and placed them in front of the nest, and made a pathway along which he could creep later to spear Emu. Then he made a spear, and kept watch.

Wadi Galaia, Emu Man, had also been making spears. A bundle of them was hidden by his nest, standing upright ready for use. Returning to the nest, he sat on his eggs: and one hatched. Bell Bird crept forward until he was behind the 'fence' of bushes he had put there. As he held his spear poised Emu saw him, jumped up, and grabbing his own spears threw one of them at Bell Bird. He missed. Bell Bird retreated, with Emu following him out into the open throwing spear after spear. Bell Bird dodged every one. At last Emu threw his last spear. Now he was unprotected. Bell Bird was able to spear him, and kill him. Using his club he broke off all Emu's 'fingers', except one little one. That is why the emu has only one now. As he did this he declared, 'You, Galaia, must remain an emu, you are no longer to be like a man!' Then he cooked him and carried away the meat with him. Metamorphosed emu tracks can still be seen at *gabi* Beri. So can a little hollow, representing the place where Emu's body fell after Bell Bird had thrown it across the water-hole; and Bell Bird's knee marks are there too, at the spot where he knelt down to drink.

Chicken Hawk Succeeds in Stealing Fire. Ngulugwongga, Daly River.

Little Chicken Hawk (Djungarabaja), Big Hawk (Bugaidjma), and Dog (Mojin) were camping together at Djungarabaja, a high hill at Dilg in Madngala and Maranunggu country. Dog went out and collected 'sour' yams and 'sweet' yams. Returning he said, 'Brother, break a special stick for making fire. We'll twirl it to make fire to cook this food.' Dog twirled it but broke it, tried another and broke it. He couldn't get it right. 'Better I should go out and get a live firestick, so we can have a good fire.'

He went off to a camp named Birangma, and hid behind a pandanus tree. A lot of women had been out collecting yams and bush foods, and now they came back to the camp with them. They made fire, preparing an oven, arranging the stones for baking. When the wood had burnt down they brushed aside the burnt out pieces, leaving the glowing coals. Dog jumped forward to take a firestick; but the women saw him and hunted him away, saying, 'There's no fire for you.' He returned home, and told the others, 'It's no good, I'm too big, they all saw me.' 'Try again,' they demanded. He went back to the women's camp, and hid behind the pandanus again. As before, the women returned from food-collecting and began to make an oven. Dog tried again to get fire but again they drove him away. He returned to the others: 'No, I'm too big. They always see me.' Dog's hands were sore from twirling the firesticks: 'You go, Djungarabaja!'

So Little Chicken Hawk went to the women's camp, and hid behind the pandanus. The women returned from the bush as before, and began to prepare an oven. But this time they looked around for Dog; and knowing that he lived with Big Hawk, Bugaidjma, they looked for him too. The presence of Djungarabaja escaped them: he was small. Satisfied, they continued with their oven making: they scraped out the wood, and placed the large glowing logs to one side. As soon as they did this Djungarabaja swooped down and took up a piece of glowing wood, crying out, '*Diiid . . . Diid*!' The women rushed forward, but he flew off with it. As he went he dropped some charcoal, broken by his beak as he held the firestick: today there are charcoal patches stretching from Birangma toward Djungarabaja Hill (almost parallel to the Dilg hills).

Back in camp he found that Dog, impatient at waiting, had eaten his yams uncooked. 'Ah!' Djungarabaja scolded, 'you have eaten them raw, and here I've brought fire!' That is why the dog doesn't talk, as Chicken Hawks do, and eats his food raw; he could not wait. But those three still remain at that place, Dreaming: at Djungarabaja, named after Little Chicken Hawk.

Curlew and Owl. Narunga; Yorke Peninsula, South Australia (Berndt, 1940*a*).

Owl, Winda, was once a man who lived with his two large dogs in a cave in the cliffs. Each day he went out hunting. Nearby on the beach lived two Curlews (*wudlaru*), husband and wife, with several young children. These two also used to go hunting, leaving their children behind. One day Owl, seeing them gone, went to their camp and encouraged his dogs to eat the children: 'There is meat for you, my dogs!' When the Curlew parents came back and saw the remains of their children, they dropped what they were carrying and wept bitterly. This is the wail of the curlew today. They buried what was left of the children, and promised each other that they would be avenged. Curlew Man set off for the cliffs where Owl lived, and in the nearby scrub he met Kangaroo, Gudla. He persuaded Kangaroo to serve as a decoy. 'You go and feed in front of the Owl's cave, so he will see you. He will send one of his dogs out after you, but you run into the dense scrub. I'll be hiding there. Leave the rest to me.' Kangaroo did this, and Curlew emerged from his hiding place and killed the dog with a club. Next day the same arrangements were made, and the second dog killed. On the third day, Curlew Man climbed the cliff to the entrance of Owl's cave. Standing there, he called on Owl to come out and fight, but Owl would not answer. Nor would he come out. After waiting for some time, Curlew put a curse on him:

'Nobody will ever like you,
You will never go out in the daytime to get food,
You will get food only at night,
You will not be able to see in the light,
You will not be able to see the sun,
Stay there, stay there!'

So even today the owl lives in caves and dark places. Curlew returned to his camp. 'There is nothing else for us to do. Our children are gone, and we can't make any more!' he said to his wife. So they transformed themselves into curlews; but they still mourn for their dead children.

Death comes to the World. Maung.

Moon, Gurana, and Spotted Possum, Jindalbu, were once men: but they quarrelled. Possum picked up a sharp wooden yam stick and knocked Moon down. After a while Moon got up, grabbed the same yam stick and hit Possum, mortally wounding him. As he was dying Possum spoke: 'All the people who come after me, future generations, when they die they'll die forever.' But Moon said, 'You should have let me say something first, because I won't die forever. I'll die for a few days, but I will come back again in the shape of a new moon.' As for human beings—we die forever because Possum spoke first. This took place at Manggumu on the mainland, in Maung country, where there are high rocks near Sandy Creek.

There are many such stories in Aboriginal Australia about the origin of death. Warner (1937/58: 523-4) gives one about the Moon and the Parrot Fish. Other examples are mentioned in Kaberry (1939: 128), Berndt (1945; 1948*a*), Spencer and Gillen (1938: 564-5). Here is another example, a children's story or 'play story' (*wogal dau*).

Punishment for Greedy Children. North-eastern Arnhem Land.

As the story opens, Moon's two wives are out gathering food. Malarei was of the *ngaridjan* subsection, Gudjiringu was *goidjan*, but they called each other 'sister' because they were married to the same man. Their language was Wulgara. Moon, Ngalindi, was *bulain*, and he spoke Wonguri. Their two little boys called each other 'brother'.

The women got great quantities of yams, 'sweet' ones that can be cooked and eaten straightaway, and 'sour' ones that need special treatment. They filled their bags, tipped all the yams out in a heap near the fire, and put some among the hot coals to bake. Then they went for more, brought them back, and set off again. This time they were looking for lilies. They gathered lily roots and stems, and said to each other, 'Let's pick these lily flowers for a plaything for those two children waiting at home!' The fire was a large one, plenty of food cooking in it.

In the meantime the two boys had been sitting in the camp waiting. Presently the smaller boy said, 'Elder brother, let's go and spear stingray and fish!' They told their father, 'You sit here, we'll go for fish!' They speared many fish, strung them on sticks, carried them all back to camp and sat down by the fire. Their father was pleased. 'Yes, my sons, there's fish for us, we'll eat. They'll taste good.' The two boys set about cooking and began to eat. First they ate the little fish. One said, 'Give some to father.' The other said,

Djunggawon novices painted to represent the mythical Wawalag sisters (see Chapter VII). They wear sacred armbands: Yirrkalla (1947)

Above: *Julunggul* didjeridu being blown over a row of prostrate novices in the *djungga-won* sequence: the Rock Python symbolically swallows the Wawalag, represented by the novices (see Chapter VII). Milingimbi (late 1930s)

(photo: courtesy H. Shepherdson)

Left: Tall *jelmalandji* structures of the Kunapipi rituals, one representing the Rock Python, the other a wild cabbage palm (see Chapter VIII). Milingimbi (late 1930s)

(photo: courtesy H. Shepherdson)

'No, this is mine!' They both ate, and finished it all. 'Finished, father!' 'Yes, well, all right, you can eat.' 'Birds now, father.' 'All right.' 'Sit there, father, we'll go for geese.' They killed a goose and brought it back, goose eggs too, and cooked them. They plucked out the feathers, threw them away, cut the goose open, took out the stomach, and began to eat. They ate the legs, belly, liver, heart and other organs, and finished them all. 'Father, would you like some body?' 'Yes.' They took it from the fire, and began to cut it up. Good. The elder brother said, 'Give father some eggs!' He wouldn't. 'We two can eat.' They cut up the bird's body and ate it. The elder brother said, 'Give father some!' 'No, you give him.' 'No, this is mine!' The two of them ate it completely. 'Finished, father.' 'Good, you two eat. Go on, you two, go and spear some birds! [He named a list of birds, including the *lindaridj* parakeet.] I'll wait here.'

The two children set off. Left to himself Moon set to work on a fish net, making it bigger and bigger, so big that he himself could go inside it. Then he called out to the two boys, looking around for them. 'Where are you, you two? When are you coming back? Listen, you two—come back!' He finished making the net, then waited for them, lying down. He was lying down for a long time, waiting, and then he heard them coming. They got firewood. He said, 'Hurry up, you two, cook those birds, then come back here for a plaything!' 'Wait, father, first we'll eat these birds.' The two of them ate the lot. 'Father, finished!' 'Come on, you two, come here!'

They came—and went inside the net—first one, then the other. Their father took it, tied it tightly, lifted it on to his shoulder. '*Wai*, father, *wai*! please! (literally, nice face!). How *can* you!' 'No. Lately you haven't given me any fish, or birds, I've only watched you two eating. (Literally, I've had only my eyes.) What am I, a wild dog? Aren't I hungry? Don't I like to eat?' He took them, and threw them into a well (waterhole). '*Wai, wai*, father, *wai*!' Yes. They filled with water—and they died, lying there in the water. Finished. He got a lot of soft grass and put it into the water, on top of them. Then he went away, back to camp, and sat down.

The two women were taking the food from the coals and putting it into their baskets, putting into their baskets the sweet yams, the lily roots and lily stems; and they wrapped up the lily flowers as a plaything for those two children of theirs. They scraped the sour roots, sliced them up, put them into baskets and left them to soak in the fresh water of the billabong. Then they went back to camp. 'Where are our children?' They couldn't hear any noise. 'Why can't we see them playing, those two? We should be able to see them, hitting their chests with their hands, happy to see us, calling out, "Oh mother, oh mother!"' They went further, and came close to camp, looking about them. 'There he is, sitting by himself. Where are those two children . . .?' They went and sat down, put down their food. 'Where are our children?' 'Over there, spearing birds.' 'When did they go, then?' 'Quite a while ago!' They searched for a long time, calling and calling. 'Come on, we're looking for you! Come here!' They kept calling, calling. 'Where are you, alas! Here's food for you both!' Those two didn't answer.

At last the women turned back. 'Let's drink water first, come on!' They hurried to drink. First the elder sister, then she stood up and the younger sister took her turn, stooping down to drink from the water. But as she drank, something cut her mouth. 'Here, what cut me in the mouth?' They felt about with their hands, took hold of something, tried to pull away the grass from on top of it: but it was too heavy. They got a stick, lifted it up with great difficulty, pulling at it. At last it came out of the water toward them. 'This is our children!' They swore, angrily, at their husband: 'Big penis! Rubbish-bones! Big testes! Nose-looking-for-sister trouble! Rough tongue! Crooked elbow! Flat buttocks! Big eye! Crooked-walk! Stinking! You corpse!' They undid the fish-net rope, pulled out one child and put it down on the ground, then the other. One mother picked up her child, the other hers. They carried them to camp, put them down on the ground; they cut two pronged poles, and straight poles, and little sticks, and got paperbark. They picked up the two bodies, those two children, put them up on the tree platform wrapped in paperbark, and put sticks in place on top of them.

Then off they went with their digging sticks, those two. One took one side, one the other, and they beat that husband of theirs, beat him with great sticks: here on this elbow—'*Dar*!' he cried. They set fire to his hut, burning it up. He jumped aside, and again he jumped aside: then he climbed up a tree. They got sticks and threw them at him, up into the tree. He climbed higher, and they kept on throwing sticks at him—he climbed far up, and still they kept throwing sticks. He was nearly to the sky: they kept on throwing sticks at him. He was high up on top among the leaves—they kept on throwing sticks at him. He climbed right up into the sky—and still they threw sticks at him. He was far away now. His belly grew big, and he spoke: '*Wiribigili*! I'm Moon!' he said. 'All you men, you husbands of those women! You won't remain alive, you'll die! I'll die, but I'll come back, I'll come up again as a new moon . . . !' He spoke the truth. Moon grows old, but he comes up new again in the sky, he shines as a new moon over the people of the western clans. The place where he lived is called Duldula, south-east of Milingimbi, shared by the Wonguri and Wulgara linguistic units.

The Orphan and the Rainbow Snake. Maung.

At Arunawanbain, meaning 'Something ate us', on North Goulburn Island, an orphan boy lived with his mother's mother. Other children were eating lily roots but would not give him any. He cried and cried. His mother's mother tried to stop him, but it made no difference. Even when everyone else went to sleep, he kept crying incessantly. The noise disturbed the Rainbow Snake, Ambidj, or Ngaljod. Gradually the great Snake drew nearer to the camp, coiled around it, and swallowed first the child, then his mother's mother, and then all the others one by one. Slowly, heavy with people, he crossed to South Goulburn Island, over the strait to the mainland at Waidbi, Sandy Creek, then inland for two or three miles to Ngudinbaidjbi. Here a number of people saw him, and preparing their spears threw them at him. In the fighting which followed a number of them were killed, but finally Ambidj was mortally wounded. The survivors cut open his belly and took out the people who had been swallowed. They were still alive. The deep groove Ambidj made, crawling inland from the coast, formed what is now called 'Number Two Sandy Creek'; and the place where he was killed became a large waterhole named Ingana.

This is one of the rare instances in which the Rainbow dies and the victims survive. Almost always, it is the other way round. In this story, too, the sex of the Rainbow is not clear: it could be either male or female.

Crow's Revenge. Maung.

In the Dreaming period South and North Goulburn Islands, now called Waruwi and Waiara, were separated by only a small creek. Here lived a man named Mandulmandul, who owned a large drum net which he placed in the creek every morning and evening and caught great quantities of fish. He would take what he wanted for himself, and give the rest to all the Bird people who assembled there. The good fish he gave to Djudjud, Seahawk Man, and Marwadi, Eagle Man; but to Crow Man, Guragag, he gave only the *umbulnga*—a species of inedible puff-ball fish. Old Crow would ask, 'Where's my fish?' Day after day he would be told, 'The *umbulnga* are for you.' At last, tired of this treatment, he went to a sacred *djang* paperbark tree and started to cut it down.

When the other Bird Men saw what he was doing they called out in consternation, 'Don't you know that tree's *djang*? If you cut it down a flood will come, and we'll all be drowned.' Crow took no notice of them, just went on cutting. At last the tree fell. From each side the sea water flowed in, filling the creek and flooding the country. 'We'll die, we'll die!' cried the Bird Men. As the flood spread and the water became deeper, they changed their shape and really became birds. Beginning to fly, they identified themselves: 'My name is *djudjud*, seahawk . . .' 'My name is *marwadi*, eagle . . .' and so on. Crow called his own name, and added that he would continue to eat any kind of food at all—'just as crows do today'. This is how the strait between the two islands was formed. In the middle, where it is rough and the waves are high, is the place where the drum net and the *djang* tree used to be. Mandulmandul 'turned himself' into a rock, which is visible today at low tide.

The Punishment of Mamuru. Bidjandjara, Great Victoria Desert.

Mamuru, the long-haired rat of the spinifex plains, was once an old man. Coming from the west, he camped at a place named Gimeri, where he cut a slab of wood from a white gum tree and made a large curved wooden dish. He carried this under his arm as he continued on his journey, putting into it the brown *mumbu* mushrooms he collected. When he arrived at Berodina he sat down and ate some of them, and went on to camp at Gudjidida, a large waterhole. While he was there he broke off short lengths of stick from a tree and put them horizontally across his dish, near each end, to straighten it. Then he continued on to Galbala, where he sat down and straightened it again. Some other people were camped there—Bilbagu, Ring-necked Parrot Men. Mamuru made friends with them.

It so happened that one Parrot Man had been out hunting. He had come upon an emu sitting on its nest, speared it, and cooked it, but left the meat there intending to return for it later. Now, feeling tired, he asked if one of the other Parrot Men would go and get it and take the eggs from the nest. He was not talking to Mamuru. Mamuru, however, was listening and spoke before any of the others had a chance to do so. He jumped to his feet, and snatching up his dish and a firestick rushed out into the bush to find the meat. When he got there he put all of it into his dish, and after eating a little went on in a southerly direction, passing many waterholes. The Parrot Men kept waiting for him to come back. After two nights, they went out to see what had happened. Only the nest was left; everything else was gone. Knowing that Mamuru was the only person who could have done this, they set out in search of him. They could see no tracks, because his long fur blurred the marks of his paws on the soft ground. But they did notice that all along the way he had pulled out mushrooms. So they followed him, and coming to his first and second camps they found emu bones and egg shells which he had carelessly thrown aside.

Eventually Mamuru, who walked slowly, came into the big waterhole called *gabi* Beri. By now the Parrot Men had almost caught up to him. They had formed themselves in a *wanmala* avenging group; and from a distance they saw him sitting there. First they sent forward, that night, two of Mamuru's sister's sons—called Buliburil, closely associated with the ring-necked parrot. The Buliburil came toward *gabi* Beri, built a fire, and stood in its light so that Mamuru could see them. Then they called out to him, 'Uncle, paint yourself with white clay! Get up, stand in the open, we're going to quarrel with you!' Mamuru, without answering, jumped up and seized his fighting shield and ran into the open: he stood holding this before him, waiting. Then the Buliburil retired, while the Parrot Men came forward and threw their spears, 'so that they fell like hail'. Mamuru dodged them all, deflecting them with his shield. The first group of Parrot Men grew tired and retreated, and a new group came forward to take their place. This went on for some time, one spear-throwing party following another. In the meantime, Mamuru's constant movement had made a depression in the ground so that he was slowly sinking downward until at last only his head showed. Still they kept flinging their spears, but they could not hit him. Finally, one old man named Dudri, leader of the Parrot Men, ran up from behind just as Mamuru's head disappeared under the ground and threw his spear with such force that it entered the earth and hit Mamuru: then all the others came forward and speared him from every side.

Gabi Beri is Mamuru's hole, and nearby are many holes made by the spears that were thrown at him. Mamuru's body is said to be still lying under the clay into which he sank, and *mumbu* mushrooms are still the main food of these rats.

The Skin Waterbag and the Flood. Bidjandjara, Great Victoria Desert.

Malgaru and Jaul were two brothers travelling south from the 'desert' country. Sometimes they are called the Two Men, the Wadi Gudjara. Margaru, the elder, had a kangaroo skin waterbag, as well as two firesticks; but he would not give the other any water. Jaul became thinner and thinner, and his throat more parched. Eventually they came to a place near the south coast—Biranbura, west of Fowler's Bay. There was nothing but dry land there. Malgaru hid his waterbag under some rocks, which were dry at that time, although the sea now breaks over them. There the two brothers quarrelled. Malgaru went out hunting, but as soon as he was out of sight Jaul rushed to the waterbag. In a hurry to get at the water he jabbed at the taut skin with his club, making a hole in it. Water poured out. Malgaru came running back and tried to save the bag, but he could not stem the onrush of water. It spread across the land, drowning them both, and forming what is now the sea.

Only the prompt action of the birds stopped it from inundating the country completely. Some of them set to work to make a barrier of kurrajong roots, while others came rushing from the north with fresh supplies. This explains why the kurrajong tree is called the 'water tree': fresh water can always be obtained from its roots, because the water from the skin bag soaked into them. And the rocky coastline and cliffs are the metamorphosed kurrajong roots, piled one on top of another to stop the oncoming waters. All the birds who flew down with roots were women. They were the *ngeni* (finch or small red-breasted bird), *wadawada* (species of laughing jackass), *bulin* (like the *wadawada*), *djindadjinda* (wagtail), *didarara* (a yellow bird), *idjididjidi* (black bird, like wagtail), *djinbun* (small brown bird), *djildjil* (red-breasted black or blue bird), *balbal* (parrot), *badalbadal* (lorikeet), *gilgilga* (budgerigah), *banban* (bell bird) and *dudu* (big blue bird). Collectively they are often called the Minmara(ra), the group of women associated with Njirana. (See Chapter VII.)

Abduction of a Novice. Bidjandjara, Great Victoria Desert.

Two Spider Women (Minma Gudjara Imbu; tarantula), sisters, were camping at a waterhole with other Spider people. Not far away a *djunjunba* or *wongaba* circumcision novice, a young Spider, was segregated in the bush. Each day the sisters would cook meat and take it out into the bush, but when they were still a little distance from him they would light a fire and leave the meat beside it. The novice was not permitted to see or speak to any women during his period of seclusion. But the younger Spider sister kept thinking of the boy, and one day she decided, 'I shall make myself into a wife.' She went out to look for him but could not find him: he lived in a hollow tree. Next day she went out again; but the novice, who was killing a goanna, saw her and scurried back into his tree. Now she had found out where he lived. Returning, she asked her sister to catch him, telling her where to go. The elder sister went off to the tree, but the novice was not there. She cut off the ladder leading to the hole, and waited nearby. When the boy came back and tried to climb into the tree she sprang out and seized him. Then she dug a hole and told him to lie, down in it, keeping quite still. He did so. The younger sister, who had been waiting out of sight, came hurrying up and was overjoyed when she saw him. She lay down in the hollow beside him, with legs apart, and tried to lift him on to her; but he was too heavy. She played with him there all day, while her elder sister kept watch, but he evaded actually copulating with her. At last she grew tired. Leaving the boy lying there, she went off hunting with her sister. While they were away a group of adolescent boys (*didji mudili*) came past and saw him, and persuaded him to run away. He got up and went with them, leaving a few of the *mudili* to wait for the return of the sisters. When the girls came back and found the boy gone, they were angry. First they chased the *mudili*. Then they searched for the boy's tracks, and followed them into a large initiation camp where they sat down with the boy's mother. The youngest sister still wanted him. All the time, sitting there, she kept watching him as he lay by the fire in the smoking rite. (See Chapter V.) Then came the moment when all the novices were told to get up and run from the ground. As the boy sprang up to go, the younger sister also jumped to her feet. Before he was out of the camp she had seized him, and lifting him on to her shoulders took him into the sky. All the other people threw spears at them, but could not reach them. They are still up there in the sky, as stars.

Guruwelin, the Cannibal Giant (sometimes called Biwubiwu). Maung.

Long ago, in the Dreaming Era, there were two sisters named Wararawundji. One day the younger said to the elder, 'Sister, let us go and get some nuts.' They went to a jungle not far from Brogden Point, near Sandy Point Creek, where they found the right kind of tree. The younger sister said she would get the nuts for them both, but the other wanted to help. The younger girl tried to dissuade her, because she was pregnant, but in the end they both climbed up. Sitting in the tree, they began to crack the nuts. Guruwelin heard them. He came near and saw them, and hurled a large yam which he carried as a club. It hit the elder sister, killing her, and stunned the younger. Both fell to the ground. He picked them up, put them into his net bag, and carried them off to his camp, then put them down and went off to find a shell to use as a knife. He left this alongside the bag and went off to collect some firewood. As he moved away he spoke to himself, 'I'll go a long way to get this firewood.' Actually, he remained quite close. He collected a heap of wood and then set off again, saying to himself, 'I'll just go a short distance', but this time he went a long way. Next he wanted some termite mound, used in cooking to keep the heat. Again, after declaring that he would go a long way, he did the opposite. This went on for some time. During one of his long absences the younger girl recovered consciousness, saw the shell knife nearby, stretched out her arm for it, and cut a large hole in the net bag. She tried to awaken her sister, but found she was dead. Guruwelin returned with termite mound and left again, and while he was away she crept out and made her escape. As soon as Guruwelin came back he noticed she was missing but he did not go after her. Instead he made a big fire, topping it with termite mound. Then he set to work cutting up the elder sister. In the process he found the foetus, and so he prepared a separate fire for cooking that. After the big fire had died down he scraped out a depression in which he put the severed pieces of her body. He arranged the red-hot chunks of termite mound around and on it, covered it completely with paperbark to retain the heat, and left it to cook. Then he did the same with the foetus. When all this was ready he took out the meat and ate it, but he did not break up the bones; he stacked them separately in two heaps. Presently he had diarrhoea: he built a special bough shelter in which to relieve himself, and when this was full he moved on to another. Still he could not stop. He built one shelter after another. This went on for several days.

In the meantime, the younger sister had told her story, and her family sent out two men to search for Guruwelin. One was Wiriwirijag (a grey bird with a black head), the other Wuruddurid (a brown bird with a spear-like tail). They came to the first shelter, but its branches and leaves were dry. 'This is only an old camp, let us move on to the next.' They went from one to another, until they came to a newly built shelter: 'He must be here!' Guruwelin was lying in the shade: he saw their shadows and jumped up, but they had disappeared. When they got home they reported what they had seen. Then two other men went to look: Nabaraminmin (bat) and Djigeridjigerid (willy wagtail). They saw Guruwelin, but he did not see them. Then all the men gathered their weapons and set off, in great numbers. They threw spear after spear at Guruwelin, but all that happened was that many of them were killed. Finally they were able to kill him. To make certain he was dead, they built a fire and burnt his body. They recovered the elder sister's bones, and her baby, and a native doctor (*margidjbu*) put them together and made them come alive again. But now, in this particular area, people have to dig deeply before they can find yams—just as Guruwelin himself used to do.

The Resentful Namarudu. Gunwinggu, but said to have belonged to the now extinct Waramungguwi people.

A *namarudu*, lightning spirit, was going along looking for a place to live in when he saw an old man in the jungle, on his way to find fish. The old man looked around, and seeing Namarudu coming said to himself, 'Oh! he's coming up to me, that dangerous fellow! He'll kill me—I can't do anything about it.' He ran to hide in the densest part of the jungle. But Namarudu came closer and closer, and at last saw him. 'Why are you afraid of me?' he asked the old man, 'I won't hurt you, let's go and look for fish together.' The old man said, 'No, I won't go with you, because I'm afraid. I'm looking for people, many people living together. They are the same as I am; but you're Namarudu, you might kill me.' He left him, went off to where those people were camped among the rocks; they were eating fish and meat and wild honey, killing goanna and watersnake. Afterward the old man went hunting again. But he heard Namarudu coming, running, making a noise like wind. 'Maybe he's coming after me again!' Well, Namarudu came chasing him, he came running to where that man was standing. The man fled, saying, 'Go away! (Literally, 'Keep going!') I don't like you to come running up to me, I don't want you!' He went back, that Namarudu. And that man went back too, back to the others, where they were camping among the rocks.

Namarudu said to himself, 'Shall I go and shut them up, where they're sleeping in the caves? Then they'll come into Dreaming for ever!' He was alone. But that man was back with the others eating meat and vegetable foods; and afterward they slept. In the night, Namarudu came up to where they were sleeping. He heard a little boy calling out, crying and crying, and he said, 'That's their little boy crying! I'll go and look at them!' He went, he looked at the place, where they were all asleep. Well, he closed them in the caves, sealing them up. They couldn't do anything about getting out; he shut them in for ever. They slept, they tried to get up, they looked about —no, there was no hole anywhere, where before they used to leave the cave, because Namarudu had sealed them in. They got up, and one man called out: but they just came into Dreaming. They stand there in spirit, turned into stone. They remain there for ever, among the rocks where before Namarudu shut them in, at Mandjawaindjau, just west of Cannon Hill, not far from the East Alligator River. There they came into Dreaming for ever.

The Unwary Elder and the Mamu. Bidjandjara.

In the Western Desert there are many stories about *mamu*, malignant spirits. Sometimes, people say, they resemble human beings. At other times they assume various shapes, such as that of the *ngeni* bird, a small finch. They are described as being usually tall and heavily built, with massive heads and hair growing to a peak; their teeth are long and bloody from biting and eating human beings, their nails long like claws. The males carry large clubs. They are said to pounce on lone wanderers, bite them and carry them off to their own camps or down into their caves, strewn with human bones. They are particularly fond of small children, who may be frightened by the mere mention of the word. The *mamu* are believed to have existed from earliest times, from the ancestral Dreaming period. (See Berndt, 1945.)

One afternoon an old man *mamu* came to a waterhole where an ordinary person, an elder, sat meditating. The *mamu* joined him and they began to tell each other *djugubi* Dreamtime myths, tracing waterhole routes in the sand before them. Presently the *mamu* took the lead, and told a long story about imaginary *djugubi* happenings until in sheer boredom the old man dozed off to sleep. The *mamu* had been awaiting his chance. He pulled out of his anus a stone knife, and cut a horizontal line across the man's eye sockets, from cheek-bone to cheek-bone: then he killed the man, cooked and ate him.

The groove or depression across the eyes under the brow-ridge, with the crow's-feet at the corner of each eye, is a characteristic somewhat more accentuated in Desert Aborigines than in Europeans; the *mamu* made it, for the first time, for all subsequent generations.

The Mamu Revenge. Bidjandjara.

Tulina, a giant spirit being, an old man, lived at *gabi* Bagalin with his wife and two children. Out hunting one day he saw two *mamu* children and tried to kill them, but one escaped with a broken leg. He cooked the other and took the meat back to his family. Breaking off one of the hands he gave it to one of his own children, who showed it to his mother. But Tulina's wife was a *mamu* herself: and she recognized it as the hand of her own sister's child. She knocked the roasted hand from her son's grasp, and disappeared. In the mother's absence, Tulina himself grew large breasts and suckled his children. One day he left them alone in the camp while he went in search of the lame *mamu* child. After many adventures he reached a big cave at Wedranbidal, the home of many *mamu*. He poked a spear down the entrance of the cave, and trampled on other holes in which the *mamu* were living. But with a great rush all the *mamu* emerged, breaking his spear and swarming over him until they dragged him down full length on the ground. They squeezed his breasts, so that milk flowed, then cut off his genitalia and gave them to the lame *mamu* child. When they had killed Tulina they set off in search of his children. The two were eventually saved by their mother's brothers, who were also *mamu*. In the process, however, many *mamu* perished. Their bodies were metamorphosed as stones along the track from Bagalin to Nundon and on to Wedrunbi, near Wedranbidal.

Revenge of the Magic Child, Windaru. Bidjandjara.

Windaru Child lived in the hilly country beyond the spinifex north of Ooldea with his grandmother, Gandjilu, the name of a kind of possum or bandicoot. While Windaru was out hunting his grandmother visited her husband Wadi Wiril, Possum Man, who lived in a different place, and persuaded him to come back with her. When Windaru returned from hunting she told him to make his own camp so that she and Wiril could be together. Windaru was angry about this. Next morning, after Gandjilu had gone out to collect food, he killed Wiril by setting fire to his windbreak. Gandjilu saw the smoke and hurried back, arriving just in time to see her grandson leaving the scene. She tried to hit him with her yam stick, but he got away. Going to a particular waterhole Gandjilu summoned all the *mamu* to her aid, and when they were assembled told them what had happened. In the distance they could hear Windaru Child laughing. This infuriated them, and at once they set out to kill him. When they found him they tried to grasp him, but he kept dodging away. At last he began to climb a tree. The *mamu* all clustered around its base, waiting to catch him. His grandmother was there too. But Windaru Child had magic powers. He sang the tree so that it rose up into the sky with all the *mamu* clinging to it. When it was high enough he caused it to shake and all of them, including his grandmother, fell to the ground and were killed. Their bodies were metamorphosed into granite boulders; smaller stones are their knives and their teeth which were knocked out in the fall. Windaru Child went on into the sky and remained there.

The Death of Marsupial Mole Woman. Bidjandjara.

Old Minma Jaradu, Marsupial Mole Woman, came from the east toward Ooldea. She sat down in the shade of a *gogulba* kurrajong tree near a large sandhill, cutting the roots of this tree and eating them. While she was doing this she saw a firestick in the distance, coming in her direction. Someone was carrying it. As he came closer, she saw that he was a young man. He sat down with her, and she gave him some of the roots to eat. That night they slept separately. Next morning he made ready to continue his journey. Old Jaradu watched him climb the large sandhill and disappear over the other side. Then she picked up a round stone and, taking aim, threw it at him. The stone hit the back of his neck and killed him. She went over, picked him up, and carried him back to her camp, where she cooked and ate him. In this way she killed a number of people. But one day the Two Men, the Wadi Gudjara, arrived. At first, everything happened in the same way as it usually did. She gave them *gogulba* roots, they slept, and next morning got ready to leave. But this time things were different. During the night the Two Men had been warned in a dream about what the old woman might do. They climbed the sandhill, but as soon as they came to the other side they stopped and waited. When the round stone came flying in their direction they dodged it, then hid behind a bush. Old Jaradu came along, singing to herself, happy at the thought of fresh meat; and as she came near them they speared her through the heart, killing her instantly. Then they left her body there and continued on their way . . .

The Trickster and the Girl. North-eastern Arnhem Land.

Jalmarida and Baiangun were two sisters who lived at Dalingur by Arnhem Bay during the *wongar* Dreaming era. They belonged to the Wonguri linguistic unit of the *jiridja* moiety. One day they went out to collect cycad palm nuts, filling their dilly bags with them. They dried them in the sun for two or three days, then pounded them, replaced them in the bags, and left them soaking in fresh water so they would be fit to eat. In the meantime, while they were waiting they went to Gudjidnga and made a camp there. Then they went down to a mangrove swamp to collect *binanggu* periwinkles from the mangrove roots.

Nearby there lived a man named Namaranganin, of the Gwulamala linguistic unit, *dua* moiety. He saw the two sisters, and followed them, watching them move across the swamp. Then he made rain, to force them to turn back so he could catch one of them. Rain clouds gathered, lightning flashed, and the two sisters asked each other, 'What has happened? Perhaps that man who followed us has made rain. What shall we do?' They decided to collect their periwinkles quickly and go back. Namaranganin, hiding behind a mangrove tree, kept watching them. The rain came down heavily and the thunder rumbled; they gathered up their belongings and ran toward the camp. Namaranganin thought, 'Those two are coming now, I'll grab them and take them away.' As they passed the tree he jumped out and tried to grasp them, but the elder sister, Baiangun, escaped. He managed to keep hold of Jalmarida, the younger. 'This will be my wife, I'll take her away.' He carried her off into the jungle. But Baiangun ran back to the main camp and told everyone, 'Namaranganin has taken Jalmarida into the jungle . . . Namaranganin, the trickster, with his long penis!' All the men hurried off, following their tracks.

While this was happening Namaranganin, far in the jungle, had chosen a good place for a camp. 'What are we going to do?' the girl asked. 'We're going to make a big fire and a hut,' he told her. He made a stringy bark house and built a fire inside, but Jalmarida would not talk to him. He kept trying, in one way and another, but still she refused to speak. At last he caused the fire to smoke, so that the hut was full of it. They lay down to sleep, but still Jalmarida was silent. The smoke continued to collect. During the night it became so dense that at last the girl awakened and asked, 'Why does that fire make so much smoke, why doesn't it escape?' Namaranganin replied, 'Yes, this is the reason, so that you will speak to me. I want to copulate now.' But Jalmarida answered, 'No, you can't do it, Dagurura is inside me, closing my vulva.' (Dagurura, or Dugururu, is a stone and a totemic emblem.) Namaranganin got a stick, sharpened it, and wedged out the stone. As it emerged, a roaring sound came from the sacred Wonguri totemic waterhole associated with it. Bursting out, the stone travelled to the waterhole, entering it, while Namaranganin called the sacred invocations relating to it. The Dagurura became a sacred emblem, *rangga,* for the Wonguri people. The removal of the stone made it easy for human women to have intercourse. (See Warner, 1937/58: 554.)

By now the other men who were tracking them had reached their jungle camp. They surrounded it with a ring of fires, preventing Namaranganin from escaping, then speared him and burnt him in a huge fire. But Jalmarida did not go home with them. She turned herself into a fly (*buwad*).

Such stories are called *bialmag dau,* funny story, or *wogal dau,* play story. The matter of the *dagurura* is taken up in sacred mythology too.

Namaranganin is equivalent to the trickster Bomaboma, who has a number of erotic adventures: some of these are recounted by Warner (1937/58: 545-65). He may be called Gwingul or Wanabwingu (stone spear). In one version he is Wabalu, Black Eagle, who tries to seduce his classificatory sister's daughter, a young girl called Bunba, Butterfly. In another the girl is his actual sister's daughter. In yet another Bomaboma injures a young girl, Jii (a small white duck), whom he calls father's sister's daughter's daughter (a relationship of constraint); he is thus seducing a female whom he should normally avoid. Bomaboma's exploits, so some people say, show that a man who flouts tribal tradition is 'abnormal' like this trickster, whose ill-deeds bring him, in the stories, only social condemnation and death. One of the worst insults a woman can offer a man who presses his unwelcome attentions on her is: 'Are you Bomaboma?' Warner writes that he is a 'crazy man' who performs anti-social acts and cannot be disciplined: he not only breaks the laws of exogamy but acts in an unpredictable way: 'he runs around like a dog'. The listeners always laugh at such tales, even while in the same breath they express disapproval. The trickster is a figure of derision, but at the same time he is appreciated as an amusing fellow, exemplifying the local tradition of slightly scandalous humour.

The Adventures of Balalngu. A dramatic sequence from Northeastern Arnhem Land. (See C. Berndt, 1952: 216-39, 275-89.) This is only a brief outline.

Balalngu, with two companions, goes out turtle hunting. Almost at once his wife is seduced by his younger brother who, through magic, causes his canoe to be cast up on the beach of a strange island. Hungrily they search for food and water, and eventually find some. Balalngu explores the island and finds some odd canoes made from large turtle shells; he returns to his companions and they go in search of the local people. In the meantime, two girls see the three strangers and rush back to tell their father. Balalngu and his companions are hospitably received, and provided with food and young girls, one each. During the night, however, the mother of the girl assigned to Balalngu prevents him from copulating with her; he is annoyed, and the three men with the girls leave the camp, go down to their canoe and paddle away. In the morning their absence is discovered, and the mother of Balalngu's girl causes a gale to rise and force the disappearing canoe back to the island. Eventually they push off again, but without the girl; she cries bitterly. They reach their home country. In the meantime, Balalngu's wife has been living with his younger brother and is pregnant by him. On their arrival Balalngu asks for his wife, and is told what has happened: he kills her. Then he goes after his brother, who in fear escapes into the jungle, but is finally killed by sorcery through eating 'poisoned' eggs. He is buried, while Balalngu sings over his grave, clapping his sticks and calling invocations to the spirits. Later, Balalngu is grieving for the brother he has killed. But the brother's spirit has taken the shape of a crocodile to seek revenge, and succeeds in killing him, in his turn. Balalngu's other wives wait for him in his camp, worrying about his absence: going in search of him, they discover his partly eaten body. They bury him and notify his clansfolk and a mortuary feast is held.

* * * * *

Whatever the characters in these stories—ancestral, totemic or spirit beings, or more or less human—the social and cultural environment in which the action takes place is considered to be contemporary and familiar. Often, the events they relate are pushed back into the distant past; and odd things happen occasionally, such as people do not expect to encounter in their own experience. But essentially the setting is very much what the story-tellers and their audience are used to: the background and the relations between the characters are, to them, ordinary and predictable—however strange they may seem to non-Aboriginals accustomed to living in a very different world. This ordinariness extends even to the actions which are deprecated or regarded as wrong: they are part of that situation, just as is right behaviour.

CHAPTER XII

Art and Aesthetic Expression

(*Continued*)

VISUAL ART

Because media and style differ from one part of Aboriginal Australia to another, it is possible to distinguish schools of Aboriginal art—not as professional centres in which methods and techniques and motifs are taught, but in the sense of traditional patterns and procedures being handed on informally. In some respects each tribe or cultural bloc could be said to have its own distinctive aesthetic expression marking it off from the next, and this is true too for song and myth; but we can also speak of art areas which may include a constellation of tribal units. (Elkin, Berndt and Berndt, 1950: 15-19; Elkin, 1954: 223-34; McCarthy, 1957*a*, 1938/58.) Within such art areas a number of art-types or techniques may be available. But over and above this, allowing for variation, are basic similarities which permit us to speak of Australian Aboriginal art in contrast to the art of other peoples.

The main materials are rock facings, shelters and caves (as in the case of cave paintings, incisings or carvings on rock outcrops and so on), wood (carving and incising: figures of human beings and other creatures; pipes; bobbins; and ceremonial objects of many kinds), sheets of bark (for example, paintings on stringy bark), hard beeswax (moulded), occasionally clay (moulded), the ground and sand (as in ground 'drawings'), and other substances which may be used to make items such as baskets, feathered string, pearlshells. There is a fairly wide range of objects which may come into the category of visual art.

Throughout the Continent techniques are limited, and very much dependent on the tools or materials available. For bark paintings, the inner surface of sheets of stringy bark is used; the brushes, fine or heavy, are pieces of twig flattened at one end, or feathers or human hair mounted on small sticks; the pigments are red and yellow ochres, pipeclay and charcoal, sometimes a black rock, mixed with water and ground at intervals during the painting on a flat stone; an adhesive, but an unsatisfactory one, can be supplied by rubbing the bark first with an orchid root. For large wooden carvings like the human figures of north-eastern Arnhem Land, the grave posts of Melville and Bathurst islands, and the profusion of emblems of western Arnhem Land, scrapers and shark-skin 'sand' paper were traditionally used, as well as the stone axes, chisels and other tools found elsewhere in Aboriginal Australia. The introduction of iron on the north coast, particularly in Arnhem Land, enabled the local people to produce beautifully finished objects much more easily than they could otherwise have done.

Looking at specimens of Aboriginal art we must remember how much the Aborigines were handicapped in that direction. At the same time, this is only one factor. It is even more important to ask what they were trying to do when they prepared these specimens. Before considering this, let us glance at what has been written on the topic.

Grey's (1841) reference to what have now become the famous Wondjina paintings of the northern Kimberleys possibly stimulated initial interest in this general subject. The paintings he illustrated were re-examined by, for instance, Worsnop (1897) and Mathew (1899), who used them as a basis for speculation about Asian contacts with Australia. The most meticulous of the earlier recorders were Spencer and Gillen (1938), Spencer (1914, 1928), and Basedow (1925). The first contains a wealth of material. Much of it is open to criticism in the light of more recent findings. In view of the fact that Sir Baldwin Spencer was an untrained anthropological observer, and Gillen a perceptive layman, the results are outstanding. They must be used with caution, a point which is especially significant when we consider that Durkheim (1915/1954) and many subsequent writers have relied almost entirely on Spencer and Gillen. Nevertheless, to the student of Aboriginal art the work of these two men is indispensable. Basedow is by no means so prolific, nor for that matter so detailed, but he does give a fairly comprehensive although rather superficial account. (For example, 1925: 297-358; 1907: 54-9 plus plates.) Among the principal writers Davidson (1936, 1937 and later 1952) came next, and McCarthy's first work in 1938: Elkin, during that year, dealt with some aspects of Aboriginal art in his first edition of *The Australian Aborigines;* Mountford, too, began writing on this topic at about that time, while McConnel had published an interesting paper in 1935*a* (pp. 49-68, with coloured plates). The systematic study of Aboriginal art was beginning.

In the years which followed, although other writers have made contributions, those by Mountford, McCarthy, Elkin, and Berndt are the most significant. McCarthy (1938/1958) has provided the only general study. (See also his 1957*a* volume: pp. 167-85; 1960-1; in 1958 he made an overall survey of Aboriginal rock art.) Elkin 1954: 222-43) also has a good total view. Elkin, Berndt and Berndt (1950) concentrated primarily on Arnhem Land, which is one of the most colourful art areas of Australia, although McCarthy (1957*b*) and Berndt (1958*b*: 26-43) have considered some general implications. Mountford who, with McCarthy, pioneered the study of Aboriginal art, has produced two important works: one concerns Arnhem Land art (1956) and the other refers to Melville and Bathurst islands (1958). There are also two catalogues of exhibitions (one held in Perth, with an introduction by R. and C. Berndt, 1957; the other, an Australia-wide one, with an introduction by McCarthy, 1960-1).

Since all Australian Aboriginal art is basically utilitarian, designed to have some direct or indirect purpose or effect, this blurs the usual distinction between craft and art. McCarthy (1957*a*: 81-97, 167-85) makes such a division on the basis of weapons and everyday articles, or matters of technology, as contrasted with decorative expression. This is rather forced, because many such objects as spearthrowers, dilly bags, pipes, and paddles are aesthetically important, comparable to bark and cave paintings and totemic emblems. Art is inseparable from its cultural and social setting. An artist's production is not just an individual response to an aesthetic urge: it must have social significance and use, it must mean something to others and not simply to himself, and it must also conform to traditionally established expectations. An Aboriginal artist certainly finds pleasure in what he does, but this is not an end in itself.

In Aboriginal Australia the artist is always confined to a set of rules, over and above the limitations of material and technique. These are traditionally defined in terms of both design and choice of subject matter. 'Creative' sense is restricted and conservative, rather than directed toward experimentation. Art is a form of communication—it has something specific to say in terms of design, whether this be a conventionalized or a naturalistic representation: and it also has something to say over and above this, either in symbolic terms or more generally. What is the Aborigines' idea of an adequate or satisfactory representation? They do not, as a rule, want an exact photographic representation, of such a kind that almost anyone anywhere will be able to recognize it for what it is.

Being semi-nomadic, they ordinarily move within only a limited radius: and although tribes come together at ceremonial times, this again is only within a limited radius. People who come into contact are usually those who share very much the same mythological and ritual background, who can communicate with one another even though they do not always speak the same language. There is really no need to communicate outside that range. A symbol may have a certain meaning, or meanings, within a community: outside it other groups may attach different meanings, but this does not matter. The Aborigines do not normally attempt to enforce their own interpretation on other groups. The main thing is that there should be agreement within the group itself, in relation to any particular symbol or design, although the meaning may vary in relation to circumstances: for example, in certain rituals in western Arnhem Land, men and women may interpret designs differently. In some cases the group concerned may be very small indeed: among the Aranda, a few men own a certain totemic site, and know the esoteric or secret meanings of the designs on the sacred objects associated with it. In such cases the designs need not be realistic: they can stand for certain mythological events or persons, and it does not matter that they do not provide a straightforward picture of either.

In fact, over a great part of Aboriginal Australia the designs are not, or were not, realistic. Like many of the songs, they are highly stylized. They cannot be understood by looking at them, just as the songs cannot be understood simply by hearing the literal meanings of the words. It is the hidden or symbolic meaning, not the surface meaning, if any, which is the important thing. For example, the symbol ⊂ among the Aranda often means a man sitting down; ⊂o⊃ can be a fire or a tree with two persons; these must be interpreted by people who know. Concentric circles, spirals and so on are popular. A circle incised on an object from the Western Desert may be interpreted as a rockhole or a place; but on the other hand it can be almost anything else, depending on the significance attached to it by the person who put it there, and his immediate group. Meandering designs may represent tracks of various kinds, travels of ancestral beings, creeks and so on. In reference to these simple designs see Basedow (1925: 337, 338-55), McCarthy (1958: 15, 25, 58), and particularly Mountford (1937*a*: 21-6; 1938*a*; 1939*a*).

A painting may be understood immediately in terms of its subject matter: for instance, it may represent human beings, animals, trees, or some abstract symbols—which are understood by all those socially involved—for clouds, rain, camps, and so on. But it will possibly still be necessary to explain the context or situation in which these representations and symbols appear in combination—to append a story, as it were, which may be a myth. This explanation may be available only to a select company: to men rather than to women, to initiates rather than novices or uninitiated, to members of a local descent group or clan rather than to 'outsiders' and so on. Or the symbolic meanings of various designs may be revealed, or change their context, in accordance with a man's progression through age-grading rituals, or with his ritual and ceremonial position in adult life. Significance of designs, for whom, and prepared by whom, is vital in understanding Aboriginal art right through this Continent.

When it comes to more realistic designs it might seem that interpretation is straightforward, but even here we need the assistance of the artist, or of people who knew what the artist intended to convey. In many parts of Australia today this is no longer possible. Carvings on rocks and paintings in caves have remained in places where there are no longer Aborigines, or at least none with traditionally derived information about them. Generally speaking, much of Aboriginal painting and carving has mythological significance. At the same time, a certain amount is concerned with everyday affairs, with hunting and food-collecting, the ordinary round of camp life, relations between the sexes, and so on, with no mythical or ritual connotation. This is perhaps more noticeable in the north than in the south. Even in a mundane situation, most Aboriginal art is planned to achieve something. There are cases when a design is said to be 'pretty' or merely for decoration, having no special significance, just as there are cases of doodling; but on the whole it is incised, carved, pecked or painted with some purpose in mind. For instance, the zigzag design incised on Western Desert spearthrowers often represents a snake—a snake strikes swiftly, as a spearthrower should propel a spear.

There are several ways of discussing Aboriginal art. The most useful, perhaps, is to talk in terms of art areas—except that within any one of these several types are discernible. Here, however, we shall look more directly at the productions themselves.

Cave and rock paintings

The richest galleries are in the northern part of the Continent. In the south they are still extremely interesting, but perhaps mainly to the specialist: the techniques are elementary and the designs and figures relatively simple. The best overall surveys have been made by Davidson (1936, 1952) and and by McCarthy (1958: 30-66, including a reasonably good bibliography). As McCarthy has mentioned, "it is quite impossible to estimate the number of cave paintings in Australia": the figure would run to "tens of thousands". The Anthropological Society of Western Australia has been making (1960) a survey of Aboriginal sites in that State, and in the process has recorded a great many of these. Its report says: "Without any fear of exaggeration, we can say that literally hundreds more sites are waiting to be recorded, some of which must be of the utmost importance."

Over much of the Continent, especially in the south, it is no longer possible to find out the traditional meanings of such designs. This is true even for parts of the north. Father Worms, for instance, could not get interpretations for all the incised and painted figures he found on rocks and caves in northern Kimberley. Some of the most sacred cave paintings are said to be of non-human origin, although human beings may touch them up for certain purposes. The usual claim is that they have been there since mythological times: a mythical being may have 'become a painting', settling down in the cave while perhaps his spirit travelled to some other site, or into the sky. In other words, they have 'always' been there—part of the mythological era, part of the Dreaming. Others again may have been painted by human beings. This does not mean that wherever there are rocks people have incised designs on them, or painted on them—only in places where there was a tradition of doing so. At the same time, these provided an extra medium, a canvas which people could use for illustrating mythical themes, among other things.

There are many outstanding sites. Ayers Rock, for instance, is well known these days. Spencer (1928: 165-76), Mountford (1948: 70-91), and Harney (1960: 63-76) have all discussed this remarkable stone monolith, with its paintings of animals and creatures and human figures. Spencer writes, of the many "shallow caves and shelters round the base of the Rock", that "their roofs were blackened with the smoke from small camp fires and their walls thickly covered with drawings". Mountford, who came along nearly fifty years after Spencer's visit in 1894, reports that a series of photographs taken at one site, "at five-year intervals, showed that many of the designs recognizable in 1930" were faint, and some indecipherable, "ten years later". McCarthy notes (1958: 60) that although "human figures are comparatively rare" in the galleries of northern South Australia, there are many such at Ayers Rock: some are shown wearing ceremonial headdress or having "a concentric circle instead of a head", others are stick-like human figures (see discussion of *mimi*, below). Here there is the contrast between types that one finds in numbers of Central Australian caves: realistic designs, side by side with highly stylized or geometrical ones. Another site complex in this general area is at Glen Cumming (Wirindjara), in the Rawlinson Ranges not far from the Giles base, in the picturesque surroundings of a large chasm. The gallery is not extensive but the designs are interesting for their mythological significance, relating particularly to Njirana and the Seven Sisters. (See Chapter VII.) In the Willeroo-Delamere region of the Northern Territory, at a Rain Dreaming centre in Wadaman tribal country, are the Lightning Brothers, said to have come from the eastern Kimberleys. The major figure has lines radiating from its head. (See Elkin, 1954: 232; and Harney, 1943, who gives an illustration, opposite p. 24.) Davidson (1936: 108-20) has discussed this and other neighbouring sites and illustrates a number of designs, including several of the Lightning Brothers. The major drawings are of the two brothers, Jagdjadbula and Djabuindji, together with a small figure signifying Gananda, the woman they both wanted. Davidson writes that "the rocky surface on which they are found constitutes one side of a huge stone mass, about sixty feet high, located about five miles northwest of Delamere": the overhang on the southern side 'protects the innumerable drawings there'. The local Wadaman deny that human beings had any hand in putting them there, and insist that 'the Lightning Brothers themselves were responsible'. The younger brother, the largest figure, is nine feet tall: the penis is as long as the legs and tipped with red, indicating subincision. McCarthy (1958: Plate 1) has an excellent coloured photograph of these remarkable drawings.

The two most colourful regions are the northern Kimberleys, and western Arnhem Land. The first is the home of the famous Wondjina paintings, the second of some of the most spectacular cave art in all Australia.

The Wondjina (or Wandjina) in the vicinity of the Prince Regent, Sale, and Glenelg Rivers, between the Drysdale River and the King Leopold Range, seem to represent a distinctive art style. They have been discussed in some detail, not only by Grey (1841) but also, among others, by Elkin (1930, 1948, 1954), Davidson (1936: 124-32), Capell (1939), Schulz (1946), Lommel (1952), Petri (1954) and McCarthy (1958: 53-8). Briefly, 'the figures are painted on a white ground. An oval band encircles the face, except for a break at the chin: from the outer edge of the head lines radiate out, a headband is shown, and eyes and nose form one unit, with lashes encircling both eyes. Conventionally, there is no mouth. The body, when there is one, is filled with parallel stripes down the arms and legs'. A glance at the illustrations of McCarthy (1957*a*, Figs. 154, 155, 182; 1958, Figs. 33, 34, 42) and Petri (1954: Plates XVI-XX) will reveal the complexity of these drawings, their variety and their interlinkage with numerous others. The Wondjina are mythical beings, male and female, the great creators and guardians responsible for the continuing welfare of the local Aborigines; and around them are drawn the totemic beings and creatures, directly associated with them, on which these people depend for sustenance. In other words, such caves and rock shelters with their clustered paintings are really increase centres, a focus of tribal religion and ritual action. They are more than mere pictures: they represent the very essence or spirit of the beings and creatures depicted. In the caves are pieces of rock symbolizing parts of their bodies, and the ritual act of painting or touching them up releases sacred energy or power: bringing on the wet season, sending out spirit children, or spirits of edible plants and natural species. Sometimes the Wondjina are related to the Rainbow. Worms (1955: 548-52) writes of them and their associates the Rainbow Snakes, Ungud. "Ungud are the creators, who appear as Rainbow Snakes. Wandjina heroes, the lawgivers, come forth from the eggs of Ungud, transform themselves into Ungud and work at the Ungud places." (Worms, 1955: 549; Petri, 1954: 97 ff.) Petri also gives different versions of the myths connected with them.

There has been much speculation about the origin or original meaning of these paintings; but, to repeat, there is no evidence at all that such paintings were inspired by alien visitors to this north-west coast. What is more, the influence of this particular kind of painting is fairly widespread: the Lightning Brothers are an example. Simplified versions are found as far south as north-western South Australia and at Ooldea. But it is most in evidence in the eastern Kimberleys extending into the Northern Territory, with a few examples in western Arnhem Land.

Outlying sites, or outposts, of the equally well-known western Arnhem Land galleries are those at Katherine (Basedow, 1925: XLVIII), Beswick (Elkin, 1952; Macintosh, 1952*d*) and St. Vidgeon's, south of the Roper River, now part of Hodgson Downs. Spencer (1914: 432) speaks of the excellent bark and rock drawings to be met with in the East Alligator-Oenpelli region—up on the rocky hill sides, "wherever there is an overhanging shelter" where a man can find protection from sun and rain. Western Arnhem Land is one of the greatest art regions in Australia. Throughout the Oenpelli-Liverpool River area, galleries of paintings give colour and life to most of the shelters and caves of the numerous hills and rocky outcrops. They are executed in ochres, pipeclay and charcoal, red, yellow, white and black, sometimes in blood, and numerous sites have never been visited by Europeans. Walls and roofs are covered with stylized or realistic designs, new ones superimposed on older and faded ones. Many are in inaccessible places, which can be reached only with the help of a notched pole or native ladder: often platforms were built for roof drawing. Some caves have been used for wet season camps when the low-lying country nearby is flooded; the drawings they contain may be blackened with smoke and the floors worn smooth.

A selection of these drawings has been illustrated and discussed by Mountford (1956: e.g. 109-78) and McCarthy (1958: 49-53): the variety and range are remarkable. Spencer (1928: 823-4) has four illustrations with a brief description: he comments that 'the slanting roofs and sides were a mass of drawings resembling those done on bark'. Although the separate art types have not all been delineated, there seem to be two basic divisions. In one are the so-called X-ray designs, first reported for bark paintings by Spencer (1914). In the other are the *mimi* or stick figures. (See Chapter I.) Mountford contrasts the polychromatic art of the first with the monochromatic art of the second. With the X-ray art some of the internal organs and skeletal structure of the creatures and human beings are shown: this, of course, reveals a fairly detailed anatomical knowledge. As McCarthy points out (1958: 50), "It is a local development of a striking nature and prolific output, enormous numbers of X-ray pictures having been done in innumerable rock-shelters, covering walls and ceilings up to 100 feet long with either scattered figures or with layer upon layer of them in a dense mosaic": fish, kangaroos, tortoises, crocodiles, snakes and so on. The *mimi* art, again, is quite distinctive and the simple linear designs of great variety are among the most vivid and charming in Aboriginal Australia: 'match-like' drawings in red ochre or blood, of human beings hunting, dancing or camping, or of spirits usually called *mimi*. The figures are slender, often only one line in breadth: movement, rhythm and grace are strikingly shown, and long stories are associated with some of them.

The *mimi* and the X-ray are the two main types, but others cannot be so easily placed and could be classified separately. One such is the Aranga spirit. Spencer illustrates a cave painting of this being (1928: Fig. 540); so does Mountford (1956: 142); the illustration in Elkin, Berndt and Berndt (1950: Plate 2) is a contemporary copy on bark. This is not a Turtle demon (as McCarthy, 1958: 51 suggests), but a malignant spirit with a Rainbow Snake head, ornaments suspended from his elbows and feathers from the end of his long penis. (The Amurag word *arangga* means 'green ant'.) R. and C. Berndt (1951*a*: 171-4) give a version of his story. The cave drawing of Aranga seems to be different to either of the main basic types. Then there are the composite and complex drawings, with head and body distortions, with extra limbs and additions, often associated with sorcery: some have been illustrated by Mountford (1956: e.g., Plates 34 C, E, 28 C, 29, 40, 42 B, 45 C, E, G, 47 A, 57 A, 58 B).

Contemporary and near-contemporary drawings in these caves are said to have been made for specific reasons. Most of them are associated with hunting and fishing magic, or the increase of natural species. Some show hunters with raised spears. In others the drawing of a creature is considered to be sufficient to stimulate that species to propagate, or become vulnerable for hunting. Then there are drawings used to illustrate a story: a spirit being, a Rainbow Snake, a monstrous creature, and so forth. These people were and still are great story-tellers, and possibly this accounts for a great number of these paintings: a drawing is used to show that a story is true. (An example is given in Elkin, Berndt and Berndt, 1950: 78-80, and others in R. and C. Berndt, 1951*a*.)

Two other reasons are sorcery and love magic. Throughout these galleries are ochre sketches of women in conventional patterning: some are drawn with human, bird or reptile heads, with several arms, accentuated breasts, elongated vulvas, with semen: there are women suckling babies, bodies of women showing foetal growth, women dancing, and men and women copulating. These are of three main kinds: imitative magic, relating to sexual intercourse or to pregnant women; those relating directly or indirectly to sorcery, designed to bring about sickness or death (we shall return to these in the section on bark paintings); and those concerning spirit beings.

Mimi figures are no longer drawn by the local people—remnants of the Mangaridji or Mangerdji, the original inhabitants of the Oenpelli region, now supplemented by Gunwinggu and Gunbalang, with some Maung, Jiwadja and others. But people still tell stories about them, and they are still believed to inhabit certain parts of the country. These figures are shown in numerous positions: for example, running females with pendulous breasts, men with prominent genitalia, some dancing or hunting with spears poised, and carrying dilly bags. In most accounts of the *mimi*, they live in caves and emerge only when no wind is blowing, because they are so thin that they fear their necks may be broken. Although some *mimi* are friendly, they are not to be depended on; they are antagonistic to human beings and capture them when they can. They eat human meat, but their staple food is a special kind of yam. In one story a human being was almost seduced by some *mimi* women, but managed to escape. (R. and C. Berndt, 1951*a*: 176-7.) Not all the cave figures of this type are *mimi*.

Both Mountford and McCarthy speak of these drawings as being the oldest variety, and certainly X-ray examples are often superimposed on them. The art type to which they belong may not represent a local tradition. They possibly have some connection with the *Giro Giro* miniatures of North Kimberley. (Worms, 1955: 554-65.) These were first reported by Bradshaw (1892). Worms speaks of them as being "delicate and fragile" and says that only fine brushes "could have produced the trim curves of the muscles, the fluttering pendants dangling from the armpits and loins, and the feathery armlets". There are also "groups of men crawling on all fours", and many other postures are depicted: most outstanding are the varied headdresses. Here again, as in the case of the western Arnhem land *mimi*, the local people have stories about the *Giro Giro*: in one example they are dwarfs, in another, possibly ghosts.

McCarthy (1958: 52-3) suggests that although this tradition reached its peak, as it were, in western Arnhem Land and the northern Kimberleys, it is widely distributed in Australia; he gives examples from the Sydney-Hawkesbury district of New South Wales, western New South Wales, Central Australia, Groote Eylandt, and so on. Worms puts forward the view that this tradition is of great age and points to a pygmanoid race, the negrito Tasmanoid people who may have been the original inhabitants of this Continent. Needless to say (see Chapter I), this is only speculation. McCarthy, more conservative here, notes that this art tradition "has a long history and a widespread distribution in Australia, surviving as a cultural element in some areas".

Other cave paintings at Chasm Island (Mountford, 1956: 102-5; McCarthy in Mountford, ed. 1960: 297-414) and Groote Eylandt have been dealt with in some detail. McCarthy records that he worked through forty-five sites containing approximately 2,400 figures, although there were over 4,000 paintings. He adds (1958: 45) that "many of the Australian styles and techniques are represented in these galleries. The silhouettes are particularly colourful." Here again the subject matter varies: there are fishing, hunting and ceremonial scenes, and the pattern of superimpositions suggests that "the stencils, silhouettes, outlines and striped styles date from the earliest period". Some stick figures appear here too, but not in such profusion nor so gracefully. Then there are the Wessel Islands caves, which contain paintings of Japanese pearlers, and others (at Groote) which show Indonesian praus (see McCarthy, 1958). The Beswick and Tandandjal caves (Elkin, 1952; Macintosh, 1951, 1952*d*) also reveal a wide range of designs, many of them symbolizing or representing sacred objects. Each cave, with its designs, is a focus of sacred religious and mortuary ritual. There are associations with the Kunapipi fertility cult; and with spirits of the dead. (Bones and hair of the dead are placed in them.)

Then there are the stencils and impressions of human hands, widely distributed; they are painted as silhouettes, by smearing the hand with paint and pressing it on to the rock surface, or holding it against the rock and spraying ochre, by mouth, over and around it. We have seen this last done simply for decoration; it is one of the motifs which appear today in tin shacks on Arnhem Land mission stations. McCarthy (1958: 35-9) notes that a wide range of things is stencilled. In some cases the local people associate such designs with ancestral beings or spirits. Basedow (1925: 321-2) reports that 'it is compulsory for men "of a certain rank" [probably religious status] among the Worora (Kimberleys) to have their hands stencilled in the caves in which the bones of their ancestors rest': Elkin and Macintosh mention the association of this practice with mourning ritual: McCarthy sums up by suggesting that it is "more than a pastime", because a person who does it wants to leave on the rock "some record of himself"—but there is not enough evidence to generalize here.

Rock engravings or petroglyphs

These have been recorded by many writers, but particularly by Davidson (1936, 1952) and McCarthy (1941-56, 1958). Other important writers on this topic have been Elkin (1949), Hale and Tindale (1925), Worms (1954). In McCarthy's view they are concentrated to a greater degree in the Sydney-Hawkesbury and eastern South Australia area than elsewhere: there are apparently none in Victoria. However, Western Australia has some very large and outstanding galleries. Various techniques are employed (following McCarthy, 1958: 14): 'abraded grooves, scratched or abraded outlines, punctured outline, punctured and abraded outline, punctured intaglio band, punctured intaglio'. Here we shall speak generally of engravings, mentioning only some of the more important sites.

The Devon Downs site (Hale and Tindale, 1929, 1930; Davidson, 1936: 46-50; McCarthy, 1958: 17) contains three types of rock carvings: sharpening marks, arranged in groups radiating from a common centre; outlined forms of various creatures, meandering lines and circles; fine scratchings rather than deep ones as in the second variety—of so-called floral design. These were analysed in conjunction with archaeological work, and each type is associated with levels: the first with the Mudukian levels, the second, early Murundian, the third, late Murundian. (See Chapter I.) However, in McCarthy's view the engravings are not as old as they seem. The Sydney-Hawkesbury carvings are found in great variety on relatively "flat or sloping rock surfaces": McCarthy mentions 4,000 figures in from 400 to 500 galleries. The designs include mythical beings, men and women, mammals, birds, reptiles, fish and a few insects. In addition there are weapons and ornaments, utensils and other implements. Some are integrated scenes depicting hunting and ceremonies. From what is known of the culture of the eastern coastal people, many of them are clearly magico-religious. Some have to do with sorcery, others with the *bora* initiation rituals, and others again with Baiami or his counterparts. (See Chapters V and VII.) The engravings are mostly rough in outline, with prominent genitalia. The western New South Wales carvings, at Mootwingie for instance, are intaglios of excellent workmanship and delicate treatment. (Davidson, 1936: 40-2, Fig. 13; McCarthy and Macintosh, 1962.) They obviously belong to an art tradition different to the Sydney-Hawkesbury one, and seem to be linked with those of eastern South Australia.

A controversial design is the famous 'Panaramittee (Yunta) Crocodile' head, discussed by Hale and Tindale (1929), Davidson (1936: 27), McCarthy (1958: 21), and Elkin (1949: 150). (See also Chapter I.)

The Flinders Ranges carvings (Basedow, 1925; Davidson, 1936) belong to the western New South Wales tradition. There is a wide range of intaglios in this series, from realistic animals to highly stylized designs: there are 'fully intagliated figures comparable to the Mootwingie ones', but less complex. Mountford (1928 and 1935) has also discussed them. Davidson mentions intaglios at Delamere, in the Northern Territory, mostly of animals, tracks and so on, interpreted by local Aborigines. Rather cruder are the designs or marks scratched on sandstone walls at this same place—said to be 'symbolic of men's ritual body paintings'. (Davidson, 1936: Fig. 2.)

The Yule River intaglios in north-western Australia reported by Worms (1954) and McCarthy (1958) are particularly outstanding, with their lively, spirited human figures—including some which have a very close parallel in the sorcery and love-magic figures of western Arnhem Land. At Red Rock (on Yarlarweelor station, near Meekatharra), said to be an important ritual centre, is a large red outcrop covered with carvings: animals, tracks, human beings, totemic designs, some fairly recent, over an expanse of many acres. Among the many other remarkable sites in Western Australia are the galleries on Depuch Island (McCarthy, 1961: 121-48) and those near Port Hedland, possibly belonging to the same art tradition. (Davidson, 1936: Figs. 26, 27; Basedow, 1925.) In Davidson's opinon they are characterized by a complexity of detail and content—realistic animals and birds, human figures in various postures—"unsurpassed by any known petroglyphic exhibitions in other parts of the Continent". Little is known of their meaning, but McCarthy (1962) recently obtained some information about them from old Aborigines living in the region.

Although in so many cases, perhaps most, meanings of the designs have been lost, in others it is not too late to record them. They may not always be the traditional interpretations, but what they mean to the local Aborigines today is significant too. Just as in the case of paintings which are assigned to the mythical era, the period of creation, so with the engravings. Unless the Aborigines have completely lost interest in such things they are likely to look for explanations, and if these are not available it will not be long before guesses are made within the framework of tradition. This possibly happened with the *mini* paintings. On the other hand, most of these sites are directly associated with ritual and myth: the engravings are shown to initiates as part of a religious revelation. In eastern New South Wales novices are (or were) taken around from one engraving to another and told of their mythical significance. Many of the Central Australian paintings are approached in the same way, but not those of western Arnhem Land. Formal instruction of this kind makes it more probable that meanings will be handed on between generations, so that even when the system breaks down under alien contact the memories may remain—at least during the lifetime of the last initiates.

Elkin (1949: 119-57) is concerned primarily with the function of petroglyphs. Underlining the sacred nature of many of them, he points out that the production of some of the larger groups, both carvings and paintings, has entailed an 'immense amount of work'; and he adds, in italics, that 'it is unlikely so much trouble would have been taken for mere amusement'.

There is no reliable information, so far, about the antiquity of any engravings in Aboriginal Australia. Some have been made within living memory. A few may well be very old indeed, like the 'extraordinary series of deeply carved pits, cup and ring motifs' and so on in the rock shelters in the Carnarvon and Drummond Ranges, Queensland. (McCarthy, 1958: Fig. 12.) But generally they were part of the culture of many Aboriginal groups up to and even long after European settlement.

Paintings on bark

Painting on sheets of stringy bark reaches its highest expression in Arnhem Land, western and north-eastern, although it is not unique to that area. It has been reported from Tasmania, Gippsland and central New South Wales. (Mountford, 1956: 8.) There are no surviving examples of similar painting used in the *bora* initiation ceremonies of south-eastern Australia. (McCarthy, 1957*a*: 172.) Petri (1954), Odermann (1959: Plate 3, No. 2), and the Frobenius Institute catalogue (1957: Plate 33) illustrate several from the Kimberleys.

Arnhem Land bark painting was first reported by Europeans in 1878 at Port Essington. (McCarthy, 1957*a*: 171.) Foelsche (1882) made a small collection there. Basedow (1907: 57-9; 1925) illustrates some from Port Essington, Katherine River and east of Darwin, and mentions that along the north coast and on Melville and Bathurst islands sheets of bark used in making huts are decorated too. Spencer collected barks from the East Alligator River-Oenpelli area, not far from Port Essington but in a different language area. (Spencer, 1914: 433-9, Figs. 79-92; 1928: 802-13; plates duplicates except for Figs. 519, 520.) Similar paintings have been done at Katherine, Adelaide River, Beswick, Roper River area, even Port Keats. They have been collected from every mission and government settlement within the Arnhem Land reserve: not only Oenpelli, but also Goulburn Islands, Maningreda, Milingimbi, Elcho Island, Yirrkalla and Groote Eylandt.

The most detailed contemporary studies have been made by Elkin, Berndt and Berndt (1950), Mountford (1956), McCarthy (1957*a*), Berndt (1958*a*, 1958*b*). They have been concerned with three art traditions: from western Arnhem Land, north-eastern Arnhem Land, and Groote Eylandt (the last by Mountford). The rather different art tradition of Melville and Bathurst islands is also considered by Mountford (1958: 38-59). The Arnhem Land barks can have no serious rival in range and variety of subject matter, and in aesthetic appeal. Despite some overlapping, they can be classified into two broad types.

On the western side, generally speaking, an artist makes no attempt to cover his bark sheet with detail: he concentrates on the main figure, or figures, not on their setting. His subjects are human beings and animals in action, naturalistic, with a minimum of stylization. There is a preference for curves and roundness, including dots, rather than for angles and straight lines. Designs are prolific, and seem to be almost inexhaustible. To some extent, there are differences in style and treatment as between the inland and coastal people—crystallized, today, in a rather artificial contrast between Oenpelli and Goulburn Islands; but these are of minor importance. Bark paintings, here, may be used specifically for illustrating stories. (See Mountford, 1956; R. and C. Berndt, 1957; *Australian Aboriginal Art, An Exhibition,* 1960-1.) In some, landscape appears: rocks, hills, countryside, coastline and sea. Ordinary, non-sacred, examples are painted on the walls of bark huts, just as sometimes in caves. Sacred barks are used on the initiation ground: they are sometimes propped up in rows along which a novice is taken, and told the meaning of each in turn. Afterward they are destroyed, or left to rot. Others relating to natural species, or to special totemic sites, are painted for increase purposes. Or a hunter is shown spearing a kangaroo, or catching fish and so on—imitative magic. Others again, covering love magic and sorcery, include some of the most vivid and aesthetically pleasing paintings of Aboriginal Australia. Some have been illustrated in Elkin, Berndt and Berndt (1950) and R. and C. Berndt (1951*a*), and they have been mentioned already in relation to cave painting. A sorcerer may sketch in ochres a composite figure with an animal, reptile, bird or human head; eaglehawk or Rainbow Snake heads are most popular. Several arms are inserted, mostly three, and stingray spines protrude from the body. When the drawing is completed the sorcerer calls the victim's name, and from that moment his (or her) death is inevitable. One example shows a pregnant woman with the head of a djabiru bird, another a man with a headcrest of cockatoo feathers. In north-eastern Arnhem Land, although there are exceptions, an artist usually tries to fill the whole surface of his bark leaving little or no open space. He tends to shape his design within a self-imposed framework, often roughly square or rectangular; this is done in body paintings too. Either the background is blocked in with cross-hatching, or as much as possible is crammed into it, even to the extent of design repetition. In fact, repetition is a marked feature of this painting. Aesthetically, blank spaces on such drawings seem to be unpleasing to artist and observer, but the material used to fill them is never meaningless. There is little in the way of movement or action in design. The tendency, much more noticeable than in the west, is to repeat central and subordinate figures as well as minor motifs, giving the effect of a pattern. There is also a playing down of naturalism; and symbolism is expressed in varying degrees of complexity. (R. Berndt, 1958*b*: 36.)

The primary concentration here, on this north-eastern side, as in body paintings and painting on sacred emblems, is on clan and linguistic group patterns. Each linguistic unit has its own series, which may be linked with others. Conventionally, these designs are fixed and invariant; but in practice there is some scope for variation, including additions or alterations on the basis of dreams. The traditional sacred patterns can be distinguished from others by their repetitive designs and extreme stylization. Special storehouses are built on the sacred ground away from the main camp for the sacred *rangga,* and within them the bark paintings may be kept for showing to initiates. This is particularly the case in the *ngurlmag* rituals.

The showing of such designs is an established part of the economic system of north-eastern Arnhem Land. People who see those of other linguistic units must pay for the privilege. A man has no option but to accept an invitation to look at someone else's sacred pattern(s), or have it painted on his chest or spear-blade. This is one of his ritual obligations. The patterns, incidentally, are associated with myths and the travels and adventures of their characters —like Laindjung's 'sea-foam' design. Non-sacred designs were, traditionally, not so plentiful here. It is true that paintings illustrating stories or everyday activities enliven the walls of wet-season bark huts, especially the stilted 'mosquito houses'. In fact it could very well be that, traditionally, nearly all non-sacred painting was expressed through this medium, and not on the tidy sheets of bark used today. The external demand for these beautiful productions, probably stimulated by our own collection of bark paintings at Yirrkalla in 1946, has been responsible both for the extension of subject matter, and for the compact shape in which it is presented. They are now used to illustrate myths and everyday stories. Some show praus, and other aspects of 'Macassan' and pre-Macassan contact, others the Lands and spirits of the Dead. Others again are hunting and fishing scenes, magical in nature—designed to ensure good hunting and a plentiful catch. Still others could be taken as having some connection with love magic or sorcery, but this is not usual.

Crayon and other drawings

Drawings and paintings by Aborigines on introduced media are becoming much more common these days. Probably the best known, and the ones that have had most publicity, are those of the Hermannsburg school of artists headed by the late Albert Namatjira, followed by drawings from native schools, especially in the southern States. Most of these are, inevitably, non-traditional in design and expression.

In contrast, there are cases where 'outsiders' have wanted to record local patterns, or local ways of depicting the social and cultural and natural environment, but there is no available medium except the fixed canvas of rocks, ground or sand. In such circumstances traditionally-oriented Aborigines have been persuaded to draw, in the way they have been used to doing, on sheets of paper or some other substance, with crayons and pencils, as well as with charcoal, and ochres. There are several early examples of this (for instance, Brough Smyth, 1879: 257; Worsnop, 1897); but the first which concern us here are five charcoal sketches from Pigeon Hole on the Victoria River, in the Northern Territory—two crows, a hopping kangaroo, a hunter and a buffalo, a man spearing a kangaroo, and ritual dancing. It is not clear whether they are direct sketches: Basedow mentions 'tracing'. (Basedow, 1925: Figs. 19, 21, 24, 25, 28.) Tindale and Mountford were the first to make systematic use of sheets of brown paper, and lumber crayons of the only colours available to the Aborigines—red, yellow, white and black. (Tindale, 1932, 1959*b*; and Mountford, 1937*a*, 1937*b*, 1937*c*, 1938*a*, 1938*b*, 1939*a*, 1939*b*.) Large numbers of such drawings are stored in the South Australian Museum. The designs in Mountford's collections are very much like those which appear on cave walls in the Western Desert and Central Australia, in sand drawings, and on sacred boards. (See, for instance, Tindale, 1959*b*.) Among their subjects are the wanderings of the Two Men, the Wadi Gudjara; totemic places belonging to the northern Aranda, and to south-western Central Australia; the Wadi Jula, or Julana, and the Gunggaranggara women, the Seven Sisters; and everyday incidents in the life of the Ngada tribe of the Warburtons.

Another large series was collected by one of us (R. M. Berndt): at Ooldea, at Birrundudu (Northern Territory), and in north-eastern Arnhem Land, among other places. All are associated with ritual and ceremonial life or with myths. The most striking are from Birrundudu, in lumber crayons, on brown paper. (See R. and C. Berndt, 1950: 183-8, 10 plates.) They range from extremely conventionalized to more or less naturalistic representations. The 'artists' were men of such tribes as the Njining, Ngari, Gugudja, Woneiga and Wailbri, which together cover, traditionally, a relatively large stretch of country from the central-west of the Northern Territory across into Western Australia. Interesting too is the variety of art styles they include—some approximating the *Giro Giro* of Worms, the Wondjina, Basedow's Pigeon Hole series, and Central Australian meandering designs, with others which are quite distinctive: two nude dancing women, or the great Rainbow Snake with native doctors astride it. Others are scenic drawings with mythical characters climbing a hill, where the side and top of the hill are both shown, in an attempt to provide perspective and detail. And there is vitality and movement in the ceremonial drawings, with their actors and singers. The north-eastern Arnhem Land drawings are mostly reproductions of bark paintings. Some relate to the Kunapipi and Djanggawul myths, others to 'Macassan' contact along the north coast, or to dreams. (See R. Berndt, 1951*a*, 1952*a*; R. and C. Berndt, 1954.)

Body painting

The Australian Aborigines have, generally, excelled in decorating themselves in ochres and other ways. Nearly all volumes on these people reproduce at least some examples of this. Almost every part of the body has been used for that purpose: most commonly the face, chest and thighs, with designs spreading across and over the shoulders to the back. As far as quality and complexity are concerned, the range extends from daubs and smearing of rough patterns to the intricate productions of north-eastern Arnhem Land. (See, for instance, McCarthy, 1957*a*: 124, 153.) These continue down the thighs and legs to above the knees, and have a shoulder band extension, leaving the neck bare. The body surface is first washed and cleaned of hair and smeared with a basis of red ochre; the actual design takes some hours to complete: during that time relevant songs are sung and the myth retold, and finally comes the ritual. Young boys being prepared for circumcision are painted in almost the same way. (See Elkin, Berndt and Berndt, 1950: 112.)

Complex patterning in ochres seems to be particularly emphasized in Arnhem Land. Elsewhere feather down is often used to achieve designs which are just as detailed. For this, the body is specially prepared, rubbed with red ochre, the basic pattern lightly outlined, and then completed with the down, or wild cotton or kapok, stuck on with blood. The main colours are white and red. The patterning usually covers thighs, chest, shoulders and back, and often extends up the neck to be integrated with an elaborate headdress decorated in the same way. (The best illustrated examples are in Spencer and Gillen, 1938; Spencer, 1928; Basedow, 1925; Strehlow, 1947; McCarthy, 1957*a*.) All of these are used in sacred totemic rites; and the men so decorated symbolize the great mythical beings of the Dreaming. Masks are atypical for Aboriginal Australia. They are reported from only two areas: around Cape York, which has had contact from New Guinea via the Torres Strait islands; and Pindan, near Port Hedland, also presumably as a result of outside contact. Instead of masks, then, the Aborigines have paid much attention to facial designs. There is a great variety of these, and the best examples (from one region, Melville and Bathurst islands) have been recorded by Basedow (1913) and Mountford (1958: 92-5, Plate 28). However, the facial patterns in this case are actually unusual for Australia; mostly they are much less complex, especially in the central regions (unless they are associated with feather down designs).

The use of feather down and of the ochre patterns of Arnhem Land is almost entirely the prerogative of men—except that in one *djarada* sequence, in the Katherine area, women are reported to frame their body designs in feather down especially prepared for them by one of the old men. But women decorate themselves in red, white, yellow and black for their own magico-religious rituals, and although these designs are much less complex they are none the less pleasing and often beautifully done. While much of men's painting relates to sacred ritual and ceremony, body designs are not confined to this. There is painting for secular or camp dancing and entertainment, for love magic, or simply for personal adornment. Different ceremonies have different patterns; mourners as well as corpses are often painted with traditional designs; and even babies and small children come in for their share. Ordinary non-sacred designs can be particularly attractive, ranging from the conventional patterns sometimes seen in cave paintings (geometric and stylized human figures, for instance) to realistic representations of natural species. And in many parts of Aboriginal Australia cicatrization, where it has no ritual or mortuary significance, is used for decoration by both men and women.

Sacred objects and emblems

This category includes a wide range of objects, some of which we have already discussed. These vary in size and shape as well as in sacredness. All have ritual and mythical associations, and are used on the sacred ground, in dancing or posturing or meditation.

The *tjurunga* of the Aranda are perhaps the best known. These flat slabs of stone or wood, of oval, pointed oval and circular shape, are often incised with complex patterning: curving and spiral lines, concentric circles, U-within-U, meandering lines, dots and tracks of animals and birds and so on. Each is virtually unique, and each totem has its own distinctive arrangement of design: each too is symbolic of an incident or scene in a relatively long myth sequence. Some are entirely plain. Others, although not in use, are painted with ochres. When in use, they are rubbed with fat and red ochre. Stone *tjurunga* are more or less confined to the Aranda area, but a few have come into the Western Desert. Davidson (1937: 98-104) illustrates some line drawings of stone *tjurunga* from north-western Australia—from the Pilbara district, from Nullagine, and one which had been traded to Ooldea in South Australia. There is little information on these. The designs are geometric, but they include interesting stylizations, and one shows a dancing human figure. Another stone *tjurunga* has recently (1961) been found in the Pilbara by Dr. W. D. L. Ride, of the Western Australian Museum. Also in the possession of that museum are several painted and worked stones, representing the body of an ancestral emu man, along with two other large flat, painted and shaped stones. Collected (1961) in the Laverton-Minnie Creek-Warburton area by R. Collard, these are comparable to the sacred stone relics noted in Chapter VIII.

More widespread than these are wooden boards, ranging in length from one to two inches (the minimum, at Balgo, southern Kimberleys) to twelve to eighteen feet and sometimes more. Made mainly for ritual purposes, they have many names. In the Great Victoria Desert they are called *inma* or *djilbilba* boards; in the southern and eastern Kimberleys they are *daragu* (sacred)—but these are general terms. Each specific type has its own name, and mythical significance. Bullroarers too come into this category. Ranging from small ones of three or four inches, used in love magic, to large ones of three to four feet in length, they are found over much of Aboriginal Australia, but seem to have been absent in Tasmania and in Bathurst and Melville islands. (Davidson, 1937: 70.) In Western Arnhem Land they are known, but not generally used. The designs on some resemble those on stone *tjurunga*. Others, especially in north-western Western Australia, have complex incised line designs with zigzag, lozenge, triangle, branching and chain patterns, sets of geometrically shaped flutings, concentric diamond, square and so on. One from Nannine, Western Australia, is carved with human figures in high relief. (See Davidson, 1937.) Another cylindrical wooden object (not a bullroarer), now in the Western Australian Museum, shows a nude woman lying with legs apart.

Some of the smaller boards are used for exchange purposes. (See Chapter IV.) One man incises the patterns of his own country and totem-complex and gives it to another, who returns one of his own. The exchange is accompanied by the relevant myth and songs, and establishes a special relationship between the two men.

The bullroarers are swung ritually. Small boards, including bull-roarers, are often used in head decorations—protruding from the top of a conical headdress, or incorporated in other ritual parapher-nalia. The first is more common. An actor dances with a sacred board headdress, perhaps holding other boards in his hands. On the conclusion of his act, onlookers and other participants place their hands upon it, receiving part of the sacred essence symbolized by the object and the actor, and drag off the headdress. On other occasions such boards are placed on the ground and the ritual act takes place before them. Or an actor postures in front of other participants and initiands holding a long board before him, revealing it. Or a board is tied to the back of a postulant, who then enacts a scene from the appropriate myth.

These designs are important, but even more so are the actual boards themselves. They represent, symbolically, the bodies of the great ancestral and mythical beings. The long boards of the Kim-berleys, the Western Desert and central-western Northern Territory nearly always have that significance. One board from Ooldea actually has stylized patterns representing a headband, eyes, navel, legs and so on. Some are male and some female boards, and some represent genitalia of the creative beings: bullroarers in the Kuna-pipi, for instance, or certain boards in the eastern Kimberleys. The best descriptions are to be found in Spencer and Gillen (1938: 128-66, illustrations and line drawings), Davidson (1937: 70-85, 89-98), Basedow (1925: 346-53), Róheim (1945: 238-44), and McCarthy (1948: 29 ff.). Spencer and Gillen (1938: 158-66) discuss the lending of *tjurunga* to a neighbouring and friendly group as a special mark of goodwill: their Fig. 23 illustrates a collection of these boards, with a platform on which they are placed during the performance of rituals; their Figs. 26 and 27 show men being rubbed on the belly with sacred stone *tjurunga* during *intichiuma* ceremonies. This rubbing of the sacred boards, whether they be of wood or stone, is widespread and particularly important: through it, men say, they obtain sacred power, coming into direct contact with the mythical beings. Most wooden boards, when used in rituals, are superimposed with ochred designs and feather down which often completely cover the original pattern.

Larger boards and other objects may also be worn on the head during ritual performances, either alone, or as the basis of a more elaborate headdress. (Spencer and Gillen, 1938: Strehlow, 1947;

Removal of the sacred Goanna Tail *rangga* from its shelter during the *dua* moiety *nara* Djanggawul rituals (see Chapter VIII). Yirrkalla (1947)

Playing the didjeridu at a symbolic sacred waterhole during a mortuary ritual. The singing concerns the *dua* moiety Land of the Dead to which the deceased's spirit will eventually go. Yirrkalla (1947)

Man on *djebalmandji*, forked stick, calling sacred invocations: Milingimbi (late 1930s)
(photo: courtesy H. Shepherdson)

and McCarthy, 1948, 1957*a*, illustrate a number of these.) One of the commonest examples is a conical headdress tipped with feathers and a *wanigi*, or *waninga*. Some *wanigi* are quite complicated. Davidson (1937: 84-7) calls them 'thread crosses'. In their simplest form they consist of string (of human hair, or animal fur) wound, web-style, around two sticks crossed at right angles. Some are decorated with bird down, feathers or grasses; and they have various totemic meanings. (See, for example, McCarthy, 1948: 31.) The simple crosses are either held in the hands or attached to a headdress. The taller variety, constructed on the basis of four or more sticks—two or more horizontal sticks forming, for instance, a double cross—is held or tied behind the back of an actor who postures with it. (Basedow, 1918: Plate XIX.) Others have a framework of four crossed sticks, leaving in the middle an open square wound about with twine, through which an actor's head is thrust: the lower horizontal bar is held between the teeth. Or the basis of the twine arrangement may be a wreath-like pad around which sticks are placed at intervals.

Ground drawings seem to be largely confined to Central Australia, although they appear in other parts as well. Spencer and Gillen (1938: 179-83), and Spencer (1928: Figs. 291, 297-308, 336), have excellent illustrations of these. Mainly they are the work of the Aranda and Waramunga tribes, but one of us (R. M. Berndt) has seen very similar ground drawings in the Victoria River country. They are made by smoothing out a piece of ground, hardened and dampened with water, and covering it with a layer of red or yellow ochre, or both, on which white and black are superimposed. The design is marked out first, then sprinkled with blood; and upon this white and red feathered down is arranged. Some designs are made up of small channels, completely lined with down. Strehlow (1947: Plate 4) gives a northern Aranda example where the ground, hardened with blood, is patterned with rings of down. Predominating designs are concentric circles and meandering lines, linked circles and so on. They have mythical and ritual significance: one such design may represent the country and travels of a particular being. Apart from the ground drawings as such, there are others which are simply marked out on the ground or at the side of a trench. The *ganala* of the Kunapipi is such an example: the walls of this crescent-shaped trench are marked with a realistic figure of the Rainbow Snake (Rock Python), in western Arnhem Land as well as in central-western Northern Territory. Mountford (1956: 288, 404-5) mentions children's drawings on sand at Yirrkalla, in north-eastern Arnhem Land, and Barrett and Croll (1943) note some for the Wessels.

While flat sacred boards preponderate over the greater part of

Aboriginal Australia, with some notable exceptions, in Arnhem Land the most sacred objects are poles, posts, slabs of wood, stylized and naturalistic objects, beautifully carved and decorated with ochred designs and often hung with feathered tassels. These perform virtually the same function as the *tjurunga* and flat boards: they are variations on a common theme—but much more complex. In western Arnhem Land the *maraiin* rituals provide ample opportunity for the use of sacred objects of totemic significance. Spencer (1914: 150-2, 183-92, 210-27) illustrates some of these. (See also R. and C. Berndt, 1951*a*: 138-9.) There are ornately decorated poles hung with feathered strings; skilfully shaped wooden figures of birds, animals, and fish, vividly painted in ochres; objects of bound grass; painted stones and lumps of hard beeswax. Many represent parts of the human body: a subincised penis showing the urethra, for example (Berndt, 1952*b*). Others 'are' slices of turtle meat, crocodile tongues, emu hearts, wallaby livers, snakes' eggs, and so on. The more durable are stored in the bush, in rock shelters, or in sacred dilly bags. Yet others are made especially for the occasion and afterward destroyed. Some of Spencer's illustrations show both realistic and highly conventionalized wooden figures of turtles, fish, birds, snakes and yams, decorated with ochred designs, some with feathers; the painted stones all represent eggs and various yams. Mountford (1956: 460-6) also illustrates a few.

Spencer (1914: 227) draws a distinction between these *maraiin* and the Central Australian *tjurunga.* The *maraiin,* he suggests, are directly totemic, they represent the natural species both in shape (even though stylized) and in the designs painted upon them; the *tjurunga* are material representations of ancestral totemic beings—the stone or board is the body, the designs on it relate to the travels and adventures of that being; also, the *maraiin* are not linked to specific living persons in the same way as *tjurunga* are; they are more impersonal; the bond is with totemic groups, its individual facets not highlighted. Both, however, have mythical associations. To put it briefly, the *tjurunga* focus on persons and their place in the eternal Dreaming: the *maraiin* focus on the natural species which are part of man's social and physical environment and upon which he depends for existence.

The *maraiin* rituals Spencer describes for the Kakadu (Gagadju) are essentially the same as one of us (R. M. Berndt) has seen among the Gunwinggu and other western Arnhem Land tribes. *Maraiin* objects are brought on to the sacred ground, and there men posture with them, in some cases writhing across the ground holding them to their chests. When this has been done with all the objects in a particular sequence, they are arranged in a rough circle and the participants dance around them. According to Spencer this is a direct appeal, or demand, to the sacred representatives of the various species to provide an adequate food supply. In the Gunwinggu case this is not so obvious, although the intention is there. One of the main aims in the ritual is to cause the natural species to propagate and increase, but the performance itself is often regarded as sufficiently compelling without direct requests.

In eastern Arnhem Land the most prominent sacred objects are the *rangga*, first discussed by Warner (1937/58) and later by Elkin, Berndt and Berndt (1950); a few are illustrated by Mountford (1956). The mythical and symbolic significance of some of these has been mentioned before. (See Chapters VII and VIII.) Traditionally the main types are wooden posts and poles and shaped planks, painted in ochres, and hung with feathered strings and tassels for ritual performances.

Rangga belonging to clans and linguistic units of the *dua* moiety are nearly all associated, directly or indirectly, with the Djanggawul. One of the most important is the *djanda* pole, usually almost five feet in length, shaped and carved to represent the backbone of the goanna. The designs on it, yellow and white on a red-ochred background, represent goanna, their tracks on the sand and dust from their scraping; parakeet feathered pendants, tipped with white eaglehawk down, hang from its jungle-twine binding. Others include the *djuda* poles, which when thrust into the ground by the Djanggawul became trees with red parakeets in their branches, and the *mawulan* and *ganinjari* which they used to make waterholes and springs. These belong to the *dua* moiety *nara* rituals.

The *jiridja* moiety *rangga* are much more varied. One pole, part of the great Laindjung-Banaidja *nara* series, symbolizes fire which in the mythical period destroyed a hut on the sacred ground: the pole itself, with red-ochred apex, is a coolibah tree, its top branches bursting into flame: diamond-shaped incising on it refers to ashes and fire. Another pole is a special tree connected with the Diving Duck totem. The carved apex is the bird's head, while the main design on the barrel commemorates its adventures; a billabong and splashing water, the tree upon which it perches, the water shaken from its feathers, a fragment of seaweed which fell from its beak on to the sacred site. Another pole is an octopus, the pendant lengths its tentacles.

There are many other designs too. Large planks with shaped tops represent, in realistic or conventionalized form, the sun, various birds, human figures, stones and so on, each an integral part of a myth, a section of which is painted on the plank itself. (See R. Berndt, 1962*a*.) Some objects used as head decorations are made of bound paperbark, with a knotted pattern of indigenous fibre to form diamonds which are painted in red, white, black and yellow:

they taper gradually to a point: the design on them represents burning paperbark trees (diamond shapes), the red ochre the fire, and the black the ashes. Other secondary *rangga* resemble the western Arnhem Land *maraiin*: they include yams, complete with feathered strings (the creepers), buds, leaves and flowers; tortoise, turtle, barramundi, emu, dugong, echidna, human genitalia, and ceremonial clapping sticks. In addition, the special drone pipes used in the Wawalag cycle of rituals, symbolizing the Julunggul python, are hung with pendants and painted with sacred references to the Wawalag myth. They range from about four to seven or even fifteen feet: the largest are carried on the shoulders of three or four men. And in eastern as in western Arnhem Land there are *uwar* and *ubar* drums or gongs, here painted with designs and sometimes hung with feathered pendants.

Carved human figures in wood

Carved human figures in the round are, today, a particular feature of eastern Arnhem Land. They were first reported and discussed by R. and C. Berndt (1948, 1949), R. Berndt (1948*b*), Elkin, Berndt and Berndt (1950: 48-60). In 1926-9 at Milingimbi, in the Crocodile Islands, Warner obtained a stylized human figure in the shape of a mortuary post. Some time prior to 1938 Chaseling collected a similar one; and in 1946, on a beach at Milingimbi, one of us (R. M. Berndt) found another. In 1946-7 we collected a series of such figures at Yirrkalla, not far from Cape Arnhem, ranging in treatment from the simple post type to the fully carved figure, with or without arms. Other figures were later brought back from the same region by Mountford (1956). It is highly likely that the post figures are traditional, and legs and arms a fairly recent development. Briefly, such figures are used (1) on graves and during mortuary rituals; (2) in certain religious rituals, when they are held during dancing, or used as standing posts; and (3) in what are known as the *wuramu* 'collection' ceremonies, when a *wuramu* figure is carried through the camp, its feathered string arms embracing and seizing any goods not securely hidden away. It is probable, too, that Macassan contact had much to do with the development of the human post-figure tradition on this coast.

Some of the sacred figures are treated in the same way as the *rangga*—the Wawalag Sisters, for example. Their bodies, carved in the round, are red-ochred, incised and painted in black, yellow and white. The elder sister's breasts are drooping to suggest that she has borne a child: other designs signify afterbirth and menstrual blood. The younger sister wears a string *maidga* girdle (shaped something like a harness) and a pubic covering.

On the *jiridja* side, a figure of Laindjung is particularly impressive. Under a thatch of black human hair his face is white from the foam which clung to it as he emerged from the water at Blue Mud Bay: at each corner of the mouth are parakeet feathers, bunched together with beeswax and stuck into the wood, as a moustache. A feathered ornament extending from the chin is the beard, and a red-ochred band extends from ear to ear across the nose—a customary facial decoration for men dancing in these sacred rituals. On his left arm Laindjung wears a parakeet-feathered armband, and the main trunk is painted with totemic patterns which he distributed to the various *jiridja* clans and linguistic groups. Most of them derive, it is said, from the dried saltwater marks seen on a man's body after coming out of the sea. Another figure is Banaidja, son of Laindjung, with a massive neck supporting a comparatively small head; except for his sacred chest design, he is completely red-ochred. Some of the more recent images of Laindjung are included among the *rangga* which serve as the 'symbols' of an adjustment movement at Elcho Island. They are partly stylized, to conform with the traditional, wholly conventionalized, plank *rangga*. The body is the plank itself, with two prongs at the top and bottom, one pair representing outstretched arms, the other legs. In more realistic examples the upright prongs have become arms, the face is delicately carved, and so are the genitalia, while the legs remain stylized. In all cases the main trunk is painted with sacred patterns referring to the Laindjung myth. The specimens now in the University of Western Australia are approximately six feet high. (One, particularly interesting, shows Laindjung in his female manifestation.)

In addition, there are representations of spirit beings. More or less typical are two figures of Guldana (Kultana), associated with the *jiridja* moiety Land of the Dead. The female has no arms: her body, face and part of the legs are painted in vertical bands of red, black, yellow and white, depicting the rain streaming down her: a shoulder length fringe of yellow bark fibre tied around her head is her hair. Her husband, slightly smaller, bears the same design. Of other *jiridja* moiety figures, the *wuramu* are not used only in 'collection' ceremonies; they often have mortuary significance. Our examples include stylized posts as well as realistic carved figures. One is a Dutchman seen at Macassar, complete with hat, round white disc representing a medal, chin-strap, and black rimmed glasses; the body design has diagonally-crossing lines, edged with yellow to form a chest band, and a white disc for a buckle or button; a belt, pistol and knife are shown; the genital organs are carved, but white lines on a red-ochred background signify the hem of short trousers. Another figure is a 'Macassan'; the head has a fez, the body a shoulder strap on a background of the conventional *wuramu* 'cloth' design, traditionally connected with early 'Macassan' trade along this coast; the genitals are carved, but black trousers are indicated too.

Mountford (1958: 118-21) illustrates some full-length human figures from Bathurst and Melville islands: these have undoubtedly been derived directly from the mortuary posts.

Other figures and heads

Wooden figure carving in eastern Arnhem Land has been extended to include heads of mythical and quasi-historical characters. Some have been illustrated in Elkin, Berndt and Berndt (1950: 58-60): typical examples are heads of the spirit Guldana, of a 'Macassan', and of a Japanese. The design painted on the Guldana head represents running water, heavy rain, and clouds: a drawing on one side of the neck is a human ghost coming to Guldana after death. The 'Macassan' head is painted in red ochre, and incised; across the forehead are bands of vertical lines—*dal* or power, referring here to thoughts and ideas, each represented by a line; across the bridge of the nose, on the cheeks, below the mouth and on the neck are maggots crawling from the head after death. The design on the Japanese head is the conventional cloth pattern, an incised and painted triangular motif in red, white, black, and yellow, which in this case signifies also clouds and rain. There are also wooden substitute skulls painted with totemic designs, some stylized, others realistic. Mountford (1956: 439-43, Plates 139, 140) gives similar examples. Petri (Frobenius Institute, 1957: Plates 1 and 2) illustrates two remarkable heads from the Njangomada (Pilbara district, Western Australia). One is of stone, partly shaped, painted, and marked with 'hair', the other of carved wood. Petri illustrates too a small human figure from the Mandjildjara tribe: some of these people have come into the Port Hedland area from the Western Desert.

Warner (1937/58) mentions images used for sorcery in eastern Arnhem Land. At Yirrkalla in 1946 we collected simple human figures of paperbark bound together and tied with fibre; these, called *bi,* were used in sorcery. Other paperbark figures, representing children, are placed beside a corpse. Mountford (1956: 443-4, Fig. 65) mentions these too, as does Worms (1942*a*: Fig. 6). In the latter case they are used in *Goranara* (*gurangara*) rituals. (See Chapter VIII.) In western Arnhem Land, *djuandjuan* 'stick' figures of paperbark or bound fibre and twine are set up near a platform or grave after a death: one arm points to the corpse, the other in the direction of the new camp to which people have moved.

Wax and clay figures

Some small figures moulded from wild beeswax are also used for sorcery in eastern Arnhem Land. There are images of men, women, or even children, either plain, or painted with the victim's clan pattern, or covered with white eaglehawk or seagull feathers. Others represent mythical characters connected with the victim in some way. Still other small wax figures are used for a very different purpose—love magic: a series collected from this region shows figures in various positions of coitus. Others are of small animals: echidna, dugong, mice, fish, tortoises and so on, as well as a penis. In addition there are sacred wax *rangga*, often hung with feathered strings and pendants, shown to postulants in the *dua* and *jiridja nara* rituals and indirectly associated with the Djanggawul and with Laindjung-Banaidja. They may be held while dancing, or carried about in men's dilly bags to help in hunting. One cylindrically moulded wax *rangga* represents wild honey and wax in a hollow tree, each section having a special name. Another has an incised and ochred design between two raised ridges, signifying mangrove goanna around a sacred waterhole from which bubbles rise; the barrel, its sides flattened, forms a slightly tapering rectangle—a fish-trap made by the Djanggawul Sisters. McCarthy (1948: 51) illustrates three small figures of a kangaroo, turtle, and goanna from Arnhem Land; Mountford (1956: 445) writes of two human figures and several wax creatures (an emu, queen fish, dugong, turtle, bandicoot, kangaroo, night bird and a fish).

Adam (1954: 163) illustrates three clay figures modelled by Djaru men near Hall's Creek (East Kimberley): a rider on horseback, an emu, and a horse. These, however, were not traditional. Interesting too are clay heads and busts from western Arnhem Land, moulded from white or red ochre and used for sorcery. (Berndt, 1951*d*: 350-3.) The face is shaped roughly to resemble the victim, and the finished product is sung over. Some are lightly incised on the surface to indicate forehead hair, beard, breast designs, and so on. An artist takes approximately a day to mould such a head, and then leaves it in the sun to dry.

Pole structures

Within this division are the massive *jelmalandji* used in Kunapipi rituals throughout Arnhem Land, the Roper River region and the central-west of the Territory. (R. Berndt, 1951*a*.) On the eastern and central coast of Arnhem Land they are about fifteen to twenty-five feet high, and about two and a half feet wide at the centre. The basis is a solid pole, around which pads of grass and paperbark are tied with twine. This outer bark covering is smeared with arm blood and red ochre, and birds' down or wild cotton stuck on to this in a meandering pattern symbolizing Julunggul, the Rock Python or Rainbow. The pole itself, tipped with a bunch of white cockatoo feathers, is the Python which swallowed the Wawalag at the sacred site of Muruwul. Usually two such structures are used (see Berndt, 1951*a*: Plate VIII), placed alongside the crescent shaped *ganala* trench: the second represents the *gulwiri* (wild coconut) palm. In the central west of the Territory the *jelmalandji* are said to represent both the Fertility Mother, Gadjeri or Kunapipi, and the Rainbow Snake; one such structure there had pearlshell eyes, and other decorations.

The *tnatantja* pole (or *nurtunja*) of the northern Aranda is a further example. The most usual type has a basis of from one to twenty spears, around which long bunches of grass are bound by means of hair girdles; rings of feather down are superimposed, stuck on with blood: occasionally a few *tjurunga* are suspended from it, and the apex is decorated with eaglehawk feathers. The feather down design varies. Spencer and Gillen illustrate some, with details of the relevant rituals. (1938: 253-5, 298-300, 345-6, 360-4, 627, particularly Figs. 63, 64, 68, 81, 82.) Strehlow (1947: 23-5 *et passim*) also discusses these poles: one, of the bandicoot totem, is covered with alternate lines of red and white down, stuck on with blood. The myth he records in connection with it tells of the experiences of the bandicoot ancestor: ". . . a great *tnatantja* was swaying above him. This *tnatantja* had sprung from the midst of the bed of purple flowers which grew over the soak of Ilbalintja. . . . It was a living creature, covered with a smooth skin like the skin of a man. . . ." (Strehlow, 1947: 7.) In another, the lines of down represent roots of the wattle trees among which ancestral women dig for ants. (Spencer and Gillen, 1938: 325.) Also among the Aranda is the *kauaua* ritual pole, which must be cut down and brought into camp without being allowed to touch the ground. (Spencer and Gillen, 1938: 364, 370, 629; Strehlow, 1947: 77, 111.) It is smeared all over with human blood, or red ochre as a substitute. Because the top of the *kauaua* represents a human head, it is adorned in the same way that postulants are.

In northern Australia generally, posts and poles are used in many rituals and ceremonies, sacred and non-sacred. In western Arnhem Land, for instance, are the sacred forked poles, often decorated, on to which men, sometimes women, climb to call invocations: the *djebalmandji* of the Kunapipi is one variety. Other poles and hollow logs appear in mortuary ceremonies all along the north coast of the Territory. The grave posts, or *bugamani* poles, of Bathurst and Melville islands are both large and heavy, some up to eighteen feet long. (Basedow, 1913; Spencer, 1914: 230-9; Mountford, 1958, 60-121.) Several such poles are erected around a grave, not as a memorial (according to Mountford), but as a 'gift to the dead'. They vary in shape, in decoration, and in the designs painted on the trunks; and Mountford reports almost total absence of any reference to myths and to totemic localities. The upper parts of these poles have been identified as 'forks or limbs of trees, women's breasts, rocks, windows and doors'; others are in the shape of human figures. Our own information suggests that the majority of pole-shapes are highly conventionalized representations of human beings, and this seems plausible when they are compared with the human figures collected by Mountford (1958: Plates 36-41).

Eastern Arnhem Land has decorated poles like the *dua* moiety Morning Star, *banumbir,* and the *jiridja* moiety 'Macassan' mast. (See Warner, 1937/58: 412-49; Elkin, Berndt and Berndt, 1950: 92-100.) The first has already been described. The second is a replica of a Malay prau mast; symbolically, the living bid the departing spirit a final goodbye, just as the 'Macassan' traders used to erect their masts and spread their sails before leaving the Australian mainland to return home. There are also bark coffins painted with the dead person's clan designs. (See Chapter XIII.) In the final mortuary rite, when the bones have been collected and cleaned and rubbed with red ochre they are put into a long hollow log, resting on one or two forked sticks: its mouth is cut to shape, and ridges carved to the required design to symbolize some particular fish, animal, natural object or feature in the relevant mythology. To name just a few, the *dua* moiety has whale, sawfish, porpoise, shark, wild honey, snake, and stone; the *jiridja,* ship's funnel, mast, cloud, another kind of wild honey, and various fish. The log is completely red-ochred, and painted with clan designs: this is done in sections by several artists, for it may be from twelve to twenty feet long. One word for it is *laragidj*; after the final ritual it is left to stand in the main camp, the bones inside it, until it falls apart. Similar log coffins are made in western Arnhem Land. (Elkin, 1954: plate opposite p. 254 shows one in use at South Goulburn Island.)

Other objects

In spite of what is often said about the paucity of Aboriginal material culture, so many items could come into this category that it is quite impossible even to list them all here.

Decorated baobab nuts in the north-western Kimberleys, used as rattles in ceremonies, are incised and painted so that their designs stand out in bold contrast to the natural brown colour of the dried nut and the lighter colour of the under surface. The designs themselves are quite varied: geometrical figures as well as naturalistic turtles, snakes, birds, plants, leaves and so on. (Davidson, 1937: 63-5; McCarthy, 1948: 51.)

The incised pearlshells are outstanding. Most, although not all, come from the Kimberley coast and find their way (via the medium of trade routes) to far distant places in southern Australia, the Victoria River district, Central Australia, and Darwin. (Davidson, 1937: 60-3; McCarthy, 1939*a*: 92-8; Mountford and Harvey, 1938: 115-35). The wholly traditional designs are mainly geometric, but there are also many realistic animals, and so on; and these days Roman Catholic symbols, horses, windmills, and stockmen's boots are common. They are worn as pendants or pubic tassels, sometimes only by fully initiated men; sometimes given to novices after circumcision; or used by native doctors and sorcerers, or for ceremonial decoration. Incised shells are used in the Cape York area too.

Here and there over the Australian Continent are some unique developments, not specifically variations on a common theme. An example of this is the *toa* associated with the Dieri and other adjacent and neighbouring tribes in the Lake Eyre region (South Australia). According to Stirling and Waite each *toa* represents and "serves as an indicator or sign-post to some particular locality": "their shape, colours, patterns or appendages depict, realistically or ideographically", conspicuous or peculiar features of the relevant localities: they refer also to the mythical wanderings of certain *muramura*. (See Chapter VII.) When a person leaves his camp he prepares a *toa* to indicate the place he is making for, so that anyone seeing it will know where to find him. (Stirling and Waite, 1919: 105-55, Plates XI-XX.) These writers record 322 examples, each called by a particular place name, and each differing from others in design and shape; the collection is now in the South Australian Museum.

Then there are the painted skulls of north-central Arnhem Land. A few have been illustrated by McCarthy (1948: 44), Elkin, Berndt and Berndt (1950), Mountford (1956: 316), McCarthy (1957*a*: 157). Such a skull is carried about by close relatives of a dead person, either thrown over the back as a kind of necklet when travelling, or hung in the camp or on an adjacent tree: it is usually red-ochred, and the top painted with the appropriate design. After a year or so it is deposited either in the waterhole from which the dead person's spirit came before birth, or in a cave.

Another object peculiar to Arnhem Land is the 'Macassan' pipe, from one to four feet long, and usually made from the pithy stem of the *lungin* (pipe) bush. It is scraped clean and smooth, the mouthpiece tapered and ridged, and the whole covered with red ochre. Then the barrels are incised, often in fine and careful workmanship, with sacred or secular patterns like those on the bark paintings. The ordinary everyday pipe is an incised decorated cylinder. But some, made from wood, are carved to represent sacred *rangga*, such as the Goanna Tail emblem associated with the Djanggawul; others, smaller copies of the 'Macassan' mast pole used in mortuary rituals, are made only for presentation to a close relative or friend leaving his home camp. Pipes shaped as sacred *rangga*, or bearing sacred designs, are always wrapped up when men are smoking them in the main camp. (Elkin, Berndt and Berndt, 1950, and Mountford, 1956: 389-400 give illustrations.) In addition, there are painted headbands, spearthrowers, paddles, clapping sticks, dancing posts, bobbins, spears, boomerangs, clubs, and such things as the wooden anchors and birds' heads designed for love magic.

Bathurst and Melville islands are as rich in material culture as the Arnhem Land coast, but even less characteristically Aboriginal. Much of it bears little resemblance to anything on the mainland. Spencer has some illustrations (1914: Plates I, VIII, IX, XXIX, XXX, XXXI, XXXII, XXXIII, and text), Mountford others (1958: 97-8, Plate 31). Initiation regalia include belts made of alternate panels of human hair and banyan bark string, their edges sewn with split cane: loops at each end, covered with wax, are whitened with pipeclay, and the whole painted with a conventional design. There are red-ochred cane back-pendants: a stick bent into a semicircle with a horizontal bar painted and decorated with abrus seeds; or an elaborate hanging pendant of banyan bark strands, red seeds, and discs, terminating in a ball of light soft brown feathers. Women wear chaplets of human hair string with wild dog tail tips: or a ball pendant of feathers, stained orange from red and yellow ochres, held between the teeth when dancing. And there are painted bark mortuary armlets with projecting decorations of feathers and sometimes red seeds, as well as discs, painted and decorated, held in mortuary dancing, and intricately carved and ornamented male and female spears, made, as Mountford notes, as gifts to the dead.

Another rather unusual feature, this time mostly from the south and east of Australia, is tree-carving. Best known, perhaps, is the type which is fairly widespread in New South Wales and adjacent Queensland. (Davidson, 1937; McCarthy, 1948: 24-5.) These dendroglyphs, as they are called, have received special attention from Etheridge (1918) and Elkin. They were used in initiation rites, and as grave posts; the designs were of mythical significance. Typical examples have geometric as well as curvilinear patterns, cut into the wood and framed, as it were, in a long oval of natural bark. Eylmann (1908: Plate 17) shows human and animal figures, crocodiles, and goanna on trees near the Daly River, Northern Territory: carving on a baobab tree on the Victoria River is sketched by Dahl (1926: 181, Fig. 5). At Jigalong (near Lake Disappointment, in Western Australia) a tree with a lively carving of a spirit was recorded and photographed in 1957.

Then there are shields, varying in overall shape and in patterning, painted or incised, or both. Davidson (1937: 33-46) and McCarthy (1948: 16, 17, 18, 25, 27-30) illustrate some. Several types can readily be distinguished. The Western Desert type is found over most of western South Australia and Western Australia, excluding the upper part of the Kimberleys. Essentially, the basic theme is a zigzag (sets of vertical lines with a central panel of diagonal lines). Within this same area are other designs too: concentric circles, for instance, or a herring-bone pattern. The Kimberley type is mainly plain or with a fluted face, but some specimens are painted. Most of these are spear shields; but in the area around Broome are parrying shields—also found in the south-west of Western Australia, and commonly in south-eastern Australia. In some regions, such as north-eastern Arnhem Land, no shields are used. In others, such as the Daly River, fighting or parrying sticks may take their place. Central Australian type shields are found over a wide area. One was recently obtained at Balgo, in the southern Kimberleys. They are broad and fluted, painted with designs, and on ritual occasions decorated with feather down. (See Spencer and Gillen, 1938: 584-8.) Some, illustrated by McCarthy (1948: 29), have designs of fish and snakes. The Queensland shield types are perhaps the most remarkable: most are fairly wide, with vivid ochred designs. (Davidson, 1937: 38-41, 46; McCarthy, 1948: 25, 27, 28-9; McConnel, 1935*a*.) The Gulmari shields are highly stylized, while those of north-eastern Queensland are large oval pieces of wood painted with bands of many patterns: some of the motifs are (from McConnel) 'axes, boomerangs, leaves of the tree from which the shield was made, bark water-bag, various leaves, bean pods and seeds, grubs, fish, stars, rainbow' and so on. Roth (1897: Plate XXI) and Davidson (1937: 40) have other illustrations.

The bark and wooden shields of eastern and south-eastern Australia represent a collective type, which can be further subdivided. The broad heavy bark shield of the Lower River Murray has a design of single or two or three concentric arcs, extending toward the centre of the shield but not overlapping. Shields from Adelaide, Victoria and New South Wales are gracefully 'bow-shaped'. (Davidson, 1937: McCarthy, 1948.) They are basically of three sub-types.

Receptacles or bags are used extensively throughout the Continent. In the desert areas of the centre and north wooden dishes are common, but not usually decorated, although some are smeared roughly. A few (illustrated by Davidson, 1937: 48) bear ochred designs, as among the Wadaman of the Northern Territory, although these would hardly have lasted long if the dishes were in everyday use. In the Kimberleys as well as at Bathurst and Melville islands, bark containers are used. (Davidson, 1937: 51-2; McCarthy, 1948: 39; Spencer, 1914: Plates XXV, XXXIV, XXXV; Mountford, 1958.)

These last are embellished with vivid and highly stylized patterns. The specially treated bark is bent double, the sides sewn with split cane, and a coating of wax or resin added so that it will hold water. Among the Gunwinggu of western Arnhem Land baskets are made of fresh green palm leaves, carefully folded, the end of the stalk tucked in and loose ends sewn. Some are decorated. There are rough paperbark baskets too.

More durable, and calling for more skill, are coiled and twined baskets. The first are, traditionally speaking, made only in the south-east and east of Australia, such as along the Lower River Murray. The second are common in the Northern Territory, particularly in Arnhem Land; but also (according to Davidson, 1937: 53) from the Kimberleys to the central coast of Queensland, and formerly in New South Wales, Victoria and Tasmania. The Arnhem Land baskets are decorated: Spencer (1914: 381-6 and plates) illustrates some from the western side. They differ from one another in shape, and the designs range from simple bands to geometric forms and stylized human figures: some are hung with feathered pendants, or the feathers are worked into the bags as part of the design. In eastern Arnhem Land decorated pandanus baskets, or bags, are used by both men and women. (Elkin, Berndt and Berndt, 1950: 103-6.) Men's sacred baskets have an overstitching of pandanus fibre and red parakeet feathers or white down, depending on the moiety, woven or stuck in as part of the patterning. Human hair may be stitched on and outlined with feathers, or possum fur twine arranged as an edging for a band of diamonds. Two or more pendants of feathered string may be attached, some having joints or knobs of beeswax encasing their owners' foreskins or those of close relatives. These 'spirit' bags, as they are called, are highly valued, and are made ritually on the sacred ground to the accompaniment of special songs. Women's baskets also have designs, both conventionalized and naturalistic, of mythical significance: for instance, one has a design in white, red and black on a yellow background signifying seaweed lying on the beach near the sacred site of the Turtle Man. Another shows two mangrove goannas, horizontal lines representing their tracks, a broad red vertical band a large tidal river flowing among the mangroves, and vertical yellow lines small tidal creeks.

There are also 'knitted' bags, as in the central west of the Territory. Spencer (1914: 388-9) mentions some for women and men in western Arnhem Land: men use the ball-like fighting bag, worn around the neck with the string long enough so that the ball can be gripped tightly between the teeth during fighting, or other times of stress or excitement. These bags are used in eastern Arnhem Land too, as an alternative to a beard or a spirit bag: horizontal bands are a common design. There are also net bags (see Davidson,

1933), widely used in the north of the Continent, but usually with no decoration apart from occasional feathers, or a banded appearance.

Finally, there are message sticks. (Roth, 1897: 136-8, Plate XVIII; Howitt, 1904: 691-710; Spencer and Gillen 1938: 141-2; Davidson, 1937: 108-10; Mountford, 1956: 466-75; 1958: 98-107.) An Aboriginal message stick does not consist of writing, as a set of agreed-upon symbols which can be interpreted by itself, but in most cases is sent with a messenger who explains its meaning. The design or marks on the stick, usually a small flat slab of wood or a cylinder tapering at both ends, may help to identify the messenger and so validate his communication. Roth gives a variety of examples; so does Howitt, pointing out that the marks are an aid to memory, or a tally. The message sticks from Arnhem Land discussed by Mountford have vertical, horizontal and diagonal lines, diamond patterns and so on, with human figures: like those from western Arnhem Land, most refer specifically to economic transactions, and are accompanied by verbal messages. Ceremonial message sticks, in contrast, are distinctively shaped, bearing sacred designs, or take the form of *rangga* emblems, sometimes hung with feathered pendants and sometimes made of hard beeswax. Mostly they refer to approaching rituals, or to ceremonial trade relations. Those on Bathurst and Melville islands are perhaps a little more elaborately carved, but also usually constitute an invitation to a ceremony or to a mortuary rite—or notification of a death.

* * * * *

COMMUNICATION AND STYLE

Apart from the matter of aesthetic appeal, all art—songs and poetic expression, oral literature, dancing and dramatic performances, visual manifestations—is a medium through which messages and ideas are communicated. The way in which this is done and the form it takes vary as between one Aboriginal society and another. Generally speaking, the range of expected participants or audience or spectators is a limiting factor: attempts are made to say something to certain people—to women and to children, to all those of a specific social unit, to initiated persons only, to those of a particular age and status, and so on. It may be designed for one or more of these categories, although it may be understood by others within limited degrees.

In Aboriginal Australia, as we have seen, a man does not paint or carve simply for enjoyment or self-expression. He does it with a purpose in mind, and what he does will need to be understood by some other persons. Certain limitations are inevitable. Most noticeable are the techniques and the materials available. But, in addition, there are the traditional modes of expression which must be taken into account—just how an object, creature, or human being must be depicted, and for that matter what can or should be presented in visual form. In other words, there are certain agreed-upon ways of doing things. Realistic and naturalistic representations are widespread throughout the Continent—even in Central Australia, where conventionalization is a major emphasis: moreover they are present contemporaneously, one alongside the other. One does not necessarily preclude the other. But stylization is probably more general.

Much Aboriginal art is not uniform in quality: it is difficult to assess, or evaluate. Some Aboriginal productions are mere daubs, not intended as anything more than this by the people responsible for them. Some are rough drawings and carvings depicting distorted creatures and human beings, with ill-formed bodies and limbs. These cannot really be classified as artistic examples. Where we have a large series of one particular art form, we are in a much better position to evaluate qualitatively—a series of stone *tjurunga* or wooden boards, of Bathurst or Melville islands grave posts, of bark paintings from eastern or western Arnhem Land, and so on: these provide clues for this purpose.

The same problem must be faced in examining poetic songs, oral literature and dancing, and dramatic performances. Like graphic art, these are means of communicating ideas and values, often through symbolic statements. It is not that Aborigines are more mythically-inclined, or think only in these terms; it is simply that these are areas of culture in which we can expect to find this kind of expression.

Most important is the question of style in relation to the aesthetic forms mentioned here. All art, naturalistic or stylized, whatever its particular medium, is an abstraction from reality— from the empirical situation. It is a statement about something, expressed in a specific way; and these ways vary, as do languages and other aspects of culture generally. But within a particular society, although variation takes place through time as well as through the impact of others, an art style (using the term 'art' broadly) may provide a key to its value orientations.

As far as graphic art or the 'language of objects' is concerned, this is a fascinating field which has been little explored in Aboriginal Australia. It might be suggested, for instance, that the differences between western and eastern Arnhem Land bark painting correspond to other, less immediately obvious, differences in social organization and in values generally. (See Berndt, 1958*b*.) In broad terms, as compared with the east, there is a more obvious directness in the west, a dislike for detail except where it has direct relevance, as in treatment of the central figure of a design, or in an X-ray drawing. Greater preciseness in language and in kinship terminology, lack of involved symbolism, co-exist here with naturalism in art style, movement and action in representation, and a straightforward approach to the subject, unhampered by a crowded setting in which it might be in danger of losing to some extent its individual identity. There is a certain degree of 'fit' between the social and cultural context and style in each of these cases. More than this needs to be said, of course; and although there are pitfalls as well as rewards in such an enquiry, the topic deserves more careful scrutiny than it has so far received.

But contrasting and complementary art styles may exist side by side in one region at the same time (the X-ray, sorcery and *maraiin* art of western Arnhem Land, for instance), or over a period (as in the case of cave paintings and carvings in western Arnhem Land, the Kimberleys and elsewhere). While we would not expect to isolate a separate style for each tribal or linguistic unit, except in a sketchy or superficially plausible way, it is possible to speak of broad culture areas encompassing a number of such units in Aboriginal Australia; but within these further, and perhaps more subtle, differences may be distinguished. Identifying culture areas on the basis of aesthetic expression, especially in the preliminary stages of such an enquiry, need not mean that all social units so classified are similar in all other respects. It is important not to consider only outward expression, or appearance. Similar designs in two or more widely separated or even adjacent areas cannot necessarily be taken to be the same, or to mean the same to the people concerned; and this is particularly the case with highly conventionalized representations. There is so such thing as universal symbolism in Aboriginal Australia. The closest approach to it is the spread of some religious cults, diffusing key concepts through symbols which may be identified by postulants over extensive areas (for example, the Kunapipi and its core of basic ritual). The rule is, mostly, local identification, especially for visual art forms.

For oral literature and poetic songs there is the same question of style or the structure of presentation, and the context of ideas: ways of saying things, choice of vocabulary, and so on. But beyond statements about obvious differences between, for example, the long songs of eastern Arnhem Land and the short succinct ones of Central Australia, there has been little systematic analysis in this direction; and this is true too as far as story-telling and mythology are concerned. Any discussion of style here would involve detailed treatment of language and dialect, both structurally and semantically.

Art style offers one sort of key to the broad patterning of social relations and their cultural content. In one respect, we could view art style as a kind of shorthand summary of the particular society and culture in which it flourishes.

CHAPTER XIII

Death and the Afterlife

Death, the final crisis of the life cycle, is almost everywhere in Aboriginal Australia associated with some ritual. Apart from anything else there is the disposal of the body to be considered—and the reorientation of the family, and to a lesser extent of other social units, which have lost a member. Almost everywhere, too, there is a linkage, explicit or otherwise, with religion. There is the question of a person's spiritual essence, or soul. The mortuary rites which normally take place after the death of an Aboriginal, although they seem to focus on his material remains, are nearly always most vitally concerned with his spirit and what will become of it. They are designed to help it, directly or indirectly, to adjust itself to changed circumstances—and to keep it away from the living.

The inevitability of death is emphasized in myth. In the beginning, people say, during the mythological or Dreaming era, something could have been done about it: but now it is too late. Someone who lived in that period took a fatal step, and set a precedent for all time. This does not mean that people voluntarily take measures to hasten on the event where they themselves are concerned. There seems to be no evidence of suicide in purely traditional situations. The nearest approximations to it are these: (*a*) Loss of will to live, on learning that one has been selected as a sorcery victim. There has been, to date, no systematic study of this phenomenon in Aboriginal Australia. (*b*) Deliberate self-exposure to danger for a variety of reasons. In local terms such a person might be regarded as under the influence of sorcery, in other words, of pressures outside his control. (*c*) Mythological examples from western Arnhem Land when one of the characters deliberately breaks a tabu stone or performs a forbidden action, for the specific purpose of bringing about the destruction of others as well as himself. Generally speaking, (*a*) and (*b*) might be viewed as examples of compulsive suicide: the other (*c*) is not common in Aboriginal Australia and there are no contemporary cases available. In that area, western Arnhem Land, people sometimes talk about taking this step, but only in a figurative or exaggerated way: in some 'Gossip' songs (see Chapter XI) a person threatens to commit suicide if he is jilted, or declares that he (or she) 'might die' from brooding about an absent sweetheart. In many parts of the Continent certain cases of elopement, or of flagrant disregard for the proprieties, may be 'suicidal'; they may be carried out in full awareness of the inevitable, or almost inevitable, consequences. Since there is an element of chance, the possibility that the persons concerned may get away with it, this cannot be regarded as direct self-destruction and therefore it is not, properly speaking, suicide: but it is very close to it.

Certain risks, of course, are inherent in everyday living in this physical and cultural environment. Droughts account for some deaths, especially in the deserts. Floods account for others, especially on the northern coasts and rivers—or drowning, as in eastern Arnhem Land, where people have often tried to cross rough waterways in frail bark canoes as well as in larger or more solid dugouts. Apart from old age, and from deliberately inflicted injuries in the course of fights, illness and accident take more toll in a situation where medical treatment is elementary and based to a large extent on magical knowledge. And European contact, bringing new and more efficient medical skills, has introduced also new hazards in the way of disease. But in any case, there are varying degrees of human intervention. At the one extreme, independent of human agency, are deaths caused by such Acts of God as lightning, striking suddenly to select, for no apparent reason, one person rather than another. At the other extreme, a death may result more or less directly from some human action, either purposefully designed to achieve that end, or doing so through carelessness or neglect: for instance, when a child or a blind or crippled person is allowed to stray, or a baby accidentally dropped from its carrying dish, or a new-born infant gobbled up by a dog while the midwives concentrated on its mother. (But these last two examples are very rare indeed.)

SOME SOCIAL IMPLICATIONS OF DEATH

Notwithstanding the expectation of a future life, a specific death is usually an upsetting event. Unless the victim is a baby too young to have made much of an impact as a separate person, it is not simply a family affair. It affects everyone living in a camp where it occurs. After it all members of the camp must, traditionally speaking, move to another site. As a man or woman lies dying his kin surround him, or watch nearby or from a distance. There may be silence or casual talk until the last breath is drawn. Or the mourners, including his wife, may wail or chant, and gash themselves on the head and on other parts of the body to draw blood, the women using stones and sharpened bones or digging sticks. Some may throw themselves on the dying person, embracing him, entreating him to remain with them. At the moment of death the wailing is intensified and taken up by others, as conventional behaviour which serves to express both genuine and simulated grief. Sometimes the chief mourners appear to reach a state of near-frenzy. This may be compounded of a reaction to the fact of death itself, both to the immediate loss and to the reminder that this can happen to anyone, and perhaps, as well, to the assumption that the malignant forces of sorcery have succeeded once again: here is proof that nobody is really safe. But nothing may be done about this until there has been time for the disturbance to calm down. We have heard accusations made immediately after a death, in the heat of the moment, and seen men grab their spears and women their digging sticks clamouring for vengeance at once. But more often a special 'inquest' takes place some time later.

The social implications of death are many. For one thing, the composition of the family unit is shattered. After the appropriate period of mourning the widow or widows must be re-allocated. The degree of choice permitted them varies a great deal. But there is usually a range of eligible men, including in many cases husbands' brothers, and if they are young and attractive or still of childbearing age they will be in some demand. A widower's case is less pressing, except that if he has no other wives and is left with young children he will probably have to remarry, or allow the children to be taken over by near relatives. Apart from this, almost any death is likely to have repercussions on all other members of the camp, particularly if there is talk of sorcery. Usually a scapegoat is sought outside the social group(s) to which the deceased belonged. But suspicion may fall on a relative who has neglected his kinship obligations, an undutiful son or daughter, an unfaithful or careless wife or a jealous husband, or on someone who had previously quarrelled with the deceased. The shadow of his death will be present until, firstly, the matter is entirely resolved and a victim chosen, or the affair dropped: and, secondly, all the subsequent rites have been performed. This could go on for a couple of years or so. Then again, as part of the mortuary sequences, there is the exchange or handing over of gifts: this economic aspect is particularly important in northern areas.

The behaviour of near kin is much the same whatever the status or the personality of the dead person, or for that matter the nature of his death. Exceptions are found in the case of newly born or premature children, or when a man or woman is killed for infringing tribal or religious 'law'. Then there may be little or nothing in the way of public mourning—in the first place because the matter is of limited interest; in the second, because any such manifestations may have been discouraged or forbidden.

Not all deaths, of course, are attributed to sorcery, but in many cases it must be taken into account. Further, because a body is lost in drowning this does not mean that no mortuary rite can be held. In north-central Arnhem Land, for instance, where the skull after death may be painted with appropriate totemic designs, a wooden substitute skull may be made if the other is not available.

News of a death is communicated as soon as possible to other camps whose inhabitants may be interested, directly or in a more casual way. In some cases, this is done conventionally by special messengers (in Arnhem Land) bearing decorated emblems referring to the deceased's totemic and clan affiliations; these may be carved sticks, feathered strings, carved birds' heads, and so on. Arriving at a camp they sing at its outskirts, referring only indirectly to the dead person, to indicate his identity. Mock fights may occur between them and the deceased's relatives. When a death occurs in north-eastern Arnhem Land, no formal wailing is supposed to take place until the whole camp has been officially notified of this event by a close relative of the deceased, singing his special clan songs. As Warner (1937/58: 415) puts it, 'after the first wailing a stillness comes over the camp, and it is at this time that people express the desire to retaliate: a near relative throws a spear on the ground, to indicate that the death will be avenged.'

In most areas, traditionally, the name of a newly dead person may not be spoken except in unusual circumstances. In some the tabu remains in force for years, and words in ordinary speech which resemble any of his personal names may be dropped from the language. Generally, however, they are not forgotten. They may persist in a sacred context, such as a song, and re-appear in a generation or so. Personal names, except for nicknames, are mostly inherited through the paternal (occasionally maternal) line, or associated with particular myths or particular localities; they are not usually invented.

The living are subjected to other restraints and prohibitions, too, in consequence of a death. People who have been closely associated with the dead person are expected to observe various tabus, relating to food, to remarriage, to a period of silence in the case of a Dieri widow, who must rely on hand signs until the end of her mourning. (Siebert, 1910.) The camp in which the death took place is abandoned or destroyed, or both; and the deceased's possessions may be formally disposed of or destroyed. This last may be associated with the preparation of the corpse—which may be painted with its 'clan' designs (eastern Arnhem Land), or smeared completely with red ochre. The hair too may be plucked and made into a hair waistband or, as in eastern Arnhem Land, into a length of parakeet-feathered string which is then regarded as a sacred *rangga*. In some areas, as on the Adelaide and Daly rivers, a dead person's goods are publicly burned. This happens in western Arnhem Land too. The Maung of Goulburn Islands have fairly elaborate rites for cleansing the widow, or widower. Clothing and minor possessions are destroyed by fire, in a specially prepared hole in the ground; but good clothes are kept, after they have been ritually washed in the same hole, with the same water, that the widow(er) uses during the cleansing sequence. The hole is later filled in with earth to form a mound, a pole erected on it, and nobody permitted to set foot there for an unspecified period.

Among the Yuin (south-eastern New South Wales) 'the body is wrapped in an opossum rug and articles of dress or ornament formerly owned by the dead man, but not his weapons, are placed at his head'. Among the Chepara (around Brisbane) all his possessions are buried, except for a few given to near kinsfolk. (Howitt, 1904: 462, 469 *et seq*.) Generally too a widow, more often than a widower, smears herself with faeces and clay. Roth (1897: 164), referring to the Boulia district of Queensland, speaks of widows and close relatives plastering themselves with *kopi*, a variety of gypsum, or with grease, ashes, and mud. A widow among the Dieri wears a special cap of gypsum about three-quarters of an inch thick, fitted over the head. (Horne and Aiston, 1924: Fig. 89.) Basedow (1925: 213) reports similar skull-caps on the Murray River in South Australia. In many cases a widow's hair is cut and she wears a chaplet. Among the Aranda such a chaplet is specially prepared from animal bones and locks of hair from certain relatives of the deceased; it is used in the final rites and eventually torn to pieces and put in the grave. (Spencer and Gillen, 1938: 501-9.) Apart from self-mutilation during wailing, scars may be made more conventionally on the arms and shoulders or other parts of the mourners' bodies; the position and number varies in accordance with their relationship to the dead person. Basedow mentions cutting of thighs among the Katherine River people, laceration of arms and thighs among the Laragia.

Some of the paraphernalia connected with burial and mourning rites have been mentioned in the last chapter. This aspect is particularly rich at Melville and Bathurst islands, and to a lesser extent in Arnhem Land. Apart from grave posts, there are painted skulls carried round as necklets; hanks of the deceased's hair; or mourning rings in the Western Desert. (Berndt and Harvey Johnston, 1942: 192.) Among the Kurnai of Gippsland, one or both hands are cut from the corpse and wrapped in grass and dried: this is the *bret*. (Howitt, 1904: 459-60.) Made into a necklet, it is believed to warn its wearer of approaching danger.

A corpse, especially a fresh corpse, is regarded with a mixture of fear, revulsion, and affection, the proportions varying in accordance with the closeness of kinship or other ties. The more intimate the bonds, the more intense the grief—and the more marked the ambivalence toward the remains. For a virtual stranger, or an enemy, the response is fairly straightforward, not complicated by personal involvement. For someone who has been in close and prolonged association with the deceased, readjustment is often painful, and particularly so if the break has been sudden. Spirits of the dead may appear to living relatives in dreams, offering advice or reassurance, or revealing songs, dance-steps or rites, and so on. This does not happen, as a rule, until some little time after death, in other words until the first wave of emotion has subsided and the relationship has been re-established on a revised basis. Dream messages from the spirit during the initial mourning period are likely to be of a more urgent kind, relating especially to the circumstances of the death, and the problem of 'who is to blame'.

Except in regard to the very young or the very old, or from the viewpoint of a person deliberately responsible for the killing, the impression is that any given death is unnatural: that it should not have happened, and would not have happened had it not been for some departure from the normal course of events, some active malevolence on the part of another human being. (See Chapter IX.) Yet in overall terms death is viewed as entirely natural; in a way, it is part of ordinary living. The Aborigines, as a hunting people, are well acquainted with the physical facts of death and bodily decay—of all living things, including human beings. This is something they learn in childhood, from personal observation as well as from hearsay. Children are not sheltered from experiences of this sort. Death is not the concern of adults only, or of specialists to whom the bereaved persons must delegate all the tasks connected with the corpse or the soul, or both. There is no mystery about it here. In this respect, at least, the Aborigines are realistic, however optimistic some of their other assumptions may seem. The information which children acquire about death, in the course of growing up, covers not only the material aspect, the question of the corpse as such, but also the conventional and actual ways in which the living respond to it. They learn about the appropriate social behaviour at the same time that they become familiar with the practical details.

DISPOSAL OF THE CORPSE

Where the body is available after a death, there are various customary ways of disposing of it: burial; exposure on a platform or tree; desiccation, or mummification; cremation; placing in a hollow tree; use of what could be called coffins; and burial cannibalism. These categories are not mutually exclusive. For instance, some time after burial the bones may be collected, and later reburied or carried about as relics. Or the body may be left on a platform until it has decomposed, and the bones finally placed in a hollow log or in a cave.

Desiccation

This is found in various forms over parts of northern and eastern Queensland, the Darling and Murray River basins, the Lakes district of the Lower River Murray, and the middle north of South Australia. (See Elkin, 1954: 313.) In 1941 one of us saw such a corpse as far west as Ooldea: it had presumably come from eastern Australia. In some cases the internal organs are removed through an incision, the cavity packed with grass and so on, and the body dried in the sun or over a fire. It is then bound and usually painted, carried around by mourners, and finally placed on a tree platform or in a cave—or buried, cremated, or put into a hollow tree.

The Lower River Murray and Encounter Bay people smoke-dry some of their corpses. (Taplin and Meyer, in Woods, 1879: 20-1, 198-200.) Taplin mentions that a special bier is constructed, a slow fire made under it, and the corpse arranged on it in a sitting posture with arms outstretched. When the skin blisters the hair is removed, and all body apertures are sewn up. Certain men, who hold this position by hereditary right, now attend to the smoke-drying. The corpse is rubbed with grease and red ochre and placed in the same position on a platform, this time inside a hut. It dries gradually over a slow fire, while wailing mourners with long whisks brush away the flies, eating and sleeping under or alongside the platform. Once dry, it is wrapped in a specially prepared mat and kept in the hut. Meyer notes that the corpse is placed between two fires: from these, and the heat of the sun, the skin loosens after a few days. At that point the corpse is called by the term used for Europeans, because it resembles them in colour. Meyer's description of the rest of the process is much the same as Taplin's. After it is dry the body is carried around for several months and finally left on a platform to disintegrate. Later the skull is taken by a close kinsman, and used as a drinking vessel. (Tindale, 1938; Massola, 1961.)

Howitt (1904: 467-8) reports that the Maranoa people first dry their corpses and then carry them about for a long time. The drying is done on a platform over a fire, while the juices are collected and rubbed over the bodies of young men "to impart the good qualities of the deceased to themselves". Howitt mentions too (*ibid.*, 459) that the Kurnai wrap a corpse in a possum skin rug, tie it up in a sheet of bark, then build a hut over it. Inside this the relatives gather to mourn, wailing and cutting themselves. Several days afterward the body is unwrapped and examined, and its hair plucked and preserved by close kin—father, mother or sisters. Then it is re-wrapped, and not opened again until far gone in decomposition, when the fluids are used for anointing. Sometimes the body is opened and the intestines removed to hasten the drying process. Later it is carried about until it is nothing more than "a bag of bones", then either buried or put into a hollow tree.

Roth (1907: 366-403, with plates) discusses this topic in some detail for north Queensland. (See also Harris, 1912.) On Cape York Peninsula, corpses are temporarily preserved by disembowelling and desiccation. (McConnel, 1937: 350-7.) Mourning dances follow, until the final settlement of food dues after the cremation. These food payments are made by a dead man's widow and her brothers and sisters to his brothers and sisters and father, to the accompaniment of rhythmic movements and the singing of mourning songs. On the day of the cremation, wrestling matches take place between 'brothers'. Finally the corpse is placed on a pyre, and the mourners turn their backs as it is consumed by the flames.

Fairly typical of the procedures followed in the upper parts of Cape York is the binding of a corpse, particularly of a young man, to a pole erected on two forked sticks; it may be covered with bark or exposed with a dilly bag over the head. Finally it is burned, with the exception of certain parts which are kept and carried around as relics, or eaten ritually. On the Russell River desiccation is quite an elaborate process, and the 'mummy' is ornamented. In other areas (such as Miriam Vale) it is sun-dried on a platform, and finally placed in a hollow tree through a specially cut aperture. Elkin (1954: 292-4, 313, 317) notes that 'the classic form of mummification was practised in the Torres Strait region and possibly spread down into eastern Australia'. In other parts of the world, he says, 'the purpose was to preserve the corpse indefinitely so that the spirit would not be deprived of its bodily home. In Aboriginal Australia, however, the dried corpse is kept only as a temporary measure. Once the mourning period with its associated rites is over, once the death has been avenged, the corpse can be finally disposed of, leaving the spirit completely free to go to the Land of the Dead, or wherever else it is traditionally expected to reside.'

Interment and/or reburial

This is by far the commonest procedure in Aboriginal Australia, although sometimes only as one stage in a recognized sequence. In the Ooldea region, the body is doubled up and bound after the hair has been cut and made into the quoit-shaped object already mentioned (Berndt and Harvey Johnston, 1942; R. and C. Berndt, 1942-5). In the case of a man, the spear arm is carefully tied at his side to prevent him from throwing spears in the afterlife. The body is carried to a site already selected, and laid in a round shallow grave on a bed of leaves, with head to the east. It is not covered with sand or earth, merely with leaves and bushes, and finally with logs. A conical mound is built nearby, named after Moon, the first man to be killed in the Dreaming era. After an interval, which can be as short as three months or as long as two years, the same burial group returns and removes the remains. Its members may clean and replace the bones, or simply uncover the decomposing corpse and rub the fluids over themselves. The grave is finally filled with earth and sand, and covered with heavy logs.

Grave mounds are set up in south-eastern Australia, New South Wales, Victoria, and eastern South Australia. The bones are sometimes transferred later to another site. There are instances of burial in a side-chamber of the grave. In north-western New South Wales and south-eastern Queensland, and among a few tribes in south-western Australia, trees around the graves are marked with conventional designs of mythical significance. In western Arnhem Land grass or paperbark figures (mentioned in Chapter XII) are placed near a deserted camp after a death, one arm pointing to the new camp, the other to the corpse—usually on a platform. In the Adelaide, Gawler, and Gumeracha districts of South Australia the corpse is stood upright, wrapped in a wallaby rug, and packed comfortably with leaves and boughs; a crescent of earth or stone is arranged at the head of the grave. (Howitt, 1904: 434-75.) Among the Tongaranka (western New South Wales) the dead person is buried in a sitting position, together with his (or her) belongings. 'Before the grave is filled in,' says Howitt, 'the nearest male relative stands over the grave and is struck several times with the edge of a boomerang, letting the blood flow on to the corpse.' This is perhaps a propitiatory rite, both to appease the spirit and to assure it of innocence should there be any accusations of sorcery. Also, blood is a symbol of life—so that this may suggest eventual rebirth, at least in spirit form. The Wiimbaio, on the Upper River Murray near the Darling, wrap a corpse in a rug or blanket, pack it about with twigs and bark in a six-foot hole, and cover it with sand. 'A pile of wood is raised over the grave, and on top of this a heap of rushes or soft grass tapering at the top and held together with old netting or string.' Fires are left burning on each side so that the dead person can keep warm.

According to Howitt, too, a headman of the Wathi-wathi, on the Upper Murray near Swan Hill, was buried in a cleared area, fenced in by logs and brush; 'the grave itself was covered with sheets of bark resembling a hut, with a central ridge pole'. The Wotjobaluk (western Victoria) tie up their corpses, with 'knees drawn up to the chest and arms crossed'; a dead man's spear-thrower is placed on his chest before he is rolled up in his possum fur rug. 'The grave is oblong. The bottom layer is a sheet of bark, then come leaves covered with strands of possum pelt, and then the corpse. More leaves and pelt, and more bark, are placed on top and finally earth, with logs to prevent dogs from interfering. Again a fire is kept burning nearby. On the following day an oval clearing is made around the grave, with internal parallel ridges of soil.' Worsnop (1897: 57-69) describes interesting earthworks over certain graves, although it is not clear how far these can be taken as accurate reports. Among the Laragia, a corpse is buried horizontally, usually on its right side, with legs doubled up against the trunk and head resting on its hands. It is covered with layers of grass and sheets of bark, then with earth, but a small passage is left at one side, for the spirit to come and go as it pleases. (Basedow, 1925: 205.) The Dieri place food at the grave for a man 'of influence', and in winter light 'a fire to keep him warm'. A corpse is placed in a rug, or net, with its big toes tied together; before being buried, it is asked to name the person responsible for its death. (Howitt, *ibid.*, 448.) Quoting Collins, for the Port Jackson tribes, Howitt mentions canoe burial: a man's body is placed in a specially cut canoe 'together with a spear fishing spear and spearthrower, and waistband, and two persons carry it on their heads to the grave'.

Among the Aranda a corpse is seated in a round hole, knees drawn up to the chin. Then the hole is filled with earth, built up to form a mound with a depression on one side facing the deceased's totemic territory, specifically the sacred site associated with his or her conception. This makes access easy for the spirit, 'which is believed to spend part of the time until the final mourning ceremony watching over close relatives, and part in the company of its *arumburinga* or spirit double, which lives at its Dreaming site'. (Spencer and Gillen, 1938: 497-8.)

One of the most spectacular burial rites is still found on Melville and Bathurst islands, where the body is buried in the ground beneath a mound heaped with sheets of stringy bark. (Spencer, 1914: 228-9; Mountford, 1958: 63-8.) Large grave posts (see Chapter XII) are carved from tree trunks, three or four being erected during the first mourning ceremony several months after burial, and perhaps a dozen or so others added at intervals.

Among the Gagadju (Kakadu) the body, wrapped in paperbark, is taken into the bush, then removed from the paperbark and laid in a trench on a thick bed of grass and leaves, on its right side with legs bent back at the knees. (Spencer, *ibid.*, 240-9.) It is covered with more grass and leaves, then with earth heaped up into a small mound, and finally stones to discourage dogs. The dead person's belongings are wrapped in the paperbark which was used to carry the body, brought back to camp, and placed in a tree. Subsequently there is a purificatory rite. In this the belongings of all the camp members affected by the death are smoked, and water poured over the men's heads; the burial covering and the deceased's possessions are burnt, men are painted with charcoal, and older men eat lily-seed cake. In the second sequence everyone's personal belongings are placed in two heaps, one for each sex; women wear armlets; again, lily-seed cakes are brought in and eaten by the older men; and, except for the dead person's immediate kin, all the men who previously painted themselves black now paint themselves white. A third sequence takes place some time later; again belongings are brought, as well as food; everyone is painted in red ochre; men speculate as to who is responsible for the death; after women and children have returned to the camp, the men eat, then arrange on the ground bundles of spears which are finally bartered.

Platform and tree disposal

This is associated with what may be called delayed disposal.

In north-eastern and north-central Arnhem Land, a body immediately after death is covered with red ochre; then the chest, abdomen and face are painted with the deceased's clan and linguistic unit totemic patterns. Most of the hair is cut, to be made later into a hairbelt interwoven with feathers, while the rest is covered with white clay. The painting is done clearly, so 'that the spirit beings in the Land of the Dead may see at a glance to which sacred well or clan the deceased belongs'. (Warner, 1937/58: 416.) During the first mortuary ceremony all his (or her) belongings are arranged about him, together with sacred feathered string and carved objects which the death messengers will afterward take to other areas to notify distant kinsfolk. There is also a feast; and because no share is set aside for the dead person's spirit this is believed to compel it to leave its familiar earthly surroundings. The mourners brush themselves with smoking green leaves to purify themselves and drive away the spirit. Then the body is carried out into the bush and placed face upward on a specially constructed platform. For a woman, paperbark or bound grass models of her children, grandchildren or other close relatives are placed at each side. The fluids which fall to the ground are interpreted as revealing the identity of the 'murderer'. Other rites follow later. (See Warner, 1937/58: 412-33.)

In the upper Georgina district (Queensland) the dead person, wrapped in a net, is laid on a platform, covered with sticks and bushes together with his possessions. (Roth, 1897: 165-6; 1907.) Platform disposal is sometimes practised by the Brisbane people too, especially those who are 'unimportant'. After the genitalia have been removed—to make sure, says Roth, that the spirit does not have "sexual relations with the living"—the body is tied up in bark and placed on a platform in the bush, feet toward the west. Underneath a small fire is made, and the dead person's belongings stuck into the ground, so that the spirit can hunt for itself and cook its own food. Next day the surrounding ground is inspected for footprints, to reveal the 'murderer'. Two or three months later the bones are collected, some of them burnt and others subjected to a special test to confirm the 'murderer's' identity. Among the Wollaroi (northern New South Wales) people sit under the platform when fluids fall from a corpse, and rub these over themselves to give them strength: after the flesh has left the bones they are buried. (Howitt, 1904: 467.) Spencer (1914: 249-52) gives examples of tree and platform disposal, and in several of these too the bones are finally buried. The Waramunga make a platform in the boughs of a tree, and eventually bury all but the smaller arm bones, which are used in sorcery. (Spencer and Gillen, 1938: 498.) In the eastern Kimberleys, too, the corpse on its tree platform, covered with paperbark, branches and stones, is left until the flesh has rotted away. (Kaberry, 1939: 212-14.)

Elkin (1954: 305 *et seq.*) observes that this form of disposal is found throughout the north-western part of the Continent, from Wyndham to Darwin (and into Arnhem Land), south to about the centre and into Queensland, always associated with bone-collection and subsequent mourning rites, and with rites of inquest.

Cremation

This may be the only rite, or the final one of a sequence. Roth (1907) gives several examples from various parts of north Queensland. In the north of Cape York Peninsula a young man who has met his death through drowning, but whose body has been recovered, is finally burnt, with the exception of the head and fibula and certain other parts: there is now no longer any danger of the spirit returning. On the Lower Tully River the corpse is tied up in a special way and cremated—or buried, or desiccated, or parts of it eaten. Cremation is accompanied by specific ritual only, it seems, when the dead person was someone of high status. Ordinarily the body is thrown on to a specially built pyre, and afterward 'female relatives pick over the remains in search of relics'.

There may also be more complicated procedures. For instance, a corpse with skin and hair removed and hands tied together is carried on a man's shoulders, with other participants following behind. At the special ground it is propped up against a tree while they prepare a heap of wood. Then they join in a ceremony, including a song about the forthcoming inquest. The corpse is carried to another place nearby, and placed on its back. The native doctor 'sits astride it', and after making a number of incisions removes the stomach and wraps it in paperbark, or in the deceased's bark blanket: using this, he 'divines' the identity of the 'murderer'. The stomach is buried, and the corpse placed on the funeral pyre to be consumed. Howitt (1904: 443-4, 456, 458, 464), quoting other sources, speaks of cremation at Kew and Geelong (Victoria), of burning the dead when there is no time to dig a grave, when the corpse was a married woman, or an elderly person who was strangled on account of being no longer physically useful. (Regarding this last point, if this is a reliable statement it is unusual for Aboriginal Australia. There are few cases of old people being killed simply because they were old or infirm.)

Speaking of Victorian tribes, Howitt (quoting Dawson) mentions that a body may be laid on a funeral pyre, its head to the east, together with the belongings which were associated with it in life. In the case of a woman, the widower later collects her bones and pounds them to powder, which he puts in a small possum skin bag; 'he wears this on his chest until he remarries or until the bag is worn out, when it is burnt'. In another example, presumably relating to a dead headman, after the bones of the lower leg and the forearm have been taken out and cleaned, the body is tied up in a flexed position and wrapped up in a rug. It is kept for a time in a special hut with a smoking fire, where it is fanned to keep away flies, then on a tree platform. Later it is burnt on a funeral pyre, and finally the remains are pounded up and kept in small bags. Howitt also reports that the people of Mt. Macedon, the King, Ovens and Murray rivers burn their dead, and afterward 'gather the bones and put them in hollow trees'. The Port Jackson tribes (Katungal, associated with the Yuin) also practise cremation. Stillborn or very young babies are often disposed of by burning.

Other forms of disposal

Among the Mukjarawaint (Grampians, Victoria), a dead person is 'left lying in his camp for two or three days, then tied with knees drawn up and elbows fastened to the sides and hands to the shoulders, and put in a hollow tree'. (Howitt, *ibid.*, 453, 459.) The Kurnai do the same, but only after the corpse-bundle has been carried around for some time. The Yerkla-mining (Eucla), according to Howitt (*ibid.*, 450), "never bury their dead": a dying person is left alone beside a fire, while all members of that group leave the area and move to another camp. On the Keppel Islands rock shelters are used instead of trees. Some people on the smaller islands about Broadsound are said to 'take their dead out to sea in canoes and throw them overboard'. (Roth, 1907: 398.)

In the northern Kimberleys, should an 'unauthorized trespasser be killed by local people the corpse is placed in a hole scooped in a termite mound, and covered up'. (Basedow, 1925: 206.) In a few hours the termites repair the damage, effectively concealing the 'evidence' from any avenging party. We ourselves heard of this procedure in East Kimberley. In western Arnhem Land a dead baby may be buried in a termite mound so that its bones will disintegrate quickly and its spirit will return to the same mother to be reborn. Or the mother may carry at least some of the bones, such as fingers and jawbone, about with her for the same purpose.

Collins (quoted by Howitt, *ibid.*, 464) reports that in the Port Jackson area, if a nursing mother dies the child is buried alive with her, 'a large stone being thrown on it and the grave immediately filled in'. Roth (1897: 165; 1907: 395) records (presumably for the Boulia district, Queensland) that a person killed by general tribal consent, 'in punishment for some serious offence, must first dig his own grave'. In tribal fighting the dead may be left on the ground, 'with broken spears or boomerangs lying nearby to show how they met their death'. In parts of the Northern Territory, on the Daly River and in Arnhem Land, an offender against the sacred 'law' may be speared and his body left where it fell, deprived of all the usual mortuary rites.

On the Lower River Murray in South Australia, a body is treated as if it were animated or repossessed by the spirit after smoke-drying, and when it is used in inquest rites. Among the

Wakelbura, in Queensland, the remains are carried about by close relatives; but during a ceremony it may be placed against a tree, with a red band tied round that part of the bundle where the head is, as if watching the dancers. (Howitt, 1904: 473.)

More active participation is demanded, conventionally, among the Gadjalibi and their neighbours in north-central Arnhem Land. A dead man (or occasionally woman) may be painted and decorated, as if about to take part in a ceremony, with designs of white pipeclay on his face, his little sacred basket hanging from his neck. His body is propped up and fastened to a pole, in a sitting or standing position, while all his relatives who have come together for the mortuary rites sing and dance before him. They cry out to him, urging him to join in. Those who call him mother's mother's brother or sister's daughter's son, particularly, joke and laugh at him: 'Get up, quickly! Why do you sit there while we are all dancing?' He sits watching them, making no response. This is his last opportunity to return; but it is only a symbolic opportunity, and so is his rejection. The inference is that they are willing to re-accept him; it is he who wants to go. A day or so later they wrap him up, preparing for the burial (or platform disposal). Afterward the bones are collected and kept for a time, before the final ceremony in which they are formally shown and presented to his immediate relatives, and perhaps to his wife.

Cannibalism

The Australian Aborigines are not, generally speaking, cannibals who kill other human beings for the specific purpose of eating them. Nevertheless, if the available accounts are to be relied on, burial cannibalism in one form or another is (or was) fairly common. Elkin (1954: 313) concludes that it was practised 'in connection with mummification in parts of Queensland, that it preceded the exposure of the body on a platform, as among the tribes to the south-west of the Gulf of Carpentaria and occasionally in the northern Kimberleys, and was part of the interment ritual in north-east South Australia'. (See also Elkin, 1937: 283-5.) Only a small part of the flesh may be eaten, by certain specified relatives, as in the Liverpool River area of western Arnhem Land. On the other hand, the Maung of Goulburn Islands and the adjacent mainland are reported to have occasionally cut up a corpse. The inedible organs are placed in one hole and a fire built over them: when they are destroyed, a low mound is raised over the place. In another hole the heart, kidneys and liver are buried. A third and larger hole serves as an oven for cooking the flesh. This is shared among certain kin—but not among those

Men from the sacred ground surround women crouched under conical *ngainmara* mats and blankets in the main camp, while old women call the names of foods forbidden to them at this time. A section of the Kunapipi rituals: Milingimbi (late 1930s)

(photo: courtesy H. Shepherdson)

Two posts being shown before use in a *djunggawon* ritual; these represent the two Wawalag sisters, with bark 'hair' (see Chapters V, VII, VIII). Elcho Island (1961)

of the deceased's territorial group, the *namanamaidj*. (See Chapter III.) The assumption is that by this means the participants gain strength. Dried pieces of the flesh are also carried about in order to improve a man's hunting ability. The head is left to dry on top of a post, and later carried about as a memento. In Central Australia and East Kimberley a mother may consume the flesh of a stillborn child, or one dying soon after birth, in the hope that its spirit will be born again through her. Elkin notes (1954: 313) that the custom of anointing mourners with fluids from the decomposing corpse (as in parts of the Northern Territory, northern Queensland, western South Australia and eastern Australia) bears some resemblance to cannibalism.

According to Roth (1897: 166), cannibalism extends throughout north-west central Queensland: parts of a child's corpse, for instance, may be eaten by its parents and siblings. Several of Roth's accounts are not well documented. He mentions that in the Leichhardt-Selwyn district the Kalkadoon eat any corpse, 'even where the flesh is visibly affected with venereal disease'. But he does say that to the best of his knowledge no adult male or female is specifically killed for food. On the Pennefather River, in north Queensland, before the cremation of a young man the soles of the feet and the fleshy front part of the thighs are cut off, baked in the ashes, cut into small pieces and eaten gradually, over a period of two to three months, by one or more of his sister's sons. (Roth, 1907.) During this period the eater must not talk until he discovers the identity of the 'murderer', revealing the name as he regains his power of speech. A death charm of bone needles is made from the dead man's fibula and used by his sister's son or mother's father's brother's son.

Among the Brisbane people a body may be carried to a place where a large fire has been made; there its hair is singed off, except for the head and beard, by a native doctor, while other members of the group sit around their own fires. Three other doctors, each holding a stone knife in his mouth, dance forward to where the corpse, if a man, is lying on its stomach: if a woman, on its back. Roth (1907: 398-401) details the cutting up procedure. First the skin is removed in one piece with toes, fingers, ears, and so on, and arranged on spears in front of the fire to dry. Entrails, heart and lungs are removed, and the body dismembered and shared. This is roasted and eaten, but certain parts are destroyed by burning. Later the bones are collected and kept by, for instance, the mother, widow or sister. The pelvis is put in a log and used to reveal the 'murderer'. The skin is carried around with the bones, and pieces distributed as relics. Finally, the bag containing the remaining bones and skin is placed in a hollow tree. The reason given for this treatment is twofold. Firstly, the participants are not afraid of the deceased's spirit and so can dispose of the body immediately. Secondly, by this means it is prevented from decomposing. Lumholtz (1889: 271-9) has a few comments, which appear to be open to question. The flesh of dead relatives is ritually consumed on the Daintree and Mossman rivers on the eastern coast of Cape York Peninsula. (McConnel, 1937: 346-8.) Those eligible to eat are the deceased's immediate family, and members of the same clan or moiety—but not of the opposite moiety. In one case a man is said to have eaten some of the flesh of his dead sister, a skilful yam-collector, in the belief that this ability would thereby pass to himself. McConnel also gives a further example of a different kind, relating to a mythical rock python named Oiyangopan, with 'flesh-eating habits', the cult ancestor of a certain clan; because of the precedent he set, members of that clan were said to eat the flesh of strangers.

Howitt reports that the Mukjarawaint killed a man who eloped with a woman of the same totem; the flesh of the thighs and upper arms was roasted and eaten, but the rest of the body was chopped up and left lying on a log, to be eaten by fellow totemites, including his brothers. (Howitt, 1904; e.g. 247, 443, 448-50, 457-8, 470, 749-56.) Ritual cannibalism is practised also among the Dieri and adjacent tribes. 'An old man follows the corpse into the grave, cuts off all the fatty parts of the face, thighs, arms and stomach, and passes it up to close relatives, who swallow pieces of it.' There are special rules relating to who eats the flesh of whom. Other tribes (the Tangara, for instance, located by Howitt above the eastern sector of the Transcontinental Railway, in South Australia; but this may not be the correct tribal name) carry the deceased about in a bag and eat parts of the flesh until only the bones remain. These are eventually pounded up, kept for a time, and then thrown into flood waters under the name of "fish seed"—possibly for increase purposes. Dawson notes that in Victoria (no specific locality mentioned), when a person is killed by violence, the genitalia and intestines are burned, together with the bones, but the flesh is roasted and eaten by adult relatives as a gesture of respect for the dead.

Howitt draws a distinction between eating one's own dead, 'ritual burial cannibalism', and eating the flesh of slain enemies, associated with revenge. He draws a further distinction relating to the eating of caul and kidney fat, for magical reasons. The Kurnai, for instance, ate only their enemies, and then only certain parts. Spencer (1914: 253-5) mentions eating of the dead among coastal tribes on the Gulf of Carpentaria. Specifically, he discusses a practice among the Mara and by extension among a number of other south Arnhem Land, Roper River and north-eastern central tribes. The corpse, he says, is cooked by men. Those who remove it from the oven and cut it up are mother's brother's sons to the deceased. Again there are rules governing who may eat whom. Later the bones are wrapped in bark and left for some time on a tree platform. Among the Aranda and central tribes, says Spencer (1928: 203), only children are eaten, and then rarely, in the belief that the flesh will give strength to a weakly elder child.

The prevalence of killing and eating the very young has been both grossly exaggerated, and also underestimated—for instance by Basedow (1925: 21). Infanticide does seem to have been practised occasionally almost all over Aboriginal Australia, but it cannot have been so frequent as Taplin, in Woods (1879: 13-15) and Bates (1938) suggest. Nor is infanticide invariably followed by eating the flesh: where this is done, the idea behind the action is the hope that the child will be born again, or that strength will accrue to another child. Children are not killed indiscriminately: bad seasons in desert areas account for some, the spacing of children for others. Howitt reports that new-born children are killed during hard summers, or in times of drought, or when a mother has other young children to care for. Rarely, too, children have been killed in anger or in fighting, but in such cases not deliberately.

There is very little reliable information available on this subject of infanticide. To some extent the same is true for cannibalism in a more general sense. There is no doubt that it was practised; but undoubtedly, too, many instances have been exaggerated and embroidered. Numerous myths and stories throughout the Continent also contain references to this topic, including, in some areas, accounts of cannibalistic spirits which kill human beings for food. It is not unusual to hear Aborigines of one tribe speak of the people in the next as cannibals, without any real evidence. Fact and fancy are not always easily separated, and evidence of this nature becomes more difficult to obtain as the traditional Aboriginal world recedes into the past. However, it seems clear that burial cannibalism was fairly widespread, and that in most cases, with some obvious exceptions, only parts of the body were eaten. The expressed aims were to absorb some of the dead person's qualities or attributes; to identify publicly with him and so ward off sorcery accusations; to show respect; or to give a child an opportunity to be reborn, from the same or a different mother. But there were exceptions in this respect too, and the reasons put forward are not always consistent with actual behaviour.

THE RITUAL OF DEATH

In some parts of South Australia and of the north 'chants of a dying person's totemic cult lodge are sung, to comfort him and to reconcile him to his return to the spirit world'. (Elkin, 1937: 285; 1954: 299.) In north-eastern South Australia mourners camp near the grave; the dead man's kin "sing his sacred songs daily", adding small quantities of earth, "until the totemic cycle has been completed and the grave filled in".

In north-eastern and north-central Arnhem Land, as well as further west, such ceremonies are especially complex and spectacular. Some of them have been described by Spencer (1914), Warner (1937/58), Elkin, Berndt and Berndt (1950). In eastern Arnhem Land, at one stage, members of the deceased's clan and moiety, other close relatives, and the husband or wives and their kin, gather about a symbolic waterhole and stretch of country, marked out on the ground with low mounds and depressions. The ceremonial leader of the relevant clan and linguistic unit, beating his clapping sticks, directs the singing and invokes the sacred names of the dead man's waterhole and country, with its mythological associations. Some of the songs which are sung at this time have already been mentioned in Chapter XI. Women sing them in a characteristic wail, interspersing the conventional words with informal comments about the person who has died, or angry accusations of blame. The main *dua* moiety cycle relates to the island of Bralgu, the main *jiridja* moiety sequence to Badu. There are further subsidiary cycles such as the *dua* Nganug series, telling of the Paddle Maker for the dead man's spirit canoe. Then there is also the 'Macassan' mast ceremony. Just as the 'Macassans' departed from the mainland, setting off across the sea to their homeland, so the spirit leaves on its long journey to the Islands of the Dead. Here is the translation of part of one song in this cycle.

> The sail at the mast head dips from side to side,
> As the boat comes up from the south . . .
> The sail unfurled at the mast head flaps in the wind,
> It stands upright and flaps, as the boat goes on.
> The wind tosses the sail, up on the mast,
> And the mast head moves, dipping from side to side.
> The sail on the mast flaps, dancing, and 'talks' in the wind . . .
> (from C. Berndt, 1952: 283.)

For the *dua* moiety, here is a section from the Bralgu cycle, telling how various creatures move to and fro between the corpse and the Land of the Dead: in this case, blowflies.

. . . Ah, the blowfly is whining there, its maggots are eating the flesh.
The blowflies buzz, their feet stray over the corpse . . .
Who is it, eating there, whose flesh are they eating?
Ah my daughter, come back here to me!
Ah, our daughter was taken ill . . .
Ah, my lost, sick child—ah, the blowflies!

(C. Berndt: women's wailing; Yirrkalla.)

In these big mortuary rituals, close relatives put goods such as clothing, spears, and tobacco into or around the symbolic waterhole. The rites and the singing take place not only in the camp where the death occurred, but also in other camps where such relatives are living at the time. These people talk to the spirit of the deceased both before and after the body is buried, or otherwise disposed of, and continue to do so until the bones have been exhumed or collected from the platform. At that stage they are cleaned and red-ochred, to the accompaniment of singing and dancing, and placed in a small bark coffin or container painted with totemic designs. This is put in the fork of a tree. The keeper of the bones watches them for two or three months, then before the final mortuary rites they are brought to the edge of the camp and red-ochred again. A large hollow log post has been prepared and painted with sacred designs associated with the dead person. (See Chapter XII.) It is set up aslant, and held in place by a forked stick. As singing continues, various people dance up with the bones. These are broken up and put into the log, which is finally stood upright and left to rot. In some cases the skull and other bones are taken to the deceased's waterhole, the source of his spirit; or the skull, specially painted, may be carried about and finally deposited in a cave.

Earlier on, a grave post, *wuramu*, may have been placed over the grave if the corpse is buried, or if it is exposed on a platform the *wuramu* may be erected in the main camp. This may be a stylized image of the dead person, or a representation of a spirit associated with his moiety home of the dead. The 'Macassan' mast or the *dua* moiety Morning Star pole or similar construction set up during the mortuary rituals, and afterward left standing in the camp, is said to be like the dead person's body: 'we look at the post, and remember the departed spirit'.

On Bathurst and Melville islands (Spencer, 1914: 229-39; Mountford, 1958: 60-118; Goodale, 1959: 3-13) the burial is followed, later, by an inquest. About two months after the burial the *bugamani* ceremonies begin. (Hart and Pilling, 1960: 88-9.) The first of these, the *ilania*, arranged in a series, include ritual jumping over a fire. The mourners sing short songs, especially composed for the occasion. (See C. Berndt, 1950*b*.) Then men are detailed to make the burial poles, and generally attend to matters relating to the grave and the kind of poles to be prepared. The second *ilania* include the return and feeding of the pole-makers, a mock fight between these men and the mourners *(bugamani)*, singing and dancing, and the *bumadi* (in which married men and women beat their affinal relatives with boughs), as well as ritual fire-jumping. Message sticks are sent to other camps to let them know that the final *bugamani* will take place about a month afterward. Other *ilania* are held in the meantime. The final *bugamani*, approximately three months after the burial, extends over a couple of days and is divided into five phases (Mountford). All the participants are painted, and special *bugamani* ornaments are worn. (See Chapter XII.) The fire-jumping rite is performed again, with a basket dance. They all rush to the grave and fling themselves on the covering of bushes, then return to the special dancing ground for a series of dances and songs. The second phase consists of more songs and dances; the third, payment of the pole-makers. In this last, goods are placed on top of each pole; some men climb these poles and sing about how generous and wealthy they are to give so much to the workers. In the fourth phase the poles are carried to the grave and erected. Finally the bushes covering the grave are pulled away and the mourners throw themselves upon it, wailing. Traditionally, the beards of the chief mourners are now plucked and the painted decorations washed from their bodies.

Apart from any question of propitiation as one aim of such ceremonies, and the assuagement of sorrow on the part of those intimately concerned as another, the immense amount of work involved represents a significant aspect. It might be said that a death allows much scope for economic exploitation. Objects must be made, and goods must be used for various purposes; and this inevitably involves consideration both of resources and of personal commitments, in a complex of debtor-creditor relationships. The use of 'wealth' is also directly relevant to the enhancement of prestige. Therefore, viewed over and above immediate mortuary issues, such rituals provide further avenues through which essentially mundane aspirations can be achieved.

INQUEST

The best descriptions of divination are to be found in Spencer and Gillen (1938), Howitt (1904) and Elkin (1945, 1954). An inquest (see Chapter X) is held in order to find a scapegoat, a person or group which can be held responsible for a death.

It is not always considered necessary. For instance, the victim may have been killed in an open fight by someone clearly identified.

Even so, the person who inflicts what appears to be a fatal injury is not always designated as the 'real' culprit. He may be regarded only as an agent, and an unwitting one, of the sorcerer on whom the main blame must rest. In the case of an infant or young child, the death may be attributed to some irregularity of conduct on the part of its parents or near kin: carelessness about food or other tabus, for instance, if not actual physical neglect; then little or nothing may be done, apart from gossip. The holding of an inquest depends to some extent on the social status of the deceased and the willingness or ability of his immediate kin to proceed in the matter, because it could be seen as a challenge, inviting reciprocal action either immediately or at some future date.

In any case, an inquest is not necessarily followed by an attempt at revenge: it may be considered enough simply to know the answer. One factor here is the strength of group feeling, which straight after a death may be running high, and is more easily controlled and diffused if it is directed against one specific target. It is partly for this reason that inquests usually take place some time afterward when people have had an opportunity to think things over more calmly and there is less likelihood of rash or impetuous action. Rumour and speculation are common enough in the first wave of emotion. There are accusations, specific and otherwise, not always taken (or intended) seriously, nor acted on later. In fact, they may be an expected part of the mourners' response. In south Western Australia women mourners would pause in their wailing to chant abuse against the supposed sorcerers, trying to goad their menfolk to seek revenge. (See Elkin, 1954: 297.) Reactions of this kind may help to deflect any feelings of guilt which trouble the mourners themselves. They also provide a way of expressing grief, in personal terms, without wallowing in self-pity. But they need not be translated into formal action.

An inquest may take a variety of forms even within one tribe. Most commonly (as we saw in Chapter X), it involves examination of the ground immediately near or on the grave, which may therefore be cleaned and levelled at the time of interment. Native doctors look for the presence of signs, which they can interpret: a small hole, for instance, or the tracks of some animals, bird or reptile. They may not specify a particular person, but merely locate a 'murderer' socially. Collective responsibility may be sufficient; or individual responsibility may be inferred from further clues, or from circumstantial evidence—consideration of grudges or ill-feeling, if not actual threats. In western Arnhem Land the 'murderer's' moiety or phratry is ascertained by small objects or signs found about the corpse. Where tree platforms are used, juices from the decomposing body are often expected to supply some indication. On the Lower River Murray, in South Australia, the liver and intestines are removed after death and examined for such signs by a native doctor. 'In some northern Queensland tribes the viscera are removed and buried, and an older male relative of the deceased is expected to have a vision of the "murderer".' As Elkin points out (*ibid.*, 308), 'surgical post-mortem seems to be confined to northern and eastern Queensland and the Darling-Murray rivers, where it is apparently associated with desiccation'. Alternatively, a native doctor may see the 'murderer' in a vision, 'rendering any such inquiry unnecessary'.

Delayed inquest is common in the Forrest River district of north-western Australia and in the Northern Kimberleys: 'small stones, each representing a possible "murderer", are set up around a grave, and drops of blood from the buried body are supposed to appear on one'. Several tribes of Cape York Peninsula 'conduct the inquest on an exhumed body a few days after interment, looking for signs of a magical wound or object' (Roth, 1907). In many tribes (such as north-eastern South Australia and the Lower River Murray: see Chapter X) the corpse, or rather the spirit remaining nearby, is asked to indicate the 'murderer'. In parts of north-western Australia 'the dead man's hair is pulled while the names of various local groups are called, the hair being said to come out at the mention of the guilty one'. Among the Maung in western Arnhem Land, before a dead woman's clothing is destroyed or ritually purified it may be carried about in a large bag by her mother or sister, who hangs it up at night on a post near where she sleeps. Faint noises from inside the bag indicate that 'the dead woman is trying to tell us something'—which can be interpreted on the basis of what people already know, or assume, about the circumstances of the death.

Apart from these relatively impersonal means of establishing guilt, more direct procedures may be used either after a formal inquest or in place of it. The identity of a suspect may be tentatively settled, to begin with, by watching a likely person's behaviour during the mortuary rites. If he does not seem genuinely upset, if he is cautious in gashing himself or appears to mourn in a perfunctory way, there is a strong presumption of guilt. Further proof may or may not be required. Among the Malngin in the eastern Kimberleys this may take the form of a test, or ordeal. Some of the victim's bones, finely pounded, are surreptitiously mixed with wild honey and given to the suspect: if this chokes in his throat as he eats, his guilt is confirmed. In the Daly River area a dead man's brother may cut off the corpse's forefinger from its right hand, the spear hand, and put this in a hole at the top of a banyan tree. The suspect is watched; and if, among other things, the forefinger of *his* right hand becomes clenched and twisted, no more evidence is needed.

Revenge expeditions actually take place, as far as one can tell, in only a small percentage of cases. In Central Australia, northwestern South Australia and the middle eastern side of Western Australia, they are not so common as in parts of Arnhem Land. There they either precipitate or reinforce local feuds. (See Chapter X, and Warner, 1937/58: 155-90.) In the first areas mentioned, a revenge expedition may not be sent out for days, weeks, or even months later. Then much attention is paid to choosing participants, and performing magical ritual to give them courage, protection and success. (See Elkin, 1954: 311.)

Even in times of acute emotional stress, such as after a death, Aboriginal social life is controlled to a very large extent by tradition and the demands of conventional behaviour. Any disorganization which results from a death is permitted to go only so far, and mechanisms of limitation and control are apparent in most situations of this kind.

COMMENT

Generally speaking, the various types of mortuary ritual in Aboriginal Australia, including the treatment of the corpse, indicate a pervasive belief in life after death, or rather in the persistence of life as known on earth but at a different level or in a different form, as another facet of human existence. Death is viewed as a transition, through which a person passes to another life not entirely unlike the one he has left—even in cases where he is believed to have more than one spirit, or soul. In ordinary life a man plays many roles, and in this respect the new situation is not altogether dissimilar. One part of him in spirit form may be a trickster, another may go on to the Land of the Dead, or return to a nucleus of spirit children awaiting rebirth, merge with the great ancestral and creative beings, and so on.

The transition is foreshadowed in the symbolic death and rebirth which are the central focus of so much initiation ritual. This is a matter of practical experience for men, hearsay and vicarious experience on the whole for women; but for all of them it is conceptually, among other things, a preparation for actual bodily death and subsequent spiritual re-emergence. Conversely, mortuary rites are themselves in a sense equivalent to initiation, drawing attention to a person's moving on to another phase of existence. In the process, they deliberately force him away from his past life by proclaiming his distinctness from living people, the fact that his old ties are severed for all general purposes. He does not, it is believed, always leave willingly; the bonds of affection and habit are not so easily abandoned. The break must be made ritually and, with some qualifications, irrevocably.

The opposition between life and death, as manifested in human beings, is a fundamental one which the Aborigines can hardly fail to recognize. The fact of bodily decomposition is obvious enough, overwhelmingly so in the warmer regions of the north; even such measures as desiccation can arrest it only to a limited degree. Certainly some sort of life is actively present in the course of this, but it is life in very different and altogether non-human forms. The body which formerly had the shape of a person is no longer what it was, just as the intangible facets of the relationships in which that person was involved are no longer the same. But there is enough recollection of both, and generally speaking enough regret on the part of at least a few of the living, to ensure that they themselves are hesitant in acknowledging the inevitable. This hesitation, this unwillingness to accept the breach as final even while realizing that there is no alternative, is reflected in statements about the presence-and-absence of the spirit, the ambiguity of its position, the different forms which facets of it can occupy simultaneously. Those people most intimately affected cling emotionally to the corpse, as the last tangible representation of the person they knew, even while in some contexts they express rejection of it. A Goulburn Island woman, affirming a preference for platform disposal as against burial, gave as a two-fold reason, 'It's cleaner on a tree than under the ground, and we can go back and look at them sometimes.'

This reluctance to lose touch is manifested in a wide range of situations, typified perhaps in the carrying about of bones over long periods. Against it is the insistence on the danger of trying to maintain too close an association, which can keep the spirit from proceeding with its own affairs, upset the mourners so that they take a long time to settle down again to ordinary life, and have disastrous repercussions generally on the living who can be harrassed by it. Hence the Gunwinggu practice of stuffing the ears and nostrils of a corpse with soft paperbark, 'to stop him from thinking of us, so he will go for ever', and the corresponding local term for any newly dead person, 'he (or she) who is far away'. A widow washes her body after her husband's death, so that none of his sweat will remain on her; and the purificatory rites here, as elsewhere on the Continent in a mortuary context, have a similar end in view: association between the living and the recently dead, without ritual precautions, entails too much risk for ordinary persons to engage in it on a casual basis. Only a native doctor can handle it safely.

The contrast between living and dead is striking; and although in organic terms it is merely a transient one, the progression from the first to the second is one-way and irreversible. But the Aborigines endeavour to resolve the contradiction, or opposition, by transposing it on to a different plane in which physical limitations are not irrelevant, but subsidiary. They do not ignore the physical aspects: if anything, in some areas they appear to be preoccupied with them. But they set these within a ritual, or symbolic, framework which denies the finality of death even while it underlines the need to accept the changes which it entails. Thus, in a further sense, through the appropriate rites the participants express their united antagonism toward death as such, and the way it disrupts the ordinary course of events. They reaffirm, collectively, their own status: the living are more important than the dead. The elaborate and extended mortuary rituals which take place in some parts of Aboriginal Australia, and the fact that only in rare cases is a body disposed of unceremoniously, express not a preoccupation with death but an emphasis on life.

The immediate practical concern, then, is to sever connections with the spirit and to send it on its way, whatever that may be. A disgruntled and unsatisfied spirit can do harm to near kin and to others. Performing the relevant mortuary rituals adequately may not be sufficient to avert this. Where the cause of the death is in question, this must be resolved by inquest and revenge; or at least something must be done to placate the watchful spirit, which otherwise may be even more reluctant to leave its old haunts. But it may, itself, so it is believed in many cases, help to settle the matter by revealing where the responsibility lies.

The spirit of a dead person may continue to treat its former body as a home—but only for as long as it remains in the vicinity, before finally taking its leave. Hence a corpse is often tied up to prevent the spirit from assuming its shape and causing trouble because it has not been immediately avenged. The common practice of burying, or placing with an exposed corpse, or burning, a dead person's material possessions reflects a belief that the spirit may use them, in essence, in the afterlife: or, alternatively, that it may have temporary need of them before it leaves for the Land of the Dead. Placing a fire near the grave is an example of this, or putting weapons within easy reach so the spirit may use them in hunting, or making a hut over the grave for it to shelter in, or placing bark representations of kinsfolk with the corpse 'so it won't be lonely'; or so that the ghost will be deceived and not attempt to take them, too, with it in death (for example, a dead mother trying to claim a living child). When different forms of disposal are practised in one area, this means that the choice of one rather than another depends on the social status of the deceased, on the cause of death, or on the pressure for revenge. Preservation of the material remains, carrying around a bundle containing some of the corpse, or isolated relics, may be done for a variety of reasons—having to do with the inquest, with propitiating the spirit, or as a token of sorrow; or in the belief that part of the spirit is still present in them and can magically assist the bearer.

However much of the spirit remains to help or molest the living, and opinions on this score differ over the Continent, an appreciable part of it eventually finds its way to what is conceived to be the Land of the Dead. In so doing it achieves some measure of immortality—not so much in terms of separate personal identity, but in the sense of merging into the traditional background of the culture, returning to the sacred world of the Dreaming.

LAND OF THE DEAD

Ngurunderi, mythical hero of the Lower River Murray (see Chapter VII), after his earthly travels went westward with his children. (Meyer and Taplin, in Woods, 1879: 55-62, 200-1, 205-6.) Missing one of them, he threw a spear with rope attached in the direction where he supposed the boy to be: the boy caught hold of it and his father drew him to safety. Since that time, Ngurunderi's sons have thrown a similar rope to the spirits of dead Aborigines of Encounter Bay and the Lower River Murray, and in this manner they too find their way safely to the Land of the Dead. Once there the dazed newcomer is aroused and, weeping, approaches Ngurunderi, who allocates to him a place to live. 'If tears flow from one eye, it signifies that he has left one wife behind; from both, that he has left two; if tears stop flowing from one eye but not from the other, he has left three, and so on. Ngurunderi provides him with new wives, to the appropriate number. Old people become young, and the infirm sound, in the company of Ngurunderi.' In other versions, before going into the sky (*waieruwar*) Ngurunderi dived into the sea on the western end of Kangaroo Island to cleanse himself of the old life (Berndt, 1940*b*: 182) after telling all the people: 'I am going first, you will come after me.' Therefore spirits of the dead follow Ngurunderi's track, staying for a while on Kangaroo Island, then cleansing themselves before going into the sky to dwell with him. The burial platform used in that area is in the shape of a raft, which these spirits are said to use in crossing from the mainland to Kangaroo Island.

A rock on the eastern side of the Coolangatta mountain is the jumping off place for spirits of the dead. (Mathews, 1899: 5, 30-5, mentions that this story is also "current among the Natives occupying the south-east coast from Botany Bay to the Victorian boundary".) An invisible tree extends from there to the Land of the Dead, and in crossing this bridge the spirit must undergo several tests, most notably by fire. There are further tests on the other side, as he continues along a track, until eventually he settles down with his own kin who have predeceased him.

Over much of eastern Australia, and parts of the west and north-west, the spirit is said to go into the sky, where it remains with the creative beings. Howitt (1904: 434-42) gives some examples. The Wiimbaio, at the juncture of the Darling and Murray rivers, on the Victorian side, believe the spirit follows a particular path into the sky. So do the Theddora (New South Wales). Their neighbours, the Ngarigo, tell of the spirit of the dead going into the sky and meeting Daramulun—or Baiami. (See Chapter VII.)

The Wuradjeri and neighbouring tribes believe that a spirit after death uses a cord to climb up into the Sky-world of Baiami, Wantanggangura, the abode of the totemic and ancestral beings. (Berndt, 1947.) To enter it the spirit must pass through a fissure, just as the mythical beings did in the beginning. This has two walls which are continually revolving, revealing from time to time a small aperture. Within sit two guardians, Moon Man on one side, Sun Woman on the other. Moon's penis is so long that it is wound around his waist; Sun has a long clitoris, covering the fire which is the source of sunshine and daylight. If the spirit remains unafraid he can pass on, to be accosted by two ancestral men, Ngintungintu and Gunababa. They cross-question him, but if he wants to get into the Sky-world he must remain silent: then they dance in front of him with erect penes, singing humorously, but he must not smile or flicker an eyelid. If he passes this test, women come before him and dance erotically: again, he must remain unmoved. (This resembles the experiences reported by native doctors who claim to have entered the Sky-world.) Later the spirit meets Baiami and his wife, Guriguda, whose body is like rock crystal. (See Chapter VII.)

The Wuradjeri hold that a person has two spirits. One, the *warangun*, is harmless, and eventually goes to the Sky-world. The other, *djir*, is malignant and continues to live an independent existence; it can affect the *warangun*, and is connected with the initiation of native doctors. Howitt (*ibid.*, 438-9) speaks of the spirits of the Kulin and Wotjo ascending into the sky on "the bright rays of the setting sun". In the Kamilaroi view, the spirit goes "to the dark patch in the Magellan clouds", called Maianba, the endless water or river. On the Herbert River in north-east Queensland, 'the Milky Way is the road along which ghosts of the dead travel to the sky'. (Howitt, *ibid.*, 431.) The Dieri, too, although they distinguish three spirits or souls in each person, believe that one goes into the sky. For the eastern Kimberleys, according to Kaberry (1939: 210-11), "the Land of the Dead lies to the west". The spirits "occasionally return to their own country, to their graves or to the gorges where their bones have been hidden": but life after death "does not offer compensations and benefits to those who have been denied them during their lifetime". On Melville and Bathurst islands the spirits of the dead, *mobadidi*, return to the place of their birth at the various totemic sites, where they make up self-contained communities and continue to behave in much the same way as living people. (Mountford, 1958: 61-3.) A small child which dies remains as a *mobadidi* for the duration of mourning, then becomes a *budabuda*, entering its former mother to be reborn. Adults however, says Mountford, after death become young again. (It is possible, although Mountford does not specifically say so, that they too are reborn.)

Among the Gunwinggu of western Arnhem Land the spirit or ghost goes into the Sky-world, sometimes called Manidjirangmad. (R. and C. Berndt, 1951*a*: 107-8.) There he (or she) meets a powerful being, called by the general terms Gunmalng or Margidjbu, which proceeds to knock out his middle teeth. If the gums bleed, Gunmalng sends the spirit back to its body, which revives. If the person is really dead there is no blood. The spirit then goes further up into Manidjirangmad along a special roadway, disturbing a white cockatoo. The wife of the guardian of the road, hearing the cockatoo, knows that a new spirit has arrived. She is sorry for him, and distracts her husband's attention by offering to delouse him. As she does this the spirit slips by. She assures her husband she can see the spirit coming, but at the same time waves her free hand signalling him to take another road. Then she tells her husband she has seen him. He jumps up grasping his spears, but it is too late.

Next the spirit comes to a large camp of people, all eating fish: seeing the new spirit, they weep for him. Nearby another guardian sits resting: he hears their cries and asks what is the matter, but they say they are crying for fish. He returns to his sleep. They are protecting the new spirit; if the guardian knew he was there, he would cut off his legs. Eventually the spirit reaches a river and calls out for a canoe. If the spirit is a man, the canoe keeper brings only an old canoe and beats him all the way to the opposite shore, the real Land of the Dead. If it is a woman he brings a nice new canoe, lifts her gently into it, and paddles slowly across the water without beating her—because, unlike men, women will pay him with coitus for taking them across. On the opposite shore the spirit finds a large camp, with many people.

In Maung accounts, the ghost goes to a billabong named Andjumu, near the site of the present mission station, where he waits for a canoe to take him to North Goulburn Island. There, walking along the beach, he comes to two great sandhills, one for men and the other for women. He climbs one of these, and facing toward Wulurunbu Island, far in the sea to the north-east, cries out, 'We are here!' A giant named Jumbarba (sometimes identified with a falling star) hears the cry and brings over his canoe, carrying with him a fighting club. If the spirit is a man he puts him into his canoe and beats him all the way. If it is a woman he treats her gently, and expects her to pay him with coitus. But after death all spirits regain their youth, no matter what age they may have reached in life.

This is the conventional picture of what happens to the most consistently personal part of the spirit of a dead human being. But other Maung and Gunwinggu accounts assume that part, at least, remains in its own country. There is much uncertainty on this score. In rites and invocations of various kinds it is taken for granted that a person's spirit returns to its home site, the waterhole or other Dreaming centre to which it really belongs—whether this is the place of conception, or of birth, or the paternal *namanamaidj* country: ideally, the first two are subsumed in the third. But unattached or wandering spirits of the dead are different. They are not only malicious, or potentially so, like the various non-human spirits which inhabit the region along with its Aboriginal population. They are also undependable in their responses. There are several words for them. One, the Gunwinggu *mam*, is sometimes applied to non-human spirits; but it can also refer to a corpse. They are often said to smell like decaying bodies; and although opinions about their appearance differ, in many accounts they resemble skeletons with little if any flesh remaining. This accounts for their lack of predictability, the impossibility of coming to satisfactory terms with them: they have nothing left to think with; all the soft organs, including the brain, have been lost. New spirits, ghosts of the newly dead, are the most dangerous of all, because they are said to resent strongly their changed state. What annoys them more than anything else is the sight of human beings enjoying each other's company, and especially the sight of a man and wife making love. In a jealous fury, they will try to destroy the offending pair, to shut them up in a cave or burn them, for no other reason than that.

There is some similarity between this overall picture and the range of views current on the north-eastern side of Arnhem Land, except that there each of the moieties has its own separate Land of the Dead. Here, too, detailed information is contained in many stories and songs: and again, they do not always agree. A human spirit after death is often said to take three shapes, or divide into three parts. One returns to its totemic centre, to wait for rebirth. One, the *mogwoi*, is a trickster spirit which is much more mobile but still remains locality-bound. The third goes to the appropriate Land of the Dead, to join and then merge with the creative beings and spirits already there. According to Warner (1937/58: 280-1), souls of the newly dead are present at the *djunggawon* rituals (see Chapter V), and in fact are *in* the *rangga* objects which are used. 'Even though they go to the islands of the dead, or a whale takes them on its back to a totemic site, they will come back to the *rangga*.' This is the case with women as well as with men. As Warner notes, when a woman dies she too, in local belief, becomes a *birimbir* spirit *wongar* (Dreaming): she may go to the same well as a man does, and she too may return to the *rangga*.

For people of the *jiridja* moiety, the main Land of the Dead is 'Badu'—a collective name for several of the Torres Strait islands and for the southern coast of New Guinea. (Berndt, 1948*b*.) Some versions emphasize Mudilnga, an unidentified island north-east of the Wessels, usually as part of the 'Badu' complex. It is a land of villages, coconut palms, and exotic foods, and the beaches fringing the islands have running fresh water streams and coral reefs. The spirits living there and looking after the dead have many names. One is Duriduri, who also goes by such names as Duradjini, Giluru, Wuramala, and Babajili. She is associated with turtles and her body, decorated with cloud designs, is distended from over-eating. Then there are the two Guldana (Kultana), husband and wife, each known by several names, who light large fires on Mudilnga to attract spirits of the dead on their way to Badu. The husband, when he is not supervising the journeying spirits, hunts for stingray in the shallow waters of the mangrove swamps and scratches his mosquito bites; his wife gathers wood, collects jungle-fowl eggs, and generally spends her time in the jungles fringing the beach. At the end of the wet season, when the north-west monsoon has ceased to blow but it is too early yet for the south-east trades, coconuts, pandanus cones, long unidentified seed pods, breadfruit, and timber, with occasional canoes, are washed up on to the mainland beaches around Cape Arnhem and Yirrkalla. These are said to have been sent by the *jiridja* spirits to their living relatives, together with the north-east winds and clouds. In return the living people send their dead, in spirit form, by performing the mortuary rites and singing the appropriate songs.

At the *dua* Land of the Dead, the island of Bralgu, which the Djanggawul visited on their way to the mainland (Berndt, 1952*a*), live some of the important *dua* moiety beings, who provide tests for each new spirit of the dead before he, or she, is fully accepted there. Nganug, the paddle maker, ferries the newcomer across the water to Bralgu. On the island itself the spirits dance, sending out Morning Stars to different parts of Arnhem Land. They use a large pole with feathered strings, and balls of seagull feathers to represent the stars; their actions are imitated by human beings in the *dua* moiety mortuary ritual of the Morning Star. (See Chapter XI.) Each night the spirits send out their stars attached to strings, which they pull in again as it becomes light, and as they dance at Bralgu large billows of dust rise from their stamping feet, forming clouds which move over toward the mainland. On reaching Bralgu the newcomer must pay the canoe man. Then he follows a track through the *bualgu* swamp yams, on which the local spirits subsist. A *birgbirg* bird (bustard), watching for new spirits, calls out to the local guardians, who prepare to receive and test him. His teeth are examined to make sure that one has been removed, his nasal septum to make sure that there is a clear aperture. If not, he is sent back. He is threatened with spears, through which he must pass unflinchingly; and two spirit women, who have been digging *bualgu,* leave their work to tempt him. Finally, after a number of adventures, he reaches the other spirits and ancestral beings and makes his home among them.

As in some other parts of Aboriginal Australia, there are reports of living people who have been to the Land of the Dead, voluntarily or otherwise. On the Lower River Murray, in South Australia, there was the story of Red Man—so called because he had been red-ochred after his 'death', and placed on a platform with a slow fire underneath; but he revived the next day and recounted his travels to the home of Ngurunderi. (Howitt 1904: 436) gives another example. Native doctors are believed to visit the Land of the Dead from time to time. (Elkin, 1945.) For eastern Arnhem Land, Warner (1937/58: 524-8) tells how a man named Jalngura visited Bralgu. We heard the same story at Yirrkalla in 1946, and at Elcho Island in 1961. Briefly, it goes like this.

Jalngura was sitting down one day when a yam leaf, blown on the *dua* wind from Bralgu, came to rest on the ground beside him. Looking at it, he decided to make the journey to the Land of the Dead. He made a canoe, fitted it out, and prepared to leave, telling his wives and children where he was going. He started from Bremer Island and after paddling for several days reached Bralgu. He rubbed himself with sweat, to give himself extra power. Then, taking up his basket and his special spearthrower—cylindrical, with a human hair fringe at one end, a type originally made by these spirits—he began to walk over the island. The spirits saw him and hailed him as their friend: a bird flew across his path and called out in his language. They gave him yams to eat. When he had finished they gave him clapping sticks, and he sang for them as they danced. Then they gave him three young girls, and he slept with them. The spirits offered to show him the Morning Stars, and how they were sent up into the sky. An old woman, who kept them hidden in a basket, refused to reveal them to him. Jalngura kept asking her, and at last persuaded her by singing a magical song. She took out the feathered balls and their strings, and showed him. He recognized them: they were the same as those used in the Morning Star rituals in his home camp, and he sang the Morning Star song cycle. As he did so, the old woman sent out the 'ball' stars to various places on the mainland, Jalngura naming them one by one. Finally, as the light grew stronger, she pulled back the string and put it away in her basket. He made ready to return home. The old woman promised to keep on sending the Morning Stars, and Jalngura promised to return eventually with his wives and children. His spirit wives came down to the beach and cried for him: and he started off, with his canoe full of things the spirits had given him. Eventually he arrived on the mainland shore where his family was awaiting him. That evening he chose one of his wives and they had intercourse together, but in the process he broke his back and died. It was said that his back was weak from too much paddling: but his spirit wives had taken his soul.

TRANSITION

Although each of these last examples is part of a relatively coherent body of belief, more or less the same ideas are current over a wide area of Aboriginal Australia. (See Elkin, 1954: 319.) There are, however, a number of differences. The Land of the Dead may be fairly consistently defined, located either in the sky, or in a certain direction, such as the west, or in a specific place, such as some distant island, real or imagined. Spirits of the dead may reside or merge with the great creative or ancestral beings. Or they may return to a totemic site intimately associated with them. This is the case with many Central Australian tribes, whether or not there is a belief in the plurality of the soul or spirit after death. Strehlow (1947: 42-6) suggests that, where an Aranda person is concerned, "death is, to him, the last great catastrophe which leads to the eventual complete destruction of his own body and of his own spirit". Among the western Aranda, 'the soul goes to the northern ocean, to the island of the dead, and is finally destroyed by lightning during a thunderstorm'. Strehlow emphasizes that the Aranda have "no hope of a future life". Nevertheless, every person is in effect an incarnation of a totemic being: death means the destruction of the material body but not of the spirit, which returns to its source. It is indestructible, like the totemic beings themselves. Although these were sometimes 'killed' or 'died' in the myths, they did not die in spirit: they remained part of the Eternal Dreaming stream—to which human beings also belong. As regards the Aranda, there is still the spiritual essence which is believed to reside in the sacred *tjurunga* possessed by each person: there is still the nucleus of unborn spirits awaiting rebirth. Among the Bidjandjara too, a dead person's spirit, or part of it, goes to its totemic site to await rebirth.

While there is no single uniform belief about a future life

throughout Aboriginal Australia, there are certainly basic similarities. There is no suggestion that wellbeing in the afterlife hinges on the goodness or badness of a person's actions prior to his death. Moral issues appear to be irrelevant in this connection. The supernatural sanctions which are so important in the maintenance of social control do not, as far as we know, take this shape. There is no threat of punishment in the next world for sins committed in this. Where there is reference to discrimination it is not framed in terms of moral behaviour, but points specifically to items of ritual action such as whether the dead person shows the appropriate physical signs of having undergone certain rites, or whether the mourners have attended properly to the mortuary procedures. Even then, the issue of sanctions is usually left vague.

Moreover, despite occasional remarks to the contrary, there seems to be some agreement on the indestructibility of the human spirit. Immediately after death it may retain its individual identity, but generally speaking this is no more than a temporary matter. Loss of personal distinctiveness, or separateness, is not viewed as annihilation of the spirit. Rather, it represents one kind of approach to the concept of immortality, whether or not it involves belief in reincarnation. All over Aboriginal Australia, the concept of the Eternal Dreaming is basic to people's view of the world and of man's relationship to his social and physical environment. The meaning of human existence is not sought only in terms of the brief span in which any given person lives on earth, even though that span serves as a framework for the varying explanations which are provided. These are expressed, fairly generally, through a more or less systematized body of belief centring on birth and rebirth, with death as a form of transition rite ensuring the continuance of a cyclical process, in which the main emphasis is on an essentially unchanging panoramic view of life.

CHAPTER XIV

The Aborigines Today

Can we speak of one way of life as better or more satisfying than another? Is it possible to make such a comparison, except in a superficial or impressionistic way? Many people would answer in the affirmative: philosophers, economists, missionaries, and perhaps almost anyone who has had at least a glimpse into another social and cultural world and has contrasted it at all thoughtfully with his own. Their reasons are not necessarily identical. Nor are they equally systematic in working these out. And assessment in terms of moral and religious principles looms larger for some than for others. What is the local religion? they may ask, and judge accordingly. Or, how much value is placed on human life in that society: in what circumstances can one person take the life of another, and what are the probable consequences? Some pay more attention to points which can be tabulated in a relatively objective way: What are the conditions in which those particular people live? What material equipment do they have, what resources? What limitations or restraints, what areas of freedom? Others are more concerned with the subjective side: What would it feel like to live in that situation? How happy are those people? How would I feel, myself, if I were caught up in that set of circumstances rather than this?

These two dimensions, of course, are not antithetical. How people feel in a situation cannot be divorced entirely from the external realities of that situation. There are basic needs which must be met if an organism is to remain actively alive. But over and above these, people's views of what is necessary for reasonably satisfactory living vary immensely, as part of the complex of assumptions and expectations which helps to differentiate one society from another. What is adequate for one group of people may appear to another as hopeless poverty. Such views are not immutable. They are open to reinterpretation, under pressure. In fact, this is a fundamental premise in the commercial world today with its demands for increasingly higher standards of living, taking into account bare subsistence-level needs only as a base-line, an essential minimum which must be achieved before the real business of selling and buying can begin. To sustain industry and employment, it is said, there must be creation of new needs as well as consolidation of old ones. Possession of more and more consumer goods is presented as not simply desirable, but essential. 'Better living', in this view, rests overwhelmingly on tangible considerations. Such features as houses for shelter and privacy, chairs for sitting on, beds for sleeping on, knives and forks for eating with, clothing for concealment and display as well as for protection from the weather, are often cited as an intrinsic part of Western European culture. Possession of these is an important criterion, but even more important is agreement on the necessity for them. Elaborations on this basic theme, and additions to it, are growing in number. Not only automobiles, television sets, washing machines, but also a host of small items, are widely acclaimed as indispensable.

Considerations of this sort are directly relevant to the Australian Aborigines, who appear to have so little in comparison with many other peoples: who lack what are frequently regarded not merely as luxuries but as basic necessities. The Central desert tribes, in particular, are depicted as being almost as close to bedrock in this respect as any group of people could be. And this aspect of their lives is highlighted in the literature, in discussions of their place among the world's peoples.

Claims to the contrary notwithstanding, it has been demonstrated conclusively that proliferation of material goods does not lead automatically to happiness, or to satisfaction—any more than material poverty does. More crucial in this respect is the matter of level of aspiration: what people want, or consider they ought to have, or be, as contrasted with their actual position; what goals they are aiming at, and how realistic is their appraisal of the possibility of achieving them. In the Aborigines' case, the total range of material things was relatively small. There was not a wide gap between persons on this score. Land was, generally speaking, not a commodity to be assessed in that way; and, despite some discrepancies, other forms of material wealth were fairly evenly distributed. For the most part, too, they had no means of knowing how they stood in this respect in comparison with other peoples. It was only contact with Europeans which made them aware of such possibilities, discontented with what they had, and anxious for more.

THE IMPACT OF THE OUTSIDE WORLD

The coming of Europeans altered the traditional picture drastically, in almost every respect, until today no Aboriginal society has been able to maintain its former integrity and independence. Open resistance was not lacking, but it was intermittent and short-lived. With their poor technology, simple weapons, and elementary notions of both strategy and tactics, the Aborigines were no match for the invaders in any clash of interests between them.

The reasons for their rapid disorganization and relatively easy collapse are to be found not only in the nature of the contact itself. It is true that in many cases, given the disparity in power, the ignorant or unsympathetic approach of Europeans was itself in very large measure responsible for this. But the reasons are to be sought, as well, in the structure and organization of Aboriginal social life and belief, with its heavy emphasis on non-change, on the emotional satisfaction to be derived through extreme dependence on the great mythical beings, through the concept of the Eternal Dreaming. The impact of the outside world came as a rude shock. Things were happening outside the framework of what the Aborigines conceived to be the established order of life, both physical and social: things which were not provided for within that framework, and could not be pigeon-holed into any known category. The traumatic experience of first contact should not be under-estimated. The first Europeans, almost all over the Continent, were regarded as returning spirits of the dead—perhaps frightening and even to some extent unpredictable, but at least beings who could be fitted into the local scheme of things, explained in terms of the local people's own experience, if not assumed to be related to them through kinship. This image of them did not last long. Other terms were used for them too: malignant spirits, strangers, inhuman creatures, and a variety of nicknames which underlined the suspicion and resentment with which they were viewed.

On nearly all counts, the Aborigines were a conservative people. There are many apparent exceptions, especially in the northern part of the Continent, and in the matter of trade—the transmission of rites, songs, stories, and ideas, as well as material objects. On the whole, however, their opportunities for communication with the outside world were restricted and spasmodic. Even allowing for the pre-European impact, which affected only small areas, they were for the most part and for most practical purposes geographically isolated. And inter-tribal exchanges, inter-tribal gatherings, were not on a sufficiently large scale, nor diversified enough, to encourage any but minor or gradual changes. As a further, and crucial, factor there were the limited resources the Aborigines had at their disposal for economic and technical exploitation of their enviroment.

These were all elements which made for conservatism. As far

as our information goes, there were no serious challenges to the established order. Protests, such as they were, took place within the framework of the existing system and did not attempt to overthrow or destroy it. There were rules and sanctions to cope with individual dissenters, or rebels. The simple machinery of government was reasonably adequate for the tasks which confronted it. It was, in general, admirably suited to dealing with problems of law and order in traditional Aboriginal society, where territorial conquest was virtually unknown and warfare spasmodic, more or less localized, and always restricted. But it was ill-equipped to withstand concerted pressures from a complex and politically-oriented society, bent on exterminating, evangelizing, exploiting, incorporating, or adjusting the Aborigines, as the case might be in varying situations and at different times.

These were 'repetitive' societies: their members emphasizing the unchanging quality of life, the importance of tradition, rather than the desirability of change as such. When they were faced with alternative modes of action and choice, as a direct result of contact, they were very ready to accept what they considered to be tangible benefits. But as far as we know, they accepted these at first without any intention of changing their own ways and their own beliefs. They wanted to have both, at the same time, and did not find out until it was too late that this was impossible. They expected the same treatment which they gave, or would have given in such circumstances. They were soon disillusioned: it did not take them long to realize that their values were not those of the newcomers.

In the religious, political, ideological, technical and economic fields, in almost everything, there appeared to be extreme incompatability, with little or no possible rapprochement between the two peoples. This was brought home to each of them, Aborigines and Europeans alike, as contact proceeded, spreading and intensifying over the whole Continent. Today this incompatability has become an underlying assumption of government policies of complete, one-way assimilation, State and Commonwealth alike.

The effect on traditional life

The first British settlement at Port Jackson, in 1788, set in motion a chain of events which have been far-reaching in their effects. What Elkin (1951, 1954) calls a process of "dispossession and de-population of the Aborigines" has been going on ever since that time, as Europeans, or Australian-Europeans, have been pushing forward their frontiers, developing or exploiting the natural resources of the country.

Before this decisive step there had, of course, been isolated visitors, particularly explorers. Dampier, for instance, pausing on the north-west coast in 1688 with his damaged ship, the *Cygnet*, was able to leave for posterity his unfavourable impressions of the Aborigines he met there. Some time after the middle of the sixteenth century the northern part of Australia became known to the Western world through the discoveries of the Dutch and Portuguese. (R. and C. Berndt, 1954; Hart and Pilling, 1960.) From Timor, the Portuguese are said to have raided Melville Island for slaves, especially boys and young men, up to the beginning of the nineteenth century. (Hart and Pilling, 1960: 97-100.) Flinders (1814), anchoring in 1803 in the Malay Road, on the Arnhem Land coast near Elcho Island, met a fleet of praus from the East Indies under the direction of a captain named Pobassoo—the first indication, for most European-Australians, that this seemingly isolated coast had its own source of contact with the wider world outside.

Nevertheless, the popular view of the Aborigines has persisted, as a people remote and secluded from all others from the time they arrived on this Continent until they were disturbed by Europeans. On the whole this is possibly true for the greater part of Australia. It was only a few regions, like Cape York Peninsula, Arnhem Land, particularly the eastern side, and perhaps the north-west coast, which had any substantial contact with non-Europeans.

The Arnhem Land case is especially important, because it was not simply a matter of an exploratory visit or two. First the Bajini, and later the 'Macassans' or Bugis from the Celebes, are said to have maintained their settlements on the coast for a couple of seasons at a time without going home. Their interest in the land, and the people, was almost solely an economic one. The 'Macassans' wanted products like trepang, pearlshell, tortoiseshell and timber. Bartering centres were established. Local Aborigines who collected these products received, in return, goods such as rice, cloth, tobacco, knives, various sweets, or sugared foods. They learned to make large dug-out sea-going canoes, to use iron in making knives, spear blades and axes, and to play various card games. These skills did not lapse, as others did, when the Macassans finally left the coast. Pottery, for example, was not of much use to the Aborigines: they did not need it for cooking, and for water-carrying they had other receptacles. But they had an irregular supply of iron in the nails they found in driftwood that came in with the tides at certain seasons, and these they would beat into shape for their knives and their 'shovel-bladed' or 'shovel-nosed' spears. Occasionally, Aborigines went back to 'Macassar' on the praus as crew, and a few settled down there with local wives. (R. and C. Berndt, 1954.) And on the Arnhem Land coast itself, some of the Aborigines trace close relationship to women who had married locally but, they say, had originally been kidnapped by Macassans from areas some distance away—Borroloola, and other places beyond the Roper River. Other tangible evidence of the visitors survives indirectly in ritual paraphernalia such as grave posts and *wuramu* figures. Less concretely, there are the songs and actions associated with them; and 'play stories', like the tale of Dog, Djuraindjura, who rejected the 'matches' and other benefits the Macassar-men offered him—and so destined the Aborigines to a subsistence-level economy in the bush, in place of what they might have had. (Warner, 1937/58: 536-38, has two variants of this. It is still a popular story at Milingimbi.) Not all the traders seem to have been strict Muslims. Some of them were perhaps indigenous people from the Celebes and neighbouring islands. Several of the coastal sites known by Malay names are pointed out today as places where the traders left offerings to spirits: *garei*, 'king', rocks, as they were called. Also, they are said to have brought arak, especially during the last phase of contact. At the end of each trading season, before the praus sailed for home, there would be ceremonies, with arak-drinking: and this is said to have degenerated into drunkenness and fighting toward the end of the Indonesian period.

After Flinders, other Europeans began to explore the Arnhem Land coast, and to express concern about the riches the traders were taking home with them. A Customs depot was set up, to receive dues. The 'Macassans' resented the move, on the grounds that this trade, which had been going on for such a long time, was their own business. As Europeans tried to exploit the coast for themselves, demanding preferences and some sort of protection, relations between Aborigines and 'Macassans' deteriorated, until finally the visits were prohibited altogether. Some of the eastern Arnhem Landers still tell how the last of the traders severed their ties with the English Company Islands people and said farewell, forced away from their legitimate trading territory by Europeans. Older people look back to the 'Macassan' period as a kind of Golden Age, but the younger folk are forgetting what they have heard of those days; there are so many new things now to capture and hold their interest. But even apart from the Bajini and Macassans, and stories of 'spirit canoes' washed up by the tides, sometimes with people aboard, the eastern Arnhem Landers delight in telling of wrecked canoes or ships which they plundered. Up to the late 1930's they had the reputation of being a fierce and intractable people. Their traditional methods of fighting, for instance, were not typically Aboriginal. (See Chapter X.) On the western side there was trouble with Chinese timber cutters, and also with Japanese: but it was the eastern Arnhem Landers who were mainly involved with the Japanese pearlers: they killed a number of Japanese as well as Europeans in the period up to the early 1930's. In the meantime, the missions had been establishing stations.

To the extent that the eastern Arnhem Landers were conditioned to alien impact, they were in a much better position than Aborigines in other parts of Australia, except, perhaps, Cape York. They had had experience with people unlike themselves, with different ideas and different ways of behaving. To them, therefore, Europeans were not returning spirits of the dead. Contact with the outside world did not come in a sudden tidal wave, or flood, as it had in the south; and because there was no attempt at political control they could adapt their behaviour, and resist some aspects of alien influence while accepting others. What was more, in 1931 Arnhem Land was declared an Aboriginal Reserve. And the Methodist Mission, responsible for the chain of stations along the northern coast, unlike the Church Missionary Society at Oenpelli in the west and Groote Eylandt on the east, was making earnest attempts to build on the native culture instead of destroying it, to learn the local languages, and to take the local people's point of view seriously into account. (C. Berndt, 1961*b*.) All this meant that they retained a good deal of their traditional life, over a longer period than most other Aboriginal groups have been able to do.

Notwithstanding the fact that this traditional life was modified in the process, we can, nevertheless, view it as Aboriginal in contrast with European. Even though during World War II they came into sharp contact with large numbers of Service personnel they kept their independent outlook, and the attitude that they themselves could choose what they wanted, and how far they would co-operate. This cushioning, then, has served them very well up to the present: but today's situation is scarcely comparable. In the 1930's, these people could have the illusion that they were essentially in control of their own affairs. Now they realize that they are not: and this realization itself will certainly affect their future. It has been one of the reasons for the Elcho Island movement, concerned with bringing about a closer rapprochement between traditional and introduced ways of life. (R. Berndt, 1962*a*.)

Generally, the aliens with whom the Aborigines have had dealings of one sort or another fall roughly into three categories: government officials, including police; missionaries, including Fijians attached to the Methodist Overseas Mission; and private persons, including traders. Most of the non-Europeans would come under this last heading: Chinese; Japanese; Indonesians, including Malays on the north-west coast; 'Afghans' in the central areas; and probably South Sea Islanders in Queensland. Many of these aliens were instrumental in altering the lives of the Aborigines they encountered. Some did so deliberately. They wanted to civilize or Christianize them, or turn them into Europeans in all except physical characteristics—and would have altered those, too, if they could. Others had only short-term intentions. They wanted something from the Aborigines, or wanted the Aborigines to do something for them, regardless of the effect this might have on other aspects of Aboriginal life. A few people thought the Aborigines should be shut away in reserves and left to their own devices, but these were very much in a minority.

The very fact that Europeans came to settle on this Continent, with a view to living and making a living here, meant that the Aborigines could not continue to go on as they had been doing.

The European settlers wanted land. Because the Aborigines did not cultivate the ground or make permanent dwellings or settlements, the newcomers did not realize, or care, that the land *was* owned and occupied and used—although on quite a different basis to their own: and so the question of Aboriginal rights to that land hardly concerned them. There were few treaties, as there were in New Zealand, for example, and in North America. The Batman treaty, involving two large tracts of land around Port Phillip Bay, in Victoria, was no more than "a piece of grotesque trickery" (Foxcroft, 1941: 32-8): and there are other similar instances. The Aborigines were landholders, landowners in the broadest sense. To the newer Australians who have supplanted them, land is a source of wealth and of livelihood, a token of security and stability. It was this to the Aborigines too; but because they approached it from a different perspective, because they were semi-nomadic, and because they did not divide up that land into parcels, individually owned, their title to it was not acknowledged. In other words, most of them lost the only tangible asset which had any real value in the new situation of contact; and those who have not, those who still live in Aboriginal reserves, do so virtually on sufferance. More than that, because of the close tie between locality and religion, alienation of territory meant more than a straightforward economic loss.

To the newcomers the land had no meaningful association. Those among them who set a value on the things of antiquity did so in terms of buildings, objects, man-made artefacts, not of natural sites. The Christianity which some of them brought was not locality-bound. The parallel between sacred sites of the Holy

Land or Lands of the Bible and those of the Aborigines was too remote to affect their attitude here—especially since to many of them the indigenous religion was nothing more than a jumble of animistic beliefs and practices which should be superseded at the earliest opportunity. For the settlers, too, these places were not sacred. Some of the most important waterholes were selected as homestead sites, or used for watering cattle, and the Aborigines often driven away from them by force. A few resisted; others submitted, in the hope of salvaging some benefits from the disaster; others again fell back into the country of neighbouring tribes. In any case, in such circumstances their sacred rites were interrupted. Up to a point that did not matter, because these could be performed from a distance—provided the group concerned had some cohesion, and continued to believe in their efficacy. But both these aspects were affected too.

Further, traditionally the whole system of maintaining authority, within a community and in relations between communities, depended on the older men's being able to control the younger people. (See Chapter X.) Contact with aliens altered this, in a wide range of ways. For one thing it led to a cleavage between the generations, a divergence in perspective. And interference with ceremonies, or sacred rites, directly undermined the influence of the older men. This was not so obvious on pastoral or sheep stations. So long as the Aborigines did as they were told and avoided being a nuisance, the station people did not normally care a great deal about their private life. If ceremonies were held some distance away from a station and did not interfere with the Aborigines' capacity or willingness to work, they were not usually prohibited as such. There was not a direct attempt to suppress them on moral or religious grounds. Many of these people ill-treated the Aborigines, or exploited them in other ways; but they did not as a rule deliberately interfere with ritual life, although in the long run their actions indirectly had that effect. Missionaries, in contrast, rarely subjected the Aborigines to physical maltreatment, and frequently had the best of intentions; but they did, almost inevitably, undermine the principles and the assumptions on which Aboriginal life was based.

The rights and wrongs of this do not concern us here. However, missions, and missionaries, are far from uniform in either policy or practice. Some are intent on stamping out Aboriginal culture entirely, even to the extent of calling for police assistance in breaking up initiation camps, and speaking of all traditional practices and beliefs as devil-sponsored, leading inexorably to hell and eternal damnation. Even ordinary camp singing may be included in this category. (See R. and C. Berndt, 1951/2.) With this extreme attitude go other aspects, handled with greater or less rigidity: forcibly taking children into dormitories and forbidding or restricting access to parents; interfering with marriage customs; undermining the authority of older people, for instance by overriding or even openly mocking at their attempts to influence the young; holding up sacred objects to ridicule, and displaying to children or to women things which are not only sacred but conventionally secret to adult men. This negative approach was more prevalent in the past than it is today. In contrast, and more in accordance with humanitarian ideals, are those missions which try to find a firm basis for their teaching in the local culture itself; to make use of its potentialities instead of flatly asserting that there are none; to learn the local language; and generally, with varying degrees of conviction and varying success, to understand the Aborigines' point of view.

Missions aside, the very presence of Europeans in the land was in itself sufficient to change the whole tenor of Aboriginal life. There was no practical way to evade the pressures which stemmed from it. Some escaped them for many years. Others felt them quite early in the history of settlement. Since the spread of settlement was not uniform throughout the Continent, numbers of Aborigines were able not simply to go on living, but to do so in almost the same way as before. But this was no more than a breathing space. From present indications it is only a matter of time before they too relinquish their traditional heritage, and the life which they or their forefathers knew becomes only a memory, a thing of the past.

In its early phases, even around the southern settlements and much more so in 'frontier' regions, contact was relatively uncontrolled—and continued that way for a long period in parts of the north. Gradually, missionaries and government welfare officers began to have some effect. Questions of humanity came to have a more practical meaning. Maltreatment and violence declined; only here and there, in a few isolated pockets, they were held up as the only 'language' the Aborigines could understand. There were signs that a happier relationship between the two peoples might be possible, after all. But although the nature of the approach was changing, the goal itself was, if anything, more tightly defined—and still in one-way terms, conditional on the disappearance of all Aboriginal cultural and social life, as a going concern. It may be that this is the only solution to the problem. But in considering that point, let us look at the situation from a slightly different angle, and in somewhat greater detail.

The trend toward assimilation

One of the most striking features of first contact between Aborigines and Europeans, wherever and whenever it took place, was the highlighting of the differences between them. The Aborigines themselves have left no adequate records of what they thought about this contact, in the southern part of the Continent, although some stories have been handed down through the generations by word of mouth. There are scattered references in the literature to what individual Aborigines said of their own response when they saw Europeans for the first time. But most early writers record frankly what they and other Europeans thought of the Aborigines. Mostly it was unfavourable. (Hasluck, 1942; Turnbull, 1948.)

Responsibility for this lies partly with the particular period during which first settlement took place—the whole climate of opinion which influenced the settlers at that particular time. Christian ideals were balanced, if not outweighed, by materialistic notions of progress, by preoccupation with property and wealth. The situation was much too complex to be summed up in a few words: but in some respects the range of tolerance was narrower than today, the conventional rejection of foreign ideas and behaviour less vulnerable to challenge or doubt. Of course, there were exceptions (Flanagan, 1888: reprinted from articles published in 1853-4; Haygarth, 1850; Massary, 1861—to name only three). But contact with the Aborigines highlighted this tendency to intolerance. On the whole, the European settlers did not regard the Aborigines as being seriously important in their scheme of things. They had their own ideas of how human beings should behave, the kind of life they should lead, and they judged other human societies in the light of these standards. In fact, the Aborigines seemed to them so different that many considered them scarcely human. It was not simply that these people were dark in colour and wore no clothes. They were semi-nomadic too, a wandering people, who practised no agriculture, had no domesticated animals, other than dogs, and few material possessions. Worse still, they did not seem to attach great weight to much of what they did have: they showed no interest in accumulating wealth, in acquiring and keeping a wide range of material objects. To the settlers, who were property-conscious, strongly aware of the importance of wealth, even when they themselves owned little or none, accustomed to assessing the status and the merits of others in such terms, this outlook was hardly comprehensible. It was almost enough, apart from anything else, to damn the Aborigines in the eyes of the settlers.

Of course, there was an element of rationalization present too. It was easier for the settlers to take over the country if they regarded the Aborigines in this way. As the member for Geraldton (Western Australia) said in 1892: "It will be a happy day for Western Australia and Australia at large when the natives and kangaroos disappear . . . in dealing with this matter all maudlin sentiment should be abolished. The time has come for drastic, exact and positive measures, administered not with a light hand." (Reported in Hasluck, 1942: 192.) Attitudes like this were nothing out of the ordinary; and they are far from uncommon even today.

Aboriginal culture, complex as it was, did not lie in the direction of material wealth, permanent settlements or elaborate clothing. Oriented about rather different values, it was not of a kind to be immediately obvious to strangers, or to people who were content to judge others on the basis of external appearances. Where the Aborigines' social arrangements were concerned, it was the same story. Lacking an abundance of material things, they concentrated their attention on relations between man and his natural environment, and between human beings themselves. Especially, they elaborated on the topic of social relations.

Because the population in any given area was relatively small, its density relatively low, with contacts largely on a primary, face-to-face, basis, those relations were oriented for the most part along the two intersecting planes of kinship and locality. But the people who were introducing a new way of living to this Continent, building up a new nation, did not conceptualize their social world in that way. Kinship was, to them, largely a personal matter, confined to the domestic sphere—not something to span a whole society. Inter-personal relations outside the elementary family were framed in more impersonal terms: the secondary, Gesellschaft-type relationships which predominate in the Western world today. Even in regard to the elementary family itself, differences in context made for differing ideas about the relations between that unit and its social environment. Much that the Aborigines took for granted was not only unfamiliar but also unacceptable to the newcomers: the classificatory system of kinship, with its extension of primary terms (father, mother, brother, sister) to a wide range of persons outside the immediate family; the widespread recognition of parent-surrogates; polygyny; the limiting of marriage choices in accordance with specified rules; infant and child betrothal; emphasis on the role of kinsfolk in arranging and sustaining a marriage; absence of elaborate marriage rites—perhaps because safeguards and checks were envisaged as lying in the set of marriage rules and in the active concern of kin on both sides, in a small-scale society where local horizons were limited and people could not easily escape from the system. Points like these, and many others, contrasted sharply with what was to become known, in time, as the Australian way of life—or, more properly, a Western European and quasi-British way of life, modified in an Australian setting.

This is not the place to dwell on comparisons, or contrasts, relevant as they are to the story of Aboriginal-white contact. Basic similarities were overlaid by such striking divergences that the total effect of the impact, through time, has been devastating. The Aborigines could hardly have been subjugated by a people more unlike themselves, and less in sympathy with their whole orientation toward living. They became exiles in their own land, or what had been their own land. They could not return to their own familiar environment: it was becoming remote from them in time, not in space. With the growth of settlements, even the contours of the land they knew were becoming strange to them. As their world broke up around them, and they turned for support to the newcomers who had brought this about, so their dependence in more than an economic sense increased. The state of affairs which ensued reinforced, as in a vicious circle, the charges of inferiority already levelled against them.

Active and alert in the traditional scene, since their survival rested on being so, in this new situation they were accused of being inherently lazy and prone to idleness. Settled in static camps, laden with cast-off clothing which they had no means of maintainin good order and repair, they were reproached with dirtiness as an inherently Aboriginal attribute. Accustomed as they were, traditionally, to relying on memory for transmitting and reproducing detailed genealogies, myth, and song material, and the minutiae of 'natural history' information necessary to everyday living, now they were claimed to have a short span of attention, to lack the ability to concentrate. Because their rhythm of everyday living was based on a different time-perspective, dependent on natural sequences (sun and moon, the cycle of the seasons) rather than on a rigid pattern of chronological reckoning, they were accused of being shiftless, having no sense of time. Capable of sustained effort in hunting and ritual affairs, responsible in attending to their own economic and social obligations, they were censured now as undependable, unwilling to work, basically irresponsible.

These are popular stereotypes, pervasive, and difficult to eradicate. Despite many examples to the contrary, they continue to assert not simply that the Aborigines 'are like that', but that this state of affairs is quite independent of their environment: that it persists, like a racial or tribal memory, among people of Aboriginal descent in whatever degree, ready to reappear at the least sign of encouragement, or the least weakening in measures designed to combat it.

The popular folklore which has grown up in Australia about

Two *wuramu* posts, one not fully painted. These are used in mortuary ceremonies and represent 'Macassans': the triangular designs are clouds (see Chapters XII and XIII). Elcho Island (1961)

The Kunapipi *nanggaru* pit; this represents the uterus of the Mother, and also the sacred waterhole into which various totemic animals (symbolized by the postulants) dived after escaping from the two Wawalag sisters. The Python design is etched around the walls of the *nanggaru*. (See Chapters VII and VIII.) Oenpelli, western Arnhem Land (1949-50)

the Aborigines rests only in small part on an informed understanding of their traditional life. It is a patchwork of exaggerations, distortions, half-truths, compounded on the basis of emotional prejudice, and supported by evidence from contact situations in which Aborigines have made, from that point of view, a poor showing.

Attitudes such as these are more than a faint echo from a dead past. On the contrary, they are still very much alive, although not quite so blatantly as they were. In outback regions the Aborigines in many cases did not know enough English to understand what was being said about them, and often *to* them, any more than they realized the connotation of the 'swear' words and obscenities they imitated from the speech of the people around them. Learning English helped to sharpen their perception of Aboriginal-white relations, to become more aware of the low esteem in which they were held. But even in places where first contact lies several generations back, where such statements are now more politely phrased, the memory and the anticipation of them linger on among the people most directly affected by them, to influence their behaviour today.

The same criteria as before are used in judging people such as the Aborigines: the same points are still brought up in evaluating their traditional life. We are more likely to treat individual Aborigines as human beings, to express concern for their health, education, employment and general wellbeing; but one question which confronted the early settlers still remains. How far can we live side by side, in harmony, with a people whose way of living diverges radically from our own? Is there room for such differences in one community, or one small nation? The question was not phrased explicitly in these terms, to begin with: but it was asked, nevertheless, and it points to the core of the problem which concerns us today.

The answer was never really in doubt, notwithstanding dissent and even active opposition. There was some hesitation in framing it, and political pressures were less obtrusive: but it was, essentially, the same answer which is put forward now in relation not only to this indigenous minority but to immigrant minorities as well. To begin with, it was expressed as a matter of straightforward conviction, not open to doubt: that the Aborigines' only hope for the future lay in Europeanization; that it would be inhumane or short-sighted to leave them alone, especially once the first contact had been made. There was some argument about whether this was in fact the best thing for them, whether the alternative of leaving them alone might not be possible away from the settled areas; but the main trend, in actions even more than in words, was unmistakably against this. Today the answer of 'inevitable Europeanization' is uttered with more conviction, and even less room for contrary opinion; and while it is presented as being, undeniably, to the advantage of the people concerned, the overriding reason is couched in terms of the interests of the country as a whole. Now that so much emphasis is placed on building up the Australian nation, as a single people with a relatively homogeneous way of life, the notion of a plural society, or of several distinct societies within the same Continent, has become even less acceptable than it was. Officially, opinion on this score has hardened noticeably in the years since World War II, and measures for achieving that goal have been intensified accordingly.

In the early days of settlement, even where the same aim was acknowledged, or at least latent, a major source of difficulty was how it should be implemented: the practical issue of 'what should be done with the Aborigines, now'.

Two broad approaches stand out in the attempts to find solutions, in respect of both goals and means. People some distance away from the actual situation, provided they are reasonably well informed about it, are in a better position to see it in context, to consider alternative courses of action, to suggest what should be or should have been done there, to be critical of mistakes. Looking back into the past from the vantage point of the present, for instance, without being personally embroiled in it, we can see this particular set of circumstances in wider perspective. We know more, today, about the Aborigines, more about our own kind of society—and more about what can be expected to happen when a semi-nomadic people with a subsistence economy comes into collision with an infinitely more numerous and powerful immigrant population. In the same way, when control was exercised by the Colonial Office in London it was relatively easy for the officials there to issue instructions that Aboriginal rights should be safeguarded, that they should be accorded all the benefits of British subjects. Most of them, however, had never seen an Aboriginal; and they were so remote from the Australian scene, in terms of physical distance, experience, and total environment, that their suggestions appeared unrealistic to people actually on the spot. These people on the spot represent the second broad approach to the question. The problems which confronted them from day to day were usually more pressing from their point of view than welfare ideals. Their response was very largely conditioned by these difficulties, by the frequent need for immediate decisions, immediate action. In this approach short-range expediency prevailed, even though altruistic considerations may have been present in the background.

Throughout the Continent, in these early days, official plans for dealing with the Aborigines were haphazard and inconsistent. There was no comprehensive policy; and no one was competent to deal with the question as a whole, taking into account both humanitarian ideals and the practical needs of all sections of the local population. The social sciences, including anthropology, were ill-developed: they could offer little help. The record of early European contact with Aborigines is shadowed by blunders, mistakes and shortcomings, muddling and self-interest. Violence, too. The period between 1840 and 1880 was, as Elkin (1951, 1954) has called it, one of 'clash'; following it, or concurrent with it, came 'pacification by force'. Among the better known examples are the 'rising' of 1842-4 in New South Wales (Flanagan, 1888: 130-54) and the 'Battle of Pinjarra' in 1835, in Western Australia (Hasluck, 1942: 50; Crowley, 1960: 30). Even more notorious is the first clash between Tasmanians and Europeans in 1803, and the 'Black Drive' of 1830 when the colonists there endeavoured to capture at one blow the entire Aboriginal population. (Melville, 1851: 364-8.) From a population of several thousand at first settlement, the last person was dead by 1876. (Melville, 1851: 345, gives a figure of 'nearly twenty thousand'. Turnbull, 1948: 5, notes that "it has been placed as high as eight thousand and as low as seven hundred".)

Less spectacularly, and on a smaller scale, much the same story can be told for every State. In Victoria, between 1835 and 1839, the number of Aborigines fell by two or three thousand. (Foxcroft, 1941: 53.) In Queensland there 'were cruel killings on both sides'. (Bleakley, 1961: 74.) In parts of South Australia (R. and C. Berndt, 1951/2), Western Australia, and the Northern Territory, brutality of various kinds was still taking place right up to the early 1940's. All this is no secret. But while there is no need to labour the point, it cannot be simply dismissed as irrelevant to the present.

The process of dispossession and depopulation which commenced with the first European settlement of Australia is not yet concluded. It took place quickly in the southern half of the Continent, in places where the newcomers found country and climate not too different from what they were accustomed to and therefore established themselves in greater numbers. The accounts of what happened in these places, divergent as they are in detail and local colour, all have the same familiar ring. The same scenes are being enacted, with the same ending.

From Perth, in 1834, there are reports of natives being made drunk, and of interference with women; in 1842, of venereal disease; in 1857, of growing drunkenness among them, and of sexual associations between convicts and native women, whose husbands were paid in drink. (Hasluck, 1942: 22.) Haygarth (1850: 102) speaks of 'the debased specimens that are to be met with in the streets of Sydney', 'the state of demoralization into which they have fallen', and the scenes around the 'public houses'. Lancelott (1853: 205) writes that Aborigines, camped in the Adelaide park-lands, are useful to the colonists as wood-choppers and light porters. They hold noisy 'corrobories', he says, have no sense of shame, are arrant beggars and inveterate smokers, 'jabber English', delight in 'profane oaths'; and their huts are 'dens of filth'. And so on.

Comments such as these could be multiplied for one area after another. The conditions in which the Aborigines found themselves gave them little opportunity either to keep up their traditional practices, or to obtain more than a precarious foothold in the world which had supplanted them. Introduced diseases came into the picture too. Wherever Europeans settled in any numbers, the trend was the same. The Aborigines around them began to die out. Sometimes others came in to take their place, and suffered the same fate.

Not only did the Aboriginal population in the south decline. The survivors were beginning to adopt some European ways, at least superficially. And there was a growing number of half-castes, offspring of European or other alien fathers and Aboriginal mothers. This dual process has continued all through the southern part of the Continent: diminishing 'Aboriginality', in physical as well as in cultural traits; and on both these scores a growing resemblance to Europeans. Decrease in the full-blood population and the disappearance of most aspects of Aboriginal culture have been paralleled by a rise in the number of part-Aborigines, people only partly Aboriginal in descent; and by more complete and more widespread acceptance of Australian-European habits of living.

Some of these part-Aborigines are not accepted on equal terms by the people about them. They are regarded as being different, in fact as inferior, to the rest of the community: they live in separate sections of it, or are conspicuous in other ways. A few, the lighter ones especially, have been absorbed into the wider society; but the environment most favourable to this is the larger cities where, generally speaking, personal antecedents and family background count for less than individual behaviour and individual performance. They have learned to be semi-nomadic in a new and different sense—the mobility of an industrial society, where it is becoming increasingly less common for people to remain all their lives in the place where they were born, or to express deep attachment to one piece of land rather than other. And they have been learning a new kind of economic interdependence, not framed in the close person-to-person terms of Aboriginal tradition: the large-scale interdependence of a society in which specialization of occupational skills makes co-operation between its component parts even more pressing, and the prospect of failure in this respect even more hazardous for personal and social survival.

In the rest of the Continent, in the north and in areas which Europeans found less inviting, the story has been almost identical. The Aborigines' tribal lands were occupied, with the consequence that they were expelled from these entirely, or allowed only limited access to them. Even where this did not happen, even when they were sheltered to some extent by the provision of separate reserves, they have been drawn into the settlements, through curiosity or the desire for new foods and new goods. From Arnhem Land, too, the middle 1940's saw a sharp increase in the westward drift to Darwin and other settlements along the north-south road. People from as far east as Yirrkalla made their way there, by canoe or overland, in search of novelty and excitement. The Methodist mission stations along this coast, in particular, offer some economic and social security in the shape of employment possibilities, medical treatment, trade stores where various handcrafts are purchased, and schools which have improved immeasurably in the post-war period. They serve as buffers between the local people and the more impersonal, often less friendly, world outside. Through them new ideas are being introduced, but also new needs; and the means of satisfying them are not always available. It is often in search of these that people leave their homes, not because they are looking for food to keep them alive, nor even because they are attracted by the freedom a new environment might seem to offer.

Apart from the wider range of employment possibilities, the townships afford more opportunities for observation of Europeans if not for intimate association with them; for a wider range of foods; for the illusion of being able to dispense with personal ties, or to shake free of kinship obligations, to select sweethearts or marital partners from a larger population and with more attention to personal choice. Also, an important consideration for people from mission stations which frown on these, there is the chance to join in card games where gambling is the rule, and, however surreptitiously, to obtain liquor. Where traditional activities have been suppressed, or are gradually lapsing, the hiatus cannot always, or easily, be filled by education and employment. Even if opportunities for these are present, there is still the problem of entertainment, or relaxation.

All over the centre and north, Aborigines have been moving out of their 'tribal' territories. This drift is almost as compulsive as if they were deliberately rounded up, except that they have an appearance of choice which is lacking when they are brought in to gaol, for instance, or, especially in the past, to a leper hospital. Today, the great Aboriginal Reserves stretching across the centre of the Continent, into South and Western Australia and the Northern Territory, are almost empty. People have drifted west into Wiluna and Laverton and Kalgoorlie, south to the Transcontinental Line. Some have come eastward to Oodnadatta, although there were attempts to block this a few years ago. West of Oodnadatta, pastoral and sheep stations extend as far as the Everard Ranges. One reason for the establishment of Ernabella Mission was that it should deflect the movement of bush people from the Musgraves and the Petermann Ranges into these stations and so on to the township. The argument was two-fold: the Aborigines must be protected from the kind of contact they would be subjected to in those places, and the settlers must be protected from the Aborigines—who were spearing stock, camping around the waterholes, and damaging windmills by taking metal to use in making spearheads. But Ernabella failed to stem the drift entirely. The government, therefore, tried additional measures of a more repressive kind. Every now and then, up to a few years ago at least, police based at Oodnadatta led patrols through the region, driving bush Aborigines back to the Central Reserve. This procedure is less necessary than it was. The demarcation between station and bush people is becoming blurred. Sometimes, so-called bush people turn out to be simply station people 'on walkabout'—people who spend part of the year in employment, and the rest in the bush: but most of them are coming to spend more of their time around the stations or other centres.

No such obstacles stood in the way of the southward movement from the Central Reserve to the Transcontinental Line. Before the Maralinga base was established there was no European settlement between the Musgraves and Petermanns on the north and the Transcontinental Line on the south, except on the eastern and western fringes. Apart from occasional travellers no Europeans were occupying tribal territories there, or interfering with sacred sites, or disrupting game or food supplies. No direct pressure was exerted on the Aborigines to leave their own lands, and no direct inducements were offered them to do so. Nevertheless, they came. The Transcontinental Line, and the mission station at Ooldea, now abandoned, appear to have been an irresistible attraction to these people from the spinifex country and the central ranges; and the local tribes, scattered and virtually extinct, offered no obstacle.

It seems indisputable that most of them had at first no intention of giving up their own familiar habits of living. They simply wanted the novelty of something different—exotic goods, new comforts and luxuries. They did not realize the implications. A major attraction was food. When they could get even small quantities of this around the settlements with little trouble, as compared with the ways in which they usually obtained it, they tended to hang around the centre of supply without moving away, to make fewer and fewer hunting trips. But this in itself—accepting the food, or the easy rewards of begging along the Line, or of prostitution—altered their whole outlook. They grew more and more dependent on this kind of situation in which they could get rations, or food, tobacco, or other goods, with a minimum of effort. Once they have become used to this kind of life they rarely go back to their former environment, or their former ways of obtaining food. They have new needs now, which cannot be satisfied there. Inevitably, then, they cluster around the settlements, accepting spasmodic employment, of a sort, depending on what skills they have been able to acquire, and gradually coming to feel more at home there than anywhere else.

This does not mean that traditional life has entirely come to an end. The people of the Western Desert, just as in some other central and northern areas, have kept up many of their rituals even when they have lost their economic and political independence. But their attention is shifting. And even for the few who consciously resist the pull of the settlements, trying to keep their accustomed ways intact, the shape of their world is not the same as it was—if only through the gaps left by their less conservative kinsmen or fellow countrymen. On the western side, the 'desert' people have given a new impetus to traditional beliefs and ideas: their reputation is acknowledged in areas where these have no counterpart in actual practice. In the long-settled Murchison, for instance, 'desert law' is still conceived of as a force to be reckoned with. Around Port Hedland too, and north to the Fitzroy River, religious rituals and sorcery attributed to the 'desert' still have power to disturb people who are well on the way to being acculturated—who have taken as a 'model for living' the European-Australians and others around them.

Outside the towns and cities, and apart from missions, cattle and sheep stations have been probably the most important focal points of contact from almost the first period of settlement. They vary considerably, of course, in size, wealth, staffing arrangements, authority patterns (resident owner, visiting owner, working manager responsible to a company with headquarters in the south), and not least in their relations with Aborigines. But here we are interested in the general picture rather than in particular situations.

The association between settlers on outback stations and the

Aborigines whose country they were occupying often had an unhappy beginning. In closely settled areas the local people were caught up more quickly and brusquely in the new order; but there were officials fairly close at hand whose business it was to maintain law and order, however much they diverged in practice from abstract ideals of justice for all. In outback regions there were not; or if there were, circumstances were such that Aboriginal welfare was not their first consideration. And although the settlers were few and scattered, this lack was sometimes made up in another way: the whole area might be heavily stocked with cattle instead of people. As the stock spread across the country, eating out indigenous foods, driving away game, monopolizing waterholes, the Aborigines were forced to compete with them. Their source of livelihood was directly affected. Some attacked the stations or the settlers, or speared the cattle: and the settlers often responded with violence. This was warfare, small-scale, as Aboriginal warfare usually was—small parties harassing the settlers, and the settlers determined to put a stop to this at all costs, or almost so. It was in this kind of context that punitive or 'pacificatory' expeditions took place. The record here is not a pleasant one. In some areas an atmosphere of bitterness persists, crystallized in the memory of various hostile incidents: and sites of massacres or even of single killings are landmarks for present-day Aborigines and, often, part-Aborigines.

In more isolated regions, especially on the larger holdings, something very much like a feudal situation developed: an overlord, with a circle of serfs over whom he had almost absolute power. The Aborigines, whether full-time employees or simply dependants ('hangers-on'), were allowed to remain there on sufferance. They owned neither the huts in which they lived nor the land on which these were built, they had no rights of tenure, and in some cases have been sold or transferred with the property. Their security depended on the new landholders—a precarious security at times and in places where there were few, if any, checks or curbs on the treatment accorded these people who had, for a long period, no effective rights at law. There were humane men among the settlers; but there were others, too. In coping with these circumstances the Aborigines made use of the approach which had served them so well in their traditional environment. They did not try to change their surroundings, human and otherwise; instead they tried to exploit them, to adapt to them while deriving from them all the benefits they could. As part of this approach they learned, of necessity, to be submissive, even ingratiating. The more truculent among them, persistently 'cheeky' or slow to recognize their place, were summarily taught their lesson: or banished, 'sent bush' as 'bad niggers', and so cut off from the material things they had come to find almost indispensable. They served as examples, and warnings, to those who might be tempted to respond in the same way. For numbers of owners, managers, stockmen, cooks, and station people generally, this seems to have been the only discipline they knew how to exercise. Others, more subtly, drew on the mutual needs which linked them with the Aborigines: the need for labour; and the need for goods, reinforced by the fact that many of the Aborigines, reluctant to move away into strange territory, had nowhere else to go.

The presence of white women was not enough in itself to improve the position. For many of them, too, firmness meant rough handling when necessary; but the point at which it became 'necessary' was much earlier for some than for others. Nevertheless, indirectly, as the number of white women on the stations increased so the rawness of conditions there was moderated. Through their demands for more amenities, they eventually brought about improved communications with the world outside and, consequently, better opportunities for outside supervision of local affairs. And by establishing families they helped to restore a more normal flavour to station living and so to reduce, although not to eradicate, the incidence of sexual associations between white men and Aboriginal women—which in fact, in such regions, were widely acclaimed as normal and natural. In a very few instances liaisons of this kind may have had their source in genuine affection between the man and the woman concerned. More often they were asymmetrical arrangements, which flourished as they did because the Aborigines' demand for material goods and introduced foods, including beef, outstripped their ability to satisfy it through other means, such as employment: and because their traditional permissiveness in regard to some extra-marital relations provided a loophole which could be expanded without too much difficulty. What it amounted to in many cases was a triangular situation in which a young woman lived almost simultaneously with her Aboriginal husband and with a white man, who had in practice more rights over her than her husband did because of the tremendous discrepancy in status between the two men.

Aboriginal women were regarded as ideal go-betweens for mediating between their menfolk and the settlers: more docile, more submissive, more amenable to reason. The men were often kept at arm's length, allowed much less latitude, treated less familiarly. This was especially marked in areas where women and young girls were associating with the settlers not so much from choice, or a desire for goods, but because they had been demanded under threat of deprivation or violence from their husbands, fathers, or brothers who had made a show of resistance. The influence of white women, blunting the edges of this picture and minimizing some of its crudities, at least on the surface, nonetheless perpetuated the theme of Aboriginal woman as intermediaries. In this case the emphasis was on the domestic sphere but without the sexual connotations: and although it did not undermine family life in the same way, it reinforced the disparity in status between the sexes. Aboriginal women, in this situation, had more avenues open to them than their menfolk did to enhance their status: not merely through straightforward employment but also through sexual association and even, occasionally, marriage with members of the dominant population.

Partly because of developments in the southern areas, partly because of pressures in the international sphere, conditions on these stations have been gradually changing. At the same time, everywhere traditional Aboriginal beliefs and activity are giving way to what passes as European. The centre of interest has been shifting from the camp, and from the sacred ground, to the station and its activities—and, through these, to the wider society. The same shift in focus has been taking place on government and mission stations, as 'half-way houses' or halting places on the road to Europeanization.

Elkin (1951: 164-86) has outlined this process as a series of phases leading to the goal of assimilation; but it is slow, and fraught with difficulties. The sequence is reversible, and variable, according to local circumstances at a particular time. Set-backs include pauperism, depopulation, disillusionment, resentment, or reaction. A few Aborigines try to recapture the 'good old days', only to find that it is impossible to recreate the life their parents or grandparents knew. In any case, even if that were feasible they themselves, brought up in a different environment, with different assumptions and aspirations, could not easily adjust to it. Some, less ambitiously, attempt a partial or even a complete withdrawal. Petri speaks of people in the Ninety Mile Beach area of Western Australia, who have endeavoured to turn their backs on European life, especially station life and all that goes with it. Others have found release from the exigencies of their workaday world in magico-religious activity—such as what Lommel (1950) calls the 'cult of despair', the *gurangara* of the Kimberleys. Elkin (1951: 177) points to manifestations of resentment on the north coast of New South Wales, where Aboriginal religion was acclaimed as equal to Christianity, and there was a revival of the local Aboriginal language.

An example in a more positive vein is the Pindan Co-operative in the Port Hedland area of Western Australia. Its members, almost entirely Aboriginal or part-Aboriginal in descent, have been engaged largely in surface mining, selling what they get to southern markets on a collective basis. (See J. Wilson, 1962; K. Wilson, 1961.) They are concerned with holding their own economically, with improving their position, and with ensuring that their children have enough education to help them to do better still. At the same time, in the structuring of their social relations, in sanctions and rules, in means of maintaining group cohesion, they draw heavily on the various tribal backgrounds which are represented among them. In social organization they make use of the section system, and of kin-based and locality-based affiliations. Their ritual and ceremonial complex includes secret-sacred objects, jealously guarded. And so on. Although the co-operative has split now into two groups, one under the leadership of a white Australian whose encouragement was first responsible for its taking the shape that it did, there is still the same attempt at blending, at drawing on the total social and cultural environment, Aboriginal and European, to form a cohesive and satisfying whole.

More traditionally Aboriginal in quality, the Elcho Island 'adjustment movement' symbolizes a people's struggle to retain something of their own culture, and at the same time to have fuller representation and more independence of action and decision in matters which directly concern them.

Generally, however, excluding such exotic exceptions, the majority of these people are today becoming more and more like those in the south—who are already, both in appearance and in manner of living, European in all but physical characteristics, and often very largely so in that respect as well. The concerted efforts of organizations directly interested in Aboriginal welfare, formally and otherwise, are designed to draw them all more closely into the orbit of the wider community: not simply to do away with unfavourable discrimination, but also to eradicate differences which point to their Aboriginal ancestry.

Nearly all people whom we now call Aborigines are inevitably involved in processes which *could* lead to assimilation. Those nearest that goal are to be found in the cities and in the large towns. Few of them have any coherent knowledge of their Aboriginal traditions. Most of them are under-privileged, handicapped by restrictive legislation, poorly trained and educated, often living in semi-slum conditions alongside other Australians of low socio-economic status. Partly on these grounds, there has been a widespread reluctance, in the community in general, to accept them socially on equal terms—despite exceptions on both sides. In some cases the formal granting of citizenship, as a privilege to be applied for, depended until very recently on whether a person cut himself away from all his Aboriginal associates, including relatives outside his immediate family. Reaction to all this, and reluctance to become caught up in a status-improvement cycle which would entail effort out of all proportion (some say) to the rewards it might bring, lead many of them to resist, at least for the time being, the pressures directed against them for complete absorption. (R. Berndt, 1961*a*: 39-42.)

* * * * *

In this final chapter we have been concerned primarily with the effect European settlement has had on Aboriginal traditional life as a whole, rather than with local details. This is not the place to dwell, even in summary, on problems of adjustment to changing conditions, or of welfare, or such issues as citizenship, or the right to drink or to vote. In one form or another these are Continent-wide today. Most of what we have been discussing in the main body of this volume is no longer in existence, no longer open to observation, or only in a modified form. There are virtually no Aboriginal groups which have not had some contact with Europeans, by hearsay or repute if not through direct face-to-face association.

People whom we call traditionally-oriented are harder to find than they were a few years ago. Including those in outback areas, on fringe settlements or mission stations, it is doubtful whether they could number any more than seven thousand or so. Most of them, these days, have some kind of relationship with Europeans; they have been influenced considerably by forces outside their traditional Aboriginal world; nevertheless, for ordinary purposes of living that traditional world, reformulated as it is in varying ways, is still more real to them than all the rest. Just how long this orientation can be sustained is a matter for conjecture; but taking into account the rate of change in the past decade, a conservative estimate would possibly be no more than ten years or so. (See Strehlow, 1959; R. Berndt, 1959*b*.) This is not to say that traditional elements will cease to survive in some form or other, but that Aboriginal life, as a way of life, will have ceased to exist.

Even if it were desirable to stem the trend, that would not be possible. The Aborigines' chance of survival as a traditionally-oriented minority would be very remote indeed. Nor, in the circumstances, can we speak realistically of integration, in contrast to one-way assimiliation, or absorption. Certainly there are many examples of blending in cultural and social terms, but this is not the end of the process. The inevitable outcome, everywhere, is that the Aboriginal elements are pushed further and further into the background. Artificial plans to achieve integration, or pluralism, could be successful only with some measure of political or at least economic independence; and this is not feasible.

Segregation is out of the question too, except as a temporary measure designed to protect the Aborigines until they are able to acquire enough in the way of occupational skills and bargaining power to cope with other Australians on their own terms. It is largely because this extra help was not available to them in the past, or not systematically so, that such numbers of them are at a disadvantage today. In some areas where Aboriginal minorities have emerged, informal restrictions have led to segregation of a sort; but this is envisaged as a transient state of affairs, lacking majority approval, frowned on by governments, and anxiously deplored by welfare organizations. Aboriginality, on an Australia-wide basis, means no more than a common identification in physical terms, the accident of Aboriginal descent: and acknowledgment of this is not encouraged because it works against formal policies of assimilation.

While many people of part-Aboriginal descent know little or nothing of their past, the past as such still plays a significant part in their lives. It is still important to know something of the background of contact, if we want to understand their present-day problems. For many others, knowledge of their immediate past, their traditional Aboriginal heritage, is essential if we are to avoid the mistakes which have dogged Aboriginal administration and European-Aboriginal relations since the early days.

We are in no position to evaluate traditional Aboriginal life, as better or worse than any other. It was a way of life which was intimately attuned to the Australian environment. It was restricted and circumscribed in certain respects, as are all ways of life. Its closeness to the natural environment and its view of the world made it inevitable that when European contact came the Aborigines would find immense difficulty in adapting to living conditions which were diametrically opposed to their own. Their almost complete isolation in the past, their lack of communication with the outside world, their preoccupation with survival in a relatively harsh environment, and their virtually closed religious system: all these served to handicap them in their relations with the aliens. They were not receptive, except in a limited sense—mainly at the level of material things, and then only so far.

Responsibility for this rests, in part, on the manner in which they were introduced to the new order: the kind of people who associated with them, the kind of teaching meted out to them. Even when goodwill was there, as often it was not, the impression persisted that this goodwill was enough. In some quarters even today, the assumption is that there is no need to divert the best trained people to this sphere: that because it is hard to interest them in such work, or because it is less significant than other work they could be engaged in, welfare and teaching programmes for people of Aboriginal descent must make do with volunteers, or people lacking in special experience, or people with limited skills. The exceptions, growing in number, merely point up the state of this field as a whole.

It is not to be wondered at that many Aborigines were passively resistant, and except for superficial responses remained so. Many considered their way of thinking and acting to be the right and only way, just as the Europeans did in respect of their own. Even when faced with the fact of tribal disintegration and the curtailment of their accustomed activities, many Aborigines brought up in a traditional atmosphere refused to believe that their way of life had gone for ever. Those who are at present still traditionally-oriented cannot envisage this either: but for them, as for the others before them, this realization is merely a question of time.

APPENDIX

The Genetic Picture[1]

Table 1 sets out a list of the more important genetic systems, together with the symbols commonly used to describe the genes involved in their control. During the last twenty years a considerable body of data has been collected on the distribution within Australia of these markers. Unfortunately, most of the studies have not recorded the tribal affiliations of the persons sampled. In consequence, with a few exceptions, only comparisons on a regional basis can be made.

TABLE 1

MODERN GENETIC SYSTEMS USED FOR STUDYING DIFFERENCES BETWEEN HUMAN POPULATIONS

SYSTEM	COMMONEST GENE SYMBOLS
Blood Groups	
ABO	A_1 (p_1), A_2 (p_2), B (q), O (r).
Rhesus	R_1 (CDe), R_2 (cDE), R_z (CDE), R′ (Cde), R″ (cdE), R_0 (cDe), r (cde).
MNS	MS, Ms, NS, Ns or M, N, S, s.
P	P_1, P^k, P_2, or P, p.
Lewis	Le^a, Le^b.
Lutheran	Lu^a, Lu^b.
Kell	K, k, Kp^a.
Duffy	Fy^a, Fy^b.
Kidd	Jk^a, Jk^b.
Diego	Di^a.
Sutter	Js^a.
Secretion of ABO blood group substances	Se, se.
Serum Protein Groups	
Haptoglobins	Hp^1, Hp^2, Hp^{2-1}(mod).
Transferrins	Tf C, Tf B, Tf D, etc.
Gamma Globulins	Gm^a, Gm^b, Gm^x; Gm-like, InV^a, InV^b.
Group Specific	Gc^1, Gc^2.
Ability to taste Phenyl-thio-Carbamide (P.T.C.)	T, t.
Abnormal Haemoglobins	Hb A, Hb S, Hb C, Hb D, etc.
Red Cell Enzyme Defects	
Glucose-6-Phosphate Dehydrogenase Deficiency	GP, gp (sex-linked).

[1] This Appendix has been kindly prepared by Dr. Robert L. Kirk, Reader in Human Genetics, University of Western Australia. (See also main text, under *Physical Homogeneity-Heterogeneity*: (*a*) *The Genetic Picture*.)

THE BLOOD GROUPS

The blood group data have been summarized by Mourant (1954), Simmons (1956 and 1958). Earlier studies were tabulated by Birdsell and Boyd (1940). A detailed tabulation of ABO blood groups only is given by Mourant and others (1958).

If all the blood group systems are considered together, the Australian Aborigines have certain associations which distinguish them as a group from other populations in the world. The gene B of the ABO blood group system is completely absent, except in Cape York, the east coast of Queensland and sporadically in Arnhem Land. The following genes too are not present in unmixed Aborigines: A_2 of the ABO system, S of the MNS system, R'' and r of the Rh system, Fy^b of the Duffy system, k of the Keil system, Lu^a of the Lutheran system, Di^a of the Diego system, and Js^a of the Sutter system. It is possible that still other blood group genes, not yet adequately tested, may be completely absent.

Within the ABO system the O and A_1 genes show wide variation. There is an increase of frequency of the A_1 gene from under 10 per cent along the west coast of Cape York to nearly 40 per cent over most of South Australia, with a peak value of nearly 50 per cent among the Bidjandjara. Intermediate values between 20 and 25 per cent prevail in both the west and east coastal areas.

The frequency of the M gene throughout Australia is low, ranging from 5 to 40 per cent. The lowest values, which correspond to almost 100 per cent in the N gene, are found in the Western Desert group stretching from the Laverton-Warburton Range area in Western Australia into South Australia, including representatives of the Mandjindja and Ngadadjara language groups. Another area of low M gene frequency is in north-eastern Queensland. Elsewhere in Queensland, the Northern Territory and north-west Australia the value of M ranges between 20 and just over 30 per cent. The M gene reaches its highest frequency of nearly 40 per cent in a group sampled at Alice Springs. To repeat, the S gene of the MNS system is absent in Aboriginal Australia.

Of the known blood group systems, the most complex genetically is the Rhesus or Rh system. Here the abbreviations as defined by Race and Sanger (1958) will be used for designating the various complex antigens. The commonest Rh gene in Australia is R_1, having a frequency of about 60 per cent, but ranging from 56 per cent in Central Australia to 73 per cent in Cape York. The genes R_2 and R_0 show considerable variation. R_2 has a value between 6 and 11 per cent in Cape York, Arnhem Land and Bathurst Island, but increases to 25 per cent at Haast's Bluff, and reaches a value of 41 per cent in one series from Yuendumu. R_0, on the other hand, increases from 1 per cent at Yuendumu to 29 per cent on Bathurst Island.

Australia is remarkable in having in some areas a high frequency of the gene R_z. It achieves a frequency of about 7 per cent in south-east Queensland, and in a group of 47 persons at Jigalong Mission in Western Australia has a value of nearly 20 per cent.

Some problems in the Rh system as observed in Australia remain to be clarified. Persons classified as R'R' have been reported in a series from Queensland, and similarly the gene R' is reported from Western Australia. Almost certainly the R' genes of the earlier studies are in fact variants of the type R_1^u. Many other variants for the Rh antigens have been reported recently from various places in Australia. Further work may indicate that some of these variants are useful markers for studying the rate of genetic interchange between neighbouring tribal groups.

The remaining blood group systems have not been tested adequately enough to enable detailed statements on the gene frequencies to be made. P positive individuals occur, and a value of about 25 per cent has been found in Western Australia. In unmixed Aborigines in Western Australia reported on by Simmons (1958), 6·9 per cent of 1,536 persons were Le (a+), 99·7 per cent of 903 persons were Fy (a+), and there were no reported cases of K+, He+ or Lu (a+) out of 903, 34 and 94 persons tested respectively. In only one survey have tests for the secretion of blood group substances been carried out. Ninety seven per cent were secretors, only 3 per cent being non-secretors (se/se).

SERUM PROTEIN GROUPS

Recently surveys have been undertaken to determine the frequencies in Australian populations of the genes controlling inherited differences in serum proteins. For the haptoglobin groups, relatively high values of the Hp_2 gene have been found in Aborigines from the Western Desert, with somewhat lower values in the Kimberleys and Cape York. Work is still proceeding on the frequency of this gene in other parts of Australia. So far the Hp 2-1 (mod) phenotype has not been encountered in Australia, and the incidence of ahaptoglobinaemia (Hp O) is low (1 per cent). A much more interesting picture is presented, however, by the distribution of the transferrin genes. The Tf D variant is common, and in the Western Desert the frequency of the gene Tf D reaches a value of 30 per cent, much higher than anywhere else in the world. In the Kimberleys and Cape York the Tf D frequency is lower, around 10 per cent.

Preliminary studies have been started also on the distribution of the gamma globulin groups. Again in Western Australia very significant differences occur between the Western Desert group and the Kimberleys. In both areas all the samples are Gm (a+). Gm (b) is absent in the Western Desert, but 30 per cent are Gm (b+) in the Kimberleys. The corresponding frequencies for Gm (x+) are 47 and 45 per cent respectively. The Gm (like) character is absent in Australia.

Preliminary studies on the Group Specific protein system using the technique of immuno-electrophoresis suggest a very high incidence of the Gc^1 gene among the Aborigines. It is possible that a different allele, found only rarely in Caucasians, may occur moderately frequently in some areas.

OTHER GENETIC SYSTEMS

Of the other genetic systems studied, one of the most significant perhaps is the complete absence in Australia of the sickle cell trait, or, when appropriate tests have been made, of any abnormal haemoglobin. Another character which seems to be absent in Australia is deficiency in the red cell enzyme glucose-6-phosphate dehydrogenase (G-6-P.D.). Only limited surveys for this character have been carried out in Australia. No deficient individuals were encountered in tests carried out by Kidson on over 700 adults from the west coast of Cape York, Central and Western Australia. An earlier report had suggested that there might be a few individuals with red-cell enzyme deficiency in this area.

Light-coloured or tawny hair is found in some parts of Australia. Birdsell (1950: 297) has postulated that this condition is controlled by a partially dominant gene. Two types of light hair-colour may be distinguished. The most common is characterized by moderate concentration of melanin and an absence of red-gold pigment when viewed by transmitted light. Its appearance by reflected light is lustreless, dark medium-brown. The less common phenotype is light-brown to medium-brown in colour when viewed by reflected light, has a lower melanin concentration, and is also deficient in red-gold pigment. Before adulthood is reached there is progressive pigmentation, which makes the differentiation between these types difficult. Birdsell suggests that if a single gene is involved, the heterozygote is manifested by the intermediate melanin values. Using this hypothesis he has mapped the gene frequencies for tawny hair on the Australian Continent. The highest frequencies are found in the Western Desert; the incidence falls rapidly in all directions away from the Centre, to low or zero in other parts of the Continent. Abbie and Adey (1954: 339-59) have discussed also the genetics of light hair-colour. Birdsell has also mapped the phenotypic distribution of two other characters, total facial height and the possession of 4th distomolar teeth.

Again the desert tribes reveal extreme values, the lowest facial height occurring in the Bidjandjara and the Mandjindja. For 4th distomolar teeth Birdsell found eight cases from among 900 adult Aborigines examined. All of these eight were concentrated in the Ngadadjara and four adjacent tribes, a frequency of 11 per cent in the persons examined from this group.

Simmons and others (1954) tested 152 persons for their ability to taste phenylthio-carbamide. Approximately 50 per cent were tasters and 50 per cent non-tasters, but there were considerable fluctuations between the groups included in the survey. Simmons and his colleagues at a later date found the same test difficult to interpret at Haast's Bluff in Central Australia. The data are too scanty to draw any firm conclusions on this particular characteristic.

ANTHROPOLOGICAL SIGNIFICANCE OF GENETIC MARKERS

It is clear from the foregoing outline that a substantial body of data exists on the frequency of many genetic markers in Australian Aborigines. It is important therefore to ask whether this information can be used to answer questions relating to the origin of the Australian Aborigines, or to relationships between groups within Aboriginal Australia itself. In the past, similarity in gene frequencies in two populations has been taken to imply common origins, or, alternatively, intermediate values in gene frequencies have been taken to imply hybridization between two distinct populations. The application of similar methods to problems concerning the Australian Aboriginal, however, is beset with difficulties. These difficulties are of two types. The first is the effect of natural selection —involving the favouring of certain gene combinations which confer greater immunity to disease or increased fertility on the persons possessing them, in contrast to other gene combinations. The second is variation in gene frequency through the operation of chance in small breeding populations, a process called random genetic drift.

Australian Aborigines over large areas of the Continent have been substantially isolated from contact with outside populations for possibly 500 generations (10,000 years). During this time relatively minor selection will have been able to produce marked changes in gene frequencies, even to the extent of eliminating some genes entirely from the population. In addition, the Australian Aboriginal is a member of a 'tribal group', the mean size of which is about 500 persons, and the reproductive size of which is frequently very much less. Although inter-tribal marriage is fairly common, tribal organization has the effect of greatly reducing gene flow, and thus making more likely fluctuations in gene frequencies between neighbouring tribes due to the operation of random genetic drift. Birdsell, Simmons and Graydon in a detailed survey of nearly 2,000 persons in Western Australia as quoted by Dunn (1959: 131), have shown, for instance, that the blood group gene O has a maximum difference between adjacent isolates of 30 per cent, and that the blood group gene M similarly varies in frequency from 2 to 37 per cent; similar abrupt differences were found for some of the Rh genes. Dunn quotes Birdsell as follows:

> At all three loci, the frequencies seem under broad clinal control and presumably hence are responsive to adaptive differences. Even so, in each instance, some isolates deviate widely and significantly from their expected position in the clinal topography, and suggest that such abrupt fluctuations may locally represent isolates in which drift has occurred. The data do not suggest one or the other process working exclusively, but rather that in the Australian isolate the drift may occasionally produce regionally localised fluctuations from expected values. These do not seem due to sampling error in all cases and suggest that drift may sometimes be a minor factor in the evolution of populations of this structure.

TABLE

FREQUENCY OF SELECTED GENETI

MARKERS		AUSTRALIAN ABORIGINES	MELANESIANS (NEW GUINEA)	MICRONESIANS (MARSHALL Is.)	POLYNESIANS (COOK Is. EASTER Is. & N.Z.)	MALAYS (INDONESIA)	SENOI (MALAYA
ABO Blood Groups	A_1	10–50	7–24	12–16	34–50	13–18	6
	A_2	0	0	0	0	0	0
	B	Sporadic	10–16	7–19	0	13–18	23
	O	50–90	64–78	67–79	50–66	64–74	71
MNS Blood Groups	M	5–40	4–17	18–27	40–53	44–63	72
	N	60–95	83–96	73–82	47–60	37–56	28
	S	0	1–32	12	12–18	?	11
Rh Blood Groups	R_1	56–73	80–95	95	40–52	81–84	92
	R_2	6–30	2–13	4	46–54	9–13	8
	R_o	1–29	2–7	1	1–3	4–7	0
	R_z	0–7+	0	0	0	2	0
	r	0	0	0	0	0	0
	R'	0?	0	0	0	0	0
	R''	0	0	0	0	0	0
	D^u	Localized & variable	Very localized	?	Sporadic	?	?
Diego Blood Groups	Di^a +ve	0	0	0	0	?	?
Lewis Blood Group	Le^a +ve	7	?	26	14–29	40	?
Hapto-globins	Hp^1	15–25	66	58	58	24	47
	(Hp 0)			0		1	10
Trans-ferrins	Tf D	5–30	11	0	0	3	2
	Tf B	Sporadic	0	0	0	0	0
P.T.C. Tasters		27–50	54	?	84–92	66–84	96

Bearing these limitations in mind, it is possible to look at the broad picture of gene frequencies in the Australian Aboriginal and compare them with those prevailing in neighbouring populations. In Table 2 available information for the frequency of genetic markers in 12 ethnic groups in addition to the Australian Aborigines is listed. In some cases an ethnic group is represented by a single investigation only, so that no indication of the range of values for the marker involved can be given.

For the ABO blood groups, the most significant feature in Aboriginal populations is the absence of gene B, except in the Northern Territory and Queensland. Elsewhere the B gene is found with high frequency in Asia, and it occurs throughout the Pacific area, except in Polynesia. The presence of the B gene in the north-east section of Australia suggests relatively recent gene inflow from Papuan and Malay sources. Its absence in Polynesians (and also in American Indians), as well as in the main group of Australian Aborigines, suggests that this gene is readily lost by natural selec-

ARKERS IN VARIOUS POPULATIONS

CHINESE (MALAYA)	AINU (HOKKAIDO)	TAMILS (SOUTH INDIA)	VEDDAHS (CEYLON)	VEDDOID TRIBES (S. INDIA)	BANTU (AFRICA)	BUSHMEN (AFRICA)
16–21	28	13–16	2–7	16–19	10	15
0	0	3–4	0	1–6	8	5
13–14	21	19	10–45	24	11	2
66–69	51	61–65	54–85	55	70	78
49–67	40	69	42–65	54–71	58	59
33–51	60	31	35–58	29–46	42	41
5	29	?	20–29	30–43	14	8
76	56	57	72–86	69	3	9
20	21	14	4–11	7	4	2
4	}	4	0	0	74	89
1	} 4 (No R_z)	1	Sporadic	0–4	0	0
0	}	24	4–28	7	12	0
0	0	0	2–5	17	7	0
0	18	0	0	0	0	0
?	?	?	?	?	10% D genes	9% D genes
5	?	0	0	0	0	0
16–24	35	?	?	9		?
28	?	9–14	19	12	53–63	29
1	?	2	6	5	3–25	2
4	?	0	8	0	?	10
0	?	0	0	0	?	0
84–94	94	86	?	62	?	?

tion under certain conditions where small isolated populations are involved. In the MNS blood group system, the Australian Aborigines resemble the Melanesians in having high frequencies of the N gene. But they also contrast strikingly with Melanesia, where the gene S has a frequency varying between 1 and 30 per cent, in not possessing the S gene at all.

Similar contrasts are found within the Rh blood group system. The R_1 gene is not as high in Australia as in New Guinea and Micronesia; but the R_z gene, which is found occasionally in Caucasians and Indonesians and in the Veddoid tribes of South India, achieves relatively high frequency in parts of Australia. On the other hand, the R_0 gene, which in Africa has a frequency of 75 per cent or higher, has moderate frequencies in Australia and is low or absent in Mongoloid peoples and throughout Oceania.

The more recently discovered, and still incompletely studied, serum groups reveal the same kind of contrasts between the Australian Aborigines and surrounding peoples as do the blood groups already discussed. In the western half of the Continent, where the most reliable studies have been made, the haptoglobin gene Hp_2 has a moderately high frequency. Kirk and Lai (n.d.) have found similar frequencies in people of Mongoloid stock, and even high frequencies in South India, including the Veddoid tribes of the Nilgiri Hills and the Veddahs of Ceylon. The Hp_2 frequency in New Guinea and throughout Oceania, however, is significantly lower. Many African populations are characterized by low values of Hp_2 and the presence of the Hp 2-1 (mod) phenotype and a high frequency of ahaptoglobinaemia. The Hp 2-1 (mod) phenotype is absent or extremely rare throughout Asia, Oceania and Australia, and the cases of ahaptoglobinaemia in these populations may frequently be a consequence of environmental factors.

The transferrin gene Tf D was first discovered in Australian Aborigines from Queensland. It achieves its highest frequency for any population in the world in the Aborigines of the Western Desert. But it is common also in New Guinea, and has a frequency of nearly 5 per cent in Mongoloid peoples; it appears to be absent in India, including the Nilgiri Hills area, with its Veddoid Irula and Kurumba tribes. On the other hand the Tf D gene reaches a value of 10 per cent among the Veddahs of Ceylon. It appears to be absent, or to have a low frequency, in Polynesia.

For the gamma globulin groups the Gm (a) phenotype is nearly 100 per cent for all the Mongoloid and Australian peoples tested; but in many groups, except those from the Western Desert, the Gm (b) phenotype is also nearly 100 per cent. This suggests that the newly postulated allele Gm (ab) is present throughout the greater part of this area, in addition to the alleles Gm (a) and Gm (b).

Finally, it has already been pointed out that the Australian Aborigines possess no abnormal haemoglobins. These are found elsewhere, in various places in Asia. Haemoglobin S has a high frequency in the Veddoid Irula and Kurumba tribes, and Haemoglobin E is present in the Veddahs of Ceylon. Haemoglobin E, together with the Thallasemia gene, is also common in South-east Asia and Indonesia, and Thallasemia is present in New Guinea. The absence of these genes in Australia suggests that the selective factors which have maintained these genes in other populations have not been operative here. Since it is now commonly accepted that malaria may be the principal selective agent for maintaining abnormal haemoglobins or the Thallasemia gene in a population, it suggests that endemic malaria has never been a serious health hazard for Aboriginal populations in Australia. Even if the original migrants brought such genes with them, they have been completely eliminated through the operation of natural selection.

Bibliography[1]

ABBIE, A. A., 1951. The Australian Aborigine, *Oceania,* Vol. XXII, No. 2.

ABBIE, A. A., 1958. The Aborigines of South Australia, in *Introducing South Australia* (R. J. Best, ed.), A.N.Z.A.A.S., Adelaide.

ABBIE, A. A., 1960. Curr's Views on How the Aborigines Peopled Australia, *The Australian Journal of Science,* Vol. 22, No. 10.

ABBIE, A. A., 1961. Recent field work on the physical anthropology of Australian Aborigines, *Australian Journal of Science,* Vol. 23, No. 7.

ABBIE, A. A. and W. R. ADEY, 1953. Pigmentation in a Central Australian Tribe, *American Journal of Physical Anthropology,* n.s., Vol. 11.

ADAM, L., 1954. *Primitive Art,* Pelican, London and Melbourne.

ANGAS, G. F., 1846-7. *South Australia Illustrated,* 2 vols. folio, London.

ANGAS, G. F., 1847. *Savage Life and Scenes in Australia and New Zealand,* London (Vols. I-II).

ANTHROPOLOGICAL SOCIETY OF WESTERN AUSTRALIA, 1960. A Preliminary Report of a survey being carried out by the Anthropological Society of Western Australia relevant to the preservation of Australian Aboriginal sites in W.A., Perth (typescript: mimeographed).

ASHLEY-MONTAGU, M. F., 1937. *Coming Into Being Among the Australian Aborigines,* Routledge, London.

ASHLEY-MONTAGU, M. F., 1937. The Origin of Subincision in Australia, *Oceania,* Vol. VIII, No. 2.

ASHLEY-MONTAGU, M. F., 1940. Ignorance of Physiological Paternity in Secular Knowledge and Orthodox Belief among the Australian Aborigines, *Oceania,* Vol. XI, No. 1.

[1] Not all references set out here are noted in the main text. The list is not intended to be exhaustive.

BARRETT, C. and R. H. CROLL, 1943. *Art of the Australian Aboriginal,* Bread and Cheese Club, Melbourne.

BASEDOW, H., 1907. Anthropological Notes on the Western Coastal Tribes of the Northern Territory of South Australia, *Transactions of the Royal Society of South Australia,* Vol. 31.

BASEDOW, H., 1913. Notes on the Aborigines of Melville and Bathurst Islands, *Journal of the Royal Anthropological Institute,* Vol. XLIII.

BASEDOW, H., 1918. Narrative of an Expedition of Exploration in North-Western Australia, *Transactions of the Royal Geographical Society of Australasia, South Australian Branch,* Vol. XVIII, Session 1916-17: Adelaide.

BASEDOW, H., 1925. *The Australian Aboriginal,* Preece, Adelaide.

BASEDOW, H., 1927. Subincision and Kindred Rites of the Australian Aborigines, *Journal of the Royal Anthropological Institute,* Vol. LVII.

BATES, D., 1938 (1949). *The Passing of the Aborigines,* Murray, Melbourne and London.

BERNDT, C. H., 1950*a*. *Women's Changing Ceremonies in Northern Australia,* L'Homme, Hermann et Cie, Paris.

BERNDT, C. H., 1950*b*. Expressions of Grief Among Aboriginal Women, *Oceania,* Vol. XX, No. 4.

BERNDT, C. H., 1951. Some Figures of Speech and Oblique References in an Australian Language (Gunwinggu), *Southwestern Journal of Anthropology,* Vol. 7, No. 3.

BERNDT, C. H., 1952. A Drama of North-Eastern Arnhem Land, *Oceania,* Vol. XXII, No. 3.

BERNDT, C. H., 1958. Review: U. McConnel, *Myths of the Mungkan, Oceania,* Vol. XXVIII, No. 4.

BERNDT, C. H., 1960. The Concept of Primitive, *Sociologus,* Vol. 10, No. 1.

BERNDT, C. H., 1961*a*. Art and Aesthetic Expression, Conference on Aboriginal Studies, Canberra, May 1961: data paper.[2]

BERNDT, C. H., 1961*b*. The Quest for Identity: the case of the Australian Aborigines, *Oceania,* Vol. XXXII, No. 1.

BERNDT, C. H., 1962. The Arts of Life. An Australian Aboriginal Perspective. *Westerly,* Vol. 1, Nos. 2 and 3.

BERNDT, C. H., n.d. *Marriage in Aboriginal Australia* (manuscript).

BERNDT, C. H., n.d. *Children's Stories from Western Arnhem Land* (manuscript).

[2] Included in volume of Conference Papers published for the Australian Institute of Aboriginal Studies by Oxford University Press, London, 1963, under the title *Australian Aboriginal Studies.*

BERNDT, C. and R., 1951. An Oenpelli Monologue: Culture Contact, *Oceania*, Vol. XXII, No. 1.

BERNDT, R. M., 1940*a*. A Curlew and Owl Legend from the Narunga Tribe, South Australia, *Oceania*, Vol. X, No. 4.

BERNDT, R. M., 1940*b*. Some Aspects of Jaralde Culture, South Australia, *Oceania*, Vol. XI, No. 2.

BERNDT, R. M., 1940*c*. Aboriginal Sleeping Customs and Dreams, Ooldea, South Australia, *Oceania*, Vol. X, No. 3.

BERNDT, R. M., 1941. The Bark Canoe of the Lower River Murray, South Australia, *Mankind*, Vol. 3, No. 1.

BERNDT, R. M., 1947. Wuradjeri Magic and 'Clever Men', *Oceania*, Vol. XVII, No. 4; Vol. XVIII, No. 1.

BERNDT, R. M., 1948*a*. A Wonguri-Mandjikai Song Cycle of the Moon-Bone, *Oceania*, Vol. XIX, No. 1.

BERNDT, R. M., 1948*b*. Badu, Islands of the Spirits, *Oceania*, Vol. XIX, No. 2.

BERNDT, R. M., 1951*a*. *Kunapipi*, Cheshire, Melbourne.

BERNDT, R. M., 1951*b*. Ceremonial Exchange in Western Arnhem Land, *Southwestern Journal of Anthropology*, Vol. 7, No. 2.

BERNDT, R. M., 1951*c*. Influence of European Culture on Australian Aborigines, *Oceania*, Vol. XXI, No. 3.

BERNDT, R. M., 1951*d*. Aboriginal Ochre-Moulded Heads from Western Arnhem Land, *Meanjin*, Vol. X, No. 4.

BERNDT, R. M., 1952*a*. *Djanggawul*, Routledge and Kegan Paul, London.

BERNDT, R. M., 1952*b*. Subincision in a Non-Subincision Area, *American Imago*, Vol. 8, No. 2.

BERNDT, R. M., 1952*c*. Circumcision in a Non-Circumcising Area, *International Archives of Ethnography*, Vol. XLVI, No. 2.

BERNDT, R. M., 1952*d*. Surviving Influence of Mission Contact on the Daly River, Northern Territory of Australia, *Neue Zeitschrift für Missionswissenschaft*, Vol. VIII, 2/3.

BERNDT, R. M., 1953. A Day in the Life of a Dieri Man before Alien Contact, *Anthropos*, Vol. 48.

BERNDT, R. M., 1955. 'Murngin' (Wulamba) Social Organization, *American Anthropologist*, Vol. 57, No. 1.

BERNDT, R. M., 1957. In Reply to Radcliffe-Brown on Australian Local Organization, *American Anthropologist*, Vol. 59, No. 2.

BERNDT, R. M., 1958*a*. The Mountford Volume on Arnhem Land Art, Myth and Symbolism: A Critical Review, *Mankind*, Vol. 5, No. 6.

BERNDT, R. M., 1958*b*. Some Methodological Considerations in the Study of Australian Aboriginal Art, *Oceania*, Vol. XXIX, No. 1.

BERNDT, R. M., 1959*a*. The Concept of 'The Tribe' in the Western Desert of Australia, *Oceania*, Vol. XXX, No. 2.

BERNDT, R. M., 1959*b*. Areas of Research in Aboriginal Australia which demand Urgent Attention, *Bulletin of the International Committee on Urgent Anthropological and Ethnological Research*, No. 2, Vienna.

BERNDT, R. M., 1959*c*. Two Love Magic Objects from Laverton, Western Australia, *Mankind*, Vol. 5, No. 8.

BERNDT, R. M., 1960. Review: C. W. M. Hart and A. R. Pilling, *The Tiwi of North Australia*, *Oceania*, Vol. XXXI, No. 2.

BERNDT, R. M., 1961*a*. Problems of Assimilation in Australia, *Sociologus*, Vol. 11, No. 1.

BERNDT, R. M., 1961*b*. Surviving Groups with Minimum Association with Europeans, Conference on Aboriginal Studies, Canberra, May 1961: data paper.[3]

BERNDT, R. M., 1962*a*. *An Adjustment Movement in Arnhem Land*, Cahiers de L'Homme, Mouton, Paris and The Hague.

BERNDT, R. M., 1962*b*. Tribal Marriage in a Changing Social Order, *Law Review*, Vol. V, Perth.

BERNDT, R. M., n.d. Traditional Life of the Australian Aborigines, *L'Encyclopédie de la Pléiade*, Paris.

BERNDT, R. M., n.d. Marriage and the Family in North-Eastern Arnhem Land: Chapter for a volume on comparative family systems edited by M. F. Nimkoff.

BERNDT, R. M., n.d. The Wuradilagu Song Cycle of North-Eastern Arnhem Land: Chapter for a volume on mythology edited by M. Jacobs.

BERNDT, R. M., n.d. *Love Songs of Arnhem Land* (manuscript).

BERNDT, R. M., n.d. *Daughters of the Sun* (manuscript).

BERNDT, R. and C., 1942-5. A Preliminary Report of Field Work in the Ooldea Region, Western South Australia, *Oceania Bound Offprint*, 1945, Sydney (*Oceania*, Vol. XII, No. 4; Vol. XIII, Nos. 1-4; Vol. XIV, Nos. 1-4; Vol. XV, Nos. 1-3).

[3] See footnote 2.

BERNDT, R. and C., 1946 (1944-46). Native Labour and Welfare in the Northern Territory, privately distributed manuscript (Sydney).

BERNDT, R. and C., 1946. The Eternal Ones of the Dream, *Oceania*, Vol. XVII, No. 1.

BERNDT, R. and C., 1948. Sacred Figures of Ancestral Beings of Arnhem Land, *Oceania*, Vol. XVIII, No. 4.

BERNDT, R. and C., 1949. Secular Figures of Northeastern Arnhem Land, *American Anthropologist*, Vol. 51, No. 2.

BERNDT, R. and C., 1950. Aboriginal Art in Central-Western Northern Territory, *Meanjin*, Vol. IX, No. 3.

BERNDT, R. and C., 1951*a*. *Sexual Behaviour in Western Arnhem Land*, Viking Fund Publications in Anthropology, No. 16, New York.

BERNDT, R. and C., 1951*b*. Discovery of Pottery in North-Eastern Arnhem Land, *Journal of the Royal Anthropological Institute*, Vol. LXXVII.

BERNDT, R. and C., 1951*c*. The Concept of Abnormality in an Australian Aboriginal Society, *Psychoanalysis and Culture*, International Universities Press, New York.

BERNDT, R. and C., 1951/1952. *From Black to White in South Australia*, University of Chicago Press, Illinois; Cheshire, Melbourne.

BERNDT, R. and C., 1952-4. A Selection of Children's Songs from Ooldea, Western South Australia, *Mankind*, Vol. 4, Nos. 9, 10, 12.

BERNDT, R. and C., 1952/54. *The First Australians*, Ure Smith, Sydney.

BERNDT, R. and C., 1954. *Arnhem Land, Its History and Its People*, Cheshire, Melbourne.

BERNDT, R. and C., 1957. Introduction to *Australian Aboriginal Art, Arnhem Land Paintings on Bark and Carved Human Figures*, Western Australian Museum, Perth.

BERNDT, R. and T. H. JOHNSTON, 1942. Death, Burial, and Associated Ritual at Ooldea, South Australia, *Oceania*, Vol. XII, No. 3.

BERNDT, R. and T. VOGELSANG, 1941. The Initiation of Native Doctors, Dieri Tribe, South Australia, *Records of the South Australian Museum*, Vol. VI, No. 4.

BIRDSELL, J. B., 1947. New data on racial stratification in Australasia, *American Journal of Physical Anthropology*, n.s., Vol. 5, No. 2.

BIRDSELL, J. B., 1950. Some implications of the genetical concept of race in terms of spatial analysis, *Cold Springs Harbor Symposia Quantitative Biology*, Vol. 15.

BIRDSELL, J. B. and W. C. BOYD, 1940. Blood Groups in the Australian Aborigines, *American Journal of Physical Anthropology*, Vol. 27.

BLEAKLEY, J. W., 1961. *The Aborigines of Australia*, Jacaranda Press, Brisbane.

BOYD, W. C., 1950. *Genetics and the Races of Man. An Introduction to Modern Physical Anthropology*, Blackwell, Oxford.

BRADSHAW, J., 1892. Notes on a recent trip to Prince Regent's River, Kimberley District, Western Australia, *Transactions of the Royal Geographical Society of Australia* (Melbourne), Vol. 9.

CAPELL, A., 1939. Mythology in Northern Kimberley, North-West Australia, *Oceania*, Vol. IX, No. 4

CAPELL, A., 1940. The Classification of Languages in North and North-West Australia, *Oceania*, Vol. X, Nos. 3 and 4.

CAPELL, A., 1942. Languages of Arnhem Land, North Australia, *Oceania*, Vol. XII, No. 4; Vol. XIII, No. 1.

CAPELL, A., 1952. The Wailbri Through Their Own Eyes, *Oceania*, Vol. XXIII, No. 2

CAPELL, A., 1956. A New Approach to Australian Linguistics, *Oceania Linguistic Monographs*, No. 1, Sydney.

CAPELL, A., 1960*a*. The Wandarang and Other Tribal Myths of the Yabuduruwa Ritual, *Oceania*, Vol. XXX, No. 3.

CAPELL, A., 1960*b*. Myths and Tales of the Nunggubuyu, South-eastern Arnhem Land, *Oceania*, Vol. XXXI, No. 1.

CHEWINGS, C., 1936. *Back in the Stone Age*. Angus and Robertson, Sydney.

CLELAND, J. B., 1928. Disease amongst the Australian Aborigines, *Journal of Tropical Medicine and Hygiene*.

CLELAND, J. B., 1940. Some Aspects of the Ecology of the Aboriginal Inhabitants of Tasmania and South Australia, *Papers and Proceedings of the Royal Society of Tasmania*, 1939.

CLELAND, J. B., 1957. Our natives and the vegetation of Southern Australia, *Mankind*, Vol. 5, No. 4

COLLINS, D., 1804. *An Account of the English Colony in New South Wales*, London.

CROWLEY, F. K., 1960. *Australia's Western Third*, Macmillan, London.

CURR, E. M., 1886-7. *The Australian Race*:......(4 vols., Vols. I and II, 1886; Vols. III and IV, 1887), Government Printer, Melbourne (Trübner, London).

DAHL, Knut, 1926. *In Savage Australia*. . . . Allan, London.

DAMPIER, W., 1688. *A New Voyage Round the World,* Chapter XVI.

DAVIDSON, D. S., 1933. Australian Netting and Basketry Techniques, *Journal of the Polynesian Society,* Vol. 42, No. 4

DAVIDSON, D. S., 1936. Aboriginal Australian and Tasmanian Rock Carvings and Paintings, *American Philosophical Society, Memoir V,* Philadelphia.

DAVIDSON, D. S., 1937. A Preliminary Consideration of Australian Aboriginal Decorative Art, *American Philosophical Society, Memoir IX,* Philadelphia.

DAVIDSON, D. S., 1938. Stone Axes of Western Australia, *American Anthropologist,* Vol. 40.

DAVIDSON, D. S., 1941. Aboriginal Australian String Figures, *Proceedings American Philosophical Society,* Vol. 84, Philadelphia.

DAVIDSON, D. S., 1952. Notes on the Pictographs and Petroglyphs of Western Australia, *Proceedings American Philosophical Society,* Vol. 96, Philadelphia.

DAVIDSON, D. S. and F. D. McCARTHY, 1957. The Distribution and Chronology of Some Important Types of Stone Implements in Western Australia, *Anthropos,* Vol. 52.

DAVIES, E. H., 1927. Aboriginal Songs, *Transactions of the Royal Society of South Australia,* Vol. 51.

DAVIES, E. H., 1932. Aboriginal Songs of Central and Southern Australia, *Oceania,* Vol. II, No. 4.

DAVIES, E. H., 1947. Music in Primitive Society, *Occasional Publications of the Anthropological Society of South Australia,* No. 2.

DAWSON, J., 1881. *Australian Aborigines,* Melbourne.

DOUGLAS, W. H., 1958. An Introduction to the Western Desert Language, *Oceania Linguistic Monographs,* No. 4, Sydney.

DOUGLAS, W. H., 1959. *Illustrated Topical Dictionary of the Western Desert Language. . . .* United Aborigines Mission, Perth.

DUNN, L. C., 1959. *Heredity and Evolution in Human Populations,* Howard University Press, Cambridge.

DURKHEIM, E., 1915/54. *The Elementary Forms of the Religious Life* (Swain, trans.), Allen and Unwin, London.

ELKIN, A. P., 1930. Rock Paintings of North-West Australia, *Oceania,* Vol. I, No. 3.

ELKIN, A. P., 1931*a*. The Kopara: the settlement of grievances, *Oceania,* Vol. II, No. 2.

ELKIN, A. P., 1931*b*. The Social Organization of South Australian Tribes, *Oceania,* Vol. II, No. 1.

ELKIN, A. P., 1932. The Social Life and Intelligence of the Australian Aborigine, *Oceania,* Vol. III, No. 1.

ELKIN, A. P., 1933. Studies in Australian Totemism, *Oceania Monographs,* No. 2, Sydney (*Oceania,* Vol. III, Nos. 3 and 4; Vol. IV, Nos. 1 and 2).

ELKIN, A. P., 1934. Cult-Totemism and Mythology in Northern South Australia, *Oceania,* Vol. V, No. 2.

ELKIN, A. P., 1937. Beliefs and Practices connected with death in North-Eastern and Western South Australia, *Oceania,* Vol. VII, No. 3.

ELKIN, A. P. (ed.), 1938. Studies in Australian Linguistics, *Oceania Monographs,* No. 3, Sydney.

ELKIN, A. P., 1938-40. Kinship in South Australia, *Oceania Bound Offprint,* 1940, Sydney (*Oceania,* Vol. VIII, No. 4; Vol. IX, No. 1; Vol. X, Nos. 2-4).

ELKIN, A. P., 1945. *Aboriginal Men of High Degree* (John Murtagh Macrossan Memorial Lectures for 1944), Australasian Publishing Co., Sydney.

ELKIN, A. P., 1948. Grey's Northern Kimberley Cave-Paintings Re-Found, *Oceania,* Vol. XIX, No. 1.

ELKIN, A. P., 1949. The Origin and Interpretation of Petroglyphs in South-East Australia, *Oceania,* Vol. XX, No. 2.

ELKIN, A. P., 1950*a*. The Complexity of Social Organization in Arnhem Land, *Southwestern Journal of Anthropology,* Vol. 6, No. 1.

ELKIN, A. P., 1950*b*. Ngirawat, or the sharing of names in the Wagaitj Tribe, Northern Australia, *Beiträge zur Gesellungs- und Völkerwissenschaft, Festschrift zum achtzigsten Geburtstag von Professor Richard Thurnwald,* Mann, Berlin.

ELKIN, A. P., 1951. Reaction and Interaction: A Food Gathering People and European Settlement in Australia, *American Anthropologist,* Vol. 53, No. 2.

ELKIN, A. P., 1952. Cave-Paintings in Southern Arnhem Land, *Oceania,* Vol. XXII, No. 4.

ELKIN, A. P., 1953-6. Arnhem Land Music, *Oceania,* Vol. XXIV, No. 2; Vol. XXV, Nos. 1-2, 4; Vol. XXVI, Nos. 1, 2, 3.

ELKIN, A. P., 1954 (1st ed. 1938). *The Australian Aborigines: How to Understand Them,* Angus and Robertson, Sydney.

ELKIN, A. P., 1959. *Aborigines and Citizenship,* Association for the Protection of Native Races, Sydney.

ELKIN, A. P., 1961*a*. The Yabuduruwa, *Oceania*, Vol. XXXI, No. 3.

ELKIN, A. P., 1961*b*. Maraian at Mainoru, 1949, *Oceania*, Vol. XXXI, No. 4; Vol. XXXII, No. 1.

ELKIN, A. P., 1961*c*. Art and Meaning: A Review Article, *Oceania*, Vol. XXXII, No. 1.

ELKIN, A. P., R. and C. BERNDT, 1950. *Art in Arnhem Land*, Cheshire, Melbourne; University of Chicago Press, Chicago.

ELKIN, A. P., R. and C. BERNDT, 1951. Social Organization of Arnhem Land, I. Western Arnhem Land, *Oceania*, Vol. XXII, No. 1.

ELKIN, A. P. and T. A. JONES, 1958. Arnhem Land Music, *Oceania Monographs*, No. 9, Sydney.

ETHERIDGE, R. Jr., 1918. The Dendroglyphs or Carved Trees of New South Wales, *Geological Survey of New South Wales, Memoir, Ethnological Series*, III.

EYLMANN, E., 1908. *Die Eingeborenen der Kolonie Südaustralien*, Dietrich Reimer, Berlin.

FALKENBERG, J., 1948. *Et Steinaldersfolk I Var Tid: Australias Innfodte*, Olaf Norlis, Oslo.

FALKENBERG, J., 1962. *Kin and Totem. . . .* Oslo University Press, Oslo.

FENNER, F. J., 1939. The Australian Aboriginal Skull: Its Non-Metrical Morphological Characters, *Transactions of the Royal Society of South Australia*, Vol. 63.

FIRTH, R., 1938/56. *Human Types*, Nelson, London.

FIRTH, R., 1951. *Elements of Social Organization*, Watts, London.

FISON, L. and A. W. HOWITT, 1880. *Kamilaroi and Kurnai*, Robertson, Melbourne.

FLANAGAN, R. J., 1888. *The Aborigines of Australia*, Flanagan and Robertson, Sydney.

FLINDERS, M., 1814. *A Voyage to Terra Australis*, etc. Nicol, London (2 vols.).

FOELSCHE, P., 1882. Notes on the Aborigines of North Australia, *Transactions of the Royal Society of South Australia*, Vol. 5.

FOXCROFT, E. J. B., 1941. *Australian Native Policy*, Melbourne University Press, Melbourne.

FRASER, J., 1892. *The Aborigines of New South Wales*, Sydney.

FROBENIUS INSTITUTE, 1957. *Ferne Völker: Frühe Zeiten*, des Museums für Völkerkunde und des Frobenius-Institutes an der Johann Wolfgang Goethe-Universität, Frankfurt am Main.

FRY, H. K., 1934. Kinship in Western Central Australia, *Oceania*, Vol. IV, No. 4.

FRY, H. K. and R. H. PULLEINE, 1931. The Mentality of the Australian Aborigine, *The Australian Journal of Experimental Biology and Medical Science,* Vol. VIII.

GATES, R. R., 1960. The Genetics of the Australian Aborigines, *Acta Geneticae Medicae et Gemellologiae,* Vol. 9, No. 1.

GENNEP, A. van, 1905. *Mythes et Légendes d'Australie,* Paris.

GENTILLI, G., c. 1953-7. Le Condizioni Etnologiche Attuali Dell' Oceania, from *Le razze e i popoli della terra* (ed. R. Biasutti), Vol. IV, Chap. VIII, Torin (2nd ed.).

GLUCKMAN, M., 1955. *The Judicial Process Among the Barotse of Northern Rhodesia,* Manchester University Press, Manchester.

GOODALE, J. C., 1959. The Tiwi Dance for the Dead, *Expedition,* Bulletin of the University Museum of the University of Pennsylvania, Vol. 2, No. 1.

GRÄBNER, Fr., 1906. Wanderung und Entwickelung socialer Systeme in Australien, *Globus,* Vol. 90.

GRÄBNER, Fr., 1909. Zur australischen Religionsgeschichte, *Globus,* Vol. 96.

GRÄBNER, Fr., 1915-16. Totemismus als Kulturgeschichtliches Problem, *Anthropos,* Vols. 10-11.

GREY, G., 1841. *Journal of two expeditions of discovery in North West and Western Australia,* 2 vols. Boone, London.

HADDON, A. C., 1901-8, 1938. *Reports of the Cambridge Anthropological Expedition to Torres Straits,* Vols. I-VI, Cambridge.

HAEKEL, J., 1950. Zum Individual und Geschlechtstotemismus in Australien, *Acta Ethnologica et Linguistica,* No. 1, Herold, Vienna.

HALE, H. M. and N. B. TINDALE, 1925. Observations on the Aborigines of the Flinders Ranges, and Records of Rock Carvings and Paintings, *Records of the South Australian Museum,* Vol. III.

HALE, H. M. and N. B. TINDALE, 1929. Further notes on the Aboriginal Rock Carvings of South Australia, *South Australian Naturalist,* Vol. 10.

HALE, H. M. and N. B. TINDALE, 1930. Notes on some Human Remains in the Lower Murray Valley, *Records of the South Australian Museum,* Vol. IV.

HARNEY, W. E., 1943. *Taboo,* Australasian Publishing Co., Sydney.

HARNEY, W. E., 1960. Ritual and Behaviour at Ayers Rock, *Oceania,* Vol. XXXI, No. 1.

HARNEY, W. E. and A. P. ELKIN, 1943. Melville and Bathurst Islanders: a short description, *Oceania,* Vol. XIII, No. 3.

HARNEY, W. E. and A. P. ELKIN, 1949. *Songs of the Songmen,* Cheshire, Melbourne.

HARRIS, R. H., 1912. Mummification and other Similar Customs as Practised by the Queensland Aborigines, *Memoirs of the Queensland Museum,* Vol. 1.

HART, C. W. M., 1930*a*. The Tiwi of Melville and Bathurst Islands, *Oceania,* Vol. I, No. 2.

HART, C. W. M., 1930*b*. Personal Names Among the Tiwi, *Oceania,* Vol. I, No. 3.

HART, C. W. M. and A. R. PILLING, 1960. *The Tiwi of North Australia,* Holt, New York.

HASLUCK, P., 1942. *Black Australians, A Survey of Native Policy in Western Australia, 1829-1897,* Melbourne University Press, Melbourne.

HASLUCK, P., 1957. *Our Aborigines,* Department of Territories, Canberra.

HAYGARTH, H. W., 1850. *Recollections of Bush Life in Australia,* Murray, London.

HERNÁNDEZ, T., 1941*a*. Social Organization of the Drysdale River Tribes, North-West Australia, *Oceania,* Vol. XI, No. 3

HERNÁNDEZ, T., 1941*b*. Children Among the Drysdale River Tribes, *Oceania,* Vol. XII, No. 2.

HIATT, L., 1959. Social Control in Central Arnhem Land, *South Pacific,* Vol. 10, No. 7.

HOEBEL, E. A., 1954. *The Law of Primitive Man,* Harvard University Press, Cambridge, Mass.

HOOKER, J., 1869. On Child-bearing in Australia and New Zealand, *Journal Ethnological Society,* London, n.s. i.

HORNE, G. and G. AISTON, 1924. *Savage Life in Central Australia,* Macmillan, London.

HOWELLS, W. W. and W. L. WARNER, 1937. Anthropometry of the Natives of Arnhem Land and the Australian Race Problem, *Papers of the Peabody Museum of American Archaeology and Ethnology, Harvard University,* Vol. XVI, No. 1.

HOWITT, A. W., 1904. *The Native Tribes of South-East Australia,* Macmillan, London.

IRVINE, F. R., 1957. Wild and Emergency Foods of Australian and Tasmanian Aborigines, *Oceania,* Vol. XXVIII, No. 2.

JOHNSTON, T. H. and J. B. CLELAND, 1933-4. The History of the Aboriginal Narcotic, *Pituri*, *Oceania*, Vol. IV, Nos. 2 and 3.

JONES, F. Wood, 1934. *Australia's Vanishing Race*, Angus and Robertson, Sydney.

JONES, T. A., 1956-57. Arnhem Land Music, Part II. A Musical Survey, *Oceania*, Vol. XXVI, No. 4; Vol. XXVIII, No. 1.

KABERRY, P. M., 1935. Death and Deferred Mourning Ceremonies in the Forrest River Tribes, North-West Australia, *Oceania*, Vol. VI, No. 1.

KABERRY, P. M., 1939. *Aboriginal Woman, Sacred and Profane*, Routledge, London.

KIRK, R. L. and L. Y. C. LAI, n.d. The Distribution of Haptoglobin and Transferrin Groups in South and South East Asia, *Acta Genetica et Statistica Medica* (in press).

KLAATSCH, H., 1907. Schlussbericht über Meine Reise nach Australien in den Jahren 1904-1907. *Zeitschrift für Ethnologie*, Bd. 39.

KLUCKHOHN, C., 1953. Universal Categories of Culture, in A. L. Kroeber (ed.) *Anthropology Today, An Encyclopedic Inventory*, University of Chicago Press, Chicago.

KOPPERS, W., 1955. Diffusion: Transmission and Acceptance, *Yearbook of Anthropology–1955*, Wenner-Gren, New York.

KROEBER, A. L. (ed.), 1953. *Anthropology Today, An Encyclopedic Inventory*, University of Chicago Press, Chicago.

LANCELOTT, F., 1853. *Australia As It Is. . . .* Vol. II, Hurst and Blackett, London.

LANG, A., 1905. *The Secret of the Totem*, Longmans Green, London.

LAWRENCE, W. E. and G. P. MURDOCK, 1949. Murngin Social Organization, *American Anthropologist*, Vol. 51, No. 1.

LEACH, E. R., 1951. The structural implications of matrilateral cross-cousin marriage, *Journal of the Royal Anthropological Institute*, Vol. LXXXI.

LEICHHARDT, L., 1847. *Journal, Overland Expedition in Australia from Moreton Bay to Port Essington*, 1844-5, London.

LÉVI-STRAUSS, C., 1949. *Les Structures Élémentaires de la Parenté*, Presses Universitaires de France, Paris.

LOMMEL, A., 1949. Notes on Sexual Behaviour and Initiation, Wunambal Tribe, North-Western Australia, *Oceania*, Vol. XX, No. 2.

LOMMEL, A., 1950. Modern Culture and the Aborigines, *Oceania*, Vol. XXXI, No. 1.

LOMMEL, A., 1951. Traum und Bild bei den Primitiven in Nordwest-Australien, *Psyche*, part 3 (Stuttgart).

LOMMEL, A., 1952. Die Unambal. Ein Stamm in Nordwest-Australien, *Monographien zur Völkerkunde*, Hamburg.

LOVE, J. R. B., 1936. *Stone Age Bushmen of Today*, Blackie, London.

LUMHOLTZ, C., 1889. *Among Cannibals*, Murray, London.

MACINTOSH, N. W. G., 1948. A Survey of Possible Sea Routes available to the Tasmanian Aborigines, *Records of the Queen Victoria Museum, Launceston*, Vol. II, No. 3.

MACINTOSH, N. W. G., 1951. The Archaeology of Tandandjal Cave, South-West Arnhem Land, *Oceania*, Vol. XXI, No. 3.

MACINTOSH, N. W. G., 1952*a*. The Cohuna Cranium. History and Commentary. . . ., *Mankind*, Vol. 4, No. 8.

MACINTOSH, N. W. G., 1952*b*. The Cohuna Cranium: Teeth and Palate, *Oceania*, Vol. XXIII, No. 2.

MACINTOSH, N. W. G., 1952*c*. Stature in some Aboriginal Tribes in South-West Arnhem Land, *Oceania*, XXII, No. 3

MACINTOSH, N. W. G., 1952*d*. Paintings in Beswick Creek Cave, Northern Territory, *Oceania*, Vol. XXII, No. 4.

MACINTOSH, N. W. G., 1953. The Cohuna Cranium: Physiography and Chemical Analysis, *Oceania*, Vol. XXIII, No. 4.

MACGILLIVRAY, J., 1852. *Narrative of the Voyage of H.M.S. "Rattlesnake" during the years 1846-50*, London.

MALINOWSKI, B., 1913. *The Family Among the Australian Aborigines*, University of London Press, London.

MALINOWSKI, B., 1926. Magic, Science and Religion, in *Science, Religion and Reality* (J. Needham, ed.), Sheldon Press, London.

MASSARY, I. (by a Resident), 1861. *Social Life and Manners in Australia*, Longmans Green, London.

MASSOLA, A., 1961. A Victorian Skull-cap Drinking Bowl, *Mankind*, Vol. 5, No. 10.

MATHEW, J., 1899. *Eaglehawk and Crow, A Study of the Australian Aborigines . . . .*, Nutt, London; Melville, Mullen and Slade, Melbourne.

MATHEW, J., 1910. *Two Representative Tribes of Queensland*, Fisher Unwin, London.

MATHEWS, R. H., 1897. The totemic Divisions of Australian Tribes, *Journal of the Royal Society of New South Wales,* Vol. 31.

MATHEWS, R. H., 1899. *Folklore of the Australian Aborigines,* Hennessey Harper, Sydney.

McCARTHY, F. D., 1938/58 (1948 ed. used and quoted from). *Australian Aboriginal Decorative Art,* Australian Museum, Sydney.

McCARTHY, F. D., 1939*a*. "Trade" in Aboriginal Australia, and "Trade" relationships with Torres Strait, New Guinea and Malaya, *Oceania,* Vol. IX, No. 4; Vol. X, Nos. 1 and 2.

McCARTHY, F. D., 1939*b*. The Grooved-Conical Stones of New South Wales, *Mankind,* Vol. 2, No. 6.

McCARTHY, F. D., 1940. Aboriginal Australian Material Culture: its Composition, *Mankind*, Vol. 2, Nos. 8 and 9.

McCARTHY, F. D., 1941-56. Records of the Rock Engravings of the Sydney-Hawkesbury District, *Mankind,* Vols. 3-5, and *Records of the Australian Museum,* Vol. XXIV.

McCARTHY, F. D., 1949. The Prehistoric Cultures of Australia, *Oceania,* Vol. XIX, No. 4.

McCARTHY, F. D., 1953. The Oceanic and Indonesia Affiliations of Australian Aboriginal Culture, *Journal of the Polynesian Society*, Vol. 62, No. 3.

McCARTHY, F. D., 1957*a*. *Australia's Aborigines, Their Life and Culture,* Melbourne, Colorgravure Publications.

McCARTHY, F. D., 1957*b*. Theoretical Considerations of Australian Aboriginal Art, *Journal and Proceedings of the Royal Society of New South Wales,* Vol. 91, Part 1.

McCARTHY, F. D., 1958. *Australian Aboriginal Rock Art,* Australian Museum, Sydney.

McCARTHY, F. D., 1960-61. Introduction to an *Exhibition of Australian Aboriginal Art,* State Art Galleries of Australia.

McCARTHY, F. D., 1961. The Rock Engravings of Depuch Island, North-East Australia, *Records of the Australian Museum,* Vol. XXV, No. 8.

McCARTHY, F. D., 1962. The Rock Engravings at Port Hedland, Northwestern Australian, *Papers, Kroeber Anthropological Society,* University of California, No. 26.

McCARTHY, F. D. and N. W. G. MACINTOSH, 1962. The Archaeology of Mootwingee, Western New South Wales, *Records of the Australian Museum,* Vol. XXV, No. 13.

McCARTHY, F. D., H. V. V. NOONE and E. BRAMELL, 1946. The Stone Implements of Australia, *Memoirs of the Australian Museum,* Vol. 9.

McCONNEL, U. H., 1931. A Moon Legend from the Bloomfield River, North Queensland, *Oceania,* Vol. II, No. 1.

McCONNEL, U. H., 1934. The Wik-Munkan and Allied Tribes of Cape York Peninsula, *Oceania,* Vol. IV, No. 3.

McCONNEL, U. H., 1935*a*. Inspiration and Design in Aboriginal Art, *Art in Australia,* Sydney.

McCONNEL, U. H., 1935*b*, Myths of the Wikmunkan and Wiknatara Tribes, *Oceania,* Vol. VI, No. 1.

McCONNEL, U. H., 1936. Totemic Hero-Cults in Cape York Peninsula, North Queensland, *Oceania,* Vol. VI, No. 4; Vol. VII, No. 1.

McCONNEL, U. H., 1937. Mourning Ritual Among the Tribes of Cape York Peninsula, *Oceania,* Vol. VII, No. 3.

McCONNEL, U. H., 1939-40. Social Organization of the Tribes of Cape York Peninsula, North Queensland, *Oceania,* Vol. X, Nos. 1 and 4.

McCONNEL, U. H., 1950. Junior Marriage Systems: Comparative Survey, *Oceania,* Vol. XXI, No. 2.

McCONNEL, U. H., 1957. *Myths of the Mungkan,* Melbourne University Press, Melbourne.

MEAD, M., 1950. *Male and Female,* Gollancz, London.

MEGGITT, M. J., 1955. Djanba among the Wailbri, Central Australia, *Anthropos,* Vol. 50.

MEGGITT, M. J., 1957. Notes on the Vegetable Foods of the Wailbri of Central Australia, *Oceania,* Vol. XXVIII, No. 2.

MEGGITT, M. J., 1962. *Desert People,* Angus and Robertson, Sydney.

MELVILLE, H., 1851. *The Present State of Australia. . . . ,* Willis, London.

MITCHELL, S. R., 1949. *Stone-Age Craftsmen,* Tait Book Co., Melbourne.

MITCHELL, T. L., 1839. *Three Expeditions into the Interior of Eastern Australia,* Vol. II, Boone, London.

MOUNTFORD, C. P., 1928 and 1935. Aboriginal Rock Carvings in South Australia, *Reports, Australasian Association for the Advancement of Science,* Vols. XIX, XXII.

MOUNTFORD, C. P., 1937*a*. Aboriginal Crayon Drawings from the Warburton Ranges in Western Australia. . . . , *Records of the South Australian Museum,* Vol. VI, No. 1.

MOUNTFORD, C. P., 1937*b*. Aboriginal Crayon Drawings. . . . , *Transactions of the Royal Society of South Australia*, Vol. 61.

MOUNTFORD, C. P., 1937*c*. Aboriginal Crayon Drawings, II. . . . , *Transactions of the Royal Society of South Australia*, Vol. 61.

MOUNTFORD, C. P., 1938*a*. Aboriginal Crayon Drawings, III. . . . , *Transactions of the Royal Society of South Australia*, Vol. 62 (2).

MOUNTFORD, C. P., 1938*b*. Contrast in Drawings made by an Australian Aborigine Before and After Initiation, *Records of the South Australian Museum*, Vol. VI, No. 2.

MOUNTFORD, C. P., 1939*a*. Aboriginal Crayon Drawing, IV. . . . , *Transactions of the Royal Society of South Australia*, Vol. 63 (1).

MOUNTFORD, C. P., 1939*b*. Aboriginal Crayon Drawings, Warburton Ranges, Western Australia, *Oceania*, Vol. X, No. 1.

MOUNTFORD, C. P., 1939*c*. Phallic Stones of the Australian Aborigines, *Mankind*, Vol. 2, No. 6.

MOUNTFORD, C. P., 1948. *Brown Men and Red Sand*, Robertson and Mullens, Melbourne

MOUNTFORD, C. P., 1956. *Records of the American-Australian Scientific Expedition to Arnhem Land, Vol. 1, Art, Myth, and Symbolism*, Melbourne University Press, Melbourne.

MOUNTFORD, C. P., 1958. *The Tiwi–their Art, Myth and Ceremony*, Phoenix House, London.

MOUNTFORD, C. P. (ed.), 1960. *Records of the American-Australian Scientific Expedition to Arnhem Land, Vol 2, Anthropology and Nutrition*, Melbourne University Press, Melbourne.

MOUNTFORD, C. P. and R. M. BERNDT, 1941. Making Fire by Percussion in Australia, *Oceania*, Vol. XI, No. 4.

MOUNTFORD, C. P. and A. HARVEY, 1938. A Survey of Australian Aboriginal Pearl and Baler Shell Ornaments. *Records of the South Australian Museum*, Vol. VI, No. 2.

MOUNTFORD, C. P. and A. HARVEY, 1941. Women of the Adnjamatana Tribe of the Northern Flinders Ranges, South Australia, *Oceania*, Vol. XII, No. 2.

MOURANT, A. E., 1954. *The Distribution of the Human Blood Groups*, Blackwell, Oxford.

MOURANT, A. E., A. C. KOPEC and K. DOMANIEWSKA-SOBSZAK, 1958. *The ABO Blood Groups—Comprehensive Tables and Maps of World Distribution,* Blackwell, Oxford.

MULVANEY, D. J., 1961. The Stone Age of Australia, *Proceedings of the Prehistoric Society,* Vol. XXVII.

NEEDHAM, R., 1962. Genealogy and Category in Wikmunkan Society, *Ethnology,* Vol. I, No. 2.

ÖBERLANDER, R., 1863. Die Eingeborenen der australischen Kolonie Victoria, *Globus,* Vol. 4.

ODERMANN, G., 1957. Das Eigentum in Nordwest-Australien, *Annali Lateranensi,* Vol. XXI.

ODERMANN, G., 1958. Heilkunde der Njangomada, Nordwest-Australien, *Paideuma,* Vol. VI, Part 7.

ODERMANN, G., 1959. Holz- und Steinsetzungen in Australien, *Paideuma,* Vol. VII, Part 2.

PACKER, A. D., 1961. The Health of the Australian Native, *Oceania,* Vol. XXXII, No. 1.

PALMER, E., 1884. Notes on Some Australian Tribes, *Journal of the Anthropological Institute,* Vol. XIII.

PARKER, K. L., 1896. *Australian Legendary Tales,* Nutt, London and Melbourne.

PARKER, K. L., 1898. *More Australian Legendary Tales,* Nutt, London and Melbourne.

PARKER, K. L., 1905. *The Euahlayi Tribe,* Constable, London.

PETRI, H., 1954. *Sterbende Welt in Nordwest-Australien,* A. Limbach, Braunschweig.

PETRI, H., 1960*a*. Anthropological Research in the Kimberley Area of Western Australia, Anthropological Society of Western Australia (mimeographed).

PETRI, H., 1960*b*. Die Altersklassen der Vorinitiation bei Eingeborenengruppen Nordwest-Australiens, *Ethnologica,* Bd. 2, Köln.

PIDDINGTON, R., 1932*a*. Totemic System of the Karadjeri Tribe, *Oceania,* Vol. II, No. 4.

PIDDINGTON, R., 1932*b*. Karadjeri Initiation, *Oceania,* Vol. III, No. 1.

PINK, O., 1936. The Landowners of the Northern Division of the Aranda Tribe, Central Australia, *Oceania,* Vol. VI, No. 3.

PORTEUS, S. D., 1931. *The Psychology of a Primitive People,* Arnold, London.

PORTEUS, S. D., 1933. Mentality of Australian Aborigines, *Oceania,* Vol. IV, No. 1.

RACE, R. R. and R. SANGER, 1958. *Blood Groups in Man,* Blackwell, Oxford.

RADCLIFFE-BROWN, A. R., 1913. Three Tribes of Western Australia, *Journal of the Royal Anthropological Institute,* Vol. XLII.

RADCLIFFE-BROWN, A. R., 1918. Notes on the Social Organization of Australian Tribes, *Journal of the Royal Anthropological Institute,* Vol. XLVIII.

RADCLIFFE-BROWN, A. R., 1930-1. The Social Organization of Australian Tribes, *Oceania,* Vol. I, Nos. 1-4 (*Oceania Monographs,* No. 1, Sydney).

RADCLIFFE-BROWN, A. R., 1945. Religion and Society, *Journal of the Royal Anthropological Institute,* Vol. LXXV, Parts I and II (reprinted in *Structure and Function in Primitive Society,* by A. R. Radcliffe-Brown, 1952, Cohen and West, London).

RADCLIFFE-BROWN, A. R., 1951. Murngin Social Organization, *American Anthropologist,* Vol. 53, No. 1.

RADCLIFFE-BROWN, A. R., 1952. *Structure and Function in Primitive Society,* Cohen and West, London.

RADCLIFFE-BROWN, A. R., 1956. On Australian Local Organization, *American Anthropologist,* Vol. 58, No. 2.

RADCLIFFE-BROWN, A. R., U. McCONNEL, A. P. ELKIN, R. PIDDINGTON, 1930. The Rainbow Serpent. . . . *Oceania,* Vol. I, No. 3.

RIESMAN, D., 1955. *The Lonely Crowd,* Doubleday Anchor, New York.

RÓHEIM, G., 1925. *Australian Totemism, A Psycho-Analytic Study in Anthropology,* Allen and Unwin, London.

RÓHEIM, G., 1933. Women and Their Life in Central Australia, *Journal of the Royal Anthropological Institute,* Vol, LXIII.

RÓHEIM, G., 1945. *The Eternal Ones of the Dream,* International Universities Press, New York.

RÓHEIM, G., 1950. Dreams of Women in Central Australia, *The Psychiatric Quarterly Supplement,* Vol. 24 (Utica, New York).

ROSE, F., 1960. *Classification of Kin, Age Structure and Marriage Amongst the Groote Eylandt Aborigines,* Deutsche Akademie der Wissenschaften zu Berlin, Berlin.

ROTH, W. E., 1897. *Ethnological Studies Among the North-West-Central Queensland Aborigines,* Government Printer, Brisbane.

ROTH, W. E., 1907. North Queensland Ethnography Bulletin No. 9: Burial Ceremonies, and Disposal of the Dead, *Records of the Australian Museum,* Vol. VI, No. 5, Sydney.

SCHMIDT, W., 1909. Die soziologische und religiös-ethische Gruppierung der australischen Stämme, *Zeitschrift für Ethnologie,* Bd. XLI.

SCHMIDT, W., 1926-35. *Ursprung der Gottesidee,* Münster.

SCHMIDT, W., 1952. Der Konzeptionsglaube Australischer Stämme, *International Archives of Ethnography,* Vol. XLVI, No. 1.

SCHNEIDER, D. M., 1941. Aboriginal Dreams (unpublished M.A. thesis, Cornell University).

SCHNEIDER, D. M. and L. SHARP, 1958. Yir Yoront Dreams (unpublished MS.) (our copy obtained 1956, undated: entitled 'An Analysis of Yir Yoront Dreams', by D. M. Schneider: pp. 1-88).

SCHULZ, A., 1946. North-Western Australian Rock-Paintings, *Memoirs National Museum of Victoria,* Vol. 20.

SERVICE, E. R., 1960. Sociocentric Relationship Terms and the Australian Class System, in *Essays in the Science of Culture in Honour of Leslie A. White* (G. E. Dole and R. L. Carneiro, *eds.*) Thomas Y. Crowell, New York.

SHARP, R. L., 1934*a*. Ritual Life and Economics of the Yir-Yoront of Cape York Peninsula, *Oceania,* Vol. V, No. 1.

SHARP, R. L., 1934*b*. The Social Organization of the Yir-Yoront Tribe, Cape York Peninsula, *Oceania,* Vol. IV, No. 4.

SHARP, R. L., 1935. Semi-Moieties in North-Western Queensland, *Oceania,* Vol. VI, No. 2.

SHARP, R. L., 1939. Tribes and Totemism in North-Eastern Australia, *Oceania,* Vol. IX, Nos. 3 and 4.

SHARP, R. L., 1943. Notes on Northeast Australian Totemism, in *Studies in the Anthropology of Oceania and Asia,* C. S. Coon and J. M. Andrews, IV, eds., *Papers of the Peabody Museum of American Archaeology and Ethnology,* Harvard University, Vol. XX, Cambridge, Mass.

SHARP, R. L., 1958. People Without Politics. The Australian Yir Yoront, in, Systems of Political Control and Bureaucracy in Human Societies, *Proceedings of the 1958 Annual Spring Meeting of the American Ethnological Society,* Seattle.

SIEBERT, O., 1910. Sagen und Sitten der Dieri. . . . , *Globus*, Vol. 97, Nos. 3 and 4.

SIMMONS, R. T., 1956. A Report on Blood Group Genetical Surveys in Eastern Asia, Indonesia, Melanesia, Micronesia, Polynesia and Australia in the Study of Man, *Anthropos*, Vol. 51.

SIMMONS, R. T., 1958. A Review of Blood Group Gene Frequencies in Aborigines of the Various Australian States, *Proceedings of the 7th Congress International Society Blood Transfusion.*

SIMMONS, R. T., J. J. GRAYDON and N. M. SEMPLE, 1954. A Blood Group Genetical Survey of Australian Aborigines, *American Journal of Physical Anthropology*, n.s., Vol. 12.

SMITH, Ramsay W., 1924. *In Southern Seas*, Murray, London.

SMYTH, R. Brough, 1878. *The Aborigines of Victoria. . . .* 2 vols., Government Printer, Melbourne.

SPENCER, B., 1914. *Native Tribes of the Northern Territory of Australia*, Macmillan, London.

SPENCER, B., 1928. *Wanderings in Wild Australia*, 2 vols., Macmillan, London.

SPENCER, B. and F. J. GILLEN, 1904. *The Northern Tribes of Central Australia*, Macmillan, London.

SPENCER, B. and F. J. GILLEN, 1912. *Across Australia*, 2 vols., Macmillan, London.

SPENCER, B. and F. J. GILLEN, 1927. *The Arunta. A study of a stone age people*, 2 vols., Macmillan, London.

SPENCER, B. and F. J. GILLEN, 1938. *The Native Tribes of Central Australia*, Macmillan, London.

SRINIVAS, M. N. (ed.), 1958. *Method in Social Anthropology: selected essays by A. R. Radcliffe-Brown*, the University of Chicago Press, Chicago.

STANNER, W. E. H., 1933*a*. The Daly River Tribes, A Report of Field Work in North Australia, *Oceania*, Vol. III, No. 4; Vol. IV, No. 1.

STANNER, W. E. H., 1933*b*. A Note Upon a Similar System Among the Nangiomeri, *Oceania*, Vol. III, No. 4.

STANNER, W. E. H., 1933-4. Ceremonial Economics of the Mulluk Mulluk and Madngella Tribes of the Daly River, North Australia, *Oceania*, Vol. IV, Nos. 2 and 4.

STANNER, W. E. H., 1936*a*. A Note on Djamindjung Kinship and Totemism, *Oceania*, Vol. VI, No. 4.

STANNER, W. E. H., 1936*b*. Murinbata Kinship and Totemism, *Oceania*, Vol. VII, No. 2.

STANNER, W. E. H., 1937. Modes of Address and Reference in the North-West of the Northern Territory, *Oceania,* Vol. VII, No. 3.

STANNER, W. E. H., 1958. The Dreaming, in *Reader in Comparative Religion: an Anthropological Approach* (W. A. Lessa and E. Z. Vogt, eds.) Row, Peterson, Evanston, Illinois.

STANNER, W. E. H., 1959-61. On Aboriginal Religion, *Oceania,* Vol. XXX, Nos. 2 and 4; Vol. XXXI, Nos. 2 and 4; Vol. XXXII, No. 2.

STIRLING, E. C., 1896. *Report on the work of the Horn Scientific Expedition to Central Australia, Part IV, Anthropology,* Dulau, London; Mullen and Slade, Melbourne.

STIRLING, E. C. 1911. Preliminary Report on the discovery of native remains at Swanport, River Murray; with an enquiry into the alleged occurrence of a pandemic among the Australian Aboriginals, *Transactions of the Royal Society of South Australia,* Vol. 35.

STIRLING, E. C., 1914. Aborigines, in *Handbook of South Australia,* Adelaide.

STIRLING, E. and E. R. WAITE, 1919. Description of Toas, or Australian Aboriginal Direction Signs, *Records of the South Australian Museum,* Vol. I, No. 2.

STOKES, J. L., 1846. *Discoveries in Australia, with an account of the coasts and rivers explored and surveyed during the voyage of H.M.S. Beagle. . . . ,* London.

STREHLOW, C. and M. von LEONHARDI, 1907-21. *Die Aranda- und Loritja-Stämme in Zentral Australien. Mythen, Sagen, und Märchen des Aranda-Stammes in Zentral Australien,* Veröffentlichungen des Frankfurter Museums für Völkerkunde, Frankfurt.

STREHLOW, T. G. H., 1933. Ankotarinja, An Aranda Myth, *Oceania,* Vol. IV, No. 2.

STREHLOW, T. G. H., 1942-4. Aranda Phonetics and Grammar, *Oceania Monographs* No. 7, Sydney.

STREHLOW, T. G. H., 1947. *Aranda Traditions,* Melbourne University Press, Melbourne.

STREHLOW, T. G. H., 1955. Australian Aboriginal Songs, *Journal of the International Folk Music Council,* Vol. VII.

STREHLOW, T. G. H., 1959. Anthropological and Ethnological Research in Australia, *Bulletin of the International Committee on Urgent Anthropological and Ethnological Research,* No. 2, Vienna.

SWEENEY, G., 1947. Food Supplies of a Desert Tribe, *Oceania*, Vol. XVII, No. 4.

THOMAS, N. W., 1906*a*. *Kinship Organisations and Group Marriage in Australia*, University Press, Cambridge.

THOMAS, N. W., 1906*b*. *Natives of Australia*, Constable, London.

THOMSON, D. F., 1933. The Hero Cult, Initiation and Totemism on Cape York, *Journal of the Royal Anthropological Institute*, Vol. LXIII.

THOMSON, D. F., 1934. The Dugong Hunters of Cape York, *Journal of the Royal Anthropological Institute*, Vol. LXIV.

THOMSON, D. F., 1936. Fatherhood in the Wik-Monkan Tribe, *American Anthropologist*, Vol. 38.

THOMSON, D. F., 1949. *Economic Structure and the Ceremonial Exchange Cycle in Arnhem Land*, Macmillan, Melbourne.

TINDALE, N. B., 1925-6. Natives of Groote Eylandt and of the West Coast of the Gulf of Carpentaria, Parts 1 and 2, *Records of the South Australian Museum*, Vol. III, Nos. 1 and 2.

TINDALE, N. B., 1932. *Manuscripts*, a Misc. of Arts and Letters, Adelaide.

TINDALE, N. B., 1935. Initiation Among the Pitjandjara Natives of the Mann and Tomkinson Ranges in South Australia, *Oceania*, Vol. VI, No. 2.

TINDALE, N. B., 1936. Legend of the Wati Kutjara, Warburton Range, Western Australia, *Oceania*, Vol. VII, No. 2.

TINDALE, N. B., 1937. Native Songs of the South-East of South Australia, *Transactions of the Royal Society of South Australia*, Vol. 61.

TINDALE, N. B., 1938. Prupe and Koromarange, a Legend of the Tanganekald, Coorong, S.A., *Transactions of the Royal Society of South Australia*, Vol. 62.

TINDALE, N. B., 1940. Results of the Harvard-Adelaide Universities Anthropological Expedition, 1938-39: Distribution of Australian Aboriginal Tribes: A Field Survey, *Transactions of the Royal Society of South Australia*, Vol. 64 (1). At present being revised (1963).

TINDALE, N. B., 1940-1. Survey of the Half-Caste Problem in South Australia, *Proceedings of the Royal Geographical Society, South Australian Branch*.

TINDALE, N. B., 1941. The Antiquity of Man in Australia, *Australian Journal of Science,* Vol. 3, No. 6.

TINDALE, N. B., 1950. Palaeolithic *Kodj* Axe of the Aborigines and its Distribution in Australia, *Records of the South Australian Museum,* Vol. IX.

TINDALE, N. B., 1951. Palaeolithic *Kodj* of the Aborigines: Further Notes, *Records of the South Australian Museum,* Vol. IX.

TINDALE, N. B., 1957. Culture Succession in South Eastern Australia, *Records of the South Australian Museum,* Vol. XIII.

TINDALE, N. B., 1959*a*. Ecology of Primitive Aboriginal Man in Australia, *Biogeography and Ecology in Australia, Monographiae Biologicae,* Vol. VIII.

TINDALE, N. B., 1959*b*. Totemic Beliefs in the Western Desert of Australia, Part I. Women Who Became the Pleiades. *Records of the South Australian Museum,* Vol. XIII, No. 3.

TINDALE, N. B. and J. B. BIRDSELL, 1941. Results of the Harvard-Adelaide Universities Anthropological Expedition, 1938-39: Tasmanoid Tribes in North Queensland, *Records of the South Australian Museum,* Vol. VII, No. 1.

TURNBULL, C., 1948. *Black War: the Extermination of the Tasmanian Aborigines,* Cheshire, Melbourne.

VOGELSANG, T., 1942. Hearts of the Two Sons of the Mura Mura Darana—Ceremonial Objects of the Dieri Tribe, South Australia. *Records of the South Australian Museum.* Vol. VII, No. 2.

WAGNER, K., 1937. The Craniology of the Oceanic Races, *Norske Videnskaps-Academie, Math. Nat. Klasse,* 1.

WARNER, W. L., 1937/58. *A Black Civilization,* Harper, New York.

WASHBURN, S. L., 1953. The Strategy of Physical Anthropology, in A. L. Kroeber (ed.), *Anthropology Today, An Encyclopedic Inventory,* University of Chicago Press, Chicago.

WASHBURN, S. L., 1955, in Hoebel, Jennings and Smith (eds.). *Readings in Anthropology,* McGraw-Hill, New York.

WHEELER, G. C., 1910. *The Tribe and Intertribal Relations in Australia,* London.

WILSON, J., 1962. Authority and Leadership in a 'New Style' Australian Aboriginal Community, Pindan, Western Australia (M.A. thesis, University of Western Australia).

WILSON, K., 1961. The Allocation of Sex Roles in Social and Economic Affairs in a 'New Style' Australian Aboriginal Community, Pindan, Western Australia (M.Sc. thesis, University of Western Australia).

WILSON, M., 1954. Nyakyusa Ritual and Symbolism, *American Anthropologist,* Vol. 56, No. 2.

WILSON, T. B., 1835. *Narrative of a Voyage round the World,* etc., London.

WOODS, J. D. (ed.), 1879. *The Native Tribes of South Australia* (including papers by Taplin, Wyatt, Meyer, Schürmann, Gason and Bennett), Wigg, Adelaide.

WORMS, E. A., 1940. Religiöse Vorstellungen und Kultur einiger Nord-Westaustralischen Stämme in Fünfzig Legenden, *Annali Lateranensi,* Vol. IV.

WORMS, E. A., 1942*a*. Die Goranara-Feier im Australischen Kimberley, *Annali Lateranensi,* Vol. VI.

WORMS, E. A., 1942*b*. Sense of Smell of the Australian Aborigines. A Psychological and Linguistic Study of the Natives of the Kimberley Division, *Oceania,* Vol. XIII, No. 2.

WORMS, E. A., 1950. *Djamar,* the Creator. A Myth of the Bād (West Kimberley, Australia), *Anthropos,* Vol. 45.

WORMS, E. A., 1952. Djamar and his Relation to other Culture Heroes, *Anthropos,* Vol. 47.

WORMS, E. A., 1953. Australian Ghost Drums, Trumpets and Poles, *Anthropos,* Vol. 48.

WORMS, E. A., 1954. Prehistoric Petroglyphs of the Upper Yule River, North-Western Australia, *Anthropos,* Vol. 49.

WORMS, E. A., 1955. Contemporary and Prehistoric Rock Paintings in Central and Northern North Kimberley, *Anthropos,* Vol. 50.

WORMS, E. A., 1957. The Poetry of the Yaoro and Bad, Northwestern Australia, *Annali Lateranensi,* Vol. XXI.

WORSLEY, P., 1955*a*. Early Asian Contacts with Australia, *Past and Present,* No. 7.

WORSLEY, P., 1955*b*. Totemism in a Changing Society, *American Anthropologist,* Vol. 57, No. 4.

WORSLEY, P., 1961. The Utilization of Food Resources by an Australian Aboriginal Tribe, *Acta Ethnographica* (Budapest), Vol. X, Parts 1-2.

WORSNOP, T., 1897. *The Prehistoric Arts, Manufactures, Works, Weapons, etc., of the Aborigines of Australia,* Government Printer, Adelaide.

Forthcoming

BERNDT, R. M. (ed.), 1964. *Australian Aboriginal Art* (containing articles by A. P. Elkin, C. P. Mountford, F. D. McCarthy, T. G. H. Strehlow, J. A. Tuckson, R. M. Berndt), Ure Smith, Sydney.[4]

BERNDT, R. M. and C. H. BERNDT (eds.) 1964. *Aboriginal Man in Australia*: Festschrift to honour Emeritus Professor A. P. Elkin. (Containing chapters by J. Bell, A. Capell, R. Fink, P. Hasluck, Trevor Jones, N. W. G. Macintosh, F. D. McCarthy, M. Meggitt, M. Reay, W. E. H. Stanner, T. G. H. Strehlow and R. M. and C. H. Berndt), Angus and Robertson, Sydney.

[4] This volume contains 73 colour plates illustrating various aspects of Aboriginal art, and for this reason no such illustrations on the subject of Aboriginal art have been included in *The World of the First Australians.*

Index

R01138 21415

65-87227 572.994

R01138 21415

'73

HOUSTON PUBLIC LIBRARY

HOUSTON TEXAS

This book may be kept for FOURTEEN DAYS. With due notice, it may be renewed once for the same period. Fine for overtime is two cents a day.

Book pocket S-8-65-60M-1

M